New York Real Estate

for

SALESPERSONS

Third Edition

JVNotebuyers.com

Marcia Darvin Spada

THOMSON
SOUTH-WESTERN

Australia · Canada · Mexico · Singapore · Spain · United Kingdom · United States

THOMSON
SOUTH-WESTERN

New York Real Estate for Salespersons, Third Edition
Marcia Darvin Spada

VP/Editorial Director:
Jack Calhoun

VP/Editor-in-Chief:
Dave Shaut

Sr. Acquisitions Editor:
Scott Person

Developmental Editor:
Sara Froelicher

Marketing Manager:
Mark Linton

Production Editor:
Todd McCoy

Production Manager:
Patricia Matthews Boies

Manufacturing Coordinator:
Charlene Taylor

Printer:
West Group
Eagan, Minnesota

Cover Designer:
Tippy McIntosh

Printed in the United States of America
2 3 4 5 06 05 04

ISBN: 0-324-19145-6
ISBN: 0-324-22463-X

Library of Congress Control Number: 2003111739

For more information, contact
South-Western
5191 Natorp Boulevard
Mason, Ohio 45040

Or you can visit our Internet site at:
http://www.swlearning.com

Brief Contents

For a complete table of contents, see page v.

Contents

CHAPTER 2 LAW OF AGENCY 44

CHAPTER 6 CONTRACTS 142

CHAPTER 8 TITLE CLOSING AND COSTS 184

Preface

People learn best by participating in the learning experience. Every chapter in this textbook provides a variety of activities so that this type of learning takes place. Learning activities include:

- *Putting It To Work* applications that give students the opportunity to handle typical problems faced by real estate agents, including:
  - Answering questions typically asked by clients and customers
  - Working with various real estate–related documents such as completing a comparative market analysis, lease, and contract of sale, or identifying parts of a deed
  - Role playing different scenarios to provide a forum for students to work together and generate ideas
- *You Should Know* boxed text, which highlights important laws, regulations, and concepts
- *Chapter Reviews* that put it all together, giving students a chance to practice what they have just learned in each chapter, using *How Would You Respond?* questions along with key term review and multiple choice questions

Other features that will assist the student in absorbing the material presented include:

- *Key Terms* lists that open each chapter and help students identify important terminology
- *Learning Objectives* that outline the Department of State's priorities for the material presented in each chapter
- *Case Studies* that exemplify the Department of State's stance on a variety of issues
- *Important Points* that synopsize each chapter so that students can easily review the material
- A comprehensive *Sample Salesperson Exam* that concludes the book, ideal for use as a diagnostic tool to assist students in pinpointing areas needing further study
- A detailed *Glossary* of all key terms presented in the book and related real estate terminology

Each chapter's activities are specifically relevant to the material within the chapter. They are enjoyable for both student and instructor as they provide for lively class discussions and an opportunity for the instructor to interact with students. Answers to all the chapter learning activities and chapter review questions are conveniently located at the end of each chapter.

This accurate and well-researched textbook completely covers the New York–mandated syllabus. In addition to providing an excellent source of information required for the New York real estate licensee, it will prepare students for the state licensing exam using an interactive learning experience that, first, promotes retention and understanding and, second, gives practice in applying the concepts.

SUPPLEMENTS

This new edition includes classroom and distance learning support!

- **Cram for the Exam: Salespersons.** Students excel at exam time with the aid of this handy study guide.
- **SmartLink™.** This computerized study guide and practice question tool supports independent learning.
- **Audio CD-ROM.** These content reviews reinforce learning while your adult learners commute or stay at home.
- **Instructor's Manual.** A complete set of support materials for guiding learning inside your classroom and from a distance.
- **Computerized Test.** This easy-to-use computerized test generator saves you time and ensures a confidential testing environment.

Contact your Thomson Learning representative for more details by calling 1-800-423-0563.

ABOUT THE AUTHOR

Marcia Darvin Spada is the former owner of the Albany Center for Real Estate Education, a New York licensed proprietary school. A professional educator, Marcia teaches real estate and has developed curricula for numerous real estate courses widely used in colleges, real estate–related organizations, and proprietary schools throughout New York. She has also developed and produced distance learning courses for salespersons, brokers, and appraisers. In addition to *New York Real Estate for Salespersons,* she is author of *New York Real Estate for Brokers, Cram for the Exam: Your Guide to Passing the New York Real Estate Salesperson Exam, Cram for the Exam: Your Guide to Passing the New York Real Estate Broker Exam, Environmental Issues and the Real Estate Professional*, and *The Home Inspection Book: A Guide for Professionals.* Spada holds a B. A. and an M. A. in English from the State University of New York at Albany and a B. S. in Real Estate Studies from Empire State College. She continues to update the material in this textbook and would welcome all comments. Her email address is marleedare@aol.com.

ACKNOWLEDGMENTS

It would have been impossible to cover the breadth of material in this book without the assistance and support of many capable and knowledgeable people. First, I would like to thank my daughter-in-law, Kimberly MacFawn Spada, Coordinator of the Albany Center for Real Estate Education, to staff members Vanessa Gonzalez and Mary Sofia.

Thanks to Noreen Baker for her overall assistance and for her review of the math chapter; to Mary Jo Cosco, John DiIanni, Hal Zucker, Jay Percent, Pat Binzer, Tony Spada, Vince Donnelly, and Vic DeAmelia, all of whom reviewed portions of the book; and to Claudia Zucker, who furnished information. Also a very special thank you to Rita Scharg, who contributed to the writing of the *Law of Agency* chapter. I also thank Seymour J. Baskin, owner of Goodman Realty in Rochester, New York, Tom Cusack, president of Cusack Sales Training Center; and Mark L. Schulman.

I am especially grateful to reviewers Alexander Frame of the Real Estate Education Center; James D. Kirby, Learning Link; Frank D'Agostino, Jr., Greater Syracuse

Association of REALTORS®; Anthony Anglieri and Sheila Margolis, Margolis Appraisal Service; and also to Milton Pachter, Esq., Arthur Elfenbein, Esq., Sal Gulino, and Wendy Tilton of the NYU Real Estate Institute. I am also indebted to reviewer Linda J. Fields, director and owner of the Professional Institute for Real Estate Training in Watertown, New York.

For assistance with the legal aspects of this book, my heartfelt appreciation to the attorneys in my family: my husband, Eugene R. Spada; my sister, Iris M. Darvin; my father, Leonard Darvin; and my daughter, Justine L. Spada. Thanks also to Martin Lazarow, Steve Lubbe, David Pollitzer, Karen Gneuch, Karen Sideri, and April Pruiksma.

Professionals from a number of New York State and other governmental agencies also provided information for this book. The following people provided their expertise: James D. Decker, Charles M. Hudson, James R. Covey, Gregory Smead, Kevin Scheuer, Desmond C. Gordon, Stephen Lukowski, Lee C. Kiernan, Richard M. Cowan, Barry A. Bechtel, Charles Lockrow, Patricia Riexinger, Peter Shugert, Richard Tyksinsky, and Elizabeth Smiraldo. Thanks also to Eileen Taus of the Westchester Board of REALTORS®.

For their help on current lending policies, thanks to John Biszick, Timothy T. Sherwin and Thomas P. Tokos. Thanks also to Stuart Sillars for his expertise on the subject of electricity. I also appreciate the assistance of Anne Groski, Rita Merith, Kevin LaPointe, Patrick Reilly, and Priscilla S. Toth, all of the New York State Association of REALTORS®.

I am indebted to the following individuals, organizations, and publishers who allowed me to reprint information or use their forms and illustrations: James A. Ader, Executive Vice President of the Greater Capital Association of REALTORS®, and the *Albany Times Union* for permission to reprint portions of Mr. Ader's column, "Real Estate Spotlight," in some of the question and answer portions of the book; Bob Kelly, Executive Director, *New York Star,* for allowing me to reprint portions of the *NY–Star Builder Field Guide;* South-Western for permission to reprint portions of *Practical Real Estate Math* by Betty J. Armbrust, Hugh H. Bradley, and John W. Armbrust; the National Association of REALTORS® for permission to reprint the role-playing exercises in the human rights chapter; Huguette Bushey and James A. Ader of the Greater Capital Association of REALTORS®; Lynnore Fetyko and the Greater Syracuse Association of REALTORS®; Marlene A. Sayers and the Greater Rochester Association of REALTORS®; Michele B. Stoeger and the Otsego-Delaware County Board of REALTORS®; Gary Sikkema and Pathfinder Realty, Inc.; James D. Kirby and Gallinger Real Estate; BlumbergExcelsior, Inc.; and Tuttle Law Print, Publishers, who furnished the real estate forms that appear in the textbook.

Greatly appreciated is the permission to reprint illustrations from the following: *Electrical Wiring,* fourth edition, American Association for Vocational Education of Winterville, Georgia; *Residential Electrical Wiring,* tenth edition, Ray C. Mullin, Delmar Publishers of Albany, New York; *Houses*, second edition by Henry Harrision, Real Estate Graphics DBA, Forms and Worms, Inc.; *Basics for Builders: Framing and Rough Carpentry,* Scot Simpson, the R. S. Means Company.

A very special thank you to editor Elizabeth Sugg and to Gay Pauley. Finally, for their ongoing help and support, thanks to editors Scott Person and Sara Froelicher, and editoral assistants Allison Abbott and Jennifer Warner, all of Thomson Learning.

—*Marcia Darvin Spada*

To The Student

In each chapter, you will find a variety of features and activities to help you understand and learn the material covered in this book. As you come to these in your reading, refer back to these instructions for using the features and completing the activities.

KEY TERMS

To prepare yourself for the information in the chapter, first look over the list of key terms at the beginning of each chapter. This will help focus your attention on important terminology throughout the chapter.

PUTTING IT TO WORK

In most chapters, you will be presented with questions and activities to stimulate your understanding and retention of the material you are studying. Some are practice problems involving filling out or identifying the sections of a sample real estate document; others are role-playing activities that involve answering a buyer or seller question. Instructions for each activity are given within the chapter, and the *Answer Key* at the end of the chapter contains possible responses to the activities.

YOU SHOULD KNOW

In most chapters, you will see small sections of boxed text. These boxes highlight either important key terms, laws, or concepts. The topics for this feature are chosen because of their special importance to your real estate career and also for the probability of these topics appearing on your exams. When studying for your exams, be sure to review the material in the "You Should Know" feature.

CASE STUDIES

Discussions of certain administrative hearings of the New York State Department of State, Division of Licensing Services, regarding alleged violations of license law, codified rules and regulations, or legal precedent in New York are found in several chapters. The events and determinations of these cases will help you understand how violations can occur. You will see how the Department of State (DOS), Division of Licensing Services, interprets certain behaviors on the part of licensees.

The facts described in each case study are from administrative hearings within DOS. The accused party is the respondent. DOS, as the party bringing forth the action, is the complainant. The complete text of the hearing is the decision. The decision of the hearing is divided into four sections:

1. The first section of the case deals with the allegations or complaints. These allegations are the reason the hearing was initiated. They deal with what the complainant (in these cases DOS) states the respondent might have done.
2. This second section deals with the findings of fact. This is a recital as to what the court believes to have happened.
3. The third section contains the conclusions of law. This section explains what violations were committed by the respondent and also includes the supporting case law to back up the determination.
4. The last section of the case is the determination of the court. This includes the penalty, if any, that is imposed upon the respondent for unlawful behavior.

IMPORTANT POINTS

Each chapter contains an *Important Points* list that summarizes the main points covered in the chapter. Review this list carefully and use it to help you determine what you need to study further.

CHAPTER REVIEW

Each chapter contains a *Chapter Review,* which is a self test to give you an opportunity to review the material you have learned. The answers appear at the end of each chapter. Your completed review will servc as a study guide and will help you prepare for your course and New York State licensing exam.

Chapter Reviews contain the following types of questions:

How Would You Respond? These questions are hypothetical situations that you may encounter in your real estate career. They are designed to stimulate thinking and discussion. Although we provide possible responses for these questions at the end of each chapter, no single response is the only "correct" answer. As you will see in your real estate career, each situation gives rise to a variety of responses.

Key Term Review and Multiple Choice Questions. These self-test questions test your understanding of the information you have studied, your retention of the important points covered in the chapter, and your ability to interpret the meaning of key terms. After studying the chapter and completing other learning activities, answer the key term and multiple choice questions and check your answers using the *Answer Key* provided at the end of the chapter.

REAL ESTATE MATHEMATICS

Understanding basic math is part of the New York syllabus. You will spend time in your course just working on math skills. Chapter 16 contains explanations for computing problems with regard to commissions, area and square footage, finance, closing costs, and ad valorem taxes, as well as practice problems. The *Chapter Review* in this chapter contains more practice math topics. The correct answers, along with the steps used to arrive at the correct answers, are given at the end of the chapter.

SAMPLE NEW YORK STATE LICENSING EXAM

After completing the chapters in the text and reviewing them with the chapter activities, you are ready to prepare for your class and state exams. This sample exam supplied in the appendix is diagnostic, meaning it will help you pinpoint areas in which you may need further study. It is divided into subject sections so that, once you have completed it and checked your answers in the *Answer Key,* you can see where you need review.

As you take the exam, make sure you know the meaning of each answer choice, even if it is not the correct answer. Alternate choices may be the correct answer for some other exam question.

A FINAL WORD

All of the activities are structured to help you learn and to allow you to self-test your understanding. Don't feel uncomfortable if at first you don't do as well as you think you should. For most students, this is new material, and it will take some time to absorb it. These activities can be completed individually, in small groups, or with the whole class participating, whichever seems most helpful for your particular class and instructor. Don't hesitate to do the activities more than once if you feel you need the practice. You will be gratified to see your proficiency level increase as you progress through the course!

New York Real Estate

for

SALESPERSONS

Third Edition

Introduction

KEY TERMS

Code of Ethics and Standards of Practice

listing contract

National Association of REALTORS® (NAR)

New York State Association of REALTORS® (NYSAR)

REALTOR®

Your Career in Real Estate

IN THIS CHAPTER Real estate plays an enormous role in national and local economies. The price for real estate is greater than that of virtually all other ownable assets. Many related industries and services profit through real estate, providing jobs and overall economic growth. The permanence of real estate makes it a desirable investment in the future. Which asset will hold its value or appreciate most for a buyer 10 years after purchase: a $30,000 vacant lot, a $30,000 car, or $30,000 worth of clothing and furniture?

As you study the topics in this textbook, you will begin to understand how they relate to one another and about their usefulness to you as a licensee. Your on-the-job experience, yet to come, will reinforce the information and applicability of your studies. This introduction answers some questions regarding real estate as a career and provides an overview of the real estate business.

YOUR CAREER IN REAL ESTATE

You may be thinking about a career in real estate because of the income you will receive—and this is a valid reason! If you are considering a career in sales, why not sell one of the biggest-ticket commodities on the market? You will also find out, however, that a career in real estate, whether part- or full-time, has many other benefits. You will meet interesting, dedicated professionals like yourself; you will gain the satisfaction of helping people realize their dreams in both residential housing and commercial ventures. You will learn new things about yourself, professionally and personally. The following section addresses some typical questions. Further information about a career in real estate can be obtained from the Department of State (DOS), the New York State Association of REALTORS®, local boards of REALTORS®, real estate brokerage businesses located in your community, and at the place where you take your 45-hour course.

What do real estate salespersons do?

With a salesperson license, under the sponsorship and supervision of a licensed broker, you may perform a number of professional activities involving real property. For other people, you may:

- list and sell
- rent and manage
- exchange
- auction
- relocate

In addition to learning about specific real estate activities, you will study other related challenges. For example, you might seek a management position or become a broker and own your own business. Eventually, you may desire to teach and train others. You can become active in your local and state boards where there are political action, education, and other community service opportunities. A real estate career is also enticing to people from diverse backgrounds because it encompasses such a variety of skills, talents, and interests.

What is the difference between a salesperson and a broker?

In most cases, you must work as a salesperson full-time for a minimum of one year before you can obtain a broker license. Salespersons may work only under the sponsorship and supervision of a licensed broker. Brokers may operate their own company or work under the supervision of another broker, as salespersons do. Some individuals choose to become brokers because they want to be owners, partners, or shareholders in a brokerage company, and New York law prohibits salespersons from holding such positions.

If I have real estate experience, can I become a broker without first becoming a salesperson?

Yes. If you have a total of two or more years' experience as an investor, developer, or a property manager, or a combination of these and other real estate experiences, you may apply for a broker license without first becoming a salesperson. You may also combine your salesperson experience of less than one year with other real estate experience to equal the two-year requirement. It is up to the DOS, the regulatory agency in New York that oversees the licensure process, to evaluate your experience and determine your eligibility for broker licensure.

What is a typical income for a beginning real estate salesperson?

Your income as a real estate salesperson depends on several factors: where you work, for what type of company you work, whether you work part- or full-time, whether you have prior real estate experience, as well as your motivation and the scope of your expertise. If you work full-time, you will typically make more money than a part-timer. During the first year, a full-time salesperson might earn an average of $12,000 to $15,000. Part-timers often average $10,000 to $12,000. It usually takes about six months before you realize your first income in real estate. The harder you work and the more you put into it, whether you work part-time or full-time, the more money you will make! Some highly motivated part-timers can earn more than a less-motivated full-timer. Do not feel limited by these figures. Numerous real estate salespersons working *either* full- or part-time have earned as much as $40,000 to $50,000 during their first year in business.

Will I be paid a commission or a flat fee?

No set fee exists for selling a property or for representing a buyer. Brokers typically are paid a certain percentage of a property's selling price. Salespersons involved in the transaction then receive a portion of that percentage from their broker. Since no set percentages exist either, your income may vary from transaction to transaction and from place to place. Sellers or buyers may also make agreements for compensation to be paid as a flat fee. You should discuss this with the broker for whom you intend to work.

Must I have some background in real estate to be licensed?

Most people who obtain a real estate license for the first time do not have a prior real estate background, and it is not necessary. A real estate career appeals to a wide range of people, including career changers, people already employed who want extra income and are willing to work two jobs, retirees, and students. The advantage of the real estate field for many people is that their schedule is flexible and they do not have to give up their current job or studies.

Whether you are a household engineer or have worked outside the home, you can still realize another income in real estate. The 45-hour qualifying course introduces you to the laws you must follow. The real estate brokerage firm you select trains you in its marketing, sales, rental, or other activities. The skills required are often similar to those needed for any type of profession: perseverance, hard work, and the desire to succeed.

How do I get started?

The best way to launch your real estate career is first to take the 45-hour qualifying course. This course is required for anyone who wishes to obtain a real estate license in New York. Even if you have real estate experience and plan to pursue earning a broker license, you still must first take the 45-hour salesperson qualifying course. (To obtain a broker license, you must also complete the 45-hour broker qualifying course.) The course is offered throughout New York State at colleges, real estate boards, and proprietary schools. You can obtain a list of approved institutions where the course is taught by calling DOS at (518) 474-4429.

How do I select a broker?

When you plan to take the 45-hour qualifying course, you might also use this period as an ideal time to think about selecting a broker for whom you wish to work. Your local newspaper often carries ads that seek to recruit real estate salespersons. Also, explore your neighborhood and research the real estate offices in your community. Many people prefer to work near where they live because they are familiar with their neighborhood and its people. It is usually easy to find a broker who will sponsor you. When interviewing with brokers, you will want to ask them about how many hours they expect you to work in the office (floor duty); whether you can work full- or part-time; what start-up fees are required; whether they have a training program and the cost of the training, if any; what type of supervision and leads they will provide to help you begin; and the nature of the commission or fee arrangement.

What are the startup expenses?

To become a real estate salesperson, you must incur some expenses to get started. The fee for the 45-hour qualifying course varies from place to place but can cost $250 or more. In some cases, sponsoring brokers will pay for or reimburse the new licensee for the 45-hour course. In addition, it currently costs $15 to take the New York State exam and $50, payable to New York State, for your license, which is renewable every two years. Depending on where you live and the firm you choose, you will generally have to pay yearly national, state, and local board dues and multiple listing services fees. Each county or specific area has a multiple listing service that identifies the inventory of properties for sale by all the member brokerage firms. (Not all brokers belong to a real estate board or multiple listing service, but most do.) Your brokerage firm also may require you to pay for training and for certain items such as a calculator or business cards.

Do I have to pass an exam?

New York State requires that you pass two exams to obtain a real estate license. First, all 45-hour qualifying courses must include an exam. New York also requires you to pass a multiple-choice state exam. Your 45-hour qualifying course will prepare you for both exams.

Do I need a separate license for residential and commercial sales?

Your New York license allows you to sell both residential and commercial properties. Most people, especially those who do not have a prior real estate background, begin in residential sales. Commercial transactions often involve the analysis of complicated income and operating expense statements and other related information. Most beginning real estate salespersons do not have sufficient experience and education to start out in commercial sales. If your goal is to work in commercial sales, you might wish to seek out a mentor in the field to help you learn this end of the business.

What are related career opportunities in the real estate profession?

In addition to residential, commercial, industrial, and farm brokerage, real estate-related activities include property management, appraisal, government service, land development, urban planning, mortgage financing, syndication, and counseling. Many other types of businesses are also related to real estate, including title search and abstract companies, and those in construction, insurance, renovating, and remodeling.

THE REAL ESTATE BUSINESS

The business of real estate is *big business*—big because of the number of people it touches and because of the money it generates. For most people, buying and selling real estate represents the most significant monetary transactions of their lives. The sale of real estate, known as *real estate brokerage,* is organized at local, state, and national levels. Various real estate organizations promote and police the real estate business, while fostering professionalism and specialization.

National Association of REALTORS®

The largest association is the **National Association of REALTORS®** (NAR), first organized in 1908. To be a full member of this association, a person must be licensed in an individual state to sell real estate and must join the local board, which is a member of the **New York State Association of REALTORS® (NYSAR),** which in turn is a member of NAR. In most areas, this organization is called the Board or Association of REALTORS®. To be an affiliate member of the NAR, a person must hold a job closely affiliated with the real estate business, such as an attorney, a lender, or an abstractor. Only members of the NAR are REALTORS®. The term REALTOR® is a registered trademark owned and controlled by the NAR, indicated by the symbol ® that accompanies every use of the term. A **REALTOR®** is a professional in real estate who subscribes to a strict set of rules known as the **Code of Ethics and Standards of Practice,** a document that is available through NAR.

At the local level, the NAR promotes the real estate business. The local board or association may sponsor seminars on home ownership, civil rights, recycling, or other issues of public concern. The local board is also instrumental in policing the local real estate business. The goal of local NAR boards is to promote the highest ethical standards in the brokerage business. Also, cooperative agreements between brokers to share information, such as a multiple listing service (MLS), usually are established at the local level. At the state and national levels, the NAR lobbies in the state legislatures and Congress regarding matters specific to the real estate business.

The NAR has developed special institutes that provide designations and certifications in specialized areas of real estate. This function of the NAR has added to the professional image of the real estate business. Some of its institutes and designations are listed in Figure I.1. Holding a real estate license does not make one a REALTOR®. A licensee must apply to and join the association of REALTORS® to become a member and to be allowed to use the designation and logo. This process involves membership fees, orientation classes, and induction into the Board.

Association of Real Estate License Law Officials

Another organization that impacts on the real estate business is the Association of Real Estate License Law Officials (ARELLO). ARELLO was established in 1929 by license law officials on the state commissions to assist one another in creating, administering, and enforcing license laws. The first licensing laws were passed in 1917 in California. Through the efforts of ARELLO, each state now has licensing laws. In addition, each state has uniform legislation to protect the consumer's rights in cases of misrepresentation and fraud.

Real Estate Licensees

As discussed above, individuals who are licensed and engaged in the real estate business are not limited to selling residential real estate. People licensed to sell real estate may specialize in one or more of several fields, including farmland, multifamily dwellings, commercial, retail, or industrial sales. In the real estate market, properties have substantial exposure, particularly at the local level. Properties are available for inspection by prospective buyers, and these buyers have the opportunity to inspect several properties before making a final selection.

Effective real estate salespersons and brokers must have a clear picture of their role in a real estate transaction. Successful real estate licensees do not use hard-sell techniques. Rather, they are agents working diligently to assist buyers, sellers, and renters of real estate. Because a home's sale and purchase often involves the seller's most important financial asset and creates long-term financial obligations for the buyer, licensees have to be thoroughly knowledgeable and competent in their duties.

The Fundamentals of a Real Estate Transaction

The basic stages of a real estate transaction are the listing, the contract for sale, financing, and settlement (see Table I.1). Each is described briefly below and discussed in more detail in later chapters.

Listing Contract

A **listing contract** is *a contract in which a property owner employs a real estate firm to market a property.* The parties to the contract agree to various terms, including the price the property will sell for (list price) and the duration of the contract. Under this contract the real estate firm becomes the seller agent. Listings represent the inventory of a real estate brokerage and are the lifeblood of the business. With-

FIGURE I-1

Some of the many real estate institutes, societies, and councils, together with their related designations.

NATIONAL ASSOCIATION OF REALTORS®

REALTOR® Institute
- —Graduate, REALTOR® Institute (GRI)
- —Certified International Property Specialist (CIPS)

American Society of Real Estate Counselors (ASREC)
- —Counselor of Real Estate (CRE®)

Commercial-Investment Real Estate Institute (CIREI)
- —Certified Commercial-Investment Member (CCIM)

Institute of Real Estate Management (IREM)
- —Accredited Management Organization® (AMO®)
- —Accredited Residential Manager® (ARM®)
- —Certified Property Manager® (CPM®)

REALTORS® Land Institute (RLI)
- —Accredited Land Consultant (ALC®)

REALTORS® NATIONAL MARKETING INSTITUTE (RNMI®)
- —Real Estate Brokerage Council: Certified Real Estate Brokerage Manager (CRB®)
- —Residential Sales Council: Certified Residential Specialist (CRS®)

Society of Industrial and Office REALTORS® (SIOR®)
- —Professional Real Estate Executive (P.R.E.)

Women's Council of REALTORS® (WCR)
- —Leadership Training Graduate (LTC)

New York Association of REALTORS®

NATIONAL ASSOCIATION OF RESIDENTIAL PROPERTY MANAGERS

Residential Management Professional (RMP)
Master Property Managers (MPM)
Certified Residential Management Company (CRMC)

NEW YORK ASSOCIATION OF REALTY MANAGERS

Offers the New York Accredited Realty Manager (NYARM) designation recognized and approved by New York State Division of Housing and Community Renewal (DHCR) and the New York City Department of Housing Preservation and Development (HPD)

ASSOCIATED BUILDERS AND OWNERS OF GREATER NEW YORK (ABO)

Offers HUD-certified courses leading to the Registered in Apartment Management (RAM)

BOMI INSTITUTE

Offers education for professional property managers, facility managers, and building engineers

APPRAISAL INSTITUTE

MAI —Appraisers experienced in commercial and industrial properties
SRA —Appraisers experienced in residential income properties
SRPA —Appraisers experienced in valuation of commercial, industrial, residential, and other property
RM —Appraisers experienced in single-family dwellings and two-, three-, and four-unit residential properties (recognized but no longer given)
SREA —Appraisers experienced in real estate valuation and analysis (recognized but no longer given)

TABLE I.1
Steps in a real estate transaction.

Real estate transactions vary in complexity; however, all of them generally proceed through these basic steps:

Step 1	Listing	Real estate agent employed
Step 2	Contract of sale	Written offer and acceptance between buyer and seller
Step 3	Financing	Buyer obtains monies to purchase the property
Step 4	Closing	Deed delivered to buyer; seller paid; broker receives commission

out listings, a real estate firm is limited to marketing only the listings belonging to other real estate offices.

As agents for the seller, real estate brokers and their associates are empowered to act as negotiators to market the listed property. The listing contract does not authorize licensees to bind the seller in a contract to sell the property. The licensees' purpose is to find a ready, willing, and able buyer—a financially qualified buyer. The seller has the right to accept, reject, or counteroffer all offers to purchase.

With the advent of buyer brokerage, a listing may also be a contract between an agent and a purchaser.

Contract for Sale (Offer to Purchase)

A binding contract to buy and sell real property results from the written acceptance of a written offer to purchase or counteroffer. In presenting the offer, real estate licensees must always remember for whom they work. In many cases, real estate licensees work for the seller and are required to always give the seller the benefit of all information regarding the buyer's qualifications and the quality of the offer.

In other instances, however, real estate licensees establish a contract for services with the buyer called *buyer brokerage.* Under buyer brokerage, real estate agents must represent the best interests of the buyer rather than of the seller.

Financing

Most buyers do not have cash funds available to purchase property; therefore, most real estate transactions cannot be completed without financing. If the property cannot be financed, it usually cannot be sold.

Because financing is so important, real estate licensees need a day-to-day working knowledge of the various loan programs available through local lending institutions. Real estate licensees must continuously keep in touch with and establish cordial working relationships with lenders. Lenders are interested in placing the loan to make the sales transaction possible, but licensees have to know the lenders' guidelines in order to qualify the buyer and the property. New salespersons should personally call on local lenders to establish a mutually supportive relationship.

When institutional financing is difficult to obtain at favorable interest rates, real estate agents may need to look to the seller as the primary source of financing, typically for all or a portion of the purchase price in the form of a contract for deed or purchase money mortgage. Real estate licensees must also be familiar with existing mortgages that might restrict any type of seller financing.

Final Settlement

A real estate transaction is completed at closing or final settlement. At this time the buyer receives the deed, the seller receives compensation from the sale of the property, and the real estate broker receives the commission. Prior to closing, the real estate salesperson often coordinates various activities, including inspections, appraisals, and so on.

In New York, the real estate agent may attend the closing, along with an attorney, loan officer, buyer, and seller. In some states, although generally not in New York, the final settlement is handled by an escrow agent who, pursuant to written instructions, processes all closing documents and distributes the sale's proceeds.

In conclusion, real estate licensees' ability to serve the parties in a real estate transaction will determine their success. Real estate licensees can find satisfaction in their career both from serving the needs of others and from reaping financial rewards. Successful real estate licensees draw on their knowledge, practice ethical conduct in all dealings, and, above all, provide service to others.

IMPORTANT POINTS

1. The price for real estate is greater than that of virtually all other ownable assets. In addition, many related industries and services profit through the real estate industry.
2. With a salesperson license, under the sponsorship and supervision of a licensed broker, salespersons may perform a number of professional activities involving real property. For other people, they may list and sell, rent and manage, exchange, auction, or relocate.
3. If you have a total of two years' experience as an investor, a developer, a property manager, or a combination of these and other real estate experience, you may apply for a broker license without first becoming a salesperson.
4. No set fee exists for selling a property or for representing a buyer. Sellers or buyers may also make agreements for compensation to be paid as a flat fee.
5. The best way to launch your real estate career is first to take the 45-hour qualifying course. This course is required for anyone who desires a real estate license in New York. During the course period is an ideal time to think about selecting a broker for whom you wish to work.
6. The New York license covers the sale of both residential and commercial properties.
7. In addition to residential, commercial, industrial, and farm brokerage, real estate–related activities include property management, appraisal, government service, land development, urban planning, mortgage financing, syndication, and counseling.
8. The real estate business is organized at local, state, and national levels, primarily through the National Association of REALTORS®. The New York State Association of REALTORS® (NYSAR) is the umbrella board for all local real estate associations in New York.
9. A REALTOR® is a professional in real estate who subscribes to a strict set of rules known as the Code of Ethics and Standards of Practice, a document that is available through NAR.
10. The NAR has developed special institutes that provide designations and certifications in specialized areas of real estate.
11. Successful real estate licensees do not use hard-sell techniques. Rather, they are agents who work diligently to assist buyers, sellers, and renters of real estate.
12. The basic stages of a real estate transaction are the listing, the contract for sale, financing, and settlement.

Chapter 1

KEY TERMS

administrative discipline
apartment information vendor
apartment sharing agent
appraiser
Article 12–A
Article 78 proceeding
associate real estate broker
blind ad
commingling
escrow account
kickback
misdemeanor
mortgage banker
mortgage broker
multiple listing service
net listing
pocket card
real estate broker
real estate salesperson
reciprocity
revocation
sponsor
suspension
uniform irrevocable consent and designation form

LEARNING OBJECTIVES

Classroom hours: 3

1. Identify the three classifications of real estate licensure and the requirements for obtaining each license.
2. Identify the responsibilities of each license category.
3. Identify who is required to be licensed.
4. Identify the rules and regulations promulgated under Article 12–A of the Real Property Law.
5. Describe the responsibilities of the real estate salesperson to the broker.
6. Identify exemptions from licensure.
7. Identify the educational responsibilities of licensure.
8. Identify the procedures DOS uses to bring disciplinary proceedings against licensees.
9. Identify the causes of complaints that are generated by the public and DOS by reviewing specific cases.

License Law and Regulations

10. Identify basic guidelines on advertisements.
11. Describe some of the duties of unlicensed assistants and limitations of their functions.

IN THIS CHAPTER New York is committed to upholding high standards of efficiency and trustworthiness and to minimizing fraudulent practices within the real estate industry. The New York Department of State, Division of Licensing Services is the regulatory agency that oversees and administers the licensure process. *Most of the law pertaining to salespersons and brokers is contained in* **Article 12–A** *of the Real Property Law.*

Other New York laws, codified rules and regulations, and legal precedent also define the licensure process. New York's authority to require licensure falls under its *police power* to protect the health, safety, welfare, and property of its citizens. Part of the purpose of the license law is to protect the public from dishonest dealings by brokers and salespersons and from incompetency on the part of real estate licensees.

CATEGORIES AND RESPONSIBILITIES OF LICENSURE

In New York, three categories of licensure exist: real estate broker, associate broker, and salesperson. In most cases, individuals first receive licensure as salespersons. If they have experience in real estate prior to licensure, they can obtain a broker or an associate broker license without first becoming a salesperson. A license generally is required to transact real estate for another individual and for a fee, although certain exemptions are allowed. A **real estate broker** is *any person, partnership, association, or corporation who, for another, and for compensation of any kind, negotiates any form of real estate transaction*. Real estate brokers supervise and are responsible for the activities of associate brokers and salespersons in their employ. A broker's responsibility is to serve the public with honesty and competency.

An **associate real estate broker** is *a licensed real estate broker who may perform the acts described for a broker but chooses to work under the name and supervision of a licensed broker.* The licensed broker may be an individual, a corporation, partnership, or trade-name organization. The license allows an individual to retain broker status while functioning as a salesperson. Associate brokers follow the same guidelines applicable to salespersons except that, as an identifying term, the words "broker associate" must be used. A **real estate salesperson** is *any person who performs any of the acts set forth in the definition of a real estate broker for compensation of any kind, but does so only while associated with and supervised by a licensed broker who is his* **sponsor.** These definitions illustrate that a salesperson can engage in the real estate business only when associated with and supervised by a broker. Therefore, *a salesperson or an associate broker working for another broker cannot operate independently.* Both the associate broker and the salesperson have a duty to the broker and to the public to act with honesty and competency.

REQUIREMENTS FOR LICENSURE

The New York DOS, Division of Licensing Services governs the licensure process and has the power to approve all real estate licenses. DOS is also empowered to deny, fine, suspend, or revoke a salesperson or broker license if the licensee violates any license law.

Salesperson and broker applications may be obtained from DOS by phone, written request, or through its website: *http://www.dos.state.ny.us*. The applications may also be available from entities that are approved by DOS to give the 45-hour qualifying courses. Completed applications must be sent to the following address: New York Department of State, Division of Licensing Services, 84 Holland Avenue, Albany, NY 12208-3490. The automated telephone voice response system of DOS, which provides general and licensing exam information by category, may be accessed by calling (518) 474-4429. DOS representatives are available to answer individual questions. Figure 1.1 lists DOS offices that have information and applications available to the public.

General Requirements

English language requirement. Article 12–A specifically states that *applicants must demonstrate a fair knowledge of the English language.* Dictionaries and other language aids are not available during the licensing exam. However, arrangements can be made to assist individuals who have hearing or visual impairments. DOS must be notified in advance to make such arrangements.

Citizenship requirement. Applicants for the broker license must be U. S. citizens or lawfully admitted permanent residents. A permanent resident is one who has the status of having been lawfully accorded the privilege of residing permanently in the United States as a non-citizen in accordance with immigration laws. Salespersons may fall into one of four categories: citizenship status; permanent residency; a work authorization card obtained from the Immigration and Naturalization Service; or a work permit that may be obtained by individuals who are sponsored by their employers.

Certificate of Relief from Disabilities. Individuals who have been convicted of a felony, either in New York or elsewhere, must show evidence of an Executive Pardon, a Certificate of Good Conduct, or Certificate of Relief from Disabilities in order to be eligible for licensure. A *felony* is any serious crime above a misdemeanor and is gen-

FIGURE 1.1 Locations of the Department of State's Division of Licensing Services offices.

84 Holland Avenue Albany, NY 12208-3490	Veterans Memorial Highway Hauppauge, NY 11788-5501
164 Hawley Street Binghamton, NY 13901-4053	123 Williams Street New York, NY 10038-3813
65 Court Street Buffalo, NY 14202-3471	333 East Washington Street Syracuse, NY 13202-1428

erally punishable by imprisonment. This certificate is an order from a court to release a convicted felon from certain prohibitions imposed because of a past crime.

Age requirement. A broker applicant must be at least 19 years old; a salesperson applicant must be at least 18 years old.

Education and Experience Requirements

To obtain a salesperson license, one must successfully complete a New York-approved 45-hour qualifying course, pass the New York licensing exam, and obtain broker sponsorship. Broker licensure involves the successful completion of 90 hours of approved qualifying education (including the salesperson qualifying course), passage of the New York broker exam, and demonstration of either one year's experience as a salesperson, two years' equivalent real estate experience, or a combination of the two. An associate broker applicant must obtain broker sponsorship. All broker applicants must complete the New York State-approved 45-hour broker qualifying course prior to licensure *and must have first completed the 45-hour salesperson qualifying course.* A high school diploma is not required for licensure. However, an applicant who became a salesperson prior to November 1, 1979 may use 45 hours of continuing education instead of the salesperson qualifying course together with the broker qualifying course to fulfill requirements for broker licensure.

You Should Know

The New York licensure examination

All applicants must pass the New York exam to obtain a license. The exam is walk-in and you can take it at any time during the licensure process; however, it is preferable to take the exam upon completing the qualifying courses. The passing grade for both exams is 70 percent. You will need two #2 pencils, a silent calculator, a photo ID, and a check or money order payable to the New York Department of State for $15. A government issued photo ID includes a driver's license, state issued identification (example: non-driver ID), military ID, U.S. passport, U.S. INS issued ID, or certificate of U.S. citizenship. You will also be thumb printed before the exam. Cash is not accepted at the exam site. You will receive the exam results within approximately two weeks. If you do not pass, you may take the exam as many times as necessary; the $15 fee will be charged each time. Exam applicants for both salesperson and broker licenses who take the test at the Albany, New York City, and Rochester test centers may receive the results and obtain their license on the same day if they bring their completed applications with them to DOS. Applications for broker licenses will be reviewed for compliance with the license law, including education, experience, business name approval, and so on. If the information is acceptable, a broker license will be issued. For applicants who do not become licensed immediately, the state exam pass grade is valid for two years.

Figure 1.2 lists the names and addresses of the 13 statewide test centers. Contact DOS for a current schedule of exam dates and times. Table 1.1 summarizes New York's licensure requirements.

45-Hour Qualifying Course

The topics and duration of time devoted to each subject in the 45-hour qualifying courses are mandated by DOS and are uniform throughout the state. Each qualifying course includes an exam.

Topics included in the salesperson qualifying course are: License Law and Regulations (3 hours), Law of Agency (8 hours), Real Estate Instruments and Estates and

Interests (10 hours), Real Estate Finance (Mortgages) (5 hours), Land Use Regulations (2 hours), Introduction to Construction (3 hours), Valuation Process (3 hours), Human Rights and Fair Housing (4 hours), Environmental Issues (3 hours), Real Estate Mathematics (3 hours), and Real Estate Salesperson–Independent Contractor/Employee (1 hour).

Topics included in the broker qualifying course are: The Broker's Office–Operation, Management and Supervision (10 hours), Real Estate Agency Disclosure (Review) (4 hours), Real Estate Finance II (5 hours), Real Estate Investments (5 hours), General Business Law (5 hours), Construction and Development (4 hours), Conveyance of Real Property and Title Closing and Costs (Review) (3 hours), Real Estate Property Management (5 hours), Taxes and Assessments (2 hours), and Local Concerns (2 hours).

The Bureau of Educational Standards within the New York Division of Licensing Services oversees the approval of all qualifying and continuing education courses for real estate licensure. The bureau will accept a degree in real estate in lieu of the qualifying courses; also acceptable is a course taken in New York or elsewhere if the bureau deems it equivalent in form and content to its qualifying courses. Applicants who wish to apply for equivalency credit should send official transcripts indicating successful completion of coursework and an outline of the course to the Bureau of Educational Standards at the Holland Avenue address given earlier for DOS.

FIGURE 1.2 Salesperson and broker walk-in examination sites.

ALBANY
State Office Building
84 Holland Avenue, "A" Wing Basement
Albany, NY 12208-3490

BINCHAMTON
State Office Building
44 Hawley Street, 15th Floor
Binghamton, NY 13901-4053

BUFFALO
State Office Building
65 Court Street
Main Floor Hearing Room, Part 5
Buffalo, NY 14202-3471

FRANKLIN SQUARE
VFW Hall Basement
68 Lincoln Road
Franklin Square, NY 11010

HAUPPAUGE
State Office Building
250 Veterans Highway
Basement Conference Room 1
Hauppauge, NY 11788-5501

NEWBURCH
Newburgh Orange Ulters BOCES
Adult Education Center
Federal Building
471 Broadway, 2nd Floor
Newburgh, NY 12550-5318

NEW YORK CITY
123 Williams Street, 19th Floor
New York, NY 10038-3813

PLATTSBURCH
Clinton County Community College
Lake Shore Drive, Route 9 South
Plattsburgh, NY 12901

ROCHESTER
Monroe Developmental Center
620 Westfall Road
Rochester, NY 14604-1197

SYRACUSE (broker only)
State Office Building
333 East Washington Street, Main Floor,
Hearing Room A
Syracuse, NY 13202-1418

SYRACUSE (salesperson only)
American Postal Workers Union Hall
407 East Taft Road
North Syracuse, NY 13212-3734

UTICA
State Office Building
207 Genesee Street, 1st Floor, Room 110C
Utica, NY 13501-2812

WATERTOWN
State Office Building
Department of State Office
317 Washington Street, 11th Floor
Watertown, NY 13601-3744

TABLE 1.1
Licensure requirements.

REQUIREMENT	SALESPERSON	BROKER/ASSOCIATE BROKER
Age	at least 18	at least 19
Citizenship/permanent residency	yes/other choices	yes
Qualifying course	45 hours	90 hours
Experience	none	1 year as salesperson or 2 years' equivalent
Fee and term of licensure	$50 every 2 years	$150 every 2 years
Number of exam questions	50	100
Continuing education	22.5 hours every 2 years	22.5 hours every 2 years
Broker sponsorship	yes	associate broker only

DUTIES THAT REQUIRE LICENSURE

Types of real estate transactions for others and for compensation of any kind covered under real estate licensure include:

1. listing or offering to list real estate for sale
2. selling or offering to sell real estate
3. purchasing or offering to purchase real estate
4. negotiating the exchange of real estate
5. leasing, renting, or offering to rent real estate
6. negotiating or attempting to negotiate a commercial mortgage. A residential mortgage loan must be negotiated by a person or entity licensed by the New York Banking Department as a mortgage broker in accordance with Article 12–D, Section 590 of the Banking Law
7. selling or purchasing real estate at an auction
8. arranging and coordinating for a fee the relocation of commercial or residential tenants from buildings or structures that are to be demolished, rehabilitated, remodeled, or somehow structurally altered (done by a *tenant relocator*)
9. performing any of the above functions with regard to the *sale* of condominium and cooperative property. Licensed real estate brokers and salespersons who are not acting as *dealers* are not required to register with the Department of Law with respect to the sale of securities that constitute real estate cooperatives, condominiums, and interests in homeowners' associations. A dealer may be a *person, association, or corporation* who is the original owner for the first-time sale of these security interests to the public.
10. negotiating the sale or exchange of lots or parcels of land
11. negotiating the sale of a business for which the value of the real estate transferred is not merely incidental to the transaction, but is a significant part of it (if the transaction involves the sale of securities, state or federal laws governing the sale of securities must be adhered to)

Property owners are free to engage in real estate transactions on their own behalf without a license.

Exemptions to Licensure

Certain individuals, acting on behalf of various governmental agencies or in a private capacity, may perform those acts permitted to salespersons and brokers without obtaining a real estate license:

1. *Attorneys admitted to practice in the New York courts* are exempt from licensure. Although attorneys may act as brokers without obtaining a broker license, they must obtain a license *if they employ salespersons to work under their supervision.*
2. *Public officers* are also exempt while performing official duties. (Example: a condemnation proceeding in which New York acquires land, employing a state agency to undertake the proceeding.)
3. *Persons acting in any capacity under the judgment or order of a court* do not need a real estate license. These persons might include trustees in a bankruptcy, guardians, administrators, or executors. (Example: an executor may be empowered through a decedent's will to sell property included in the estate.) Trustees in a bankruptcy may also have the legal right to sell real property included in the bankruptcy.
4. *Tenants' associations and nonprofit corporations* are exempt from licensure. These agencies may be either residential neighborhood or rural preservation companies that are authorized in writing by the commissioner of the New York Department of Housing and Community Renewal or by the New York City Housing Authority to manage residential property owned by the state or the city. The agencies may also be appointed by a court to manage residential property.
5. *Building superintendents or maintenance workers* who perform tasks such as rent collection for one owner, company, or entity, do not require licensure, nor do persons employed and empowered by one owner to act on the owner's behalf with regard to various real estate transactions. (Example: an individual who works for one owner might be a property manager who runs an apartment complex or commercial enterprise.)

THE SALESPERSON APPLICATION

In most cases, salesperson applicants obtain the form from the school or organization where they complete the 45-hour qualifying course. (The school must certify directly on the application that the applicant successfully completed the course.) The salesperson application must include the following: the name and address of the applicant, the name and principal business address of the broker with whom the salesperson is to be associated, a statement of association and signature by the sponsoring broker, and a certificate of completion indicating that the applicant has successfully completed the 45-hour salesperson qualifying course. This section of the application is signed and sealed by representatives of the agency that offers the course. Both the salesperson and broker applications contain a question as to whether the applicant is responsible for child support.

A finalized salesperson license application should include the following: the completed front of the form, including the name and address of the sponsoring broker and the child support statement; the completed back of the form, including certification that the 45-hour course has been completed, with the school's name, date of course completion, authorized signature by a school official, the school seal, the applicant's signature, and that of the sponsoring broker; the exam "Passed" slip; and a $50 check made out to the New York Department of State. The salesperson application is shown in Figure 1.3.

THE BROKER APPLICATION

The broker application details all necessary information for receiving a broker or an associate broker license. It is useful to obtain a current application from DOS to apply for this licensure.

The application is divided into several parts. After filling in their name, home address, and business name and address, applicants then provide background data regarding age, criminal offenses, if any, and whether they are an attorney, a corporate

FIGURE 1.3 The salesperson license application.

OFFICE USE ONLY	CLASS	KEY	UNIQUE ID NUMBER	CASH NUMBER	FEE
	4				$ 50

E W S ____ / ____ B ____ / ____

Real Estate Salesperson Application

Read the Instruction Sheet for details before completing this application form. You must answer each question and TYPE or PRINT responses in ink.

APPLICANT'S LAST NAME | FIRST NAME | M.I. | SUFFIX

HOME ADDRESS -NUMBER AND STREET (P.O. BOX MAY BE ADDED TO ENSURE DELIVERY) | APT/UNIT

CITY | STATE | ZIP+4 | COUNTY

SPONSORING BROKER OR FIRM NAME (EXACTLY AS IT APPEARS ON THE BROKER'S LICENSE)

OFFICE ADDRESS WHERE APPLICANT WILL BE PERMANENTLY STATIONED - NUMBER AND STREET

CITY | STATE | ZIP+4 | COUNTY

DAYTIME TELEPHONE NUMBER ( ) | SOCIAL SECURITY NUMBER OR FEDERAL ID NUMBER (*SEE PRIVACY NOTIFICATION*)

E-MAIL ADDRESS (IF ANY)

1 BACKGROUND DATA

1. What is your date of birth? ______________

YES **NO**

2. Have you ever been convicted in this state or elsewhere of any criminal offense that is a misdemeanor or a felony? . . . . ____ ____

   ➔**IF "YES,"** submit a written explanation giving the place, court jurisdiction, nature of the offense, sentence and/or other disposition. You must provide a copy of the accusatory instrument (e.g., indictment, criminal information or complaint) and a Certificate of Disposition. If you possess or have received a Certificate of Relief from Disabilities, Certificate of Good Conduct or Executive Pardon, you must provide a copy of same.

3. Are there any criminal charges (misdemeanors or felonies) pending against you in any court in this state or elsewhere? . . . . ____ ____

   ➔**IF "YES,"** you must provide a copy of the accusatory instrument (e.g., indictment, criminal information or complaint).

4. Has any license or permit issued to you or a company in which you are or were a principal in New York State or elsewhere ever been revoked, suspended or denied? . . . . ____ ____

   ➔**IF "YES,"** you must provide all relevant documents, including the agency determination, if any.

5. Have you ever applied for or been issued a real estate broker's or salesperson's license in this state? ____ ____

   ➔**IF "YES,"** in what year? ________ Under what name? ______________

   UID # (if applicable) ______________

DOS-0022 (Rev. 11/02) PAGE 1 OF 3

(continued)

FIGURE 1.3 Continued.

Real Estate Salesperson Application

2 Certification of Satisfactory Completion

(Name of School)

Real Estate Salesperson Course (Code) #S-________________

This certifies that ______________________ (Name of Student) has satisfactorily completed a 45-hour salesperson qualifying course in real estate approved by the Secretary of State in accordance with the provisions of Chapter 868 of the Laws of 1977; that attendance of the student was in compliance with the law and that a passing grade was achieved on the final examination. The course was completed on ________________.

Authorized Signature

X______________________ *Date* ____________

(School Seal)

3 Child Support Statement — *You must complete this section. If you do not complete it, your application will be returned.*

"X" A or B, below

I, the undersigned, do hereby certify that (You *must* "X" A or B, below):

A. [ ] **I am not under obligation to pay child support**. (SKIP "B" and go directly to **Applicant Affirmation**).

B. [ ] I am under obligation to pay child support (You must "X" any of the four statements below that are true and apply to you):

[ ] I do *not* owe four or more months of child support payments.

[ ] I am making child support payments by income execution or court approved payment plan or by a plan agreed to by the parties.

[ ] My child support obligation is the subject of a pending court proceeding.

[ ] I receive public assistance or supplemental social security income.

4 Applicant Affirmation — I affirm, under the penalties of perjury, that the statements made in this application are true and correct. I further affirm that I have read and understand the provisions of Article 12-A of the Real Property Law and the rules and regulations promulgated thereunder.

Applicant's Signature

X______________________ *Date* ____________

DOS-0022 (Rev. 11/02) PAGE 2 OF 3

(continued)

FIGURE 1.3 Continued.

Real Estate Salesperson Application

5 Association Statement — I am sponsoring this application in accordance with the Real Property Law, §441.1(d).

Broker Name ______________________ Date ____________

Broker Signature ______________________

Broker Print Name ______________________

Please remember to include with this application any required explanations and statements along with your application fee (payable to NYS Department of State).

It is important that you notify this division of any changes to your business address so you can continue to receive renewal notices and any other notifications pertinent to your license.

DOS-0022 (Rev. 11/02) PAGE 3 OF 3

Source: New York Department of State.

officer, and so on. Associate broker applicants must have their sponsoring broker sign the application; all applicants must sign an applicant affirmation.

Supplements detailing the accumulated points applicants earn for experience follow. (The point system is also discussed later in this chapter.) Salesperson experience applicants must fill out Supplement A and provide relevant employment history. The salesperson's sponsoring broker at the time she attained the experience must verify the information and sign the application. Supplement B is completed by individuals claiming equivalent experience in general real estate along with information about relevant employment history; Supplements A, B, and C are filled out by applicants claiming combined salesperson and general real estate experience.

Although applicants do not have to submit proof of experience with the application, DOS reserves the right to investigate applicants prior to or after licensure. It is particularly important that salespersons take note of the *scope* of the broker application. *All salespersons should keep detailed chronological records of all of their real estate activity so that this material will be available if they decide to become a broker.*

A completed broker application should include the following: the completed application form (incomplete applications will be returned); original certificate of completion for the 45-hour qualifying courses (salesperson applicants need not submit salesperson certificates of completion since these documents are already on file with DOS); D/B/A, corporate, or partnership certificates if applicable; the "Passed" broker exam slip, and a check made out to DOS for $150.

Classes of Licensure for Brokers

Before applying for a broker license, applicants must decide the *class* of licensure they wish to obtain. DOS offers several classes of licensure for brokers.

Individual broker (Class 35). This class is for individuals who will be doing business under their individual name *only.* For this license, brokers may add the words "Licensed real estate broker" after their name for use on signage, business cards, or other forms of advertising. This class of licensure does not allow the brokers to represent themselves as being associated with any firm or company. Even though brokers may be licensed in their own names, they still must have a business address even if the business is operated from their homes. Home offices, however, must comply with zoning requirements as to use and signage (discussed later).

Associate broker (Class 30). Individuals applying for an associate broker license must be sponsored by a broker and therefore must have their supervising broker sign the association statement contained in the broker application.

Trade-name broker (Class 37). Trade-name brokers conduct business as a sole proprietorship, using a name other than their personal name. A Certificate to Do Business Under an Assumed Name (D/B/A Certificate) must be filed with the county clerk in the county where the applicant does business. For example, the certificate might state: *Alinda Rodriquez doing business as (d/b/a) Own Your Home Realty.* A copy of the business certificate must be submitted with the application.

Partnership broker (Class 33). A partner or partners in a partnership may apply for the broker license under the partnership name. Each partner who wishes to be licensed as a real estate broker must file an application and individual fee. A partnership certificate must be filed with the county clerk in the county where the business is located, and a copy of the certificate must be filed with the application.

Corporate broker (Class 31). An officer of a corporation may be issued a license to conduct business as a real estate brokerage under a corporate name. A copy of the corporate filing receipt must be submitted with the application for new corporations only. Each officer of a corporation or member of a co-partnership who is involved in any form of the real estate brokerage must be licensed as a broker. Salesperson licenses are not issued to officers of corporations or members of co-partnerships. Salespersons and associate brokers may not be principals in the brokerage firm and may not own voting stock in the licensed brokerage corporation.

Limited liability company (LLC) or limited liability partnership (LLP) (Class 49). A member or manager of an LLC or LLP who meets the qualifications for licensure, may be issued a license to conduct real estate brokerage under the LLC or LLP name. Applicants must be a member or manager prior to licensing. New limited liability companies *only* must file a copy of the articles of organization with the Division of Corporations or the company filing receipts must be submitted with the broker application.

Individuals who are not licensed brokers *can* be principals in real estate brokerage firms. They cannot, however, perform any of the duties allowed by licensure; for example, listing and selling real estate for others. Unlicensed principals of a brokerage corporation may hold up to 100 percent shares of voting stock; however, at least one of the corporate principals must be a licensed real estate broker.

All business names, including trade, partnership, and corporate names, must first be submitted for approval in writing to DOS, Division of Licensing Services. Submitting this information must be done prior to filing a certificate of partnership and/or incorporation. Established business names that will be submitted for licensure must also go through the same clearance process. In the case of a new corporation, once a corporate name is cleared by the Division of Licensing, the corporation must be set up. Name clearance is also required by DOS, Division of Corporations. Once the name is cleared, the corporate papers may be filed with New York Department of State, Division of Corporations, 41 State Street, Albany, NY 12231, (518) 473-2492.

The Point System

DOS has implemented a point system to clarify real estate experience required for a broker license. A certain number of points is allotted for various types of experience. For example, 250 points are allotted for the sale of a single-family residence, a condominium, a cooperative unit, a multifamily dwelling (two to eight units), or a farm (under 100 acres). The applicant must multiply the allotted points in each category by the number of completed transactions per category, then total the points from each category. *Experience for a broker license may be obtained through one type of experience only, such as residential sales; or through a variety of experiences, such as residential and commercial sales, property management, rentals, and leasing.* The three types of acceptable experience are one year as a salesperson and the accumulation of 1,750 points; two years' equivalent experience in general real estate and the accumulation of 3,500 points; and combined experience, that includes work as a salesperson and general real estate activity as well as the accumulation of 3,500 points. Figure 1.4 shows the broker point system. For the combined experience licensure, the applicant multiplies by two the experience gained as a salesperson. (Salesperson experience requires only half the time in the business as equivalent experience.)

MAINTAINING A LICENSE

All licensees are expected to be familiar with license law and rules and regulations. If DOS officials deem that a licensee has violated some part of the license law, they do not accept ignorance of wrongdoing as an excuse.

FIGURE 1.4 The broker point system.

Category	*Point Value X*	*Number of Transactions Performed*	=	*Total Points Earned*
Residential Sales:				
1. Single Family, condo, co-op unit, multi family (2 to 8 unit), farm (with residence, under 100 acres)	250 X		=	
2. Exclusive listings	10 X		=	
3. Open listings	1 X		=	
4. Binders effected	25 X		=	
5. Co-op unit transaction approved by seller and buyer that fails to win Board of Directors approval	100 X		=	
Residential Rentals:				
6. Rentals or subleases effected	25 X		=	
7. Exclusive Listings	5 X		=	
8. Open Listings	1 X		=	
9. Property Management - Lease renewal	2 X		=	
- Rent collections per tenant/per year	1 X		=	
Commercial Sales:				
10. Taxpayer/Storefront	400 X		=	
11. Office Building	400 X		=	
12. Apartment Building (9 units or more)	400 X		=	
13. Shopping Center	400 X		=	
14. Factory/Industrial warehouse	400 X		=	
15. Hotel/Motel	400 X		=	
16. Transient garage/parking lot	400 X		=	
17. Multi-unit commercial condominium	400 X		=	
18. Urban commercial development site	400 X		=	
19. Alternative sale type transaction	400 X		=	
20. Single-tenant commercial condo	250 X		=	
21. Listings	10 X		=	
Commercial Leasing:				
22. New Lease - aggregate rental $1 to $200,000	150 X		=	
23. New Lease - aggregate rental $200,000 to $1 million	250 X		=	
24. New Lease - aggregate rental over $1 million	400 X		=	
25. Renewal - aggregate rental $1 to $200,000	75 X		=	
26. Renewal - aggregate rental $200,000 to $1 million	125 X		=	
27. Renewal - aggregate rental over $1 million	200 X		=	
28. Listings	10 X		=	
Commercial Financing (includes residential properties of more than four units):				
29. $1 to $500,000	200 X		=	
30. $500,000 to $5,000,000	300 X		=	
31. Over $5,000,000	400 X		=	
Miscellaneous:				
32. Sale vacant lots, land (under 100 acres)	50 X		=	
33. Sale vacant land (more than 100 acres)	150 X		=	
34. Other, must be fully explained	___ X		=	
Total Qualifying Points	➢			

Source: New York Department of State.

License and Pocket Card

When licensure is approved, DOS issues both a license and a pocket card. The broker license must be conspicuously displayed in the principal place of business and at branch offices at all times. A broker may not display an expired license. Salesperson licenses need not be displayed but must be stored in a safe and accessible place. Salespersons and brokers receive a **pocket card** *that specifies their name and business address.* The pocket cards of salespersons and of associate brokers also include the name and business address of the broker with whom they are associated. *Pocket cards must be carried at all times and shown on demand.* If desired, the pocket card may be laminated. If the card is lost or destroyed, DOS will issue a duplicate card for a $10 fee.

Change of Address, Status, or Name

If the broker moves a principal or branch office to a different address, the broker must notify DOS within five days. Failure to do so renders the broker subject to license suspension. It is prudent, in some cases, to have the location preapproved, especially if the location is in a cease and desist zone. Brokers must first cross out the former address on their license and the licenses and pocket cards of the salespersons and associate brokers who are employed by them, and the new address must be printed on all licenses and pocket cards. Then the broker must complete a broker change of address form and send it to DOS with a $10 fee. Each salesperson or associate broker affiliated with the broker must also submit a salesperson/associate broker change of address form and pay a $10 fee.

If salespersons or brokers decide to change the *status* of their license from, for example, associate broker to broker, the fee is $150. Changes of *name* may be filed for a fee of $50 for a salesperson and $150 for individual or company broker name changes. (Example: A woman who marries during a licensure term may wish to have her married name appear on the license.)

Fees, Branch Office Requirements, and Term of Licensure

A broker must pay a $150 fee and a salesperson a $50 fee for each licensure term. If a broker license is issued to a corporation or co-partnership, the officers or co-partners must also pay $150 for their individual licenses. Additional licenses for each branch office cost $150. Both the salesperson and the broker license must be renewed every two years. If licensees fail to renew by the expiration date that appears on their license, they have a two-year grace period from that expiration date during which they may renew. If applicants do not renew within this time period, DOS requires them to retake and pass the exam and complete continuing education requirements. Table 1.2 summarizes most of the fees that are charged by DOS for various services.

Termination or Change of Association

When salespersons or broker associates *terminate* association with their broker, the broker must forward a salesperson/associate broker *termination of association* form to DOS along with a $10 fee and return the license to the salesperson or associate/broker. If desired, the broker may send a letter to DOS stating the reason for termination.

To *change* association, the new sponsoring broker must send a salesperson/broker *change of association form* signed by the salesperson or associate broker and the new broker, to DOS along with a $10 fee. The salesperson or associate broker must cross out

TABLE 1.2

A summary of licensure fees. Most forms required for salespersons and brokers to do business may be downloaded from the DOS website.

LICENSURE	FEE
Salesperson license	$ 50
Associate broker/broker license	$150
Each broker branch office	$150
Exam fee	$ 15
Change of salesperson name	$ 50
Change of broker name or status	$150
Change of address	$ 10
Termination of association	$ 10
New association	$ 10
Duplicate license/pocket card	$ 10

the name and address of the former broker and print the name and address of the new broker on the front of the license. DOS will then issue new licenses and pocket cards.

Dual Licensure—Broker and Salesperson

Licensees may hold more than one license at a time. A separate application and fee must be submitted to DOS for each license. For example, a broker may hold two broker's licenses. A licensed broker may also become an associate broker with another firm. A salesperson or an associate broker can work under the association and supervision of more than one broker. Associate brokers and salespersons who wish additional licenses must submit a statement to DOS from each sponsoring broker indicating acknowledgment of each licensure.

Renewal Requirements and Responsibilities of Sponsoring Brokers

As discussed above, all real estate licenses are renewable every two years. Approximately one to two months before renewal, DOS sends the licensee a renewal application. Licensees may renew their licenses online at the DOS website using their registration number and a password obtained through calling the Department of State. If the licensee is a salesperson or an associate broker, the renewal application *must be signed by the broker, attesting to the fact that the licensee is sponsored by that broker.* The renewal application also asks if continuing education requirements have been completed. Although DOS does send the licensee the renewal application, it is still the licensee's responsibility to complete the renewal form and pay the appropriate fees *before* license expiration (see Table 1.2). A licensee who does not receive a renewal application should call DOS to obtain one.

You Should Know

Continuing education requirements

Unless exempt, licensees must complete the required *continuing education* courses within the required time frame. Licensees must successfully complete 22.5 hours of approved continuing education every two years upon license renewal. The salesperson qualifying course may not be used for the 22.5 hour continuing education requirement. Salespersons must complete an additional 22.5 hours of continuing education during their two-year license period. Salespersons may use the broker qualifying course for *one* two-year period to fulfill this requirement. New York allows alternative distance learning formats for continuing education such as online delivery, CD–ROM, and video cassettes. Check with your course provider for more information on these learning choices. Individuals *exempt* from completing continuing education requirements are licensed brokers who are engaged in the real estate business full-time and who have been licensed with no lapse in licensure for 15 years. The licensed broker need not have been a broker during the entire 15 years but could have been licensed as a salesperson for part of that time. Attorneys are also exempt from continuing education requirements.

Licensure of Nonresident Brokers and Salespersons

In order to be licensed in New York, salespersons and brokers who live in other states (nonresidents) must take the New York exam and work in or maintain an office in New York. Under reciprocity regulations, however, nonresident licensees desiring New York licensure who live in states that do *not* require New York salespersons and brokers to have an office in their state or pass their exam do not have to do so in New York. This arrangement is called **reciprocity.** New York has reciprocal licensure arrangements with

Arkansas	Broker only—two years licensure and current. (Business and Residence must be in Arkansas.)
Connecticut	Broker and Sales—current licensure only. (Business and Residence must be in Connecticut.)
Georgia	Broker and Sales—current licensure only (business and residence must be in Georgia). Must have obtained their license by passing Georgia exam.
Massachusetts	Broker only—two years licensure and current. (Business and Residence must be in Massachusetts.)
Nebraska	Broker and Sales—two years licensure and current. (Business and Residence must be in Nebraska.)
Oklahoma	Broker and Sales—two years licensure and current. (Business and Residence must be in Oklahoma.)
West Virginia	Broker and Sales—current licensure. (Business and Residence must be in West Virginia.)

FIGURE 1.5
New York reciprocity with other states.

seven other states. For a list of the states with which New York has reciprocity, see Figure 1.5. The states listed allow licensees from New York to obtain a nonresident license, and New York allows residents from these states to obtain licensure here in New York.

All nonresident applicants must adhere to and complete the following guidelines:

1. Maintain a current (dated within six months) certificate from the real estate authority where they obtained their license.
2. Submit a New York application with the appropriate fees.
3. Submit a signed **uniform irrevocable consent and designation form.** *This form gives the New York courts jurisdiction over unlawful actions of applicants who conduct business in New York and allows the courts to serve a summons or other legal documents on the New York secretary of state in place of personal service on the applicant.*
4. Applicants seeking a reciprocal salesperson's license must be sponsored by their home-state broker who must hold a current New York State broker's license.
5. Applicants seeking a corporate real estate broker license must file the corporation with the New York DOS, Division of Corporations, as a foreign corporation.
6. Broker applicants from nonreciprocal states must also submit Supplement B of the New York broker application, two character witness statements, a New York resident's reference, licensing requirements from the state where the broker is licensed, and real estate course transcripts.

OTHER LICENSES OR REGISTRATION RELATED TO REAL ESTATE

The following summarizes other types of licenses. None of them requires either a salesperson or broker license. However, individuals applying for a mortgage broker license may use their real estate broker license as qualifying experience. Licensed salespersons and brokers may hold these licenses in addition to their real estate license. Care must be taken, however, in the course of business, to not engage in activities that pose a conflict of interest between the duties inherent in each of the licenses.

An **apartment information vendor** is *an individual who, for a fee, engages in the business of furnishing information concerning the location and availability of residential real property, including apartment housing.* The housing may be rented, shared, or subleased. The license fee is $400 for a one-year term (branch office fee: $250) and the apartment information vendor must maintain a trust account in the amount of $5,000 plus an additional $2,500 for each additional office.

An **apartment sharing agent** is *an individual who, for a fee, arranges and coordinates meetings between the current owners of real property, including apartment housing, who wish to share their housing with others.* The license fee is also $400 per year for a one-year term (branch office fee: $250), and the apartment sharing agent must maintain a trust account in the amount of $2,500 plus a fee of $1,250 for each additional office. Like salesperson and broker licenses, licenses for apartment information vendor and apartment sharing agents are issued by the DOS, Division of Licensing Services.

An **appraiser** *estimates the value of real property.* Individuals who appraise properties related in any way to federal transactions in which the transaction value is $250,000 or more must have an appraisal *license* or *certification.* Four levels of licensure exist: (a) NYS Appraiser Assistant, for individuals who have little or no appraisal experience; (b) NYS Licensed Real Estate Appraiser; (c) NYS Certified Residential Appraiser; and (d) NYS Certified General Appraiser. Except for the appraiser assistant license, the other levels of licensure require two years of appraisal experience. DOS also oversees the appraisal licensure process. All levels of licensure require a $300 fee for a two-year term.

A bank is a type of institution that acts as a "general store" of money. It assists in obtaining and making loans and services customers with savings, checking, and other types of accounts. Banks offer credit cards, life insurance, and other services. Federal and state licensed banks that make mortgage loans are exempt from having to obtain a mortgage banker license. Other individuals or entities who make more than four mortgage loans per year must obtain a mortgage banker license.

A **mortgage banker** is *an individual or an entity licensed by the New York Banking Department to engage in the business of making residential mortgage loans.* Mortgage bankers, who are also called mortgage companies, make mortgage loans for the construction of housing and purchase of existing housing. They often specialize in FHA-insured loans and VA-guaranteed loans. A mortgage banker can act as a mortgage broker.

The requirements for a mortgage banker license are as follows: a net worth of at least $250,000; an existing line of credit of at least $1 million provided by a banking institution, insurance company, or similar credit facility approved by the superintendent of banking; the filing of a surety bond in the amount of $50,000 or the execution of a deposit agreement coupled with a pledged deposit of securities or other assets in the amount of $50,000; five years' experience making residential mortgage loans or conducting similar transactions; demonstration of good character; a background report, provided by a selection of agencies chosen by the banking department; a set of fingerprints; a $74 fingerprint fee; and a $1,000 investigation fee. The license is for a one-year term and costs $1,000. A surety bond or deposit agreement are monies held by a third party who promises to be liable for the payment of another person's debt. The surety bond or deposit agreement, in this case, is used by the Banking Department to reimburse improperly charged consumer fees or to cover banking department fees in the event of liquidation by the licensee.

A **mortgage broker** is *an individual or an entity registered by the New York Banking Department to engage in the business of soliciting, processing, placing, or negotiating residential mortgage loans.* A mortgage banker and a mortgage broker are quite different. A mortgage banker makes and services mortgage loans. A mortgage broker brings together a lender and a borrower for a fee paid by the borrower, just as a real estate broker brings together for a fee a buyer and seller of real property.

To apply for a mortgage broker registration, an applicant must have good standing in the community and two years of credit analysis experience, underwriting experience, or other relevant experience or education. Licensed New York real estate brokers and attorneys do not have to demonstrate their experience. Licensed salespersons must have actively participated in the residential mortgage business for two years. The application also requires a credit report provided by a selection of agencies chosen by the Banking Department, a set of fingerprints, a $74 fingerprint fee, and a $500 investigation fee. The license is for a one-year term and the registration fee is $500 per term. Individuals employed by either licensed mortgage bankers or mortgage brokers are not required to have a license themselves. For further information and an application for either of the above, contact the Banking Department, State of New York, 2 Rector Street, New York, NY 10006-1894; (212) 709-5574 or access an application online: *http://www.banking.state.ny.us*. Table 1.3 shows other licenses related to real estate.

DOS REGULATIONS

The laws governing real estate licensees are a combination of laws in Article 12–A of the Real Property Law, other sections of the Real Property Law, codified DOS rules and regulations, and other areas of law in New York, such as agency, contract, torts, and human rights laws.

Business Sign

Brokers must post a sign conspicuously outside their place of business that is easily readable from the sidewalk. The sign must include the broker's name and business address and indicate that the individual or corporation is a licensed real estate broker. If the brokerage office is located inside a building where the sign would not be visible from the street, the sign must be posted in the building directory where the names of businesses are displayed and it must include the broker's name and the words "licensed real estate broker." In many towns and municipalities, various zoning ordinances exist that prohibit or restrict signage and also designate certain areas for either residential or business use, but not both. A broker is not allowed to violate license law in order to comply with local zoning ordinances and, conversely, a broker may not violate zoning laws to comply with the license law.

PUTTING IT TO WORK

Jeannine decides that her house, that includes a den in the front room with a picture window facing the street, would make an excellent brokerage office. She discovers two problems, however. First, her town zoning ordinances will not allow her to put a sign on the front lawn or in her picture window indicating that she is a licensed real estate broker. Second, her house is in a neighborhood zoned for residential use only. Although she applied for a variance for both of the above problems and none of the neighbors complained about her proposed project, the variance was denied. In short, Jeannine's plans to open a brokerage firm in her home failed.

TABLE 1.3
Other licenses related to real estate.

LICENSE	NYS REGULATORY AGENCY	TERM	FEE
Apartment information vendor	Department of State	1 year	$ 400
Apartment sharing agent	Department of State	1 year	$ 400
Appraiser licensure/certification	Department of State	2 years	$ 300
Mortgage banker	Banking Department	1 year	$ 1,000
Mortgage broker	Banking Department	1 year	$ 500

Compensation and Fee Splitting

Salespersons may not accept any compensation except from their sponsoring brokers. Brokers may share compensation only with salespersons employed by them or with other New York brokers and brokers from another state. Brokers may, however, share compensation with individuals who are exempt from the license law, for example, attorneys.

Kickbacks

If brokers improperly pay any part of a compensation to anyone who is not licensed or who is not exempt from the license law, they are in violation of the license law. This payment is called a **kickback.** An example of a kickback is a situation where a broker pays an unlicensed person for procuring a listing.

Lawsuits for Commissions

An unlicensed person, co-partnership, or corporation cannot bring about a lawsuit to collect compensation for real estate services rendered because only a licensed real estate broker or salesperson is entitled to a judgment by the courts.

Violations of Real Estate License Law

The following list summarizes possible violations of real estate law in New York:

1. Making a material misstatement in the application for a license. Examples include not checking the appropriate spaces that ask about age, criminal records, or previous license revocations.
2. Committing fraud or fraudulent practices. *Fraudulent practices* are acts meant to deceive or misrepresent that result in giving one person an advantage over another. One example is if a broker does not disclose his knowledge of a persistent termite problem with the property. Another includes a broker who has knowledge of a new zoning variance allowing industrial activity in a residential neighborhood and not passing this information on to prospective home buyers.
3. Demonstrating untrustworthiness or incompetency to act as a real estate broker or salesperson.
4. Making any substantial and willful misrepresentations. It is illegal for a licensee to make an intentionally false statement regarding an important matter in a real estate transaction for the purpose of inducing someone to sign a contract. Although it is not the duty of the broker to verify all representations made by the owner, if the broker knows or has reason to know that the owner has made misrepresentations or has failed to disclose *material defects,* then the broker must make such misrepresentations known.

   A material defect is one that has:

   - a material adverse effect on the value of the property
   - materially and adversely impair the health or safety of the future of the occupants
   - significantly shorten or adversely affect the expected normal life of the premises, if not repaired, removed, or replaced

   Examples include leaky roofs, skylights, and windows; high levels of radon; a malfunctioning well or septic system; or malfunctioning wiring or heating.

   Moreover, if representations could be considered crucial to the sale, the broker has a duty to verify the accuracy of the representation.

   Under a new law, real estate licensees must inform their client-sellers of the obligation to provide a signed statement disclosing information regarding the condition and status of their residential one-to-four-unit property. The Property

FIGURE 1.6 Page 1 of a seller's property condition disclosure form.

NYS Department of State
Division of Licensing Services
84 Holland Avenue
Albany. NY 12208-3490
(518) 474-4429
www.dos.state.ny.us

Property Condition Disclosure Statement

Name of Seller or Sellers: ______________________________

Property Address: ______________________________

____

General Instructions:

The Property Condition Disclosure Act requires the seller of residential real property to cause this disclosure statement or a copy thereof to be delivered to a buyer or buyer's agent prior to the signing by the buyer of a binding contract of sale.

Purpose of Statement:

This is a statement of certain conditions and information concerning the property known to the seller. This Disclosure Statement is not a warranty of any kind by the seller or by any agent representing the seller in this transaction. It is not a substitute for any inspections or tests and the buyer is encouraged to obtain his or her own independent professional inspections and environmental tests and also is encouraged to check public records pertaining to the property.

A knowingly false or incomplete statement by the seller on this form may subject the seller to claims by the buyer prior to or after the transfer of title. In the event a seller fails to perform the duty prescribed in this article to deliver a Disclosure Statement prior to the signing by the buyer of a binding contract of sale, the buyer shall receive upon the transfer of title a credit of $500 against the agreed upon purchase price of the residential real property.

"Residential real property" means real property improved by a one to four family dwelling used or occupied, or intended to be used or occupied, wholly or partly, as the home or residence of one or more persons, but shall not refer to (a) unimproved real property upon which such dwellings are to be constructed or (b) condominium units or cooperative apartments or (c) property on a homeowners' association that is not owned in fee simple by the seller.

Instructions to the Seller:

a. Answer all questions based upon your actual knowledge.
b. Attach additional pages with your signature if additional space is required.
c. Complete this form yourself.
d. If some items do not apply to your property, check "NA" (Non-applicable). If you do not know the answer check "Unkn" (Unknown).

Seller's Statement:

The seller makes the following representations to the buyer based upon the seller's actual knowledge at the time of signing this document. The seller authorizes his or her agent, if any, to provide a copy of this statement to a prospective buyer of the residential real property. The following are representations made by the seller and are not the representations of the seller's agent.

GENERAL INFORMATION

1. How long have you owned the property? .... ______________
2. How long have you occupied the property? .... ______________
3. What is the age of the structure or structures? .... ______________
   Note to buyer – If the structure was built before 1978 you are encouraged to investigate for the presence of lead based paint..
4. Does anybody other than yourself have a lease, easement or any other right to use or occupy any part of your property other than those stated in documents available in the public record, such as rights to use a road or path or cut trees or crops? .... ☐ Yes ☐ No ☐ Unkn ☐ NA
5. Does anybody else claim to own any part of your property? *If Yes, explain below* .... ☐ Yes ☐ No ☐ Unkn ☐ NA

____

____

DOS-1614 (1/02) PAGE 1 OF 6

Source: New York Department of State.

Condition Disclosure Act, (Article 14 of the Real Property Law), requires that the disclosure statement (Figure 1.6) be provided to the buyer or buyer's agent prior to the seller's acceptance of the purchase offer. The statement includes 48 questions related to the property's condition, patent and latent defects, structure, and status with respect to occupancy and its location in a flood plain. Failure to provide the form to a buyer before the buyer signs the contract results in a $500 credit from the seller to the buyer at the closing.

5. Failing to provide adequate disclosure regarding any or all of the following: (a) if licensees purchase property listed by their firm, they must make their position clear to the seller; (b) if licensees buy or sell property for a client and they have an ownership interest, the licensees must disclose their interest to all parties. In addition, licensees must make clear their position regarding the party for whom they are acting in a residential real estate transaction—seller, buyer, or both. In certain transactions (discussed more fully in Chapter 2), licensees must have all prospective buyers and sellers read, understand, and sign specific disclosure forms mandated by Article 12–A explaining the position of each salesperson or broker in the real estate transaction.
6. Receiving compensation from more than one party in a real estate transaction without the knowledge and consent of all parties.
7. Negotiating the sale, exchange, or lease of any property with an owner or a lessor if the licensee knows that the owner or lessor has an existing written exclusive contract with another broker. A licensee also may not interfere with a lease or contract of sale that a principal has with another broker.
8. Offering a property for sale or lease without the authorization of the owner.
9. Placing a sign of any kind on a property without the consent of the owner.
10. Failing to deliver duplicate instruments relating to any type of real estate transaction in which the broker is a participant.

PUTTING IT TO WORK

Licensees must follow certain prescribed rules in handling purchase offers and other documents. Licensees must:

- Always give the seller a copy of the listing contract.
- Present all offers, whether they are written or not, to the seller. It is the seller's prerogative to accept or reject any offer.
- Immediately deliver duplicate copies to all parties who sign the documents.
- Provide the buyer and seller with copies of all documents executed by buyer, seller, or both. The buyer must receive a copy of the offer and both buyer and seller must receive copies of the executed contract. In addition, copies of any other documents such as options, contracts for deed, or contracts for lease, must be provided to the parties.

11. Accepting the services of any salesperson who is employed by another broker. A broker may not compensate another broker's salesperson without the knowledge of that salesperson's broker. The salesperson may not represent another broker without the knowledge and consent of the broker with whom the salesperson is associated.
12. Retaining listing information upon termination of association. If licensees terminate their association with a real estate broker, they must turn over all listing information obtained during their association with the broker whether the information was given to them by the broker, copied from the broker's records, or acquired by the licensee.

13. Being a party to an exclusive listing contract that contains an automatic continuation of the listing beyond the specified termination date. Listing contracts are renewed by the signing of a written renewal agreement. This agreement must be signed by the seller and the agent. If the property is listed through a *multiple listing service (MLS)* (described later in this chapter), the broker must notify MLS of the renewal.
14. Drawing up legal documents such as deeds or mortgages; giving an opinion as to the legal validity of any document, or the legal rights of others; performing a title examination; rendering an opinion as to the quality of the title. In essence, *a licensee may not perform any service that is performed by an attorney.* In all legal matters affecting buyers and sellers, the licensee should recommend that the parties retain the services of a competent attorney.

    In 1978, a landmark decision by the New York Appellate Division, *Duncan & Hill Realty, Inc. v. Department of State* (62 AD2d 690, NYS 2d 339) determined that real estate brokers may not insert detailed legal agreements into contracts and must alert buyers and sellers to see an attorney before signing a contract. In the Duncan & Hill case, the brokerage firm, which represented the seller, described the terms of a purchase money mortgage in a contract of sale. The court found that this activity constituted an unauthorized practice of law. The purchase form contained no warning alerting the parties that, when signed, the instrument became a binding contract. The form also did not caution the parties that it would be preferable for them to consult an attorney before signing.
15. Failing to account for and remit funds belonging to others that have come into the licensee's possession. *All brokers must maintain a separate trust* or **escrow account** *in a federally insured bank account.* The broker must deposit any monies as promptly as practicable. A broker need not have an interest-bearing account. If there is such an account, accrued interest may *not* be retained for the benefit of the broker. However, with the consent of all the parties to the transaction, this interest may be applied toward monies owed to the broker for the commission. Brokers are prohibited from **commingling** or *mixing the funds of others with their business or personal funds and are required to maintain adequate records regarding the deposit and disbursement of funds from their accounts.* A broker should have at least two accounts: an office escrow account for client deposits and an operating account for business expenses. If a broker uses deposit money which is not yet his, places it into the operating account, and spends it, he may be guilty of conversion. *Conversion* is the apportionment of other people's money from one use to another. In the above example, it is illegal and may be classified as a felony. Article 36–C of the General Business Law further clarifies that the broker need not establish a *separate* escrow account for each transaction deposit as long as he keeps adequate records of each individual deposit in the one separate escrow account.

    The General Business Law also addresses deposits for new residential construction. The vendor, for example, the builder, can either: (1) post a bond in the amount of the deposit with the chief fiscal officer in the locality where the property is located; or (2) establish a separate interest bearing account in the name of each of the vendees (purchasers) in the amount of the deposit. *Salesperson licensees are required to remit promptly to their supervising broker all funds belonging to others that come into their possession.*
16. Entering into a net listing contract. A **net listing** *occurs when a seller authorizes a broker to procure a specified amount for the property and then allows the broker to keep as a commission any money above the specified amount obtained from the sale.*
17. Discriminating because of race, creed, color, national origin, age, sex, disability, or familial or marital status in the sale, rental, or advertisement of housing or commercial space covered by law. (New York City has other discrimination restrictions, discussed in Chapter 13.) Licensees also are prohibited from engaging in the prac-

tice of *blockbusting;* that is, the solicitation or the sale or lease of property initiated because of a change in the ethnic composition of a neighborhood.

18. Failing to provide definitions of exclusive right to sell and exclusive agency listings. This requirement is necessary in the sale of one- to three-unit dwellings, but does not apply to condominiums and cooperatives. In all listing agreements the broker must provide a printed explanation of the difference between the two listings. The explanation must be initialed or signed by the homeowner. (See the exclusive right to sell agreement in Chapter 2, which depicts this explanation.)
19. Failing to provide a list of **multiple listing service** members. *A multiple listing service is a system that pools the listings of all member companies.* If the listing broker is a member of a multiple listing service, he must provide this list. In addition, the listing contract should give the homeowner the option of having all offers to purchase submitted through the listing or selling broker.
20. Failing to maintain records. In the sale or mortgage of one- to four-unit properties, brokers must maintain records of transactions for three years. Records must include the names and addresses of the seller, buyer, and mortgagee, if any; the purchase price and resale price, if any; the amount of deposit paid on the contract; and the commission paid to the broker or the gross profit realized by the broker if purchased by him for resale. Instead of other types of records, the broker can keep, for each transaction, a copy of the contract of sale; commission agreement; closing statement; and statement showing disposition of the proceeds of the mortgage loan.

Guidelines for Advertisements

Advertisements placed by real estate brokers must not in any way mislead the public. *All ads placed by a broker must indicate that the advertiser is a broker and give the name and telephone number of the broker.* Ads that do not contain this information are called **blind ads**. In addition, advertising stating that a property is in a certain geographical vicinity must identify the exact name of the geographical area. Figure 1.7 shows examples of correct and incorrect copy.

FIGURE 1.7 DOS guidelines for broker advertising.

BLIND AD

19NYCRR RULE 175.25(a) requires that all advertisements placed by a broker must indicate that the advertiser is a broker, or give the name and telephone number of the broker.

Correct Copy	*Incorrect Copy*
House, 1/2 acre, $90,000 John Doe, Broker (or) John Doe, XXX Realty 518-XXX-1000	House, 1/2 acre, $90,000 518-XXX-1000

GEOGRAPHICAL LOCATIONS

19NYCRR Rule 175.25(b) requires that all advertisements placed by a broker which state that property is in the vicinity of a geographical area or territorial subdivision must include as part of such advertisement the name of the geographical area or territorial subdivision in which such property is actually located.

Correct Copy	*Incorrect Copy*
House, 1/2 acre, $90,000 New Concord John Doe, Broker 518-XXX-1000	House, 1/2 acre, $90,000 Vicinity Berkshire Mts. John Doe, Broker 518-XXX-1000

Advertisements should also state the exact name under which a license is issued. Confusion occurs when brokerage firms that are part of large franchises have the same name or in cases when individuals in large communities have the same or similar name. Advertising guidelines may be obtained from the DOS; the guidelines also include the correct copy, typesetting, and other details necessary for licensee business cards.

PUTTING IT TO WORK

The following sample ads illustrate the elements of correct ad copy. Analyze them to understand why they adhere to DOS regulations.

SUNRISE
Overlooking beautiful Lake George. 3 bedroom, 2 bath bungalow with full view of lake. Includes boat slip. 1/4 acre lot, Bolton Landing. $200,000.
Rustic Realty, Inc.
Glens Falls, New York
Ahmad Mir, Salesperson
(518) 678–9999

Cityscape Properties
Prime Location
East 80s, Fifth Avenue
Gorgeous 3 bedroom condo; 2.5 baths. Full service building. $450K.
Contact Richey Riche, Broker.
891–2222

New beginnings
Near schools and shopping. Adorable cape. 2 bedrooms, front porch, AC, screened sunroom Must see. Yonkers, New York. $150,000
J. C. Meckler, Broker
call and ask for
Byung Lee, Salesperson
(914) 943–4444

Buyer Representation Only
Let us find you the best properties for the lowest price. We negotiate price and terms for you.
Buyer Brokerage Unlimited
Bill Blue, Broker
370–9472

GARDEN APARTMENT
(Duplex), Queens
Co-op in established community. Union Turnpike and Main Street. 2 bedrooms, 2 baths, A/C, hardwood floors.
103–24 Gardenway Road.
$120,000
Shelly Duval, Broker
Gardenpark Management
(718) 383–9876

Unlicensed Assistants

Many real estate businesses utilize unlicensed employees or personal assistants to help with routine tasks. The assistants may legally engage in any office activities that are not specified in Section 440 of Article 12–A. Some office activities that may be performed by a person who does not hold a license include the following: answering the phone, taking messages, arranging appointments, assembling documents for closing, writing ad copy and typing contract forms for broker approval, computing commission checks, preparing fliers and other promotional material, and gathering information for comparative market analysis. This list of duties is not all-inclusive. The broker is responsible for the supervision and control of an assistant's activities; however, unlicensed assistants' duties are mostly clerical in nature. They should not show apartments, houses, or other real property or discuss the real estate in question either with clients or customers.

Unlicensed assistants may be paid directly by either the licensed broker or salesperson. The method of reimbursement for unlicensed activities is best handled on an hourly, per activity, or salaried basis. If compensated on a completed transaction, the assistant must be licensed as a real estate salesperson and must receive compensation

You Should Know **Liabilities and penalties for violations of the license law**

Unlawful acts committed by licensees violate Article 12–A and fall under the jurisdiction of DOS. Persons who violate any part of Article 12–A of the Real Property Law are guilty of a **misdemeanor.** *Under the penal law in New York, a misdemeanor is punishable by a fine of not more $1,000 and/or imprisonment for not more than one year.* **Administrative discipline** *by DOS may include a reprimand to the licensee. DOS may also deny, revoke, or suspend the license of a salesperson or broker for as long as it deems proper.* DOS may also impose a fine not to exceed $1,000.

Article 12–A empowers all state courts to hear and try, without indictment, anyone who violates the license laws. In addition, criminal matters such as felonies and civil matters can be prosecuted in the public forum. The state attorney general is empowered to prosecute all criminal actions. Civil actions are heard in New York Supreme Court.

directly from the licensed broker. Complete guidelines for allowable activities for unlicensed assistants are available from the DOS.

DOS Hearings and Appeals

If the DOS receives a complaint or has reason to believe that a licensee may be in violation of the law, it will investigate the allegations and notify the licensee in writing of the charge and the penalty. Licensees may then request a hearing to contest the charges and penalty. If all parties agree, the charge may go to voluntary mediation; if not, a hearing is scheduled. If DOS decides to deny a license application, the applicant will be notified in writing. The applicant may then ask for a hearing within 30 days of receiving the denial notice. Applicants and licensees may bring an attorney to any DOS hearing. DOS administrative law judges preside over each hearing. DOS also has its own attorneys.

An appeal of a decision made by DOS at a hearing may be heard through a proceeding under the NYS Civil Practice Law and Rules (CPLR) called an **Article 78 proceeding.** This proceeding is *the method for appeals against regulatory agencies such as DOS.*

The **revocation** or **suspension** of a broker's license *suspends the licenses of the salespersons and associate brokers affiliated with the broker.* The suspension is lifted if the salesperson or associate broker affiliates with another broker or when the designated suspension period ends. If a salesperson or broker license is revoked, the licensee loses his license and must wait *one year* from the date of revocation to be eligible for relicensure.

New York State Real Estate Board

The New York State Real Estate Board consists of fifteen members including the Secretary of State and the Executive Director of the Consumer Protection Board together with thirteen additional appointed members from the real estate brokerage community and the public at large. The board has the power to promulgate rules and regulations affecting real estate licensees with certain exceptions.

CASE STUDIES

The following examples of DOS cases brought to administrative hearings illustrate how DOS makes determinations regarding a real estate licensee's duties and responsibilities under license law and regulations. See *To the Student,* "Case Studies," on page *xxvi,* which explains the terms and format of the following DOS administrative hearings.

Department of State, Division of Licensing Services, Complainant, against Jo Ella Robinson, Respondent.

Notifying DOS about a new business address or a change in business name may seem unimportant to real estate practice, but under the law, New York licensees must at all times inform the state of their location and the name of their business.

Allegations. Respondent failed to notify the Division of Licensing Services of a change of business address, operated a real estate brokerage business under an unlicensed name, and permitted unlicensed persons to conduct real estate brokerage activities.

Findings of fact. Respondent is licensed as a real estate broker in her individual name. However, Respondent filed a Certificate to Conduct Business Under an Assumed Name (D/B/A), J. Merchant Realty. Respondent Robinson conducted the real estate brokerage at a different address from that on file with the Division of Licensing, and under the name J. Merchant Realty, without notifying the Division of Licensing of the new business address and without obtaining approval for use of the assumed name. Also, on three occasions, individuals came to the offices of J. Merchant Realty to rent apartment space. First, Respondent gave a rental deposit to an unlicensed, temporary employee of the brokerage firm. The prospective tenant then did not rent the apartment, but the deposit was not refunded. During the DOS hearing, Respondent promised to make restitution. On the second occasion, an unlicensed temporary employee received a deposit, but the tenant never received a lease and the deposit was not refunded. On the third occasion, Respondent's husband, who was unlicensed, received a deposit; the prospective tenant did not obtain an apartment and received a settlement in small claims court from Respondent. Respondent states that she was unaware of the wrongful acts of the unlicensed employee on the first two rental occasions and learned of the third rental only when a lawsuit was filed.

Conclusions of law. The court found that two of the above allegations constituted technical violations of the Real Property Law, including failure to notify the Division of Licensing Services of a change in the address of the brokerage firm (Section 441–a) and operating a business under a name other than the name licensed by DOS (Section 440–a). Although the evidence did not prove that Respondent Robinson either had knowledge of the wrongful acts of the unlicensed persons or received any benefit or retained any proceeds from the wrongful transactions of the unlicensed persons, the evidence did establish that Respondent did not directly supervise the operations of the office. However, in this instance, Respondent was not charged with failure to supervise. The evidence in the case was also insufficient to establish that Respondent permitted unlicensed persons to engage in the brokerage business.

Determination. Respondent Robinson demonstrated incompetence by violating the Real Property Law. Respondent was reprimanded and ordered to present proof by a certain date that she conducted the brokerage at the principal address and under the name licensed by the Division of Licensing. If the material was not provided by the deadline, Respondent's license would be suspended until presentation of such evidence.

Department of State, Division of Licensing Services, Complainant, against Donald J. DuBois, d/b/a DuBois Realty, Respondent.

The judiciary law in New York prohibits the practice of law by anyone not admitted to the bar in New York courts. Licensees must never draw up legal documents or give legal advice. The following case study illustrates this point.

Allegations. Respondent DuBois breached the fiduciary duties of reasonable care, skill, diligence, and judgment, and of full and fair disclosure by failing to inform the sellers, or principals, that a lawyer should be consulted before accepting the buyer's purchase offer. Respondent also engaged in the unauthorized practice of law by preparing a purchase offer contract that established the payment terms and did not contain a clause subjecting the contract to review and approval by the parties' attorneys.

Findings of fact. One of Respondent's salespersons negotiated the listing and purchase offer for the sale of two adjoining properties. Respondent prepared a preprinted offer to purchase form contract, which established a purchase price of $100,000; a brokerage fee of $8,000; buyer's deposits of $500 at time of execution, $4,500 (5 percent of the purchase price) on or before a designated later date, and $99,500 (an obvious error) in cash at the closing. The down payment of 5 percent of the purchase price was to be paid in two installments, an arrangement negotiated by the salesperson because the buyer was not able to make the customary 10 percent down payment (or any down payment) at the time of the offer.

The seller and buyer of the properties signed the preprinted form. The signed, preprinted form is a binding contract and does not indicate that it was approved by the bar association and the board of REALTORS® in the county where Respondent engaged in the brokerage business. The contract called for a $500 deposit upon execution and $4,500 more in deposit money prior to a designated date. On the date the buyer signed the contract, the $500 deposit check was not received. The purchase offer was then presented to and signed by the seller, who was unaware that the $500 deposit had not been paid. Subsequently, the $500 deposit was made. The sellers did not negotiate directly with the buyer; negotiations were conducted with the buyer by the salesperson on behalf of the sellers. The salesperson did not collect the $4,500 balance of the down payment, and the sale did not occur.

Conclusions of law. Agency law and Article 12–A of the Real Property Law require the licensee to make full disclosure of all information known by the licensee that might affect the principal's interest in the transaction. In this case, the salesperson controlled the channels of communication. The sellers did not negotiate directly with the buyer. The sellers were not aware that the amount of the down payment contracted for was 50 percent less than the usual down payment; that when they signed the contract, the initial $500 payment had not been made; and that the salesperson accepted payment after the seller accepted the offer. Neither the broker nor the salesperson advised the sellers to consult an attorney prior to the execution of the contract prepared by the broker.

A purchase offer must either contain a provision making the contract subject to the approval of the respective parties *or* must use a form that is approved by the National Conference of Lawyers and REALTORS® or by a joint committee of the county's bar association and REALTOR'S® association where the brokerage is located. The offer must also contain a boldface caveat that the document is a legal contract and recommend that the parties consult with their attorneys before signing. The above case was a result of the landmark 1978 case on this issue, discussed previously (*Duncan & Hill Realty, Inc. v. Department of State,* 62 AD2d 690, NYS 2d 339).

Determination. Respondent demonstrated untrustworthiness and incompetence. His license was suspended for three months and all commissions were forfeited.

IMPORTANT POINTS

1. License laws are an exercise of the police power of New York, and the purpose of these laws is to protect the public and elevate the standards of the real estate industry.
2. A real estate broker is a person or an organization who, for compensation of any kind, performs or offers to perform aspects of real estate transactions for others.
3. Real estate salespersons perform acts that a broker is authorized to perform, but salespersons do so on behalf of a broker with whom they are associated.
4. Associate real estate brokers must fulfill the same requirements as a broker, but their status in the firm is equivalent to that of salespersons.
5. Attorneys do not have to be licensed to engage in real estate brokerage unless they employ licensees to work under their supervision.
6. The New York Department of State, Division of Licensing Services, oversees the licensure process.
7. DOS has the power to deny, revoke, fine, or suspend a license.
8. The term of licensure for both real estate salespersons and brokers is two years.
9. New York has reciprocal arrangements with seven other states for the licensure of nonresident licensees.
10. Real estate salespersons and associate brokers may not be officers of real estate brokerage corporations, hold voting stock in the company, or be a partner in the company.
11. Other licenses and registrations related to real estate include mortgage bankers and mortgage brokers, apartment information vendors, and licensed or certified appraisers.
12. Under a new law, real estate licensees must inform sellers that a disclosure statement be provided to the buyer or buyer's agent prior to the seller's acceptance of the purchase offer.
13. DOS has specific guidelines for real estate advertising by brokers and also for the employment and duties of unlicensed real estate assistants.
14. Net listings, kickbacks, and commingling of funds are illegal.
15. Violation of the license law is a misdemeanor and is punishable by a $1,000 fine and/or a maximum sentence of one year in jail.
16. The revocation or suspension of a broker real estate license also suspends the license of the salespersons and associate brokers in the broker's employ.

How Would You Respond? CHAPTER REVIEW

Analyze the following situations and decide how the individuals should handle them in accordance with what you have just learned. Check your responses using the Answer Key at the end of the chapter.

1. Lucy is president of Alovely Day Brokerage, Inc. Her husband, Dominic, is employed full-time in the company as an associate broker. Lucy decides that Dominic should become secretary of the corporation. What steps must Lucy and Dominic take so that Dominic can lawfully assume his new role in the company?

2. Marco has moved to Walton, New York, from Puerto Rico to work in the real estate company of his childhood friend, Fernando. Marco does not have a broker license but has been a successful real estate investor. He has bought and sold more than 20 apartment buildings in San Juan over the last seven years. Fernando is a licensed broker who owns Rural Beauty Real Estate in Walton. What type of license is Marco eligible for in New York and how can he become licensed?

3. Jewel is an attorney practicing in Manhattan. She has bought, rehabilitated, rented, and sold a number of buildings in lower Manhattan. Lately, Jewel has felt overwhelmed by the volume of legal work plus the burden of managing her investments. She has decided to set up a brokerage company under a trade name, Bijoux Associates, and hire several sales agents. What must Jewel do to set up her new company?

4. Obadiah has been a licensed broker for four years and lives in Pittsfield, Massachusetts. Pittsfield is not far from the New York border. Obadiah has many friends and business contacts in New York and wants to sell some lots of subdivided land in New Lebanon, New York, which is near Pittsfield. How can Obadiah obtain a broker license in New York?

5. Gloriana is frantic. Her license is up for renewal in just 30 days and she is so busy, she doesn't want to take a continuing education course. Gloriana has been an associate broker with Queen's County Real Estate in Jamaica, New York, for six years. Before that, Gloriana worked as a salesperson for 11 years in Whitehall, New York. She has never had a lapse in her licensure. Does Gloriana need to take continuing education courses? Why or why not?

KEY TERM REVIEW

Fill in the term that best completes each sentence and then check the Answer Key at the end of the chapter.

1. The section of the New York Real Property Law that applies to salespersons and brokers is ____________________.
2. Brokers who do not separate their business or personal bank accounts from their real estate deposit accounts are guilty of ____________________ the funds.
3. An illegal arrangement where a seller allows a broker to procure a fixed amount for property and allows the broker to keep as commission any money obtained above this amount is called a(n) ____________________.
4. A(n) ____________________ is a form of advertising by a licensee that does not indicate the name of the broker or brokerage firm.
5. A(n) ____________________ is an appeal brought forth because of a decision by an administrative agency.
6. An individual who fulfills the license requirements for a real estate broker but whose status in the firm is that of a salesperson is called a(n) ____________________.
7. The arrangement with several other states that allows nonresident licensees to be licensed in New York (if their state allows New York licensure under the same terms and conditions) is called ____________________.
8. An illegal commission or fee paid to an unlicensed individual who may have helped with a real estate transaction is called a(n) ____________________.
9. A(n) ____________________ is registered by the New York Banking Department to process or negotiate mortgage loans for others.
10. A licensed individual who, for a fee, makes lists of apartment space available to the public is called a(n) ____________________.

MULTIPLE CHOICE

Circle the letter that best answers the question and then check the Answer Key at the end of the chapter.

1. Which of the following is NOT specifically exempted from the licensure requirements?
   A. trustees in a bankruptcy
   B. attorneys
   C. receivers
   D. individuals under age 21
2. The legal authority of a state that requires real estate brokers and salespersons to be licensed is derived from:
   A. enabling power
   B. executive power
   C. commission power
   D. police power
3. A seller is so pleased with the manner in which a salesperson has handled the listing and sale of her property that she decides to pay an extra commission to go entirely to the salesperson. The salesperson:
   A. may receive part of the extra monies if it is paid through the sponsoring broker and then given to the salesperson through the broker
   B. may not accept this extra commission
   C. must first ask permission from the supervising broker
   D. may have the seller give the commission to a friend who will in turn give it to the salesperson

4. Which licensee activity violates the license law?
   A. marketing one's own property through one's real estate office
   B. charging varying rates of commission for several different listings
   C. advising a seller as to the validity of a warranty deed of trust taken by the seller from the buyer in a real estate transaction
   D. completing a comparative market analysis

5. Which of the following is typically exempt from real estate licensure?
   A. a person who lists only property for sale for others
   B. a person acting for another as a rental agent for one property
   C. a person who negotiates only leases for others
   D. a person engaged in the real estate brokerage business for only a few months a year

6. In an effort to induce a prospective buyer to enter into a contract to purchase a home, a real estate broker tells the buyer that the home is only four years old although it is actually eight years old. The broker knows the true age of the home. Relying on the broker's statement, the prospect enters into a contract to purchase the property. Given this information, which of the following statements is FALSE?
   A. the broker is in violation of the license law
   B. the broker has committed an act of willful misrepresentation
   C. the buyer can have the contract set aside
   D. the seller and not the broker is unconditionally responsible for any misrepresentation

7. The maximum time allowed to renew a license without having to retake the state exam is:
   A. within two years from the expiration date of the license
   B. no later than the expiration date of the license
   C. six months prior to the expiration date
   D. one year from the date the license was issued

8. A real estate salesperson license is:
   A. kept by the salesperson
   B. kept by the broker
   C. conspicuously displayed by the broker
   D. void unless put in a safe deposit box by the broker

9. According to license law and regulations, which of the following is required by a real estate broker?
   A. open at least one branch office
   B. conspicuously display license
   C. hire other salespersons
   D. close at least ten transactions a year

10. Which of the following is NOT exempt from taking continuing education?
   A. a broker licensed for 15 continuous years
   B. a salesperson licensed for 15 continuous years
   C. an attorney licensed to practice law in New York
   D. a broker licensed for 20 continuous years

ANSWER KEY

How Would You Respond?

1. Dominic must change his status in the firm from an associate broker to a broker as only a broker may be an officer of a corporation. He will have to file his change of status with DOS, Division of Licensing Services, and pay a $150 fee.
2. Based on his experience, Marco is eligible for a broker license. He will become an associate broker in Fernando's firm. He may submit transcripts from courses for credit that he has taken in the past to see if the Bureau of Educational Standards will accredit them. If they are not approved, he must take 90 hours of qualifying courses. He must also take the broker exam and submit the broker application to DOS. He must fill out Supplement B, Statement of Equivalent Experience to that of a Salesperson, indicate his equivalent work experience, and submit a $150 fee with his application. He may also apply for a salesperson license.

3. Jewel must file for a broker license with DOS and pay a $150 license fee since she will have salespersons working under her who will be transacting real estate for others. She must first clear her proposed name with DOS, Division of Licensing, and then file a doing business under an assumed name form with the county clerk in her county. She does not need to take an exam or fulfill any educational requirements.
4. Fortunately for Obadiah, New York and Massachusetts share reciprocal arrangements for licensure. Obadiah must file a broker application with DOS, pay a $150 license fee, and sign and submit a uniform irrevocable consent and designation form.
5. Because Gloriana is a broker and has 15 years of continuous licensure, she is exempt from taking continuing education courses.

Key Term Review

1. Article 12-A
2. commingling
3. net listing
4. blind ad
5. Article 78 proceeding
6. associate broker
7. reciprocity
8. kickback
9. mortgage broker
10. apartment information vendor

Multiple Choice

1. D
2. D
3. A
4. C
5. B
6. D
7. A
8. B
9. B
10. B

Supplemental Information

Salesperson and Broker License Law pamphlet, printed by New York Department of State, may be obtained by writing to DOS. Access the Department of State website at *http://www.dos.state.ny.us*; the e-mail address is info@dos.state.ny.us. Forms including applications, frequently asked questions, and other information may be accessed at the DOS website.

Chapter 2

KEY TERMS

agency disclosure form
agent
broker's agent
buyer agent
client
cooperating agent
customer
disclosure
dual agent/dual agency
estoppel
exclusive agency
exclusive right to sell
express agency
fiduciary
fiduciary duties
first substantive contact
general agent
implied agency
informed consent
misrepresentation
open listing
price fixing
principal
self-dealing
seller's agent
single agent
special agent
subagent
undisclosed dual agency
undivided loyalty
vicarious liability

LEARNING OBJECTIVES

Classroom hours: 8

1. Explain the basic nature of agency.
2. Describe how agency is created.
3. Describe the rights, duties, and responsibilities of each party in an agency relationship.
4. Identify the role of a salesperson when acting as a subagent of the principal broker.
5. Describe the various forms of agency.
6. Identify the relationship of the salesperson to the principal broker.
7. Identify the relationship of the salesperson to the client.
8. Identify the relationship of the salesperson to the customer.

Law of Agency

9. Determine and understand the dangers of dual agency.
10. Describe the proper procedures and explanations of properly disclosing agency relationships.
11. Describe the concept of buyer brokerage.
12. Explain the interaction that will be required between the agent for the seller and agent for the purchaser.
13. Explain the fiduciary responsibilities of an agent.
14. Explain key terms related to the law of agency.
15. Identify and describe the steps that a licensee must take to ensure proper agency disclosure.
16. Explain basic antitrust laws.

IN THIS CHAPTER Understanding agency relationships and the corresponding disclosure requirements is of primary importance to all real estate licensees in New York. This chapter covers the creation of agency, types of agencies, obligations of a licensee as agent, New York disclosure requirements and antitrust laws, and the brokerage industry. This chapter is divided into two sections: agency and antitrust.

SECTION 1 AGENCY

When one person is hired to act on behalf of another person, an agency relationship is created. The person hired on another's behalf is the **agent.** An agency relationship is consensual; the parties willingly enter into the agreement. Upon creation of the relationship, the agent is placed in a position of trust and loyalty to the principal.

The *person who selects the agent to act on his behalf* is the **principal** or **client.** The **customer** of an agent is *the party whom the agent brings to the principal as a seller or buyer of the property*. For example, an agent can represent a seller in a real estate transaction. The seller then becomes the client of the agent. If the seller's agent finds a prospective purchaser for the seller's property, the purchaser is the agent's customer. This particular example raises the issue of a dual agency relationship, that is allowable in New York with informed consent and disclosure. The issue of dual agency is discussed later in this chapter.

SCOPE OF AGENT'S AUTHORITY

Most agency relationships are contractual relationships. Few are simply implied by law. Thus, the agent's authority must be expressed in the brokerage contract. The principal controls the extent of authority delegated to the agent through the language in the brokerage contract. Two important classifications of agents exist: general and special. The differences between the two revolve around the authority given to the agent by the principal and the services provided.

General

A **general agent** is *someone authorized to handle all affairs of the principal concerning a certain matter or property,* usually with some limited power to enter into contracts. An example is a person who has been appointed property manager of an apartment complex by the owner of the complex. The property manager may collect rent, evict, enter into leases, repair the premises, advertise for tenants, and perform a range of activities on behalf of the principal concerning the specified property. This type of agency also may be established through power of attorney, but this is not always required. Someone who has been given the complete power of attorney over another's affairs is called an attorney-in-fact. A *power of attorney,* which is a relationship that allows one individual to handle the affairs of another within the scope of a predetermined arrangement, can be either a general or special agency.

Special

A **special agent** is *someone who has narrow authorization to act on behalf of the principal.* An example is a real estate broker who has a property listing. The broker can market the property for sale but cannot make decisions as to price, repairs, financing, and so on. A special agent cannot bind a principal to a contract. The range of authority is specialized and limited, and the services provided are specifically defined.

FIDUCIARY RESPONSIBILITIES

An agency relationship is basically a contractual relationship to provide services. The person hired is the agent. The person who hires is the principal. As a result of the agency agreement, a fiduciary relationship then exists between the agent and the principal. The term **fiduciary** means *a position of trust.* Fiduciary responsibilities should not be taken lightly by licensees. *A breach in fiduciary duties can jeopardize an agent's commission as well as render the agent liable for his acts or omissions.*

Agent's Responsibilities to Principal

Every agency creates a fiduciary relationship between principal and agent. The agent has certain obligations to the principal as required of every agent by law. The agent's **fiduciary duties** and responsibilities include *obedience; loyalty; disclosure of information; confidentiality; accountability; and reasonable care, skill, and diligence.*

Obedience

The agent must act with *obedience* and obey reasonable and legal instructions from the principal. For example, a seller, as principal, may specify that the property be shown only during certain times of the day or, for instance, not on a seller's religious holiday. The buyer being represented may instruct the broker not to disclose the buyer's identity to the parties without the buyer's consent. Of course, the principal cannot require the agent to perform any illegal acts, such as violating fair housing laws. If the principal insists that the broker commit an illegal act, the broker must withdraw from the relationship.

Loyalty

An agent must demonstrate *loyalty* to the principal and must work diligently to serve the best interests of the principal under the terms of the employment contract creating the agency. The agent may not work for personal interest or for the interest of others adverse to the principal's interest. The agent cannot legally represent any other person who directly affects the principal without disclosing this fact to the principal and obtaining the principal's consent in writing. A real estate agent cannot represent both buyer and seller in the same transaction and the broker cannot receive a commission from both without the knowledge and consent of both buyer and seller.

Disclosure of Information

Agents are required to keep the principal fully aware of all important matters through *disclosure of information.* They must promptly communicate to the principal all information material to the transaction for which the agency is created. As an example, the requirement for disclosure of information requires that a broker present every offer to the seller (principal) with information about all circumstances surrounding the offer, even after a contract exists or is believed to exist. The seller has the prerogative to decide whether to reject or accept any offer for purchase of the property. If the agent is a buyer agent, the agent should indicate to the buyer the property's market value and use all possible negotiating techniques to obtain the most favorable terms and price for the buyer.

New York also has specific disclosure and informed consent requirements regarding whom the agent represents in a real estate transaction. (This subject is explored in more depth later in this chapter.)

Confidentiality

Because of the fiduciary relationship, the principal is owed faith, trust, and confidentiality by the agent hired. For example, if a seller's agent represents principals who are selling their home because of a divorce, this information should not be given to prospective purchasers without the seller's permission.

Accountability

Accountability generally refers to *financial accountability.* An agent must account for and promptly remit as required all money or property entrusted to the agent for the benefit of others. The agent is required to keep adequate and accurate records of all receipts and expenditures of other people's money in order to provide a complete accounting. For example, a real estate broker must maintain a special account for depositing other people's money. This account should be labeled either "trust account" or "escrow account" and be maintained in an insured banking institution. An agent is violating the law of agency for real estate brokers if the agent commingles funds or property, held in trust for others, with the agent's own personal or corporate money or property, or with the operating account of the business. Handling other people's money is one of the most serious fiduciary responsibilities of licensees.

Reasonable Care, Skill, and Diligence

In offering services to the principal, agents assert that they possess the necessary skill and training to perform the requested services. Agents must exercise the *reasonable skill, care, and diligence* to which the public is entitled in all real estate transactions.

If an agent's principal incurs a financial loss as a result of the agent's negligence and failure to meet the standards of skill, care, and diligence, the agent is liable for any loss the principal incurs.

You Should Know **Agent's fiduciary responsibilities to the principal**

It helps to remember them if you think of the words OLD CAR:

O Obedience
L Loyalty
D Disclosure of Information
C Confidentiality
A Accountability
R Reasonable Care, Skill, and Diligence

Agent's Responsibility to Third Parties

The broker and the principal are the first two parties in an agency relationship. Other individuals who are involved in any way with the principal and broker are called *third parties.*

Even though one of the agent's obligations to the principal is not to disclose certain confidential information to other parties that could be injurious to the principal, the agent may not engage in any way in misrepresentation of fact to a third party. Agents must disclose any material facts of which they have knowledge or should have had knowledge regarding the condition of any service or item provided. For example, a seller broker must disclose to prospective buyers any information about any aspect of the property that may be defective, such as a wet basement or an unresolved boundary dispute. Liability may be imposed upon the agent for concealing defects in the property or for failing to disclose the existence of defects they know about.

The basis for imposing liability in a case of **misrepresentation** consists of (a) *a false representation of a material fact;* (b) the fact that the person making the false representation knew or should have known it to be false; (c) the fact that the misrepresentation was made with an intent to induce the party to act or refrain from acting in reliance upon the misrepresentation; (d) the fact that the party relied upon the misrepresentation in acting or failing to act; and (e) the fact that there was damage to the party who relied upon the misrepresentation in acting or not acting.

A *positive misrepresentation* by a seller broker occurs when the broker conceals a defect in the property from the buyer or misrepresents to the buyer the existence of a defect. A positive misrepresentation occurs by omission of facts about the property even if the buyer does not ask. Positive misrepresentation may also take place when an agent engages in **self-dealing.** *Illegal self-dealing can occur when a broker has an undisclosed interest in a property.*

An *unintentional misrepresentation* occurs when the seller broker makes a false statement to the buyer about the property and the broker does not know whether the statement is true or false. In either situation the broker is liable to a customer who suffers a loss as a result of acting or failing to act in reliance upon the misrepresentation. The broker is not excused from liability for making a misrepresentation based upon statements the principal makes to the broker. The broker is required to make a personal, diligent investigation before passing on any information. Brokers are liable for what they know from disclosure by the principal, what they should know because of their skill and training, and what they should know by an inspection of the property.

Principal's Responsibility to Agent

Under an agency agreement, the principal is obligated to the agent for cooperation, compensation, and indemnification. The agency agreement should clearly set out the amount of compensation to be paid and the conditions that must be met to earn the compensation.

Because an agency agreement is for providing services to the principal by the agent, the principal must not hinder the agent's efforts in providing services. For example, the seller of listed property must not refuse to allow the broker to show the property to prospective buyers in accordance with the terms of the listing.

For compensation, a typical listing agreement might provide that the seller will pay the broker a set percentage of the accepted sales price of the property when a ready, willing, and able buyer is produced. If the broker brings a buyer with an offer completely in accordance with the listing agreement, the broker is entitled to the commission whether the seller does or does not accept the offer or is later unable to close the transaction.

Finally, the agent is entitled to be free from liability if the principal has withheld information that causes the agent to make incorrect representations to third parties. If the agent is found liable to the third parties for the principal's misrepresentation, the agent is entitled to repayment from the principal for all monies paid. The repayment from the principal is indemnification to the agent and makes the agent financially whole. For instance, the seller of listed property may know of a *latent defect.* Latent defects are generally structural problems that a seller may know about but are not obvious to the purchaser. Examples include hidden water damage, faulty wiring, a malfunctioning heating system, or termites. If the seller fails to disclose this information to the agent, legal action may be brought by an innocent buyer against the broker and then the broker may in turn bring action against the seller for failure to disclose.

Principal's Responsibility to Third Parties

The principal in an agency agreement has no express contract with anyone except the listing broker and agent. The principal, however, does have a common-law duty of disclosure and fairness to any third parties. This duty complements the duty the principal has to the agent for *revealing all information that affects the agency agreement.* This duty is owed to any person who may be affected directly or indirectly by any of the terms of the agency agreement. This duty also requires that the principal disclose completely all information that has a bearing on the agency agreement.

The seller's duty to disclose to the broker knowledge of any and all hidden defects also runs to any buyer brokers, prospective buyers, and subagents of the listing broker. A property condition disclosure form (discussed in Chapter 1), completed by the seller, is a means through which defects may be disclosed. If sellers fail to disclose correctly, they can be held liable for the statutory penalties.

REAL ESTATE BROKERAGE AND AGENCY

Brokerage refers to the business of bringing buyers and sellers together and assisting in negotiations for the terms of sale of real estate. A brokerage firm or company may be owned by a single licensed broker (sole proprietor) or by more than one licensed person, such as in a partnership or corporation. A brokerage firm is considered an independent broker if the brokerage is not associated with a national or local real estate franchise organization. Association with a real estate franchise organization licenses the brokerage firm to use the franchise's trade names, operating procedures, reputation, and referral services. The franchisee still owns and operates the brokerage firm. Brokerage firms usually employ or have other licensed salespersons or brokers working there. The listing contracts are shared between the sellers and the brokerage firm. The brokerage firm owns the listing contracts.

The sales associates affiliated with the brokerage firm are agents of the broker and subagents of the brokerage firm's principals (clients).The fiduciary duty of sales associates therefore extends both to their employing brokerage firm and to the firm's principals. Thus, the broker has two separate agency relationships. The broker is the agent under the listing agreement. The broker is also the principal of the sales associates under a subagency agreement in the brokerage firm. Therefore, the broker is responsible for the actions of the sales associates even though the sales associate almost always is an independent contractor. As subagents of the broker in reference to the listing agreements, the sales associates are required to comply with the terms of the listing and all rules of the brokerage firm.

Vicarious Liability

In any discussion of employment arrangements in the brokerage business, it is important to understand the meaning of **vicarious liability.** The term means that *one person is responsible or liable for the actions of the other.*

According to Section 442–c of the New York Real Property Law, a broker is vicariously liable for a salesperson's actions only if "the broker had actual knowledge of such violations or if the broker retains the benefits from the transaction after he knows that the salesperson has engaged in some wrongdoing." If, however, while acting as an agent (salesperson), the agent is negligent and causes damage and/or injury to another, the employer (broker) can be held liable and be required to pay damages. Furthermore, DOS *can* penalize a broker even if the broker did not know of the wrongdoing by imposing a fine or a reprimand.

Brokerage Contracts

A brokerage contract is created when the principal, usually the owner of real estate, hires a broker (agent) to perform services relating to the real estate. The services typically involve selling or renting real estate that the principal owns. Under the listing agreement, the principal and the agent have expressly agreed to the terms of the agency relationship. Although the real estate listing contract is the most common brokerage contract, a brokerage contract also can be created between a prospective buyer and the broker. Under that agency agreement, the buyer is the principal. The typical brokerage contract is a special agency with narrow authority.

Agency and Brokerage—Are They Synonymous?

With the advent of strict disclosure regulations in New York, real estate agents must clearly define to buyers and sellers whom they represent in the real estate transaction. It is possible in some situations for buyers or sellers to request that a licensee *not* represent them as an agent. Under certain conditions, a licensee may also suggest this relationship. The licensee then may become a *finder* or *facilitator* in the real estate transaction. In this role, the licensee may bring together individuals who will communicate, negotiate, and contract directly. This relationship is permissible under New York agency and disclosure law. However, in any kind of relationship between a licensee and a buyer or seller, it is easy for a licensee to cross the line into the role of agent or fiduciary. Finders are not common—in residential real estate, particularly. Agency and brokerage are generally synonymous.

DETERMINATION OF COMPENSATION

The fee or rate of commission paid to a real estate broker is strictly negotiable between the broker and the seller or buyer. Federal and state laws are violated if any person or organization even recommends a commission schedule to a broker or group of brokers. It is also illegal for two or more brokers to agree to charge certain commission rates to listing sellers. This is called **price fixing** and is an act in restraint of trade that violates the Sherman Antitrust Act (discussed later). Brokers are typically paid by a percentage commission of the final sales price or, less often, by a flat fee for services rendered.

Percentage of Final Sales Price

The most common type of commission arrangement in listing contracts is for the broker to receive a specified percentage of the final sales price of the property. For example, the contract may call for the broker to be paid 7 percent of the property's sales price. Real estate firms generally establish their own individual office policy regarding the level of commission charged. The fee decided upon by the broker is frequently tied to the amount of services being offered, such as in-house services, agent support systems, or advertising.

Net Listing

Another type of commission arrangement is the net listing, in which the seller specifies a net amount of money to be received upon sale of the property. All monies above the net amount are designated as the broker's commission. *This type of commission arrangement is illegal in New York.* Net listings can be unfair to a seller if the seller's property sells for substantially more than the listed price; one of the broker's responsibilities is to establish a fair market price for the property. A net listing leaves open an opportunity for a broker to take advantage of a property owner by putting the broker's own interests above the interests of the principal, thus breaching the fiduciary duty inherent in the agency relationship.

Flat Fee

Under the flat fee listing arrangement, the broker takes the listing based on a specified payment by the seller at the time of the listing. This is called an up front fee. The broker is entitled to retain this fee for efforts to market the property. Compensation under this listing does not depend on the sale of the property; thus the flat fee typically is substantially less than the fee for a percentage of the final sales price. Under this arrangement, the broker usually advertises the property but may not be involved in showing the property or negotiating terms of the sale between seller and buyer. Under a flat fee arrangement, if a seller wants a broker to open the listing to other brokers, the commission usually becomes a combination of a flat fee (to the listing broker) and a small percentage (to cooperating brokers).

Commission for Sales Associates

Commission splits paid to sales associates in real estate brokerage firms are established by the owner of the firm and the sales associates. Under the usual commission split agreement, the entire commission is paid directly to the broker, who then pays a portion to the sales associate who listed the property and a portion to the sales associate who sold the property. If a sales associate sells a listed property, the associate receives both portions. Some brokers use an incentive program, raising the proportion paid to the sales associate in relationship to the dollar volume produced by the sales associate.

Franchise Firms

A franchise is the right to use the name of a parent company along with certain operating procedures. Generally, this right is paid for by the franchisee through a percentage of the profits or outright fees or a combination of both. In some franchise firms, the franchise fee portion is deducted from the final commission due the sales associate.

Real estate franchises are popular because they offer name recognition, referral services on a nationwide level, and methods of operation that have proven track records. In many cases, a real estate firm can keep its own name in conjunction with the franchised name.

Commission for Cooperating Brokers

Upon the sale of real estate through the cooperating efforts of two real estate firms, the commission paid pursuant to the listing agreement is paid to the listing broker by the property owner. This commission then is shared by the listing broker and the selling broker on a prearranged basis. Often each broker invoices the seller for his or her share.

Through the publication of cooperative commissions reflected in multiple listing services, some listing offices offer two forms of cooperating commission. One amount is payable to a subagent of the seller and another amount is payable to a buyer agent as a cooperative agent who does not represent the seller.

Referral Fees

Brokerage firms often pay a referral fee to licensees from other localities when the licensee refers prospective buyers or sellers. *In New York, however, such fees may be payable to the broker only with the informed consent of the party being referred.* Referral fees are then distributed to the licensee who originates the referral in accordance with the in-house policy of commission split. Certain franchises offer a referral fee for relocation. Some real estate firms seek referral through offerings made through the directory published by the National Association of REALTORS® or the New York State Association of REALTORS®. Mortgage brokers, especially those affiliated with the firm originating the referral, must sign a disclosure to dual agency and an acknowledgment of prospective buyer and seller.

CREATION OF AGENCY

Express Agency

An *agency relationship created by an oral or a written agreement between the principal and agent* is called an **express agency.** A typical example is the written listing agreement between the seller of real estate and the broker.

Implied Agency—Ratification and Estoppel

An agency also may be created by the words or actions of the principal and agent indicating that they have an agreement. This is called an **implied agency.**

> EXAMPLE: Juanita, a real estate agent, places an ad in the paper for the sale of her friend Savannah's house, even though she has no express agreement with Savannah. This could be construed as an implied agreement.

Let's take this implied agency a step further:

Juanita has an implied agency with Savannah. It is not in writing. Savannah does not stop Juanita from advertising and marketing the house. Juanita later brings her a written offer to purchase the property. Savannah finds the contract acceptable and signs it. The signature on the contract *ratifies* or *confirms* the previously understood implied contract. *This is known as agency by ratification.* Ratification should restate an earlier understood contract, including an agreement or contract of sale.

Ostensible and estoppel agency refer to the principal in the relationship. *Ostensible agency* occurs when a principal allows a third party to believe that an agency relationship exists; there is an appearance of relationship between the parties.

EXAMPLE: Assume that Savannah needs to rent her house and Juanita takes the liberty to show the house to a prospect. Savannah does not want to be represented by Juanita, but she does not mention this to her. Juanita brings Savannah an offer to rent. Savannah begins to negotiate some of the points in the offer. Neither Savannah nor Juanita disclose to the tenant (third party) that Juanita is not representing Savannah, the owner/landlord. The tenant (third party) believes that Juanita is Savannah's representative. Later, the case goes to court and Savannah claims that Juanita was not her representative. The court may declare than an ostensible agency existed because the tenant believed that Juanita was Savannah's representative. Ostensible agency can be intentional or unintentional.

An agency by **estoppel** *exists when a principal does not stop an individual from representing his interests, thus creating an agency relationship between the two.*

EXAMPLE: Juanita calls Savannah. Through their recent discussions, Juanita knows that Savannah wants to rent the house. Savannah allows Juanita to bring her prospects to the property and does not make it clear to the prospect that she is not represented by Juanita. In this relationship, the principal, Savannah, fails to estop an individual, Juanita, from representing her interests.

In New York, implied real estate agency agreements are not easily enforced by the courts because, according to the Statute of Frauds, all real estate contracts, except listings contracts and leases of less than one year's duration, must be in writing. However, other New York laws may affect the determination of the courts.

AGENCY ALTERNATIVES

Agents, as fiduciaries, cannot offer absolute loyalty to both seller and buyer in the same transaction, yet New York law does not prohibit dual agency (discussed later). Once agents choose, they must always fully represent the principal, whether that is the seller or buyer.

SELLER AND SUBAGENCY

Subagency can be created when a seller and broker agree, usually by means of a multiple listing service, that other agents will also work for the seller.

In the distant past, placing a property in MLS automatically created subagency. In other words, all the agents showing the listed property became subagents for the listing broker and principal. Today, however, primarily because of the prevalence of buyer brokerage and other choices, the listing in MLS does not create a blanket unilateral offer of subagency. The principal can agree to accept or reject the option of subagency when signing the listing agreement.

A buyer agent cannot be a subagent of the seller broker. Licensees acting as buyer agents must make their agency status clear to the listing broker before showing the property. Brokerage, therefore, can be conducted without a unilateral offering of sub-

TABLE 2.1 Possible roles of real estate agents.

TYPE OF AGENT	REPRESENTATION	DEFINITION	LIMITATIONS
1. Single agent	Buyer or seller	The agent works for the buyer or seller.	The agent never represents both. Firms that represent solely the buyer or seller may reject subagency and dual agency. The broker should counsel, but not advise the principal as to the limitations of this relationship. If a situation arises to compromise the relationship, the broker could suggest that another broker from a referral firm be utilized.
2. Seller agent	Seller	A listing agent who acts alone or cooperates with other agents as a subagent or broker's agent.	The agent works in the best interests of the seller but must deal fairly and honestly with buyers.
3. Subagent	Seller or buyer	An agent of the principal under the agency relationship of the primary broker.	The agent must be hired with the principal's informed consent. The principal may be vicariously liable for the acts of the subagent.
4. Buyer agent	Buyer	The agent represents the buyer as principal and enters into a listing agreement with the buyer. Locates a property and negotiates for the buyer.	The agent works in the best interests of the buyer but must deal fairly and honestly with sellers.
5. Dual agent	Buyer and seller	Represents both buyer and seller in the same transaction; undisclosed dual agency is a breach of fiduciary duty and violation of license law.	This arrangement is allowable only with disclosure and written informed consent. The agent cannot give undivided loyalty to either party.
6. Broker's agent	Broker (who may represent either buyer or seller)	An agent is hired through a broker to work for that broker. The broker alone has hired the agent and accepts liability. Although a broker's agent does not work directly for the principal, the agent still owes a fiduciary duty to that principal because an agency relationship has been established through the broker that hired the broker's agent.	The agent owes a fiduciary duty to the broker's principal.

(continued)

TABLE 2.1 Continued.

TYPE OF AGENT	REPRESENTATION	DEFINITION	LIMITATIONS
7. Cooperating Agent	Buyers or sellers	Representation includes seller agents, subagents, buyer agents, and broker's agents. These agents work to assist the listing broker in the sale of the property. Cooperating agents may or may not work through MLS.	The principal can designate those agents that work as broker's agents, subagents, or buyer agents. The principal may choose to reject subagency arrangements.

Real estate agents, in cooperation with the principal may assume different roles within the agency relationship. The principal can designate those agents that work as broker's agents, subagents, or buyer agents. One or more defined roles may apply to an agent within the transaction. For example, a seller agent may also be a subagent and a cooperating agent.

agency by using the services of an MLS and offering a commission share to all cooperating agents even when the cooperating agents have been employed by buyers.

When cooperating brokers accept the offer of subagency associated with a seller's listing, however, they work through the listing broker and are therefore the principal's subagent, as are the sales associates in the listing agency's office. Cooperating subagents have the same responsibility to work for the best interests of the seller. The advantage to this arrangement is that cooperating subagents from other firms and in-house subagents have more offerings, and sellers have more licensees working on their behalf.

EXAMPLE: Melissa, who works for Sellquick Realty, shows the Millers' house, which is listed by Tom, another agent at Sellquick. Tom is the subagent of the seller (principal), the Millers. Melissa is also the Millers' subagent because both Melissa and Tom are employed by the same broker, the primary agent listing the property. The Millers' house is also listed in the multiple listing service. Matthew, an agent for Payless Realty, also shows the Millers' house to some of his customers. Because Matthew's firm, through the MLS, has agreed to a subagency arrangement, Matthew, although an agent from another firm, is also the subagent of the Millers. All the individuals who have accepted subagency owe the same fiduciary responsibilities to the principal and to the primary seller agent. The principal, however, may be held liable for the action of agent and subagent alike in cases of misrepresentation or any acts that result in damages to any other party in the real estate transaction. Subagents must also deal honestly and ethically with the buyer or customer and must disclose any pertinent information that may affect the value of the specific property.

Broker's Agent

The concept of the broker's agent can be understood if it is compared with that of the subagent. In the case of the subagent, the principal accepts vicarious liability for the acts of the agents and subagents. In the case of the broker's agent, the broker accepts vicarious liability for the acts of the agents working for his principal through him.

EXAMPLE: Ricardo hires Sellquick Realty to market his house. However, he does not want to accept vicarious liability for the acts of agents working on his listing. Avita, his broker, still wants to list the property and have the cooperation of other agents. Avita agrees to take any responsibility for liability problems that may arise because of other agents' activities. The agents who assist with the sale of the property according to this arrangement are known as broker's agents.

Cooperative Sales

Cooperative sales, either those handled by a seller agent from another real estate firm as subagent of the listing broker and owner (seller), or those handled by a buyer agent from another real estate firm, are either processed through MLS or between cooperating offices. When a cooperating office arranges to show a listed property, the role of the cooperating agent must be identified immediately. The cooperating agent must indicate if the prospective buyer is a client or a customer.

When the seller real estate firm takes a listing, the owner must be informed that some agents will be acting as representatives of the buyer. Arrangements can then be made in advance of any showing as to whether or not the owner wants the listing agent to accompany any appointments made by the buyer agents to protect the best interest of the seller.

Who Represents the Buyer in Seller Agency?

In dealing with seller agents, buyer customers may gain the mistaken impression that their broker is representing them against the seller. However, the broker is working for the seller; this should be made clear to the buyer at the outset. The buyer customer can tell nothing to the selling broker or agent in confidence, such as how much the buyer is willing to pay for the property, since the broker is required to pass on all pertinent information to the seller client or seller's broker.

When the broker represents the seller, the buyer customer does have rights. Although the broker is working on behalf of the seller, the buyer can expect honest disclosure from the broker, including full property disclosure outlining any problems the seller has experienced. The broker must accurately and completely answer any questions from the buyer concerning the property. Furthermore, the buyer can expect that the broker will comply with all local, state, and federal discrimination laws. The buyer, however, cannot expect the broker to disclose confidential information concerning the seller's reasons for selling, the seller's lowest sales price, the seller's original purchase price, or any other information that might give the buyer an enhanced negotiating position with the seller. Conversely, the buyer customer's duties should include fair and honest dealings with the seller and seller agents.

DUAL AGENCY

A **dual agency** *exists when a real estate firm or agent attempts to represent both the buyer and seller in the same transaction.* Dual agency can occur not only when one sales associate is involved with both buyer and seller but also when the salesperson representing the seller and the salesperson representing the buyer both work for the same broker. In such cases, only one firm (one agent) is involved despite the fact that two separate associates are working independently with the two parties.

Single licensee dual agency occurs when a sales agent attempts to represent the interests of both a seller client and a buyer client in the same transaction. A licensee may not engage in any form of dual agency without the informed consent of the listing broker and all other parties to the transaction.

Broker dual agency can occur if agents of the broker represent both buyer and seller in the same transaction, as stated above, or if the broker offers services to a buyer, such as finding or negotiating a mortgage for the buyer, when the broker already represents the seller. Another example of broker dual agency would be if the broker who represents the seller offers to negotiate the purchase agreement for the buyer.

Dual agency may be intended or unintended.

Intended Dual Agency

An *intended dual agency* arises when a listing broker acts as a buyer's broker and shows an in-house listing with the seller's full knowledge and consent. The real estate firm then represents both the buyer and the seller in a dual agency capacity and owes both the seller and the buyer confidentiality. In this situation, it is important to convey to both buyer and seller that neither can receive full representation. In certain cases, maintaining neutrality may be difficult because the responsibilities to both buyer and seller are complex and multifaceted.

Unintended Dual Agency

An *unintended dual agency* occurs if the *buyer believes by the agent's actions and/or representations that the buyer is being represented by that broker.* This implication can arise, for example, when a broker gives the buyer advice on negotiations or suggestions of what price to offer when in fact the broker is representing the seller. Confusion may also occur when a seller successfully sells her property with the broker as the agent and then enters the market as a buyer. The seller may assume that the broker then automatically represents her in the new transaction, but this is not the case unless this individual establishes a new agency relationship in her new role as buyer.

Obligation of Informed Consent

Dual agency must be disclosed to both buyer and seller, and both must agree to that dual relationship in writing. Undisclosed dual agency is a breach of a broker's fiduciary duty and a violation of New York license law. In the sale or rental of certain residential property (defined later) in New York, licensees must present a written disclosure form at the first substantive meeting with prospective sellers or purchasers (discussed later).

Undisclosed Dual Agency

Undisclosed dual agency occurs when a *subagent or seller agent is working with a buyer customer and agrees to negotiate for that buyer customer rather than working in the best interests of the other client, the seller.*

Consensual Dual Agency

The law of agency in New York permits consensual dual agency with **disclosure** and **informed consent** of all parties to the transaction. DOS generally interprets dual agency as a lawful alternative as long as informed consent includes *timely and complete disclosure of the nature and consequences of the dual agency.*

In certain circumstances, consensual dual agency may pose problems since both the *seller and purchaser must release the portion of the fiduciary agent relationship known as* **undivided loyalty.** The goals of the seller and purchaser are adverse. The sellers want to receive the highest price for their property under the best financial terms, whereas the buyers want to pay the lowest price for a property under the most favorable financial terms for them. In many instances, however, with proper disclosure and informed consent, the agent may effect an agreement acceptable to all parties.

Company Policies and In-House Sales

New York real estate offices can provide consensual dual agency representation for in-house sales. A seller client should be made aware when the listing agreement is signed that a dual agency arrangement could occur if a buyer agent affiliated with that same firm has a buyer client who may be interested in purchasing the seller's property. Because a dual agency situation must be disclosed at the time that it arises and informed consent must be obtained at that time, the seller client should not agree to dual agency at the date of listing but has the option to accept it should it occur.

Brokerage firms whose primary business is representing buyers will, at the time of listing the buyers, inform them that a prospective property may be available through an in-house listing. At that time, the buyers may choose to relinquish their status as clients and choose an alternative status (discussed below).

- The broker and buyer could dissolve their agency relationship. The buyer can then retain another broker, an attorney, or represent himself. The broker then would continue to act as the agent for the seller.
- The broker and the seller could dissolve their agency relationship. The seller could find another broker, attorney, or represent himself. The broker then would continue to act as the agent for the buyer.
- With informed consent, the buyer and seller may elect to continue with the brokerage firm serving as consensual dual agent.

The Designated Agent

Recently, DOS has defined an alternative for handling a dual agency with a brokerage firm. With full disclosure and informed consent, one sales agent in the firm can be designated to represent the buyer and another agent designated to represent the seller.

For example, if a buyer expresses interest in a property listed with a firm, consent must be obtained by both parties to proceed as a dual agent. The agency disclosure form is used for that purpose. At the same time, the benefits of appointing a *designated agent* for the buyer and another for the seller is explained. If, after full disclosure, the buyer and seller agree to this arrangement, designated agents may be appointed. The firm continues as dual agent representing both the buyer and the seller in the same transaction. The designated agents, however, by virtue of the new agreement with the buyer and seller, function as single agents giving undivided loyalty to their respective clients. If proper procedures are carried out, this arrangement does not violate Article 12–A or any other DOS regulations. While not mandatory, both DOS and NYSAR recommend that the buyer and the seller enter into a Designated Agent Agreement. A form has been drafted by NYSAR and adopted by many real estate firms (see Figure 2.1).

Consequences of Undisclosed Dual Agency

An undisclosed dual agency can result in a violation of the Real Property Law and regulations. Violators may be guilty of a misdemeanor. DOS may reprimand a licensee, or deny, revoke, or suspend the license of a salesperson or broker for as long as DOS deems proper to impose a fine up to $1,000. A civil court may also require that monetary damages be paid to a buyer, seller, or other injured party. *The legal process may result in rescission of any contracts involving the real estate transaction.*

Obtaining Informed Consent of Both Parties

Section 443 of the Real Property Law specifically provides for informed consent and written acknowledgment of dual agency by both a prospective buyer or tenant and a seller or landlord. Certain procedures are undertaken in the presentation of the disclosure form when listing the seller's property or entering into a buyer agency agreement. When the listing takes place, the licensee should give a full explanation of dual agency although neither party should sign an acceptance of dual agency at this time.

FIGURE 2.1 A designated agent agreement.

Central New York's
#1 Residential Real Estate Company

DESIGNATED AGENT AGREEMENT

We, the undersigned, Buyer and Seller, regarding the purchase and sale of premises known as ____________________________, New York, acknowledge our consent to ____________________("Broker") acting as a dual agent with respect to this transaction. We acknowledge that the Broker will be working for both the Buyer and the Seller in this transaction and we understand that we are giving up our respective rights to the Broker's undivided loyalty. We have carefully considered the possible consequences of a dual agency relationship and understand that instead each of us could have engaged our own agent as a seller's agent or buyer's agent, respectively.

We hereby agree that ______________________________ is appointed to represent only the Buyer (the "Buyer's Designated Agent") and ______________________________ is appointed to represent only the Seller (the "Seller's Designated Agent") in this transaction. We understand that the Broker continues to be a dual agent representing both of us in this transaction with honesty and fairness, but that the Buyer's Designated Agent and the Seller's Designated Agent will each function as a single agent providing each of us, respectively, with undivided loyalty.

SELLER:

__________________________ **Date** ______

__________________________ **Date** ______

BUYER:

__________________________ **Date** ______

__________________________ **Date** ______

FormD002 - 5/98

Source: Gallinger Real Estate.

If at any time in the transaction process an in-house listing results in the possibility of a dual agency, it should be clarified with all parties. If the seller and buyer both agree to accept dual agency, then the acknowledgment of the prospective buyer or tenant and the seller or landlord to dual agency sections of the disclosure form must be signed and acknowledged (refer to Figure 2.7). *The dual agency relationship, applies only to one transaction at a time.*

TERMINATION OF AGENCY

An agency relationship ends in accordance with the terms of the agency contract. An example is the expiration of a listing contract for the sale of real estate. When the contract terminates, so does any authority of the agent to act on behalf of the principal. Another means of terminating an agency relationship is by completing the terms of the agency; for example, when the sale of listed real estate is complete and the seller has paid the commission. In some cases, an agency relationship may be terminated by operation of law. For instance, a power of attorney terminates automatically at the death of either principal or agent. Another example is the termination of a listing contract held by a broker whose license is revoked.

BUYER BROKERAGE: BUYER AS PRINCIPAL

Although some buyers are most comfortable with customer status, real estate buyers increasingly are hiring brokers to represent them. This relationship is referred to as *buyer brokerage:* a buyer employs a broker to locate a certain type of property for purchase. In such cases, the agency relationship exists between the buyer and the broker; the buyer is the principal and the broker is the agent.

Why Is Buyer Brokerage So Popular?

Buyer brokerage is common in both commercial and residential real estate transactions. Buyers moving into a new area recognize the advantages of broker representation in locating a house for purchase: using the broker's technical expertise to negotiate a better price and gaining the broker's fiduciary confidentiality and trust. Buyers naturally want assurance that they are paying a reasonable and fair price for a property. A buyer's broker may perform a market analysis and advise the buyer on an offer. A buyer's broker also may be able to suggest creative financing that is in the buyer's interest.

With the establishment of buyer agency, the direction of agency responsibility is reversed from the seller agency situation. When a buyer hires a broker, the broker owes all duties of loyalty and disclosure to the buyer, not to the seller. A written buyer broker agreement signed by both buyer and broker is used to prevent any disputes; however, verbal agreements are common in a certain percentage of cases. Typically, a disclosure of this relationship is made to the seller prior to any showing of the property.

Does Everyone Need an Agent?

Buyers represented by their own agent may encounter properties listed by sellers who have a real estate agent and sellers who do not. A buyer agent may arrange to show properties that may or may not be listed with MLS, but in which a seller agent represents the property owner. A buyer agent may also arrange to show a buyer property that is for sale by owners. These owners may or may not have representation.

Buyer's Broker Compensation

The buyer broker is compensated through a variety of methods. One way is payment by the buyer upon the purchase of property through terms in the buyer/purchaser listing agreement. In this case, the buyer broker must inform the seller and the seller's broker that compensation is being directly paid; therefore the buyer broker rejects any offer of a cooperative agency commission. The more common method of compensation, however, is when a broker shares in the commission according to the traditional arrangement between listing broker and cooperating broker. This method occurs when the seller of the property offers a commission upon sale through MLS. The seller is notified and agrees to the commission split between the listing broker and the buyer broker. The buyer in this scenario does not pay an additional fee, which keeps the transaction simple and avoids any restructuring.

Should the broker receive any up-front guarantee of compensation, then the buyer is credited on purchase; therefore the transaction requires some restructuring. An example is a buyer listing agreement that reflects a payment due to the buyer broker on completion of the agency transaction, a sum equal to 3 percent of the purchase price. The cooperating commission offered through the MLS is 2.75 percent. The balance then due from the buyer client is 0.25 percent. A buyer's broker commonly accepts a fee equal to the cooperating offer in the MLS, thereby allowing the buyer to have client representation without any additional cash outlay.

In some cases, the buyer broker can receive a nonrefundable up-front fee that would not be credited at the closing to the monies owed to the buyer broker. In this case, the buyer broker is paid the balance due according to the arrangement between the buyer broker and the principal.

Buyers as Clients

Once the purchaser accepts the role as client or principal of a firm, a buyer/purchaser listing agreement is signed (see Figure 2.2). As in all consensual contracts in real estate, both parties must agree to the terms of the listing agreement, including the services provided by the broker. The agreement also delineates the obligations of the broker and affiliated agents as well as the principal, the means of compensation, and the length of time of the listing. Legal obligations are outlined in a standard listing contract. Most other terms are negotiated, established, or determined by the office policy of the buyer broker's firm with the acceptance of the client. As in seller agency, the client of the buyer's broker now has a fiduciary relationship with the broker and agent.

Buyers as Customers

Some agencies specializing in buyer brokerage do accept listings from seller clients. After disclosure, a prospective buyer may elect customer status as to the properties

PUTTING IT TO WORK 1

Now that you have an idea of the different agency relationships, respond to the following scenario.* Then compare your response to the model in the Answer Key at the end of the chapter.

We've worked with an agent for some time now (as customers, not in a buyer–broker relationship) and have found a home we would like to purchase. Now we find out that an acquaintance has a real estate license. Can our friend submit the offer for us?

*Source: James A. Ader, "Real Estate Spotlight." Copyright © The Albany *Times Union*. Reprinted by permission.

FIGURE 2.2 An exclusive buyer/purchaser agency agreement form.

CAPITAL REGION MULTIPLE LISTING SERVICE, INC.

REALTOR®

THIS IS A LEGALLY-BINDING CONTRACT. IF NOT FULLY UNDERSTOOD, WE RECOMMEND CONSULTING AN ATTORNEY BEFORE SIGNING.

EQUAL HOUSING OPPORTUNITY

EXCLUSIVE BUYER/PURCHASER AGENCY AGREEMENT

AGREEMENT

The BUYER/PURCHASER ______________________ (hereinafter called the "CLIENT") retains and authorizes as Buyer's Broker (hereinafter called the "BROKER") ______________________ ______________(firm) represented by______________________(agent) to locate and/or negotiate for the purchase of real property of the general nature shown below.

AGREEMENT PERIOD

This Agreement begins upon signing and ends on ______________, 19 ____ or upon closing of a property purchased under this Agreement.

BROKER'S OBLIGATIONS

The BROKER will:

(1) use diligence in locating a property on price and terms acceptable to the CLIENT;
(2) use professional knowledge and skills to negotiate for CLIENT's purchase of the property;
(3) assist CLIENT throughout the transaction and act in the CLIENT's best interest at all times; and
(4) personally present the purchase offer to the Seller unless otherwise directed by the CLIENT.

CLIENT'S OBLIGATIONS

The CLIENT will:

(1) work exclusively with the BROKER during the period of this Agreement in all matters pertaining to the purchase of real property located within the Capital Region market area with the following exceptions:

____

____

____; and

(2) furnish the BROKER with all requested personal and financial information necessary to complete this transaction.

COMPENSATION

The CLIENT agrees to compensate the BROKER if the CLIENT, or any other person acting on the CLIENT's behalf, buys, exchanges for, or obtains an option on any real property.

The amount of compensation shall be:

(1) If the property is listed with a real estate company or licensee, BROKER will accept a fee equal to the fee being offered to cooperating agents; but in any event not less than ________ % of the purchase price of the property, or a flat fee of $ ______________.
If such fee, or any portion thereof, is paid by the Seller or the Seller's agent as a convenience of the transaction, then CLIENT will be credited by BROKER for the amount so paid.

(2) If the property is not listed with a real estate company or licensee, a fee of ________ % of the purchase price, or a flat fee of $ ______________ will be paid.
If such fee, or any portion thereof, is paid by the Seller as a convenience of the transaction, then CLIENT will be credited by BROKER for the amount so paid.

(3) Other Compensation Agreement: ____

____

____.

NOTE: If the CLIENT within ________ months of the termination of this Agreement, without the services of a licensed agent, purchases real property shown to the CLIENT by the BROKER during the term of this Agreement compensation as set forth in this Agreement shall apply and a fee shall be due the BROKER.

ADVICE ON TECHNICAL MATTERS

BROKER will not counsel CLIENT on legal, home inspection, public health, surveying, tax, financial or other technical matters. Upon request, BROKER will assist CLIENT in engaging qualified professionals to consult in such fields.

FAIR HOUSING

BROKER is committed to the philosophy of Fair Housing for all people. Therefore, BROKER will present properties to CLIENT in full compliance with local, state and federal fair housing laws against discrimination on the basis of race, color, religion, sex, national origin, handicap, age, marital status and/or familial status, children, or other prohibited factors.

PROPERTY LISTED WITH BROKER

If CLIENT becomes interested in acquiring any property for which BROKER has a listing contract, CLIENT may:

(1) elect customer status as to the property for which there is a conflict; or
(2) terminate this contract as to the property for which there is a conflict; or
(3) with knowledge and informed consent in writing of both CLIENT and Seller, CLIENT may agree to dual agency. CLIENT understands that in such a dual agency situation, the agent will not be able to provide the full range of fiduciary duties to the CLIENT and Seller and that by consenting to the dual agency relationship, CLIENT and Seller are giving up the right to undivided loyalty.

BROKER ______________________ CLIENT ______________________

By ______________________ CLIENT ______________________

[C-BUYERAGENCY] 1/15/92 Date ______________________

listed with that firm. As in other examples, this arrangement constitutes a consensual agreement. Company policy will determine whether or not a buyer brokerage firm will agree to work with a customer rather than for a buyer client.

DISCLOSURE AND LISTING FORMS

In New York, all real estate listing agreements for the sale or rental of one-to-four-unit residential property must be accompanied by the disclosure regarding real estate agency relationships form shown later in Figure 2.7. The form must be explained by the agent and read, acknowledged, and signed by the principal prior to signing the listing agreement.

The Exclusive Right to Sell Agreement

Under the **exclusive right to sell** listing contract (Figure 2.3), the *property is listed with only one broker.* If anyone else sells the property during the term of the listing contract, the broker is legally entitled to the commission. This form could contain or have an addendum attached that includes a statement regarding in-house sales that offer options available to a principal should dual agency occur.

The Exclusive Agency Agreement

In an **exclusive agency** listing (Figure 2.4), the *property is listed with only one broker as the agent.* If the broker effects sale of the property, the broker is legally entitled to the commission agreed upon; but if the owner sells the property, the broker earns no commission. Again, the agreement should include or have an addendum attached with a statement regarding in-house sales.

Upon listing with either the exclusive right to sell contract or the exclusive agency agreement, the agent must fully disclose the difference between the two contracts and allow the sellers to choose. In addition, a termination date for the listing must be assigned. New York prohibits automatic extensions of listings. All listings last for a specific time and are renegotiated or renewed after the contract expiration.

The Open Listing Agreement

Under an **open listing** (Figure 2.5), the *seller allows a property to be shown by one or more brokers.* The broker effecting the sale is entitled to the commission. If the owner sells the property to a prospect not generated by any broker, however, the owner owes no commission. In an open listing, the same rules of disclosure apply as in other listing contracts.

The Exclusive Right to Rent Agreement

This contract (see Figure 2.6) is between an owner or a lessor and a broker or agent in the rental of residential property. The contract is similar to the exclusive right to sell listing agreement discussed earlier. The rental fee is paid to the listing agent even if the owner or another party rents the property. In New York, disclosure is required with listing agreements for rental or lease just as it is with listing agreements for the sale of residential property.

AGENCY DISCLOSURE

Section 443 requires that licensees present a written **agency disclosure form** that *details consumer choices about representation at the* **first substantive contact** *with a*

FIGURE 2.3 An exclusive right to sell contract form.

REALTOR®

Greater Rochester Association of REALTORS®, Inc.

EXCLUSIVE RIGHT TO SELL CONTRACT

THIS FORM IS FOR USE BY MEMBERS OF THE GREATER ROCHESTER ASSOCIATION OF REALTORS®, INC. ("GRAR") ONLY FOR THE PLACING OF PROPERTY LISTINGS IN THE GENESEE REGION REAL ESTATE INFORMATION SERVICES, INC. MULTIPLE LISTING SERVICE ("GENRIS MLS").

REALTORS® EXCLUSIVE RIGHT TO SELL, EXCHANGE OR LEASE CONTRACT. COMMISSIONS OR FEES FOR REAL ESTATE SERVICES TO BE PROVIDED HEREUNDER ARE NEGOTIABLE BETWEEN REALTOR® AND OWNER. IT IS UNDERSTOOD THAT GRAR AND THE GENESEE REGION REAL ESTATE INFORMATION SERVICE, INC. ("GENRIS") IS NOT A PARTY TO THIS LISTING AGREEMENT.

1. OWNERSHIP OF PROPERTY AND POWER TO SIGN CONTRACT. I, ______________________________, am the Owner(s) of the property located at ______________________________ (the "Property"). I have complete legal authority to sell, exchange or lease the Property. I have not entered into any other agreement which would affect the sale, exchange, lease, or transfer of the Property; except as follows: (name or specify agreement) ______________________________. For purposes of this Contract, any reference to a "sale" or "purchase" of the Property shall be deemed to include any "exchange" of the Property.

2. EXCLUSIVE RIGHT TO SELL OR LEASE. (Check and complete either (a) or (b), or both).

(a) ____ I hereby hire ______________________________ (REALTOR®) to sell the Property and I hereby grant to REALTOR® the Exclusive Right to Sell the Property for the price of $ ______________________ or any other price that I later agree to, and upon such terms and conditions as I may agree to.

(b) ____ I hereby hire ______________________________ (REALTOR®) to lease the Property and I hereby grant to REALTOR® the Exclusive Right to Lease the Property for a rent of $ ______________________ per ________ or any other rent that I may later agree to, and upon such terms and conditions as I may agree to.

3. MULTIPLE LISTING SERVICE/INTERNET. I authorize REALTOR® to submit the information contained in this listing agreement and the applicable GENRIS Data Sheet relating to the Property to the GENRIS MLS. REALTOR® will submit such information to GENRIS **within 24 hours** of my signing this Contract. REALTOR® shall retain this listing agreement and the Data Sheet for at least six years. I agree that REALTOR® will provide GENRIS with information, including the selling price, about the Property upon final sale of the Property. I further agree that REALTOR® will provide GENRIS with information, in addition to the list price, prior to final sale of the Property. All information submitted becomes the property of GENRIS and may be published by GENRIS including, without limit, on the Internet.

4. PAYMENT TO REALTOR®. (Check and complete either (a) or (b), or both).

(a) _____ I will pay REALTOR® a commission of ___ % of the gross sale price of the Property as set forth in the purchase and sale contract that I sign, or $ ______________________ .

(b) _____ I will pay REALTOR® a commission of ___ % of the gross rent for the Property as set forth in the lease contract that I sign, or $ ______ .

5. AUTHORIZATION REGARDING OTHER BROKERS. I authorize REALTOR® to cooperate with other brokers, including brokers who represent buyers (with the understanding that such "buyer's brokers" will be representing only the interests of the prospective buyers), to appoint subagents, and to divide with other licensed brokers such compensation in any manner acceptable to REALTOR®, such other brokers and me. In the event that there is a participating subagent broker or buyer's broker, I authorize that the following compensation be paid out of the commission provided in Paragraph 4 above to such subagent broker or buyer's broker: (Complete both)

Subagent broker will be paid ______% of the gross sale or rent price, or $____________.

Buyer's broker will be paid ______% of the gross sale or rent price, or $____________.

6. PAYMENT OF COMMISSION. I agree to pay to REALTOR® the commission set forth in Paragraph 4 on the "closing date" specified in the purchase and sale contract or when I sign a lease for the Property. I will pay this commission to REALTOR® whether I, REALTOR®, or anyone else sells or leases the Property during the life of this Contract. REALTOR® has earned the commission when I am provided with a written purchase offer which meets the price and other conditions I have set or when the purchase and sale contract becomes a binding legal commitment on the buyer, or when I sign a lease for the Property.

7. SUBMISSION OF OFFERS TO PURCHASE. I agree that any offers to purchase or lease the Property shall be submitted through REALTOR® or, with my REALTOR®'s consent, through any cooperating broker. **Check One**

8. FOR SALE, FOR RENT SIGN. I authorize REALTOR® to install a "**For Sale**"/"**Sold**" or "**For Rent**" sign on the Property. ______ Yes ______ No

9. LOCKBOX. I authorize REALTOR® to use a lockbox. I understand that neither REALTOR®, any cooperating broker, the GRAR nor GENRIS shall be responsible for any theft, loss or damage attributed to the use of a lockbox. ______ Yes ______ No

10. DUTIES OF REALTOR®. REALTOR® will use best efforts to procure a buyer. REALTOR® will physically inspect the interior and exterior of the Property prior to submission of the listing to the GENRIS MLS. REALTOR® will list the Property in full compliance with local, state and federal fair housing laws against discrimination on the basis of race, creed, color, religion, national origin, sex, familial status, marital status, age, or disabilities. REALTOR® will bring all offers to purchase or lease the Property to me. REALTOR® will assist in negotiating any and all offers to purchase or lease the Property.

________________ Owner's Initials

________________ Broker's/Salesperson's Initials

Revised GRAR 11/00 **Exclusive Right to Sell Contract** **Page 1 of 2**

(continued)

prospective seller or buyer (Figure 2.7). This contact is defined as when some detail and information about the property is shared with interested parties. The law is part of Article 12–A of the New York Real Property Law. *Section 443 applies to the sale and rental of residential one- to four-unit properties.* The law does not cover vacant land or condominium and cooperative apartments in buildings containing more than four units.

The law's purpose is to make consumers aware of the agency relationship of a real estate agent with whom they come into contact and of the choices available to them. For example, a prospective buyer may attend an open house and discuss matters regarding the property with the agent who is present and who holds the listing on the property. This agent represents the seller. However, the prospective purchasers may

FIGURE 2.3 Continued.

11. OBLIGATIONS OF OWNER/PROPERTY INFORMATION. To the extent within my possession, I agree to furnish to REALTOR® complete information reasonably necessary for processing this listing in the GENRIS MLS and for closing the sale or lease of the Property. All information about the Property I have given REALTOR® is accurate and complete, and REALTOR® assumes no responsibility to me or anyone else for the accuracy of such information, except as otherwise provided by law. I authorize REALTOR® to obtain other information about the Property. REALTOR® will use sources of information REALTOR® believes to be reliable, but is not responsible to me for the accuracy of the information REALTOR® obtains, except as otherwise provided by law. I authorize REALTOR® to disclose to prospective purchasers and any other persons, including other brokers, any information about the Property REALTOR® obtains from me or any other source. I understand that New York law requires me to give certain information about heating and insulation to prospective purchasers if they ask for it in writing before a purchase and sale contract is signed. I agree to refer all inquiries about the Property to REALTOR® and conduct all negotiations through REALTOR®. I agree to cooperate with REALTOR® in showing the Property to possible buyers or renters at any reasonable hour. I agree that REALTOR® and GENRIS may photograph the Property listed for sale or lease and may use the photographs in promoting its sale or lease. If the Property becomes vacant, I understand it is my obligation to continue to maintain the Property, including but not limited to, lawn care, snow plowing, utility service continuation, interior and exterior maintenance, until transfer of title unless otherwise agreed in the purchase and sale contract.

12. AUTHORIZATION OF REPRESENTATIVE TO PAY COMMISSION. Without in any way limiting any provision of Paragraph 6 above, I authorize my closing representative (such as my attorney) to pay to REALTOR® the commission agreed to in Paragraph 4 from the proceeds of the sale of the Property upon recording of the closing of the sale of the Property. If the proceeds of sale are insufficient to pay the entire commission due, I agree to pay the balance of commission to REALTOR®.

13. LIFE OF CONTRACT; SALE OR LEASE OF PROPERTY AFTER CONTRACT ENDS TO A PERSON WHO WAS SHOWN THE PROPERTY DURING THE LIFE OF CONTRACT. This Contract will last until midnight on ________________, 20 _____. However, if I sell or lease the Property within _______ days after this Contract ends (the "Effective Period") to a person who was shown the Property by Owner(s). REALTOR®, or anyone else during the life of this Contract, I will pay REALTOR® the same commission agreed to in Paragraph 4 of this Contract. I will not owe any commission to REALTOR® if such sale or lease occurs during the life of another Exclusive Right to Sell Contract I enter into with another REALTOR® after this Contract ends but before the expiration of the Effective Period.

14. NON-DISCRIMINATION. I understand that the listing and sale or lease of the Property must be in full compliance with local, state and federal fair housing laws against discrimination on the basis of race, creed, color, religion, national origin, sex, familial status, marital status, age, or disabilities.

15. RENEWAL AND MODIFICATION OF CONTRACT. I may extend the life of this Contract by signing another Exclusive Right to Sell Contract. If I renew this Contract, REALTOR® will notify GENRIS of the renewal. All changes or modifications of the provisions of this Contract must be made in writing, signed by Owner(s) and REALTOR®.

16. OWNER'S LIABILITY FOR CONTRACT TERMINATION. In the event this Contract is terminated prior to the time specified in Paragraph 13 for any reason other than REALTOR®'s fault, I will be liable for and agree to pay all damages and expenses incurred by REALTOR®, including without limitation costs for advertising the Property and any commission due hereunder.

17. ATTORNEY'S FEES. In any action, proceeding or arbitration arising out of this Contract, the prevailing party shall be entitled to reasonable attorney's fees and costs.

18. RESPONSIBILITY OF OWNER(S) UNDER THIS CONTRACT. All Owners must sign this Contract. If more than one person signs this Contract as Owner, each person is fully responsible for keeping the promises made by the Owner.

19. OTHER. ____

____

In consideration of the above, REALTOR® and Owner accept this Contract and agree to its terms and conditions as of _____________, 20___.

Owner(s) Signature	Owner(s) Signature
Print Owner(s) Name	Print Owner(s) Name
Property Address	Broker or Salesperson Signature
Print Name of REALTOR® Firm	Print Name of Broker or Salesperson

EXPLANATION

The Secretary of State, State of New York, requires that the following explanation be given to homeowners and acknowledged by them in the listing of property:

An *"exclusive right to sell"* listing means that if you, the owner of the property, find a buyer for your house, or if another broker finds a buyer, you must pay the agreed commission to the present broker.

An *"exclusive agency"* listing means that if you, the owner of the property find a buyer, you will not have to pay a commission to the broker. However, if another broker finds a buyer, you will owe a commission to both the selling broker and your present broker.

Owner(s) understands that this Contract grants REALTOR® the exclusive right to sell the Property.

Owner(s) Signature	Owner(s) Signature

Revised GRAR 11/00 **Exclusive Right to Sell Contract** **Page 2 of 2**

Source: Copyright © Greater Rochester Association of REALTORS®, Inc. Reprinted with permission.

erroneously think that this agent is considering *their* best interests. The duty of the agent, when details about the property are discussed, is to inform the prospective purchasers that he represents the seller. A disclosure form must be signed to verify that disclosure has taken place. Section 443 includes the actual text of the New York required disclosure form. Brokers may copy this text and use it. Most of the real estate boards in New York have printed copies available to members.

In addition to the Real Property Law, New York also has codified rules and regulations that govern the behavior of licensees. Regulation 175.7 limits compensation as follows: *"A real estate broker shall make it clear for which party he is acting and he shall not receive compensation from more than one party except with the full knowledge and consent of all the parties."*

This regulation bears a direct relationship to Real Property Law Section 443 covering one-to-four-unit residential properties. This regulation states that licensees must disclose whom they represent in a real estate transaction. This mandatory disclosure reveals the party whom the agent represents, explains the choices available to the consumer, and provides written proof of the disclosure.

FIGURE 2.4
An exclusive agency listing agreement form.

REALTOR®

EXCLUSIVE AGENCY CONTRACT
Approved as to form by the Multiple Listing Service
OTSEGO-DELAWARE BOARD OF REALTORS, INC.

EQUAL HOUSING OPPORTUNITY

_______________ Listing No.

COMMISSIONS OR FEES FOR REAL ESTATE SERVICES TO BE PROVIDED ARE NEGOTIABLE BETWEEN REALTOR AND CLIENT.
THIS IS A LEGALLY BINDING CONTRACT. IF YOU HAVE QUESTIONS CONCERNING THIS CONTRACT, YOU SHOULD CONSULT AN ATTORNEY BEFORE SIGNING IT.

DATE:_______________________________, 19 ___________

GRANT OF EXCLUSIVE AGENCY/TERM OF LISTING

TO ____

I the undersigned OWNER (the word OWNER refers to each and all parties who have an ownership interest in the property) hereby give you the Broker the exclusive agency to sell my property located at:

____

more fully described as:

____

for $__________________________ until 12:00 o'clock midnight on ______________________________. It is understood and agreed that you will submit this listing within 48 hours to the MULTIPLE LISTING SERVICE of the Otsego-Delaware Board of Realtors, Inc., (MLS) for circulation to all member participants in the MLS and to make an offer of subagency and cooperating agency to all members of the Otsego-Delaware Board of Realtors MLS, and any other cooperating agent authorized under the law to receive a commission. The Owner grants the Broker exclusive For Sale Sign privileges on said property, consents that said property may be shown at any reasonable hour, and agrees to refer any and all inquiries concerning said property to Broker.

COMPENSATION/BROKER PROTECTION PROVISION

I agree that if my property is sold to or exchanged with any person during the term of the listing I will pay broker a commission of ________percent (%) of the gross selling price, or ____________________ dollars ($), unless I am the procuring cause for the sale or exchange of my property, then no commission is due.

If within_____________ days after the expiration of the term of this listing, my property shall be sold to or exchanged with any person to whom the property has been shown by a Broker, subagent, or cooperating Broker during the term of listing, I will pay broker the commission stated in this agreement as if broker, subagent or cooperating Broker had made the sale.

If after the term of this listing the seller enters into a new Exclusive Right to Sell Listing Agreement with another licensed real estate agency, the above protection period will become null and void and the seller will have no obligation to pay commission to this listing agency.

If the Owner must remove the above described property from the market during the duration of this agreement and subsequently the property is sold within _________________days or within the original duration of this agreement, whichever is longer, the Broker will be entitled to a full commission,unless the property is sold or exchanged by the owner to a person or persons who previously had not viewed the property during the the term of this agreement.

Should the owner desire to rent the property during the period of this agreement, the Broker is hereby granted, irrevocably, the sole and exclusive right to rent the property, the exclusive "for rent" sign privilege and the Broker rental commission of $ ______________.

ONE COMMISSION

In utilizing subagency, cooperating agency, and/or buyer agency as described below, I will not be liable for more than one (1) commission totaling ____________percent (%) of the gross selling price.

SUBAGENCY

I am aware that this MLS listing is an offer of subagency made by me through you to the participants in the MLS. I am further aware that I could be liable for the misrepresentations, if any, of subagents. If I incur a loss,as a result of misrepresentations of subagents, I may be entitled to bring legal action against the responsible subagents, for reimbursement of such loss.

I agree with you that the compensation to the selling subagent or cooperating broker in a transaction shall be_________percent (%) of the gross selling price or __________________________dollars ($).

BUYER AGENCY

I authorize you to cooperate with brokers who represent buyers with the understanding that such buyers' brokers will be representing only the interests of the prospective buyers, unless I agree otherwise in writing.

I agree with you that the compensation to the buyer's agent in a transaction shall be_______ percent (%) of the gross selling price or __________________________dollars ($).

TERMINATION

I understand that if I terminate the listing Broker's authority prior to expiration of its term, that the listing Broker shall retain its contract rights to a commission and recovery of advertising expenses and any other damages incurred by reason of my early termination of this agreement.

PROPERTY INFORMATION

I direct you to furnish a copy of the signed profile sheet (Schedule A), which you have completed, to participants of the MLS.
I have____ or have not _____ completed and delivered to you a signed Seller's Disclosure of Property Condition Statement, and I certify that the information furnished is accurate to the best of my knowledge, and may be disseminated to interested customers.

NON-DISCRIMINATION

It is agreed that my property is listed in full compliance with local, state and federal fair housing laws against discrimination on the basis of race, creed, color, religion, national origin, sex, familial status, marital status, age, or disabilities.

SUBSEQUENT PURCHASE OFFERS

Owner should consult an attorney regarding subsequent purchase offers because a binding contract for the property may already exist and owner could incur additional liabilities to buyers and/or Brokers.

FOR SALE SIGN, INTERNET, LOCKBOXES, PHOTOGRAPHS (Please initial for authorization)

______ I authorize the placement of a " For Sale" sign on my property.
______ I authorize placing my property on the Internet.
______ I hereby authorize the use of a lockbox, and I accept any responsibility for any damage or loss arising from the use of the lockbox
______ I authorize the photographing of my property and the use of such photographs in promoting its sale.

MLS COMPANIES

I also confirm that I have received a list containing the names and addresses of all MLS companies.

ACCEPTANCE

By signing this contract, each party agrees to be bound by all of the terms of this contract and each party further acknowledges that he or she received a fully signed duplicate of this contract.

Owner ______________________________ Broker ______________________________

Owner ______________________________ By ______________________________

An **"Exclusive Right to Sell"** listing means that if you, the owner of the Property, find a buyer for your house, or if another Broker finds a buyer, you must pay the agreed commission to the present Broker.

An **"Exclusive Agency"** listing means a contract under which the owner appoints a real estate broker as his or her exclusive agent to sell the property on the Owner's stated terms for a commission. The owner reserves the right to sell to any buyer he procures without paying anyone a commission.

OOMLS-9/97

FIGURE 2.5 An open listing agreement.

OPEN NON-EXCLUSIVE LISTING AGREEMENT

Owner(s) have engaged _____________ Pathfinder Realty to act as agent for the sale of property known as _____________ and located at _____________ New York.

In return Agent will use his/her best efforts to sell the property. The Owner(s) agree to grant the agent the Open Listing to sell this property under the following terms and conditions.

1. Time Period of Agreement: This agreement shall be in effect from _____________ until the property is sold or Agent is notified that the property is no longer available.

2. Price of Property: The property will be offered for sale at the list price of $ _____________ and shall be sold subject to negotiations at such price and terms which the Owner(s) may agree.

3. Commission to be Paid to Agent: The agent shall be entitled to one commission of ______ % of the selling price. Agent is due one month's rent if property is rented by Agent for Owner. All commissions are Negotiable.

4. Owner(s) Obligation after Expiration of Agreement: Owner understands and agrees to pay commission of ______ % if this property is sold or transferred, or is the subject of a contract of sale within 120 days of this agreement, expiring to anyone who was offered, quoted, shown the property by the Agent or subagent during the time period of this Agreement. Owner will not however be obligated to pay such a commission if the owner enters into an Exclusive Listing Agreement with another licensed real estate broker after the expiration of this agreement or if the owner(s) sells the property themselves without any assistance from the Agent.

5. Negotiations and Deposits: Owner(s) agree to have all negotiations submitted by this Agent with buyers shown the property with this agent or subagent. Further, all deposits shall be held by _____________ Pathfinder Realty in its escrow account at _____________ Bank in _____________ New York. Any forfeiture of the deposit by the buyer shall go 1/2 to Owner, 1/2 to _____________, Pathfinder Realty not to exceed the commission due in #3.

6. Marketable title owners shall cooperate with the marketing of this property and shall provide at the time of sale a good marketable title. All information given by the owners is correct to the best of their knowledge and they give authorization to the Agent to place a For Sale sign on the property; to take interior and exterior photos of the property; and to give listing information to buyers and subagents.

7. Nondiscrimination: It is agreed that the property is listed in full compliance of all local, state and federal fair housing laws against discrimination on the basis of race, color, creed, religion, national origin, sex, familial status, marital status, age, or disabilities.

8. Acceptance: This is a legal and binding contract. No change, amendment, or termination of this agreement shall be binding unless in writing and signed by both parties. By signing this agreement each party agrees to be bound by the terms of this agreement and acknowledges that they have received a copy.

Owner _______________________________ Date _____________

Owner _______________________________ Date _____________

Address ____

Phone# _______________ Attorney _______________________

Acceptance by Pathfinder Realty _____________________ Agent Date _____________

An "Open Listing" means that if you, the seller of the property, find a buyer for your property without assistance from the broker you will not owe the agreed commission to the present broker. However if a purchase offer is accepted by you from anyone that has been sent to you, told about your property, or shown your property by the broker you must pay the agreed upon commission to the broker.

Further, you agree that if you, or another broker, find a buyer and enter into a purchase agreement, you will notify _____________ Pathfinder Realty immediately.

Source: Pathfinder Realty, Inc. East Springfield, New York. Reprinted by permission of Pathfinder Realty, Inc.

FIGURE 2.6
An exclusive right to rent contract form.

EXCLUSIVE RIGHT TO RENT CONTRACT

Approved as to Form by the Multiple Listing Service

Greater Syracuse Association of REALTORS®

Commissions or fees for real estate services to be provided are negotiable between REALTOR® and Client

________________, 200____

TO: ________________________________

I hereby give you the exclusive right to rent my property located at ________________ ________________________________ for $______________ per month. This exclusive right to rent agreement will expire at 12:00 midnight on ____________, 200____.

It is understood that you will submit this contract to the Multiple Listing Service of the Greater Syracuse Association of REALTORS®, Inc., for circulation to all members of the service.

It is agreed that my property is listed in full compliance with local, state and federal fair housing laws against discrimination on the basis of race, creed, color, religion, national origin, sex, familial status, marital status, age, or disabilities.

I agree to pay $__________ rental fee to you if my property is rented to any person to whom it has been shown during the term of this listing agreement.

In the event a contract to purchase and an offer to rent are presented simultaneously, the contract to purchase shall take precedence, and, in such case, there will be no rental fee deemed earned.

I agree with you that the compensation to the rental agent in a cooperative transaction shall be _____% of the rental fee or $__________, unless other arrangements have been made between the cooperative brokers.

______________________	______________________
Owner	Real Estate Company
______________________	______________________
Owner	By

Signed original to owner; signed original to broker; copy to MLS.

The Agency Disclosure Form

The licensee should first explain to prospective buyers or sellers that by law they have certain consumer rights. The licensee should then thoroughly explain each section of the document. The prospective clients should be given some time to read through the document privately and ask the licensee any questions. The roles of the agent, seller, buyer, client, and customer should be defined, and the consumers should be offered a choice as to the position they prefer. The form covers the following information:

- *Section 1* notifies consumers that brokers must disclose for whom they are working in an agency relationship.

FIGURE 2.7 A written disclosure form.

Disclosure Regarding Real Estate Agency Relationships

Section 443 of Article 12-A of the Real Property Law requires the real estate industry to provide the following information to prospective buyers, tenants, sellers and landlords: *Before you enter into a discussion with a real estate agent regarding a real estate transaction, you should understand what type of agency relationship you wish to have with that agent. New York State law requires real estate licensees who are acting as agents of buyers or sellers of property to advise potential buyers or sellers with whom they work of the nature of their agency relationship and the rights and obligations it creates.* 1

2

Seller's or Landlord's Agent

If you are interested in selling or leasing real property, you can engage a real estate agent as a seller's agent. A seller's agent, including a listing agent under a listing agreement with the seller, acts solely on behalf of the seller. You can authorize a seller's or landlord's agent to do other things including hire subagents, broker's agents or work with other agents such as buyer's agents on a cooperative basis. A subagent, is one who has agreed to work with the seller's agent, often through a multiple listing service. A subagent may work in a different real estate office.

A seller's agent has, without limitation, the following fiduciary duties to the seller: reasonable care, undivided loyalty, confidentiality, full disclosure, obedience and a duty to account. The obligations of a seller's agent are also subject to any specific provisions set forth in an agreement between the agent and the seller.

In dealings with the buyer, a seller's agent should (a) exercise reasonable skill and care in performance of the agent's duties; (b) deal honestly, fairly and in good faith; and (c) disclose all facts known to the agent materially affecting the value or desirability of property, except as otherwise provided by law.

3

Buyer's or Tenant's Agent

If you are interested in buying or leasing real property, you can engage a real estate agent as a buyer's or tenant's agent. A buyer's agent acts solely on behalf of the buyer. You can authorize a buyer's agent to do other things including hire subagents, broker's agents or work with other agents such as seller's agents on a cooperative basis.

A buyer's agent has, without limitation, the following fiduciary duties to the buyer: reasonable care, undivided loyalty, confidentiality, full disclosure, obedience and a duty to account. The obligations of a buyer's agent are also subject to any specific provisions set forth in an agreement between the agent and the buyer.

In dealings with the seller, a buyer's agent should (a) exercise reasonable skill and care in performance of the agent's duties; (b) deal honestly, fairly and in good faith; and (c) disclose all facts known to the agent materially affecting the buyer's ability and/or willingness to perform a contract to acquire seller's property that are not inconsistent with the agent's fiduciary duties to the buyer.

Broker's Agents

As part of your negotiations with a real estate agent, you may authorize your agent to engage other agents whether you are a buyer/tenant or seller/landlord. As a general rule, those agents owe fiduciary duties to your agent and to you. You are not vicariously liable for their conduct. 4

Agent Representing Both Seller and Buyer

A real estate agent acting directly or through an associated licensee, can be the agent of both the seller/landlord and buyer/tenant in a transaction, but only with the knowledge and informed consent, in writing, of both the seller/landlord and the buyer/tenant.

In such a dual agency situation, the agent will not be able to provide the full range of fiduciary duties to the buyer/tenant and seller/landlord. The obligations of an agent are also subject to any specific provisions set forth in an agreement between the agent and the buyer/tenant and seller/landlord. 5

An agent acting as a dual agent must explain carefully to both the buyer/tenant and seller/landlord that the agent is acting for the other party as well. The agent should also explain the possible effects of dual representation, including that by consenting to the dual agency relationship the buyer/tenant and seller/landlord are giving up their right to undivided loyalty.

A buyer/tenant or seller/landlord should carefully consider the possible consequences of a dual agency relationship before agreeing to such representation.

General Considerations

You should carefully read all agreements to ensure that they adequately express your understanding of the transaction. A real estate agent is a person qualified to advise about real estate. If legal, tax or other advice is desired, consult a competent professional in that field. Throughout the transaction you may receive more than one disclosure form. The law requires each agent assisting in the transaction to present you with this disclosure form. You should read its contents each time it is presented to you, considering the relationship between you and the real estate agent in your specific transaction. 6

(continued)

- *Section 2* pertains to seller or landlord agency and the fiduciary duties inherent in this relationship. The agent owes allegiance to the seller or landlord; however, in dealing with the buyer, the agent must use reasonable skill and care and must disclose all known facts affecting the property.
- *Section 3* defines the role of the buyer or tenant agent and the fiduciary duties inherent in this relationship. The agent owes allegiance to the buyer or tenant; however, in dealing with the seller, the agent must exercise care and skill and must disclose all known facts that may be inconsistent with the agent's fiduciary duty to the seller and may affect the buyer's ability to execute the contract.

FIGURE 2.7 Continued.

Acknowledgment of Prospective Buyer/Tenant. (1) I have received and read this disclosure notice. (2) I understand that a seller's/landlord's agent, including a listing agent, is the agent of the seller/landlord exclusively, unless the seller/landlord and buyer/tenant otherwise agree. (3) I understand that subagents, including subagents participating in a multiple listing service, are agents of the seller/landlord exclusively. (4) I understand that I may engage my own agent to be my buyer's/tenant's broker. (5) I understand that the agent presenting this form to me,

(name of licensee) ______________________ of *(name of firm)* ______________________

is *(check applicable relationship)* _____ an agent of the seller/landlord _____ my agent as a buyer's/tenant's agent

Buyer/Tenant Signature ______________________ *Date* ____________

7 *Buyer/Tenant Signature* ______________________ *Date* ____________

Acknowledgment of Prospective Seller/Landlord. (1) I have received and read this disclosure notice. (2) I understand that a seller's/landlord's agent, including a listing agent, is the agent of the seller/landlord exclusively, unless the seller/landlord and buyer/tenant otherwise agree. (3) I understand that subagents, including subagents participating in a multiple listing service, are agents of the seller/landlord exclusively. (4) I understand that a buyer's/tenant's agent is the agent of the buyer/tenant exclusively. (5) I understand that the agent presenting this form to me, *(name of licensee)* ______________________ of *(name of firm)* ______________________

is *(check applicable relationship)* _____ my agent as a seller's/landlord's agent _____ an agent of the buyer/tenant

Seller/Landlord Signature ______________________ *Date* ____________

Seller/Landlord Signature ______________________ *Date* ____________

Acknowledgment of Prospective Buyer/Tenant and Seller/Landlord to Dual Agency. (1) I have received and read this disclosure notice. (2) I understand that a dual agent will be working for both the seller/landlord and buyer/tenant. (3) I understand that I may engage my own agent as a seller's/landlord's agent or a buyer's/tenant's agent. (4) I understand that I am giving up my right to the agent's undivided loyalty. (5) I have carefully considered the possible consequences of a dual agency relationship. (6) I understand that the agent presenting this form to me,

(name of licensee) ______________________ of *(name of firm)* ______________________

8 is a dual agent working for both the buyer/tenant and seller/landlord, acting as such with the consent of both buyer/tenant and seller/landlord and following full disclosure to the buyer/tenant and seller/landlord.

Buyer/Tenant Signature ______________________ *Date* ____________

Buyer/Tenant Signature ______________________ *Date* ____________

Seller/Landlord Signature ______________________ *Date* ____________

Seller/Landlord Signature ______________________ *Date* ____________

Acknowledgment of the Parties to the Contract. (1) I have received, read and understand this disclosure notice. (2) I understand that *(name of real estate licensee)* ______________________

of *(name of firm)* ______________________

is *(check applicable relationship)* _____ an agent of the seller/landlord _____ an agent of the buyer/tenant

_____ a dual agent working for both the buyer/tenant and seller/landlord, acting as such with the consent of both the buyer/tenant and seller/landlord and following full disclosure to the buyer/tenant and seller/landlord.

I also understand that *(name of real estate licensee)* ______________________ of

9 *(name of firm)* ______________________ is *(check applicable relationship)* _____ an agent of the seller/landlord _____ an agent of the buyer/tenant

_____ a dual agent working for both the buyer/tenant and seller/landlord, acting as such with the consent of both the buyer/tenant and seller/landlord and following full disclosure to the buyer/tenant and seller/landlord.

Buyer/Tenant Signature ______________________ *Date* ____________

Buyer/Tenant Signature ______________________ *Date* ____________

Seller/Landlord Signature ______________________ *Date* ____________

Seller/Landlord Signature ______________________ *Date* ____________

DOS-1565 (9/01)

Source: New York State Department of State.

When the agency disclosure form should be used **You Should Know**

The disclosure form must be utilized in the following transactions involving the sale or rental of one-to-four unit residential properties:

1. A listing agent must obtain a signed acknowledgment from a seller prior to entering into a listing agreement with the seller.
2. A seller agent must present the disclosure form to a buyer or buyer agent *at the first substantive contact* and the buyer must sign and acknowledge the form.
3. An agent must provide the disclosure form to a buyer prior to entering into an agreement to act as a buyer agent.
4. A buyer agent must present the disclosure form to the seller or seller agent *at the first substantive contact* with the seller and must obtain a signed acknowledgment from the seller or the seller's listing agent.
5. When the real estate transaction reaches the point where the contract of sale is signed, all parties to the contract must sign the acknowledgment of the parties to the contract section of the disclosure form.
6. The agent must provide a copy of the disclosure form to the buyer or seller and maintain a copy for a minimum of three years.

- *Section 4* states that the consumer may authorize the agent to engage other agents (broker agents) and that these agents are bound by the same fiduciary duties. The agents must be loyal to the consumer, but the consumer has no vicarious liability for the agent's actions.
- *Section 5* defines dual agency with informed consent and warns that a dual agency causes the consumer to give up the fiduciary right of undivided loyalty.
- *Section 6* explains that other kinds of advice, such as legal advice, should be obtained as necessary from other professionals. It also clarifies that the disclosure form may be presented on more than one occasion.
- *Section 7* is the acknowledgment by the parties to the transaction. It asks the buyer or tenant or the seller or landlord to confirm an understanding of the disclosure form.

When disclosure should take place **You Should Know**

Whether a written disclosure form is required or not, the following typical situations require the agent to clarify who he represents:

1. *The open house.* Prospective buyers express a sincere interest in a property and want additional time with the agent to discuss a possible offer. Disclosure must be made prior to any substantive contact.
2. *Walk-ins.* A prospective buyer or seller may walk into a real estate office, meet an agent, and want to discuss listing or purchasing a property. At this point, disclosure must be made.
3. *Appointments.* An agent meets with a seller to discuss the possibility of listing a property for sale. Disclosure must take place at the meeting and/or before a listing agreement is signed.
4. *Viewing the property.* When the prospective purchasers and the agent meet to view the property, disclosure must take place.

- *Section 8* is an acknowledgment by the prospective buyer or tenant and/or the seller landlord to a dual agency relationship.
- *Section 9* is a reaffirmation that both the buyer and the seller have been introduced to the agency relationship. This section is used when the buyer and seller go to a contract for purchase and sale.

Licensee's Role

It is imperative that licensees thoroughly discuss the agency relationship they represent. Agents must clarify client and customer roles and enumerate the agent's fiduciary responsibilities to the client. It is equally important for licensees to explain to the client their services and define their obligation to deal fairly and honestly with the customer.

You Should Know

Agent record keeping

As illustrated above, agents will have opportunities to record information relevant to their daily activities. The recorded information can be used as factual reminders of past, present, and future activities, and is useful should a dispute arise. Diaries, journals, notebooks, and appointment books are generally admissible in court as evidence in that event. Documented statements, directives, and interactions with customers, clients, prospects, and other agents can be particularly useful in the areas of license law, agency relationships, and human rights issues (discussed later in this text).

Record keeping should include:

- Properties shown
- Communication log; parties who call and the nature of their call
- Properties suggested to prospects
- Copies of contracts and other documents
- Correspondence on offers and contracts
- Refusals to sign the agency disclosure form
- Other relevant business

Refusal to Sign Disclosure Form

If a buyer or seller refuses to sign the disclosure form, the agent should determine the reason for that decision, reinforce the idea that the document is intended to protect the consumer, and explain that the form is a notice of consumer rights and not a binding contract. Sellers are more likely to sign as part of the listing process than are buyers, who may be reluctant. Buyers often state, "I never sign anything without the approval of my attorney." If this occurs, the agent should make notes in an appointment book of the names of the prospective buyers, the time, the date, and reasons for refusal. At this point, the property may be shown. However, after returning to the office or at the earliest possible moment following this substantive contact, the agent must complete a declaration form stating all of the facts, have it acknowledged, retain a copy for the records, and provide a copy to the broker to be kept on file for a period of three years. Figure 2.8 indicates that this declaration must be completed if either a seller or buyer refuses to sign the mandated disclosure form. Additional information may be appended to the form.

Change in Agent Roles

With the consent of the principal, agents may change roles after having established, for instance, a relationship with the seller as client, a seller subagent–client relationship, or a buyer agent–client relationship. Some examples follow.

From buyer client-agent to dual agent. An agent employed to represent a buyer client may have another agent at the same firm show a listing on a property that the buyer might be interested in. The buyer agent could then approach the buyer client, review and discuss the disclosure form, and receive an acceptance by the buyer client to revert to customer status for that particular property, or with disclosure and informed consent, permit the firm to be a dual agent.

From seller client-agent to dual agent. An agent employed by a seller client to represent that client may know of another agent in the same brokerage firm who has been employed by a buyer client. This prospective buyer may have a sincere interest in the property listed by the seller agent in the same firm. The listing agent must approach and discuss with the seller a possible dual agency relationship for that particular buyer. The seller and the buyer may then accept the dual agency arrangement and the brokerage firm becomes the dual agent for buyer and seller. Designated agents may be assigned as discussed earlier. The disclosure of the agency relationship and informed consent must be made and accepted by all the parties.

PUTTING IT TO WORK 2

Do you now understand disclosure and when and how it should be made? Respond to the following scenario,* then compare your response to the model in the Answer Key at the end of the chapter.

I'm interested in buying some vacant land. The agent I've contacted refuses to let me know whether he is representing me or the seller. I thought agents had to offer this type of disclosure. The agent says not with land sales. Is he correct?

need a verbal acknowledgment.

OTHER TYPES OF DISCLOSURE

Stigmatized Property Disclosure

Article 443-a of the New York Real Property Law addresses stigmatized property disclosure. The law covers all residential property for sale or lease and addresses properties that have: (1) occupants who have AIDS or other illnesses not transmitted through occupancy or (2) properties that were a site of death due to natural causes, accidents, suicide, homicide, crime, and other reasons. Under this law, sellers and seller agents do not have to disclose this information and may or may not disclose upon written request of the buyer or buyer agent. A seller agent can disclose only with permission of the seller. A buyer or buyer agent may provide written request for disclosure to the seller or seller agent during negotiations for purchase.

---

*Source: James A. Ader, "Real Estate Spotlight." Copyright © The Albany *Times Union*. Reprinted by permission.

FIGURE 2.8 A declaration form for use if buyers or sellers refuse to sign disclosure form.

CAPITAL REGION MULTIPLE LISTING SERVICE, INC.

DECLARATION BY REAL ESTATE LICENSEE
PURSUANT TO SECTION 443(3)(F) OF THE REAL PROPERTY LAW

STATE OF NEW YORK)
) ss.:
COUNTY OF)

______________________________ (name of licensee), do hereby swear and affirm under penalties of perjury:

1. I am a principal broker/associate broker/licensed salesperson affiliated with ____(name of firm). I make this statement in compliance with Section 443(3)(f) of the New York State Real Property Law.

2. On_______________, 199_____, I presented to____(name of buyer or seller) the disclosure notice required under Section 443 of the Real Property Law. A true copy of the actual disclosure form presented to him/her is attached to this affirmation.

3. Although I indicated to the buyer/seller that New York State Law required that I request that he/she sign to acknowledge receipt of the disclosure notice, he/she refused to sign the acknowledgement to the disclosure form when presented. The reason given for this refusal was as follows:

____

____

____

Dated: ________________________, New York

__________________________, 199___.

____
Print Name Below Signature of Licensee

PUTTING IT TO WORK 3

Choose a partner to enact the following role-playing exercises. One person can be the seller or buyer agent and the other can be the seller or prospective purchaser. These exercises will help you apply agency and disclosure to real-life situations. So that the conversation is not one-sided, those who assume the role of seller or buyer should put themselves in the position of a person who must be educated in this process and who will ask questions during the course of the conversation. Compare your role-play with the model in the Answer Key at the end of the chapter.

a. *Daphne is a seller agent; Bob is a prospective buyer. Daphne reviews the disclosure form with Bob, a walk-in, who is interested in several listings available in Daphne's firm. Bob questions aspects of the disclosure form, discusses the different choices with Daphne, and then decides his status.*

b. *Daphne is a seller agent; Betina is a seller. Daphne is making a listing presentation. She describes and defines cooperating agency and subagency and explains the distribution of the commission. She discusses the possibility and implications of an in-house sale.*

c. *Bill is a buyer agent; James is a buyer client. Bill is discussing a new in-house listing as a possible purchase for James and is explaining the alternatives to James.*

Electrical Service

An individual or a company must provide written notice to a purchaser or a purchaser agent if there is no public utility electrical service available at the property being purchased.

Utility Surcharge

In New York, any individual or company who sells a property where there is a gas or an electric utility surcharge imposed to defray the costs of extending the service to that particular property must provide written notice to a purchaser or purchaser agent. The exact wording must be: "This property is subject to an electric and/or gas utility surcharge." The notice must include the amount of the surcharge and the terms of payment.

Agricultural Districts

Prior to the sale, purchase, or exchange of property located partially or entirely within a state-mandated agricultural district, a specifically worded notice must be given to the purchaser. An agricultural district disclosure form, when necessary, is appended to the contract for purchase and sale.

SECTION 2 ANTITRUST LAW

ANTITRUST LAWS AND THE REAL ESTATE BUSINESS

Under federal and New York antitrust law, independent real estate brokerage firms, real estate brokerage franchises, real estate boards, and multiple listing services *cannot combine to fix commission rates.*

Elements of an Antitrust Violation

In general, antitrust violations are any business activity in which there is *a monopoly, a contract, a conspiracy, or a combination* that negatively impacts an individual's or a company's ability to do business. This negative impact is called restraint of trade.

To violate antitrust law, the restraint of trade must unreasonably restrict competition and be against the public interest. For example, if all the broker members of a particular real estate board agreed to charge a commission of not less than 15 percent of the purchase price of a property, they would be violating antitrust law.

A History of Antitrust Laws—Common-Law Era

As the United States grew into an industrial power during the nineteenth century, large monopolies began to form that controlled business and commerce in various sectors of the economy. By the end of the nineteenth century, the status of common law, that is, nonstatutory general public policy regulations, was not broad enough to protect the public from the power and control of these monopolies. Sanctions were needed to define, regulate, and control antitrust activity. The Sherman and Clayton Antitrust Acts and the Federal Trade Commission Act, enacted over a span of 24 years at the turn of the century, provided the necessary legislation and control (see Table 2.2).

The purpose of the *Sherman Antitrust Act,* enacted July 2, 1890, was to preserve a system of free economic enterprise and *to protect the public against the activities of monopolies, contracts, or other combinations that tend to be an unreasonable restraint of trade.* The focus of the act was to allow small businesses to compete effectively with larger companies. The Sherman Act covers trade and commerce with foreign countries and between the states (interstate commerce). Congress can exempt public agencies and selected industries from the provisions of the act. An example of an exemption is

TABLE 2.2 Federal antitrust enforcement regulations.

REGULATION OR AGENCY	PURPOSE	ENFORCEMENT
Sherman Act (1890)	Protects public from monopolies or combinations that restrain trade	corporate fines up to $10 million; individual fines up to $350,000; possible felony; up to 3 years in prison
Clayton Act (1914)	Supplements sanctions in Sherman Act	allows for individual or group (class-action) lawsuits for antitrust violations
Federal Trade Commission (1914)	Declares applicable trade procedures unfair	no penal sanctions but can provide monetary relief for victims; enforces Sherman Act and indirectly enforces Clayton Act
U.S. Department of Justice	Has antitrust division that enforces the Sherman and Clayton Acts	federal court system

the baseball industry. The *Clayton Antitrust Act,* enacted October 15, 1914, supplements the Sherman Act and has the same general purpose. It was designed to cover restraints on interstate trade or commerce not covered by the Sherman Act. The Clayton Act made *it unlawful for any individual engaged in commerce to lease or sell goods or machinery on the condition that the lessee or purchaser would then not deal with the goods or machinery of another competitor of the lessor or seller.* If this were allowed, it would decrease competition in the marketplace and create monopolies.

The *Federal Trade Commission (FTC),* an administrative body, was formed through an act of Congress in 1914 and given the broad power to declare trade practices unfair, particularly with regard to practices that conflict with basic policies of antitrust legislation. The FTC has the authority to enforce compliance with the Sherman Act and certain sections of the Clayton Act. In creating antitrust legislation, Congress did not intend that the statutes themselves would decrease the practice of unfair methods of competition and the tendency to monopolize. Ultimately, it would be up to the FTC and, more importantly, the courts, to resolve these questions.

Legislative Action

Over the years, congressional regulatory power has been expanded to include *intrastate* (within a state) as well as interstate trade and commerce. Most states, including New York, have statutes against monopoly, restraint of trade, and unfair trade practices, as well as other laws that protect the consumer. Although more private antitrust lawsuits have been filed in recent years, Congress and the courts are still deciding whether an individual has legal standing to sue under antitrust law. State enforcement is generally considered synonymous with federal law. It focuses on local and intrastate offenses. If antitrust activities occur on the state or local levels, violators may be subject to both federal and state laws.

Antitrust liability under the law — You Should Know

The antitrust division of the Department of Justice enforces the Sherman and Clayton Antitrust Acts. Violators of the Sherman Act can be subject to both criminal liability and monetary damages. A 1990 amendment to the Sherman Act provides that corporations can be fined up to $10 million and individuals up to $350,000. Violators of the Sherman Act can be found guilty of a felony and can be imprisoned for a term of up to three years. The Department of Justice can also impose other fines for antitrust violations. The FTC has no penal sanctions; it has the power to enforce only the Sherman Act and to enforce the Clayton Act indirectly. The FTC may stop practices that violate antitrust laws and can act as a court of equity and apply monetary relief for violations. A court of equity decides matters of law and makes judgments based on these laws.

Section 4 of the Clayton Act allows private parties, either individually or as a group (class-action lawsuit), *to sue antitrust violators. Injured parties can recover three times the damages sustained plus court costs and attorneys' fees.* Proving damages in antitrust lawsuits is difficult. Specific or certain proof of the injury is not required; however, the lawsuit must include facts that go beyond speculation. Even if individuals are damaged, they may not have the legal standing to sue unless it can be proved that they were directly injured by the actions.

Rule of Reason Versus Per Se Illegality

In antitrust lawsuits, the courts have to determine *if the restraints of trade are unreasonable and therefore illegal.* If the activity *is* reasonable, then it is allowable under law; this is called the *rule of reason.* Certain kinds of restraints of trade, however, were so inconsistent with free competition that they were found to be *per se illegal;* that is, absolutely not allowable under the law. Under the rule of reason, the following considerations apply:

1. Was the act a reasonable restraint with a compelling rationale?
2. What are the surrounding circumstances that led to the presumption of restraint of trade?
3. What is the nature or character of the contracts involved in the restraint of trade?

A restraint of trade is per se illegal if it is arbitrary in application and is potentially harmful to free competition. Per se illegal restraints of trade include price-fixing agreements between competitors, group boycotts, market allocation agreements between manufacturers and distributors, and tie-in arrangements between sellers and buyers.

Price fixing. Illegal *price fixing* occurs when competitors in a group or an industry conspire to charge the same or similar price for services rendered. Price fixing can be engaged in by competitors at the same level, such as retailers, or by members of different levels of production, such as manufacturer and retailer. Price fixing decreases competition between businesses, when for example, all brokerage firms in a community agree to charge a six percent commission.

Group boycotts. A *group boycott* is a conspiracy in which a person or group is persuaded or coerced into not doing business with another person or group. An example of a group boycott might be if an MLS directs that all broker members not do business with a certain real estate related company.

Market allocation agreement. A *market allocation agreement* is an agreement between competitors who are dividing or assigning a certain area or territory for sales. For example, two business franchises agree that one will sell goods or services in Albany County only and the other will sell in Schenectady County only. They agree not to compete with each other in the same county.

Tie-in arrangements. *Tie-in arrangements* are agreements between a party selling a product or service with a buyer that, as a condition of the sale, the buyer will buy another product from the seller or the buyer will not buy a product or use a service of another. If a buyer brokerage firm, for example, tells a buyer that the firm must use a certain mortgage company as a condition of the exclusive buyer/agency agreement, this would be illegal.

Real Estate and Antitrust Law

The real estate brokerage industry in New York must comply with both the Sherman and Clayton antitrust laws, New York law, and court decisions. The court decree in a 1972 lawsuit, *United States v. Long Island Board of REALTORS®, Inc.* [1972 WL 584 (E.D. NY)], furnishes guidelines for proper conduct within the real estate industry:

1. Commission rates must be negotiable between board members and their clients.
2. An MLS may circulate information concerning the commission that a broker has agreed upon with a client and may also give out information as to the percentage division that a listing broker has agreed to pay a selling broker.
3. The commission rate can be altered only with the consent of both the listing and selling broker.
4. The recipient of the commission must pay the listing or selling broker the agreed-upon percentage division of the commission.

In addition, boards may *not* do any of the following:

- fix commission rates or urge board members to adhere to any prescribed schedules of commission rates or publish prescribed commission rates or amounts
- include a suggested commission rate or amount in an educational course
- limit the right of a board member to negotiate and agree to a commission with a client

- take any punitive action against a person for not adhering to a rate or schedule of commission
- adopt any rules that would prohibit a member from doing business with another
- establish fees for membership in the board or MLS that are not related to the cost of maintaining or improving the organization
- refuse to accept for multiple listing any listing because of the rate or amount of commission set forth in the listing

CASE STUDIES

The following examples of DOS cases brought to administrative hearings illustrate how DOS makes determinations regarding a real estate licensee's duties and responsibilities as an agent. See *To the Student,* "Case Studies," which explains the terms and format of the following DOS administrative hearings.

Department of State, Division of Licensing Services, Complainant, against Marc L. Winograd and Gail F. Winograd, Respondents.

The agency issues specifically addressed in this case are improper dual agency and failure to disclose to principal. Also, the broker is liable for the associate broker's acts under his duty to supervise.

Allegations. The complaint alleges that Respondent Gail Winograd, when licensed as an associate broker, acted as a double agent on behalf of a tenant and landlord without the required disclosure or failed to make clear for whom she was acting; failed to advise the tenant that because the apartment involved in the transaction was located in a cooperative building, approval of the tenancy would have to be obtained from the board of the cooperative. The complaint further alleges that Marc Winograd failed to maintain rent and security monies in an escrow account or to turn those monies over to the landlord, wrongfully retained deposit monies and/or an unearned commission, and is liable for the alleged misconduct of Gail Winograd.

Findings of fact. A renter, Hodja, spoke to Respondent Gail Winograd about locating an apartment to rent, and Winograd agreed to assist her. Sometime thereafter, Respondent Winograd was asked by a Mr. Cook to assist him in subletting his cooperative apartment. Respondent previously assisted Cook and was authorized by him to sign a sublease on his behalf. At no time did Respondent disclose to Cook that she was acting as Hodja's agent or tell Hodja that she was acting as Cook's agent. Hodja gave Respondent Winograd a security deposit and a commission and signed a sublease for the apartment. Respondents did not place the money in an escrow account and instead kept it in a locked file cabinet. Winograd did not give Hodja a copy of the sublease, and Cook never saw or signed it. Hodja subsequently decided she did not want the apartment, and Respondent returned the rent and security deposit to her. Hodja did not request that the commission be returned and it was not.

Opinion. As a fiduciary, a licensee is prohibited from serving as a double agent representing parties with conflicting interest in the same transaction without the informed consent of the principals. "A real estate agent must prove that prior to undertaking to act as a dual agent, the agent must make full disclosure to all parties so as to obtain the consent of the principals to proceed in the undertaking." This legal principle is amplified by New York Regulation 175.7, which mandates that "a real estate broker shall make it clear for which party the agent is acting" and prohibits the agent from receiving compensation from more than one party "except with the full knowledge and consent of all parties to the transaction."

New York Regulation 175.12 also provides that a real estate broker "shall immediately deliver a duplicate of any instrument to any parties executing the same, when the instrument is prepared by the broker or under his supervision and when the instrument relates to the employment of the broker." This is applicable to the associate broker. Respondent's explanation for not giving Hodja a copy of the sublease was that at the time of signing, she had not yet received permission from Cook to sign on his behalf. The applicable regulation here does not allow for such a delay in delivery.

New York Regulation 175.1 provides that a real estate broker "shall at all times maintain a separate, special bank account for deposit monies." Respondent Marc Winograd violated this regulation. Respondents kept the commission paid by Hodja in spite of the fact that Respondent had acted in the transaction as an undisclosed double agent. However, in the absence of proof of Respondent Marc Winograd's knowledge of that misconduct, he cannot be held liable for retention of the commission. Respondent Gail Winograd's conduct, because of her status as an associate broker, is governed by the laws related to salespersons. Therefore, Respondent Marc Winograd, as her broker, had the duty of supervising her conduct.

Real Property Law Section 442–c provides that no violation of Article 12–A by a salesperson shall be deemed to be cause for the revocation or suspension of the broker license unless the broker had actual notice of the violation or received some benefit. If a broker is found liable for his own acts or vicariously liable for a salesperson's act, then a revocation or suspension may be imposed.

When a broker or salesperson has received money to which she is not entitled, she may be required to return it, with interest, as a condition for retaining her license.

Conclusions of law. The activities stated in the findings of fact violated several sections of the New York law and regulations as stated above.

Determination. Respondents demonstrated untrustworthiness and incompetency. Marc Winograd's license is suspended for four months and Gail Winograd's for three months. The commission must be refunded along with accrued interest.

Department of State, Division of Licensing Services, Complainant, against George Siderakis, Helen Siderakis, and High Value Realty Corporation, Respondents.

The agency issues in this case address the following: improper dual agency and failure to disclose to principal.

Allegations. The complaint alleges that the corporation and Respondent Siderakis demanded and received an unearned brokerage fee in connection with a rental transaction between a tenant and Respondent, in which Respondent acted as undisclosed dual agent for the tenant and himself (as landlord). Also, Respondent failed to provide a legitimate brokerage service to the tenant. In addition, the corporation, acting through Respondent Helen Siderakis, continues to retain the unearned commission.

Findings of fact. In 1988, in answer to an ad, Mirett, a prospective renter, met with Respondent George Siderakis, a licensed real estate broker, to see an apartment. Respondent told Mirett that he was the owner of the two-family house in which the apartment was located and if he rented the apartment, Mirett would have to pay a commission of $820. Mirett and Respondent Helen Siderakis, a co-owner of the apartment, entered into a lease and Mirett paid the rent, security deposit, and commission. Four years later, in 1992, Mirett complained to DOS about the commission. He alleged that disclosure of Respondent's ownership was not made until just before he signed the lease.

Opinion and conclusions of law. One of the charges is that Respondent did not make timely disclosure to Mirett of Respondent's ownership of the house and his status as a dual agent or the consequences of this type of agency. The only evidence to support this charge is the hearsay testimony of Mirett, which, although admissible, is weakened by the four and one-half years Mirett waited before complaining. Therefore, the court concluded that disclosure of Respondent's ownership was made when the two parties first met.

Considering the issue of timely disclosure by Respondent, it is hard to see how Mirett could have believed that Respondent and High Value Realty were acting as his agents. Further, since Respondent and High Value could not have been acting as agents for the landlord, there can be no issue of insufficient disclosure with regard to agency.

The issue remains as to whether the commission was earned despite the timely disclosure. According to a New York court of appeals ruling, *"a broker's fee must represent charges for actual services."* According to the facts, Respondents did not provide Mirett with any brokerage services. They do not contend that they offered broker services to Mirett nor did they act as agents for a landlord. According to Section 440 of the Real Property Law, there is no agency unless one is acting for another. Accordingly, Respondent can be said to have been acting as broker, or as his own agent. In cases when a broker received money to which he is not entitled, the refund of the money together with interest may be required as a condition of the retention of the broker's license.

Determination. Respondent George Siderakis and High Value Realty demonstrated untrustworthiness and incompetence and must pay a fine of $1,000 to DOS. If they fail to pay the fine, their license will be suspended for two months. Respondent Helen Siderakis has demonstrated incompetency and shall pay a fine of $500 to DOS, or her license will be suspended for two months. Respondent must also pay back the commission money to Mirett, a total of $820, plus interest.

IMPORTANT POINTS

1. When one person is hired to act on behalf of another, an agency relationship is created. Agency is usually created with an agreement (express agency) but also can be implied by the agent's conduct. A position of trust, which is a fiduciary relationship, exists between every principal and agent in an agency relationship.
2. Real estate agents are special agents with specific authority.
3. The agent's fiduciary duties and responsibilities include obedience; loyalty; disclosure of information; confidentiality; accountability; and reasonable care, skill, and diligence.
4. A brokerage contract is created when the principal, usually a real estate owner, hires a broker (agent) to perform services relating to the real estate. Every agency relationship is consensual.
5. The principal may authorize the agent to use other people to assist in accomplishing the purpose of the agency. These people are subagents.
6. An agency relationship is not determined by the nature of the compensation (commission or flat fee) or who pays it.
7. An agent may decide to represent either the seller or the buyer in a real estate transaction.
8. A single agent works only for the buyer or seller directly and may elect to reject subagency.
9. A seller agent represents the owner of real property and accepts the employment contract of a listing agreement establishing a client relationship, which works in the best interests of the seller.
10. A buyer agent represents the buyer/purchaser of real property and accepts the employment contract of a listing agreement establishing a principal/client relationship working in the best interests of the buyer/purchaser.
11. A dual agent is an agent who attempts to represent both the buyer and the seller in the same transaction. Dual agency also occurs in real estate companies when the firm attempts to represent both the buyer and seller in the same transaction.
12. A multiple listing service (MLS) offers cooperation and compensation to participating members. It does not create an automatic subagency.

13. Cooperative sales, with seller agents from another real estate firm as subagents of the listing broker and seller, or with buyer agents from another real estate firm, are processed through the usual system of offerings published within an MLS.
14. In the sale or rental of one- to four-unit residential properties in New York, a dual agent must have the *written* approval of both parties after the agent's informed disclosure. The buyer and seller each agree to relinquish the individual, undivided loyalty in the fiduciary relationship.
15. An undisclosed dual agency can result in a violation of New York Real Property Law.
16. Currently, New York real estate firms can provide consensual dual agency for in-house sales.
17. All agents must disclose what party they represent in a real estate transaction.
18. In the sale or rental of one- to four-unit residential properties in New York, a mandatory disclosure form must be presented to all parties signing listing agreements and at other meetings and discussions between prospective buyers and sellers at the time of the first substantive contact or meeting.
19. Antitrust violations are any business activities in which a monopoly, contract, or conspiracy negatively impacts an individual's or a company's ability to do business. The negative consequence is called restraint of trade.
20. Antitrust laws are important to the real estate profession because it is unlawful for brokerage firms, real estate boards, franchises, and MLS services to conspire to fix commission rates.
21. The Sherman (1890) and Clayton (1914) antitrust acts and the Federal Trade Commission (1914) established legislation to control and regulate antitrust activity.
22. The antitrust division of the Department of Justice enforces the Sherman and Clayton acts. Violators are subject to criminal liability and monetary damages.
23. Antitrust laws prohibit price fixing, group boycotts, market allocation agreements, and tie-in arrangements.

CHAPTER REVIEW How Would You Respond?

Analyze the following situations and decide how the individuals should handle them in accordance with what you have just learned. Check your responses using the Answer Key at the end of the chapter.

1. Vita and Charles Hope call Garry, a salesperson with Better Days Real Estate. They are interested in a raised ranch that Garry had listed only a few days earlier. Garry makes an appointment to show the property that afternoon. At this point, whom does Garry represent? How should he handle the phone inquiry? At what point does disclosure take place? What must Garry tell the prospective purchasers regarding their choices in obtaining representation? How should Garry make the disclosure presentation?

   ____

   ____

   ____

2. Vita and Charles feel that Garry has shown them their "dream house." Because they are sure about the house and they don't wish to waste any time, they ask Garry to represent them, too. If Garry also represents the Hopes, how has his role changed? What type of agency relationship is now being created? What have both the buyers and the sellers given up?

   ____

   ____

   ____

3. After disclosure by Garry, the Hopes decide to accept a dual agency relationship. They also wish to make an offer on the home. What forms must be acknowledged and signed by the Hopes, the sellers, and Garry? At what point can the buyer make an offer through a contract for purchase and sale?

____

____

____

KEY TERM REVIEW

Fill in the term that best completes each sentence and then check the Answer Key at the end of the chapter.

1. The principal is also known as the ____________________ of the agent. The ____________________ of an agent is the party that the agent brings to the principal as a seller or buyer of the property.
2. A real estate agent is a(n) ____________________ agent who has narrow authorization to act on behalf of the principal.
3. The term ____________________ implies a position of trust and undivided loyalty to the principal.
4. Agents must disclose any material facts of which they have knowledge regarding the condition of a property; if they fail to disclose this information they are guilty of ____________________.
5. The principal may authorize the agent to engage other people to assist in accomplishing the purpose of the agency. These people are called ____________________.
6. An agency agreement created by a written listing contract is called a(n) ____________________. An agency created by the actions of principal and agent is called a(n) ____________________ agency.
7. Agents who do not disclose to other parties in a transaction an interest they have in a property are engaging in illegal ____________________.
8. A(n) ____________________ is any individual from another real estate office, whether a seller agent, subagent, or buyer agent, who takes part in representing any parties to the real estate transaction.
9. When one person is legally responsible for the actions of another, this is known as ____________________.
10. The ____________________ of 1890 was enacted to prevent businesses and individuals from engaging in acts that are in restraint of trade.
11. Illegal ____________________ occurs when competitors in an industry conspire to charge a similar price for goods or services rendered.
12. A(n) ____________________ is a conspiracy wherein a person or group is persuaded not to do business with another person or group.
13. An agreement between competitors dividing or assigning a certain area or territory for sales is known as a(n) ____________________.
14. ____________________ are agreements between a party selling a product or service with a buyer who determines, as a condition of the sale, that the buyer will not buy a product or use a service of another.

MULTIPLE CHOICE

Circle the letter that best answers the question and then check the Answer Key at the end of the chapter.

1. Which of the following is NOT one of the agent's duties to the principal?
   A. loyalty
   B. accounting
   C. disclosure
   D. legal advice

2. Which of the following does NOT describe an agency relationship?
   A. the relationship between a selling agent and subagent
   B. the relationship between a seller and a buyer of real property
   C. the relationship between a listing agent and a cooperating agent participating in marketing the listed property
   D. the relationship between a seller of property and the broker under a listing

3. A real estate agent advises a buyer that a property is zoned for the type of commercial use that the buyer seeks in purchasing the property. Relying upon the agent's advice, the buyer contracts to purchase the property. In discussing the zoning, the agent had not known what zoning applied to the property. The buyer subsequently learns that the zoning is such that he cannot use the property as he intended. Which of the following is correct?
   A. the agent committed an act of misrepresentation and is liable to the buyer for any loss the buyer suffers as a consequence
   B. because the agent did not know the true facts regarding the zoning, no misrepresentation of the property to the buyer took place; therefore the agent is not liable
   C. caveat emptor applies; thus the agent is not liable
   D. the agent is not liable because the property was for commercial instead of residential use

4. When a licensed real estate salesperson desires to buy property listed with her broker's office, she may:
   A. buy the property at any time and on any terms
   B. not buy the property because of the subagency relationship with the seller through her office
   C. buy the property provided her interest is made known to all parties
   D. buy the property if she informs her broker but doesn't notify the principal

5. Which of the following does NOT terminate an agency agreement?
   A. bankruptcy of the salesperson
   B. expiration of time period set out in the agreement
   C. death of the principal
   D. completion of sale of property subject to the agency agreement

6. A broker can accept compensation from both buyer and seller:
   A. only if there is a written listing from both
   B. only if the total amount is equal to the total commission
   C. under no circumstances
   D. only after disclosure and informed consent of both parties

7. When a cooperating broker accepts an MLS offer of subagency, the cooperating broker becomes an agent of the:
   A. listing agency
   B. seller
   C. buyer
   D. both a and b

8. A broker may NOT discuss which of the following with a buyer?
   A. agency relationship that exists
   B. required New York disclosure form
   C. bankruptcy the seller is facing
   D. problem with an inadequate septic system

9. Someone who has power of attorney is typically a:
   A. special agent
   B. real estate agent
   C. general agent
   D. trust agent

10. An MLS is best defined as:
    A. listings of multiple-unit properties in one area
    B. listings of properties that have multiple owners
    C. a means of sharing listings among member brokers and their agents, allowing for cooperation and shared compensation
    D. sharing lists of buyers with builders in an effort to increase the construction and magnitude of home sales

11. A salesperson is typically a(n):
    A. general agent
    B. special agent
    C. universal agent
    D. trust agent

12. A principal is one who:
    A. empowers another to act for him or her
    B. buys directly from the owner, without a broker's representation
    C. expects care, obedience, accounting, and loyalty from the buyer of his or her property
    D. is the owner of a brokerage firm

13. When taking a listing, the agent is told by the property owner that the septic system is not working. This fact is disclosed on the listing sheet or on the MLS. At a showing of the property, which of the following is true?
    A. the agent does not have to disclose this information unless the prospective buyer asks about the septic system
    B. the agent must disclose this information only if given permission by the seller
    C. the agent must disclose this information whether asked or not, because the agent is to be fair, open, and honest in all dealings
    D. the agent does not have to disclose this information unless she is in a dual agency situation, in which case she represents both buyer and seller

14. Sheryl, a real estate salesperson, has just listed the home of Mr. and Ms. Badd. They explain to Sheryl that their home is perfect for children and they want her to find only families with children. Sheryl:
    A. must obey the desires of the Badds because she is their listing agent
    B. need not obey the Badds because listing agents need not obey the principal
    C. must refuse this request because principals cannot violate laws in an agency relationship including fair housing laws
    D. can choose to obey this request because the law of agency in New York allows the principal to make these demands upon written disclosure

15. Section 443 of the New York Real Property Law regarding written disclosure applies to the sale or rental of which of the following?
    A. commercial properties
    B. residential 1–4 unit properties
    C. vacant land
    D. condominiums and cooperative buildings containing more than 4 units

16. Leonard and Sue are desperately trying to sell their home in New York because they have purchased another and cannot pay two mortgages. They tell Kirsten, their listing salesperson, that they want only $210,000 for their home and that she can keep whatever she obtains above that price for her commission. This commission arrangement is:
    A. a net listing that is illegal
    B. legal if there is disclosure on Kirsten's part and informed consent on the sellers' part
    C. legal if Kirsten does not take more than 7 percent of the selling price for her commission
    D. legal if Kirsten first obtains permission from her broker

17. Faisal, of Dundee Realty, in his role as subagent, shows a house that is listed by Trustee Realty to customers. Faisal tells his customers that he was told that the owners of the property are going through a divorce and they will accept an offer substantially lower than the listed price. Faisal's statement is:
    A. perfectly acceptable because it is his duty to obtain the best deal for his customers

B. illegal because Faisal is a subagent of the principal and may not reveal this confidential information
C. legal as long as Faisal does not reveal where or how he received the information
D. mandatory because Faisal is also an agent for the buyers and must reveal this information to them

18. Which of the following is NOT an advantage of buyer brokerage for the consumer? The buyer agent:
A. can help in negotiating a price
B. owes complete loyalty to the buyer client
C. can perform a market analysis of the property for the buyer client
D. can also negotiate for the sellers without giving up his role as fiduciary

19. If a buyer or seller refuses to sign the required New York disclosure form for covered properties, the agent must:
A. refuse to enter into a listing agreement with a prospective seller or a buyer/purchaser exclusive agency agreement with a prospective purchaser
B. fill out a prescribed declaration form describing the facts of the situation
C. refuse to negotiate for a seller or buyer if he refuses to sign
D. explain to the seller or buyer that the disclosure form is a contract that must be signed in order to purchase or sell real estate in New York

20. Which of the following is NOT a penalty under the Sherman Antitrust Act?
A. capital punishment
B. a felony charge
C. imprisonment
D. monetary damages

21. Which of the following activities is allowable under antitrust law?
A. free competition
B. tie-in arrangements
C. group boycotts
D. price fixing

22. A federal commission that may serve as a court of equity for antitrust activities is known as the:
A. Unfair Practices Commission
B. Federal Trade Commission
C. Securities and Exchange Commission
D. Urban Development Commission

23. Two neighboring county multiple listing services agree to set all commission rates for commercial properties at 10 percent so that consumers will not have to shop around for lower commission rates. This activity is:
A. an illegal restraint of trade
B. allowable for commercial properties but not for residential properties
C. helpful to consumers because they don't have to worry about higher commission rates
D. allowable under the law because the real estate industry is composed of services, not "trade"-type activity

24. Commercial Properties, a large brokerage firm, does not belong to the local board of REALTORS® or MLS. A notice is sent out from the board telling its members not to show any properties listed by Commercial Properties. Which of the following is correct?
A. the board is illegally promoting a group boycott against Commercial Properties
B. the board has the right to dictate to its members with whom they may or may not do business
C. Commercial Properties must belong to both a real estate board and a multiple listing service in order to do business with members of the MLS
D. even if the board promotes a group boycott, this is not illegal since it involves intrastate commerce

25. PDQ Realty, a commercial firm with many offices in a particular county, makes an agreement with On Your Own Realty, another commercial firm, that they will each market a specific section of the county. They arrange an even division; each company takes both active real estate locations and less active areas and they agree not to compete for business in the other's area. These companies:
    A. have every right to divide sales territories as they see fit
    B. would be guilty of restraint of trade only if they were residential companies
    C. have arranged an illegal market allocation agreement
    D. have arranged an illegal tie-in arrangement

26. Full Service Brokerage, a buyer brokerage firm, has a clause in its contract that states that as a condition of purchase, all prospective buyers who need a mortgage must apply for a mortgage with EZ Loan Mortgage Company. If EZ loan does not grant the mortgage, only then may the buyers approach another mortgage company. This activity is:
    A. legal only if full disclosure and informed consent occur on the part of the mortgage company
    B. an illegal tie-in arrangement that is in restraint of trade
    C. legal since brokerages may have mandatory tie-in arrangements with other types of service companies
    D. not allowable under New York law since financing cannot be discussed until purchasers find a property they like

ANSWER KEY

Putting It To Work

1. Your friend certainly can submit the offer to the seller through the listing broker. However, before doing this, you might consider the possible impact on the agent who has worked for you. Salespersons are not paid unless they are a part of the efforts that ultimately sell the home. And while the efforts of the first agent certainly will be considered when the commission is paid, the agent who brings in your offer will also probably want part of the commission. As a result, there could be a conflict over the commission dollars available. Most agents in your friend's position, knowing you had worked with another agent for some time, will want to be sure you are aware of the consequences before they transmit the offer for you. Unless you have hired a buyer's broker, you have no contractual ties to any agent. But you might feel some loyalty in light of the efforts the agent has put forth in helping you find a home.*
2. The agent is incorrect. He does not understand the basic laws governing licensee conduct. The law clearly requires that agents must make it known to all parties in a transaction who it is the agent represents. This applies to all real estate transactions. What is true is that the legislated written agency disclosure form need not be used by an agent in a transaction involving vacant land, but disclosure is still required.*
3. The following role-playing scenarios are only suggestions; other variations are possible. Further explanations can be validated by your instructor.
    a. Before showing Bob any listings, Daphne explains that she is an agent for the seller. Daphne clarifies that the role of an agent is one of undivided loyalty to a principal. She presents a disclosure form to Bob and explains the meaning of seller agency, buyer agency, and dual agency. She tells Bob that he is entitled to full representation in the purchase of a property and may accomplish this by choosing a buyer–agency relationship. She advises Bob that he can

*Source: James A. Ader, "Real Estate Spotlight." Copyright © The Albany *Times Union.* Reprinted by permission.

choose an agent from another company to represent him. She also explains that if he shows an interest in a listing offered by another agent from Daphne's firm, he then raises the potential of an in-house dual agency situation. After questioning Daphne further, Bob chooses to remain with Daphne in a customer status. He does not therefore have agent representation.

b. Daphne explains to Betina that as a seller agent, she will be working with other cooperating agents from other companies who are attempting to sell her listing. She tells Betina that some agents will be buyer's brokers who owe their loyalty to their buyers, and some will be subagents working for Betina, who owe their loyalty to her. Daphne explains that these agents will receive a portion of the commission. In the arrangement that is usually worked out through Daphne's office policy, cooperating brokers, who are buyer's brokers, will receive 2.5 percent of the commission and subagents of the seller will receive 3 percent of the commission. Daphne explains the in-house sales portion of the exclusive right to sell listing agreement and explains Betina's choices should a dual agency in-house situation occur. Daphne tells Betina that this situation could occur if another agent in Daphne's real estate firm represents purchasers who have an interest in Betina's home.

c. Bill explains to James that another agent in the company has listed a property that will fit James's needs exactly. Since James already has an agency relationship with the firm as a buyer client, and the seller has an agency relationship with the firm as a listing client, a dual agency situation may exist. Bill states that he is going to ask the seller agent if the seller is willing to dissolve the agency relationship with the firm. Then James could continue in the same representative role with Bill. If the seller refuses, James may choose to represent himself, ask an attorney for representation, or go to an agent in another firm. Under these circumstances, the agency contract between James and Bill would be dissolved. James could also choose customer status and remain with Bill, but he would not have representation. He could also elect to continue with Bill, who would act as a dual agent, but James would be forfeiting his right to Bill's undivided loyalty. The seller could also choose to continue with the firm and then the parties would proceed in a consensual dual agency relationship. James opts for the dual agency arrangement.

How Would You Respond?

1. Because Garry is the listing agent, he represents the sellers. He need not disclose this information on the phone, but when he shows the house to the Hopes, he must explain that he represents the sellers. Garry must explain to the Hopes that they have several options: they are entitled to their own agent, they may accept customer status, or they may elect dual agency. Garry should present the disclosure form, allow both Vita and Charles to read it, and answer any questions they might have. After the Hopes are clear about all of the points, they must acknowledge and sign the portion of the form that indicates that they understand that Garry is an "agent of the seller."
2. In this new role, Garry can no longer offer undivided loyalty to the sellers. As a dual agent, he cannot offer undivided loyalty to the prospective buyers either. His role as a fiduciary is compromised by the dual agency relationship.
3. Both the prospective buyers *and* the sellers must accept the dual agency. They must acknowledge and sign the "Acknowledgment of Prospective Buyer/Tenant and Seller/Landlord to Dual Agency" section of the required *disclosure form.* Before going to contract, the buyers and sellers must acknowledge and sign the "Acknowledgment of the Parties to the Contract" section of the *disclosure form.* In this case, both the buyer and the sellers would check the applicable relationship with Garry as a *"dual agent working for both the buyer/tenant and seller/landlord,*

acting as such with the consent of both buyer/tenant and seller/landlord and following full disclosure to the buyer/tenant and seller/landlord." Garry must explain this form and its implications to both the buyers and the sellers and make sure that they understand what they are signing.

Key Term Review

1. client; customer
2. special
3. fiduciary
4. misrepresentation
5. subagents
6. express agency; implied
7. self-dealing
8. cooperating agent
9. vicarious liability
10. Sherman Antitrust Act
11. price fixing
12. group boycott
13. market allocation agreement
14. tie-in arrangements

Multiple Choice

1. D
2. B
3. A
4. C
5. A
6. D
7. D
8. C
9. C
10. C
11. B
12. A
13. C
14. C
15. B
16. A
17. B
18. D
19. B
20. A
21. A
22. B
23. A
24. A
25. C
26. B

Chapter 3

KEY TERMS

act of waste
air rights
beneficiary
board of directors
bundle of rights
chattel
common elements
curtesy
dower
fixture
holdover tenant
homestead
illiquid
joint venture
littoral rights
parcel
partition
personal property
real estate
real property
remainder interest
remainderman
reversionary interest
right of survivorship
riparian rights
severalty
special purpose real estate
subsurface rights
trade fixture
trustee
trustor
undivided interest
unity of interest
unity of possession
unity of time
unity of title

LEARNING OBJECTIVES

Classroom hours: 2

1. Distinguish between real estate, real property, and personal property.
2. Identify the characteristics of real property and its uses.
3. Distinguish between ownership, interests, and leases.
4. Identify forms of ownership by individuals and various business organizations.
5. Identify key terms related to the rights conveyed in ownership and leasing.

Estates and Interests

IN THIS CHAPTER This chapter presents an introduction to the concept of real estate. It provides definitions of real estate, real property, and personal property, and discusses the factors affecting real estate. The various types of ownership of real property are also discussed. Real estate terminology is like a new language to many people, so you should first try to understand the meaning of the new terms and then memorize them.

ELEMENTS OF REAL PROPERTY

Bundle of Rights

The terms *real estate* and *real property* are often used interchangeably, but they have slightly different definitions. **Real estate** is *the land and all improvements made both on and to the land, whether found in nature or placed there by humans.* **Real property** is broader in meaning. It is *real estate plus all legal rights, powers, and privileges inherent in ownership of real estate.* These rights are many in number and varied in nature. They have value, are usually salable, and affect the value of the underlying real estate (land).

To understand the subtle difference between real estate and real property, visualize real property as a bundle of sticks (Figure 3.1). The sticks in the bundle include the major sticks of land, improvements, fixtures, and fruits of soil, all of which are *tangible.* The bundle also includes *intangible* rights such as air rights, water rights, mineral rights, easements, leases, mortgages, licenses, profits, and so on. This visual concept, referred to as a **bundle of rights,** illustrates that real estate licensees sell more than land and houses. They also can sell *any rights to, interests in, and title to real property that affect the value of the real property.* Every bundle of sticks (one piece of real property) can be divided in numerous ways. The division referred to here is not that of acres or lots. Instead, it refers to the various rights that can be held in real property, which will be discussed later in this chapter.

Real Property

Real property consists of land and everything permanently attached to land, as well as the rights of ownership. Ownership in land includes not only the face of the earth but also the area below the surface to the center of the earth and the area above the sur-

FIGURE 3.1 Real estate ownership as a bundle of rights.

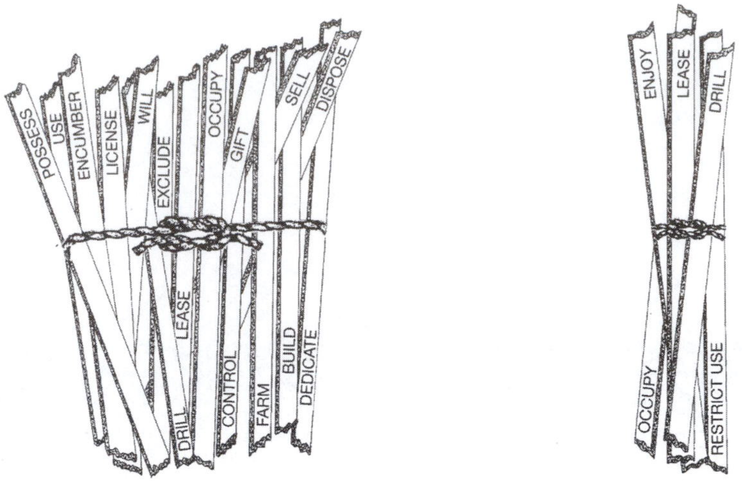

face, theoretically to outer space. Real property also includes everything that is permanently attached to the land. Therefore, the landowner owns all structures on the land as well as other improvements to the land, including items such as buildings, swimming pools, flagpoles, fences, and other structures. Improvements also refer to clearing the land, building roads, and placing utilities. Figure 3.2 illustrates the differences between land, real estate, and real property.

Personal Property

Other than real property, the only category of property defined in law is **personal property.** *Everything that is not real property is personal property. Tangible personal property is everything that is readily movable.* Personal property is your "stuff," that is, household furniture, cars, tractors, mobile homes, and jewelry. Personal property also includes the annual harvest from growing crops. *Another name for personal property is* **chattel.** Ownership of personal property is transferred and evidenced by a document called a *bill of sale.*

Land

Land is defined as the earth's surface extending downward to the center of the earth and upward to infinity, including things permanently attached by nature. Land includes the dirt and soil as well as boulders and growing entities, such as trees and bushes. Land also includes minerals located below the surface, such as oil, gold, and silver.

Air and subsurface rights. Ownership of real property includes ownership of the rights to the area above and below the earth's surface. *Rights to the area above the earth are called* **air rights.** The right of ownership of airspace enables the landowner to use that space and to lease or sell the airspace to others. For example, an owner of a building that houses retail space can sell the space above the building to allow a developer to build one or more stories of office space. As in this case and others, the right of ownership, control, and construction of airspace is limited by zoning ordinances and federal laws.

Sale or lease of airspace is becoming more common in high-density urban areas. Density is the population and/or structures per a certain area of land. The more population or structures inhabiting a given area, the higher the density. In purchasing air rights, the purchaser must obtain an easement appurtenant (see Chapter 4) over the ground if someone else controls the ground.

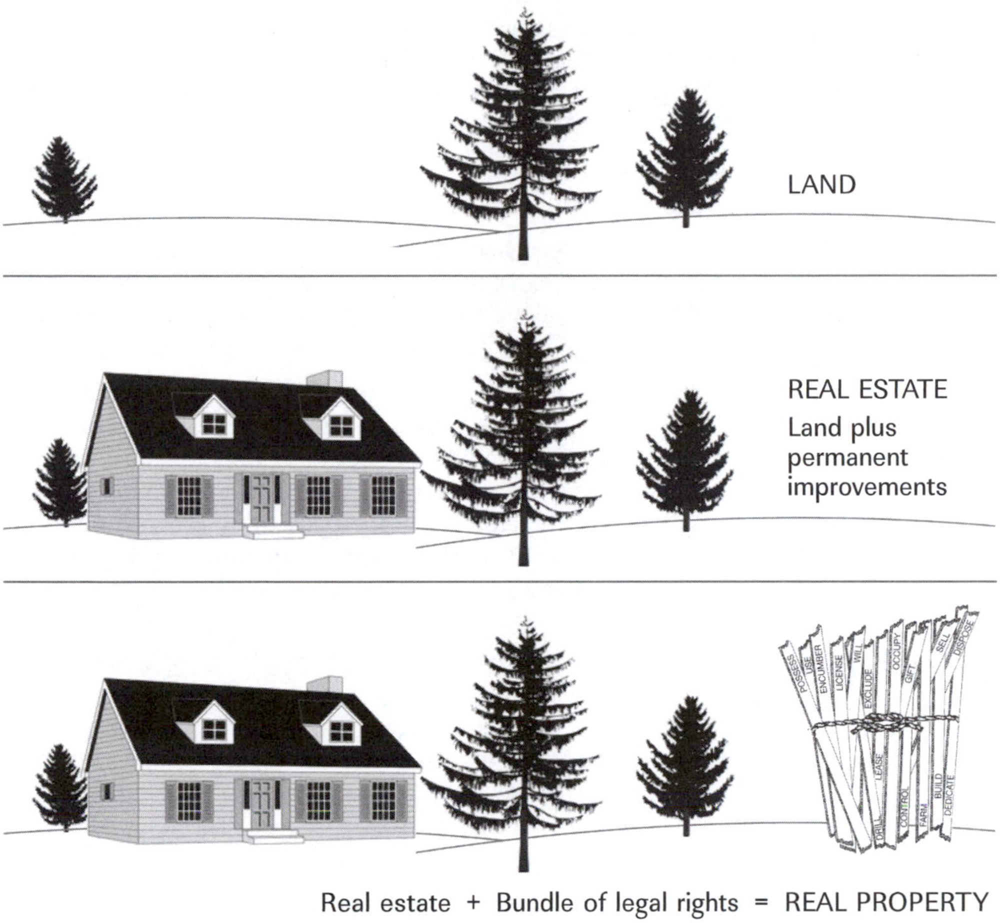

FIGURE 3.2
Land, real estate, and real property.

Rights to the area below the earth's surface are called **subsurface rights,** often referred to as mineral rights. These rights also are subject to restriction by local, state, and federal laws. The owner of mineral rights may conduct mining operations or drilling operations personally or may sell or lease these rights to others on a royalty basis.

Water rights. Water rights in real property include percolating water rights, riparian water rights, and surface water rights. Percolating water is the water underground that is drawn by wells. Landowners have the inherent right in that land to draw out the percolating water for their own reasonable use. The right of natural drainage is at the heart of surface water rights. No landowner can substantially change the natural drainage of surface water (runoff) in such a manner as to damage neighboring landowners or their property. **Riparian rights** *belong to the owner of property bordering a flowing body of water.* **Littoral rights** *apply to property bordering a stationary body of water,* such as a lake or a sea. Generally, property adjacent to a river or a watercourse affords the landowner the right of access to and use of the water. Actual ownership of the water in a flowing watercourse, however, is complex and depends on numerous factors.

Fixtures

The real estate term for improvements both on and to the land is **fixture.** The object that becomes a fixture, and therefore part of the real estate, could have been at one time a piece of personal property. Items can become a fixture and therefore a part of the real estate in one of three ways: attachment, adaptation, and agreement.

Attachment refers to the physical connection of objects to the real estate. For example, lumber to build a structure is personal property when it is delivered to the building site. By attachment and intent of the builder, however, the lumber becomes a building on the land and thus real estate. The same is true for light fixtures, showers, bathtubs, toilets, windows, and so on.

Adaptation refers to how an object specifically fits the real estate. Custom draperies or even cabinetry that is sized for a certain area, even if it is not attached, are examples.

Agreement refers to those items specified by an owner that constitute a part of the real estate and those that do not. For example, a seller might stipulate that all of his appliances will sell with the house, and are therefore fixtures, except the refrigerator, which he considers personal property.

An exception to the fixture rule is *items of personal property that a business operator installs in rented building space.* These are called **trade fixtures** and are *presumed to remain personal property.* An example would be built-in shelves for displaying merchandise. Although they are attached to the property, these fixtures remain the personal property of the rental tenant and may be removed at the end of the lease period. Residential tenants may also enter into an agreement with their landlord that they wish to remove all personal property, even if attached, upon the termination of the lease.

ESTATES IN LAND

An *estate* in real property is an interest in the property sufficient to give the holder of the estate the right to possession. The right of possession and right of use must also be distinguished. Similar to the analogy of a bundle of sticks as it relates to real property rights, the owner of an estate in land has the right of possession, or a bigger bundle of sticks than the mere bundle, or right to use or have access to the land.

The estate establishes the degree, quantity, nature, and interest a person has in real property. The word *estate* is generally interchangeable with the word *tenancy* and both imply a right to possession.

Estates in land are divided into two groups: freehold estates and nonfreehold estates. A *freehold estate* is ownership for an undetermined length of time. A *nonfreehold, or leasehold, estate* signifies possession with a determinable end. Each of these two major divisions has various groupings or subheadings. Figure 3.3 illustrates freehold and nonfreehold (leasehold) rights in real property.

FREEHOLD ESTATES

Freehold estates include (a) various types of fee simple estates and (b) life estates. Fee simple estates are inheritable; life estates are not.

Fee Simple Estates

Fee Simple Absolute

The estate of *fee simple absolute* provides the most complete form of ownership and bundle of rights in real property. This type of estate is also called fee, fee simple, or fee simple absolute. Ownership in fee simple absolute *provides certain legal rights usually described as a bundle of legal rights.* This bundle includes the right to possession of the property; the right to quiet enjoyment; the right to dispose by gift, sale by deed, or by will; the right of exclusion; and the right to control use within the limits of the law.

The owner in fee simple absolute may convey, or pass to another, a life estate in reversion or in remainder (discussed later in this section); pledge the property as secu-

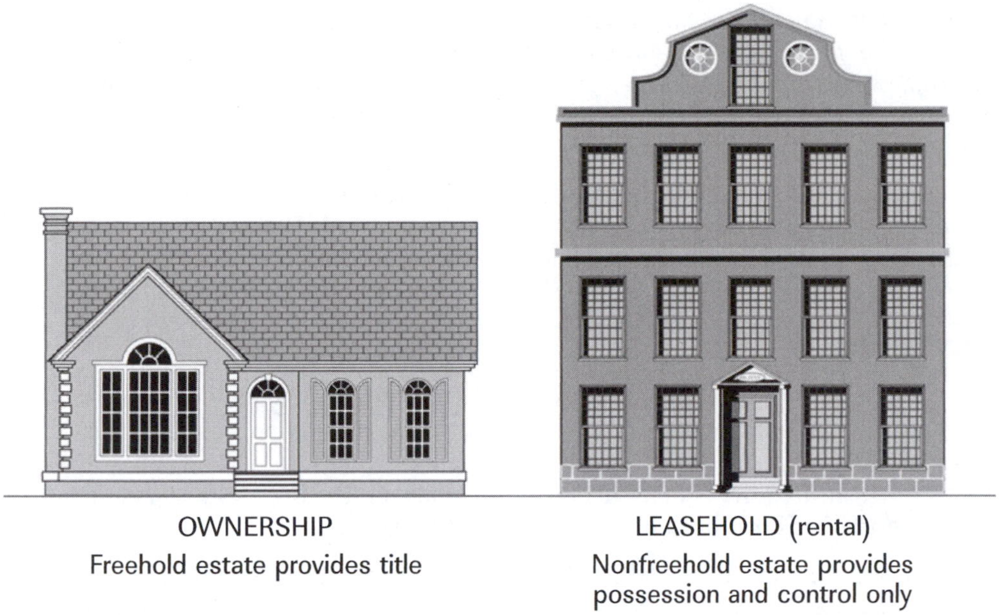

FIGURE 3.3
Freehold and nonfreehold (leasehold) rights in real property.

rity for a debt; convey a leasehold estate to another; grant an easement in the land; or give a license to conduct some activity on the property. Certain of these rights may be removed from the bundle while leaving the other rights intact. For example, if the owner pledges the title as security for a mortgage debt, the balance remaining is a fee simple title subject to the mortgage. Most real estate transfers convey fee simple absolute. No special words are required on a deed to create this freehold estate. It is the assumed estate.

Fee Simple Defeasible

Although fee simple absolute is the most complete form of ownership, some conveyances create what begins as a fee simple absolute but with a condition or limitation attached. These are termed *defeasible* estates, meaning destructible or defeatable. A common use of defeasible freeholds occurs when someone wishes to donate land to a school or community for a specific purpose. The two types of defeasible fees are (a) fee simple on condition and (b) qualified fee simple.

Fee simple on condition. The fee simple on condition can continue for an infinite time, as with the fee simple absolute. The fee simple on condition, however, can be defeated and is therefore a defeasible title. A fee simple on condition is easily recognized in the transfer by the words "but if." For example, grantor conveys 40 acres to his son, but if the son constructs houses on the land, the son's ownership terminates.

A fee simple on condition is created by the grantor specifying in the conveyance of title a use of the property that is prohibited. The deed must specifically state the condition. In the example above, the grantor conveyed property to his son with the condition that it never be used for house construction. As long as the property is not used for this purpose, the title will continue indefinitely with the initial grantee, his son, or any subsequent grantee. At any time, if the son does not adhere to the condition, the original grantor or heirs may reenter the property and take possession or go to court to regain possession. The titleholder's estate is terminated in this case because breach of the condition occurred.

Qualified fee simple. A *qualified fee simple* is another inheritable freehold estate in the form of a fee simple estate. It is also a defeasible fee, however; thus the grantor can terminate the title. This type of estate is easily recognized in the deed by the words "as long as." For example, *grantor transfers 10 acres to her daughter, as long as the property is used for educational purposes.* Title received by her daughter can be for an indefinite time. If the property is not used for the purpose specified in the conveyance, however, the title will terminate automatically and revert to the original grantor or her heirs.

In a qualified fee simple, the estate of the grantee terminates automatically in the event the designated use of the property is not continued. Defeasible fee estates are relatively rare. Most ownership positions are fee simple absolute.

Life Estates

The *life estate* is ownership, possession, and control for someone's lifetime. Ownership, possession, and control are contingent upon living and are lost at death. If the measured life is for the life of a tenant, the life estate ends with the death of the tenant. If the measured life is other than that of the tenant, the life estate can be inherited or transferred until the death of the measuring life person.

A life estate may be created for the life of the named tenant or for the life of some other named person. A life estate created for the duration of the life tenant's own life is called an *estate for life* or *ordinary life estate.* For example, B conveys 40 acres to C for C's life. When the life estate is for the life of a person other than the life tenant, however, it is called an estate pur autre vie, meaning for the life of another. For example, D conveys 40 acres to E until the death of F.

With a life estate, two outcomes are possible upon death: (a) an estate in remainder or (b) an estate in reversion. If the conveyance is from the grantor to G for life, and then to a named person or persons upon G's death, it is an estate in remainder. A **remainder interest** is a fee simple present interest. The *person or persons receiving the title upon the death of G, the life tenant,* are called **remaindermen,** and the conveyance is a *conveyance in remainder.* The remaindermen receive a fee simple title. The life tenant has only an estate or ownership for her life. Immediately upon her death or upon the death of some other person named in the conveyance, the title automatically vests in the remaindermen.

If the conveyance does not specify a person or persons to receive the title upon the death of the life tenant or other specified person, a life estate in reversion is created. Upon the death of the life tenant, the title will revert to the grantor or the grantor's heirs. The grantor has a **reversionary interest** in the estate, meaning that *possession of the property will go back to the owner at the end of the lease.* Figures 3.4 and 3.5 illustrate the differences between life estate in remainder and life estate in reversion.

Life estates are created by act of the parties, either by deed or in a will (conventional life estates), or by operation of law. In the past, the most common life estates created by law were **dower** and **curtesy,** *automatic life estates owned by a surviving spouse in inheritable property owned by the deceased spouse alone during the marriage.* If the owner of the land was the husband, the wife has a life estate called dower. If the owner of the land was the wife, the husband has a life estate called curtesy (in most states). Some states recognize a **homestead** life estate for a surviving spouse. A homestead life estate *is available only on the family home,* not on all the inheritable property. New York does not recognize a homestead life estate, and dower and curtesy have been abolished in New York.

Rights and Responsibilities of Life Tenants

In New York, the life tenant has the right to possess and enjoy the property. The life tenant may also have a right to lease the property, depending on the wording of the life

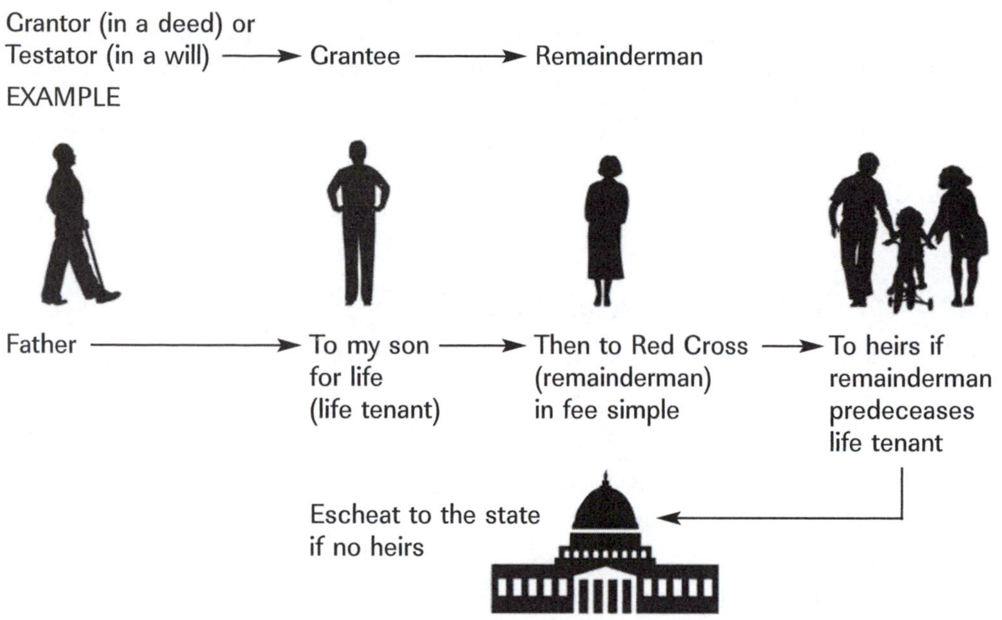

FIGURE 3.4
A life estate in remainder.

estate, and is also entitled to the net income produced by the property, if any. The life tenant also may legally mortgage the life estate (if a willing lender can be found). A life tenant has certain responsibilities to preserve and protect the estate for the benefit of the remainderman or reversionary interest. *If the life tenant abuses or misuses the property,* this is known as an **act of waste.** Examples of waste may include items such as failure to pay property taxes, converting the use of the property, or destruction of the dwelling (i.e., a fire). The life tenant, however, has a legal right called the right to *estovers.* This right provides that the life tenant may cut and use reasonable amounts of timber from the land to repair buildings or to use for fuel on the property, but not for profit.

A life tenant has an obligation to pay the real property taxes and assessments and must perform necessary maintenance on the land. If a life tenant violates these responsibilities, the tenant may be subject to a lawsuit brought by those persons having the remainder or reversionary interest and who wish to protect the real estate subject to the life estate.

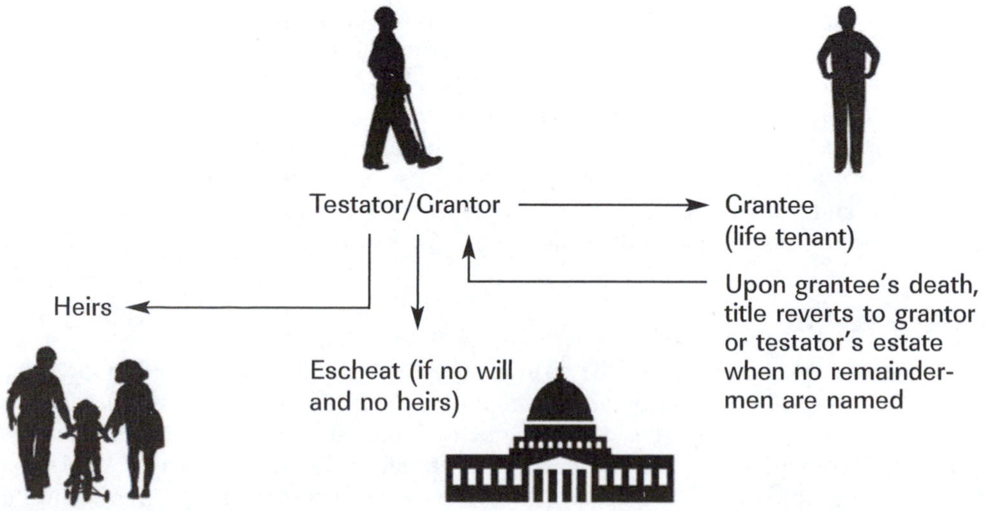

FIGURE 3.5
A life estate in reversion.

NONFREEHOLD (LEASEHOLD) ESTATES

A nonfreehold estate, also called a leasehold estate, is a less-than-freehold estate (less than a lifetime) and therefore is of limited duration. Leasehold, or rental, estates are created by a contract called a lease agreement, which provides contractual rights and duties to both parties. Leasehold estates grant possession to the tenant, but not title. Title stays with the owner. Leasehold estates create the relationship between the lessor (landlord) and lessee (tenant). These estates may be called leasehold estates, tenancies, or leaseholds.

Estate for Years (Fixed Termination)

The key feature of the *estate, tenancy, or leasehold for years is that it exists for only a fixed period of time,* which can be as short as one day. At the end of that time, the estate (rental agreement) terminates automatically without any need for either party to give notice to the other. If any uncertainty exists about the duration of the lease, it is not an estate for years. New York law requires that if this estate lasts for more than one year, the lease must be in writing.

In New York City, a lease establishing a tenancy for a term, but not specifically stating the duration of the term, continues until the first day of October after the possession. If a lease does not have to be recorded and the property is sold with a tenant in possession at the time of sale, the purchaser will have to honor the lease. At the death of either the landlord or the tenant, heirs of the deceased party are bound by the terms of the lease. The lease is considered to be inheritable because the obligations and rights of the lease pass to the estate or heirs of the decedent.

Periodic Estate (Estate from Year to Year)

The *estate from year to year* is commonly known as a *periodic tenancy.* The period length can be a week, a month, or any other negotiated time period. *The key feature of a periodic lease is that it automatically renews itself for another period at the end of each period unless one party gives notice to the other* at a prescribed time prior to the end of the lease. For example, if the required period is one year and the parties enter the last 30 days of the lease without notifying the other of any change, a new lease is automatically created for another time period equal to the previous one, with the same terms.

In New York, any lease stating that it will be renewed automatically unless the tenants give notice to the landlord that they are leaving is not enforceable unless the landlord gives the tenant written notice at least 15 to 30 days before the renewal reminding the tenant about this provision in the lease. In New York City, a monthly periodic tenancy may be terminated by notice from the landlord at least 30 days from the expiration of the term; in areas outside of New York City, the landlord's notice must come one month before the expiration of the term. In areas outside of New York City, no notice of termination is required if a definite term for the lease has been set (unless there is a lease clause requiring notice, as explained above). At the death of either the landlord or tenant, heirs of the deceased party are bound by terms of the lease, including giving notice if the heirs wish to terminate.

Estate at Will

In an *estate at will,* duration of the term is completely unknown at the time the estate is created, because either party *may terminate the lease simply by giving notice to the other party.* In this sense, the estate is open-ended. New York statute requires that notice of termination be given at least 30 days before the date upon which termination is to be effective. The notice must be served personally to the tenant or conspicuously posted on the premises. This type of leasehold is typical in a casual arrangement, such as a family setting in which a parent rents to an adult child. At the death of either the landlord or the tenant, this leasehold terminates, unlike the estate for years or the periodic lease.

Estate at Sufferance

An *estate at sufferance* describes *a tenant who is originally in lawful possession of another's property but refuses to leave after his right to possession terminates.* During this period, the occupier is called a *tenant at sufferance.* The term is used to distinguish between the tenant at sufferance who originally was in lawful possession of the property and someone who was on the property illegally from the beginning (trespasser.) A tenant *who does not leave upon expiration of the lease is termed a* **holdover tenant.** According to real property law in New York, a landlord may remove a holdover tenant by initiating an eviction proceeding. In New York, if a landlord accepts rent after the expiration of the term, a month-to-month tenancy is created.

FORMS OF OWNERSHIP OF REAL PROPERTY

Ownership of real property may be by one person alone or by many persons, or even nonnatural entities such as partnerships and corporations. Co-ownership of property may be used to control transfer of the property at death or to allow pooling monies to purchase an investment, which then will be owned by several people. When acquiring property, buyers have many options for acquiring the property, referred to as *vesting options.*

Ownership in Severalty

When *title to real property is held in the name of only one person or entity,* it is called ownership in **severalty,** because the interest is "severed" from all others. The person or entity holding title is the sole or only owner. If the titleholder is married, the property is called separate property; the owning spouse holds title separately from the other spouse.

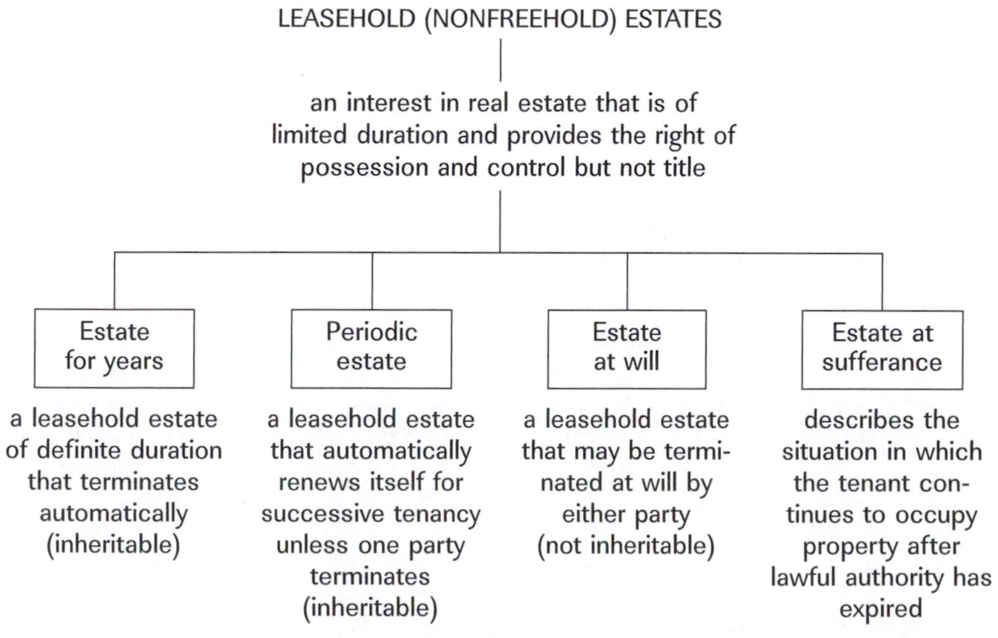

FIGURE 3.6 Leasehold (nonfreehold) estates.

FIGURE 3.7 Comparison of the forms of co-ownership.

JOINT TENANCY WITH RIGHT OF SURVIVORSHIP	TENANCY IN COMMON	TENANCY BY THE ENTIRETY
Always equal interests —each has right to possession of the whole —at death, interest of decedent passes to surviving tenants automatically (right of survivorship)	Not necessarily equal interests —each entitled to possession of the whole —each interest inheritable (no right of survivorship)	Equal interests of husband and wife —each spouse entitled to possession of the whole —divorce converts to a tenancy in common —on death, interest of decedent passes automatically to surviving tenant (right of survivorship)
Must be created on purpose —one deed —equal interests —survivorship must be specified —four unities—time, title, possession, and interest—must exist	May happen accidentally —through inheritance by more than one heir —through purchase in which shares may or may not be equal —through failure to specify joint tenancy with right of survivorship	Created by a deed to a husband and wife, without specific reference to survivorship rights
Each tenant has an undivided share in the whole property; is equally responsible for expenses and equally entitled to rents and profits	Each tenant has an undivided share in the whole property; is equally responsible for expenses and equally entitled to rents and profits	Marriage owns the whole property; is responsible for expenses and entitled to rents and profits
Terminated by sale of one co-tenant or more than one tenant —unities destroyed —new owner is tenant in common	Sale by one co-tenant does not terminate —buyer succeeds to interest; substitution occurs	One member cannot sell his or her interest —right of survivorship is not defeated by attempted sale —divorce converts ownership to tenancy in common

Concurrent Ownership

Simultaneous ownership of real property by two or more people is called co-ownership. The rights of the owners depend upon the type of ownership (see Figure 3.7). The various types of co-ownership include: tenancy in common, joint tenancy, tenancy by the entirety, and community property. To understand adequately the distinctions among types of co-ownerships, one must learn the difference between right of survivorship and right of inheritance. **Right of survivorship** means that *if one (or more) of the co-owners dies, the surviving co-owners automatically receive the interest of the deceased co-owner.* Right of survivorship defeats passing of title by will. The remaining survivor among all co-owners owns the entire property in severalty. *Right of inheritance,* by contrast, means that a co-owner's share of the real estate will pass at his death to his heirs, or in accordance with his will.

Concurrent ownerships require certain unities of ownership. The four possible unities are: *time, title, interest,* and *possession.* For the co-ownership to be recognized, the concurrent ownerships require one or more of the unities between the co-owners. The **unity of time** *exists when co-owners receive their title at the same time in the same conveyance.* The **unity of title** *exists if the co-owners have the same type of ownership, such as a life estate, fee simple, or fee simple on condition.* The **unity of interest** *exists if the co-owners all have the same percentage of ownership.* The **unity of possession** *exists if all co-owners have the right to possess or access any and all portions of the property owned, without physical division.* This type of possession is called possession of an **undivided interest.**

Tenancy in Common

Tenancy in common is characterized by two or more persons holding title to a property at the same time. The only required unity is that of possession. Each tenant in common holds an undivided interest in the entire property, rather than any specific portion of it. No right of survivorship exists; upon the death of a tenant in common, the deceased's share will go to the person's heir or as designated in the will. For example, Beth and Miguel buy property together but want to ensure that if either dies, his or her share of the property may pass by the will to whomever they designate.

Tenancies in common may occur when property is inherited by more than one person. If the will does not designate the type of co-ownership, or in the event of no will, the inheriting parties receive title as tenants in common.

A tenancy in common also is created if two or more purchasers do not request a vesting choice when they acquire property through a deed. If nothing is stated, a tenancy in common is created. A tenant in common may sell her share to anybody without destroying the tenancy relationship and without the permission of the other tenant(s) in common. Tenants in common do not need to have equal interest in the property. For example, one co-tenant may hold one-half interest and two other co-tenants may hold one-quarter each. If no fractional interest of ownership is stated, the ownership interest is assumed to be equal. *A tenant in common may bring legal action to have the property* **partitioned** *so that each tenant may have a specific and divided portion of the property exclusively.* If this action can be done equitably with a piece of land, each would receive title to a separate tract according to his or her share of interest. If it cannot physically be done to the land, the court may order the sale of the property, distributing appropriate shares of the proceeds to the tenants in common.

Joint Tenancy

The *joint tenancy* form of co-ownership *requires all four unities of time, title, interest, and possession.* Joint tenants must have the same interest in the property, must receive their title at the same time from the same source, have the same percentage of ownership, and have the right to undivided possession in the property. For example, if the property has three joint tenants, the tenants must each own one-third of its interest, receive their title from the same conveying document, own the same type of freehold estate, and have the right to possession of any and all portions of the property. A special characteristic of joint tenancy is the right of survivorship. When one joint tenant dies, his share goes automatically to the other surviving joint tenants equally, instead of passing to the heirs of the deceased. For example, Nora, Peggy, and Ed buy property together as joint tenants. Peggy dies, and her portion passes to Nora and Ed. A joint tenant therefore cannot convey ownership by will. By acquiring as a joint tenancy, each joint tenant gives up the right of inheritance.

If a joint tenant, prior to his death, sells his share of ownership, the person purchasing this share will *not* become a joint tenant with the others. The necessary four unities will not exist. The document that gives title to the new purchaser is not rendered at the same time as the document giving title to the original joint tenants. The *unity of time* has been destroyed. The new co-owner therefore will enter the relationship as a tenant in common. The remaining original joint tenants continue as joint tenants, with the right of survivorship shared among them. In New York, the new purchaser, as a tenant in common with the original joint tenants, will be able to pass his share upon dying to his heirs.

Tenancy by the Entirety

Ownership as *tenants by the entirety is limited to husband and wife.* To receive title as tenants by the entirety, they must have a legal marriage at the time they receive title to the property. Similar to a joint tenancy, tenancy by the entirety contains the right of survivorship. Upon the death of one spouse, the surviving spouse automatically receives title to the property by law. Creation of a tenancy by the entirety requires *unity of time, title, interest, possession, and marriage.*

A husband or wife owning land as tenants by the entirety may *not* legally convey or pledge property as security to a third party without the other spouse joining in the deed or pledge instrument. A spouse who is a tenant by the entirety may convey her interest to the other spouse with only the signature of the conveying spouse on the deed. No action for partition can occur regarding real estate held as tenants by the entirety. Tenancy by the entirety exists only as long as the tenants hold title to the property and are legally married. Tenancy by the entirety is abolished automatically by decree of divorce.

Community Property

Nine states (Arizona, California, Idaho, Louisiana, Nevada, New Mexico, Texas, Washington, and Wisconsin) are *community property* states. By law, in these states, *husband and wife must acquire title to real estate as community property.* A husband and wife may hold title to both real and personal property as community property. They also may hold title separately in severalty. The theory of community property is that husband and wife share equally in the ownership of property acquired by their joint efforts during the community of marriage.

Equitable Distribution

In community property states, all property acquired during the marriage is divided equally should there be a divorce. The Domestic Relations Law is the statute that governs how marital property is divided should a couple divorce in New York. Property is not necessarily divided equally as in community property states. The theory of *equitable distribution* is applied by the courts as to the division of property. Generally, property acquired either before the marriage or inherited during the marriage is treated as separate property belonging solely to the spouse who acquired it. Property acquired during the marriage is distributed *equitably,* taking into account numerous factors. These factors include the number of years married, contributions of each of the partners, possible future circumstances, and projected tax consequences. Property may need to be sold or partitioned (discussed earlier in this chapter) to divide these assets.

Trust

A *trust* is *a fiduciary relationship between the trustee and the beneficiary of the trust.* A **trustee** is *one who holds title to property for the benefit of another, called a beneficiary.* The **beneficiary** is *one who receives benefits or gifts from the acts of others given by, for example, a will or trust.* In a fiduciary relationship, the trustee must be loyal to and protect the interest of the trust beneficiary. Any assets may be held in trust. Anyone can create a trust, naming anyone, including oneself, as beneficiary or trustee, or both. A **trustor** is *one who conveys title to a trustee.* An *inter vivos trust* is a trust set up during the lifetime of the person who creates the trust. A *testamentary trust* is set up within a person's will and is effective upon the death of the person who created the trust. A *land trust* is usually an *inter vivos trust* and is created by transferring the title of the land to a trustee, who holds the title for the benefit of the beneficiaries. The beneficiary in a land trust can be the trustor. Interest in a land trust cannot be partitioned because, by law, it is not considered real estate, but personal property. Therefore real estate in a land trust is held as an *undivided interest* among all the beneficiaries. The trustee's power and duties are expressly set out in the document establishing the trust.

OWNERSHIP OF REAL ESTATE BY BUSINESS ORGANIZATIONS

Business organizations can be structured in several different ways, including sole proprietorship, partnership, corporation, syndicate, joint venture, and real estate investment trust. All of these business organizations can receive, hold, and convey title in the same ways as individuals.

Sole Proprietorship

This form of business organization is owned by one individual and may use a name other than the owner's personal name. The business title of a sole proprietorship could be, for example, Franklin Wonder doing business as (dba) Wondrous Heights Apartments. Title to real property may not be held in the name of the business alone such as Wondrous Heights Apartments but must be stated as "Franklin Wonder doing business as Wondrous Heights Apartments."

Partnerships

A *partnership* is a form of business organization that is owned by two or more partners and created by contract between the partners. The partners do not have to have the same degree of interest in the partnership or the same extent of management authority. The contract should contain the procedure for dividing ownership interest upon the withdrawal, death, or removal of a partner.

Under the Uniform Partnership Act, which has been adopted in New York, a partnership may hold title to real property in the name of the partnership as a tenancy in partnership. In addition, under common law, partnerships may hold title to real property in the names of the individual partners. In New York, a partnership doing business under an assumed name must file with the clerk of the county where the partnership does business.

The types of partners fall into two categories: general or limited. In *general partnerships,* the partners are personally liable for partnership debts exceeding partnership assets. Partners are jointly (together) and severally (separately) liable for these debts.

A *limited partnership* consists of one or more general partners who are jointly and severally liable, and one or more silent, or limited, partners who contribute money or other assets of value to the extent of their ownership interest. Limited partners are not liable for the debts of the partnership beyond the amount of money they have contributed. To retain the protected status from partnership debts, a limited partner may not participate in managing the partnership and if he does, he may lose the protection beyond limited liability. Limited partners, therefore, may incur a general partners' liability merely by their actions.

The limited partnership organization is used frequently in real estate investments. Typically, a general partner conceives of the investment opportunity, then solicits monies from limited partners to purchase, construct, or improve a property. The general partners do all of the work and management necessary to create the investment. The limited partners provide the funds to purchase the investment. The return on the investment is divided among the partners—both general and limited—on a predetermined basis, as set out in the partnership agreement. The purpose of the investment may be to provide an income stream or to improve a property and sell the improved property at a higher price.

Corporations

A *corporation* is an artificial being—invisible, intangible, and existing only pursuant to law. A corporation is a taxable legal entity recognized by law, with tax rates separate from individual income tax rates. A corporation is created by a charter granted by the state of incorporation and has the power to receive, hold, and convey title to real property for all purposes for which the corporation was created. A corporation is empowered to give a mortgage on real estate to secure a financial debt of the corporation and can hold a mortgage on real estate to secure a debt owed to the corporation. The proper method for conveying property is set out in the corporation's bylaws. The bylaws may state expressly what officers, directors, or other persons must sign conveying documents.

A *subchapter S corporation* is a type of corporate organization that is permitted to function as a corporation but is taxed as a partnership. Corporations that are not subchapter S are known as *C corporations.* A C corporation must pay corporate income tax to the IRS and the shareholders are also taxed on their dividends. Therefore, a double tax is paid; at the corporate level and the shareholder level. An advantage of a subchapter S corporation is that since it is taxed as a partnership, it does not have to pay corporate income tax, thereby avoiding the double tax a C corporation must pay. Subchapter S shareholders are taxed individually on their portion of the corporate income. The shareholder can deduct losses on their share of the corporation's losses on their individual tax returns.

Limited Liability Companies and Partnerships

Recently, other forms of business organizations have been authorized in New York. The limited liability company (LLC) may be formed by two or more persons. This form of business combines the most favorable attributes of both partnerships and corporations. Owners of an LLC (called members) are not personally liable for the obligations of the LLC; however, an LLC is taxed as a partnership.

A limited liability partnership (LLP), typically formed by professionals such as attorneys and accountants, does not have to have a general partner. Instead, all partners are limited partners who are not personally liable for the obligations of the partnership. The limited partners may participate in management, however. An LLP is taxed as a partnership.

Syndicates

Syndicates denote *multiple joint participation in a real estate investment.* They may involve joining the assets and talents of individuals, general partnerships, limited partnerships, or corporations in some combination. Although the people and entities invest in real estate, some investors are hoping to make money based solely on the efforts of another, without liability, so the organization may be considered to be dealing in securities. An investment is a security, as defined by the Federal Securities Act of 1933, if it is:

- an investment of money
- a common or joint enterprise
- undertaken for the purpose of making a profit
- one in which profit will be derived solely or substantially from the management efforts of others

Because most syndications intend to make a profit for many from the efforts of a few, they must comply with the rules and regulations of the Securities and Exchange Commission. Syndications typically are used in cases of multiple, continuing projects that require the investment of substantial amounts of money from many different sources.

Joint Ventures

A **joint venture** is *an organization formed by two or more parties for the purpose of investing in real estate or any other type of investment.* The joint venture may be in the form of a corporation or a partnership, or the parties may hold title as joint tenants or as tenants in common. Joint ventures usually are devised for only one project.

Real Estate Investment Trusts

Real estate investment trusts (REITs) were created in 1967, stemming from changes in the Internal Revenue Code. As a result, the beneficiaries were not taxed doubly on trust income. The trust can now earn income from real estate investments without paying trust income tax. To avoid the trust income tax, however, the trust must distribute 95 percent of the ordinarily taxable income to the trust beneficiaries and 75 percent of all REIT income must come from real estate. The beneficiaries then report the income for tax purposes. Congress's stated purpose for creating this trust tax advantage was to allow and encourage small investors to pool their money to participate in larger real estate transactions and help make financing available for large real estate developments. The two major investment choices for REITs are whether (a) to lend or (b) to buy, rent, or sell property. If the REIT primarily lends money for the interest return, it is called a *mortgage* REIT. If the REIT primarily owns, manages, rents, and sells property, it is called an *equity* REIT.

COMBINATION FORMS OF OWNERSHIP

Condominiums

Condominium developments are jointly controlled. Condominium statutes are called horizontal property acts because they authorize a three-dimensional property description, with a property line above and below the condominium. These horizontal property lines create a cube of air space or a volume that is the privately owned condominium. Air rights and the area below the land surface are owned as tenants in common. Condominium law in New York is contained in the Real Property Law and sets forth the manner in which a condominium is to be created and managed. The laws include a declaration (master deed), articles of association, and the bylaws, that must be recorded in the public record in the county where the property is located.

Condominiums may be residential, industrial, or commercial. They may be newly constructed or conversions of existing structures. Condominium ownership is a combination of ownerships—individual unit plus co-ownership of the common elements. **Common elements** are *those areas available to all owners and include the yard, roof, hallways, elevators, and pools.* The individual unit may be held as a fee in severalty, fee in joint tenancy, fee in common, or fee as tenants by the entireties. Common elements are owned as tenants in common. Title to the individual unit may be transferred by deed or by leaving it to an heir by will. Title to the common elements is held as tenancy in common with all other unit owners. The common elements are the responsibility of all unit owners. See Figure 3.8 for an illustration of condominium ownership.

Cooperatives

The same types of structures that house condominiums can also house cooperative ownership. Cooperatives also can be newly constructed or conversions of existing structures and can be residential or commercial. The type and form of ownership in a

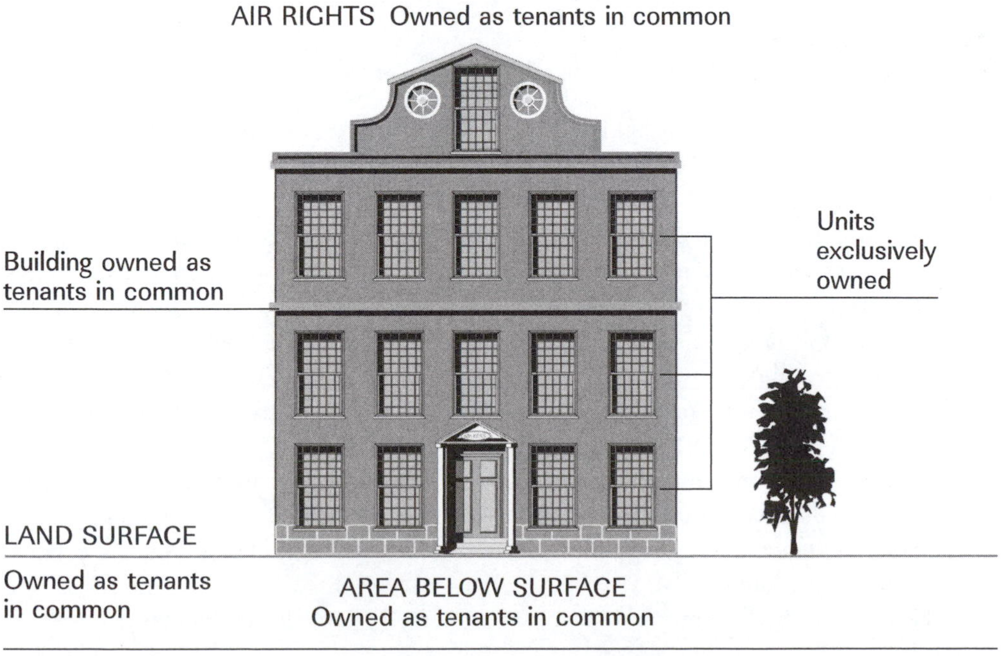

FIGURE 3.8
Condominium ownership.

cooperative, however, are vastly different from ownership in a condominium facility. In a cooperative, the buildings, land, all real property rights and interests are owned by a corporation in severalty. The title to the property, as shown on the deed, is in the name of the corporation. The shareholders of the corporation are tenants in the building. The tenants have the right of occupancy as evidenced by a *proprietary lease,* which is usually an estate for years or for a long period of time. Thus, ownership in a cooperative is really ownership of shares of stock in a corporation plus a long-term lease for the apartment or space. There is no tenancy in common ownership in the common areas, even though all tenants can use the common areas. The common areas, as all of the building, are owned in fee by the corporation.

An owner in a cooperative does not receive a deed. An owner in a cooperative does not own real estate in the typical sense, although the Internal Revenue Service considers this as ownership by recognizing the traditional benefits of home ownership, such as mortgage interest and property tax deductions (on a pro rata basis). The only real property interest the shareholders have is a leasehold estate providing the right to possession of an apartment and use of the common areas. As lessees, the shareholders pay a monthly maintenance share which is rent to cover the cost of maintaining and operating the building, real property taxes, and debt service if the corporation has placed a mortgage against the real estate. The shareholder's rights and obligations are specified in the lease and the corporation's bylaws. The business operations of a cooperative are managed by a **board of directors** *that oversees the finances, maintenance, and decision-making policy regarding the property.*

Timeshares

The timeshare is a type of ownership of a condominium or other type of ownership in fee that shares the use of the unit with many different owners. This co-ownership is based upon prescribed time intervals. It works by allowing several different individuals to purchase the condominium unit in fee and then divide the use by weeks or months. Each owner of the unit purchases the exclusive right to use the unit for a specified period of time. Timeshares are commonly used for vacation purposes. Maintenance costs, taxes, and insurance are prorated among the different owners. The percentage of expense is equivalent to the percentage of the year (time) purchased. Exchange programs are also available for some timeshares that allow an owner of a specified time at a property to trade time with the owner of another specified time at a totally different property.

IMPORTANT POINTS

1. Real property consists of land and everything attached to the land and the bundle of rights inherent in ownership.
2. Everything that is not real property is personal property.
3. Real property has the physical characteristics of immobility, indestructibility, and uniqueness, and economic characteristics based on scarcity, permanence of investment, location, and improvements.
4. Ownership in land includes the surface of the earth and the area above and below the surface, although these rights may be assigned.
5. A fixture is formerly personal property that has become attached to real property and becomes a part of the real property.
6. Estates in land are divided into two groups: freehold estates and estates of less than freehold (nonfreeholds or leaseholds).
7. Freehold estates are the fee simple estates, which are inheritable, and life estates, which are not inheritable.
8. The greatest form of ownership in real property is fee simple absolute.

9. Life estates may be in reversion or in remainder. The duration of a life estate may be measured by the life tenant or by the life of another (pur autre vie). A life tenant has the right of possession and enjoyment of the property, and the right to derive certain income from it.
10. Leasehold estates (or nonfreeholds) are estates of limited duration, providing possession and control, but not title as in the case of freehold estates. Leasehold estates are estates for years, periodic tenancy (estates from year to year), estates at will, and estates at sufferance.
11. Title held in the name of one person only is called ownership in severalty.
12. When two or more persons or organizations hold title concurrently, it is called co-ownership or concurrent ownership. The forms of co-ownership include tenancy in common, joint tenancy, tenancy by the entirety, community property, and certain aspects of condominiums and cooperatives.
13. Joint tenancy and tenancy by the entirety include the right of survivorship and require the unities of time, title, interest, and possession. Tenancy by the entirety is restricted to husband and wife and adds the fifth unity of marriage (unity of person).
14. The owner of a condominium unit holds title to the unit either in severalty or as co-owner with another, as well as title to the common elements as tenants in common with the other unit owners.
15. A cooperative requires stock ownership in a corporation that owns a building containing cooperative apartments. Stockholders occupy apartments under a proprietary lease.
16. Business organizations may receive, hold, and convey title to real property.

How Would You Respond? CHAPTER REVIEW

Analyze the following situations and decide how the individuals should handle them in accordance with what you have just learned. Check your responses using the Answer Key at the end of the chapter.

1. Terry's husband has passed away, and she does not wish to stay on their apple farm in Rhinebeck, New York, that she and her husband owned. Terry's neighbor, Mickey, owns the adjoining property, so Terry decides to convey the farm to Mickey, to be used by himself or his family as they please, for her lifetime. However, when she passes away, the property will then be conveyed to the Catholic Church. What kind of estate has Terry created? What is the nature of Mickey's tenancy? What is the nature of the church's tenancy?

   ____

   ____

   ____

2. April has been living in her apartment for two years, and her lease expired last month. She is not ready to move because she is waiting for a promised raise from her boss so she can afford a larger apartment. She does not wish to renew her lease, but her landlord wants her to sign for another year. Her landlord has asked her to move out if she doesn't sign a new lease, but April refuses. What kind of estate does April now have in the property? Is she guilty of trespassing? How can her landlord force her to move out? What is the legal name for April's tenancy?

   ____

   ____

   ____

KEY TERM REVIEW

Fill in the term that best completes each sentence and then check the Answer Key at the end of the chapter.

1. ______________________ is real estate plus all the legal rights, powers, and privileges inherent in ownership of real estate.
2. Another name for personal property is ______________________.
3. An object of improvement to the property that becomes part of the real property is called a(n) ______________________.
4. When title to real property is held in the name of only one person, it is called ownership in ______________________.
5. An individual who derives benefit from a trust is called the ______________________.
6. ______________________ apply to the rights of an owner whose property adjoins a flowing waterway, such as a river.

MULTIPLE CHOICE

Circle the letter that best answers the question and then check the Answer Key at the end of the chapter.

1. Which of the following illustrates evidence of a definite ownership right in real property?
   A. possess
   B. lease
   C. occupy
   D. sell

2. An estate in qualified fee simple is an example of a(n):
   A. freehold estate
   B. nondefeasible fee
   C. nonfreehold estate
   D. leasehold estate

3. If a widow inherits an estate by will, which grants her the right of use and possession of a parcel of land for the rest of her life with the provision that the estate go to her children in fee simple upon her death, she has received:
   A. an inheritable freehold estate
   B. a life estate in remainder
   C. a life estate in reversion
   D. a fee simple absolute

4. The highest and best form of ownership in real property is which of the following?
   A. leasehold for years
   B. defeasible fee
   C. life estate in reversion
   D. fee simple absolute

5. Linda, Sheila, and Iris own a piece of property as joint tenants. Iris decides to sell her share to Kate. Kate's share of ownership will be an owner as:
   A. tenant in common
   B. joint tenant
   C. joint tenant by the entirety
   D. in severalty

6. Which of the following types of ownership requires unity of interest, title, time, and possession?
   A. cooperative
   B. tenancy in common
   C. joint tenancy
   D. community property

7. Ownership as joint tenants by the entirety includes which of the following?
   A. the right of one owner to convey title to his or her share of ownership without the participation of the other owner
   B. the right of survivorship
   C. ownership of an unequal interest in the property with another
   D. conversion to ownership as joint tenants if the owners are divorced

8. Which of the following is a characteristic of a leasehold estate?
   A. it is for an unlimited time
   B. the holder of a leasehold estate has title to the property
   C. it is a fee absolute estate
   D. the holder of a leasehold estate has possession of the property

9. Which of the following is an estate that automatically renews itself for consecutive periods?
   A. estate at will
   B. life estate
   C. periodic estate
   D. estate for years

10. After termination of a lease, the tenant continues in possession of the property without the property owner's permission. The tenant's status is known as:
    A. tenant at will
    B. lessor
    C. trespasser
    D. tenant at sufferance

ANSWER KEY

How Would You Respond?

1. Terry has created a life estate in remainder. Mickey is the life tenant. He has an ownership interest only until Terry's death. At that time, the farm will go to the Catholic Church, which is the remainderman. The church will receive a conveyance in remainder and a fee simple title to the property.
2. April's behavior has created an estate at sufferance. She is a tenant who originally was in lawful possession of the property but now refuses to leave although her right to possession is terminated. Since she was not illegally on the property from the beginning, she is not guilty of trespassing. The landlord must bring a legal action to evict her. April is a tenant at sufferance.

Key Term Review

1. real property
2. chattel
3. fixture
4. severalty
5. beneficiary
6. riparian rights

Multiple Choice

1. D
2. A
3. B
4. D
5. A
6. C
7. B
8. D
9. C
10. D

Chapter 4

KEY TERMS

appurtenance
dominant tenement
easement
easement appurtenant
easement by condemnation
easement by grant
easement by implication
easement by necessity
easement by prescription
easement for light and air
easement in gross
encroachment
encumbrance
general lien
in rem legal proceeding
involuntary lien
lis pendens
mechanics' lien
nonpossessory
party wall
possessory
restrictive covenant
servient tenement
specific lien
tax lien
voluntary lien

LEARNING OBJECTIVES

Classroom hours: 1 1/2

1. Identify the various forms of encumbrances.
2. Distinguish between voluntary and involuntary liens.
3. Identify the types of general liens and when they are applied.
4. Identify the types of specific liens and when they are applied.
5. Describe the effects of liens on title.
6. Discuss the priority of liens.
7. List several effects of subordination agreements.
8. Distinguish between the various forms of easements.
9. Describe the effects of deed restrictions.

Liens and Easements

IN THIS CHAPTER An **encumbrance** is *anything that lessens the bundle of rights in real property*. It is a "stick" that has been given away, and therefore the remaining bundle is of less value. Most encumbrances are interests in the property that create debt or give use and/or control to another. This chapter covers liens, easements, restrictive covenants, and encroachments, all of which are encumbrances that can attach to real property.

LIENS

A *lien* is a claim or charge against the property of another. This stick in the bundle of sticks is usually security for a debt. In most cases, if the lien is not satisfied in the prescribed time, the lienholder may execute on the lien to force payment. This process is called foreclosure. Proceeds of a foreclosure sale are applied to the liens in the order of priority. *Liens may be voluntary or involuntary.* A **voluntary lien** occurs *when an individual consents to placing a security against herself or her property*. An example of a voluntary lien is a mortgage lien in which the parties voluntarily consent to place their house as security for a mortgage loan. An **involuntary lien** occurs through *a legal proceeding in which a creditor places a claim on real and/or personal property to obtain payment of a debt.* An example of an involuntary lien is a mechanics' lien in which the contractor places a lien against a property for completed work that was not paid for by the owner.

PRIORITY OF LIENS

At the execution and foreclosure of the liens, priority for payment is based upon the time (day and hour) they were recorded in the office of the county clerk. Certain liens, however, have special priority or *receive preferential treatment.* Examples of special *priority liens* are mechanics' liens and materialmen's liens. The theory given for the priority treatment lies in the nature of the services and materials provided that increased the value of the real estate. Other lienholders benefit from the work and materials of the contractors and suppliers. Therefore, the contractors and suppliers should be paid first providing a prior mortgage lien does not exist. As explained below, in New York, liens for real property taxes and special assessments receive the highest priority of all liens. Liens fall into two categories (see Figure 4.1):

1. **specific liens:** *claims against a specific and readily identifiable property,* such as a mortgage
2. **general liens:** *claims against a person and all of his or her property,* such as the disposition of a lawsuit

Specific Liens

Mortgage Liens

Mortgages are discussed fully in Chapter 9. The discussion here is limited to the type of lien created by a mortgage. A *mortgage* is a document pledging a specific property as collateral for payment of a debt. In most cases, the debt was incurred to purchase the property specified in the mortgage. The property is placed as security. If the borrower does not pay the debt as promised, the lender can foreclose the mortgage by having the property sold at public auction. Proceeds from the sale are utilized to satisfy the liens in order of priority. In some instances, the order of priority can be modified by a *subordination agreement,* whereby an earlier lender may be willing to subordinate (take a back seat) to a later lender. Typically a lender will subordinate his mortgage to another mortgage only if he is certain the property value is sufficient to pay off both mortgages should foreclosure become necessary. An example of subordination is if a lienholder on a building lot subordinates his mortgage lien to the construction mortgage lien.

Real Property Tax Liens

Taxes levied by a local government constitute a specific lien against the real estate. New York law provides that a real property **tax lien** has priority over all other liens. If the assessed real estate property taxes are not paid when due, the local official responsible for collecting the tax can bring legal action to collect the taxes. This procedure is known as an **in rem legal proceeding** and *occurs when an action is brought against the real property directly and not against an individual and his personal property.* The typical action for collection is the forced sale of the property at a tax sale.

Foreclosure of a tax lien by an action in rem. A situation may occur when a tax district holds a tax lien for more than four years (local statutes may reduce this time period). In New York, with proper notice to the property owner, and publication of the delinquent property, the tax lien is sold to the taxing district, and the enforcing officer executes a deed to the taxing district. As with any other deed, the deed is executed, delivered, and recorded. The proceeding is officially concluded two years after the recorded date of the deed. The taxing district may then sell and deed the property over to a purchaser. The timeframe for foreclosure of a tax lien may vary according to local

FIGURE 4.1 Classification of liens.

1. *Specific liens:* claims against a particular property
   a. mortgage (voluntary)
   b. real property tax (involuntary)
   c. mechanics' (involuntary)
   d. materialmen's (involuntary)
   e. lis pendens (involuntary)
2. *General liens:* claims against all assets of a person
   a. judgment (involuntary)
   b. writ of attachment (involuntary)
   c. income tax (involuntary)
   d. estate and inheritance tax (involuntary)

tax districts. This procedure is the most popular method of tax foreclosure because it is inexpensive and timely.

Mechanics' and Materialmen's Liens

A "mechanic" refers not to someone who works on vehicles but to a person who provides labor to a specific property, such as a carpenter. A "materialman" is a supplier, for instance, a lumber company that provides the wood for constructing a home. Therefore, a **mechanics' lien** is *a specific lien filed by a person who provides labor to a property;* a *materialmen's lien* is *a specific lien filed by a supplier of products required in the construction or improvement of a building.* New York law requires that a mechanics' or materialmen's lien for residential property be filed with the county clerk of the county where the property is situated within four months from the date when the labor or materials were furnished. For other types of property, the liens must be filed in the public records within eight months after furnishing the labor or materials. This limitation allows title companies and buyers of property time to ensure that no unrecorded liens are outstanding upon the purchase of a newly constructed or remodeled home. The time and date of filing determines the priority of the mechanics' or materialmen's lien. In New York, mechanics' liens must be renewed annually.

Lis Pendens

The term **lis pendens** comes from Latin, and means *pending litigation.* This filing (form) is *a legal notice that a lawsuit has been filed concerning the specific property.* The notice is filed in the office of the county or local official responsible for keeping records of pending litigation. The notice is a warning to a prospective purchaser that the pending lawsuit could result in an order that creates an enforceable claim against the property of the defendant. A court order resulting from the lawsuit will attach to the property even though the title was transferred to someone else prior to the final judgment in the suit as long as the transfer occurred *after* the lis pendens was placed on the public record. A lis pendens is also used as a means of extending a mechanics' lien against a property.

General Liens

Judgment Liens

A *judgment* is a *court decree resulting from a lawsuit.* The court decree establishes that one person is indebted to another and specifies the amount owed. The person who owes the judgment is called the judgment debtor. The person who is owed the judgment is called the judgment creditor. A judgment can be enforced against all of the real and personal property the debtor owns in the county where the judgment is recorded. A judgment lien does apply to real property owned by husband and wife by the entireties even if the lien is against only the husband or only the wife. A creditor may record the judgment in any other county in the state (and possibly in other states); then it becomes a general lien against all the property of the debtor in that county. This is called a *transcript of judgment.*

The lien takes effect at the time the judgment is entered in the court records. It also attaches as a lien to any real property the debtor acquires after the judgment and prior to satisfaction of the judgment. The lien is enforced by an execution of judgment, an order by the court instructing the sheriff to attach and seize the property of the debtor. The sheriff then sells the debtor's property. Proceeds from the sale are applied to satisfy the judgment.

A judgment lien, if renewed in the ninth year, remains in effect for 20 years in New York against personal property and 10 years against real property unless it is paid or discharged by filing a petition in bankruptcy. A judgment may be renewed and kept in force for additional periods if the creditor obtains a court order to extend it. New York law also provides for interest on the judgment at 9 percent per year.

Judgment liens have a priority relationship based upon the time of recording in the county clerk's office. The creditor who obtains a judgment and files it before another creditor will have the priority claim. The debtor's obligation to the creditor is paid in order of highest to lowest priority.

Writs of Attachment

Though similar to a lis pendens, a *writ of attachment* is stronger. It is an actual *court order that prevents any transfer of the attached property during the litigation.* Violation of the order can result in a contempt-of-court citation.

Income Tax Liens

The Internal Revenue Service (IRS) and the New York Department of Taxation and Finance may create a general lien against all of a taxpayer's property for taxes due and unpaid. The lien may be for various types of taxes owed, such as personal income tax, employee withholding tax, federal unemployment tax, FICA for employees, self-employment tax, sales tax, use tax, or any other tax relating to income. The period of time for validity of these liens depends upon the type of tax due and unpaid.

This lien is created by filing a certificate of lien against the landowner in the county where the taxpayer's land is located. Liens held by the IRS or New York do not automatically receive priority status or preferential treatment for payment purposes. Priority of the tax lien could be determined by the date the lien was placed on the real estate or against the individual and is also subject to federal and state statutes and court determinations. For example, in a 1998 U. S. Supreme Court decision, the court found that an unrecorded federal lien does *not* have priority over a (local) judgment lien.

Estate and Inheritance Tax Liens

Federal estate and state inheritance taxes are calculated and incurred at the time of death of an individual property owner. A general lien on the property in the estate is imposed to assure payment of the taxes due at death. New York imposes an inheritance tax upon the inheritance of real and personal property. This tax is a lien on all property the heirs inherit. To satisfy the tax bill, the estate is allowed to sell sufficient property.

The federal government imposes a tax on the estate of deceased persons. Called the federal estate tax, this tax creates a lien that attaches to all of the property in the estate. Both federal and New York tax laws allow property to pass to surviving spouses without taxation. Taxes owed by other heirs to the estate must be paid out of the estate proceeds before the remaining property can pass to the heirs.

Corporation Franchise Tax Liens

A corporation franchise tax is a yearly tax levied on corporations by the state for doing business in New York. The minimum tax for all corporations including a subchapter S corporation is $325. Other charges apply to inactive corporations.

The corporation franchise tax is calculated on the net profit of the corporation, and if it is not paid, it becomes a lien against the corporation's assets. The corporation's assets may then be foreclosed by the state and the assets attached. Failure to pay a franchise tax will permit the state to dissolve the corporation which will invalidate its right to do business legally in New York. (Refer to Chapter 3 for a discussion of Subchapter S and C corporations.)

Effects of Liens on Title

A lien creates an encumbrance on the property; therefore, all liens should be paid in full before transfer of title takes place on a property to avoid a foreclosure proceeding. A lien may prompt foreclosure proceedings against a property even if the lien is as small as $1,000. This could also cause a new owner to lose the property. In the case of a mortgage lien, it is possible for the new purchasers to assume the seller's mortgage on the property instead of the seller paying off the mortgage lien against the property. This can be accomplished if the mortgage is already assumable and, if not, the lender can still allow the existing mortgage to be assumed (although this is quite rare).

PUTTING IT TO WORK

A mortgage creates a voluntary specific lien against a property. The value of the lien, however, may be less than the total value of the property if sold at foreclosure. This fact poses an interesting dilemma for the owner who faces foreclosure. Respond to the following scenario,* then compare your response to the model in the Answer Key at the end of the chapter.

We've had some financial difficulties lately and expect our home to be foreclosed shortly. It is worth much more than what we owe on the mortgage. What happens to the extra money the lender gets when the property is sold?

EASEMENTS

An **easement** is a **nonpossessory** *interest in land owned by another.* Someone who owns an easement right does not own or possess the land where the easement lies. The easement owner merely owns the right to use or have access to the land. The right of ingress and egress (entry and exit) to and from real estate is one of the primary purposes of easements. Other uses for easements relate to things such as a common wall in a duplex or condominium, also known as a party wall; the right to take water from the land of another; and the right to receive light and air. If one has a **possessory** interest in a property, that individual cannot own an easement. The common terminology for easement is *right-of-way.* The real estate industry recognizes easements in gross and easements appurtenant, both of which can be negative or affirmative. Easements can be created by property owners, by law, or by use.

Easements in Gross

Easements in gross are also called commercial easements in gross. This category of easements is *usually owned by the government, an agency of the government, or a public utility.* Examples are the water and electric lines that run underground in subdivisions. The owner of the easement (the utility company) does not *own* any land adjacent to the easement, merely the right to use the land of the owner. Thus the utility company may place utility lines as well as maintain and repair the utilities. Commercial easements in gross are usually assignable by the owner. The governmental agency or utility that owns the easement right can allow other utilities to use the same easement. The owner of the commercial easement in gross also can sell or assign to others the right to use the easement. An example is if a telephone company sells to a cable television company the right to place cable television lines within the telephone easement.

Source: James A. Ader, "Real Estate Spotlight." Copyright © The Albany *Times Union.* Reprinted by permission.

The easement in gross is the most common form of easement, since virtually all urban and suburban property is subject to several government easements for items such as utilities and roadway expansion. Easements in gross also may be held by those in the private sector. Examples are the right of access allowed to a Planned Unit Development association to go onto the land of private owners to repair walls or fences.

Easements Appurtenant

The **easement appurtenant** category includes *all easements that are not easements in gross.* For an easement appurtenant to exist, two landowners must be involved; one must receive a benefit and the other must accept a burden. The *land that benefits from an easement appurtenant* is called the **dominant tenement** or estate. The *land that must suffer and allow the use* is called the **servient tenement** or estate. An example of an easement appurtenant is shown in Figure 4.2. In the illustration, if landowner B sells her property to another party, X, the easement appurtenant follows the transfer of title to the land now owned by X. *When an easement appurtenant follows the transfer of title to land from one owner to another and attaches to the land, this is called running with the land.* For an easement to run with the land, the owner of the easement must own land for which the easement is used (dominant tenement). Just as the dominant nature of the easement appurtenant runs with the land, so does the servient nature run with the land. If landowner A sells his land to another party, Z, Z must allow B the use of the easement.

The typical purpose of an easement appurtenant is to allow access to some desirable feature such as water, an access road, or other land owned by the dominant owner on the other side of the servient owner.

Negative and Affirmative Easements Appurtenant

Easements appurtenant can be divided into two categories: negative and affirmative. The easement appurtenant illustrated in Figure 4.2 is an affirmative easement. The dominant tenement or estate is given the right to physically cross the servient tenement. When a negative easement appurtenant exists, the dominant tenement does not have the right to physically enter the land of the servient tenement. Instead, the dominant tene-

FIGURE 4.2
An easement appurtenant. Landowner B may cross A's land to access the public road. This is an example of an affirmative easement.

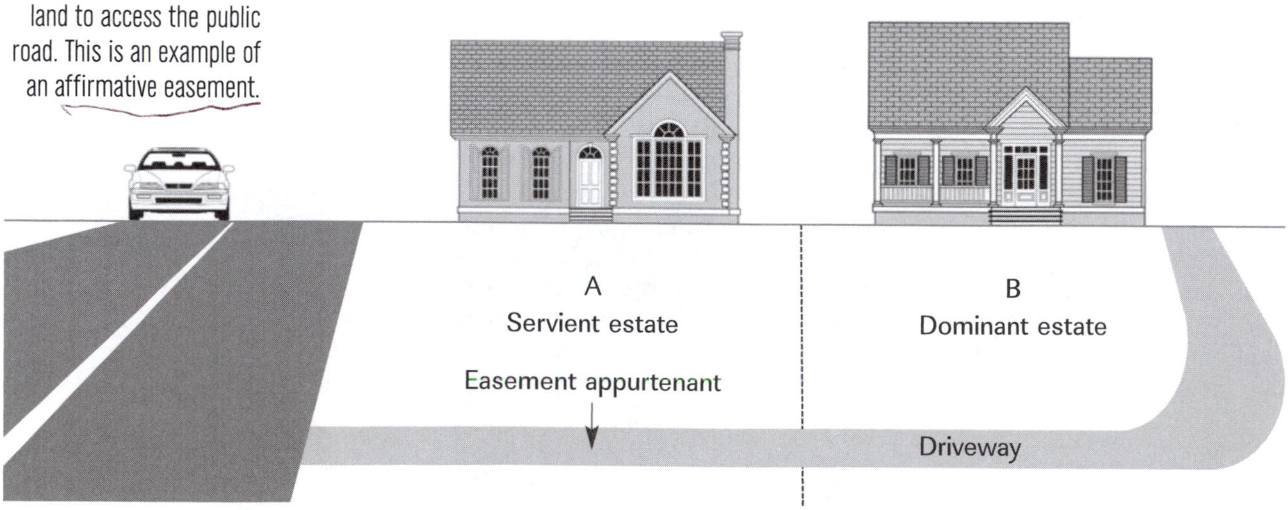

*Servient estate D is not allowed to erect a fence or landscape in such a way as to block C's view of the lake. However, C may not cross D's land for lake access.

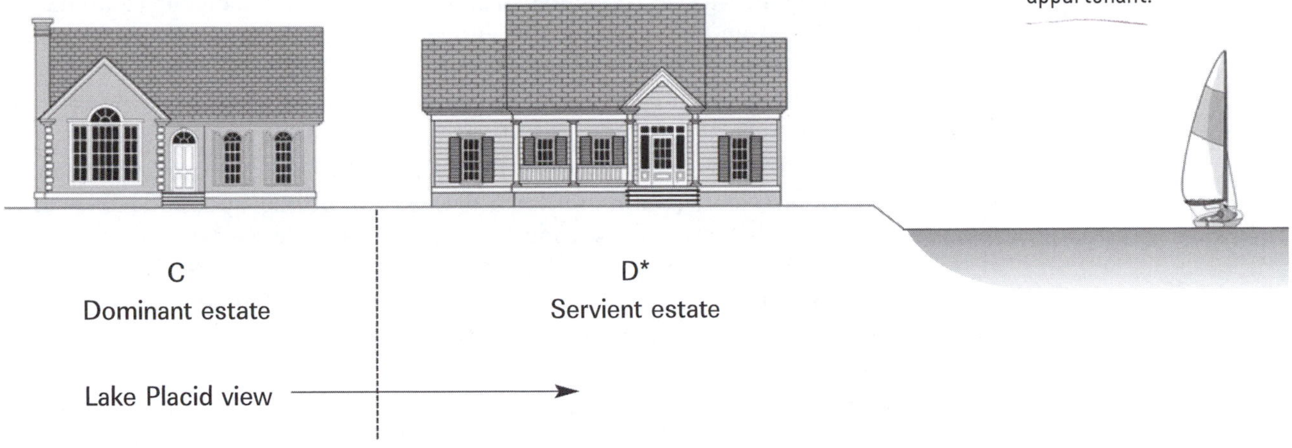

FIGURE 4.3
A negative easement appurtenant.

ment has the right to restrict some activity or use of the servient tenement. A negative easement is illustrated in Figure 4.3. Landowner D borders the lake and landowner C borders landowner D. In this case, D is prohibited from erecting a fence or landscaping that would block C's view of the lake. C is not permitted to cross D's land to get to the lake. (If C did have the right to cross the land to reach the lake, C's right would constitute an affirmative easement.) Instead, C is only allowed to restrain D in developing her land so as not to block the view. *This type of negative easement often is called an* **easement for light and air,** *or view easement.* Negative and affirmative easements both run with the land. Typical negative easements appurtenant include view easements, aviation easements, and solar easements. Figure 4.3 illustrates a view easement, in which the servient tenement cannot block the view of the dominant tenement. New York has determined that a landowner does not have a natural "right" to sunlight. In addition, a landowner generally does not have a natural "right" to a view.

Affirmative and negative easements — **You Should Know**

AFFIRMATIVE	NEGATIVE
Runs with the land	Runs with the land
Dominant tenement can physically use servient tenement	Dominant tenement can restrict servient tenement
Allows access to water, road, or other feature	Also known as view easement or easement for light and air

Creation of Easements Appurtenant

Easements appurtenant are created by:

- grant or reservation (deed)
- necessity and intent
- prescription
- implication
- condemnation

Easements by grant or reservation are those *created with the express written agreement of the landowners,* usually in a deed. The written agreement sets out the location and extent of the easement. An owner may convey land and reserve to herself an easement. This act is called the retention of an easement (retaining a stick in the bundle) on land conveyed to another. A common example of an easement by grant or deed is found when a developer in the plat sets aside a portion of the land for common area—parks, sidewalks, and so on. This practice also is called *dedication* of the land.

Easements by necessity exist *when land has no access to roads and is landlocked.* Access, also known as ingress and egress, is required by law. The servient tenement may be entitled to some compensation for the interest taken. Landowner B is landlocked. For landowner B to have access (ingress and egress) to the public road, landowner B must cross the property of landowner A. Landowner B receives the benefit of the easement. Landowner A must suffer and allow the use of access by landowner B.

Easements by prescription are *obtained by use of land without the owner's permission for a legally prescribed length of time.* In New York, the use must be open and obvious to anyone who looks, and must continue uninterrupted for a period of 10 years. The user must prove in a court action that he has satisfied all the requirements for the easement to be valid. (The easement by prescription gives only the right of continued use, not ownership of the land.) A common example of an easement by prescription is when a driveway is constructed by owner B at or near her boundary line without the benefit of a survey. After 10 or more years of using the driveway, a survey shows the driveway to be partially or completely on the land of owner C. Owner B will have an easement by prescription to use the driveway. Landowner B is the dominant tenement, and C is the servient tenement.

Easements by implication arise *by implication from the conduct of the parties.* For example, when landowner X sells mineral rights to Company Y, Company Y has an easement by implication to go onto the property of X to do mining. Company Y's use of the easement must be reasonable and only for the purpose of obtaining minerals.

An **easement by condemnation** is *created by the exercise of the government's right of eminent domain.* Through eminent domain (discussed more fully in Chapter 10), the government can take title to land (with the payment of just compensation) and take the right to use land for some purpose in the future. Most road widenings, sidewalks, and utility easements are created through eminent domain.

A **party wall** is *a wall shared by two adjoining structures.* Each owner of the structure owns his section of the wall in severalty subject to an easement by each of the owners to use the other's section of the wall for support. This is called a *cross-easement.*

Termination of Easements Appurtenant

Easements appurtenant may be terminated by:

1. release of the easement by the easement owner
2. combining the dominant and servient lands into one tract, called *merger*
3. abandonment of the easement by the easement owner
4. purpose for the easement ceasing to exist, for example, when land is no longer landlocked because a new road has been built
5. expiration of a specified time period for which the easement was created

ENCROACHMENTS

An **encroachment** is created by the intrusion of some structure or object across a boundary line. Typical encroachments in real estate include tree limbs, bushes, fences, antennae, roof lines, driveways, and overhangs. The encroaching owner is a trespasser. In most encroachment situations, the encroachment is accidental or unintentional. The only method to accurately determine the existence of an encroachment is through surveying the boundary line. Almost every subdivision in the United States has classic examples of encroachments. At the time her new home was built 12 years ago, homeowner Alice planted small trees and shrubs on or near her property's boundary lines. As the bushes and trees grew, the branches extended beyond the boundaries. One small apple tree is now dropping rotten apples into the neighbor's back yard. The roof of the garage that Alice erected within six inches of the boundary line has eaves that extend over the boundary line, and water drains onto the neighbor's yard.

In New York, an encroachment that is caused by shrubbery or garage eaves or the like, and is continuous, does not automatically become an easement by prescription or ownership in fee. If the adjoining landowner is damaged or disturbed by the encroachment, he has the right to bring legal action to remove the encroachment or to file a suit for damages (judgment by the court requires the encroacher to compensate the landowner for the encroachment). Figure 4.4 illustrates some encroachments.

APPURTENANCES

Appurtenances in real property are *the inherent or automatic ownership rights that are a natural consequence of owning property.* Not only do property owners have these rights but property owners also may sell or lease these rights to others. The most common appurtenant rights are: profit, license, air rights, subsurface rights, and water rights. The right of accession also may bear on ownership rights. Accession rights

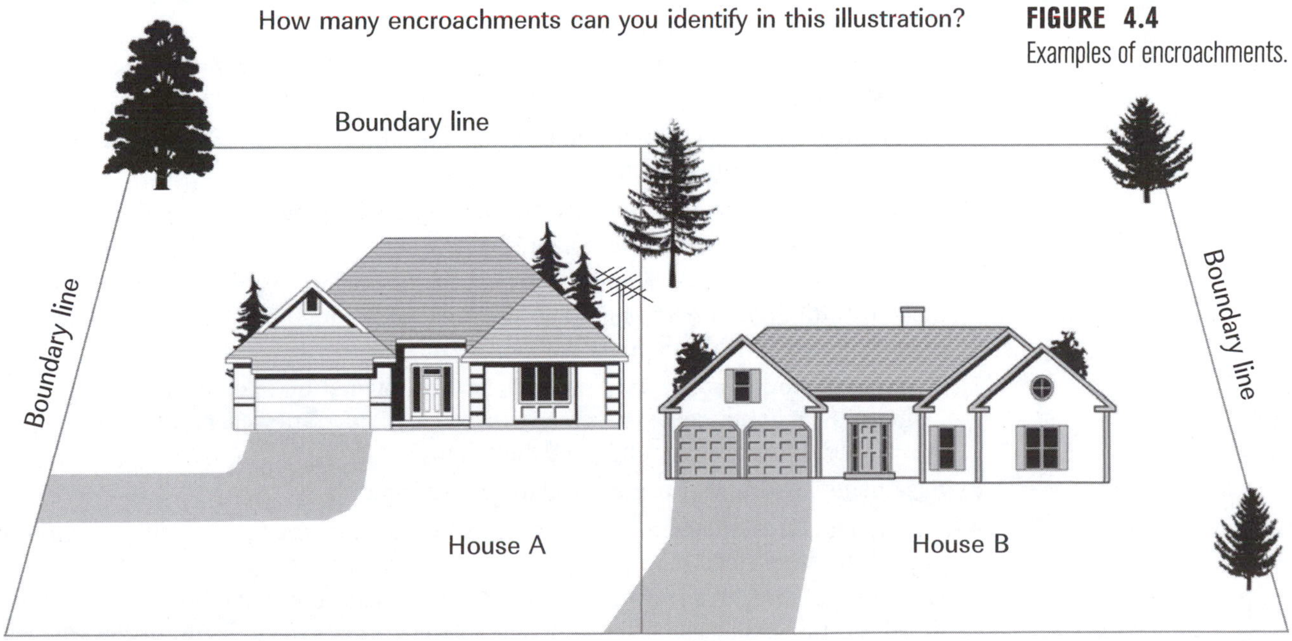

FIGURE 4.4
Examples of encroachments.

affirm that owners of real property have ownership rights to products obtained from their land, such as crops, and also have ownership rights to all that is added to their land, either intentionally or by mistake. See Chapter 3's discussion about air rights, subsurface rights, and water rights. Accession rights are discussed more fully in Chapter 5. Profit and license are discussed below.

Profit

The word *profit* is a legal term describing the right to take products of the soil from someone else's land, including soil, minerals, or timber. Profits are created in the same manner as easements: by grant or deed, by necessity, or by prescription. A profit is salable, inheritable, and transferable. A profit in land easily could be more valuable than owning the land. For example, if land in New York has timber, the right to take and sell the timber could be more valuable than use of the land for any other purpose.

License

A *license* is defined as permission to do a particular act or series of acts on another's land without possessing any estate or interest in the land. A license is a personal privilege that the licensor may revoke at any time unless the licensee has paid for the license for a specific time. For example, an individual pays for a license for the right to fish or hunt in a specified lake or forest. The licensor may not revoke the license unless the licensee has gone outside the authority of the license. A license is not assignable, not inheritable, and is a *temporary privilege.*

IMPORTANT POINTS

1. An encumbrance is a claim, lien, charge, or liability attached to and binding upon real property. Examples are encroachments, easements, liens, assessments, and restrictive covenants.
2. Specific liens are claims against a specific and readily identifiable property, such as a mortgage or a mechanics' lien.
3. The lien for real property taxes is a specific lien; in New York this lien is given the highest priority for payment.
4. Mechanics' and materialmen's liens are specific liens that may receive preferential treatment for priority of liens.
5. A lis pendens notice provides specific and constructive public notice that a lawsuit concerning certain real estate is pending.
6. General liens are claims against a person and all of his property, such as a judgment resulting from a lawsuit. The property of a judgment debtor is subject to execution and forced sale to satisfy an unpaid judgment.
7. Easements are nonpossessory interests in land owned by another. Easements can be in gross or appurtenant. Easements are created by grant (reservation), necessity, prescription, implication, and condemnation.
8. Easements appurtenant can be negative or affirmative.
9. Easements are terminated by release, merger, abandonment, necessity, or expiration of the prescribed time period.
10. An encroachment is a trespass on land or an intrusion over the boundary of land. Proof of the existence of an encroachment is evidenced by a survey of the boundary.
11. A profit in real property is transferable and inheritable. A license in real property is not transferable or inheritable.

How Would You Respond? CHAPTER REVIEW

Analyze the following situations and decide how the individuals should handle them in accordance with what you have just learned. Check your responses using the Answer Key at the end of the chapter.

1. Donna wishes to purchase a country property for weekend getaways. Her salesperson takes her to a lovely property but, as they leave the main highway, she notices that to reach her intended property, they must cross a driveway that does not belong to the parcel for sale. Donna realizes that her prospective home is landlocked and inaccessible to the highway except through the neighbor's driveway. She is now afraid to buy the property because she thinks that the neighbors will not permit her to use their driveway. Are Donna's concerns legitimate? What type of easement is required for Donna's property? Which property is the dominant tenement? Which property is the servient tenement?

   ____

   ____

   ____

2. The Clairmonts purchase an inground pool. As the contractor works on the installation, he suggests added features such as built-in lights and wrought-iron fencing. The Clairmonts enthusiastically agree to all of the suggestions, but the bill totals $5,000 more than they have budgeted. The contractor files a lien against the property for the unpaid sum. In the meantime, Ms. Clairmont's company transfers her, so they need to sell the house. What kind of lien was put on the property? Will the title transfer with the lien attached to it? Whose responsibility is the lien?

   ____

   ____

   ____

KEY TERM REVIEW

Fill in the term that best completes each sentence and then check the Answer Key at the end of the chapter.

1. Anything that lessens the bundle of rights in real property is a(n) __________.
2. A legally filed claim or charge against the property by an individual who makes repairs to a property is a(n) ____________________.
3. A mechanic's lien is a(n) ____________________ filed by a supplier of services in connection with the construction or improvement to a building.
4. A(n) ____________________ is a legal notice that a lawsuit has been filed concerning a specific property.
5. A(n) ____________________ may be needed by public utility companies for the placement of power lines.
6. The land that benefits from an easement appurtenant is called the __________.
7. The land that must suffer and allow the use of the easement appurtenant is called the ____________________.
8. A(n) ____________________ exists when a landowner has no access to roads and is landlocked.

MULTIPLE CHOICE

Circle the letter that best answers the question and then check the Answer Key at the end of the chapter.

1. Which of the following statements about easements is FALSE?
   A. an easement provides a nonpossessory interest in land
   B. a servient tenement is the land burdened by an easement
   C. a dominant tenement is the land benefited by an easement
   D. an easement appurtenant may never be terminated

2. Easements in gross are also known as:
   A. eminent domain easements
   B. appurtenant easements in gross
   C. easements by necessity
   D. commercial easements in gross

3. A property owner gives another person permission to fish in a lake on his property. The permission is a temporary privilege and exists in the form of which of the following?
   A. license
   B. easement
   C. lease
   D. appurtenance

4. The creation of an easement by condemnation results from the exercise of which of the following?
   A. prescription
   B. eminent domain
   C. dedication
   D. implication

5. If a property has liens for inheritance tax, income tax, estate tax, and property tax, which will receive priority in payment at foreclosure?
   A. inheritance tax
   B. income tax
   C. estate tax
   D. property tax

6. A merger with regard to easements occurs when:
   A. the dominant tenement is larger and more valuable than the servient tenement
   B. the servient tenement must allow the dominant tenement complete access
   C. the easement is terminated because the dominant tenement and the servient tenement are owned by the same person
   D. the easement is an easement in gross and is utilized by all of the government agencies in the jurisdiction to deliver utility services

7. The right to take sand, soil, and gravel from another's land is called:
   A. license
   B. profit
   C. easement
   D. lien

8. When a negative easement exists:
   A. the dominant tenement has the physical right to enter the land of the servient tenement
   B. the dominant tenement does not have the physical right to enter the land of the servient tenement
   C. an easement by necessity is automatically created
   D. an easement by prescription is automatically created

9. A mechanic's lien is an example of a:
   A. specific involuntary lien
   B. general involuntary lien
   C. specific voluntary lien
   D. general voluntary lien

10. A judgment against an individual is an example of a:
    A. general involuntary lien
    B. specific involuntary lien
    C. general voluntary lien
    D. specific voluntary lien

ANSWER KEY

Putting It To Work

If the property were to sell for more than the amount due the mortgage holder (the lender), then you (the borrower) would receive the excess proceeds. However, remember that there could be no other claims against the property including, but not limited to, other mortgage holders and taxing authorities. In addition, the sale expenses are paid from the excess. Also, remember that if a property sells for less than what is owed, the borrower is not relieved of this additional debt, but the lender may request a deficiency judgment that can proceed against the borrower's other assets.*

How Would You Respond?

1. Donna's concerns have no merit since her property is landlocked and it is therefore entitled to an easement by necessity through operation of law. Donna's property would be the dominant tenement because Donna would be the user of the easement. The property with access to the main road is the servient tenement because this property would provide the entry and exit to the main road.
2. The contractor attached a mechanic's lien to the property, not only for the unpaid labor but also for materials used in the construction of the pool. Before their title transfers, the Clairmonts would have to pay the lien. The payment of the lien is the responsibility of the sellers, the Clairmonts. If the buyer purchases the property with the lien attached to it, the buyer would become the responsible party, and if the lien is not paid, the new purchaser could face foreclosure proceedings against the property.

Key Term Review

1. encumbrance
2. mechanics' lien
3. specific lien
4. lis pendens
5. easement in gross
6. dominant tenement
7. servient tenement
8. easement by necessity

Multiple Choice

1. D
2. D
3. A
4. B
5. D
6. C
7. B
8. B
9. A
10. A

---

*Source: James A. Ader, "Real Estate Spotlight." Copyright © The Albany *Times Union.* Reprinted by permission.

Chapter 5

KEY TERMS

accession
accretion
acknowledgment
adverse possession
alluvion
avulsion
bargain and sale deed
conveyance
dedication
dedication by deed
deed
delivery and acceptance
executor/executrix
full covenant and warranty deed
grantee
grantor
habendum clause
involuntary alienation
land patent
public grant
quitclaim deed
referee's deed
reference to a plat
voluntary alienation

LEARNING OBJECTIVES

Classroom hours: 1 1/2

1. Discuss the definition and purpose of a deed.
2. Identify the essential elements of a deed.
3. Distinguish between the various types of deeds and when they are used.
4. Identify the various types of wills and the process that must be undertaken for a conveyance to be finalized.
5. Identify key terms that are common to understanding deeds and wills.

Deeds

IN THIS CHAPTER Transfer of title to real property is described in law as *alienation.* In a transfer, the property owner is alienated, or separated, from the title. Alienation may be voluntary or involuntary. As a licensee, you should be familiar with the laws and methods involved with title transfer as well as the various types of deeds.

During the life of an owner, title to real property may be transferred by involuntary alienation as a result of a lien foreclosure sale (discussed in Chapter 4), adverse possession, filing a petition in bankruptcy, or condemnation under the power of eminent domain. **Involuntary alienation** occurs when *an individual must relinquish title to real property against his will.* This chapter explores involuntary ownership through adverse possession. (Eminent domain is discussed in Chapter 10.)

Voluntary alienation, and transfer of title during life, is *accomplished by the delivery of a valid deed by the grantor to the grantee while both are alive.* Voluntary transfer is the most important type of alienation in the real estate business and is the primary subject of this chapter.

DEEDS

The most important document in the transfer of title to real property is the **deed,** *the document used to convey title legally to real property. A deed is also known as a* **conveyance.**

Essential Elements of a Valid Deed

Writing

As required by the Statute of Frauds (discussed in Chapter 6), every deed must be in writing. An oral conveyance is not recognized under the law. The written deed must meet New York's requirement for a valid deed.

Grantor

The **grantor,** *the person conveying the title,* must be legally competent; the individual must have the capacity to contract. The same requirement exists for all parties to a valid contract. The grantor must have reached the age of majority, that in New York is

18, and must be mentally competent. Also, the grantor must be named with certainty; that is, it must be possible to positively identify the grantor.

Grantee

The **grantee,** *the person receiving title,* does not need legal capacity; a minor or a mentally incompetent person can receive and hold title to real property. These individuals, however, cannot convey title on their own because they are not qualified to be grantors. To effect a conveyance of title held in the name of an incompetent, a guardian's deed must be executed by the incompetent's guardian as grantor. The conveyance by the guardian may be accomplished only with court authority. The grantee must be alive at the time of delivery of the deed.

Within the deed, the grantor may be referred to as *party of the first part* and the grantee referred to as *party of the second part. Also, a New York deed must include the addresses of the grantor(s) and grantee(s).*

Property Description

The deed must contain an adequate formal legal *description* of the property. Methods for providing this description are discussed later in this chapter.

Consideration

The deed must provide evidence that *consideration* (something of value, such as money) is present. In New York, the deed does not have to recite the actual amount of consideration (money) involved. The deed in New York states, "One dollar and other good or valuable consideration." This is called *nominal* consideration. A recital of consideration is shown in Figure 5.1 in conjunction with words showing conveyance.

Words of Conveyance

The deed must contain *words of conveyance* demonstrating that it is the *grantor's intention to transfer the title to the named grantee.* These words of conveyance are contained in the *granting clause.* In the case of warranty deeds, typical wording on the deed is "has given, granted, bargained, sold and conveyed" or "grants and releases."

The words of the granting indicate the type of deed: "conveys and warrants to" indicates a warranty deed; "quits any and all claims to" indicates a quitclaim deed.

In addition to the granting clause, the deed sometimes contains a **habendum clause,** *which describes the estate granted and always must agree with the granting clause. This clause begins with the words "to have and to hold."* A typical habendum clause in a deed conveying a fee simple title reads, "to have and to hold the above described premises with all the appurtenances thereunto belonging, or in anywise appertaining, unto the grantee, his heirs, and/or successors and assigns forever."

Execution

Proper execution of the deed means that it must be signed by each grantor conveying an interest in the property. Only the grantors execute the deed; the grantee does not sign unless he is assuming a mortgage.

Acknowledgment

For a deed to be eligible for recording, it must have an **acknowledgment.** A *grantor must appear before a public officer,* such as a notary public, who is eligible to take an acknowledgment, *and state that signing the deed was a voluntary act.* A deed is perfectly valid between grantor and grantee without an acknowledgment. Without the

FIGURE 5.1
A warranty deed showing consideration and words of conveyance.

FORM S 301 — Warranty Deed with Lien Covenant

© NATIONAL LEGAL SUPPLY, INC.
126 Sheridan Ave., Albany, N.Y. 12210

This Indenture

Made the 28th *day of* March *Two Thousand and* four

Between

Carolyn Butler, residing at 20 Amortization Drive,
City and County of Albany, State of New York

part y *of the first part, and*

Vanessa Dupree, residing at 5 West Avenue, City and County of Albany, State of New York

part y *of the second part,*

Witnesseth *that the part* y *of the first part, in consideration of* One and 00/100 ---------------------------- *Dollar* *($* 1.00 *)* *lawful money of the United States,* and after good and valuable consideration *paid by the party* *of the second part, do*es *hereby grant and release unto the part* y *of the second part,* her heirs *and assigns forever, all*

BEGINNING on a stake in the northeast margin of Amortization Drive, south corner of Lot No. 20 of the subdivision or a portion of the property of Mortgage Heights Land Company, Inc., and running thence North 6° 18' East 215.2 feet to a stake; thence North 8° 49' West 241.0 feet to a stake, common corner of Lot Nos. 20 and 19 of said subdivision; thence with the dividing line between said Lot Nos. 19 and 20, South 87° 50' West 138.5 feet to a stake in the east margin of a cul-de-sac; thence with the east margin of said cul-de-sac in a southwesterly direction along a curve with the radius of 50.0 feet, 61.2 feet to a stake in said margin; thence with the east margin of a drive leading to Amortization Drive, South 5° 19' West 132.8 feet to a stake in the point of intersection of said margin of said drive with Amortization Drive; thence with the northeast margin of said Amortization Drive, South 51° 17' East 84.7 feet to a stake in said margin; thence still with said margin of said drive, South 42° 27' East 47.2 feet to a stake in said margin; thence still said margin of said drive, South 29° 36' East 199.9 feet to the BEGINNING.

Intended to be the same premises as conveyed to the party of the first part by Consuela Davis by deed dated April 3, 1999 recorded in the office of the Albany County Clerk on April 10, 1999 in liber # 240, page 300.

(continued)

FIGURE 5.1
Continued.

Together *with the appurtenances and all the estate and rights of the part* y *of the first part in and to said premises,*

To have and to hold *the premises herein granted unto the part*y *of the second part,* her heirs *and assigns forever.*

And *said* party of the first part *covenant* s *as follows:*

First, *That the part* y *of the second part shall quietly enjoy the said premises;*

Second, *That said* party of the first part *will forever* **Warrant** *the title to said premises.*

Third, *That, in Compliance with Sec. 13 of the Lien Law, the grantor will receive the consideration for this conveyance and will hold the right to receive such consideration as a trust fund to be applied first for the purpose of paying the cost of the improvement and will apply the same first to the payment of the cost of the improvement before using any part of the total of the same for any other purpose.*

In Witness Whereof, *the part* y *of the first part ha* s *hereunto set* her *hand and seal the day and year first above written.*

IN PRESENCE OF

Carolyn Butler (L.S.)

(L.S.)

(L.S.)

(L.S.)

State of New York
County of Albany } **ss.**

On this 28 *day of* March *Two Thousand and* Four *before me, the subscriber, personally appeared*

Carolyn Butler

to me personally known and known to me to be the same person described in and who executed the within Instrument, and she *acknowledged to me that* she *executed the same.*

Notary Public- State of New York, County of Albany
My Commission Expires 3/30/05

Tax Map No. ______________________

Tax Billing Address ______________________

Deed
WARRANTY WITH LIEN COVENANT

TO

Dated, 19

STATE OF NEW YORK

COUNTY OF ______ *SS.*

RECORDED ON THE

day of ______ *A.D. 19* ______

at ______ *o'clock* ______ *M.*

in LIBER ______ *of DEEDS*

at PAGE ______ *and examined*

CLERK

acknowledgment, however, the grantee cannot record the deed and thereby has no protection to title against purchasers of the same property from the same grantor who records his deed. The grantee should insist upon receiving a deed that has been acknowledged.

Delivery and Acceptance

To effect a transfer of title by deed, **delivery and acceptance** must occur. *The grantor must deliver a valid deed to the grantee, and the grantee must accept the deed*. These acts constitute transfer of title. Delivery may be made directly to the grantee or to an agent of the grantee. The agent is typically the grantee's attorney, the real estate broker, or title company insuring the title. In almost every case, there is a presumption of acceptance by the grantee. This presumption is especially strong if the deed has been recorded and the conveyance is beneficial to the grantee.

Forms of Deeds

Many forms of deeds result from the various warranties of title contained in the deed, and the deed may have numerous variations based on the special purpose for which it is drawn. The most frequently used types of deed in New York are the full covenant and warranty deed with at least several covenants, the quitclaim deed, and the bargain and sale deed.

Full Covenant and Warranty Deed

The **full covenant and warranty deed** *contains the strongest and broadest form of guarantee of title of any type of deed* and therefore provides the greatest protection to the grantee. The full covenant and warranty deed usually contains six covenants, described below. Exact wording of the covenants may vary.

1. *Covenant of seisin*. Typical wording in this covenant is, "Grantor covenants that he is seised of said premises in fee." This covenant, like the others in the full covenant and warranty deed, is a specific covenant assuring the grantee that the grantor holds the title that he specified in the deed he is conveying to the grantee.
2. *Covenant of right to convey.* This covenant, that usually follows the covenant of seisin in the full covenant and warranty deed, typically reads, "and has the right to convey the same in fee simple." By this covenant the grantor provides *an assurance to the grantee that the grantor has legal capacity to convey the title and also has the title to convey.*
3. *Covenant against encumbrances.* This covenant typically states that "said premises are free from encumbrances (with the exceptions above stated, if any)." The grantor assures the grantee that *no encumbrances against the title except those set forth in the deed itself* exist. Typical acceptable encumbrances to grantees are a mortgage lien when the grantee is assuming the grantor's existing mortgage, recorded easements, and restrictive covenants.
4. *Covenant of quiet enjoyment.* This covenant usually reads, "the grantee, his heirs and assigns, shall quietly and peaceably have, hold, use, possess, and enjoy the premises." This covenant is an assurance by the grantor to the grantee that the grantee shall have quiet possession and enjoyment of the property being conveyed and will not be disturbed in the use and enjoyment of the property because of a defect in the title conveyed by the grantor.
5. *Covenant for further assurances.* This covenant commonly states, "that she (grantor) will execute such further assurances as may be reasonable or necessary to perfect the title in the grantee." Under this covenant, the grantor must perform any acts necessary to correct any defect in the title being conveyed and any errors or deficiencies in the deed itself.

6. *Covenant of warranty.* The warranty of title in the full covenant and warranty deed provides that the grantor "will warrant and defend the title to the grantee against the lawful claims of all persons whomsoever." This is the *best form of warranty for protecting the grantee* and contains no limitations as to possible claimants protected against, because the grantor specifies that he will defend the title against "the lawful claims of all persons whomsoever." The covenant of warranty is the most important of all the covenants.

Section 13 of the New York Lien Law, as stated in the lien covenant in Figure 5.1, addresses priority of liens. In a warranty deed with lien covenant, the grantor is guaranteeing the grantee that there are no outstanding liens on the property and if such a lien would appear, then it would be the duty of the grantor to satisfy that lien. A warranty deed with lien covenant is commonly used in New York and this covenant appears in other forms of deeds.

Bargain and Sale Deed

Bargain and sale deeds may be with or without covenants of warranty. In either case, there is *an implied representation on the part of the grantor that she has a substantial title and possession of the property.* Grantees of these deeds should require that the deed contain specific warranties, such as the warranty against encumbrances. A bargain and sale deed simply conveys property from one person or entity to another for a consideration. The deed includes both words of conveyance and words of consideration. A bargain and sale deed with covenants guarantees that the grantor "has not encumbered the property in any way" except what is stated in the deed itself. The deed does not address any encumbrances that may have been on the property when the grantor acquired title and does not warrant the deed for the future. A bargain and sale deed with the above stated covenants is usually acceptable to lenders because these covenants cover the areas of warranty required by lenders to loan money. A bargain and sale deed *without* covenants offers weaker protection for the grantee and is not acceptable to lenders in New York for mortgage purposes. The bargain and sale deed with covenants is used extensively in the New York City area. Figure 5.2 shows a portion of a bargain and sale deed.

Quitclaim Deed

The **quitclaim deed** contains no warranties whatsoever. It is simply a *deed of release.* It will release or convey to the grantee any interest, including title, that the grantor may have. The grantor, however, does not state in the deed that he has any title or interest in the property and certainly makes no warranties as to the quality of title. Execution of the quitclaim deed by the grantor prevents the grantor from asserting any claim against the title at any time in the future. Quitclaim deeds may be used to clear a "cloud on a title," which occurs when someone has a possible claim against a title. As long as this possibility exists, the title is clouded and therefore not a good and marketable title. To remove this cloud and create a good and marketable title, the possible claimant executes a quitclaim deed as grantor to the true titleholder as grantee. Common clouds include lingering spousal claims (particularly after a divorce), liens that appear to have been paid but not released (mortgages and mechanics' liens), and claims of relatives after estate probation. Figure 5.3 contains a portion of a quitclaim deed showing a granting clause.

Judicial Deed

Execution of a *judicial deed* results from a court order to the official executing the deed. The names of various types of judicial deeds relate to the official executing the deed: guardian's deed, sheriff's deed, referee's deed, tax deed, and administrator's or executor's deed. Judicial deeds contain no warranties except that the grantor has not done any act to encumber the property.

FIGURE 5.2
A bargain and sale deed.

T 691

Standard N.Y.B.T.U. Form 8002: Bargain & sale deed, with covenant against grantor's acts—Ind. or Corp.: single sheet

DATE CODE

JULIUS BLUMBERG, INC., LAW BLANK PUBLISHERS

CONSULT YOUR LAWYER BEFORE SIGNING THIS INSTRUMENT – THIS INSTRUMENT SHOULD BE USED BY LAWYERS ONLY

THIS INDENTURE, made the day of , nineteen hundred and

BETWEEN

party of the first part, and

party of the second part,

WITNESSETH, that the party of the first part, in consideration of Ten Dollars and other valuable consideration paid by the party of the second part, does hereby grant and release unto the party of the second part, the heirs or successors and assigns of the party of the second part forever,

ALL that certain plot, piece or parcel of land, with the buildings and improvements thereon erected, situate, lying and being in the

TOGETHER with all right, title and interest, if any, of the party of the first part in and to any streets and roads abutting the above described premises to the center lines thereof; TOGETHER with the appurtenances and all the estate and rights of the party of the first part in and to said premises; TO HAVE AND TO HOLD the premises herein granted unto the party of the second part, the heirs or successors and assigns of the party of the second part forever.

AND the party of the first part covenants that the party of the first part has not done or suffered anything whereby the said premises have been encumbered in any way whatever, except as aforesaid.
AND the party of the first part, in compliance with Section 13 of the Lien Law, covenants that the party of the first part will receive the consideration for this conveyance and will hold the right to receive such consideration as a trust fund to be applied first for the purpose of paying the cost of the improvement and will apply the same first to the payment of the cost of the improvement before using any part of the total of the same for any other purpose.
The word "party" shall be construed as if it read "parties" whenever the sense of this indenture so requires.

IN WITNESS WHEREOF, the party of the first part has duly executed this deed the day and year first above written.

IN PRESENCE OF:

FIGURE 5.3
A quitclaim deed.

FORM 559½ N. Y. DEED—QUIT CLAIM

TUTBLANX REGISTERED U. S. PAT. OFFICE
TUTTLE LAW PRINT, PUBLISHERS, RUTLAND, VT. 05701

This Indenture *Made the day of Nineteen Hundred and*

Between

part of the first part, and

part of the second part,

Witnesseth *that the part of the first part, in consideration of Dollar ($)*
lawful money of the United States,
paid by the part of the second part, do hereby remise, release and quitclaim unto the part of the second part, and assigns forever, all

Together *with the appurtenances and all the estate and rights of the part of the first part in and to said premises,*

To have and to hold *the premises herein granted unto the part of the second part, and assigns forever.*

In Witness Whereof, *the part of the first part ha hereunto set hand and seal the day and year first above written.*

In Presence of

____________________ L.S.
____________________ L.S.
____________________ L.S.
____________________ L.S.

State of New York
County of } ss. *On this day of Nineteen Hundred and*
before me, the subscriber, personally appeared

to me personally known and known to me to be the same person described in and who executed the within Instrument, and he acknowledged to me that he executed the same.

____

State of New York
County of } ss. *On this day of Nineteen Hundred and*
before me, the subscriber, personally appeared

to me personally known and known to me to be the same person described in and who executed the within Instrument, and he acknowledged to me that he executed the same.

____

Referee's Deed

A referee is an individual empowered by the court to exercise judicial power, such as in the sale and conveyance of real property if decided by court order. A referee may act for a sheriff at a sheriff's sale or act as directed by the court in a bankruptcy or similar case. A **referee's deed** (also known as a sheriff's deed) is a type of judicial deed used to convey the real property in question.

PROPERTY DESCRIPTIONS

For effective and accurate title transfers, title insurers, abstractors, and attorneys also rely on an *accurate legal description of the land.* The legal description for title transfer must be formal. Informal descriptions, such as street addresses or assessor/tax numbers, are acceptable on listings but not on documents for transferring or encumbering title.

Three acceptable types of property descriptions are discussed below: (a) metes and bounds, (b) description by reference, lot and block (plat of subdivision), and (c) monuments. The government, or rectangular, survey system of property description is used primarily in the western states, not in New York. It is used generally to transfer large tracts of real property whose shapes are rectangular or square.

Metes and Bounds

New York frequently uses the metes and bounds property description. In the *metes and bounds* description, metes are the distances from point to point and bounds are the directions from one point to another. An example of a metes and bounds description was shown in the deed in Figure 5.1.

A metes and bounds description results from a survey performed by a licensed land surveyor. One of the most important aspects of the metes and bounds description is the selection of the point of beginning. This point should be reasonably easy to locate and well established. After identifying the point of beginning, the surveyor then sights the direction to the next point, or monument. A metes and bounds description always ends at the point of beginning.

Reference, Plat, or Lot and Block (Plat of Subdivision)

A *description by reference, plat, or lot and block,* shown in Figure 5.4, is another valid legal description. Sometimes an attorney incorporates into the deed a description by reference in addition to a metes and bounds description. At other times, the description by reference is the only description in the deed. A description by **reference to a plat** *may refer to a plat (map) and lot number as part of a recorded subdivision.* The former description states the plat book and page number in which the plat or map is recorded so that interested parties can look it up and determine the exact location and dimensions of the property. A subdivision plat map is illustrated in Figure 5.5. Property may also be described by reference to section, block, and lot on the tax map or by reference to a prior recorded instrument.

ALL that certain plot, piece, or parcel of land, with the buildings and improvements thereon erected, situate, lying and being in the Town of East Greenbush, Rensselaer County, State of New York, designated as Lots 4 and 6 on a map entitled "Plat of David Minor 4—Lot Subdivision" Town of East Greenbush, Rensselaer County, New York, made by Evander Crady, Professional Land Surveyor, P.C., dated October 10, 2003, and revised June 10, 2004, and filed in the Rensselaer County Clerk's Office on October 1, 2004, in Drawer 2000 as Map No. 150.

FIGURE 5.4
A description by reference.

FIGURE 5.5
A subdivision plat map.

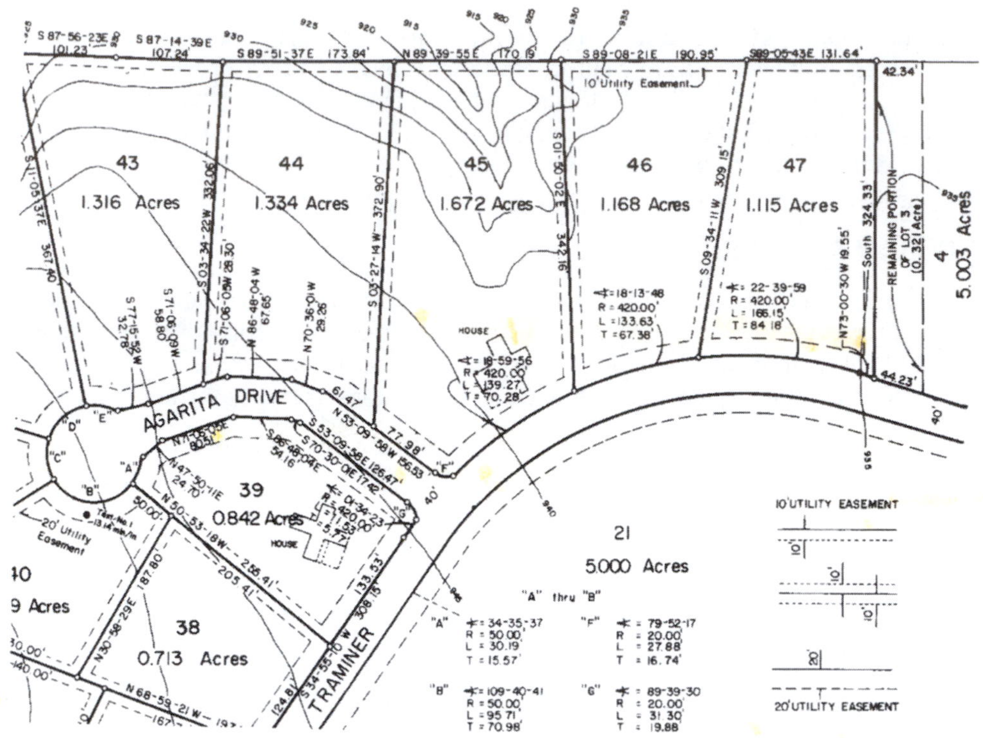

PUTTING IT TO WORK

See how well you can identify the different sections of a deed. To complete this activity, refer to Figure 5.1. Answer the questions below. If you are asked to identify a particular section of the deed, draw brackets [ ] around the actual sections of the deed shown in the textbook. Can you remember the purpose of each section? Compare your responses to the Answer Key at the end of the chapter.

a. What is the name of the grantor? ____________________
b. What is the name of the grantee? ____________________
c. Identify the phrase containing the consideration for the transaction.
d. Identify the phrase containing the granting clause.
e. Identify the description of the property. What type of description is this?

____

f. Identify the habendum clause, the covenant of quiet enjoyment, the covenant of warranty, and the lien covenant.
g. On what date was the deed executed? ____________________
h. Identify the acknowledgment.

Monument

Description by monument is used in place of the metes and bounds method and is used by surveyors when describing multiple-acre tracts of land that might be quite expensive to *survey*. The description is drawn from permanent objects such as a stone wall, large trees, or boulders.

METHODS OF TRANSFERRING TITLE

Upon an owner's death, a number of determining factors, such as whether the owner died with or without a will, can affect the transfer of real property.

Intestate Descent

When a person dies and leaves no valid will, the laws of intestacy determine the order in which the property is distributed to the heirs. The typical order of descent is: spouse, child(ren), parents, and siblings, followed by more distant relatives. Intestate successions statutes in New York determine questions of descent regarding a person who dies intestate (without a will). *Escheat* occurs when no one is eligible to receive the property of the decedent as provided by statute. In the absence of heirs, then, the state takes title to the property of the deceased. Because *the deceased has no control over the transfer of title* to the state, an involuntary alienation exists after death. No other form of involuntary alienation exists except by judicial action after death.

The person appointed by a court to distribute the intestate decedent's property, in accordance with provisions of the statute, is called an *administrator* or *administratrix*.

Testate Descent

If the deceased has left a valid will or, in the absence of a valid will, the deceased has heirs qualified to receive title to the property, the applicable term is voluntary alienation. If a person dies and leaves a valid will, he or she is said to have died *testate.* A male party who makes a will is called a *testator,* and a female a *testatrix.* A person appointed in a will to carry out provisions of the will is called an **executor** (male) or an **executrix** (female). *Probate* is the judicial determination of the validity of a will by a court of competent jurisdiction and subsequent supervision over distribution of the estate. A gift of real property by will is a *devise,* and the gift's recipient is the *devisee.* A gift of personal property by will is a *bequest* or *legacy,* and the recipient in this case is the *beneficiary* or *legatee.* Although wills are relatively simple documents, they must include certain required information or the will could be declared invalid.

Formal or Witnessed Will

A *formal* or *witnessed will* is a will signed by the testator or testatrix in front of two witnesses. The testator declares the writing to be his last will and testament and states that the document expresses his wish for the disposition of his property after death. He asks the two witnesses to sign the will and acknowledge that he has performed certain required acts and has signed the will.

Holographic Will

A *holographic will* is written entirely in the handwriting of the person whose signature it bears. A holographic will does *not* require the presence of witnesses in order to be valid.

Oral Will

An *oral will* (nuncupative will) is an unwritten will and is usually only valid if made by a member of the armed services during a war or a mariner at sea. This type of will is seldom upheld because of the possibility of fraud and because it does not usually meet the requirements of a valid oral will. The oral will is supposed to have the testator or testatrix state that it is a will; that it be put in writing by a witness as soon as possible; that a witness must prove the will; and that the witnesses are competent, disinterested parties. Oral wills usually are restricted to the granting of personal property, not real property, because of the conflict with the Statute of Frauds, which states that interests conveyed regarding real property must be in writing.

Codicil

A *codicil* is a supplement or an appendix to a will that either adds or changes some bequest in the will. It must be executed in the same form and manner as a formal will.

Dedication by Deed

A developer in the plat of subdivision may set aside a portion of the land for common area, parks, sidewalks, and so on. This practice is called **dedication,** and occurs *when land or an easement to land is given for use to the public by an owner.* A *statutory dedication* occurs when a property owner files a plat that marks or notes on the subdivision plat the specific portions of the property that are dedicated, donated, or granted to the public. A *common law dedication* involves an act or intention by the party who owns the land to allow use by the public. A common law dedication may be *express* when the appropriation is formally declared, or it may be *implied* by the owner's conduct and other facts and circumstances. An example of an express dedication is when a developer deeds the municipality a parcel of her land to use for a park. This act is a **dedication by deed** and a quitclaim deed may be used for this purpose. An example of an implied dedication is when the public is allowed access to a private road. A will also may contain a dedication of land to the public domain.

Public Grant

A **public grant** is *a grant of a power, license, or real property from the state or government to a private individual or individuals. The instrument conveying the public land* is a **land patent.** Land patent can also mean the actual land conveyed.

Adverse Possession

A *person other than the owner can claim title to real property* under **adverse possession** if that person uses the land following these conditions:

1. The possession or occupation must be open and well known to others (notorious).
2. Possession of the property must be under color of title or claim of title; that is, the occupant of the property must have some reasonable basis to believe that she is entitled to possession of the property, which typically takes the form of a defective deed or a quitclaim deed.
3. The possession must be without the permission of the true owner and must be exclusive (not shared with the true owner). Thus, co-owners cannot adversely possess against each other.
4. The possession must be continuous and uninterrupted for a period of 10 years in New York. In a claim of title, possession is based on some type of claim against the land rather than on a written document, as in the case of color of title. Individuals who inherit property and continue the adverse use legally fulfill the continuous use provision of adverse possession. An individual who takes title to the property through inheritance or otherwise also assumes the title subject to the claim of the former adverse possessor.

The adverse possessor does not automatically acquire title to the property by merely meeting the four requirements. To perfect the claim and obtain title to the property, the claimant must, in an action to quiet title, satisfy the court that the requirements of Article 15 of the New York Real Property Action and Proceedings Law (the adverse possession statute) have been met. (See Table 5.1.)

TABLE 5.1 Summary of title transfers.

TITLE TRANSFER	VOLUNTARY ALIENATION	INVOLUNTARY ALIENATION	BEFORE DEATH	AFTER DEATH
Sale	✓		✓	
Gift	✓		✓	
Dedication	✓		✓	
Grant	✓		✓	
Will	✓			✓
Descent	✓			✓
Lien foreclosure sale		✓	✓	
Bankruptcy		✓	✓	
Eminent domain		✓	✓	
Adverse possession		✓	✓	
Escheat		✓		✓

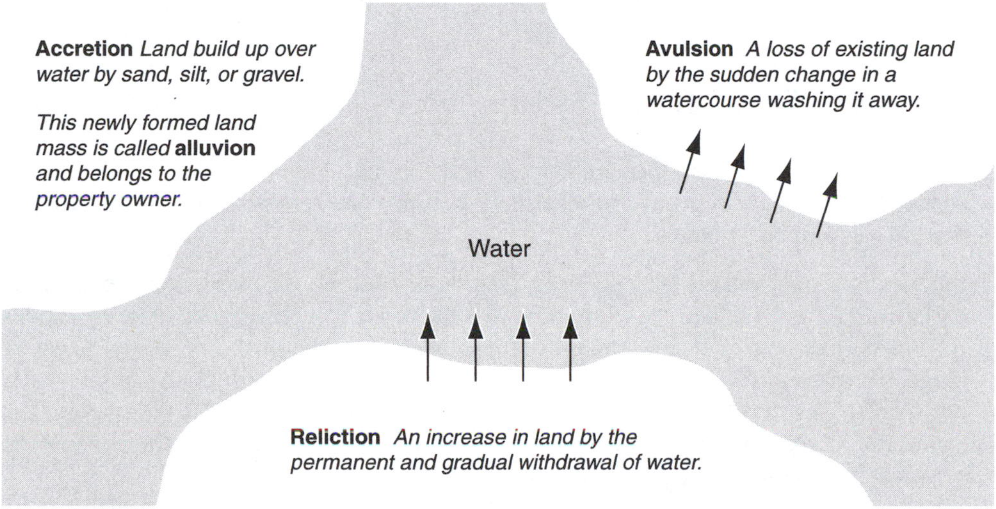
Accretion *Land build up over water by sand, silt, or gravel.*
This newly formed land mass is called **alluvion** *and belongs to the property owner.*
Avulsion *A loss of existing land by the sudden change in a watercourse washing it away.*
Water
Reliction *An increase in land by the permanent and gradual withdrawal of water.*

Accretion and reliction alter a property's boundary line.

FIGURE 5.6 Accession Rights–Property owners have the right to all that their land produces, either intentionally or by mistake.

IMPORTANT POINTS

1. A deed is the document used to convey title to real property. Transfer of title is termed alienation. Alienation may be voluntary or involuntary.
2. The requirements for deed validity are: (a) deed in writing, (b) competent grantor, (c) competent or incompetent grantee, (d) grantor and grantee named with certainty, (e) adequate property description, (f) recital of consideration, (g) words of conveyance, that sometimes contain a habendum clause, (h) proper execution by grantor, and (i) delivery and acceptance to convey title.
3. To be eligible for recording on the public record, a deed must be acknowledged. Recording protects the grantee's title against subsequent conveyances by the grantor.
4. A full covenant and warranty deed is the strongest and broadest form of title guarantee.
5. A quitclaim deed is a deed of release and contains no warranties. It will convey any interest the grantor may have. The quitclaim deed is used mainly to remove a cloud from a title.

6. A bargain and sale deed may be with or without covenants; if the bargain and sale deed contains covenants, it is acceptable to lenders.
7. Judicial deeds result from a court order to the official executing the deed. Forms of judicial deeds include sheriff's deed, referee's deed, tax deed, guardian's deed, and executor's or administrator's deed.
8. Dedication occurs when a land or an easement to land is given for use to the public. There are two types of dedication: statutory or common law. Common law dedications may be express or implied.
9. Deed descriptions include metes and bounds, lot and block (plat of subdivision), and monuments.
10. When a person dies and leaves no will, the laws of descent determine the order of distribution of property to the heirs.
11. If a person dies and leaves a will, the gift of real property through the will is a devise; a gift of personal property through a will is a bequest.
12. A person other than the owner can claim title to real property under adverse possession. In New York, the possession must be continuous and uninterrupted for a period of 10 years and a court must award title.
13. Owners have the right to all that their land produces or all that is added to the land, either intentionally or by mistake. This is the ownership right of accession.

CHAPTER REVIEW How Would You Respond?

Analyze the following situations and decide how the individuals should handle them in accordance with what you have just learned. Check your responses using the Answer Key at the end of the chapter.

1. Arne lives in Howard Beach, Long Island, and his house overlooks the Atlantic Ocean. He has decided to sell and hires a surveyor to compare the size of beachfront he has now with the amount he had when he bought the property 30 years ago. To his surprise, Arne's beachfront has increased by five feet and he proposes to his broker that they add $10,000 to the purchase price. Does Arne possess the ownership right to this newfound five feet? What is the name of the process by which Arne attained this extra frontage?

2. Jay has recently been divorced and, in the settlement, the court awarded him the ownership of the family home in Spring Valley, New York. Jay's ex-wife, Sheila, is bitter over the settlement and claims that she still has an ownership interest in the house despite the court order. Sheila refuses to sign a deed giving Jay full title. Jay decides to sell, and his broker has found an eager purchaser. What type of deed might Jay's attorney select in light of the difficulties?

KEY TERM REVIEW

Fill in the term that best completes each sentence and then check the Answer Key at the end of the chapter.

1. A(n) ______________________ is a type of document used to convey title to real property.
2. The person conveying title through a deed is the ______________________.
3. For a deed to be eligible for recording, it must have a(n) ______________________.
4. ______________________ occurs when a property owner sets aside and donates a portion of land to a municipality for public use.
5. The ownership right of ______________________ is the right of property owners to all that their land produces or all that is added to their land.
6. The loss of land when a sudden or violent change in a watercourse washes it away is called ______________________.
7. The document conveying the strongest and broadest form of guarantee of title is conveyed through a(n) ______________________.
8. An individual can claim title to real property under ______________________ in New York if the possession of the property is continuous and uninterrupted for a period of 10 years and if other legal conditions are met.

MULTIPLE CHOICE

Circle the letter that best answers the question and then check the Answer Key at the end of the chapter.

1. The words of granting in a deed indicate the:
   A. description of the property
   B. form of deed
   C. habendum clause
   D. number of heirs to the property

2. The only form of involuntary alienation after death is:
   A. dedication by deed
   B. escheat
   C. formal will
   D. public grant

3. To effect a transfer of title by deed, there must be:
   A. delivery and acceptance
   B. a legally competent grantor and grantee
   C. a full covenant deed
   D. an exchange of money

4. Which of the following covenants assures the grantee that the grantor has the legal capacity to transfer title?
   A. covenant of quiet enjoyment
   B. covenant of right to convey
   C. covenant of seisin
   D. covenant for further assurances

5. A quitclaim deed:
   A. contains full warranties
   B. contains no warranties
   C. is a special warranty deed
   D. is never used for residential transactions

6. Grantor Susie left a deed for Grantee Charlie to find after Susie's death. The title was:
   A. conveyed during Susie's life
   B. conveyed after Susie's death
   C. not conveyed, as the deed was not delivered
   D. not conveyed, as the deed was not recorded

7. The type of property description most commonly used in New York is:
   A. rectangular survey system
   B. monuments
   C. informal description
   D. metes and bounds
8. A formal will:
   A. requires two witnesses
   B. needs no witnesses
   C. may be an oral will
   D. need not be signed by the testator or testatrix
9. A claim of title by adverse possession:
   A. may be made after possession of the property for five years
   B. is not enforceable in New York
   C. must be enforced through a court order
   D. also affects the personal property of the owner
10. The land mass added to property over time by accretion is called:
    A. reliction
    B. accession
    C. avulsion
    D. alluvion

ANSWER KEY

Putting It To Work

a. Carolyn Butler

b. Vanessa Dupree

c. The phrase containing the consideration for the transaction is:

"Witnesseth *that the party of the first part, in consideration of One and 00/100 Dollar* ($1.00) *lawful money of the United States,* and other good and valuable consideration *paid by the party of the second part."*

d. The phrase containing the granting clause is:

"does hereby grant and release unto the party of the second part, her heirs *and assigns forever, all* that lot, piece or parcel of land together with the improvements thereon."

e. The description of the property starts with the phrase (found in Figure 5.1):

"BEGINNING on a stake in the northeast margin of Amortization Drive. . . ." and ends with the phrase "South 29° 36' East 199.9 feet to the BEGINNING."

The type of description is metes and bounds.

f. The habendum clause is:

"To have and to hold *the premises herein granted unto the party of the second part,* her heirs *and assigns forever."*

The covenant of quiet enjoyment is:

"And *said* party of the first part *convenants as follows:* **First,** *That the party of the second part shall quietly enjoy the said premises."*

The covenant of warranty is:

"Second, *That said* party of the first part *will forever* **Warrant** *the title to said premises."*

The lien covenant is:

"Third, *That, in Compliance with Sec. 13 of the Lien Law, the grantor will receive the consideration for this conveyance and will hold the right to receive such consideration as a trust fund to be applied first for the purpose of paying the cost of the improvement and will apply the same first to the payment of the cost of the improvement before using any part of the total of the same for any other purpose."*

g. The deed was executed on March 28, 2004.

h. The acknowledgment begins with the phrase **"In Witness Whereof,** *the party of the first part"* and ends with the notary signature and stamp.

How Would You Respond?

1. Arne possesses ownership rights to this newfound beach frontage because accession rights give an owner the right to all that the land produces. The process of reliction is the probable reason Arne has gained this extra frontage. This process occurs when the natural withdrawal of the ocean causes an increase of land.
2. Although a court has awarded legal title to the marital home to Jay, Sheila is still fighting. In this case, a quitclaim deed rather than a full covenant and warranty deed might be the appropriate solution. A quitclaim deed releases the property to the purchasers (grantees) but does not warrant the title.

Key Term Review

1. deed
2. grantor
3. acknowledgment
4. dedication
5. accession
6. avulsion
7. full covenant and warranty deed
8. adverse possession

Multiple Choice

1. B
2. B
3. A
4. B
5. B
6. C
7. D
8. A
9. C
10. D

Chapter 6

KEY TERMS

"as is"
assignment
caveat
caveat emptor
contingencies
contract
counteroffer
earnest money deposit
executed contract
executory contract
forbearance
liquidated damages
novation
offer and acceptance
power of attorney
reformation
rescission
rider
right of first refusal
specific performance
Statute of Frauds
Statute of Limitations
time is of the essence
Uniform Commercial Code

LEARNING OBJECTIVES

Classroom hours: 2

1. Discuss the definition of a contract.
2. Distinguish between an express and implied contract and a bilateral and unilateral contract.
3. List the essentials of a valid contract.
4. Illustrate the difference between a valid contract, a void contract, and a voidable contract.
5. List the provisions that are common in a sales contract.
6. Describe a simple cooperative apartment purchase and the contract provisions that will be necessary.
7. Describe the necessary elements of a lease with option to buy.
8. Identify the requirements of the Statute of Frauds with respect to real estate contracts.
9. Distinguish between a contract and a binder.
10. Discuss the contracts that directly relate to the real estate brokerage business.

Contracts

IN THIS CHAPTER Contracts are relevant to every aspect of real estate. The theory of **caveat emptor,** Latin for *let the buyer beware, does not apply when the real estate agent has a fiduciary relationship with the client.* Licensees must be aware of the obligations of parties under different types of real estate contracts. This chapter discusses the essentials of a valid contract and explains the types of contracts utilized in the real estate profession and their implications.

BASIC CONTRACTS

A **contract** is *an agreement between competent legal parties to do or refrain from doing some legal act in exchange for consideration.* (See Table 6.1.) A contract establishes both the rights and responsibilities of the parties to the contract, which can differ from contract to contract. Therefore, various classifications of contracts have evolved:

1. express versus implied
2. bilateral versus unilateral
3. executed versus executory
4. valid
5. enforceable or unenforceable
6. void or voidable

TABLE 6.1
Basic contract definitions.

TYPE OF AGREEMENT	DEFINITION
Express	parties have agreed to terms of contract
Implied	inferred from behavior of the parties
Unilateral	only one party is bound under the contract
Bilateral	two parties have agreed to terms of contract
Executory	a contract not yet fully performed
Executed	a fully performed contract
Valid	binding and enforceable on all parties to the contract
Void	no legal force or effect
Voidable	may or may not be legally enforceable

Express Contract

Under an *express contract,* the parties to the contract have definitely agreed on all the terms in the contract. An express contract can be written or oral. Among real estate contracts, which include listings, offers to purchase, mortgages, installment contracts, options, and leases, the majority are prepared in writing and therefore are express contracts. In some cases, parties have oral leases that are also express contracts.

Implied Contract

An *implied contract* is one inferred from the conduct and actions of another without express agreement. Implied contracts arise when the conduct of the parties clearly illustrates the intention to contract. An implied contract is created, for example, if Trevor, a property owner, allows Christopher, a real estate agent, to show his property to prospective buyers. Even though there is no oral or written agreement between them, an implied agency contract now exists.

Bilateral Contract

A *bilateral contract* is one in which two parties have made promises of some kind to each other. The promise could be for the payment of money or for the performance of some act such as painting a house. Because both parties make promises, both are bound or obligated under the contract from the onset of the contract. The offer to purchase a home is bilateral because it is based on the exchange of promises in which the seller will sell and the buyer will buy.

Unilateral Contract

In a *unilateral contract,* one party makes a promise in order to induce a second party to do something. The party making the promise is bound and obligated under the contract after the other party completes the contract. The other party, however, has made no promise and therefore is not bound or obligated in any way to perform or act. An example is an open listing contract in which, at any time before the broker succeeds in making the deal, the owner can withdraw the listing.

Executed Contract

A *contract that has been fully performed* is an **executed contract.** An example is an offer to purchase in which all contingencies and conditions have been met and closing takes place. After the closing, nothing more is to be performed under the offer to purchase. In addition, the term *execute* also refers to the signing of a legal document.

Executory Contract

A *contract that is not fully performed or completed* is called an **executory contract.** In real estate, most contracts begin as executory. A mortgage is a contract where the borrower pays money over a term of years to the lender. A listing contract sets a definite time period during which the real estate broker tries to sell the property, and activity continues during the term of the listing.

Valid Contract

A *valid contract* is one that is binding and enforceable on all concerned parties. It contains all the essential elements of a contract. The parties to a valid contract are legally obligated to abide by the terms of the contract.

Unenforceable Contract

An unenforceable contract is one that appears to meet the requirements for validity but would not be enforceable in court. However, unenforceable contracts may still be considered valid between the parties if they wish to complete performance.

Examples of possible unenforceable contracts include:

- verbal contracts in which one of the parties reneges on the agreement. Verbal contracts are also unenforceable when only written contracts are allowable such as most real estate contracts
- the time to enforce the contract has run out (see the Statute of Limitations discussed later)
- one of the parties has a voidable contract (discussed later) thereby rendering the other party an unenforceable contract
- contracts that are vague in meaning and/or poorly worded

Void Contract

A *void contract* has absolutely no legal force or effect even though all of the essential elements for a contract exist. The phrase "null and void" is often used to mean "does not exist in the eyes of the law." Two circumstances cause a contract to be void: if the purpose of the contract is illegal; or if the contract is impossible to complete because of an act of God or operation of law. An example of a void contract is one that provides for racial discrimination.

Voidable Contract

A *voidable contract* may or may not be enforceable between the parties. It results from the failure of the contracting parties to meet some legal requirement in negotiating the agreement. In a voidable contract situation, one party to the contract is usually the victim of wrongdoing by the other party.

The parties to a voidable contract are not required to void the contract. The parties may fulfill their obligations under the contract and receive their benefits. A voidable contract can be voluntarily performed by the parties.

ESSENTIAL ELEMENTS OF A CONTRACT

The essential elements required for the existence of a real estate contract are (a) competent parties, (b) mutual agreement, (c) lawful objective, (d) consideration, and (e) written format.

Competent Parties

For a contract to be valid, the parties to the contract must have the capacity to enter into a contract. Minors—those who have not reached the age of majority as established by the statutory law—do not have the legal capacity to contract. In New York, the age of majority is 18. Legal capacity also is determined by the party's competence, or mental and emotional ability, to enter into contracts. Contracts entered into by parties lacking legal capacity are voidable by the party lacking capacity. In the case of minors, the contract is voidable at the option of the minor. The minor may hold an adult to a contract, but the adult cannot legally hold the minor to a contract. *Individuals or other entities may give a person a* **power of attorney** *to act for them in legal transactions such as real estate contracts.*

Mutual Agreement

For a contract to be created, the parties must enter into it voluntarily and understand the terms or facts upon which the contract is based.

If a person enters into a written contract, as evidenced by the signature on the contract, the individual is presumed to have assented to the terms. Typical factors that cause lack of mutual consent are fraud, misrepresentation, mutual mistake, undue influence, and duress. Any of these factors can defeat the voluntary assent of the parties and therefore invalidate and render the contract voidable.

Lawful Objective

Lawful objective means that the contract must be used for a legal purpose. A contract for an illegal purpose is void. Examples of illegal contracts include contracts in restraint of trade or contracts to stifle or promote litigation.

Consideration

Consideration is the giving of value. For a contract to be valid, consideration must be present. Consideration includes anything of value, such as money, property, or even a promise of performance. For example, the buyer's promise to pay in an offer to buy property is sufficient consideration for a valid contract.

In Writing

Because of the potential for misunderstandings in oral contracts, all states have adopted the **Statute of Frauds,** which in New York is codified in the General Obligations Law. Section 5-703 of the General Obligations Law states that contracts involving the creation or conveyance of an interest in real property must be written to be enforceable.

You Should Know

Broker's authority to prepare contracts

Brokers and their agents have traditionally prepared real estate contracts long before their authority to do so was questioned in the courts. Because of lawsuits such as *Duncan & Hill Realty vs. Department of State* (1978) (see Chapter 1) New York law does not allow individuals to engage in the unauthorized practice of law. This includes contract preparation. Because real estate agents use a number of different contracts, however, the courts have acknowledged a limited exception. This allows the broker to fill in blanks on standardized contract forms. However, the courts require the broker, for each party to the transaction, to make the contract subject to attorney approval or use very specific standardized forms. These forms must be recommended by the American Bar Association, the National Conference of Lawyers and REALTORS®, or a joint commission of the bar and REALTOR® association of the local county. The forms must contain a warning in boldface that the parties consult their attorneys before signing. The agent cannot make insertions requiring legal expertise and must follow guidelines set forth by the American Bar Association and the National Association of Real Estate Boards.

The Statute of Frauds requires that real estate contracts be written and contain all of the essential elements for a valid contract. Oral testimony (parol evidence) is not sufficient to create a contract involving the transfer of title to real property. A primary purpose of the Statute of Frauds is to prevent presentation of fraudulent proof of an oral contract. The General Obligations Law also requires the use of "plain language in consumer transactions."

DISCHARGE OF CONTRACTS

Contracts can be discharged or terminated by (a) agreement of the parties, (b) full performance, (c) impossibility of performance, or (d) operation of law.

Agreement of the Parties

Just as contracts are created by agreement of the parties, any executory contract can be terminated by agreement. This situation is usually called a release of contract. A form of agreement that terminates contracts is **novation,** *the substitution of a new contract for a prior contract or the substitution of a new party for an old party.* Novation may involve the substitution of parties in the contract. This is also known as an **assignment** of the contractual obligations. A *new party to the contract agrees to satisfy the former contracting party's obligation*. Upon reaching the agreement to substitute parties, the novation or new contract is created, terminating the original contract and the original party's liability.

Full Performance

The usual and most desirable manner of terminating contracts is by complete performance of all terms of the contract. The contract is said to be executed when all parties fully perform all terms.

Impossibility of Performance

Generally, even if a party to a contract is unable to perform obligations under the contract, the party is still liable. One who cannot perform should have included in the contract a provision for relief in the event of impossibility.

There are exceptions to this clause, such as when the performance of an obligation under a contract becomes illegal as a result of a change in law after the contract was created; for example, contracting for the drainage of farmland that has been recently designated by law to be wetlands.

Operation of Law

The term *operation of law* describes the manner in which the rights and liabilities of parties may be changed by the application of law without cooperation or agreement of the parties affected. Contracts can be terminated or discharged by operation of law. Examples of discharge of contracts by operation of law are:

1. ***Statute of Limitations.*** If a party to a contract fails to bring a lawsuit against a defaulting party within a time period set by statute, the injured party loses the right of remedy. The mere passage of time and expiration of the statutory time period affect the injured party's right to recover. In New York, *the time limit by statute to bring legal action against a party in a real estate transaction is six years.*

2. *Bankruptcy.* The filing of a petition for bankruptcy under federal law has the effect of terminating contracts in existence as of the date of filing the bankruptcy petition.
3. *Alteration of contract.* The intentional cancellation or alteration of a written agreement has the effect of discharging the agreement.

CONTRACT REMEDIES

In some cases, a party to a contract fails to complete the contract or fails to perform, with no legal cause. This is breach of contract. The breach, however, does not terminate the contract obligations of the breaching party. The nondefaulting party has the following legal remedies against the defaulting party, which may be obtained by filing suit in a court of law. The remedies include (a) specific performance, (b) rescission, (c) compensatory damages, (d) liquidated damages, (e) reformation, or (f) injunction.

Specific Performance

Every piece of real estate is unique. As a result, a party contracting to buy a parcel of real estate does not have to accept a similar or almost identical parcel. Because of the unique nature of real estate, the remedy of specific performance is available to nondefaulting parties. An order from the court requiring **specific performance** means that *the contract will be completed as originally agreed.*

Rescission

This remedy is the opposite of specific performance. **Rescission** means *to take back, remove, annul, or abrogate.* Rescission is applied when a contract has not been performed by either party and when it has been breached by a party. Upon suit for rescission, the court orders the parties placed back in their original positions as if the contract had never existed.

Compensatory Damages

When a contract is breached, one party usually suffers monetary loss as a result. The amount of money actually lost is the amount of compensatory damages that the court will award.

Liquidated Damages

In lieu of compensatory damages, the parties to the contract can stipulate in the contract *an amount of money to be paid upon certain breaches of the contract.* Damages agreed to be paid in the contract are called **liquidated damages.**

Reformation

Reformation is *a doctrine that permits the court to rewrite a contract* which expresses the true intentions of the parties. It is most often called for when the parties to a contract sign without realizing that the contract contains a clerical error.

Injunction

An injunction is a court order stipulating that a party must discontinue a specific act or behavior.

SALES CONTRACTS AND PRACTICES

Offer to Purchase

The parties to an **offer and acceptance**—*an accepted offer to purchase*—are the buyer and the seller, also called offeror and offeree, respectively. Another term for offer and acceptance is *meeting of the minds.* Meeting of the minds is evident when the parties to the contract reach agreement on the terms of the contract. The purchase contract is a bilateral express contract and constitutes the road map for the transaction. The relationship between the parties is described as "arm's length." The parties presumably have equal bargaining power and are not related by business interest, familial relationship, and so on.

In a typical real estate purchase agreement, the buyer begins as the offeror. An offer that has not been accepted can be withdrawn at any time prior to acceptance and the notification of that acceptance. Once the offeror (or the agent) has knowledge of the acceptance, the offer may not then be withdrawn. An acceptance that varies in any way from the offer as presented will not qualify as an acceptance. An *acceptance that varies from the offer* is a **counteroffer.** If the seller makes a counteroffer, no contract exists regarding the first offer. The counteroffer terminates and destroys the original offer, similar to rejection of the offer. The seller has now become the offeror and the buyer is the offeree.

Although most offers to purchase are accompanied by earnest money, it is not legally required for a valid offer to purchase. An **earnest money deposit** (a) *shows the sincerity of the buyer,* (b) *demonstrates financial capability to raise the money called for in the agreement,* and (c) *serves as possible liquidated damages to the seller in the event of default by the buyer.*

All terms and conditions of sale of property are contained in this contract. They include sales price; type of financing; interest rate, if a mortgage is to be obtained or if seller financing is to be used; required inspections; proration of taxes and insurance; listing of personal property to be included in the purchase; designated party with risk of loss from fire, flood, and other causes; time periods for possession and transfer of title; type of deed; type of title acceptable to buyer; amount of earnest money; liquidated damages upon breach; and time period for acceptance or rejection.

In many areas of New York, a preprinted contract form is filled in and signed by the parties to the transaction and then usually reviewed by the attorneys for both the buyer and the seller. Appropriate and desired changes are made to the document and initialed by the parties. Many brokerage firms use prepared addenda or riders to cover supplemental issues of the agreement. If a broker prepares these documents, it could constitute the illegal practice of law (Chapter 1). These additions, amendments, agreements, **contingencies,** and caveats are annexed to the contract and incorporated into the terms of the contract. Some examples of *addenda* or **riders** are *personal property lists, homeowner's warranties, and presale or postsale rental agreements. A contingency generally contains provisions for inspection or remediation before the parties become obligated under the contract.* Examples of contingencies are septic system, well-water flow, and quality tests; assumption of mortgage; and Federal Housing Authority (FHA) and Department of Veteran Affairs (VA) approval for mortgage loans. **Caveat** is Latin for *a warning or caution.* In New York, properties that lie within an agricultural district must have a disclosure attached stating that fact. This is an example of a caveat. Figure 6.1 shows a contract for purchase and sale. The specific provisions of the contract are outlined below.

- *Section 1* identifies all parties to the contract, the purchaser(s) and seller(s), the addresses of each, and a description of the property being sold.

FIGURE 6.1
A contract for purchase and sale.

EQUAL HOUSING OPPORTUNITY

CAPITAL REGION MULTIPLE LISTING SERVICE, INC.

REALTOR®

STANDARD FORM
CONTRACT FOR PURCHASE AND SALE OF REAL ESTATE

THIS IS A LEGALLY-BINDING CONTRACT. IF NOT FULLY UNDERSTOOD, WE RECOMMEND ALL PARTIES TO THE CONTRACT CONSULT AN ATTORNEY BEFORE SIGNING.

1

1. IDENTIFICATION OF PARTIES TO THE CONTRACT

A. **SELLER** — The Seller is ______________________________
residing at ______________________________
(the word "Seller" refers to each and all parties who have an ownership interest in the property).

B. **PURCHASER** — The Purchaser is ______________________________
residing at ______________________________
(the word "Purchaser" refers to each and all of those who sign below as Purchaser).

2. PROPERTY TO BE SOLD

The property and improvements which the Seller is agreeing to sell and which the Purchaser is agreeing to purchase is known as ______________________________ located in the city, village or town of ______________ in ______________ County, State of New York. This property includes all the Seller's rights and privileges, if any, to all land, water, streets and roads annexed to, and on all sides of the property. The lot size of the property is approximately ______________ .

2

3. ITEMS INCLUDED IN SALE

Heating and Lighting Fixtures	Storm Windows and Screens	Television Aerials
Built-in Kitchen Appliances	Storm and Screen Doors	Smoke Detectors
Built-in Bathroom and Kitchen Cabinets	Water Softeners (if owned by Seller)	Alarm Systems
Drapery Rods and Curtain Rods	Plumbing Fixtures	Shrubbery, Trees, Plants and Fencing in the Ground
Shades and Blinds	Pumps	
Wall-to-Wall Carpeting as placed	Awnings	Fireplace insert, doors and/or screen

The items listed above, if now in or on said premises are represented to be owned by the Seller, free from all liens and encumbrances, and are included in the sale "as is," on the date of this offer, together with the following items: ______________
____
____

4. ITEMS EXCLUDED FROM SALE

The following items are excluded from the sale: ______________________________
____
____

3

5. PURCHASE PRICE

The purchase price is ______________________________
______________ DOLLARS ($ ______________) The Purchaser shall pay the purchase price as follows:

a. $ ______________ deposit with this contract and held pursuant to paragraph 17 herein.
b. $ ______________ additional deposit on ______________________________
c. $ ______________ in cash, certified check, bank draft or attorney escrow account check at closing.
d. $ ______________ ______________________________
e. $ ______________ ______________________________

4

6. MORTGAGE CONTINGENCY

A. This Agreement is contingent upon Purchaser obtaining approval of a ☐ conventional, ☐ FHA or ☐ VA (if FHA or VA see attached required addendum) or ______________ mortgage loan of $ ______________ for a term of not more than ______ years at an initial ☐ fixed or ☐ adjustable nominal interest rate not to exceed ________ percent. Purchaser agrees to use diligent efforts to obtain said approval and shall apply for the mortgage loan within ________ business days after the Seller has accepted this contract. Purchaser agrees to apply for such mortgage loan to at least one lending institution or licensed mortgage broker. Upon receipt of a written mortgage commitment or in the event Purchaser chooses to waive this mortgage contingency, Purchaser shall provide notice in writing to ______________________________ of Purchaser's receipt of the mortgage commitment or of Purchaser's waiving of this contingency. Upon receipt of such notice this contingency shall be deemed waived or satisfied as the case may be. In the event notice as called for in the proceeding sentence has not been received on or before ______________ , then either Purchaser or Seller may terminate this contract by written notice to ______________________________ . Upon receipt of such notice, this agreement shall be deemed cancelled, null and void and all deposits made hereunder shall be returned to Purchaser.

B. **Seller's Contribution:** At closing, as a credit toward prepaids, closing costs and/or points, Seller shall credit to Purchaser $ ______________ or ________ % of the ☐ Purchase Price or ☐ mortgage amount.

Buyer's Initials ________ **Seller's Initials** ________ REVISED 7/17/02

5

7. MORTGAGE EXPENSE AND RECORDING FEES

The Mortgage recording tax imposed on the mortgagor, mortgage and deed recording fees, expenses of drawing papers and any other expenses to be incurred in connection with procuring a mortgage, shall be paid by the Purchaser.

8. OTHER TERMS (if any) ______________________________
____
____
____

9. TITLE AND SURVEY

A ☐ 40-year abstract of title, tax search and any continuations thereof, or a ☐ fee title insurance policy, shall be obtained at the expense of ☐ Purchaser or ☐ Seller. (If both boxes are checked, the option of whether an Abstract of Title or fee policy is provided shall be that of the party paying for same.) The Seller shall cooperate in providing any available survey, abstract of title or title insurance policy information, without cost to Purchaser. The Purchaser shall pay the cost of updating any such survey or the cost of a new survey.

10. CONDITIONS OF PREMISES

The buildings on the premises are sold "as is" without warranty as to condition, and the Purchaser agrees to take title to the buildings "as is" and in their present condition subject to reasonable use, wear, tear and natural deterioration between the date hereof and the closing of title: except that in the case of any destruction within the meaning of the provisions of Section 5-1311 of the General Obligations Law of the State of New York entitled "Uniform Vendor and Purchaser Risk Act," said section shall apply to this contract.

A. This Agreement is contingent upon determination by a Certified Exterminator or other qualified professional that the premises are free from infestation or damage by wood-destroying organisms; this determination to be made at Purchaser's expense and to be completed by ______________________________ and, if premises are not free from infestation or damage, then Purchaser shall have the option, by written notice to be given within five (5) days after date in this paragraph, to cancel this contract.

B. This Agreement is contingent upon a written determination, at Purchaser's expense, by a New York State registered architect or licensed engineer, by a third party who is ______________________________ , or other qualified person, that the premises are free from any substantial structural, mechanical, electrical, plumbing, roof covering, water or sewer defects. The term substantial to refer to any individual repair which will reasonably cost over $1000.00 to correct. This contingency shall be deemed waived unless the Purchaser shall notify ______________________________ no later than ______________ , as called for in paragraph 22, of such substantial repair(s), and furthermore supplies a written copy of the inspection report. If the Purchaser so notifies, then this agreement shall be deemed cancelled, null and void and all deposits made hereunder shall be returned to Purchaser or, at Purchaser's option, said cancellation may be deferred for a period of ten (10) days in order to provide the parties an opportunity to otherwise agree in writing.

The following buildings or items on the premises are excluded from this inspection ______________________________
____

(continued)

FIGURE 6.1
Continued.

11. CONDITIONS AFFECTING TITLE
The Seller shall convey and the Purchaser shall accept the property subject to all covenants, conditions, restrictions and easements of record and zoning and environmental protection laws so long as the property is not in violation thereof and any of the foregoing does not prevent the intended use of the property for the purpose of ______________________________ ; also subject to any existing tenancies, any unpaid installments of street or other improvement assessments payable after the date of the transfer of title to the property, and any state of facts which an inspection and/or accurate survey may show, provided that nothing in this paragraph renders the title to the property unmarketable. 5

12. DEED
The property shall be transferred from Seller to Purchaser by means of a Warranty Deed, with Lien Covenant, or ______________ ______________ deed, furnished by the Seller. The deed and real property transfer gains tax affidavit will be properly prepared and signed so that it will be accepted for recording by the County Clerk in the County in which the property is located. If the Seller is transferring the property as an executor, administrator, trustee, committee or conservator, the deed usual to such cases shall be accepted.

13. NEW YORK STATE TRANSFER TAX AND MORTGAGE SATISFACTION
The Seller agrees to pay the New York State Real Property Transfer Tax as set by law and further agrees to pay the expenses of procuring and recording satisfactions of any existing mortgages.

14. TAX AND OTHER ADJUSTMENTS
The following, if any, shall be apportioned so that the Purchaser and Seller are assuming the expenses of the property and income from the property as of the date of transfer of title:
a. rents and security deposits. Seller shall assign to Purchaser all written leases and security deposits affecting the premises. 6
b. taxes, sewer, water, rents, and condominium or homeowner association fees.
c. municipal assessment yearly installments except as set forth in item 11.
d. fuel, based upon fair market value at time of closing as confirmed by a certification provided by Seller's supplier.

Buyer's Initials ________ Seller's Initials ________

15. RIGHT OF INSPECTION AND ACCESS
Purchaser and/or representative shall be given access to the property for any tests or inspections required by the terms of this contract upon reasonable notice to the Seller or a representative. Purchaser and/or a representative shall be given the right of inspection of the property, at a reasonable hour, within 48 hours prior to transfer of title.

16. TRANSFER OF TITLE/POSSESSION
The transfer of title to the property from Seller to Purchaser will take place at the office of the lender's attorney if the Purchaser obtains a mortgage loan from a lending institution. Otherwise, the closing will be at the office of the attorney for the Seller. The closing will be on or before ______________________ . Possession shall be granted upon transfer of title unless otherwise mutually agreed upon in writing signed by the parties.

17. DEPOSITS
It is agreed that any deposits by the Purchaser are to be deposited with the Listing Broker at ______________________ ______________ as part of the purchase price. If the Seller does not accept the Purchaser's offer, all deposits shall be returned to Purchaser.
If the offer is accepted by Seller, all deposits will be held in escrow by the Listing Broker and deposited into the Listing Broker's escrow account in the institution identified above, until the contingencies and terms have been met. The Purchaser will receive credit on the total amount of the deposit toward the purchase price. Broker shall then apply the total deposit to the brokerage fee. Any excess of deposit over and above the fee earned will go to the Seller. 7
If the contingencies and terms contained herein cannot be resolved, or in the event of default by the Seller or the Purchaser, the deposits will be held by the Broker pending a resolution of the disposition of the deposits.
If the broker holding the deposit determines, in its sole discretion, that sufficient progress is not being made toward a resolution of the dispute, that broker may commence an interpleader action and pay the deposit monies into court. The Broker's reasonable costs and expenses, including attorney's fees, shall be paid from the deposit upon the resolution of the interpleader action and the remaining net proceeds of the deposit shall be disbursed to the prevailing claimant. In the event the deposit is insufficient to cover the broker's entitlement, the non-prevailing party shall pay the remaining balance.

18. TIME PERIOD OF OFFER
Purchaser and Seller understand and agree that, unless earlier withdrawn, this offer is good until ________ a.m. ________ p.m., ______________ , ______ , and if not accepted by the Seller prior to that time, then this offer becomes null and void. 8

19. REAL ESTATE BROKER
The Purchaser and Seller agree that ______________________________ and ______________________________ brought about the sale, and Seller agrees to pay broker's commission to ______________________________ as agreed to in the listing agreement.

20. ATTORNEYS APPROVAL CLAUSE
This agreement is contingent upon Purchaser and Seller obtaining approval of this agreement by their attorney as to all matters, without limitation. This contingency shall be deemed waived unless Purchaser's or Seller's attorney on behalf of their client notifies ______________________________ in writing, as called for in paragraph 22, of their disapproval of the Agreement no later than ______________ . If Purchaser's or Seller's attorney so notifies, then this Agreement shall be deemed cancelled, null and void, and all deposits shall be returned to the Purchaser. 9

21. ADDENDA
The following attached addenda are part of this agreement:

a.	b.	c.
d.	e.	f.
g.	h.	i.

22. NOTICES
All notices contemplated by this agreement shall be in writing, delivered by (a) certified or registered mail, return receipt requested, postmarked no later than the required ate; (b) by telecopier/facsimile transmitted by such date; or (c) by personal delivery by such date. 10

23. ENTIRE AGREEMENT
This contract contains all agreements of the parties hereto. There are no promises, agreements, terms, conditions, warranties, representations or statements other than contained herein. This agreement shall apply to and bind the heirs, legal representatives, successors and assigns of the respective parties. It may not be changed orally.

Dated: ______________ Time ________ Dated: ______________ Time ________

Purchaser ______________ Seller ______________ 11

Purchaser ______________ Seller ______________

Selling Broker ______________ Listing Broker ______________

- *Section 2* specifies the items included in the sale and the items that are excluded from the sale. Some of the property's items are not considered fixtures; they are the personal property of the seller and must be delineated in the contract. Fixtures are part of the real property and pass with the deed unless specifically excluded. Examples of fixtures include a range hood or built-in bookshelves. Note the "as is" clause. Purchasers should be aware of the condition of these items when the contract is signed.
- *Section 3* states the purchase price of the property and the terms of the payment. Usually, an earnest money deposit is put down upon signing the contract, and an additional deposit might be paid upon seller's acceptance of the contract. The remaining balance is usually paid when title is transferred at the closing. An earnest money deposit becomes the consideration; however, without a deposit, the purchaser's offer to buy can be the consideration for the contract.
- *Section 4* specifies the terms for financing that must be met to complete the offer to purchase, such as cash sale; assumption of present mortgage; contract sale; or new mortgage; and, if the sale is contingent on the buyer obtaining a mortgage, the date by which the buyer must notify the seller of his inability to obtain financing.
- *Section 5* delineates who will pay the expenses of the mortgage and recording fees, the other items to be paid by each party, the title and survey requirements, and who will pay for each of these. The division of expenses between seller and purchaser of these carrying charges is known as *apportionment.* This section also indicates that the premises are sold **"as is,"** without warranty as to condition, or *in their present condition subject to reasonable use, wear, and tear between the date of the contract and the closing date.* Contingency agreements regarding termite inspection, and structural, mechanical, plumbing, and other defects are also included. Section 5 also states that the purchaser is accepting the property subject to covenants, deed restrictions, easements, and environmental protection or zoning laws, as long as the property does not violate these items or prevent the purchaser from using the property for its intended purpose.
- *Section 6* delineates the type of deed that will be conveyed. This section includes the amount of taxes and fees to be paid by each party, the tax adjustments and other fee adjustments, the right of the purchaser to inspect the property within 48 hours of transfer of title, and the date and place of transfer. If a mortgage is involved in this contract, the closing takes place at the lending institution. If not, the closing takes place at the office of the attorney for the seller. The **time is of the essence** rule is included here if desired by either party. This means that *the closing must take place on or before the exact date stipulated in the contract.* It also indicates that possession will be granted upon transfer of title unless otherwise mutually agreed upon by the parties. This is the *merger clause,* in which the contract is fulfilled and the conveyed deed supersedes the contract.
- *Section 7* indicates who will hold the deposit money and describes the terms of refund in the event that the transaction does not close. This part of the contract provides that if there is a default by the buyer or seller, the deposits will be held by the broker pending a resolution. A court would have to decide if liquidated damages are in order if the title does not transfer. Liquidated damages could be included here if agreed upon by the parties.
- *Section 8* indicates the date and time that the offer will expire if not accepted by the seller. A seller has only a limited time to accept the contract, or risks losing the offer.
- *Section 9* contains the broker's clause, which specifies that, in this case, the seller pays the commission. It also contains the attorneys' approval of the contract, and the date by which the attorneys must notify their disapproval of the contract. This section also provides space to list any addenda or riders that will be attached to the

contract, such as disclosure forms, contingencies, or other statements not included in the contract form.

- *Section 10* states that notices regarding this agreement must be given in writing and delineates the means by which notice must be given. Note that oral notices regarding the contract are not legally valid.
- *Section 11* requires the signature of all parties to the transaction—purchasers, sellers, and the selling and listing broker—as well as the date and time of the signing. The *survival clause* in this contract states that the agreement shall apply to and bind all heirs, legal representatives, and successors of the parties to the contract.

PUTTING IT TO WORK

In numerous areas in New York, you will complete a preprinted contract for purchase and sale of real estate. Using the following information, fill in the necessary information on the contract shown in Figure 6.1 or one provided by your instructor. Compare your contract to the model in the Answer Key at the end of the chapter.

The sellers are Peter W. and Anita B. Rose, residing at 105 Maple Avenue, Saratoga Springs, New York. This is also the address of the subject property to be sold. The subject property is located in the city of Saratoga Springs, in Saratoga County, New York. The lot size is 100 by 150 feet and the property is a single-family residence. The purchasers are Roger T. and Melissa A. Barter, residing at 100 Main Avenue, Memphis, Tennessee. The listing broker is James Butell of Morgan Realty, and the selling broker is Ned Stack of Chelmsley Realty. The Roses are including a riding lawn mower with the sale of the house and are excluding an antique Tiffany chandelier. The purchase price of the house is $150,000. The Barters are putting $500 down upon signing the contract; they are paying an additional $8,000 deposit on November 20, 2004, with the balance due at the closing. The contract is contingent upon the purchasers' obtaining approval of a conventional mortgage loan of $120,000 for a term of not more than 30 years at a fixed rate not to exceed 7 percent. The purchaser agrees to apply for the mortgage within five business days of seller acceptance of the contract. This contingency will be waived unless the purchasers contact the listing broker by December 15, 2004.

Other terms state that the cellar and garage shall be in "broom-clean" condition before closing. The purchasers will pay for the abstract of title and also for the termite inspection, which must be completed by November 15, 2004. Ralph Young will inspect the house for structural defects; this contingency will be waived unless the purchasers notify the listing broker by November 20, 2004. The date of the closing is January 15, 2005. Any deposits by the purchaser will be deposited with the listing broker at First Federal Savings Bank, Saratoga Springs, New York. The offer is good until 9:00 PM on November 7, 2004. The purchasers' or sellers' attorneys must notify either of their client's real estate salespersons by November 13, 2004, if they disapprove of the contract. The addenda attached to the contract is a radon inspection contingency. The contract is dated and signed at 10:00 AM November 5, 2004, by the purchasers and their real estate salesperson; it is dated and signed at 11:00 AM on November 6, 2004, by the sellers and their real estate salesperson.

Cooperative Apartment Purchase and Contract

The purchase of a cooperative apartment is different from other types of real estate purchases. In a cooperative purchase, the owner sells shares of stock in a cooperative corporation. A cooperative apartment corporation is like other corporations, in that the value of the ownership is greater or lesser depending on the number of owned shares. The number of shares assigned to a particular apartment is generally a reflection of the size of the apartment, the location within the building, and certain other features that the dwelling may have, or have access to, such as a terrace, pool, extra kitchen appliances, and so on. A cooperative apartment buyer is purchasing an interest in the corporation; therefore the ownership is not a fee simple interest. The cooperative apartment is not realty, but personalty; that is, personal property. The board of directors of a cooperative usually interviews all prospective shareholders, and in certain situations the board may decide to disallow a prospective tenant shareholder from purchasing an apartment in the cooperative. The board cannot control the share value of each apartment, but it sets and carries out policy decisions.

The transaction is similar in ways to the sale of real property. The seller decides the number of shares that the apartment is worth and the purchaser pays the dollar value of these shares as the purchase price to the seller. The shares and thereby the apartment are transferred to the purchaser along with assignment of the *proprietary lease* to the apartment.

The board of directors of the cooperative can, however, have a financial interest in the sale of any of the apartments because it may impose a flip tax. This is a revenue-producing device for the cooperative corporation. Usually, the flip tax is paid by the seller at a fixed percentage of the purchase price of the apartment. Figure 6.2 shows a cooperative contract.

Uniform Commercial Code (UCC)

Because a cooperative is bought through shares of stock and therefore considered personal property, the financing of the loan needed to purchase a cooperative apartment is governed by the rules of the Uniform Commercial Code (UCC). The **Uniform Commercial Code** *provides for the lender to retain a security interest in the personal property or chattel until the lender is paid in full.* In a cooperative transaction, the loan from the bank is secured by the shares of stock, not a mortgage on the property, as in real property transactions.

Condominium Contract

Condominium contracts are similar to other fee simple interest real estate contracts except they may contain a right of first refusal clause for the board of managers of a condominium association. This clause allows the condominium association to have the first opportunity to purchase the condo when it goes up for sale. Therefore, the seller, at the closing, may have to present a waiver of this right issued by the board of managers of the condominium association. The condominium association may also, in some instances, inquire about buyer credentials, bank references, and so on, prior to purchase.

Binder

In certain areas of New York, a written document for the purchase and sale of real property, called a *binder,* is used by licensees instead of an offer to purchase contract (see Figure 6.3). A binder is a written outline of the scope of the real estate transaction and may be signed by all the parties to the transaction. The binder does not generally contain all of the essential elements of a valid contract. It delineates a framework for the contract. It may set up a time period during which the contract must be written and

FIGURE 6.2
A contract for purchase of a cooperative. This is the first page only of the multi-page contract.

M 123—Contract of sale of cooperative apartment, 10-89.
Prepared by The Committee on Condominiums and Cooperatives of the Real Property Section of the New York State Bar Association.

Distributed by Julius Blumberg, Inc. NYC 10013

CONSULT YOUR LAWYER BEFORE SIGNING THIS AGREEMENT

Contract of Sale — Cooperative Apartment

This Contract is made as of between the **"Seller"** and the **"Purchaser"** identified below.

1. Certain Definitions and Information

1.1 The "Parties" are:

Seller:

Address:

Prior names used by Seller:

Soc. Sec. No.

Purchaser:

Address:

Soc. Sec. No.

1.2. The "Attorneys" are *(name, address and telephone)*:
For Seller:

For Purchaser:

1.3 The "Escrowee" is *(name, address and telephone)*

1.4 The "Managing Agent" is *(name, address and telephone)*

1.5 The name of the cooperative housing corporation ("Corporation") is

1.6 The "Unit" number is

1.7 The Unit is located in "Premises" known as

1.8 The "Shares" are the shares of the Corporation allocated to the Unit.

1.9 The "Lease" is the proprietary lease for the Unit given by the Corporation.

1.10 The "Broker" (see Par. 12) is

1.11 The "Closing" is the transfer of ownership of the Shares and Lease, which is scheduled to occur on at M. (see Pars. 9 and 10)

1.12 The "Purchase Price" is $

1.12.1 the "Contract Deposit" is $

1.12.2 the "Balance" of the Purchase Price due at Closing is $ (see Par. 2)

1.13 The "Maintenance" charge is the rent payable under the Lease which at the date of this Contract is in the monthly amount of $ (see Par. 4)

1.14 The "Assessment" is the additional rent payable under the Lease which at the date of this Contract is $ payable as follows:

1.15 The Party upon whom the Corporation imposes a "Flip Tax" or similar transfer fee, if any, is (see Par. 11.3)

1.16 If Par. 19 (Financing Contingency) applies:

1.16.1 the "Loan Terms" are:

Amount Financed: $ or any lower amount applied for or acceptable to Purchaser.

Payment Terms and Charges: The customary payment terms (including prevailing fixed or adjustable interest rate, prepayment provisions and maturity) and charges (including points, origination and other fees) then currently being offered to purchasers of cooperative apartments by the Institutional Lender (defined in Par. 19.5.1) to which Purchaser applies.

Security: Pledge of the Shares and Lease.

1.16.2 the period for Purchaser to obtain a Loan Commitment Letter is business days after a fully executed counterpart of this Contract is given to Purchaser.

1.17 The "Proposed Occupants" of the Unit are the following:

1.17.1 persons and relationship to Purchaser:

1.17.2 pets:

1.18 The Contract Deposit shall be held in a interest bearing escrow account. Interest shall be payable to the The escrow account shall be a type account held at (See Par. 28)

2. Agreement to Sell and Purchase; Purchase Price; Escrow

2.1 Seller agrees to sell and assign to Purchaser, and Purchaser agrees to purchase and assume from Seller, the Seller's Shares and Lease for the Purchase Price and upon the other terms and conditions stated in this Contract.

2.2 The Purchase Price is payable to Seller by Purchaser as follows:

2.2.1 the Contract Deposit at the time of signing this Contract, by Purchaser's collectible check to the order of Escrowee.

2.2.2 the Balance at Closing, only by cashier's, official bank or certified check of Purchaser made payable to the direct order of Seller. These checks shall be drawn on and payable by a branch of a commercial or savings bank, savings and loan association or trust company located in the same City or County as the Unit. Seller may direct, on not less than 3 business days' Notice (defined in Par. 17) prior to Closing, that all or a portion of the Balance shall be made payable to persons other than Seller.

3. Personal Property

3.1 Subject to any rights of the Corporation or any holder of a mortgage to which the Lease is subordinate, this sale includes all of Seller's ownership, if any, of the following "Property" to the extent existing in the Unit on the date hereof: the refrigerator, freezer, range, oven, microwave oven, dishwasher, cabinets and counters, lighting fixtures, chandeliers, wall-to-wall carpeting, plumbing fixtures, central air-conditioning and/or window or sleeve units, washing machine, dryer, screens and storm windows, window treatments, switch plates, door hardware, built-ins not excluded in Par. 3.2 and

3.2 Specifically excluded from this sale is all personalty not included in Par. 3.1 and

Source: BlumbergExcelsior, Inc. Forms may be purchased from BlumbergExcelsior, Inc. or any of its dealers. Interactive electronic forms may be purchased at *http://www.blumberg.com*. Reproduction prohibited.

FIGURE 6.3 A binder document.

ABC Real Estate Brokerage
777 Easy Street • New York, New York 10007

Receipt and Memorandum of Sale for Offer to Purchase

Name of Purchaser: ____________________

Address of Purchaser: ____________________

Phone, email, and fax number of Purchaser: ____________________

The above-named individual(s) offer to purchase the following:

Address of property: ____________________

Purchaser agrees to a purchase price of $__________ for the above-described property.

Payment shall be made as follows:

Deposit on account for purchase of the property $__________

To be paid when a formal contract is executed $__________

Subject to the Purchaser(s) obtaining a mortgage within ______ days at the prevailing interest rate in the amount of $__________

Subject to a mortgage in the amount of $__________ at ______% interest per year payable to the Owner.

Balance paid on transfer of title $__________

TOTAL PURCHASE PRICE $__________

The above transaction is contingent upon the Owner's approval and if accepted is subject to a formal contract between all parties dated not later than ______________, 2003.

Title to close on or about ______________, 2003 at the offices of ______________.

Comments: ____________________

If the Purchaser failes to purchase the above-described property, the amount paid may be retained by the Owner, as consideration for this agreement.

The Owner recognizes that ______________, Broker, brought about this sale, and agrees to pay pay the commission.

The deposit is being kept in escrow by ______________ at ______________.

I agree to the terms of the agreement set forth herein.

______________	______________
Owner	Purchaser
______________	______________
Owner	Purchaser
Name and Address of Attorney for Owner	Name and Address of Attorney for Purchaser
______________	______________
______________	______________

signed, but it may lack specifics such as mortgage contingencies. It might contain a checklist of contingencies and other items that would appear in contracts. After the binder is signed, it is submitted to an attorney who draws an offer to purchase contract based on the terms and conditions and other essential elements in the contract. A binder may or may not be enforceable in court.

Installment Sales Contract

The essence of an installment sales contract is that the buyer contracts to obtain legal title to the property by paying the purchase price in installments, and the seller agrees to transfer the legal title to the buyer by delivering a deed upon buyer's full payment of the purchase price. The seller defers receipt of payment of the purchase price from the buyer over the term of the contract. The parties to an installment sales contract are the vendor and the vendee. Under this contract, the vendor is the seller and the vendee is the buyer. The contract is an express bilateral executory contract. The vendor promises to give possession to the vendee during the contract, accept payments toward the purchase price, and convey marketable title to the vendee upon payment of the full purchase price. The vendee promises to make the agreed-upon payments, pay taxes, obtain insurance on the property, and maintain the property in good condition. The vendor's security for payment of the purchase price is retention of legal title until all payments are made. If the contract is recorded, a mortgage tax is payable. However, unlike mortgages, installment land contracts cannot be foreclosed for nonpayment since the purchaser does not generally hold title until final payment is made.

This contract has cash flow advantages to the buyer, particularly in times of tight credit (high interest rates) markets, or when the buyer does not qualify for conventional loans. In these cases, the seller may be willing to provide the financing, especially because this form of contract puts the seller in a strong position because she still maintains title to the property. The seller may also not require a down payment or, if one is required, it may be less than a lending institution requires.

An installment contract has tax advantages for the seller. The seller can still claim depreciation on the property as she is still the owner. Moreover, the seller does not have to pay any federal capital gains tax that would normally be due on the sale of a property all at one time, but can pay a percentage each year as payments are received from the buyer.

Most mortgage documents today contain a "due on sale" or alienation clause, specifying that the entire principal balance due on the mortgage must be paid in full if a transfer of the property takes place. An installment contract must never be used to circumvent these loan-assumption clauses. The lending institution holding the mortgage may declare the execution of an installment contract a transfer of the property and thereby require the seller to pay off the mortgage. In cases of an installment sales contract, a **forbearance** may be granted by the lending institution. A forbearance is simply *the act of refraining from taking legal action for payment of a mortgage despite the fact that it is due.* Usually a lender will grant a forbearance if the owner is a strong credit risk and the interest rate on the mortgage is favorable to the lender.

Lease with Option to Buy

An *option* is a contract in which an optionor (owner) sells a right to purchase the property to a prospective buyer, or optionee, at a particular price for a specified time period. An option is an express unilateral contract. Only one party to the option contract makes a promise. The optionor promises to allow the optionee the sole right to purchase the real estate during the specified time. The optionee pays for this right but makes no promise to purchase the real estate. The optionee is merely buying time to decide or arrange financing. An option is often tied to a lease. In this case, additional issues must be addressed. All or part of the rent may apply toward the purchase price of the property. The option may expire at the expiration of the lease. The date on which the lease option expires and the transfer of the property occurs must be written into the lease option. A breach of the lease may cancel the option, and all credits toward the purchase price under the lease may be forfeited.

A lease with option to buy may be a great benefit to the tenant (buyer) because less money is needed to possess the property than in the case of an outright sale. This arrangement buys time for the tenant to save enough money to purchase the property. The landlord benefits because all of the payments are rental payments and are not subject to capital gains taxes. Moreover, because the landlord retains title to the property, he retains the right to depreciate the property for tax purposes. This depreciation allowance can wipe out a portion of the rent payment. The landlord and tenant must agree about who pays the expenses associated with the property, such as taxes, maintenance, repairs, and other items.

Right of First Refusal

A **right of first refusal** is different from an option. *It allows the holder a right to purchase (or lease) a property should another purchaser (or lessee) come along.* Tenants may also desire a right of first refusal to allow an opportunity to expand into additional space before it is leased to another. This option right may be at a different rental rate than originally agreed upon. In a right of first refusal, the owner must have first put the property up for sale or lease and second have an offer from another party. The holder of the right of first refusal can either match the offer from this other third party or forfeit his claim to purchase or lease the property. At this point the owner may sell or lease the property to the third party.

With an option, the optionee or holder of the option has control over whether to exercise this right to the property. In a right of first refusal, the holder must exercise his right when another purchaser enters the picture.

CONTRACTS AFFECTING BROKERS

Contracts affecting brokers and their agents include employment contracts, leases (discussed in Chapter 7), sales contracts, binders and options, just discussed, and listing agreements (discussed in Chapter 2), and the independent contractor agreement between the salesperson and broker (Chapter 15). More detailed contracts may exist between a broker and salesperson or an associate broker that can delineate the exact amount or fee paid for work performed, a comprehensive list of each party's expenses, and a more specifically defined notice for termination of the contract.

Commission Entitlement

The broker's entitlement to commission is determined by two tests: the "ready, willing, and able" test and the "acceptance" test.

The "ready, willing, and able" test arises if the broker brings to the seller a buyer who is ready, willing, and financially able to buy under the terms and conditions of the listing contract, in which case the broker is legally entitled to the commission. The broker has done the job he was hired to do in the listing contract—find a buyer who will pay the listed price in cash or in other specified, accepted terms. The broker then earns the commission under the ready, willing, and able test. Whether the owner actually agrees to sell the property to the prospective buyer does not matter. The seller may reject any offer, but rejecting an offer that conforms to the terms of the listing contract does not remove the duty to pay the commission.

The "acceptance" test arises if the broker brings a buyer whom the seller accepts, in which case the broker is legally entitled to the commission since he has been instrumental in procuring a buyer for the property. Acceptance is based on some price or terms other than the listed price in cash. For example, the listing contract may specify $80,000 to be payable in cash. A broker may bring an offer of $78,500 to the seller. This offer may not be for payment in cash but instead may be subject to the buyer's assuming the seller's existing mortgage. If the seller accepts that arrangement, the broker is legally entitled to the commission on the basis of acceptance. The broker has brought the seller a buyer who is acceptable to the seller. Both of these tests are not required; using them is an either/or situation. The broker earns a commission either on the basis of having brought a ready, willing, and able buyer or on the basis of having brought an offer that the seller accepts.

IMPORTANT POINTS

1. A contract is an agreement between competent parties, upon legal consideration, to do or abstain from doing some legal act.
2. An express contract is spoken or written. An implied contract is one inferred from the actions of the parties.
3. Bilateral contracts are based on mutual promises. Unilateral contracts are based on a promise by one party and an act by another party.
4. An executed contract has been fully performed. An executory contract contains provisions yet to be performed.
5. A contract is created by the unconditional acceptance of a valid offer. Acceptance of bilateral offers must be communicated.
6. A voidable contract is one that may not be enforceable at the option of one of the parties to the contract.
7. The requirements for contract validity are (a) competent parties, (b) mutual agreement, (c) lawful objective, (d) consideration, and (e) in writing when required to be.
8. The Statute of Frauds, that in New York is written into the General Obligations Law, requires that real estate contracts be in writing. Leases and listing contracts for more than one year must be in writing.
9. The remedies for breach of contract are (a) compensatory damages, (b) liquidated damages, (c) specific performance, and (d) rescission.
10. An offer to purchase is the road map for the real estate transaction and is a bilateral express contract.
11. A cooperative apartment buyer is purchasing an interest in the form of shares in a cooperative corporation. In a cooperative transaction, the loan from the bank is secured by shares of stock, not by a mortgage on the property.
12. A binder is a written outline of the scope of the real estate transaction and does not usually contain all of the essential elements of a valid contract.
13. An installment land contract is a contract of sale and a method of financing by the seller for the buyer. Legal title does not pass until the buyer pays all or some specified part of the purchase price.
14. An option is often tied to a lease. In some cases, all or part of the rent may apply toward the purchase price of the property.
15. The broker is legally entitled to a commission if he produces a ready, willing and able buyer according to the terms of the listing contract and/or if the broker brings a buyer whom the seller accepts.

CHAPTER REVIEW How Would You Respond?

Analyze the following situations and decide how the individuals should handle them in accordance with what you have just learned. Check your responses using the Answer Key at the end of the chapter.

1. A contract for purchase and sale was signed by the purchasers, Vivian and Byung Osaka, on a property they wished to buy at 55 Worthington Road. A brother, who was traveling in Europe at the time of signing, and two sisters own the property. Both sisters agreed to the sale and signed the contract. The brother had told the sisters before departing on his trip that he was agreeable to selling. Do the Osakas have a legally binding contract of sale if only the two sisters sign the contract?

____

____

____

____

2. A real estate broker successfully negotiates a signed contract for purchase and sale between his client, the owner of the property, and a customer who desires to buy the property. Three weeks before the closing, the purchaser breaches the contract by informing the broker that she has changed her mind and will not be purchasing the property under contract. Has the broker earned a commission? If so, to whom would the broker look to recover his commission?

____

____

____

____

KEY TERM REVIEW

Fill in the term that best completes each sentence and then check the Answer Key at the end of the chapter.

1. A document that includes the written outline of the real estate transaction but does not contain all the elements of a valid contract is known as a(n) ______________.
2. An agreement between competent legal parties to do a legal act in exchange for consideration is called a(n) ______________________.
3. The ______________________ sets the statutory time period in New York in a case when, if a party to a contract fails to bring a lawsuit against a defaulting party, the injured party loses the right of remedy.
4. If a closing date is set for February 25, 2000, and the buyer cannot close until February 26, 2000, then the seller may legally cancel his contractual obligations if the contract states that ______________________.
5. The doctrine of ______________________ means that the contract will be completed as originally agreed upon and a buyer need not accept any substitute remedy from a seller for what was agreed upon in the original contract.
6. If a buyer offers to pay $50,000 for a home, and the seller responds that she wants $55,000, the seller has given the buyer a(n) ______________________.

7. A contract that arises because of the conduct of the parties is known as a(n) ______________________.

8. ______________________ is the right given by one party to another to perform certain acts, legally, for the other party.

MULTIPLE CHOICE

Circle the letter that best answers the question and then check the Answer Key at the end of the chapter.

1. A contract in which mutual promises are exchanged at the time of signing (execution) is termed:
   A. multilateral
   B. unilateral
   C. bilateral
   D. promissory

2. A contract may be terminated by which of the following?
   A. partition
   B. patent
   C. novation
   D. reintermediation

3. For valid contracts, in general, which of the following is NOT an essential element?
   A. competent parties
   B. mutual agreement
   C. lawful objective
   D. bilateral agreement

4. Manny has listed his house for sale for $175,000. Jane makes a written offer of $164,500, which Manny accepts. Under the terms of this agreement:
   A. Manny was the offeror
   B. Jane was the offeree
   C. there was a meeting of the minds
   D. a unilateral contract was created

5. Money awarded for losses due to breach of contract is known as:
   A. rescission
   B. compensatory damages
   C. forbearance
   D. equitable consent

6. Which of the following describes an agreement where a property owner agrees to convey title when a purchaser satisfies all obligations agreed to in the contract?
   A. lease contract
   B. listing contract
   C. implied contract
   D. installment contract

7. Upon receipt of a buyer's offer, the seller accepts all terms except the amount of earnest money; the seller then agrees to accept an amount 20 percent higher than the buyer had offered. This fact is communicated to the buyer by the real estate agent. Which of the following describes these events?
   A. the communication created a bilateral contract
   B. the seller accepted the buyer's offer
   C. the seller conditionally rejected the buyer's offer
   D. the seller rejected the buyer's offer and made a counteroffer to the buyer

8. Which of the following does NOT apply to cooperative apartment contracts of sale?
   A. they are different from other types of real estate contracts
   B. they define the transfer of shares from seller to purchaser
   C. they may impose a flip tax to be paid by the seller of the apartment
   D. they specify the type of deed used to convey title

9. A lease of more than one year with option to buy:
   A. need not be in writing
   B. may allow the lease payments to be credited toward the purchase of the property
   C. is invalid after one year
   D. must follow the rules set down in the Uniform Commercial Code

10. Which of the following is NOT a contract?
   A. deed
   B. lease
   C. mortgage
   D. option

ANSWER KEY

How Would You Respond?

1. No; *all* buyers and sellers must sign the contract or at least provide for a power of attorney to someone who would sign for the absent brother.
2. The broker brought to the seller a buyer who was ready, willing, and able to buy under the terms of the listing contract. The broker is entitled to the commission. The broker would have to look to the seller for the commission because the seller is the party who engaged him to sell the property and agreed to a specific commission.

Key Term Review

1. binder
2. contract
3. Statute of Limitations
4. "time is of the essence"
5. specific performance
6. counteroffer
7. implied contract
8. power of attorney

Multiple Choice

1. C
2. C
3. D
4. C
5. B
6. D
7. D
8. D
9. B
10. A

Putting It To Work

CAPITAL REGION MULTIPLE LISTING SERVICE, INC.
STANDARD FORM
CONTRACT FOR PURCHASE AND SALE OF REAL ESTATE

THIS IS A LEGALLY-BINDING CONTRACT. IF NOT FULLY UNDERSTOOD, WE RECOMMEND ALL PARTIES TO THE CONTRACT CONSULT AN ATTORNEY BEFORE SIGNING.

1. **IDENTIFICATION OF PARTIES TO THE CONTRACT**
   A. **SELLER** — The Seller is Peter W. and Anita B. Rose
   residing at 105 Maple Ave., Saratoga Springs, New York
   (the word "Seller" refers to each and all parties who have an ownership interest in the property).
   B. **PURCHASER** — The Purchaser is Melissa A. and Roger T. Barter
   residing at 100 Main Ave., Memphis, Tennessee
   (the word "Purchaser" refers to each and all of those who sign below as Purchaser).

2. **PROPERTY TO BE SOLD**
   The property and improvements which the Seller is agreeing to sell and which the Purchaser is agreeing to purchase is known as 105 Maple Avenue located in the city, village or town of Saratoga Springs in Saratoga County, State of New York. This property includes all the Seller's rights and privileges, if any, to all land, water, streets and roads annexed to, and on all sides of the property. The lot size of the property is approximately 100 x 150 .

3. **ITEMS INCLUDED IN SALE**

Heating and Lighting Fixtures	Storm Windows and Screens	Television Aerials
Built-in Kitchen Appliances	Storm and Screen Doors	Smoke Detectors
Built-in Bathroom and Kitchen Cabinets	Water Softeners (if owned by Seller)	Alarm Systems
Drapery Rods and Curtain Rods	Plumbing Fixtures	Shrubbery, Trees, Plants and Fencing in the Ground
Shades and Blinds	Pumps	
Wall-to-Wall Carpeting as placed	Awnings	Fireplace insert, doors and/or screen

   The items listed above, if now in or on said premises are represented to be owned by the Seller, free from all liens and encumbrances, and are included in the sale "as is," on the date of this offer, together with the following items: Riding lawn mower

4. **ITEMS EXCLUDED FROM SALE**
   The following items are excluded from the sale: antique Tiffany chandelier

5. **PURCHASE PRICE**
   The purchase price is One Hundred Fifty Thousand 00/100 DOLLARS ($ 150,000) The Purchaser shall pay the purchase price as follows:
   a. $ 500.00 deposit with this contract and held pursuant to paragraph 17 herein.
   b. $ 8,000.00 additional deposit on November 20, 2004
   c. $ 141,500.00 in cash, certified check, bank draft or attorney escrow account check at closing.
   d. $
   e. $ 150,000.00 Total purchase price

6. **MORTGAGE CONTINGENCY**
   A. This Agreement is contingent upon Purchaser obtaining approval of a ☒ conventional, ☐ FHA or ☐ VA (if FHA or VA see attached required addendum) or ________ mortgage loan of $ 120,000 for a term of not more than 30 years at an initial ☒ fixed or ☐ adjustable nominal interest rate not to exceed 7 percent. Purchaser agrees to use diligent efforts to obtain said approval and shall apply for the mortgage loan within 5 business days after the Seller has accepted this contract. Purchaser agrees to apply for such mortgage loan to at least one lending institution or licensed mortgage broker. Upon receipt of a written mortgage commitment or in the event Purchaser chooses to waive this mortgage contingency, Purchaser shall provide notice in writing to Morgan Realty (Saratoga Springs) of Purchaser's receipt of the mortgage commitment or of Purchaser's waiving of this contingency. Upon receipt of such notice this contingency shall be deemed waived or satisfied as the case may be. In the event notice as called for in the proceeding sentence has not been received on or before December 15, 2004 , then either Purchaser or Seller may terminate this contract by written notice to Morgan Realty . Upon receipt of such notice, this agreement shall be deemed cancelled, null and void and all deposits made hereunder shall be returned to Purchaser.
   B. **Seller's Contribution:** At closing, as a credit toward prepaids, closing costs and/or points, Seller shall credit to Purchaser $ ________ or _____ % of the ☐ Purchase Price or ☐ mortgage amount.

   Buyer's Initials MB/RB **Seller's Initials** AR/PR REVISED 7/17/02

7. **MORTGAGE EXPENSE AND RECORDING FEES**
   The Mortgage recording tax imposed on the mortgagor, mortgage and deed recording fees, expenses of drawing papers and any other expenses to be incurred in connection with procuring a mortgage, shall be paid by the Purchaser.

8. **OTHER TERMS (if any)** The cellar and garage shall be in "Broom Clean" condition before closing.

9. **TITLE AND SURVEY**
   A ☒ 40-year abstract of title, tax search and any continuations thereof, or a ☐ fee title insurance policy, shall be obtained at the expense of ☒ Purchaser or ☐ Seller. (If both boxes are checked, the option of whether an Abstract of Title or fee policy is provided shall be that of the party paying for same.) The Seller shall cooperate in providing any available survey, abstract of title or title insurance policy information, without cost to Purchaser. The Purchaser shall pay the cost of updating any such survey or the cost of a new survey.

10. **CONDITIONS OF PREMISES**
   The buildings on the premises are sold "as is" without warranty as to condition, and the Purchaser agrees to take title to the buildings "as is" and in their present condition subject to reasonable use, wear, tear and natural deterioration between the date hereof and the closing of title: except that in the case of any destruction within the meaning of the provisions of Section 5-1311 of the General Obligations Law of the State of New York entitled "Uniform Vendor and Purchaser Risk Act," said section shall apply to this contract.
   A. This Agreement is contingent upon determination by a Certified Exterminator or other qualified professional that the premises are free from infestation or damage by wood-destroying organisms; this determination to be made at Purchaser's expense and to be completed by November 15, 2004 and, if premises are not free from infestation or damage, then Purchaser shall have the option, by written notice to be given within five (5) days after date in this paragraph, to cancel this contract.
   B. This Agreement is contingent upon a written determination, at Purchaser's expense, by a New York State registered architect or licensed engineer, by a third party who is Ralph Young , or other qualified person, that the premises are free from any substantial structural, mechanical, electrical, plumbing, roof covering, water or sewer defects. The term substantial to refer to any individual repair which will reasonably cost over $1000.00 to correct. This contingency shall be deemed waived unless the Purchaser shall notify Morgan Realty no later than November 20, 2004 , as called for in paragraph 22, of such substantial repair(s), and furthermore supplies a written copy of the inspection report. If the Purchaser so notifies, then this agreement shall be deemed cancelled, null and void and all deposits made hereunder shall be returned to Purchaser or, at Purchaser's option, said cancellation may be deferred for a period of ten (10) days in order to provide the parties an opportunity to otherwise agree in writing.
   The following buildings or items on the premises are excluded from this inspection

11. **CONDITIONS AFFECTING TITLE**
The Seller shall convey and the Purchaser shall accept the property subject to all covenants, conditions, restrictions and easements of record and zoning and environmental protection laws so long as the property is not in violation thereof and any of the foregoing does not prevent the intended use of the property for the purpose of single family residence ____________ ; also subject to any existing tenancies, any unpaid installments of street or other improvement assessments payable after the date of the transfer of title to the property, and any state of facts which an inspection and/or accurate survey may show, provided that nothing in this paragraph renders the title to the property unmarketable.

12. **DEED**
The property shall be transferred from Seller to Purchaser by means of a Warranty Deed, with Lien Covenant, or ____________ deed, furnished by the Seller. The deed and real property transfer gains tax affidavit will be properly prepared and signed so that it will be accepted for recording by the County Clerk in the County in which the property is located. If the Seller is transferring the property as an executor, administrator, trustee, committee or conservator, the deed usual to such cases shall be accepted.

13. **NEW YORK STATE TRANSFER TAX AND MORTGAGE SATISFACTION**
The Seller agrees to pay the New York State Real Property Transfer Tax as set by law and further agrees to pay the expenses of procuring and recording satisfactions of any existing mortgages.

14. **TAX AND OTHER ADJUSTMENTS**
The following, if any, shall be apportioned so that the Purchaser and Seller are assuming the expenses of the property and income from the property as of the date of transfer of title:
a. rents and security deposits. Seller shall assign to Purchaser all written leases and security deposits affecting the premises.
b. taxes, sewer, water, rents, and condominium or homeowner association fees.
c. municipal assessment yearly installments except as set forth in item 11.
d. fuel, based upon fair market value at time of closing as confirmed by a certification provided by Seller's supplier.

Buyer's Initials MB/RB **Seller's Initials** AR/PR

15. **RIGHT OF INSPECTION AND ACCESS**
Purchaser and/or representative shall be given access to the property for any tests or inspections required by the terms of this contract upon reasonable notice to the Seller or a representative. Purchaser and/or a representative shall be given the right of inspection of the property, at a reasonable hour, within 48 hours prior to transfer of title.

16. **TRANSFER OF TITLE/POSSESSION**
The transfer of title to the property from Seller to Purchaser will take place at the office of the lender's attorney if the Purchaser obtains a mortgage loan from a lending institution. Otherwise, the closing will be at the office of the attorney for the Seller. The closing will be on or before January 15, 2005 . Possession shall be granted upon transfer of title unless otherwise mutually agreed upon in writing signed by the parties.

17. **DEPOSITS**
It is agreed that any deposits by the Purchaser are to be deposited with the Listing Broker at First Federal Savings Bank as part of the purchase price. If the Seller does not accept the Purchaser's offer, all deposits shall be returned to Purchaser.
If the offer is accepted by Seller, all deposits will be held in escrow by the Listing Broker and deposited into the Listing Broker's escrow account in the institution identified above, until the contingencies and terms have been met. The Purchaser will receive credit on the total amount of the deposit toward the purchase price. Broker shall then apply the total deposit to the brokerage fee. Any excess of deposit over and above the fee earned will go to the Seller.
If the contingencies and terms contained herein cannot be resolved, or in the event of default by the Seller or the Purchaser, the deposits will be held by the Broker pending a resolution of the disposition of the deposits.
If the broker holding the deposit determines, in its sole discretion, that sufficient progress is not being made toward a resolution of the dispute, that broker may commence an interpleader action and pay the deposit monies into court. The Broker's reasonable costs and expenses, including attorney's fees, shall be paid from the deposit upon the resolution of the interpleader action and the remaining net proceeds of the deposit shall be disbursed to the prevailing claimant. In the event the deposit is insufficient to cover the broker's entitlement, the non-prevailing party shall pay the remaining balance.

18. **TIME PERIOD OF OFFER**
Purchaser and Seller understand and agree that, unless earlier withdrawn, this offer is good until ________ a.m. 9 p.m., November 7 , 2004 , and if not accepted by the Seller prior to that time, then this offer becomes null and void.

19. **REAL ESTATE BROKER**
The Purchaser and Seller agree that Chelmsley Real Estate and Morgan Realty brought about the sale, and Seller agrees to pay broker's commission to Morgan Realty as agreed to in the listing agreement.

20. **ATTORNEYS APPROVAL CLAUSE**
This agreement is contingent upon Purchaser and Seller obtaining approval of this agreement by their attorney as to all matters, without limitation. This contingency shall be deemed waived unless Purchaser's or Seller's attorney on behalf of their client notifies that Client's agent in writing, as called for in paragraph 22, of their disapproval of the Agreement no later than November 13, 2004 . If Purchaser's or Seller's attorney so notifies, then this Agreement shall be deemed cancelled, null and void, and all deposits shall be returned to the Purchaser.

21. **ADDENDA**
The following attached addenda are part of this agreement:

a. Radon inspection	b.	c.
d.	e.	f.
g.	h.	i.

22. **NOTICES**
All notices contemplated by this agreement shall be in writing, delivered by (a) certified or registered mail, return receipt requested, postmarked no later than the required ate; (b) by telecopier/facsimile transmitted by such date; or (c) by personal delivery by such date.

23. **ENTIRE AGREEMENT**
This contract contains all agreements of the parties hereto. There are no promises, agreements, terms, conditions, warranties, representations or statements other than contained herein. This agreement shall apply to and bind the heirs, legal representatives, successors and assigns of the respective parties. It may not be changed orally.

Dated: November 5, 2004 Time 10:00 a.m.	Dated: November 6, 2004 Time 11:00 a.m.
Melissa A. Barter Purchaser	Anita B. Rose Seller
Roger T. Barter Purchaser	Peter W. Rose Seller
Ned Stack Selling Broker	James Butell Listing Broker

Chapter 7

KEY TERMS

actual eviction
assignment
constructive eviction
eviction
graduated lease
gross lease
ground lease
index lease
landlease
lease
lessee
lessor
net lease
option to renew
percentage lease
security deposit
sublease
triple net lease

LEARNING OBJECTIVES

Classroom hours: 2

1. Discuss the definition of a lease.
2. Distinguish between the types of leases.
3. Identify the main terms of a lease.
4. List the methods of terminating a lease.
5. Describe several basic methods of extending a lease's term.
6. Identify the characteristics and mechanics of an assignment of a lease.
7. Distinguish between an assignment of a lease and a sublease.
8. Identify and discuss owner's obligations to tenant.
9. Identify and discuss owner's obligations regarding security deposits.
10. Identify and discuss the concept "fixture."

Leases

IN THIS CHAPTER The lease contract defines the relationship between the owner and the tenant. This chapter describes the parties in a lease agreement; the elements of a valid lease; duties, obligations, and rights of the parties to the lease agreement; and various leasehold estates.

DEFINITION OF A LEASE

A **lease** is *a contract, in which, for a consideration (usually rent) an owner of property transfers to the tenant a property interest, or possession, for a prescribed period of time.* The *owner of the property* is called the **lessor.** The *tenant placed in possession* is called the **lessee.** The tenant is entitled to *quiet enjoyment* of the premises, and the owner is expected to receive money plus a reversionary interest in the property; that is, possession of the property will go back to the owner at the end of the lease.

Under a lease, the lessor and lessee agree to the terms of possession and the amount of rent to be paid. The benefit of the lease runs to both the lessor and the lessee, so either the lessor or lessee can demand the contracted benefit. This right is based upon privity of contract, that exists only between lessor and lessee.

Individuals who are not a party to the lease contract cannot demand to receive any benefit. For example, a guest of the lessee has no right to bring legal action against the lessor for lessor's breach of the lease; the guest does not have privity of contract. A person who receives the rights of the lessee by assignment, however, has privity of contract to bring suit against the lessor. Assignment of contract rights transfers the privity of contract necessary for suit.

STANDARD LEASE PROVISIONS

A lease is a contract. Therefore, the same laws governing contractual obligations in New York apply to creating a valid lease; the contractual requirements of offer, acceptance, legal capacity, legal purpose, consideration, and reality of assent apply. No statutory forms of leases exist in New York. The covenants in the lease, however, are extremely important because their inclusion or omission may have serious consequences for the owner or the tenant. Figure 7.1 shows an example of a standard residential lease.

FIGURE 7.1
A standard residential lease agreement.

T 8018—NLS Lease Agreement, House, Flat or small Apartment Building, 12-78 (formerly T 18 B).

JULIUS BLUMBERG, INC., PUBLISHER, ALBANY, NY

LEASE AGREEMENT

The Landlord and Tenant agree to lease the Premises at the Rent and for the Term stated on these terms:

LANDLORD: ______________________ **TENANT:** ______________________

Address ______________________ Address ______________________

Premises: ______________________

Lease date: ______________ 20____	**Term** ______________ **beginning** ______________ 20____ **ending** ______________ 20____	**Yearly Rent** $________ **Monthly Rent** $________ **Security** $________
Broker*		

1. Rent The tenant must make the rent payment for each month on the 1st day of that month at the landlord's address as set forth above. The landlord need not notify the tenant of tenant's duty to pay the rent, and the rent must be paid in full and no deductions will be allowed from the rent. The first month's rent must be paid at the time of the signing of this Lease by the tenant. If the landlord permits the tenant to pay the rent in installments, said permission is for the tenant's convenience only and if the tenant does not pay said installments when they are due, the landlord may notify the tenant that the tenant may no longer pay the rent in installments.

2. Use The tenant agrees to use the premises rented to the tenant by the landlord, to live in only and for no other reason. Only a party signing this Lease, spouse and children of that party may use the Premises. If the tenant wishes to use the leased premises for any other reason, the tenant must obtain the written permission of the landlord to do so. The landlord is not required to grant permission to the tenant to use the leased premises for any purpose other than the purpose listed above.

3. Tenant's duty to obey laws and regulations Tenant must, at tenant's expense, promptly comply with all laws, orders, rules, requests, and directions, of all governmental authorities, landlord's insurers, Board of Fire Underwriters, or similar groups. Notices received by tenant from any authority or group must be promptly delivered to landlord. Tenant may not do anything which may increase landlord's insurance premiums; if tenant does, tenant must pay the increase in premium as added rent.

4. Repairs The tenant must maintain the apartment and all of the equipment and fixtures in it. The tenant agrees, at tenant's own cost, to make all repairs to the apartment and replacement to the equipment and fixtures in the apartment whenever the need results from the tenant's acts or neglect. If the tenant fails to make a repair or replacement, then the landlord may do so and charge the tenant the cost of said repair or replacement as additional rent, which rent shall be due and payable under the terms and conditions as normal rent is due and payable.

5. Glass, cost of replacement The tenant agrees to replace, at the tenant's own expense, all glass broken during the term of this lease, regardless of the cause of the breakage. The tenant agrees that all glass in said premises is whole as of the beginning of the term of this lease.

6. Alterations The tenant agrees not to make any alterations or improvements in the leased premises without the landlord's written permission and any alterations and improvements made by the tenant after obtaining the written permission of the landlord shall be paid at the sole expense of the tenant and will become the property of the landlord and be left behind in the leased premises at the end of the term of this lease. The landlord has the right to demand that the tenant remove the alterations and installations before the end of the term of this lease. That demand shall be by notice, given at least 15 days before the end of the term, and the removals shall be at the sole expense of the tenant. The landlord is not required to do or pay for any of the work involved in the installation or removal of the alterations unless it is so stated in this lease.

7. Assignment and sublease Tenant must not assign this lease or sublet all or part of the apartment or permit any other person to use the apartment. If tenant does, landlord has the right to cancel the lease as stated in the Tenant's Default section. State law may permit tenant to assign or sublet under certain conditions. Tenant must get landlord's written permission each time tenant wants to assign or sublet. Permission to assign or sublet is good only for that assignment or sublease. Tenant remains bound to the terms of this lease after a permitted assignment or sublease even if landlord accepts rent from the assignee or subtenant. The assignee or subtenant does not become landlord's tenant.

8. Entry by the landlord The tenant agrees to allow the landlord to enter the leased premises at any reasonable hour to repair, inspect, install or work upon any fixture or equipment in said leased premises and to perform such other work that the landlord may decide is necessary. In addition, tenant agrees to permit landlord and/or landlord's agent, to show the premises to persons wishing to hire or purchase the same, during the reasonable hours of any day during the term of this Lease, tenant will permit the usual notices of "To Let" or "For Sale" to be placed upon conspicuous portions of the walls, doors, or windows of said premises and remain thereon without hindrance or molestation.

9. Fire, accident, defects and damage Tenant must give landlord prompt notice of fire, accident, damage or dangerous or defective condition. If the apartment can not be used because of fire or other casualty, tenant is not required to pay rent for the time the apartment is unusable. If part of the apartment can not be used, tenant must pay rent for the usable part. Landlord shall have the right to decide which part of the apartment is usable. Landlord need only repair the damaged structural parts of the apartment. Landlord is not required to repair or replace any equipment, fixtures, furnishings or decorations unless originally installed by landlord. Landlord is not responsible for delays due to settling insurance claims, obtaining estimates, labor and supply problems or any other cause not fully under landlord's control.

If the fire or other casualty is caused by an act or neglect of tenant or guest of tenant, or at the time of the fire or casualty tenant is in default in any term of this lease, then all repairs will be made at tenant's expense and tenant must pay the full rent with no adjustment. The cost of the repairs will be added rent.

Landlord has the right to demolish or rebuild the building if there is substantial damage by fire or other casualty. Even if the apartment is not damaged, landlord may cancel this lease within 30 days after the fire or casualty by giving tenant notice of landlord's intention to demolish or rebuild. The lease will end 30 days after landlord's cancellation notice to tenant. Tenant must deliver the apartment to landlord on or before the cancellation date in the notice and pay all rent due to the date of the fire or casualty. If the lease is cancelled landlord is not required to repair the apartment or building.

10. Waivers If the landlord accepts the rent due under this lease or fails to enforce any terms of this lease, said action by the landlord shall not be a waiver of any of the landlord's rights. If a term in this lease is determined to be illegal, than the rest of this lease shall remain in full force and effect and be binding upon both the landlord and the tenant.

11. Tenant's default

A. Landlord may give 5 days written notice to tenant to correct any of the following defaults:

1. Failure to pay rent or added rent on time.
2. Improper assignment of the lease, improper subletting all or part of the premises, or allowing another to use the premises.
3. Improper conduct by tenant or other occupant of the premises.
4. Failure to fully perform any other term in the lease.

B. If tenant fails to correct the defaults in section A within the 5 days, landlord may cancel the lease by giving tenant a written 3 day notice stating the date the term will end. On that date the term and tenant's rights in this lease automatically end and tenant must leave the premises and give landlord the keys. Tenant continues to be responsible for rent, expenses, damages and losses.

C. If the lease is cancelled, or rent or added rent is not paid on time, or tenant vacates the premises, landlord may in addition to other remedies take any of the following steps:

1. Enter the premises and remove tenant and any person or property;
2. Use dispossess, eviction or other lawsuit method to take back the premises.

D. If the lease is ended or landlord takes back the premises, rent and added rent for the unexpired term becomes due and payable. Landlord may re-rent the premises and anything in it for any term. Landlord may re-rent for a lower rent and give allowances to the new tenant. Tenant shall be responsible for landlord's cost of re-renting. Landlord's cost shall include the cost of repairs, decorations, broker's fees, attorney's fees, advertising and preparation for renting. Tenant shall continue to be responsible for rent, expenses, damages and losses. Any rent received from the re-renting shall be applied to the reduction of money tenant owes. Tenant waives all rights to return to the premises after possession is given to the landlord by a Court.

(continued)

FIGURE 7.1
Continued.

PAGE 2

12. Tenant's additional obligations Tenant shall keep the grounds and common areas of the leased premises as well as the leased premises themselves neat and clean. Tenant agrees not to use any of the equipment, fixtures or plumbing fixtures in the leased premises for any purpose other than that for which said equipment, fixtures or plumbing fixtures were designed. Any damage resulting from the misuse of such equipment, fixtures and plumbing fixtures shall be paid for by the tenant as additional rent, which additional rent shall be due and payable under the terms and conditions as normal rent is due and payable.

All furniture and other personal belongings, equipment or the like, if any, provided by the landlord and included within the terms of this lease shall be returned to the landlord at the end of the term of this lease or any earlier termination in as good condition as possible taking into account reasonable wear and tear. If the tenant vacates the premises or is dispossessed and fails to remove any of tenant's furniture, clothing or personal belongings, those items shall be considered abandoned by the tenant and the landlord shall be authorized to dispose of those items as the landlord sees fit.

13. Quiet enjoyment The landlord agrees that if the tenant pays the rent and complies with all of the other terms and conditions of this lease, then the tenant may peaceably and quietly have, hold and enjoy the premises leased hereunder for the term of this lease.

14. Lease, parties upon whom binding This lease is binding upon the landlord and the tenant and their respective heirs, distributees, executors, administrators, successors and lawful assigns.

15. Utilities and services Tenant agrees to pay for all utilities and services provided to the leased premises with the following exceptions:

____

____

____

16. Space "as is" Tenant has inspected the Premises. Tenant states that they are in good order and repair and takes the Premises "as is."

17. Tenant restrictions No sign, advertisement or illumination shall be placed upon any portion of the exterior, or in the windows of premises and no television aerials shall be installed without written consent of Landlord. Washing machine or driers or water beds are not permitted in the premises. No animal shall be permitted in these premises without the consent in writing of Landlord and Tenant will be responsible for all damages which may be caused by such animal permitted by the Landlord.

18. Security Tenant has given Security to landlord in the amount stated above. If tenant fully complies with all the terms of this lease, landlord will return the security after the term ends. If tenant does not fully comply with the terms of this lease, landlord may use the security to pay amounts owed by tenant, including damages. If landlord sells the premises, landlord may give the security to the buyer. Tenant will look only to the buyer for the return of the security.

Rider Additional terms on __________ page(s) initialed at the end by the parties is attached and made a part of this Lease.

Signatures, effective date The parties have entered into this Lease on the date first above stated. This lease is effective when landlord delivers to tenant a copy signed by all parties.

LANDLORD: ______________________ **TENANT:** ______________________

____

WITNESS: ______________________

to

Lease Agreement

No.

Dated 20

Begins

Expires

Rent

Payable

Source: BlumbergExcelsior, Inc. Forms may be purchased from BlumbergExcelsior, Inc. or any of its dealers. Interactive electronic forms may be purchased at *http://www.blumberg.com*. Reproduction prohibited.

Capacity to Contract

The parties to the lease must be competent, sane adults.

Demising Clause

A definite demising clause addresses the issue of when the lessor (owner) leases the premises and the lessee (tenant) takes possession of the property leased.

Description of Premises

A formal legal description of the property is not required. A street address or other informal reference that is sufficiently identifying to both parties is acceptable. If the lease is for a long term, a formal legal description is recommended to accommodate recordation of the contract.

Term of Lease

The term of the lease is the period of time that the lease will exist between owner and tenant. Although a lease is usually expressed in annual terms, there is no limit to the length of time the property may be leased. The term should be clear so that all parties will know the date of expiration and the method of termination. The term may be cut short prematurely by breach of the lease by one of the parties or by mutual agreement.

Specification of Rent and Payment

Rent is the *consideration* the tenant pays to the owner for possession of the premises. In addition to possession, the rent paid assures the tenant quiet enjoyment of the premises. Rent is due at the end of the lease period unless the lease agreement states otherwise. Because this is typically unacceptable to the owner, lease agreements usually require rent to be paid in advance on a month-to-month basis. Under contract law, the validity of a contract can be challenged if both parties are not bound or if both parties have not received consideration. Under a lease, the owner's consideration is receipt of rent. The tenant's consideration is possession of the premises and the right to quiet enjoyment. The owner's obligation to give possession of the premises to the tenant is directly tied to the tenant's rent payments. If one party fails in his responsibility (consideration), the other party may be relieved of his duty.

Written Term Requirements

The *Statute of Frauds,* or the General Obligations Law in New York, requires that a real estate lease be in writing if the term is for more than one year. Oral leases for less than one year are generally enforceable by the courts. If a written lease is used, both owner and tenant should sign. To be safe, regardless of the time period, any lease should be in writing.

Signatures of Lessee and Lessor

In New York, a lease may not be recorded unless it is for a term exceeding three years. If recorded, it must be signed and acknowledged by the parties. Recordation provides constructive notice of the tenant's rights in the event of property sale or the death of the owner.

Plain Language Requirement

A residential lease must be written in a clear and coherent manner, using everyday terminology. The lease must be appropriately divided and captioned.

Use Provisions

A residential lease provides that the premises be used reasonably for its intended purpose. Unless the lease prohibits it, commercial leases allow the premises to be used "for any lawful purpose" as long as it does not violate any private deed restrictions and is not substantially different from what is customary. However, a commercial lease may limit the use of the premises with a clause stating that the premises may be "for no other purpose" than set forth in the lease. For example, the lease can state that the premises may be used only for a retail clothing business. A **landlease** a*llows a lessee the right to use land for any purpose for a specified period of time.*

Renewal of Leases

Leases are usually expressed in annual terms. New York has no statutory rights to renewal. Once commercial tenants are established in a certain place, they may want options written in the lease to expand the premises or renew the terms of the lease.

An **option to renew** the lease *sets forth the method for renewal and the terms by which the renewed lease will exist.*

Rent Regulations

Rent regulations are governed by several laws including the Emergency Tenants Protection Act of 1974 (revised 1997). There are 55 municipalities that have rent control, including New York City, Albany, Buffalo, and various cities, towns and villages in Albany, Erie, Nassau, Rensselaer, Schenectady, and Westchester counties. Rent stabilization exists in New York City and municipalities in Nassau, Rockland, and Westchester counties. Rent regulation, through two programs, rent control and rent stabilization, protects tenants in privately-owned buildings from illegal rent increases and limits the rights of owners to evict tenants. Rent regulations are overseen by the New York State Division of Housing and Community Renewal (DHCR). Units with rents of $2,000 or more per month and occupied by tenants with incomes over $175,000 are subject to deregulation. In addition, tenants who are 62 years or older may qualify for a full or partial exemption from rent increases.

Rent Control

Rent control dates back to the housing shortage immediately following World War II and generally applies to buildings constructed before 1947. In New York City, rent control operates under the Maximum Base Rent (MBR) system. A maximum base rent is established for each apartment. Owners are entitled to raise rents up to 7.5 percent each year until they reach the MBR. Tenants may challenge the proposed increase if they believe that the building has violations or that the owner's expenses do not warrant an increase. In NYC, rents can be increased because of increases in fuel costs (passalongs) or to cover higher labor costs. When a rent-controlled apartment is vacated, it either becomes rent stabilized (where the building contains at least six units) or is removed from regulation.

Rent Stabilization

Rent stabilization generally covers buildings built after 1947 and before 1974, and apartments removed from rent control. In New York City, apartments are under rent stabilization if they are in buildings of six or more units built between February 1, 1947, and December 31, 1973. Tenants in buildings built before February 1, 1947, who moved in after June 30, 1971, are also covered by rent stabilization. A third category of rent stabilized apartments covers buildings with three or more apartments constructed or extensively renovated on or after January 1, 1974 with special tax benefits. Generally, those buildings are only subject to stabilization while the tax benefits continue or, until the tenant vacates. Outside NYC, rent stabilization is also known as ETPA, for the Emergency Tenant Protection Act, and applies to non-rent controlled apartments in buildings of six or more units built before January 1, 1974, in the localities that have adopted ETPA in Nassau, Westchester and Rockland counties. Some municipalities limit ETPA to buildings of a specific size—for instance, buildings with 20 or more units, or 100 or more, but not less than six.

Besides rent limitations, a lease on a stabilized unit may be renewed for a term of one or two years. The Rent Guidelines Boards (one in New York City and one each in Nassau, Westchester, and Rockland counties) set maximum allowable rates for rent increases in stabilized apartments. The Division of Housing and Community Renewal website has further information: *http://www.dhcr.state.ny.us*.

Security Deposit

Most owners require the tenant to deposit a certain *sum of money that will be refunded at the end of the lease* based upon the condition of the premises. This **security deposit** often constitutes one month's rent. The money is intended for repair of only that damage the tenant causes beyond ordinary wear and tear, and the owner is not to use it for basic cleaning and repainting. However, the owner is allowed to charge the tenant a separate sum for cleaning and repainting if both parties agree. The security deposit must be held in an escrow account, separate from the owner's personal fund. Commingling of the tenant's security deposit with other monies belonging to the owner is illegal in New York. In multiple dwellings with six or more units, the security deposit must be placed in an interest-bearing account. The interest on the security deposit belongs to the tenant.

Possession and Habitability

The owner is required to put the tenant in possession of the premises. The tenant is entitled to *quiet enjoyment*, meaning that no one will interrupt the tenancy or invade the premises without the tenant's consent, including the owner. The owner does not have an automatic right to inspect the leased premises, although the tenant may agree in the lease to the owner's right to inspect. The owner has no right to send mechanics into leased premises, to make alterations, or install new equipment unless the lease specifically authorizes the owner to do so. The owner has the right to enter the premises in an emergency, such as fire or burst water pipes, to protect the premises.

In New York, with regard to residential property, whether the lease is written or oral, the owner is obligated to lease the premises in *habitable,* or *livable,* condition at the beginning of the lease and to maintain the premises in habitable shape throughout the term of the lease. The owner also warrants that the occupants will not be subject to any conditions that would be dangerous, hazardous, or detrimental to their life, health, or safety.

Improvement

Most written leases include provisions stating who has the responsibility for maintenance and repair. In New York, if a person is physically injured on the premises as a result of defective or broken facilities, an owner can be held legally responsible for failure to make repairs. According to New York's Multiple Dwelling Law, an owner renting a multiple dwelling (housing that contains three or more units) must keep the dwelling in good repair. A tenant or his family, however, may be responsible for damage caused by their own negligence. The tenant's basic obligation under any lease (apart from the payment of rent) is to maintain the premises in the same condition as found at the beginning of the lease, with *ordinary wear and tear* excepted, that is, the *usual deterioration caused by normal living.* During occupancy, the tenant is expected to use the premises for legal purposes only and conform to all laws. The requirement for maintenance may be shifted to the tenant by agreement of the parties.

Assignment and Subletting

A negative covenant in a lease binds the tenant *not* to do certain acts, such as assigning or subletting the premises. An **assignment** of a lease involves the *transfer of the lease contract from the present tenant to the assignee.* The assignee now shares the privity of estate with the owner (lessor). In a **sublease,** the original tenant is still responsible to the owner for the lease payments under the lease contract. In a sublease arrangement, *the sublessee pays the rent to the tenant (lessee) and the tenant pays the owner.*

The owner usually includes a provision in the lease prohibiting assignment of lease rights or subleasing of the premises without the owner's approval. To sublease or assign, the tenant would have to receive written permission. In New York, if the owner unreasonably withholds consent, the tenant may legally seek release from the lease. Similarly, a tenant in a residential building with four or more units has the right to sublease *subject* to written consent of the owner. In this case, the owner cannot unreasonably withhold consent.

In commercial lease assignments in New York, the factors considered as to whether the owner's decision is reasonable regarding assignment or sublease includes the financial stability of the assignee, his experience in the business, the nature of the business, effect on other businesses in the building, and the need for any changes to the floor plan or structure of the premises.

Apartment Sharing

A lease may have restrictions regarding who can live in the apartment. According to the Real Property Law, certain lease restrictions on the number of tenants occupying a dwelling or on related tenants' occupancy may be unenforceable.

Termination and Eviction Remedies

At the end of the lease, the tenant is obligated to vacate the premises without the need for legal eviction by the owner. A lease may terminate in a variety of ways. The simplest way is for the lease term to expire. At the expiration of the lease, if no renewal agreement is reached, the duties and rights of the owner and tenant terminate. The tenant vacates the premises, and possession reverts to the owner.

The owner and tenant also can mutually agree to cancel a lease prior to expiration. Mutual cancellation terminates the parties' duties and rights, and possession reverts to the owner. Because cancellation of the lease is by mutual agreement, it may occur after a breach of the lease by either party.

The lease also can be terminated if the owner chooses to evict the tenant if the tenant breaches the lease agreement, for example, by failing to pay rent. It also can occur after the lease agreement expires and the tenant fails to vacate the premises. **Eviction** is a *legal action in the court system for removal of the tenant and his belongings and a return of possession of the premises to the owner.* In some cases, the owner requests a lien on the tenant's belongings as security for payment of rent owed. Should an owner take matters into his own hands, *without the aid or control of the court system, and removes the tenant from the premises,* this is known as **actual eviction.** Actual eviction is wrongful use of self-help. *Self-help* occurs when the owner violates statutory law by physically removing the tenants and their belongings from the premises or takes action to prevent tenant-access to the premises.

A lease also can be terminated by a tenant's claim of constructive eviction, that is mainly limited to residential properties, but can also apply to commercial properties. In some cases, the tenant can claim constructive eviction and be relieved of the obligation to pay rent.

A **constructive eviction** occurs when *the tenant is prevented from the quiet enjoyment of the premises.* In New York, unless there is an agreement to the contrary and the tenant did not cause the problem, he can leave the leased premises and forfeit his lease obligations (rental payment) if the building becomes unlivable. In such cases, through the owner's lack of care, the tenant has been evicted for all practical purposes because *enjoyment of the premises is not available.* An example is when heat and water are not available because of the owner's negligence. To claim constructive eviction, however, the tenant must actually vacate the premises while the conditions that make the premises uninhabitable still exist. The lease is then terminated under the constructive eviction claim. Such cases do not reflect an automatic right that the tenant can assume; they may have to be litigated.

Withholding Rent

Rent strikes occur in so-called slumlord situations in which the owner refuses to maintain the property; when basic needs such as heat, water, and electricity are deficient; or if life-threatening conditions, such as rat infestation, exist. Tenants are allowed to withhold rent from the owner but are required to pay the rent to the court for disbursement as the court decides.

In New York City, if an owner does not provide heat, water, electricity, or wastewater disposal facilities; if the building is infested with rodents; or if the owner has threatened the health, safety, and welfare of the occupants, they may take action. A minimum of one-third of the tenants, after five or more days of this activity, can petition the court to collect the rents rather than pay the owner. In addition, in New York City, the owner must pay compensatory and punitive damages to tenants if the utilities in a building are not available because the owner did not pay the utility bill.

Abandonment by Tenant

A lease can terminate if the tenant abandons the premises and the owner reenters to repossess the premises. This is similar to cancellation of the lease. Upon the tenant's abandonment, the owner does not have to accept return of the premises; instead, he can pursue the tenant for rent under the clauses in the lease. If the owner does accept return of the premises, he may still pursue the tenant for lost rent under the old lease. The owner must use his best efforts to re-rent the premises.

Death or Sale of Property

A lease agreement never terminates upon the death of the owner or the tenant. The type of leasehold existing between the parties determines whether the lease survives at death of one party. The lease agreement also does not terminate when an owner sells the premises. The new owner is bound by the terms of the lease. The timetable for eviction proceedings and the evidentiary requirements to prove right to eviction are governed by local court rules. An owner seeking an eviction should hire an attorney or obtain a copy of the court rules and forms to ensure compliance.

PUTTING IT TO WORK

Property rentals are another way of realizing income as a licensee. Familiarity with the requirements of a standard residential rental application will help you better serve your customer or client. Check your understanding of what is involved in residential property rental by using the following information to fill out the residential lease in Figure 7.1.

Listing and leasing broker's name: Matilda Brick
Leasing brokerage firm: Landlover Realty
Date of lease: December 10, 2004
Name of owner: Bill Tuppence, 45 Queens St., Jamaica, New York 11435
Name of tenant: Nancy Bealieux
Current address of tenant: 28-46 Parsons Blvd., Jamaica, New York 11435
Address of leased property: Garden Apts., 21-10 Jamaica Ave., Jamaica, New York 11435
Lease begins: February 1, 2005
Lease terminates: January 31, 2006
Security deposit: $850
Rent: $850 per month
Utilities: Tenant pays for all utilities except the water bill
Yard maintenance: Responsibility of tenant
Pets: Not allowed
Late charge: $10 per day; bad check fee $25
Commission paid to leasing broker by owner: $850

TYPES OF LEASES

Gross and Net Leases

The two primary classifications of leases based on arrangement of payment of expenses of the rental property are *gross* lease and *net* lease. A **gross lease** provides for *the owner (lessor) to pay all expenses,* such as real property taxes, owner's insurance, liability insurance, and maintenance. In a **net lease,** *the tenant (lessee) pays some or all of the expenses.* Sometimes net leases are referred to as net, double net, or triple net, depending upon how many property expenses the tenant pays. A lessee who contracts for a **triple net lease** *pays all the expenses associated with the property in addition to the rent.* Variations of the standard lease exist, and they can be either gross or net; the arrangement for paying property expenses is the determining factor.

Percentage Lease

Many retail commercial leases are percentage leases. A **percentage lease** has *a base rent plus an additional monthly rent that is a percentage of the lessee's gross sales.* Most commercial leases in cases when the lessee is using the property to conduct a retail business are percentage leases. This is especially true in shopping malls. The percentage lease provides the lessor with a guaranteed monthly rental plus the opportunity to participate in the lessee's sales volume on a percentage basis.

Ground Lease

A **ground lease** is *a long term lease of unimproved land,* usually for construction purposes. The ground lease normally contains a provision that the lessee will construct a building on the land. However, the owner–lessor retains his interest in the land. Ownership of the land and improvements is separated. The ground lease generally allows the lessee sufficient time to recoup the cost of improvements. This type of lease also typically is a net lease in that the lessee is required to maintain the improvements, pay the property taxes, and pay the expenses of the property. Normally, under a ground lease the owner–lessee has a right to retain and to mortgage the land (if desired), and the lessee has a right to finance the leasehold improvements.

Index Lease

An **index lease** is *a method of determining rent on long term leases.* The rent is tied to an index. An index is a value estimate and economic indicator used by banks to adjust interest rates. The consumer price index expresses the difference among the value, price, or cost of a group of items at various times. Index figures (indices) are available through the Federal Home Loan Bank Board and the Treasury Bond Index. If the index used by the owner indicates a declining economy, the rent may increase so that the owner can cover his costs. If the economy is stable, the rent may stay the same or even decrease under very good conditions. Percentage and index leases allow owners to keep pace with a changing economy which obviously fluctuates during a long term lease.

Graduated Lease

A **graduated lease** is *one in which the rent changes from period to period over the lease term.* The lease contract specifies the change in rental amount, which usually is an increase in stair-step fashion. This type of lease could be utilized for a new business tenant whose income is expected to increase with time.

This and other types of leases and even mortgages may contain an *escalation clause* which gives the lender the right to increase monthly payments or interest rates based on the Treasury Bond Index or other economic indicators.

TENANTS' GROUPS

In New York, groups and organizations exist to further and protect the rights of tenants. These groups may be specific to one apartment building or complex or may be an independent organization for the furtherance of tenants' rights in general. New York Real Property Law prohibits owners from interfering with tenants' rights to join and participate in these groups.

IMPORTANT POINTS

1. A lease is created by contract between the owner of property and the tenant. The owner is the lessor; the tenant is the lessee.
2. The owner and tenant are bound by contractual rights and obligations created by the lease agreement.
3. The transfer of the entire remaining term of a lease by the lessee is an assignment. A transfer of part of the lease term with a reversion to the lessee is a subletting.
4. Rent regulation is governed by several laws including the Emergency Tenants Protection Act of 1974 (revised 1997). Two programs, rent control and rent stabilization, are intended to protect tenants in privately-owned buildings from illegal rent increases while limiting the rights of owners to evict tenants.
5. In a lease of residential property, the owner has the duty to provide habitable premises to the tenant.
6. The tenant has a duty to maintain and return the premises to the owner, at expiration of the lease, in the same condition as at the beginning of the lease, ordinary wear and tear excepted.
7. The tenant can make a claim of constructive eviction when the premises become uninhabitable because of the owner's lack of maintenance. A claim of constructive eviction will terminate the lease.
8. Leases are terminated by (a) expiration of lease term, (b) mutual agreement, (c) breach of condition, (d) actual eviction, (e) court-ordered eviction, or (f) constructive eviction. The law does not favor actual eviction.
9. The two main classifications of leases based on arrangement for payment are the gross lease and the net lease. Under a gross lease, the owner pays the real property taxes, insurance, and costs for maintaining the property. Under a net lease, the tenant pays some or all of these expenses.
10. Types of commercial leases are the percentage lease, the index lease, and the graduated payment lease.
11. A ground lease is a long-term lease on unimproved land and is generally used for construction purposes.

How Would You Respond? CHAPTER REVIEW

Analyze the following situations and decide how the individuals should handle them in accordance with what you have just learned. Check your responses using the Answer Key at the end of the chapter.

1. Joel owns and manages 10 duplex rental units. One family to whom he rents has not paid rent for the last three months, although Joel has requested payment. In the meantime, a couple has come to Joel, desperate for an apartment; they have a security deposit and the first month's rent. One afternoon, while the family not paying rent is out, Joel enters the apartment, takes all of their possessions, puts them in a storage warehouse, and changes the locks. What is legally wrong with Joel's actions?

   ____

   ____

   ____

2. Carol, a real estate broker in Watertown, New York, is the buyer broker for Deanna, who is purchasing a residential apartment building. The building is only 60 percent occupied and is losing money. Although Deanna is getting a good deal on the purchase price, she wants to maximize her income once the property is hers. Deanna tells Carol that she will purchase the building only if she can increase all the tenants' leases by $50 per month and attach an addendum to their leases that states that they must pay rent on the first of the month rather than the fifteenth (their current payment date). It doesn't look like Carol, the broker, will make her sale. Why not?

____

____

____

KEY TERM REVIEW

Fill in the term that best completes each sentence and then check the Answer Key at the end of the chapter.

1. A(n) ____________________ is a type of contract, in which, for a consideration, usually rent, an owner of property transfers to the tenant a property interest, possession, for a prescribed period of time.
2. The owner of a property is called the owner or the ____________________ and the tenant of the property is also known as the ____________________.
3. A(n) ____________________ involves the transfer of the lease contract from the present tenant to another who takes over the lease.
4. The original tenant is still responsible to the owner for the lease payments under the lease contract in a(n) ____________________.
5. ____________________ is when a owner physically removes a tenant and his possessions from the premises.
6. A(n) ____________________ clause in a lease sets forth the method for renewing a lease.
7. A certain sum of money that will be refunded at the end of the lease based upon the condition of the premises is the ____________________.
8. A(n) ____________________ provides for the lessor to pay all expenses, such as real property taxes, owner's insurance, liability insurance, and maintenance.
9. A lease that includes a base rent and also shares in the sales volume of the business is known as a(n) ____________________.

MULTIPLE CHOICE

Circle the letter that best answers the question and then check the Answer Key at the end of the chapter.

1. The right of the lessee to uninterrupted use of the leased premises is known as:
   A. consideration
   B. quiet enjoyment
   C. succession rights
   D. peaceful coexistence

2. According to the Statute of Frauds, a real estate lease must be in writing under which of the following circumstances?
   A. for commercial properties only
   B. for residential properties if the term is more than three years
   C. only if a security deposit is required
   D. if the term is for more than one year

3. Which of the following laws has to do with rent regulations?
   A. Emergency Tenant Protection Act
   B. Fair Housing Act
   C. Landlord Tenant Law
   D. Multiple Dwelling Law

4. If a tenant abandons the leased premises, the owner may NOT do which of the following?
   A. attempt to collect the balance of the rent
   B. rent the premises to another party
   C. terminate the lease
   D. file a mechanics' lien against the tenant

5. A owner has a duty to keep a premises in habitable condition under which of the following circumstances?
   A. with regard to all residential leases
   B. only if there is a written lease
   C. only with regard to multiple dwellings
   D. only with regard to properties subject to rent stabilization

6. Don buys a building owned by Althea. Althea has leased the building to American Products Corporation for seven years. Don must:
   A. renegotiate the lease with American Products
   B. evict American Products to obtain possession
   C. share the space with American Products
   D. honor the lease agreement

7. Which of the following does NOT terminate a residential lease?
   A. abandonment by the tenant
   B. expiration of the lease term
   C. death of the owner
   D. constructive eviction

8. Under a residential lease, if the lessor does not provide habitable premises, the lessee can claim:
   A. eviction
   B. constructive eviction
   C. habitability damages
   D. mitigation of damages

9. A lease with a fixed low base rent plus an additional amount based upon gross receipts of the lessee is a(n):
   A. percentage lease
   B. gross lease
   C. net lease
   D. escalated lease

10. Louise sells her card shop business to Leslie. She also signs over her lease to Leslie so that the business can stay in the same location. What has taken place regarding the lease?
    A. a subletting
    B. a transfer of title
    C. nothing
    D. an assignment

ANSWER KEY

Putting It To Work

T 8018—NLS Lease Agreement, House, Flat or small Apartment Building, 12-78 (formerly T 18 B).

JULIUS BLUMBERG, INC., PUBLISHER, ALBANY, NY

LEASE AGREEMENT

The Landlord and Tenant agree to lease the Premises at the Rent and for the Term stated on these terms:

LANDLORD:	**TENANT:**
Bill Tuppence	Nancy Beaulieux
Address 45 Queens St.	**Address** 28-46 Parsons Blvd.
Jamaica, NY 11435	Jamaica, NY 11435

Premises: Garden Apts., 45 Queens St., Jamaica, NY 11435

Lease date:	**Term** one year	**Yearly Rent**	$ 10,200
December 10 20 04	**beginning** Feb. 1 20 05	**Monthly Rent**	$ 850
	ending Jan. 31 20 06	**Security**	$ 850

Broker* Matilda Brick, Broker, Landover Realty

1. Rent The tenant must make the rent payment for each month on the 1st day of that month at the landlord's address as set forth above. The landlord need not notify the tenant of tenant's duty to pay the rent, and the rent must be paid in full and no deductions will be allowed from the rent. The first month's rent must be paid at the time of the signing of this Lease by the tenant. If the landlord permits the tenant to pay the rent in installments, said permission is for the tenant's convenience only and if the tenant does not pay said installments when they are due, the landlord may notify the tenant that the tenant may no longer pay the rent in installments.

2. Use The tenant agrees to use the premises rented to the tenant by the landlord, to live in only and for no other reason. Only a party signing this Lease, spouse and children of that party may use the Premises. If the tenant wishes to use the leased premises for any other reason, the tenant must obtain the written permission of the landlord to do so. The landlord is not required to grant permission to the tenant to use the leased premises for any purpose other than the purpose listed above.

3. Tenant's duty to obey laws and regulations Tenant must, at tenant's expense, promptly comply with all laws, orders, rules, requests, and directions, of all governmental authorities, landlord's insurers, Board of Fire Underwriters, or similar groups. Notices received by tenant from any authority or group must be promptly delivered to landlord. Tenant may not do anything which may increase landlord's insurance premiums; if tenant does, tenant must pay the increase in premium as added rent.

4. Repairs The tenant must maintain the apartment and all of the equipment and fixtures in it. The tenant agrees, at tenant's own cost, to make all repairs to the apartment and replacement to the equipment and fixtures in the apartment whenever the need results from the tenant's acts or neglect. If the tenant fails to make a repair or replacement, then the landlord may do so and charge the tenant the cost of said repair or replacement as additional rent, which rent shall be due and payable under the terms and conditions as normal rent is due and payable.

5. Glass, cost of replacement The tenant agrees to replace, at the tenant's own expense, all glass broken during the term of this lease, regardless of the cause of the breakage. The tenant agrees that all glass in said premises is whole as of the beginning of the term of this lease.

6. Alterations The tenant agrees not to make any alterations or improvements in the leased premises without the landlord's written permission and any alterations and improvements made by the tenant after obtaining the written permission of the landlord shall be paid at the sole expense of the tenant and will become the property of the landlord and be left behind in the leased premises at the end of the term of this lease. The landlord has the right to demand that the tenant remove the alterations and installations before the end of the term of this lease. That demand shall be by notice, given at least 15 days before the end of the term, and the removals shall be at the sole expense of the tenant. The landlord is not required to do or pay for any of the work involved in the installation or removal of the alterations unless it is so stated in this lease.

7. Assignment and sublease Tenant must not assign this lease or sublet all or part of the apartment or permit any other person to use the apartment. If tenant does, landlord has the right to cancel the lease as stated in the Tenant's Default section. State law may permit tenant to assign or sublet under certain conditions. Tenant must get landlord's written permission each time tenant wants to assign or sublet. Permission to assign or sublet is good only for that assignment or sublease. Tenant remains bound to the terms of this lease after a permitted assignment or sublease even if landlord accepts rent from the assignee or subtenant. The assignee or subtenant does not become landlord's tenant.

8. Entry by the landlord The tenant agrees to allow the landlord to enter the leased premises at any reasonable hour to repair, inspect, install or work upon any fixture or equipment in said leased premises and to perform such other work that the landlord may decide is necessary. In addition, tenant agrees to permit landlord and/or landlord's agent, to show the premises to persons wishing to hire or purchase the same, during the reasonable hours of any day during the term of this Lease, tenant will permit the usual notices of "To Let" or "For Sale" to be placed upon conspicuous portions of the walls, doors, or windows of said premises and remain thereon without hindrance or molestation.

9. Fire, accident, defects and damage Tenant must give landlord prompt notice of fire, accident, damage or dangerous or defective condition. If the apartment can not be used because of fire or other casualty, tenant is not required to pay rent for the time the apartment is unusable. If part of the apartment can not be used, tenant must pay rent for the usable part. Landlord shall have the right to decide which part of the apartment is usable. Landlord need only repair the damaged structural parts of the apartment. Landlord is not required to repair or replace any equipment, fixtures, furnishings or decorations unless originally installed by landlord. Landlord is not responsible for delays due to settling insurance claims, obtaining estimates, labor and supply problems or any other cause not fully under landlord's control.

If the fire or other casualty is caused by an act or neglect of tenant or guest of tenant, or at the time of the fire or casualty tenant is in default in any term of this lease, then all repairs will be made at tenant's expense and tenant must pay the full rent with no adjustment. The cost of the repairs will be added rent.

Landlord has the right to demolish or rebuild the building if there is substantial damage by fire or other casualty. Even if the apartment is not damaged, landlord may cancel this lease within 30 days after the fire or casualty by giving tenant notice of landlord's intention to demolish or rebuild. The lease will end 30 days after landlord's cancellation notice to tenant. Tenant must deliver the apartment to landlord on or before the cancellation date in the notice and pay all rent due to the date of the fire or casualty. If the lease is cancelled landlord is not required to repair the apartment or building.

10. Waivers If the landlord accepts the rent due under this lease or fails to enforce any terms of this lease, said action by the landlord shall not be a waiver of any of the landlord's rights. If a term in this lease is determined to be illegal, than the rest of this lease shall remain in full force and effect and be binding upon both the landlord and the tenant.

11. Tenant's default

A. Landlord may give 5 days written notice to tenant to correct any of the following defaults:
1. Failure to pay rent or added rent on time.
2. Improper assignment of the lease, improper subletting all or part of the premises, or allowing another to use the premises.
3. Improper conduct by tenant or other occupant of the premises.
4. Failure to fully perform any other term in the lease.

B. If tenant fails to correct the defaults in section A within the 5 days, landlord may cancel the lease by giving tenant a written 3 day notice stating the date the term will end. On that date the term and tenant's rights in this lease automatically end and tenant must leave the premises and give landlord the keys. Tenant continues to be responsible for rent, expenses, damages and losses.

C. If the lease is cancelled, or rent or added rent is not paid on time, or tenant vacates the premises, landlord may in addition to other remedies take any of the following steps:
1. Enter the premises and remove tenant and any person or property;
2. Use dispossess, eviction or other lawsuit method to take back the premises.

D. If the lease is ended or landlord takes back the premises, rent and added rent for the unexpired term becomes due and payable. Landlord may re-rent the premises and anything in it for any term. Landlord may re-rent for a lower rent and give allowances to the new tenant. Tenant shall be responsible for landlord's cost of re-renting. Landlord's cost shall include the cost of repairs, decorations, broker's fees, attorney's fees, advertising and preparation for renting. Tenant shall continue to be responsible for rent, expenses, damages and losses. Any rent received from the re-renting shall be applied to the reduction of money tenant owes. Tenant waives all rights to return to the premises after possession is given to the landlord by a Court.

PAGE 2

12. Tenant's additional obligations Tenant shall keep the grounds and common areas of the leased premises as well as the leased premises themselves neat and clean. Tenant agrees not to use any of the equipment, fixtures or plumbing fixtures in the leased premises for any purpose other than that for which said equipment, fixtures or plumbing fixtures were designed. Any damage resulting from the misuse of such equipment, fixtures and plumbing fixtures shall be paid for by the tenant as additional rent, which additional rent shall be due and payable under the terms and conditions as normal rent is due and payable.

All furniture and other personal belongings, equipment or the like, if any, provided by the landlord and included within the terms of this lease shall be returned to the landlord at the end of the term of this lease or any earlier termination in as good condition as possible taking into account reasonable wear and tear. If the tenant vacates the premises or is dispossessed and fails to remove any of tenant's furniture, clothing or personal belongings, those items shall be considered abandoned by the tenant and the landlord shall be authorized to dispose of those items as the landlord sees fit.

13. Quiet enjoyment The landlord agrees that if the tenant pays the rent and complies with all of the other terms and conditions of this lease, then the tenant may peaceably and quietly have, hold and enjoy the premises leased hereunder for the term of this lease.

14. Lease, parties upon whom binding This lease is binding upon the landlord and the tenant and their respective heirs, distributees, executors, administrators, successors and lawful assigns.

15. Utilities and services Tenant agrees to pay for all utilities and services provided to the leased premises with the following exceptions: Tenant does not pay for the water bill.

Tenant maintains the backyard.

16. Space "as is" Tenant has inspected the Premises. Tenant states that they are in good order and repair and takes the Premises "as is."

17. Tenant restrictions No sign, advertisement or illumination shall be placed upon any portion of the exterior, or in the windows of premises and no television aerials shall be installed without written consent of Landlord. Washing machine or driers or water beds are not permitted in the premises. No animal shall be permitted in these premises without the consent in writing of Landlord and Tenant will be responsible for all damages which may be caused by such animal permitted by the Landlord.

18. Security Tenant has given Security to landlord in the amount stated above. If tenant fully complies with all the terms of this lease, landlord will return the security after the term ends. If tenant does not fully comply with the terms of this lease, landlord may use the security to pay amounts owed by tenant, including damages. If landlord sells the premises, landlord may give the security to the buyer. Tenant will look only to the buyer for the return of the security.

Additional terms:

(a) No pets allowed.

(b) A late charge of $10.00 per day will be charged for overdue rent.

Bad check fee is $25.00.

(c) Commission to leasing broker is $850.00

Rider Additional terms on above page(s) initialed at the end by the parties is attached and made a part of this Lease.

Signatures, effective date The parties have entered into this Lease on the date first above stated. This lease is effective when landlord delivers to tenant a copy signed by all parties.

LANDLORD:

Bill Tuppence

TENANT:

Nancy Beaulieux

WITNESS:

Tamara Jones

to

Lease Agreement

No.

Dated 20

Begins

Expires

Rent

Payable

Source: BlumbergExcelsior, Inc. Forms may be purchased from BlumbergExcelsior, Inc. or any of its dealers. Interactive electronic forms may be purchased at *http://www.blumberg.com*. Reproduction prohibited.

How Would You Respond?

1. Joel has performed an actual eviction, which is against the law. If a tenant does not vacate the premises willingly after the termination of a lease or does not abide by the provisions of the lease, the owner must petition the court to initiate legal eviction proceedings.
2. When title to a rental property is transferred, the new owner must honor the lease contracts as they stand. Deanna, as a new owner, may not raise rents or change the terms of a lease before the expiration of the current leases. If this is her position, then it is doubtful she will be purchasing the property.

Key Term Review

1. lease
2. lessor, lessee
3. assignment
4. sublease
5. actual eviction
6. option to renew
7. security deposit
8. gross lease
9. percentage lease

Multiple Choice

1. B
2. D
3. A
4. D
5. A
6. D
7. C
8. B
9. A
10. D

Chapter 8

KEY TERMS

abstract of title
actual notice
assessments
chain of title
closing statement
constructive notice
credits
debits
marketable title
proration
Real Estate Settlement Procedures Act (RESPA)
reconciliation
survey
title
title closing
title insurance
title search

LEARNING OBJECTIVES

Classroom hours: 1

1. Explain the significance of the closing.
2. Describe the various functions of those individuals attending the closing.
3. Identify preclosing responsibilities.
4. List the numerous potential steps or transactions that take place during the course of a closing.
5. Explain the difference between a cooperative and a condominium closing.
6. Explain closing costs and adjustments.

Title Closing and Costs

IN THIS CHAPTER The title closing is the consummation of the real estate transaction. At the closing, the buyer receives a deed and the seller receives payment for the property. This chapter covers the various methods of closing, items required at closing, and proration calculations.

WHAT IS A TITLE CLOSING?

At a **title closing,** *the parties and other interested persons meet to review and execute the closing documents, pay and receive money, and receive title to real estate.* Those present are buyers, sellers, their attorneys, real estate agents, lender representatives, and possibly title company representatives.

Functions of Those Present at Closing

The buyers attend the closing to pay for and receive clear title to the property. **Title** *is evidence of the right to possess property.* The sellers are present to grant their property to the buyers and receive payment. The real estate agent may be there to collect the commission. The role of the lenders' attorney (if there is a loan) is to examine all documents and make sure that the property for which they are giving a mortgage loan has a clear title. Sometimes representatives of the title company are present to review the documents and, if satisfied, to deliver evidence that the title is insured and answer questions concerning the title. The buyers and sellers may also each be represented by an attorney who examines all documents and works in their respective best interests. Often buyers believe that bank attorneys represent them, but they typically represent the interests of the lending institution.

The Title Closing and Recording Acts

At the title closing, the seller is paid the balance of the purchase price, and existing liens against the property are satisfied. The purchaser normally pays the balance of the purchase price with a combination of funds obtained through an acquisition mortgage and the purchaser's own funds. Before executing the closing documents and disbursing the closing funds, the parties should assure themselves that the conditions and contingencies of the purchase agreement are met. The title to the real estate is transferred upon execution and delivery of the deed. Title insurers, abstractors, and attorneys all rely on these *recorded documents* concerning the property. Some documents are not required to be recorded.

You Should Know **The difference between a condominium and a cooperative closing**

A condominium transaction is a fee simple transaction just as is the transfer involving any other residential or commercial property. The closing includes a title search, transfer of the property by a deed, and appropriate transfer fees and recordation.

The purchase of a cooperative is very different. Cooperatives are personalty, that is, personal property, and condominiums are real property. In a cooperative purchase, the purchaser becomes a stockholder in a corporation and buys shares of stock in a corporation. Upon closing, the purchaser receives stock certificates in her name. A cooperative purchaser does not obtain a deed but rather a proprietary lease issued by the cooperative corporation. Those present at a cooperative closing include the buyer, the seller, their respective attorneys, the managing agent of the cooperative, and sometimes a member of the board of directors. A financial investigation and search is conducted on the purchaser to discover any judgments or liens against the purchaser, and also to assess financial strength.

PRELIMINARIES TO CLOSING

Before closing, the parties arranging the closing must ensure that all conditions and contingencies of the offer to purchase are met. Some typical items or documents of concern for the closing agent are described next. Not all are applicable at each closing.

Deed and Other Closing Documents

To ensure accurate completion of the closing documents to transfer title and secure debt, the legal names of the parties must be identified prior to closing. *The deed is the instrument used to convey title to real property.*

Survey

In some real estate transfers, the buyer or buyer lender requires either a full staked survey or a mortgage survey to ensure that no encroachments exist. A survey is the process by which a parcel of land is measured. The final **survey** document is *a type of blueprint showing measurements, boundaries, and area of a property.* The cost of the survey is typically the buyer's responsibility. However, in certain counties in New York, such as Madison and Cayuga, the cost is the seller's responsibility.

Recording Acts

Recordation provides protection for the owner's title against all unrecorded titles. This protection is provided by the theory of **constructive notice:** *all of the world is bound by knowledge of the existence of the conveyance of title if evidence of the conveyance is recorded.* Constructive notice is contrasted with actual notice. **Actual notice** *requires that the person in fact knows about the document.* Constructive notice, provided by recording, protects the title for the grantee, and also protects against anyone with a later claim, including other purchasers of the same property from the same grantor. In New York, a recorded deed takes precedence over any prior unrecorded deed. The recording of a document determines the priority of interests in the property unless a subsequent buyer has actual knowledge of a prior unrecorded transfer.

Additional documents needed at closing **You Should Know**

Depending on the transaction, any of the following documents also may be involved in closing the real estate transaction.

- bill of sale of personal property
- Broker's commission statement
- certificate of occupancy
- closing or settlement statement (HUD Form No. 1)
- deed
- disclosure statement
- estoppel certificate
- fire alarm or smoke detector existence affidavit
- flood insurance policy
- installment land contract (contract for deed)
- lease
- lien waivers
- mortgage
- mortgage guarantee insurance policy
- note
- option and exercise of option
- original homeowner's policy or hazard insurance policy with proof of payment
- Real Property Transfer Report
- sales contract
- Sellers' and purchasers' proof of identity (i.e., driver's license)
- Transfer Gains Tax Affidavit

Title Registration/Torrens System

In addition to the regular method of recording titles, a special form of recording, called the Torrens system, is available in some states, but has not been used in New York except in Suffolk County. Under this method, the titleholder applies to the court to have the property registered. The court orders the title to be examined by official title examiners, who report the examination results to the court. If results of the examinations are satisfactory, the court issues instructions to the Registrar of Titles to record the title and provides certificates of registration of title after giving adequate public notice (allowing anyone contesting the title to have ample opportunity to appear). The certificate of registration of title states the applicant's type of title and sets forth any encumbrances against the title. One certificate is issued to the Registrar of Titles and the other to the titleholder who applied for the registration of the title. The certificate of registration provides conclusive evidence of the validity of the title, and it cannot be contested except for fraud. Title to properties recorded under the Torrens system cannot be obtained by adverse possession.

Marketable Title

Before the title can be transferred, *evidence of* **marketable title,** *or one that is reasonably free and clear of encumbrances should be provided.* (Although marketable title means salable, unmarketable title, burdened with many encumbrances, may nonetheless be very salable also.) The purpose of a title examination is to determine the quality of a title. The examination must be made by an attorney or an abstract or title company. Only an attorney can legally give an opinion as to the quality of a title.

Marketable title is not perfect title and is not necessarily free of all liens. In the case of a sale with mortgage assumption, the buyer has bargained for and will accept seller's title with the present mortgage as a lien on the title.

Evidence of marketable title through a **title search** *can be provided by a commercially hired or personal search of the records affecting real estate titles.* The records examined through a title search can include public records of deeds, mortgages, long-term leases, options, installment land contracts, easements, platted subdivisions, judgments entered, deaths, marriages, bankruptcy filings, mechanics' liens, zoning ordinances, real property and sales taxes, miscellaneous assessments for improvements, mortgage releases, and lis pendens notices.

Chain of Title

The search of the records will establish a **chain of title,** that must be unbroken for the title to be good and therefore marketable. It involves *tracing the successive conveyances of title,* starting with the current deed and going back an appropriate time (typically 40 to 60 years), and quite often back to the original title (the last instance of government ownership). The two forms of commercial title evidence most often used are the abstract of title with attorney opinion and the policy of title insurance.

Any missing links in the chain of title create uncertainty as to the path and proof of ownership. If these missing links can be bridged by obtaining proper title-clearing documents, the transaction may safely occur. If not, the sale should not close. Table 8.1 illustrates a broken chain of title.

Abstract of Title with Attorney Opinion

An **abstract of title** is a *condensed history of the title,* setting forth a summary of all links in the chain of title plus any other matters of public record affecting the title. The abstract contains a legal description of the property and summarizes every related instrument in chronological order. An abstract continuation is an update of an abstract of title that sets forth memoranda of new transfers of title. When the abstract is completed, an attorney must examine it to ensure that the chain of title is unbroken and clear. The attorney then gives a written *certificate of title opinion as to what person or entity owns the real estate and the quality of title and exceptions, if any, to clear title.*

Because title insurance binders typically are issued several days or weeks before closing, an update of the abstract or title binder should be obtained prior to closing with a date that is effective as of the day of closing. In addition, the seller may be required to sign a vendor's affidavit, a *document stating that the seller has done nothing since the original title evidence to affect the title adversely.* If title defects are found, the seller is responsible for the cost of curing or removing the defects. Until marketable title is available, closing will not likely be completed.

TABLE 8.1 A broken chain of title.

Can you identify the break in the chain of title?

GRANTORS	GRANTEES	DATE OF CONVEYANCE
Peggy and Frank Delay	Pat and Henry Bird	August 10, 1975
Pat and Henry Bird	Nancy and John Day	November 15, 1980
Nancy and John Day	Mary Jo and Bob Ray	April 19, 1995
George and Tonya Good	Sue and Mike Smith	September 20, 1998
Sue and Mike Smith	Lois and Art Giles	February 14, 2004

Title Insurance

A **title insurance** policy is *a contract of insurance that insures the policy owner against financial loss if title to real estate is not good.* Title insurance policies are issued by the same companies that prepare abstracts of title. The company issuing the insurance policy checks the same public records as abstractors do, to determine if it will risk insuring the title.

The most common title insurance policy requires the title insurance company to compensate the insured for financial loss up to the face amount of the policy resulting from a title defect (plus cost of litigation or challenge). The policy protects the insured only against title defects existing at the time of transfer of title. If a claim is filed and the title insurance company pays the claim, the company may have the right to bring legal action against the grantor for breach of warranties in the deed. The title insurance policy is issued only upon an acceptable abstract or a title opinion. A title that is acceptable to the title insurance company is called an *insurable title.* The premium for a title insurance policy is a one-time premium paid at the time the policy is placed in effect. At or before closing, the title company will require proof of identity for both seller and purchaser such as a driver's license or other official document.

PUTTING IT TO WORK

Now that you understand what constitutes a good title to property, respond to the following scenario.* Then compare your response to the model in the Answer Key at the end of the chapter.

My spouse and I have heard the term "incurable defect" associated with a home we're thinking of buying. Does this mean we should absolutely steer clear of that property?

Location of Closings

The closing most often is held at the office of the lender, the attorney for one of the parties, the title company, or at the local county clerk's office.

Structural Inspection

Usually the buyer wants to inspect the premises prior to closing. The inspection most commonly is performed by a professional inspection company. This is called a whole-house or structural inspection. The inspection report indicates any mechanical, electrical, plumbing, design, or construction defects. The buyer pays for this inspection.

Pest Inspection

Often the buyer or the buyer's lender requires proof that no wood-destroying pests, infestation, or damage exists. The cost of this inspection is typically paid by the purchaser. If infestation is present, the seller has to pay for treating and repairing any damage.

Perc, Soil, and Water-Flow Tests

If the property is connected to a private water supply (discussed in Chapter 11), the seller is required to provide the results of what is commonly called a perc test, an inspection

---

Source: James A. Ader, "Real Estate Spotlight." Copyright © The Albany *Times Union.* Reprinted by permission.

on percolation of the septic system to ensure proper functioning and drainage and to show compliance with local and state health codes. In addition, if the property is used for commercial purposes, the seller is responsible for a soil test to ensure the absence of hazardous waste or Environmental Protection Agency (EPA) violations. Water-flow tests may also be conducted if the property is not connected to a municipal system.

Role of Licensee Prior to Closing

A broker or salesperson's role prior to closing involves inspection of the property with the purchaser. In addition to the professional inspection, the buyer usually arranges for a final walk-through on the day of closing, or immediately prior to closing. This is to ensure that no damage has been done since the offer to purchase, and that no fixtures have been removed. These parties are usually accompanied by either the buyer agent (if there is one) or the seller agent.

Payment of Commission

At the closing, the broker commission is generally paid. Sometimes, all or part of the deposit money is credited toward the broker commission. The broker or agent handling the transaction generally furnishes a commission statement to the participating attorneys. See Figure 8.1. Generally, only one check is cut for the commission, and then the broker who receives the money puts it through his escrow account and disburses portions of the monies due to subagents and cooperating agents.

Homeowner's Insurance

Prior to closing, the buyer usually provides homeowner's fire and hazard insurance on the real estate being purchased. If the buyer is borrowing money for the purchase, the lender or mortgagee is listed on the policy as an additional insured. The cost of this insurance is the buyer's, and it must be purchased to protect the lender's interest.

Standardized Homeowner's Insurance Policies

Homeowner's policies exist and are identified HO-1 through HO-6. An HO-4 is a tenant's policy; an HO-6 is designed for condominiums and cooperatives. HO-1 through HO-3, and HO-5 cover owners of single-family dwellings.

Every hazard insurance policy must contain a description of the insured property. The street address usually is adequate, although some insurers require a full legal description.

Specific provisions contained in the six homeowner's policies are:

HO-1: "Named perils." Perils covered are damage or loss as a result of fire at the premises.

HO-2: "Broad form." Coverage extends to loss or damage as a result of fire, vandalism, malicious mischief, wind, hail, aircraft, riot, explosion, and smoke.

HO-3: A special "all-risk" policy. It covers loss for damage resulting from anything not specifically excluded from coverage.

HO-4: "Tenant's broad form." Its coverage is similar to HO-2's except it applies only to the tenant's contents at the premises.

HO-5: A different special "all-risk" policy. It offers automatic replacement cost for contents and dwelling.

HO-6: Similar to a tenant's broad form but applies to condominium owners and cooperative owners, covering their property's *contents.* (The actual structure would be insured by the association.)

The six HO forms are all package policies that include medical coverage and personal liability coverage for negligence.

Real Estate Settlement Procedures Act (RESPA)

Congress enacted the **Real Estate Settlement Procedures Act (RESPA)** in 1974 (revised 1996). The act applies only to residential federally financed or refinanced properties, not to commercial properties or owner financed loans. It *regulates lending activities of lending institutions in making mortgage loans for housing.* RESPA has the following purposes:

1. to effect specific changes in the settlement process resulting in more effective advance disclosure of settlement costs to home buyers and sellers
2. to protect borrowers from unnecessarily expensive settlement charges resulting from abusive practices
3. to ensure that borrowers are provided with sufficient information on a timely basis about the nature and cost of the settlement process
4. to eliminate referral fees or kickbacks, which increase the cost of settlement services; lenders are permitted to charge only for services actually provided to home buyers and sellers and in an amount equal to what the service actually costs the lender

RESPA Requirements

The act requires:

1. *Good faith estimate.* Within three working days of receiving a completed loan application, the lender is required to provide the borrower with a good faith estimate of the costs likely to be incurred at settlement. This application is shown in Figure 8.1.
2. *Buyer's guide to settlement costs.* At the time of loan application, the lender must provide the borrower with a booklet entitled *Homebuyer's Guide to Settlement Costs,* which contains the following information:
    a. clear and concise language describing and explaining the nature and purpose of each settlement cost
    b. an explanation and sample of the standard real estate settlement forms required by the act
    c. a description and explanation of the nature and purpose of escrow or impound accounts
    d. an explanation of choices available to borrowers in selecting persons or organizations to provide necessary settlement charges
    e. examples and explanations of unfair practices and unreasonable or unnecessary settlement charges to be avoided
3. *HUD Form No. 1.* In making residential mortgage loans, lenders are required to use a standard settlement form designed to itemize clearly all charges to be paid by borrower and by seller as part of the final settlement. The form (see Figure 8.2), which has become known as HUD Form No. 1, or the HUD 1, must be made available for the borrower's inspection at or before final settlement. This form is *not* required for assumptions and nonresidential loans.

    A federal rule affecting portions of RESPA allows brokers to assist home buyers in selecting and prequalifying for a mortgage and to charge a reasonable fee for those services. Any fees must be disclosed and agreed to in writing by the buyer. Brokers can even begin the loan application process. Brokers' services typically include the use of computerized loan origination (CLO) systems that list the various loan programs for lending institutions.

FIGURE 8.1 A broker commission agreement.

ABC Real Estate Brokerage
777 Easy Street • New York, New York 10007

Broker Commission Agreement

Address of Subject Property: ______________________________

This Agreement is entered into on ______________________, 20____ between ABC Real Estate Brokerage, and ______________________ Seller(s).

It is agreed by the parties herein that the, ______________________, selling broker and ______________________, listing broker obtained a ready, willing, and able individual (s) to purchase the above-named premises according to the terms of the listing agreement between the broker and seller(s) dated ______________________.

It is further agreed that the commission due to the broker(s) is __________ divided as follows:

listing broker $__________; selling broker $__________.

The commission is due to the broker from the proceeds of the sale or by certified check from the seller no later than the day of title closing and when the deed is delivered to the purchaser(s) pursuant to a contract of sale dated ______________________.

If the deed is not delivered pursuant to the said contract of sale, for any reason, except for the deliberate default of the seller, no commission is due to the broker(s). Any dispute arising from this Agreement shall be decided by arbitration according to rules set forth by the American Arbitration Association.

ABC Real Estate Brokerage

By: ______________________

Seller

____

____

Seller

This agreement is generally forwarded by the broker to the attorneys for the parties prior to closing.

FIGURE 8.2
HUD-1 Settlement Statement Costs form. More information about settlement costs can be found at the HUD website: *http://www.hud.gov.*

Homes & Communities
U.S. Department of Housing and Urban Development

Settlement Costs and Helpful Information

Buying Your Home

Settlement Costs and Helpful Information

June 1997 Disclaimer

HUD-1 Settlement Statement Costs

A. U.S. DEPARTMENT OF HOUSING AND URBAN DEVELOPMENT SETTLEMENT STATEMENT				
B. TYPE OF LOAN			6. File Number	7. Loan Number
	1. o FHA	2. o FmHA		
3. o CONV. UNINS.	4. o VA	5. o CONV. INS.	8. Mortgage Insurance Case Number	
C. NOTE: This form is furnished to give you a statement of actual settlement costs. Amounts paid to and by the settlement agent are shown. Items marked "(p.o.c.)" were paid outside the closing; they are shown here for informational purposes and are not included in the totals.				
D. NAME AND ADDRESS OF BORROWER:	E. NAME AND ADDRESS OF SELLER:		F. NAME AND ADDRESS OF LENDER:	
G. PROPERTY LOCATION:	H. SETTLEMENT AGENT: NAME, AND ADDRESS			
	PLACE OF SETTLEMENT:		I. SETTLEMENT DATE:	

J. SUMMARY OF BORROWER'S TRANSACTION		K. SUMMARY OF SELLER'S TRANSACTION	
100. **GROSS AMOUNT DUE FROM BORROWER:**		400. **GROSS AMOUNT DUE TO SELLER:**	
101. Contract sales price		401. Contract sales price	
102. Personal property		402. Personal property	
103. Settlement charges to borrower(line 1400)		403.	
104.		404.	
105.		405.	
Adjustments for items paid by seller in advance		*Adjustments for items paid by seller in advance*	
106. City/town taxes to		406. City/town taxes to	
107. County taxes to		407. County taxes to	
108. Assessments to		408. Assessments to	
109.		409.	
110.		410.	
111.		411.	
112.		412.	
120. **GROSS AMOUNT DUE FROM BORROWER**		420. **GROSS AMOUNT DUE TO SELLER**	
200. **AMOUNTS PAID BY OR IN BEHALF OF BORROWER:**		500. **REDUCTIONS IN AMOUNT DUE TO SELLER:**	
201. Deposit of earnest money		501. Excess deposit (see instructions)	
202. Principal amount of new loan(s)		502. Settlement charges to seller (line 1400)	
203. Existing loan(s) taken subject to		503. Existing loan(s) taken subject to	
204.		504. Payoff of first mortgage loan	
205.		505. Payoff of second mortgage loan	
206.		506.	
207.		507.	
208.		508.	
209.		509.	
Adjustments for items unpaid by seller		*Adjustments for items unpaid by seller*	
210. City/town taxes to		510. City/town taxes to	
211. County taxes to		511. County taxes to	
212. Assessments to		512. Assessments to	
213.		513.	
214.		514.	
215.		515.	
216.		516.	
217.		517.	
218.		518.	
219.		519.	
220. **TOTAL PAID BY/FOR BORROWER**		520. **TOTAL REDUCTION AMOUNT DUE SELLER**	
300. **CASH AT SETTLEMENT FROM/TO BORROWER**		600. **CASH AT SETTLEMENT TO/FROM SELLER**	
301. Gross amount due from borrower(line 120)		601. Gross amount due to seller (line 420)	
302. Less amounts paid by/for borrower(line 220)		602. Less reductions in amount due seller (line 520)	
303. **CASH (_ FROM) (_ TO) BORROWER**		603. **CASH (o TO) (o FROM) SELLER**	

(continued)

FIGURE 8.2
Continued.

L. SETTLEMENT CHARGES		
700. **TOTAL SALES/BROKER'S COMMISSION based on price $ @ %=**	PAID FROM BORROWER'S FUNDS AT SETTLEMENT	PAID FROM SELLER'S FUNDS AT SETTLEMENT
Division of Commission (line 700) as follows:		
701. $ to		
702. $ to		
703. Commission paid at Settlement		
704.		
800. **ITEMS PAYABLE IN CONNECTION WITH LOAN**		
801. Loan Origination Fee %		
802. Loan Discount %		
803. Appraisal Fee to		
804. Credit Report to		
805. Lender's Inspection Fee		
806. Mortgage Insurance Application Fee to		
807. Assumption Fee		
808.		
809.		
810.		
811.		
900. **ITEMS REQUIRED BY LENDER TO BE PAID IN ADVANCE**		
901. Interest from to @$ /day		
902. Mortgage Insurance Premium for months to		
903. Hazard Insurance Premium for years to		
904. years to		
905.		
1000. **RESERVES DEPOSITED WITH LENDER**		
1001. Hazard Insurance months @ $ per month		
1002. Mortgage insurance months @ $ per month		
1003. City property taxes months @ $ per month		
1004. County property taxes months @ $ per month		
1005. Annual assessments months @ $ per month		
1006. months @ $ per month		
1007. months @ $ per month		
1008. Aggregate Adjustment months @ $ per month		
1100. **TITLE CHARGES**		
1101. Settlement or closing fee to		
1102. Abstract or title search to		
1103. Title examination to		
1104. Title insurance binder to		
1105. Document preparation to		
1106. Notary fees to		
1107. Attorney's fees to		
(includes above items numbers;)		
1108. Title Insurance to		
(includes above items numbers;)		
1109. Lender's coverage $		
1110. Owner's coverage $		
1111.		
1112.		
1113.		
1200. **GOVERNMENT RECORDING AND TRANSFER CHARGES**		
1201. Recording fees: Deed $; Mortgage $; Releases $		
1202. City/county tax/stamps: Deed $; Mortgage $		
1203. State tax/stamps: Deed $; Mortgage $		
1204.		
1205.		
1300. **ADDITIONAL SETTLEMENT CHARGES**		
1301. Survey to		
1302. Pest inspection to		
1303.		
1304.		
1305.		
1400. **TOTAL SETTLEMENT CHARGES** *(enter on lines 103, Section J and 502, Section K)*		

U.S. Department of Housing and Urban Development
451 7th Street, S.W., Washington, DC 20410
Telephone: (202) 708-1112 TTY: (202) 708-1455

Source: U.S. Department of Housing and Urban Development.

The difference between the Real Estate Settlement Procedures Act (RESPA) and the Truth-in-Lending Act (TILA)

You Should Know

	RESPA	TILA
When enacted	1974 (revised 1996)	1969 (revised 1980)
Purpose	Act covers residential federally financed properties and focuses mainly on the *settlement* process (loan and closing fees) of lending institutions in making mortgage loans	Requires *disclosure* by lenders of annual percentage rate, finance charges, amount financed, and total monies to be paid toward mortgage; implemented through Regulation Z, which covers all residential mortgages.
Importance to real estate practitioners	RESPA allows real estate agents to assist home buyers in selecting and prequalifying for a mortgage	Regulation Z addresses advertisement of credit terms which may not be violated by real estate agents
How to remember the difference	RESPA deals mainly with the cost of the mortgage and calls for a closing statement, HUD Form No. 1, to be made available to purchasers prior to closing	TILA deals mainly with obtaining the mortgage and disclosure of the terms of the loan.

*TILA is discussed more fully in Chapter 9.

Closing Statement

A **closing statement** is a historical document prepared in advance. The statement is prepared before the closing, but it records what must happen at closing. The statement *sets forth the distribution of monies involved in the transaction*—who is to pay a specific amount for each expense and who is to receive that amount. A closing statement is prepared by the buyer's and seller's representatives. They could be an attorney, a broker, a lender, someone working for a title company, or an escrow agent.

CLOSING COSTS AND ADJUSTMENTS—PREPARATION OF CLOSING STATEMENTS

The first step in preparing the closing statement is to list all items in the transaction. Some of these items involve both the buyer and the seller; other items are of concern only to the buyer and others are of concern only to the seller. Items included fall into one of two categories: debits or credits. *Items that are owed* are **debits.** Those to be paid by the buyer are called buyer debits, and those owed and to be paid by the seller are seller debits. *Monies received* are **credits.** Items representing money to be received by the buyer are called buyer credits. Items representing money to be received by the seller are called seller credits.

In the RESPA settlement statement form shown in Figure 8.2, the areas for debits and credits are marked. Although real estate agents typically do not have to complete that form, they should be sufficiently familiar with the format to explain the entries to buyers and sellers. Typical debits and credits of buyer and seller are illustrated in Table 8.2.

TABLE 8.2 Typical buyer and seller debits and credits.

BUYER DEBITS	SELLER DEBITS
Appraisal fee	Attorney fee
Bank attorney and personal attorney fees	Balance due to seller at closing (this is a balancing entry only, as seller receives this money)
Broker's fee if a buyer broker agreement exists and the buyer is paying the commission	Broker's fee
Credit report	Contract for deed balance
Discount points	Deed preparation
Hazard or homeowner's insurance	Delinquent real property taxes
Loan origination fee	Existing mortgage and accrued interest
Mortgage assumption fee	Mortgage interest on assumed loan
Mortgagee's title insurance	Mortgage satisfaction fee
Mortgage insurance	Pest inspection
Overpaid (by seller) taxes	Purchase money mortgage taken back from buyer
Prepaid mortgage interest	Soil test (perc test)
Preparation of loan documents (mortgage and note)	Survey (some counties)
Purchase price	Termite inspection and treatment
Real estate property taxes paid in advance by seller	Transfer tax on transfer of real estate
Recording of deed	Unpaid real property taxes prorated
Recording of mortgage documents	Unpaid utility bills
Survey	

BUYER CREDITS	SELLER CREDITS
Assumed mortgage and accrued interest on mortgage	Escrow balance on assumed loan
Balance due from buyer at closing (this is a balancing entry only, as buyer owes this money)	Overpaid insurance premium
Contract for deed balance	Overpaid real property taxes
Earnest money deposit	Purchase price
New mortgage money	Sale of personal property
Purchase money mortgage	
Unpaid real property taxes prorated	

Handling Closing Funds

At the closing, the monies the buyer owes are received by the closing agent. The monies owed to the seller are disbursed by the closing agent. All other expenses of the sale are paid from the closing proceeds and disbursed by the closing agent. The closing agent basically begins with an empty account, receives money, disburses money, and ends with an empty account.

The money available for disbursement must equal the amount to be disbursed. The closing agent should perform a **reconciliation,** *a check of the money available and money owed prior to closing.*

Seller Closing Costs

Title Transfer Taxes (Revenue Stamps)

New York imposes a *tax on the conveyance of title to real property* and uses the term *real property transfer tax.* New York requires the seller to pay this tax. The amount of tax is based on the consideration the seller receives in selling the property.

The amount of transfer tax charged on the purchase price in New York is $4 per $1,000 of the purchase price. New York subtracts the amount of any mortgage being assumed, or "old money," and therefore charges the tax only on the "new money" brought into the transaction, above the amount of the assumed loan. In New York, an examination of tax stamps provides only an indication of the new money, which is below the sales price if a mortgage is assumed. The real estate licensee needs to learn the rate and application of this tax as well as the collection procedures.

New York City real property transfer tax. In addition to the New York State transfer tax, for the sale of residential property, New York City imposes an additional transfer tax of 1% of the selling price. If the selling price is over $500,000, the New York City transfer tax is 1.425%. For other types of property, the rate is 1.425% of the selling price, and if the consideration is more than $500,000, the transfer tax is 2.625%.

Broker Commission

In most transfers, the broker commission is a percentage of the selling price of the property. Even if a buyer's broker has been involved, she is paid a percentage of the selling broker's commission through a cooperative arrangement. The commission, therefore, is generally the responsibility of the seller. Other commission or fee arrangements are possible. (See Chapter 2.)

Attorney Fees

Sellers generally have an attorney represent their interests in the closing and must pay his fee. Attorney fees vary depending on the amount of work involved. If the buyers are giving the sellers a purchase money mortgage, the buyer generally pays the seller's attorney for its preparation.

Recording Documents to Clear Title

Depending on what is required for a particular property, the seller may have to file through her attorney a satisfaction of mortgage and/or satisfaction of other judgments. In New York, these documents are usually recorded in the office of the county clerk, and the fees for recordation vary according to county. In New York City, these documents are generally recorded in the Register's Office.

Satisfy Existing Liens

A property cannot usually transfer unless all existing liens against it have been discharged (paid). The cost of discharging the liens depends on the dollar amount of the lien. For example, if a roofer has not been paid for a $2,000 roof job and has filed a mechanics' lien, then this money plus interest must be paid before the title is transferred.

Co-op and Condo Fees

Cooperatives may have a *flip tax* imposed upon transfer. This tax, paid by the seller, is the amount assessed on the transfer of the property and is sometimes based on a fixed percentage of the purchase price of the apartment. The flip tax may be 1%–5% of the purchase price. It is not paid to any government agency, but to the cooperative corporation. According to regulations set forth in the Uniform Commercial Code, the buyer of a cooperative must also pay a $25 UCC-1 filing fee and the seller must pay a $25 UCC-3 filing fee.

Condominiums charge *special fees* called **assessments** *payable to the homeowner's or condominium association for maintenance of the common elements.* These items may include, but are not limited to, trash pickup, landscaping, and snow removal. Any outstanding seller obligations must be brought up to date by the seller and adjustments by both purchaser and seller must be made for services already paid for by the seller but to be used by the purchaser.

Purchaser Closing Costs

If the buyer is borrowing money from an institutional lender, he also needs a mortgagee's title insurance policy. The buyer usually bears the cost of this title insurance policy. Evidence of marketable title should be provided for transfer. Proof that a marketable title exists can be provided by the update of an abstract of title or by issuance of a title insurance binder. In New York, depending on the county, the buyer or seller may have to pay for the title search. As mentioned earlier, the buyer pays for the structural inspection.

Appraisal and Credit Report Fees

The purchaser is generally charged by the lender for both the appraisal of the property and the credit investigation. This is part of the application process.

Mortgage Recording Tax

In New York, the mortgage recording tax is three-quarters of a percent of the mortgage amount in certain counties. In counties where there is a public transportation system, the amount is 1 percent. In this case, in the sale of one- to six-family residential properties, three-quarters of the mortgage recording tax typically is paid by the purchaser and one-quarter is paid by the lender. If there is no outside lender involved in the transaction, then the purchaser must pay the entire mortgage recording tax.

Attorney Fees

The purchasers are responsible for the payment of the lender's attorney as well as the fees for their own attorney.

Lender Fees

Lender costs and fees may include any or all of the following:

- an escrow account for property taxes (in certain cases, interest must be paid on escrow accounts)
- discount points on a mortgage if applicable (these are negotiable between seller and buyer at contract)
- a credit check of the prospective purchaser, usually paid before closing (this may be paid for by the purchaser)
- loan origination fees (these are charged by the lender and usually paid for by the buyer)
- a survey of the property (this is negotiable between seller and buyer)

Other Recording Fees

The New York State Office of Real Property Services requires the recordation of a sworn statement of consideration paid, signed by both buyer and seller, called a real property transfer report. The form is filed with the county clerk and costs $25 to file. A copy of this form is forwarded by the county to the town, city, or village assessors. The filing fee is typically paid by the buyer.

Also required on file by the New York State Department of Taxation and Finance is a transfer gains tax affidavit, signed and sworn to by the buyer and seller. This form indicates the purchase price of the property. A *capital gain* is the amount of profit realized by the seller. The form is filed with the county clerk with a $5 fee typically paid by the seller.

ADJUSTMENTS—PRORATIONS AT CLOSING

The obligation for paying various costs is determined by local custom, New York law, and the type of financing incurred, if any.

Items Adjusted and Prorated

A closing usually involves **proration,** the *division of expenses and income between buyer and seller.* The items that are usually adjusted and divided include real estate taxes, fuel, survey, water and sewer charges, rent, security deposits, interest, homeowner's association dues, and insurance (in many cases, purchasers wish to buy their own insurance).

Proration is necessary to ensure fair apportioning of expenses between buyer and seller. Prorated items are either accrued or prepaid.

Accrued expenses are costs the seller owes at the day of closing but that the buyer will eventually pay. The seller therefore gives the buyer a credit for these items at closing. Typical accrued items to be prorated are unpaid real estate taxes, rent collected by the seller from the tenant, and interest on a seller's mortgage assumed by the buyer.

Prepaid expenses are costs the seller pays in advance and are not fully used up. At closing, these items are shown as a credit to the seller and a debit to the buyer. Typical prepaid items to be prorated are prepaid taxes and insurance premiums, rent paid by the seller under lease assigned to the buyer, utilities billed and paid in advance, and heating oil in the tank.

Arithmetic of Proration—Rules and Methods

1. Either the buyer or the seller may pay the costs on the day of closing. For purposes of the calculations in this book, the seller will pay the costs on the day of closing. Local practices in certain areas of New York provide that beginning with the day of closing all expenses are borne by the purchaser, and all income goes to the purchaser.
2. Mortgage interest, taxes, insurance, and similar expenses usually are prorated on the basis of 360 days per year (30 days per month). However, lenders, attorneys, and closing agents also may base the prorations on a 365-day year, using the exact amount of days in each month. Mortgage interest generally is paid in arrears, so the parties must understand that the mortgage payment for August will include interest not for August but for July. In many areas, taxes are paid in advance. This means the seller will receive reimbursement at closing for the remaining days of the tax year following closing.
3. Accrued real estate taxes that are assessed but not yet due are normally prorated to the day of closing, with the seller assuming a debit and the buyer a credit for the amount owed as of the day of closing.
4. In prorating rent, the seller typically receives the rent for the day of closing.
5. Personal property taxes may be prorated between buyer and seller, or they may be paid entirely by the seller. In the calculations used here, personal property taxes are not prorated.
6. Basically, the computation involves determining a yearly, monthly, or daily charge for the item being prorated. This charge then is multiplied by the number of months or days of the year for which reimbursement or payment is to be made.

PUTTING IT TO WORK

Read through the two exercises in Figure 8.3 and track how the prorated costs were determined. For a further explanation of, and practice with, proration computations, see Chapter 16.

FIGURE 8.3
Exercises for determining prorated costs.

EXERCISE 1

Accrued Items: The closing of a property is to be held on October 14. The real estate taxes of $895 for the year have not been paid and are due at the end of the year. What entry will appear on the seller's and buyer's closing statements?

January 1 —— October 14 / —— December 31

Accrued period of taxes owed by seller at closing:

895 ÷ 12 = $74.58 taxes per month
74.58 ÷ 30 = $2.49 taxes per day

74.58	plus	2.49		
× 9 full months		× 14 days		
$671.22	plus	$34.86	=	$706.08

Thus, the accrued taxes owed by seller at closing are $706.08. This will be a seller debit and a buyer credit at closing.

EXERCISE 2

Prepaid Items: The closing of a sale of a rental is to be held March 10. The seller has received the rent for March in the amount of $500. What entry will appear on the seller's and buyer's closing statements?

March 1 —— March 10 / —— March 30

500 ÷ 30 = $16.67 rent per day
16.67
× 20 days not used
$333.40 unused rent

Prepaid period not earned by seller prior to closing and assigned to buyer at closing.

Thus, the prepaid rent credited to the buyer at closing is $333.40. This will be a seller debit and a buyer credit at closing.

IMPORTANT POINTS

1. At a title closing, all interested parties meet to review closing documents and transfer title to real estate. The deed is the document that conveys the title from seller to purchaser (grantor to grantee).
2. Recordation of a deed provides protection for the owner's title against subsequent claimants. Deeds and other closing documents are recorded in the county clerk's office of the county where the property is situated, and in New York City, the Registrar's Office.

3. The purpose of a title examination is to determine a title's quality. The examination must be made by an attorney or a title company. Only an attorney can legally give an opinion about the title's quality.
4. A title insurance policy protects the insured against financial loss caused by a title defect.
5. Various types of tests and inspections of the property take place prior to closing. A real estate agent may take a prospective purchaser to a "walk through" of the property immediately prior to closing.
6. The Real Estate Settlement Procedures Act (RESPA) regulates lending activities of lending institutions that take mortgages for housing.
7. The closing statements set forth the distribution of monies involved in the transaction. Seller closing costs may include New York title transfer taxes, broker commission, attorney fees, costs of document preparation and the satisfaction of existing liens, if any. Purchaser costs may include a title search and title policy, survey fees, the mortgage recording tax, lender fees, recording fees, and, if relevant, the broker commission.
8. The basic difference between the purchase of a cooperative and a condominium and other types of property is that a cooperative purchase involves the purchase of shares in the cooperative corporation. The purchase of a cooperative gives the buyer a proprietary lease for the apartment purchased. In a condominium purchase, the buyer is conveyed title through a deed. In a cooperative purchase, the buyer receives shares of stock.
9. Prorations are the division of expenses and income between the purchaser and seller at closing.

CHAPTER REVIEW

KEY TERM REVIEW

Fill in the term that best completes each sentence and then check the Answer Key at the end of the chapter.

1. A meeting where interested parties assemble to transfer title to real estate is a(n) ______________________.
2. A blueprint that illustrates the measurements and boundaries of a property is a(n) ______________________.
3. Recordation of a deed provides ______________________ that a particular party has title to a property.
4. The title to a property is searched to check that there are no breaks in the ______________________ so that the property is marketable.
5. A condensed history of the title setting forth all public records that affect the title is called a(n) ______________________.
6. A document that is prepared in advance setting forth the distribution of monies at the time of title transfer is a(n) ______________________.
7. At a closing, monies owed by a buyer or seller are called ______________________; monies that are to be received or have been received by a buyer or seller are called ______________________.
8. The mathematical apportionment of expenses between a buyer and a seller at the closing are called ______________________.

MULTIPLE CHOICE

Circle the letter that best answers the question and then check the Answer Key at the end of the chapter.

1. A basic difference between the purchase of a condominium and a cooperative is:
   A. a cooperative is always an apartment in a building and a condominium never is
   B. a cooperative involves the transfer of shares of stock in a corporation and a condominium purchaser receives a deed
   C. attorneys must be present at cooperative closings, but not at condominium closings
   D. a board of directors must consent to the purchase of a condominium, but not a cooperative

2. A title insurance policy protects the:
   A. broker
   B. owner
   C. seller
   D. grantor

3. The successive conveyances of a title are called:
   A. releases
   B. remises
   C. chain of title
   D. warranty of title

4. Title to real estate is transferred upon:
   A. execution and delivery of a deed
   B. title search
   C. filing of a transfer tax affidavit
   D. payment of the real estate commission

5. Under RESPA requirements, which of the following is NOT required by lenders?
   A. buyer's guide to settlement costs
   B. good faith estimate
   C. standard settlement form
   D. three day right of rescission

6. The amount of the earnest money deposit appears as a:
   A. seller debit
   B. seller credit
   C. buyer debit
   D. buyer credit

7. If a lot was listed for sale at $30,000 and sold for $28,500, the 6 percent broker's fee would appear in the seller's statement as a:
   A. debit of $1,800
   B. credit of $1,800
   C. debit of $1,710
   D. credit of $1,710

8. If the closing date is June 30 and the seller's real property taxes of $664 for the calendar year are unpaid, the appropriate entry on the buyer's statement would be a:
   A. credit of $332
   B. debit of $664
   C. debit of $332
   D. credit of $664

9. Recording a deed protects the:
   A. grantor
   B. grantee
   C. vendor
   D. seller

10. The broker commission is usually paid:
    A. prior to closing
    B. at least two weeks after closing to ensure that the deed has been recorded
    C. at the closing
    D. by the seller as soon as there is a meeting of the minds

ANSWER KEY

Putting It To Work

Contrary to its name, "incurable defect" does not mean that the house is not a good home or a good buy. It simply indicates that there is some defect that cannot be corrected. Facing a noisy railroad track or being located on a busy highway are examples. Another example might be a property with a utility easement running through it, or a property that is landlocked, with its entrance through an easement on someone else's property. If the property and the neighborhood are otherwise satisfactory, such properties can sometimes be attractive purchases on favorable terms. Many people learn to live with the incurable defect. Don't avoid consideration of such properties until you've investigated them carefully.*

Key Term Review

1. title closing
2. survey
3. constructive notice
4. chain of title
5. abstract of title
6. closing statement
7. debits; credits
8. prorations

Multiple Choice

1. B
2. B
3. C
4. A
5. D
6. D
7. C
8. A
9. B
10. C

*Source: James A. Ader, "Real Estate Spotlight." Copyright © The Albany *Times Union.* Reprinted by permission.

Chapter 9

KEY TERMS

acceleration clause
adjustable rate mortgage (ARM)
alienation (due on sale) clause
amortization
assignment
buydown
default
discount points
grace period
inflation
loan-to-value ratio
margin
mortgage
mortgagee
mortgagor
negative amortization
payment cap
prepayment penalty clause
promissory note
rate cap
release clause
satisfaction of mortgage
usury laws

LEARNING OBJECTIVES

Classroom hours: 5

1. Discuss the simple definition of a mortgage.
2. Identify and distinguish between the types of mortgages.
3. List the basic types of loans available and the payment options for each.
4. Identify the lender's basic criteria for granting loans.
5. Explain how the borrower must have the ability to repay loans.
6. Discuss the common terms relating to real estate financing.
7. Explain the broker responsibilities in truth in lending.
8. Describe the influence of the secondary market on mortgage lending.

Real Estate Finance (Mortgages)

IN THIS CHAPTER To help buyers choose the most advantageous method of financing, today's real estate practitioner must have a thorough understanding of finance. Knowledge of mortgages, down payments, and methods of structuring the best possible deal is essential. Topics include financing principles, including types of mortgages, payment options, and lender criteria for granting a loan. This chapter is divided into two sections: Section I—Mortgage Basics and Section II—The Loan Process.

SECTION 1 MORTGAGE BASICS

MORTGAGES

A **mortgage** is *a loan that constitutes a lien against the real property.* The mortgage is a two-party instrument between the lender and borrower. The mortgage *pledges a described property as security for the repayment of a loan under certain terms and conditions.* The *borrower who gives the mortgage* is called the **mortgagor.** The *lender who receives the mortgage* is known as the **mortgagee** (see Figure 9.1). The borrower (mortgagor) retains title (ownership) to the property, but this title is encumbered by the lien created by the mortgage in favor of the lender (mortgagee). If the lender is not paid according to terms of the mortgage and note, the lender can foreclose the lien.

The borrower's personal promise to pay the debt is often not enough security for the large amount of money involved in a mortgage loan. The lender therefore requires the additional security of the property itself as collateral for the loan. *Pledging property as security for the loan* (hypothecating) is accomplished through the mortgage. Therefore, every mortgage loan has two instruments: (a) the note (a personal IOU), and (b) the mortgage. Pledging the property does not require the borrower to give up possession except in case of **default,** or *failure to perform an obligation.*

Mortgage Clauses and Covenants

Examples of the various clauses and covenants (see Figure 9.2) that may be included in a mortgage are as follows:

1. The mortgage is dated and contains the names of mortgagor and mortgagee.

FIGURE 9.1 An illustration of a mortgage transaction.

MORTGAGOR
The *borrower gives* a mortgage to the lender.

MORTGAGEE
The *lender receives* a mortgage from the borrower.

The borrower (mortgagor) must give the lender (mortgagee) a mortgage lien and a promissory note or bond in return for the borrowed funds.

2. The note or bond executed by the borrower is reproduced in the mortgage. The note includes an **acceleration clause** *enabling the lender to declare the entire balance remaining immediately due and payable if the borrower is in default.*
3. The note may provide a **prepayment penalty clause** stating either that *the borrower is permitted to pay off the loan at any time prior to expiration of the full mortgage term without incurring a financial penalty for the early payoff,* or that a prepayment penalty *will be imposed on the borrower if the debt is satisfied prior to expiration of the full term.* Most loans, however, including FHA, VA, and conforming loans (discussed later in this chapter) cannot have a prepayment penalty, so this clause is more often found in owner financing or commercial loans. How-

FIGURE 9.2 A summary of note and mortgage clauses.

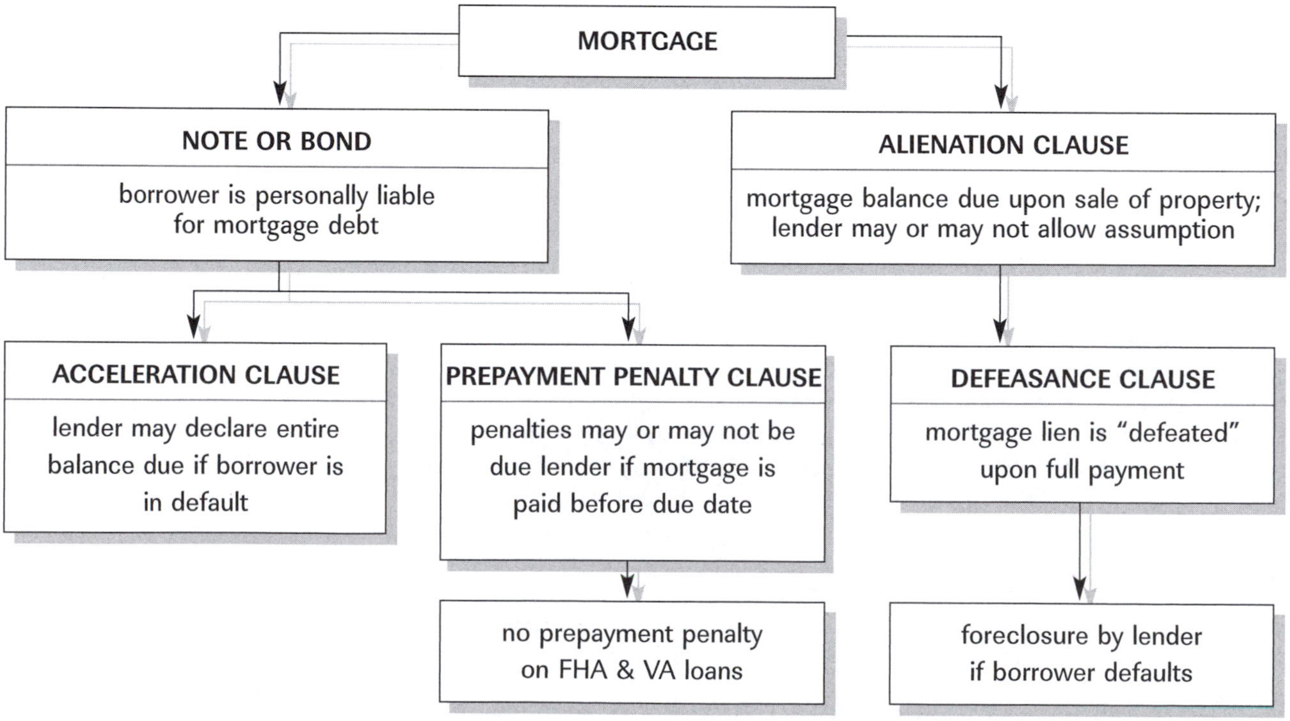

ever, residential mortgages given to institutional lenders may provide for a prepayment penalty if the mortgage is paid within the first year.

4. The mortgage contains a defeasance clause *giving the borrower the right to defeat and remove the lien by paying the indebtedness in full.*
5. The mortgage provides the right of foreclosure to the lender if the borrower fails to make payments as scheduled or fails to fulfill other obligations as set forth in the mortgage.
6. In the mortgage, a covenant always specifies that the mortgagor has a good and marketable title to the property pledged to secure payment of the note.
7. The mortgage may contain an **alienation clause** (due-on-sale clause) entitling *the lender to declare the principal balance immediately due and payable if the borrower sells the property during the mortgage term and makes the mortgage unassumable* without the lender's permission. Permission to assume the mortgage at an interest rate prevailing at the time of assumption can be given at the discretion of the lender. The alienation clause may provide for release of the original borrower from liability if an assumption is permitted. This release is sometimes referred to as a *novation.*
8. The mortgage always provides for execution by the borrower.
9. The mortgage provides for acknowledgment by the borrower to make the document eligible for recording on the public record for the lender's protection.

Note or Bond

In making a mortgage loan, the lender requires the borrower to sign a **promissory note,** or bond. The *note, that must be in writing, provides evidence that a valid debt exists.* The note contains a promise that the borrower will be personally liable for paying the amount of money set forth in the note and specifies the manner in which the debt is to be paid. Payment is typically in monthly installments of a stated amount, commencing on a certain date. The note also states the annual rate of interest to be charged on the outstanding principal balance. The note and mortgage are generally part of the same document. Figure 9.3 shows a bond and mortgage.

PUTTING IT TO WORK

Your buyers will have to deal with a number of documents that are new to them. Respond to the following scenario,* then compare your response to the model in the Answer Key at the end of the chapter.

I want a mortgage, not a bond. How should I clarify the difference between a bond and a mortgage?

Principal, Interest, and Payment Plans

Interest is the money paid for using someone else's money. The mortgage principal is the amount of money borrowed on which interest is either *paid* or *received.* In the case of an interest-bearing note, principal is the amount of money the lender has lent the borrower and on which the borrower will pay interest to the lender.

The note can be an interest-only note on which interest is paid periodically until the note matures and the entire principal balance is paid at maturity. (Most construction notes are interest-only notes.) The note also can be a single-payment loan that requires no payments on either principal or interest until the note matures, and the

*Source: James A. Ader, "Real Estate Spotlight." Copyright © The Albany *Times Union.* Reprinted by permission.

FIGURE 9.3
A bond and mortgage.

FORM 547X N. Y. BOND AND MORTGAGE, FULL COVENANT AND LIEN

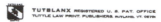

TUTBLANX REGISTERED U. S. PAT. OFFICE
TUTTLE LAW PRINT, PUBLISHERS, RUTLAND, VT. 05701

This Bond and Mortgage,

Made the day of

Nineteen Hundred and

Between

the mortgagor , and

the mortgagee

Witnesseth. *That the mortgagor , do hereby acknowledge to be indebted to the mortgagee in the sum of Dollars, ($) lawful money of the United States, which the mortgagor do hereby agree and bind to pay to the mortgagee*

to secure the payment of which the mortgagor hereby mortgage to the mortgagee

AND the mortgagor

covenant with the mortgagee as follows:

1. That the mortgagor will pay the indebtedness as hereinbefore provided.
2. That the mortgagor will keep the buildings on the premises insured against loss by fire for the benefit of the mortgagee ; that will assign and deliver the policies to the mortgagee ; and that will reimburse the mortgagee for any premiums paid for insurance made by the mortgagee on the mortgagor default in so insuring the buildings or in so assigning and delivering the policies.

3. That no building on the premises shall be removed or demolished without the consent of the mortgagee

4. That the whole of said principal sum and interest shall become due at the option of the mortgagee : after default in the payment of any installment of principal or of interest for days; or after default in the payment of any tax, water rate or assessment for days after notice and demand; or after default after notice and demand either in assigning and delivering the policies insuring the buildings against loss by fire or in reimbursing the mortgagee for premiums paid on such insurance, as hereinbefore provided; or after default upon request in furnishing a statement of the amount due on the bond and mortgage and whether any offsets or defenses exist against the mortgage debt, as hereinafter provided.
5. That the holder of this bond and mortgage, in any action to foreclose the mortgage, shall be entitled to the appointment of a receiver.

6. That the Mortgagor will pay all insurance premiums, taxes, assessments or water rates, and in default thereof, the legal holder of this mortgage shall have the right to cause such property to be so insured in the owner's name, and to pay such taxes and assessments, adding the proper expense thereof to the principal sum secured under this mortgage.

7. That the mortgagor within days upon request in person or within days upon request by mail will furnish a written statement duly acknowledged of the amount due on this bond and mortgage and whether any offsets or defenses exist against the mortgage debt.
8. That notice and demand or request may be in writing and may be served in person or by mail.
9. That the mortgagor warrant the title to the premises.
10. That, in Compliance with section 13 of the Lien Law, the mortgagor will receive the advances secured by this mortgage and will hold the right to receive such advances as a trust fund to be applied first for the purpose of paying the cost of improvement, and that the mortgagor will apply the same first to the payment of the cost of improvement before using any part of the total of the same for any other purpose.

Source: Reprinted with permission of Tuttle Law Print, Inc., Rutland, VT 05701.

entire principal and interest is paid at maturity. This occurs more frequently in short-term notes. The note also can be an amortized note in which periodic payments are made on both principal and interest until such time as the principal is completely paid. Most mortgage loans are of this type. The original principal is the total amount of the note. This amount remains the same in an interest-only or a one-payment loan until the entire principal is paid.

Mortgage loan interest almost always is calculated in arrears, although it sometimes is calculated in advance. If interest is calculated in arrears, a monthly payment due June 1, for example, includes interest for use of the money during May, the previous month. If interest is calculated in advance, a monthly payment due on June 1 includes interest for use of the money in June. When paying off or assuming a loan, one must know if the interest is paid in advance or in arrears in order to determine the amount of interest owed or to be prorated at closing. Interest must be paid in arrears on all loans sold in the secondary mortgage market.

A mortgage may provide for a **grace period** *that allows a specified time frame in which the payment may be made.* For example, a mortgage may allow a payment due on the first of the month to be paid up until the 15th day of the month without the borrower being in default. This mortgage payment, therefore, has a 15-day grace period. However, it is important to note that although there may be provisions for a grace period, the payment is still due on the first of the month. Some lenders regard use of grace periods as payments in default, and continual use could affect the mortgagor's credit standing in the future.

Tax deductible expenses involved in home ownership are *mortgage interest* (not principal) and *ad valorem real property taxes* paid to local taxing authorities.

Deed of Trust

A type of financing used in other states, and not generally in New York, requires the mortgagor (borrower) to convey title to the property to a trustee, a type of third-party referee, through a deed of trust. When the mortgagor completes paying off the debt, the trustee is required to return title to the trustor, the borrower, by executing a deed of release. If the borrower defaults in her obligation to pay back the funds, the lender (mortgagee) may instruct the trustee to sell the title to recover the lender's funds. Because the lender therefore benefits from the trust title, the lender is also known as the beneficiary.

FORECLOSURE

If the borrower (mortgagor) does not make the payments as required, he is in default on the loan. The lender's ultimate power is to foreclose. *Foreclosure* is the process leading to the sale of real property pledged to secure the mortgage debt.

Foreclosure by action in equity and sale is the standard type of foreclosure in New York in which the owner of the property is the mortgagor. A lawsuit is brought against the mortgagor by the lender, the property is sold at auction, and the proceeds are distributed among parties who have mortgages or other types of liens against the property.

Equity of Redemption

After default, and up to the time a foreclosure sale is held, the borrower has an equitable right to redeem his property by paying the principal amount of the debt, accrued interest, and lender costs incurred in initiating the foreclosure. The borrower's *equity of redemption* cannot be defeated by a mortgage clause. This right is terminated by the foreclosure sale.

Deed in Lieu of Foreclosure

In a measure sometimes called a friendly foreclosure but more formally a deed in lieu of foreclosure, a borrower in default simply *conveys the title to the property to the lender,* to avoid record of foreclosure. The disadvantage is that it does not eliminate other liens against the property. Furthermore, the lender may lose the right to claim against mortgage insurance or guarantee programs such as FHA or VA.

Deficiency Judgment

The borrower in a mortgage loan is personally liable for payment of the note. Therefore, if the proceeds of a foreclosure sale are not sufficient to satisfy the balance due the lender, the lender can sue for a deficiency judgment on the note. A *deficiency judgment* is a court order stating that the borrower still owes the lender money.

In New York, a lender can obtain a deficiency judgment only if the fair market value of the property at the time of the foreclosure auction is less than the amount due the bank. For example, if the fair market value is $100,000 and the amount due the lender is $110,000, the lender can obtain a deficiency judgment. Conversely, if the highest bid at the auction is only $75,000 and the fair market value is $100,000 and the bank is owed $96,000, the lender is not entitled to a deficiency judgment on the property.

DUTIES AND RIGHTS OF BORROWER (MORTGAGOR)

In addition to paying the debt insured by the mortgage, the mortgage requires the borrower to pay all real property taxes and assessments on a timely basis, keep the buildings in a proper state of repair, and protect against loss by fire or other casualty by an insurance policy written in an amount at least 80 percent of the value of the structure. Many lenders also require insurance for 100 percent of the loan value minus the lot value.

Rights of the borrower include: (a) the borrower has the right to possession of the property during the mortgage term as long as the borrower is not in default, and (b) the defeasance clause gives the borrower the right to redeem the title and have the mortgage lien released at any time prior to default by paying the debt in full.

RIGHTS OF LENDER

1. The lender has the right to take possession of the property (after foreclosure) if the borrower defaults in mortgage payments and the lender is the purchaser at the sale.
2. The lender has the right to foreclose on the property if the borrower defaults in the payments.
3. The lender has the right to assign the mortgage. This enables the lender to sell the mortgage and thereby free up the money invested. The right of **assignment** provides liquidity to mortgages because *the lender can sell the mortgage at any time and obtain the money invested rather than wait for payment* of the loan over an extended time.

SALE OF MORTGAGED PROPERTY

Sale Free and Clear (Cash Sale)

Although cash sales are the exception in real estate, they are perhaps the simplest real estate transaction to process. The seller provides a deed and the buyer provides the cash. Unfortunately, cash transactions may cause an inexperienced real estate agent to make costly mistakes. No lender is involved in the transaction to demand an appraisal, a survey, a wood-destroying insect inspection, a structural inspection, deed recordation, payment of taxes or transfer fee, title search, and so on.

Sale "Subject To" a Mortgage

If property is sold and title is conveyed subject to the lien of an existing mortgage (but that lien is not actually assumed), the lender can still foreclose against the property in the event of a default in mortgage payments. In taking title subject to a mortgage, the purchaser does not become liable for payment of the note. Therefore, the lender cannot sue the purchaser for a deficiency judgment but may obtain only a deficiency judgment against the seller, who remains personally liable for paying the debt, as evidenced by the note.

Sale in Which Buyer Assumes Mortgage Debt

Although most conventional fixed-rate real estate loans are not assumable, some are, along with some FHA-insured and VA-guaranteed loans. When a purchaser assumes the seller's existing mortgage, the purchaser assumes liability for the mortgage and personal liability for payment of the note. Therefore, purchasers who default on mortgage payments are subject to losing their property as a result of a foreclosure sale and also are subject to a possible deficiency judgment obtained by the lender.

In a mortgage assumption, the *seller whose mortgage was assumed remains liable for the mortgage and payment of the note* unless specifically released from liability by the lender. The seller's attorney has a responsibility to inform the seller of a property sold under a loan assumption of any liability and to recommend that the seller obtain a release of liability from the lender at the time of sale, if possible.

RECORDING THE MORTGAGE

Recording the mortgage establishes order in the system of land ownership and transfer. Mortgages should always be recorded. This protects those with any present or future interest in the property by providing constructive notice to the general public of ownership and any other interest in the property. If mortgages are not recorded, someone obtaining and recording a future interest in the property may have an interest superior to that of the person who gained an interest earlier but did not record the document.

Junior Mortgage

A junior mortgage describes the priority rather than the type of mortgage. A junior mortgage refers to *any mortgage that is subordinate (lower in priority) to another mortgage.* A junior mortgage may be a second mortgage, a third mortgage, or a fourth mortgage. Each of these is subordinate to any prior mortgage securing the same property. Junior mortgages are usually for a shorter term and at a higher interest rate than first mortgages because they pose a greater risk to the lender. Second mortgages, the most common form of junior mortgages, are often used to finance part of the difference between the purchase price of a property and the loan balance being assumed in a purchase involving assumption of the seller's existing mortgage.

Priority and Subordination

Priority of mortgage liens usually is established by the time (date and hour) the lien is recorded. In the event of a foreclosure sale, the holder of the first lien has the first claim against the sale proceeds, and that debt must be fully satisfied before the holder of the second lien is fully satisfied, and so on down the line of priorities. In some instances, the order of priority can be modified by a subordination agreement, whereby an earlier lender may be willing to subordinate (take a back seat) to a later lender. Typically lenders will subordinate their mortgage to another mortgage only if they are certain the property value is sufficient to pay off both mortgages should foreclosure become necessary. An example of subordination is if the lien holder on a building lot subordinates a mortgage lien to the construction mortgage lien.

Releases

Recording a release of a mortgage is as important as recording the original document. *When the mortgage is paid in full, an instrument called a* **satisfaction of mortgage** is drawn up by the mortgagee (lender). This document is also recorded and is called a discharge of mortgage. Failure to record may cloud the title to the property.

MORTGAGE LOANS AND PAYMENTS

Mortgage loans that may be obtained from lending institutions are divided into two groups: conventional loans and government loans. Conventional loans involve *no participation by an agency of the federal government.* Many kinds of conventional mortgage loans exist that are either insured or uninsured. Government loans are guaranteed, insured, or funded by a government agency and discussed later. Types of mortgages are described below.

Straight-Term Mortgage

In a *straight-term mortgage,* the borrower pays interest only for a specified term and at the end of the term, the borrower is required to pay the principal. Today, interest-only loans are common for investors looking for short-term financing.

Adjustable Rate Mortgage (ARM)

A *fixed rate loan* carries the same rate of interest for the entire term of the loan. In contrast, with an **adjustable rate mortgage,** *the mortgage rate floats based on the fluctuations of a standard index.* Common indices include the cost of funds for savings and loan institutions, the national average mortgage rate, and the more popular one-year rate for the government's sale of treasury bills. The ARM or variable rate mortgage is one solution to the uncertainty of future financial rates.

For an ARM, the lender designates an index and then adds a **margin** (*measure of profit*) above this index. For example, if the treasury bill (T-Bill) index were 7 and the lender's margin were 2.50, the ARM would call for an interest rate of 9.5. (Margins sometimes are expressed in terms of basis points, each basis point representing 0.01 of a percent, or 250 basis points in the above example.)

ARMs are structured with **rate caps** *(ceilings), which limit both the annual adjustment and the total adjustment during the lifetime of the loan.* For example, annual increases could be limited to perhaps 1 or 2 percent interest, and the lifetime of the loan cap might be no higher than perhaps 5 or 6 percent. A **payment cap** may also be offered by the lender. If the interest rate on the loan changes and therefore the monthly payments increase, *the lender allows a payment cap, in which the monthly payment remains the same and the money for the higher interest rate is added to the principal.* This interest then accumulates onto the principal that eventually will have to be paid. This is an example of negative amortization. Many modern ARMs prohibit negative amortization.

A significant concern in an ARM is the possibility of **negative amortization.** When the index rises while the payment is fixed, it may cause the payments to fall below the amount necessary to pay the interest required by the index. This *shortfall is added back into the principal, causing the principal to grow larger after the payment.*

Balloon Mortgage

The *balloon mortgage* provides for installment payments that are not enough to pay off the principal and interest over the term of the mortgage, so the final payment (called a balloon payment) is substantially larger than any previous payment and satisfies the remaining principal and interest.

If the balloon payment is a substantial amount of money, the note may provide for refinancing by the lender to provide the funds to the borrower if he cannot otherwise make the final payment.

Amortized Mortgage

FHA will insure only *amortized mortgages* (mortgages that retire the debt). As a result of this and of the potential hardship for borrowers under the term mortgage, the typical home mortgage loan today is the amortized mortgage, whether the loan is FHA, VA, or conventional.

Amortization *provides for paying a debt by installment payments.* A portion of each payment is applied first to the payment of interest; the remainder reduces the principal. The interest always is applied against only the outstanding principal balance unpaid at the time of an installment payment. The rate of interest is an annual percentage rate as specified by the note and mortgage. The interest rate is calculated by multiplying the annual percentage rate by the unpaid principal balance and dividing the result by 12 to determine the amount of interest due and payable for each monthly installment.

After deducting the interest, the remainder of the payment goes to reduce the principal balance. Therefore, the amount of interest paid with each installment declines because the interest rate is applied against a smaller and smaller amount of principal. In this way, the loan is amortized, so the final payment in a fully amortized mortgage will pay any remaining interest and principal. (See the mortgage amortization chart, Table 16.2, Chapter 16, p. 380.)

Pledged Account Mortgage

In a *pledged account mortgage,* the purchaser's down payment is deposited in a savings account with the lender. The borrower makes escalating payments to which are added withdrawal forms from the savings account in the early years. Over time the account is exhausted, but by then the mortgagor's payments increase enough to amortize the remaining balance.

Another type of pledged account arrangement can include a third party. For example, Arthur does not have the collateral he needs for a mortgage loan. His friend, Mariah, agrees to allow the lender to use her account for this purpose. Mariah, in turn, may charge Arthur for the use of her account.

Graduated Payment Mortgage (GPM)

In the *graduated payment mortgage (GPM),* the monthly payments are lower in the early years of the mortgage term and increase at specified *intervals* until the payment amount is sufficient to amortize the loan over the remaining term. The monthly payments are kept low in the early years by not requiring the borrower to pay all the interest, which is then added to the principal balance. The purpose of this mortgage is to enable individuals to buy homes, because they are able to afford the lower initial monthly payments.

Open-End Mortgage

With an *open-end mortgage,* a popular form of junior financing, the borrower has the right to demand that the lender advance additional funds without rewriting the mortgage or charging additional closing costs. The original mortgage provides the security for additional funds to be advanced to the borrower after the loan balance has been reduced to a specified amount and sometimes functions as a line of credit. This is not the typical residential first mortgage; home equity loans are relevant to this category.

Blanket Mortgage

In a *blanket mortgage,* two or more parcels of real estate are pledged as security for payment of the mortgage debt. The blanket mortgage usually contains a **release clause** *that allows certain parcels of property to be removed from the mortgage lien if the loan balance is reduced by a specified amount.* The mortgage always should provide that sufficient property value remain subject to the mortgage lien to secure the remaining principal balance at any given time.

Real estate developers often use blanket mortgages with release clauses. In this way, the mortgagor can obtain the release of certain parcels from the lien of the mortgage and convey clear title to purchasers to generate a profit and provide the funds to make future mortgage payments.

Wraparound Mortgage

A *wraparound mortgage* is a type of seller financing. It is a subordinate mortgage that includes the same principal obligation secured by a superior mortgage against the same property. This mortgage "wraps around" the existing first mortgage, which stays in place. The seller of the property makes a wraparound loan to the buyer, who takes title to the property subject to the existing first mortgage. The seller continues to make the payments on the first mortgage, and the buyer makes the payments to the seller on the wraparound.

The wraparound mortgage can be beneficial to both seller and buyer. The seller makes payments on the existing first mortgage at an old and often lower interest rate and on a smaller initial loan amount. The seller receives the buyer's payments on a substantially larger loan amount at a higher rate of interest than the seller is paying on the existing first mortgage. In this way, the seller receives principal payments on the second mortgage and earns interest income on the amount by which the interest received on the wraparound exceeds the interest being paid on the existing first mortgage. In addition, the wraparound may enable the seller to effect a sale that otherwise may not have been accomplished, in times of high interest rates and tight money. The benefits to the buyer in this situation include purchasing the property with a small down payment and obtaining seller financing at a rate usually several percentage points below the prevailing market rate for new financing at that time.

Purchase Money Mortgage

The *purchase money mortgage,* another type of seller financing, is a mortgage given by a buyer to the seller to cover part of the purchase price. Here, the seller becomes the mortgagee and the buyer becomes the mortgagor. The seller conveys title to the buyer, who immediately reconveys or pledges it as security for the balance of the purchase price. The seller is financing the sale of his property for the buyer in the amount of the purchase money mortgage. The purchase money mortgage may be a first mortgage, a typical junior mortgage, or a junior mortgage in the form of a wraparound. See Figure 9.4.

Swing Loan

A *swing loan* (also known as an *interim* or a *bridge* loan) is usually not secured by a mortgage. A borrower uses the equity that she has in one property to obtain the money necessary to buy another property. When the property borrowed against is sold, the money from the sale is used to pay back the loan. A solid credit background is usually needed and the loan is generally for a short time. It can be used as interim financing before a permanent loan is obtained.

Construction Mortgage

The *construction mortgage* is a form of interim, or temporary, short-term financing for creating improvements on land. The lender makes the construction loan based on the value resulting from an appraisal of the property and the construction plans and specifications. The loan contract specifies that disbursements will be made as specified stages of the construction are completed, for example, after the foundation is laid or upon framing. Interest is not charged until the money has actually been disbursed. Upon completion, the lender makes a final inspection and closes out the construction loan, which is then converted to permanent, long-term financing or replaced by financing obtained by a buyer of the property. Permanent financing on a short-term construction loan is known as a *take-out loan* or an *end loan*.

Often the lender requires the builder to be bonded for completion of the property. The bond is made payable to the lender in the event the builder goes bankrupt and is unable to complete the construction. In this way, the lender can obtain the funds to complete the construction and have a valuable asset to sell and recover the monies extended under the construction loan.

FIGURE 9.4
A Purchase Money Mortgage.

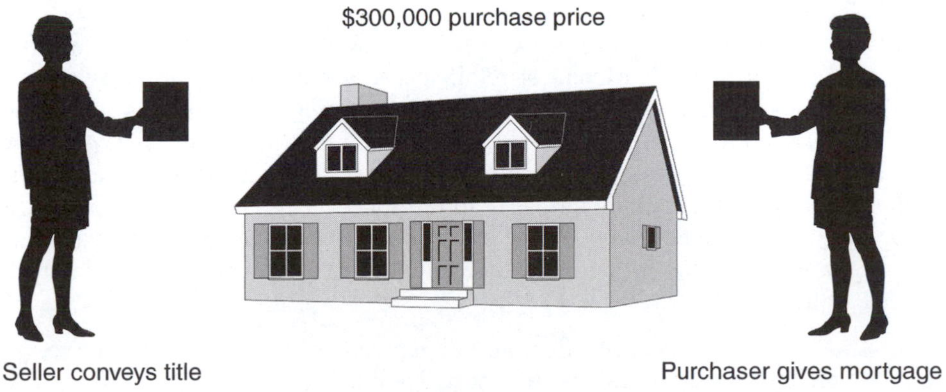

Structure of purchase

$200,000 loan from Sunny Bank (first mortgage)
$ 50,000 purchase money mortgage to seller (second mortgage)
$ 50,000 personal funds

In this scenario, the purchase money mortgage is subordinate to the bank mortgage.

Shared Equity Mortgage

A *shared equity mortgage* is *a type of participation mortgage* sometimes used in commercial lending. The lender participates in the profits generated by a commercial property used to secure payment of the debt in the mortgage loan. The borrower agrees to the lender's participation in the net income as an inducement for the lender to make the loan. This allows the lender to receive interest as well as a share of the profits.

A shared equity mortgage can also be arranged for residential financing. In this case, the lender or another participating party who initially loaned funds to the borrower, receives a portion of the profits when the property is sold.

Home Equity Loan

A home equity loan is a loan against the equity in a home. It can be a first mortgage, if the property is owned free and clear, or second (junior mortgage), if there is an existing first mortgage. Usually, the interest rates are higher on a home equity loan because the loan is for a shorter term than other types of mortgages. Some home equity loans are term loans for which one pays interest only at first; the later payments are attributable to the principal.

Reverse Annuity Mortgage

The *reverse annuity mortgage* is often used by older people who need income and want to put to use the equity in their homes. The lender makes payments to the borrower for a contracted period of time. Upon the death of the homeowner or upon the sale of the property, the lender recaptures the equity or amount paid during the mortgage term.

Package Mortgage

In a *package mortgage,* personal property in addition to real property is pledged to secure payment of the mortgage loan. Typical examples of these items are the large household appliances. The package mortgage is used in the sale of furnished condominium apartments and includes all furnishing in the unit. This method is also common in commercial real estate lending where the business assets are offered as collateral.

Sale and Leaseback

In real estate financing, long-term leases have greater significance than do short-term leases, such as renting an apartment or retail space. Some types of property are quite difficult to finance. An alternative way to obtain financing is to find a purchaser who would be interested in buying the property and leasing it back to the seller. A *sale and leaseback* is a transaction in which a property owner sells a property to an investor who immediately leases back the property to the seller as agreed in the sales contract. This type of transaction normally is used by an owner of business property who wishes to free up capital invested in the real estate and still retain possession and control of the property under a lease.

The sale and leaseback also offers an alternative to a mortgage. It, in effect, provides 100 percent financing, whereas the mortgage might provide 70 or 80 percent. The purchaser–investor in this arrangement obtains the income tax benefits of ownership and the security of owning the property. The seller pays rent, which may include real estate taxes, insurance, and maintenance for a fixed, predetermined number of years.

PRIMARY METHODS OF FINANCE

The *primary mortgage market* consists of lending institutions that make loans *directly* to borrowers. These loans consist of conventional loans and government loans.

Conventional Loans

In the uninsured conventional loan, the borrower's *equity* in the property, which is the difference between the value of the property and its liabilities, provides sufficient security for the lender to make the loan. Therefore, insurance to protect the lender in case of the borrower's default is not required. In most cases, the borrower obtains a loan that does not exceed 75 to 80 percent of the property value and has an equity of 20 or 25 percent.

An insured conventional loan typically is a conventional loan in which the borrower makes less than a 20 percent down payment and therefore borrows 90 to 95 percent of the property value. In these cases, insuring repayment of the top portion of the loan to the lender is necessary in the event the borrower defaults. The top portion of the loan is the amount that the mortgage insurance covers which in most cases is the top 25 or 30% of the loan. The insurance is called *private mortgage insurance (PMI),* and private insurance companies issue the policies. Today, private mortgage insurance companies insure more mortgage loans than does the FHA.

The Homeowner's Protection Act of 1998 (PMI Act) enable mortgagors with new loans originated after July 29, 1999 and who meet specified requirements to have their PMI canceled. The two cancellation situations are when the homeowner's equity position reaches 22 percent of the original value of the property, the mortgage servicer must automatically cancel the PMI or by request from the mortgagor when his equity position reaches 20 percent of the original value of the property.

Government Loans

FHA-Insured Loans

The Federal Housing Administration (FHA) was created in 1937 for the purpose of *insuring mortgage loans to protect lending institutions in case of borrower default.* FHA is an agency of the U. S. Department of Housing and Urban Development (HUD).

FHA does not make mortgage loans. Instead, *FHA-insured loans protect lenders against financial loss.* The buyer pays for this insurance protection by paying an up-front *mortgage insurance premium (MIP)* at closing and an annual mortgage insurance premium prorated monthly and paid with the monthly mortgage payment. This insurance enables lenders to provide financing when the loan-to-value ratio is high. **Loan-to-value ratio** *compares the loan amount to the property value.* With a high ratio, the borrower has made only a small down payment. The amount of insurance protection to the lender is always sufficient to protect the lender from financial loss in the event of a foreclosure sale because these loans are insured for 100 percent of the loan amount.

The FHA 203(b) loan that allows an owner-occupant to purchase a one- to four-family home only requires a minimum of 3% from the borrower and permits 100% of their money needed to close to be a gift from a relative, non-profit organization, or government agency. It also insures loans for the purchase or construction of owner-occupied one- to four-family dwellings. FHA does not set a maximum sales price, only a maximum loan amount. A buyer may purchase a home for more than the FHA maximum loan amount, but he will have to pay anything above the maximum loan amount in cash. Effective January 1, 2003, FHA is insuring single-family home mortgages up to $154,896 in low cost areas and up to $280,749 in high cost areas. There are also higher loan limits for two-, three- and four-unit dwellings. The maximum loan amount is based on acquisition cost, which is the combination of the FHA-appraised price or sales price, whichever is lower, plus the buyer's closing costs that FHA will allow to be financed. Figure 9.5 shows a home mortgage qualifying example.

The FHA 234(c) loan is similar to the FHA 203(b) loan except that it insures loans for individual condominium units. A condominium complex must meet FHA requirements for construction, number of units, owner occupancy, and homeowner association structure. The FHA 203(k) mortgage allows homeowners and homebuyers to purchase

FIGURE 9.5 Home mortgage qualifying example.

Single borrower's gross annual salary	$ 31,500
Total monthly income ($31,500 divided by 12)	$ 2,625
Monthly gross income	$ 2,625
Multiply by 28%	× .28
Allowable monthly housing costs	**$ 735**
Home purchase price	$75,000
Down payment	− 5,000
Mortgage loan amount	**$70,000**
30-year loan/7% interest—monthly payment (PI)	$ 466
Monthly taxes and insurance	+ 155
Total monthly housing costs	**$ 621**
Monthly gross income	$ 2,625
Multiply by 36%	× .36
Allowable total monthly debt	**$ 945**
Other monthly debts	
Car payment	$ 220
Credit cards	+ 50
Total other monthly debts	**$ 270**
Total monthly housing costs	$ 621
Total other monthly debts	$ 270
Total monthly costs	**$ 891**

Source: Fannie Mae Foundation

or refinance existing homes and finance 110% of the costs needed to improve the home. The mortgagor can borrow up to 110% of the "after-completed" value and the borrowed amount must be a minimum of $5,000. Although the loan applies to many property types, it must be owner occupied.

FHA mortgage insurance. FHA insured mortgages require mortgage insurance. The mortgage insurance, referred to as mutual mortgage insurance (MMI), charges 0.5% per year of the loan amount. Fifteen-year mortgages where the homebuyer makes a down payment greater than 10% of the purchase price do not have to pay the monthly mortgage insurance.

In addition to the mutual mortgage insurance that is charged to the purchaser each month, FHA charges an upfront mortgage insurance premium (MIP) that is 1.50% for 30- and 15- year fixed rate mortgages originated after January 1, 2001. The upfront mortgage insurance premium is calculated on the base loan amount and paid at closing or added to the loan amount.

VA Guaranteed Loan Program

While the FHA programs insure loans, the Department of Veteran Affairs (VA) offers a loan that *guarantees repayment of the top portion of the loan to the lender in the event the borrower defaults.* Due to secondary market requirements, a veteran who has not previously used the benefit may be able to obtain a VA loan up to $240,000 depending on the borrower's income level and the appraised value of the property.

The *VA-guaranteed loan* is a 100 percent loan; therefore no down payment is generally required. The loan amount may be for 100 percent of the VA appraisal of the property set forth in the VA's certificate of reasonable value (CRV) or for 100 percent of the sales price, whichever is less. The VA provides this certificate, sometimes informally called the VA appraisal, to the lending institution as a basis for making the loan. VA-guaranteed loans are available for the purchase, improvement, or construction of one- to four-family dwellings. There is no monthly mortgage insurance premium to pay and the borrower has the right to prepay the loan without penalty. The VA does not have a program for loans in which the veteran borrower will not occupy the property being purchased or constructed. (If the veteran is on active duty, the spouse must occupy.) If the property is a multifamily dwelling (maximum of four units), the veteran must occupy one of the apartments.

Veterans who had a VA loan before may still have "remaining entitlement" to use for another VA loan. The current amount of entitlement available to each eligible veteran is $36,000. Veterans who are using entitlement for a second or subsequent time who do not make a down payment of at least 5 percent are charged a funding fee of 3 percent. For borrowers to be eligible for a VA-guaranteed loan, they must qualify as veterans under requirements of the Department of Veteran Affairs.

Rural Housing Service (RHS)

The Rural Housing Service is an agency of the U. S. Department of Agriculture (USDA). The agency operates federal loan programs designed to strengthen family farms, finance new and improved rural housing, develop community facilities, and maintain and create rural employment. RHS makes direct loans, guarantees loans made by private lenders, and provides a limited number of grants primarily to low-income individuals. It has two major housing programs: Section 502, for guaranteed loans for single family housing, and Section 515, for multirental housing that provides funds directly to the owners for the benefit of the low-income tenants. Eligible borrowers must reside in rural areas having fewer than 10,000 people or in counties outside a metropolitan area with a population of 10,000 to 20,000, where mortgage money is scarce. There is no maximum loan amount, and the interest can be as low as 1 percent per year (plus taxes, insurance, and amortization) or 20 percent of family income (for mortgage principal/interest, taxes, and insurance), whichever is greater.

The advantages and disadvantages of an FHA mortgage — **You Should Know**

Advantages:
- Credit criteria for a borrower are not as strict as FNMA or FHLMC (conventional loans).
- Borrower's allowable costs can partially be wrapped into the loan.
- 100% of the down payment and closing costs can be gifted.
- Loans are assumable, allowing a person to take over the mortgage without the additional cost of obtaining a new loan

Disadvantages:
- On a 30 or 15 year FHA home loan, the upfront mortgage insurance premium (MIP) equals up to 1.50% of the loan amount in addition to the 0.5% annual renewal premium that a borrower pays for the life of the loan.
- FHA limits the amount that can be borrowed

TABLE 9.1 A summary of government mortgage loans.

NAME	AGENCY	WHAT IT DOES	SPECIAL REQUIREMENTS
Federal Housing Authority (FHA)	U.S. Department of Housing and Urban Development	insures loans	buyer qualification upfront mortgage insurance premiums maximum loan amounts
Department of Veteran Affairs (VA)	Department of Veteran Affairs	guarantees loans	buyer must be veteran guarantees up to 100% of appraised value on sales price no maximum loan amount no down payment
Rural Housing Service (RHS)	U.S. Department of Agriculture	makes direct loans guarantees loans makes some grants	borrowers must reside in rural areas loan up to 100% appraised value
State of New York Mortgage Agency	State of New York Mortgage Agency	makes loans	percentage of loans go to buyers in target areas (SONYMA) nontarget area loan can be made to first time buyers or borrowers who have been nonowners for 3 years, insured by private mortgage insurance

State of New York Mortgage Agency (SONYMA)

SONYMA (also known as Sonny Mae) raises money from the sale of New York tax-free bonds and applies the money toward mortgage loans. Sonny Mae mortgages are available through participating lenders at lower interest rates than are most conventional loans. A percentage of the mortgage money available through Sonny Mae has to be used for certain target or economically distressed areas in New York. Sonny Mae mortgages are insured by private mortgage insurance. Sonny Mae mortgages contain a variety of restrictions both for target and nontarget areas. To obtain a Sonny Mae mortgage in a nontarget area, the purchaser must be a first-time buyer or must not have owned a residence for the prior three years. These restrictions do not apply to target areas. SONYMA mortgages also define maximum purchase prices as well as purchaser income limits. These amounts vary from county to county in New York. For example, in 2003, for a new one-family home in a target area in Queens, the maximum loan amount is $303,800, and in a nontarget area in Queens, $248,500. Sonny Mae mortgages are generally set at a fixed rate that runs 2 to 3 percentage points less than conventional rates. Sonny Mae mortgages have a *recapture clause* that requires the borrower to pay a percentage of the profits on the sale of the mortgaged property to IRS if the sale is made within 9 years of purchase. This IRS payment is calculated according to the income of the borrower. Table 9.1 summarizes various government mortgage loans.

SECTION 2 THE LOAN PROCESS

SECONDARY MORTGAGE MARKET

The *secondary mortgage market* is necessary to the loan process. It buys and sells mortgages created in the *primary mortgage market.* A mortgage is generally assignable if not stated otherwise and must be assignable to qualify. Assignability allows the original lender to assign or sell the rights in the mortgage to another; therefore, the money invested in the mortgage is freed without waiting for the borrower to repay the debt over the long mortgage term.

A sale of a mortgage by the lender does not in any way affect the borrower's rights or obligations. The original mortgagor may not even be aware that the mortgage has been sold, because the original lending institution often continues to service the loan. The mortgagor continues to make the necessary mortgage payments to the same lending institution. If the purchaser of the mortgage prefers to collect the mortgage payments directly, the original lender simply notifies the mortgagor to make payments to the new lender at a different address.

Secondary Market Activities

Some lending institutions limit their mortgage loans to their own assets (known as in-house loans) rather than participate in the secondary mortgage market. For lenders that do participate in the secondary market, two types of markets are available: (a) the purchase and sale of mortgages between lending institutions, and (b) the sale of mortgages by lending institutions to three organizations that provide a market for this purpose—FNMA, GNMA, and FHLMC, discussed below. (See Table 9.2.)

Federal National Mortgage Association (FNMA) (Fannie Mae)

It is the oldest secondary mortgage institution and the single largest holder of home mortgages. Fannie Mae was created in 1938 as a corporation completely owned by the federal government to provide a secondary market for residential mortgages. By 1968, it had evolved into a privately owned corporation. FNMA is a profit-making organization and its stock is listed on the New York Stock Exchange.

To create liquidity in the mortgage market, Fannie Mae purchases both conventional and government issued mortgage loans and mortgage backed securities (MBS). Mortgage-Backed Securities are securities backed by mortgage loans. MBS' entitle an investor to an undivided interest in the underlying mortgage loan pool. Thus, an investor receives a pro rata share of the interest and principal on the underlying mortgage loans.

Government National Mortgage Association (GNMA) (Ginnie Mae)

An agency of HUD established in 1968, Ginnie Mae guarantees (insures) the timely payment of principal and interest from government insured mortgages including those

TABLE 9.2 Secondary mortgage market organizations.

NICKNAME	FULL NAME	OWNERSHIP	TYPES OF LOANS PURCHASED
Fannie Mae (FNMA)	Federal National Mortgage Association	Privately owned corporation	purchases VA, FHA, RHS, and conventional loans
Ginnie Mae (GNMA)	Government National Mortgage Association	U.S. Department of Housing and Urban Development	purchases VA, FHA, and RHS mortgages only
Freddie Mac (FHLMC)	Federal Home Loan Mortgage Corporation	owned primarily by savings and savings and loan banks	purchases loans from any member of the Federal Home Loan Bank or any bank where deposits are insured by an agency of the federal government

insured by the FHA, VA and RHS. Although Ginnie Mae does not issue, sell, or buy mortgage-backed securities, or purchase mortgage loans, its primary function is to operate its Mortgage-Backed Securities program that increases the liquidity and efficiency of mortgage loan funding.

Federal Home Loan Mortgage Corporation (FHLMC)

Like the other organizations, FHLMC has a nickname, Freddie Mac, and exists also to increase the availability of mortgage credit and provide greater liquidity for savings associations. FHLMC purchases mortgages and packages them into securities that can be sold to investors. Freddie Mac was created by Congress in 1970 primarily to establish a reliable market for the sale of conventional mortgages. Any member of the Federal Home Loan Bank and any other financial institution, whose deposits or accounts are insured by an agency of the federal government, is eligible to sell mortgages to Freddie Mac.

Conforming Loans

Primary lenders wishing to sell mortgages to Fannie Mae or Freddie Mac must use uniform loan documents that meet criteria established by FNMA and FHLMC. Loans *processed on uniform loan forms and according to FNMA/FHLMC guidelines* are called *conforming loans.* For example, the involved organizations will not purchase any mortgage containing a prepayment penalty. The prohibition of this clause is particularly advantageous to individual borrowers, who avoid the prepayment penalty when they are required to pay off their mortgage as a condition of a contract of sale. In some cases, prepayment penalties on nonconforming loans are extremely high and therefore pose a real hardship to sellers.

TRUTH-IN-LENDING ACT (TILA)

The Truth-in-Lending Act, Title I of the *Consumer Credit Protection Act* (1980), is aimed at promoting he informed use of consumer credit by requiring disclosures about its terms and costs. TILA requires four chief disclosures: annual percentage rate, finance charge, amount financed, and total amount of money to be paid toward the mortgage in both principal and interest payments. The Federal Reserve Board implemented these regulations by establishing Regulation Z. *Regulation Z* does not regulate interest rates but instead provides specific consumer protections in mortgage loans for residential real estate. It covers all real estate loans for personal, family, household, or agricultural purposes. The regulation does not apply to commercial loans. Regulation Z also standardizes the procedures involved in residential loan transactions and requires that the borrower be fully informed of all aspects of the loan transaction. In addition, the regulation addresses any advertisement of credit terms available for residential real estate. (See Chapter 8, that defines the differences between TILA and RESPA.)

Disclosure

At the time of application or within three days thereafter, the lender must provide the borrower with a *disclosure statement.* The disclosure must set forth the true, or effective, annual interest rate on a loan, called the annual percentage rate (APR). This rate may be higher than the interest as expressed in the mortgage. For example, when certain fees and discount points charged by the lender are subtracted from the loan amount, the result is an increase in the true rate of interest. As a result of the subtraction, the borrower receives a smaller loan amount and pays interest on a larger amount. Therefore, the effect is to increase the interest rate.

The disclosure statement must specify the finance charges, that include loan fees and interest and discount points. Finance charges do not include fees for title examination, title insurance, escrow payments, document preparation, notary fees, or appraisals.

Cooling-Off Period

If the borrower is refinancing an existing mortgage loan or obtaining a new mortgage loan on a residence already owned, the disclosure statement must provide for a cooling-off period, or three-day right of rescission for the loan transaction. The borrower has the right to rescind, or cancel, the loan prior to midnight of the third business day after the date the transaction was closed. The three-day right of rescission *does not* apply to the purchase of a new home, construction of a dwelling to be used as a principal residence, or refinancing of an investment property.

Advertising

Regulation Z also applies to the advertised credit terms available. The only specific thing that may be stated in the advertisement without making a full disclosure is the annual percentage rate, that must be spelled out in full, not abbreviated as APR. If any other credit terms are included in the advertisement, they must also be fully disclosed. For example, an advertisement mentioning a down payment triggers the requirement to make a complete disclosure of all of the following credit terms: purchase price of the property, annual percentage rate, amount of down payment, amount of each payment, date when each payment is due, and total number of payments over the mortgage term. If the annual percentage rate is not a fixed rate but is instead a variable rate, the ad must specify this variable or adjustable rate.

Effect on Real Estate Licensees

Statements of a general nature about the financing may be made without full disclosure. Statements such as "good financing available," "FHA financing available," and "loan assumption available" are satisfactory. Real estate licensees must take special care not to violate the advertising requirements of Regulation Z.

Penalties

Violators of Regulation Z are subject to criminal liability and punishment by a fine of up to $5,000, imprisonment for up to a year, or both. If borrowers suffer a financial loss as the result of the violation, they may sue the violator for damages under civil law in federal court.

EQUAL CREDIT OPPORTUNITY ACT (ECOA)

The *Equal Credit Opportunity Act (ECOA)* (1975) is a federal law to to prevent lending institutions from discriminating in the loan process. The act requires financial lending institutions to make loans on an equal basis to all creditworthy customers without regard to discriminatory factors. The ECOA is implemented by Regulation B of the Federal Reserve Board. This act makes it unlawful for any creditor to discriminate against any loan applicant in any aspect of a credit transaction, including:

1. on the basis of race, color, religion, gender, national origin, marital status, or age (unless the applicant is a minor and, therefore, does not have the capacity to contract)
2. because part of the applicant's income is derived from a public assistance program, alimony, or child support
3. because the applicant has in good faith exercised any right under the Federal Consumer Credit Protection Act of which the Truth-in-Lending Law (Regulation Z) is a part

Compliance with the ECOA is enforced by different agencies depending on which agency has regulatory authority over which type of financial institution.

LENDER CRITERIA FOR GRANTING A LOAN

The Economy

The state of the economy has an impact on the loan process. An important consideration is **inflation.** This is defined as *an increase in money and credit relative to available goods, resulting in higher prices.* Inflation causes governments to borrow more to meet current debts, businesses to borrow more to meet costs of operations, and individuals to borrow more to pay for the higher cost of goods and services. When there is a high demand for housing, causing a high demand for mortgages, and the demand is coupled with rapid inflation, the demand for credit then accelerates to abnormal highs. Inflation generally is not good for the real estate market because not only will the price of real estate be higher but the cost to borrow will also increase. However, real estate purchased prior to inflationary trends provides an attractive hedge against inflation as once inflation kicks in, the return on investment is greatly increased.

Investment Quality of the Property

Some of the considerations the lender must include in the evaluation process are: neighborhood and location, site analysis, condition of the property, improvements, economic life, and comparable value to other similar properties. The *sales price* that the purchaser has agreed to pay should be comparable with the recent sales prices of other similar properties in an area or neighborhood as close to the subject property as possible. An appraisal, which is an estimate of value that the lender must evaluate, is performed for the subject property. Based on the gathered data, the appraiser makes a final reconciliation of value. This is the appraised value, and the lender, after reviewing the appraisal, makes a conclusion as to the actual value.

Loan-to-Value Ratio

Loan-to-value (LTV) is the ratio of the loan amount to the property value. The value of the property for mortgage purposes is either the appraised value or the purchase price, whichever is less. For example, a loan of $200,000 on a property valued at $400,000 is at an LTV of 50%. Loan-to-value ratios are determined by the primary lender, Fannie Mae, or the secondary mortgage market. The importance of a prevailing loan-to-value ratio is in determining the down payment amount. A down payment is the difference between the purchase price and the amount of the loan. In New York, if the loan-to-value ratio is greater than 80 percent, a purchaser must obtain *private mortgage insurance (PMI).*

Type of Property

In a one- to four-unit rental property, the lender can add in a percentage of the rent as the borrower's income, qualifying the buyer for a higher loan amount. With owner-occupied property, the lender may require less money for a down payment. From a lender's perspective, there is less risk involved because the property is likely to be much better maintained with an owner-occupant. A nonowner-occupied rental property would most likely require a larger down payment.

Loans for Cooperative Purchase

In purchasing a single-family home or condominium, the purchaser usually attains a fee simple absolute ownership. In the purchase of a cooperative apartment, the purchaser is buying shares of stock in a corporation that owns the cooperative.

Presale. Depending on the bylaws, the board of directors of the cooperative corporation may have the right to interview potential purchasers and to approve or disapprove their purchase. This board may be able to set financial qualifications for purchasers, which possibly bear no relationship to lender requirements. For example, the board may require 40 percent of the purchase price as a down payment and request financial and personal references.

Pro rata and square footage of specific units. Cooperative purchasers obtain a pro rata share of the corporation. Pro rata shares are usually based on the square footage of the individual unit and other factors such as location in the building and access to other amenities. The square footage of specific units is part of the description contained in the proprietary lease. Each proprietary lease includes a pro rata share of the mortgage indebtedness of the building, and any equity in the building. Special assessments for *maintenance* and other costs may also be pertinent. Maintenance includes payment towards the mortgage indebtedness of the building together with upkeep of the common areas. These assessments are allocated on a per-share basis. When considering a loan for a cooperative purchase, the lender must consider not only the loan for the individual shareholder but also look at other indebtedness for which the borrower–shareholder has responsibility. For example, if a $1 million mortgage exists on the building, the cooperative shareholder takes on a pro rata share of that mortgage. Moreover, if the loan-to-value ratio is, for example, 70 percent to 30 percent, part of the 70 percent of the loan might include a portion of the mortgage for the entire building as well as the pro rata share of each of the units.

To finance the purchase of a cooperative, the cooperative purchaser uses both the shares of stock assigned to the apartment as well as the proprietary lease as collateral for the loan. In this sense, the loan is different from a mortgage since the security for it is not real estate, but personalty. This type of loan is known as a collateralized security loan. Some of the purchaser's indebtedness, as explained above, includes a portion of the mortgage on the entire building. Therefore, if a cooperative purchaser has an obligation of $1,000 per month, $300 may go to the lender for repayment of the collaterized security loan while the remaining $700 goes toward maintenance and is paid to the cooperative corporation.

Sponsor declaration. The individual or entity that either constructs a cooperative or converts a building into a cooperative corporation must file a declaration and disclosure statement with the New York attorney general's office. The first part of the declaration includes the scope of the project, a description of the corporate setup and other required information. This first part of the review process is called the preliminary prospectus, or red herring. At this point, the attorney general can suggest any changes to the project except for the price of shares. Once the prospectus is accepted for filing by the attorney general, it is a black book, or offering plan. The cooperative units may now be offered for sale to the public. In the initial declaration, a schedule is drawn that describes the price of units, the pro rata indebtedness of each unit, and the amount of predicted tax deductions.

Phases. The presale phase of the cooperative begins with the declaration to the attorney general. Prospective purchasers may view the units but may not purchase them. The sale of units occurs during the black-book phase, when the offering plan has been accepted for filing by the attorney general's office. In some cases, a presale law allows units to be sold with the approval of the attorney general.

Floors. The height of a cooperative and the number of floors generally should be in accordance with zoning requirements for that area. It is possible that in some areas, because of view, units on upper floors have a greater pro rata share value per square foot than do units on lower floors.

Borrower's Ability to Repay Loan

The buyer's ability to pay consists of the following considerations:

1. *Income/salary.* Even if employment is stable, income may not be. Borrowers must submit signed federal income tax returns from the prior two years. Income reported on past tax returns is averaged with current verified income to reflect a stable income figure. Self-employed or commissioned employees with declining incomes are evaluated against offsetting factors.

Overtime and bonus income usually is not relevant unless the borrower verifies stability over the prior two years. Part-time income can be counted if the borrower has held the job continuously for the prior two years and seems likely to continue. Seasonal employment is valid if it is uninterrupted over a two-year history and if continued employment is likely.

2. *Qualifying ratios.* The underwriter must calculate the borrower's two debt ratios: (a) monthly housing expense to income, and (b) total payment obligations to income. These ratios determine the borrower's ability to meet home ownership responsibilities.

   Monthly housing expense includes principal and interest of mortgage payment plus escrow deposits for hazard insurance premium; real estate taxes and mortgage insurance premium; owner or condominium association charges, less the utility charge portion; any ground rents or special assessments; and payments under any secondary financing on the subject property.

   These ratios do not constitute absolute requirements. A borrower's excellent credit history or capability for future increased earnings and savings may be considered.

3. *Employment history.* Borrower employment for the prior two years is verified as evidence of ability to pay. The lender also determines the probable stability and continuance of that employment. Changing jobs frequently without advancement does not reflect stability. However, recent college graduates and individuals specially trained and beginning work in their respective fields often indicate continued and stable employment to lenders.

4. *Sole proprietorship, partnership, corporation.* If the borrower's income comes from a business enterprise, the lender must know if the operation is organized through a sole proprietorship, partnership, or corporation. If the business is a sole proprietorship and the borrower is the owner, all the income falls under the control of the borrower. If the business is a partnership, other parties have an income interest. The income of the business is *not* under the full control of the borrower. The business of a corporate enterprise is controlled by a majority vote of the stockholders, and if the borrower receives no salary or dividends, then the borrower's income is questionable. These factors must be considered by the lender in approving a loan.

5. *Verification and documentation.* At the time of loan application, the borrower is required to sign the following authorization forms, so the lender can verify the data the borrower gives on the loan application:
   - verification of employment (if the borrower is self-employed, the most recent two or three years' tax returns [personal and business] are usually required in place of this verification)

TABLE 9.3

Mortgage qualification table.

INTEREST RATES	ANNUAL INCOME											
	$15,000	$20,000	$25,000	$30,000	$35,000	$40,000	$45,000	$50,000	$55,000	$60,000	$65,000	$70,000
5.5%	$55,000	$73,400	$91,700	$110,100	$128,400	$146,800	$165,100	$183,500	$201,800	$220,200	$238,500	$256,800
6.0%	52,100	69,500	86,900	104,200	121,600	139,000	156,400	173,700	191,100	208,500	225,900	243,200
6.5%	49,400	65,900	82,400	98,800	115,300	131,800	148,300	164,800	181,300	197,700	214,200	230,700
7.0%	47,000	62,600	78,300	93,900	109,600	125,300	140,900	156,600	172,300	187,900	203,600	219,200
7.5%	44,600	59,600	74,500	89,400	104,300	119,200	134,100	149,000	163,900	178,800	193,700	208,600
8.0%	42,600	56,700	70,900	85,100	99,300	113,500	127,700	141,900	156,100	170,300	184,500	198,700
8.5%	40,600	54,100	67,700	81,200	94,800	108,300	121,900	135,400	149,000	162,500	176,100	189,600
9.0%	38,800	51,700	64,700	77,700	90,600	103,500	116,500	129,400	142,400	155,300	168,200	181,200
9.5%	37,200	49,500	61,900	74,300	86,700	99,100	111,400	123,800	136,200	148,600	161,000	173,400

Rather than using the normal 28 percent ratio, this chart uses a 25 percent ratio and assumes that the amount needed to set aside to pay for taxes and insurance would amount to approximately the three percent difference.

Source: Fannie Mae Foundation

- verification of rent or mortgage
- verification of bank account balance
- verification of outstanding loans
- verification of sales contract deposit
- verification of pension (if applicable)
- authorization to release information
- consent to credit check and verification

Sometimes substitute documentation may be used in place of verifications. For example, pay stubs or employee year-end W-2 statements may be used in place of employment verification; bank statements for two months prior to loan application may substitute for bank account verification. The verified borrower's deposit on the sales contract plus verified bank balances must equal the down payment plus closing costs and prepaid items. The underwriter must look for the possibility that the borrower wishes to use last-minute unsecured borrowed funds for all or part of the required closing costs (evidenced by large, unexplained recent bank deposits).

6. *Liquid assets and closing funds.* Borrowers have to show sufficient funds on hand to close the mortgage transaction. Gift funds from a family member are acceptable to meet cash requirements for closing FHA or VA loans if they are actually transferred to borrowers and verified. With conventional loans, borrowers must invest 5 percent of the sales price from their own funds; a family member may put up additional money required above that 5 percent. Stocks and bonds also are acceptable as closing funds if the market value can be verified and the borrowers make a 5 percent cash down payment. Securities must be separately appraised, and a property record search must be conducted to verify ownership.
7. *Monthly obligations, history of repayment, and credit reports.* The buyer's willingness to pay is reflected by credit history that can be demonstrated by the borrower's mortgage payment record, number and amount of outstanding credit obligations, and payment history on other credit obligations.

DISCOUNT POINTS

Lending institutions may charge **discount points** in making mortgage loans. *Each point that the lender charges costs someone* (either the buyer or the seller, depending upon the situation) *1 percent of the loan amount,* paid at the time of loan closing. Lenders may charge discount points in conventional loans. At times of high interest rates and short supply of money for making mortgage loans, lenders often charge one or two points in making 90 percent and 95 percent conventional loans. New York has **usury laws** that *fix a maximum allowable interest rate.* This maximum rate is subject to fluctuation. Borrowers sometimes volunteer to pay discount points to **buy down** or *reduce a mortgage interest rate at the time the loan is made.*

PUTTING IT TO WORK

Prequalifying your buyer is one of the most important steps in closing a real estate transaction. However, for new licensees, the methods of qualifying and understanding loan payments may seem mystifying at first. Use the amortization chart in Chapter 16 (Figure 16.2) as you study Figures 9.6 and 9.7 to enhance your understanding of the processes involved. Work with your instructor or another student. The answers appear in each exercise.

FIGURE 9.6
Exercises for qualifying income for a conventional loan.

Before approving a conventional mortgage loan, the lender must determine if the borrower will be able to meet the financial obligation of monthly mortgage payments. Most often, the lender requires that the monthly mortgage payment not exceed 28% of the borrower's gross monthly income and that the total of all long-term obligations not exceed 36% of this income; this is referred to as the 28/36 rule.

For example, assume a sales price of $125,000, a loan amount of $100,000* and an annual interest rate of 8.5% with a 30-year loan term. (Please use the amortization chart in Figure 16.2 if you don't have a financial calculator.) Tax and insurance escrow numbers are given. In this case, the formula would be applied as follows:

1. The lender will first calculate the total monthly payments:

$769.00	(P & I)
116.80	for tax escrow (T)
54.00	for insurance escrow (I)
$939.80	total monthly payment for principal, interest, 1/12 annual real property taxes, 1/12 annual property insurance (PITI)

2. Next the borrower's gross monthly income will be calculated by dividing the annual household salary by 12:

   $55,000 ÷ 12 = $4,583.33

3. The ratio of mortgage payment to gross monthly income is then determined by dividing the payment by monthly income:

   $939.80 ÷ $4,583.33 = 20.5%

   The first part of the 28/36 rule has been satisfied since this ratio is under 28%.

4. All other long-term expense payments are then added to determine the borrower's other long-term debt:

$340.00	car payments
75.00	credit card payments
100.00	personal loan payment
$515.00	total monthly payment for long-term debt

5. Add this total to the mortgage payment:

   $ 515.00
   939.80
   $1,454.80

6. Divide this total by monthly income to determine the ratio of long-term debt:

   $1,454.80 ÷ $4,583.33 = 31.7%

The borrower will qualify for the loan since this ratio is under 36%.

*This is an 80% loan-to-value ratio; therefore, it requires no private mortgage insurance (PMI). A higher loan-to-value ratio requires PMI to be included in payments.

FIGURE 9.7
Exercises for understanding loan payments.

(a)
Using the amortization chart.

Example: Assume a home purchase price of $87,500 with a conventional mortgage of 80% of the sales price at an annual interest rate of 8.5% for 30 years.

1. Calculate the amount of the loan:
   $87,500 × 80% = $70,000
2. Figure 16.2 lists a factor for each $1,000 of a loan. Divide $70,000 (our loan amount) by $1,000 to determine the number of units of $1,000, which is 70. Jot down this figure before completing step 3.
3. Go to the 8.5% row (our annual interest rate) on Figure 16.2. Read across to the 30-year column (our loan term). The factor listed is 7.69. This is the payment per month per $1,000 of the loan.
4. Multiply the 70 from step 2 by the 7.69 figure from step 3 to arrive at $538.30. This is the monthly payment of principal and interest (P & I) needed to amortize (pay off) a loan of $70,000 at 8.5% for 30 years.

(b)
Calculating interest paid per month.

Use the data from (a) to calculate how much of the payment (P & I) went toward interest (I).

1. Interest (I) equals the principal (P) times the rate (R) times the period of time (T) you have had the money, or:
   I = P × R × T
2. In our example,
   I = $70,000 × 8.5% × 1⁄12 of one year, or
   I = $70,000 × 0.085 = $5,950.00 ÷ 12 = $495.83
3. Therefore, of the total payment of $538.30 in the first month, $495.83 went to interest.

(c)
Calculating principal reduction per payment.

How much did this monthly payment of $538.30 reduce the loan principal?

Subtract the amount that went toward interest from the total payment amount; the remainder went to principal:

$538.30	(P & I)
− 495.83	(I)
$ 42.47	(P)

(d)
Calculating principal balance after one payment.

1. Calculate the amount that went to principal: $42.47
2. Subtract this amount from the previous balance:
   $70,000.00
   − 42.47
3. The remainder is the new principal balance: $69,957.53

(e)
Calculating total interest paid over the life of this loan.

1. Calculate the monthly payment: $538.30
2. Calculate the total number of months to be paid; in this case:
   30 (years) × 12 (months per year) = 360 payments
3. Multiply the monthly payment times the total number of months to be paid to calculate the total of the payments:
   $538.30 × 360 payments = $193,788 total payback
4. Subtract the amount of the loan borrowed from the total payback to calculate the amount that went toward interest:
   $193,788.00
   − 70,000.00
   $123,788.00 total interest paid

IMPORTANT POINTS

1. The purpose of a mortgage is to secure the payment of a debt. A mortgage creates a lien against the property.
2. If a borrower defaults on a loan, a lender may institute foreclosure proceedings. If the sale proceeds available to the lender are insufficient to satisfy the debt, the lender may sue for a deficiency judgment.
3. The borrower's rights are: (a) possession of the property prior to default, (b) defeat of lien by paying debt in full prior to default, and (c) equity of redemption.
4. The lender's rights are: (a) possession of the property after foreclosure, (b) foreclosure, and (c) right to assign the mortgage.
5. A buyer assuming a seller's mortgage assumes liability on both the mortgage and the note. The seller remains liable on the note unless specifically released by a mortgage clause or by the lender. A buyer taking title subject to an existing mortgage has no liability on the note.
6. Conventional loans are not required to be insured if the loan amount does not exceed 80 percent of the property value. Most conventional insured loans are 90 percent and 95 percent loans. The insurance is called private mortgage insurance (PMI). The premium is paid by the borrower.
7. A fully amortized mortgage requires payments of principal and interest that will completely satisfy the debt over the mortgage term.
8. Various types of mortgages and loans include term, adjustable or variable rate, balloon, amortized, pledged account, graduated payment, open-end, blanket, wraparound, swing (or bridge), purchase money, construction, shared equity, home equity, reverse annuity, and package.
9. FHA and VA loans are made by specifically qualified lending institutions.
10. The FHA-insured programs include 203(b). FHA mutual mortgage insurance and the upfront mortgage insurance premium protect the lender from financial loss in the event of foreclosure. FHA establishes a maximum loan amount.
11. VA loans are guaranteed. VA loans may be made for up to 100 percent of the sales price or of the property value.
12. The primary mortgage market is the activity of lending institutions making loans directly to individual borrowers. The secondary market is the activity of lending institutions selling and buying existing mortgages. The secondary market consists of the purchase and sale of mortgages between lenders and the sale of mortgages by lenders to Fannie Mae (FNMA), Ginnie Mae (GNMA), and Freddie Mac (FHLMC).
13. Methods of financing include insured and uninsured conventional mortgage loans, FHA-insured loans, VA-guaranteed loans, SONYMA mortgages, RHS loans, and the various types of private financing.
14. Regulation Z of the Truth-in-Lending Act provides for disclosure by lenders and truth in advertising.
15. Lender criteria for granting a loan include investment quality of the property, sales price and appraised value, loan-to-value ratio, types of property, and purchaser's ability to pay.
16. Cooperative purchasers buy pro rata shares of a corporation. Therefore, a lender's considerations for financing are different from those of other residential or condominium property buyers.
17. Income, qualifying ratios, employment history, the nature of the borrower's business organization (if any), liquid assets, monthly obligations, and credit history are considered by the lender in the loan qualification process.

CHAPTER REVIEW

KEY TERM REVIEW

Fill in the term that best completes each sentence and then check the Answer Key at the end of the chapter.

1. The borrower who gives the mortgage is called the ____________________ and the lender who receives the mortgage is known as the ____________________.
2. The note on the mortgage includes a(n) ____________________ enabling the lender to declare the entire balance remaining immediately due and payable if the borrower is in default.
3. In a(n) ____________________ loan, every payment is applied toward a portion of the interest and the principal.
4. When the mortgage is paid in full, an instrument called a(n) ____________________ is drawn by the mortgagee.
5. Adjustable rate mortgages are structured with ____________________, which limit both the annual adjustment and the total adjustment during the lifetime of the loan.
6. The right of ____________________ allows the lender to sell the mortgage and obtain the money invested rather than wait for payment of the loan over an extended time.
7. A mortgage may allow a payment due on the first of the month to be paid up until the 15th day of the month without the borrower being in default. This span of time is known as a(n) ____________________.
8. A mortgage that contains an extra charge for paying off a mortgage sooner than specified in its terms has a(n) ____________________.
9. Borrowers sometimes volunteer to pay discount points to ____________________ a mortgage interest rate at the time the loan is made.
10. The ____________________ compares the loan amount to the property value.

MULTIPLE CHOICE

Circle the letter that best answers the question and then check the Answer Key at the end of the chapter.

1. Which of the following statements does NOT apply to promissory notes?
   A. they must be written
   B. the borrower is personally liable for payment
   C. they provide evidence of a valid debt
   D. they are executed by the lender

2. A second mortgage for an amount larger than the existing mortgage on the same property is a:
   A. blanket mortgage
   B. balloon mortgage
   C. straight-term mortgage
   D. wraparound mortgage

3. The clause that makes a mortgage unassumable is which of the following?
   A. defeasance
   B. alienation
   C. mortgaging
   D. payment

4. Which of the following gives the borrower the right to pay the debt in full and remove the mortgage lien at any time prior to default?
   A. defeasance
   B. alienation
   C. equity of redemption
   D. foreclosure

5. If the sale proceeds available to the lender are insufficient to satisfy the debt, the lender may sue for:
   A. disintermediation
   B. strict foreclosure
   C. deficiency judgment
   D. release of liability

6. A deed in lieu of foreclosure conveys a title to which of the following?
   A. lender
   B. borrower
   C. trustee
   D. mortgagor

7. A foreclosure is a(n):
   A. equity of redemption
   B. buydown
   C. deficiency judgment
   D. liquidation of title to real property to pay the mortgage debt

8. A deficiency judgment may be available to a:
   A. mortgagee
   B. mortgagor
   C. vendor
   D. trustor

9. A buyer assumed the seller's mortgage without procuring a release of liability. The seller subsequently defaulted. Which of the following is correct?
   A. only the buyer is personally liable for payment of the note
   B. only the seller is personally liable for payment of the note
   C. both the buyer and the seller may be personally liable for payment of the note
   D. neither the buyer nor the seller is personally liable for payment of the note

10. Lending institutions making mortgage loans directly to individual borrowers are called the:
    A. secondary mortgage market
    B. money market
    C. institutional market
    D. primary mortgage market

11. Which of the following is a government-owned corporation that is limited to the purchase of VA, FHA, and RHS mortgages only?
    A. Fannie Mae
    B. Ginnie Mae
    C. Freddie Mac
    D. Sonny Mae

12. Insurance for the protection of lending institutions making conventional loans is called:
    A. mutual mortgage insurance
    B. conventional mortgage insurance
    C. institutional insurance
    D. private mortgage insurance

13. Under ECOA, which of the following may a lender consider in making consumer loans?
    A. age
    B. occupation
    C. gender
    D. marital status

14. Which of the following statements about discount points is FALSE?
    A. points increase the lender's yield on the loan
    B. each point charged by the lender costs 1 percent of the loan amount
    C. buyers can pay points on VA, FHA, and conventional loans
    D. they violate usury laws

15. Which of the following statements about Regulation Z is FALSE?
    A. it applies to commercial loans
    B. it requires lenders to furnish a disclosure statement to the borrower
    C. it provides for a three-day right of rescission if a residence already owned is pledged
    D. it regulates the advertising of credit terms of property offered for sale

16. The type of mortgage requiring the borrower to pay interest only for a specified duration of time is:
    A. balloon
    B. open
    C. straight term
    D. closed

17. The amount of interest paid in an amortized mortgage for a month in which the principal balance is $73,000 and the rate is 12 percent is:
    A. $600
    B. $730
    C. $876
    D. $1,369

18. A mortgage that is not on a fully amortized basis and therefore requires a larger final payment is called a(n):
    A. graduated mortgage
    B. balloon mortgage
    C. open mortgage
    D. wraparound mortgage

19. A mortgage in which two or more parcels of land are pledged is called:
    A. blanket
    B. package
    C. all-inclusive
    D. wraparound

20. A mortgage that is subordinate to another is called:
    A. leasehold
    B. blanket
    C. junior
    D. participation

ANSWER KEY

Putting It To Work (page 207)

A bond is a contract to pay money, indicating one party's indebtedness to another. The mortgage document establishes that a property has been pledged to ensure payment of the bond. The mortgage details the obligations and rights of the borrower and lender. If you are borrowing money from a lending institution to purchase a home, you will be a party to both a bond and a mortgage. Often these are consolidated into one document.*

Key Term Review

1. mortgagor, mortgagee
2. acceleration clause
3. amortized
4. satisfaction of mortgage
5. rate caps
6. assignment
7. grace period
8. prepayment penalty clause
9. buydown
10. loan-to-value ratio

Multiple Choice

1. D	6. A	11. B	16. C
2. D	7. D	12. D	17. C
3. B	8. A	13. B	18. B
4. A	9. C	14. D	19. A
5. C	10. D	15. A	20. C

*Source: James A. Ader, "Real Estate Spotlight." Copyright © The Albany *Times Union*. Reprinted by permission.

Chapter 10

KEY TERMS

abutting land
accessory apartment
accessory uses
area variance
census tract
cluster zoning
condemnation
cul-de-sac
deed restriction
demography
doctrine of laches
eminent domain
escheat
family
group home
home occupation
infrastructure
lead agency
moratorium
New York State Office of Parks, Recreation, and Historic Preservation (OPRHP)
police power
setback
spot zoning
"taking"
topography
transfer of development rights
use variance
variance

LEARNING OBJECTIVES

Classroom hours: 2

1. Identify the federal, state, county, and local government agencies that regulate the use of land.
2. Describe how and where to learn what land use regulations affect a particular parcel, neighborhood, or community.
3. Describe the legal definition and guidelines for a special use permit, an area variance, and a use variance.
4. Define the key terms usually referred to for the subject of land use regulations.

Land Use Regulations

IN THIS CHAPTER As a licensee, you must be aware of existing public and private land use controls within your market area. It is impossible to market property responsibly and competently without a substantial understanding of the factors that affect land use. This chapter covers public and private control of land including deed restrictions, federal and state laws, and zoning ordinances.

PLANNING FOR THE FUTURE

As you study land use, you will learn that the use of land encompasses a number of issues that may not have been considered as recently as forty to fifty years ago. Concerns related to land use are continuously tested in our local, state, and federal courts. Decisions made today will impact land use and the real estate market in the future. It is essential to know how these controls affect the community where you hold your license.

PRIVATE LAND USE CONTROLS: DEED RESTRICTIONS, COVENANTS, AND CONDITIONS

Individual owners have *the right to place private controls on their own real estate.* These restrictions may exist on individual deeds or may take the form of restrictions affecting an entire subdivision. **Deed restrictions** are in the form of covenants or conditions. These restrictions, or covenants, run with the land (move with the title in any subsequent conveyance). Restrictions providing for a reversion of title that are violated are called *conditions.* If a condition is violated, ownership reverts to the grantor.

Restrictive covenants can also be limitations placed on the use of land by the developer of a residential subdivision. The covenants are promises by those who purchase property in the subdivision to limit the use of their property to comply with these requirements. The deeds conveying title to these properties contain references to a recorded plat of the subdivision and references to the recording of the restrictive covenants; or the restrictions may be recited in each deed of conveyance. Restrictions must be reasonable and they must benefit all property owners.

Subdivision Regulations

Subdivision regulations are restrictions that often address issues to maintain quality and consistency of the subdivision. A typical private restriction is that dwellings must have **setback** requirements; that is, *specified distances from the front property line to the building line, as well as from the interior property lines.* Covenants may be enforced by property owners within the subdivision by taking appropriate court action. If property owners do not act to enforce restrictive covenants on a timely basis, the violators will not be restricted by the courts and the covenant will be terminated. Termination of a covenant in this manner is an application of the **doctrine of laches,** which *states that if landowners are lax in protecting their rights, they may lose the rights.* (See Figure 10.1)

PUBLIC LAND USE CONTROLS

Public control of land by the government covers a broader range of jurisdiction than does private control. **Police power** *empowers government to fulfill its responsibility to provide for the public health, safety, and welfare of its citizens.* Government may exercise this power even if it restricts the fundamental freedoms of its citizens. Exercise of police power, however, must be in the best interests of the public. The following sections describe some of the laws and government agencies that are involved in land use regulation in New York.

State and Local Controls

New York State Article 9-A of Real Property Law

Article 9–A is regulated by the New York Department of State (DOS) and is designed to protect the residents of New York in the purchase or lease of vacant subdivided lands. The land can be located either within New York or in another state. Article 9–A covers subdivided lands *within and without New York only when sold through an installment land contract. The law, when applicable, covers a sale made by a sales-*

FIGURE 10.1
Private control of land.

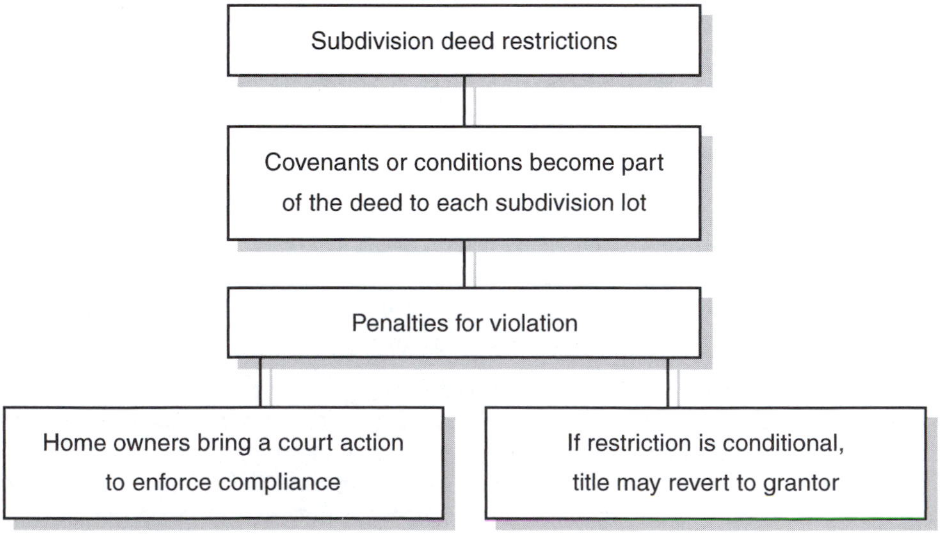

The private control of land is in the form of deed restrictions. Subdivisions use restrictions to maintain quality standards and uniformity.

Source: From *The Home Inspection Book: A Guide for Professionals,* by Marcia Darvin Spada. © 2002. Reprinted with permission of South-Western Publishing.

person, broker, owner, or any other individual empowered to sell the land. To comply with Article 9–A, certain documentation describing the land to be sold and a filing fee must be filed with the New York DOS. All advertising, before publication, must be submitted for DOS approval. If the subdivision is sold before the offering plan is approved, the offeror is guilty of a felony. If the offering statement is violated after the subdivision is approved, the offeror is guilty of a misdemeanor.

Environmental Impact Statements

In New York, environmental impact statements fall under the State Environmental Quality Review Act (SEQRA). This act requires a state environmental quality review (SEQR), that is a process mandating all levels of state and local government to assess the environmental significance of actions for which they have discretion to approve, fund, or undertake.

The environmental impact statement (EIS) is the process that describes and analyzes a proposed action that may significantly affect the environment. The EIS is available to the public for review and comment. In land use policy, which includes environmental considerations, a number of federal, state, and local governmental agencies may undertake evaluation. *The agency that oversees the entire issue and makes final decisions* is called the **lead agency.**

Transportation

Transportation planning is important because thoroughfares and other transportation facilities support and provide access to residential and commercial areas as well as to public places such as recreational areas, hospitals, schools, and other facilities. The New York State Department of Transportation (NYS DOT) builds, oversees, and maintains roadways, bridges, and overpasses on state-owned roads. Counties, cities, or towns may have a local highway department under its jurisdiction. New York City has its own department of transportation.

New York State Office of Parks, Recreation, and Historic Preservation (OPRHP)

The Field Services Bureau of the **New York State Office of Parks, Recreation, and Historic Preservation,** *administers federal and state programs for park lands and historic sites.* New York has a state register of historic places and receives federal preservation funding grants for historic preservation. The Field Services Bureau oversees the Certified Local Government Program (CLG). CLG is a nationwide program that supports local preservation and provides a link between the communities and state and federal preservation programs. The New York State Department of Environmental Conservation also oversees park lands and open space.

Federal Controls

Various federal agencies have control and jurisdiction over different areas of land use within the municipalities.

Interstate Land Sales Full Disclosure Act

This act (1968) regulates interstate (across state lines) sale or lease of unimproved lots. The act is administered by HUD and is designed to prevent fraudulent marketing schemes that may be used to sell land sight unseen. Before offering lots for sale by mail or phone, a developer must register subdivisions of 100 or more non-exempt lots with HUD. The purchaser must be provided with a disclosure document called a Property Report before signing a contract. The act allows several exemptions, such as subdivisions consisting of fewer than 25 lots, and provides certain penalties for violation.

U. S. Department of Housing and Urban Development (HUD)

HUD administers the funding of federal money to municipalities and private individuals within New York for projects related to housing. Grant money is funded to the larger cities on an annual basis. The amount is set by formulas based on factors such as the local economy, population density, and housing poverty levels. These grants or entitlements must be expended in accordance with federal guidelines. A major portion of the funding comes through the Community Development Block Grant Program.

U. S. Army Corps of Engineers

The Army Corps of Engineers is a division of the U. S. Army. Much of the corps' activities are mandated through the EPA. The corps oversees navigation, water resource activities, flood control, beach erosion, and dredging projects. It also has the authority to permit or deny a variety of water-related activities and to issue permits for waterfront development and rights of entry into waterways under its jurisdiction. One of the Corps' functions is to determine who is responsible for contamination.

Power of Taxation

Exercise of the power of taxation is one of the inherent burdens on private ownership of land. Taxes levied by a local government constitute a specific lien against the real estate. In New York, real property tax liens take priority over all other liens.

Eminent Domain

The right or power of **eminent domain** is *the power of the government or its agencies to take private property for public use.* The actual *taking of property under the power of eminent domain* is called **condemnation.** In New York, the condemning authority may be the state including authorized agencies, municipalities, school districts, public utilities, railroads, and the federal government. The right of eminent domain can be used only if (a) the property condemned is for the use and benefit of the general public, and (b) the property owner is paid the fair market value of the property lost through condemnation. Property owners have the right to trial if they are not satisfied with the compensation.

"Taking" as Defined by the New York Courts

A **"taking"** *occurs when private property is regulated by a government authority to the economic detriment of the owner, without compensation.* In a lawsuit decided by the New York Court of Appeals in 1989, *Seawall Associates v. City of New York* (542 NE2d 1059 74 NY2d 92), the court found that the regulation of the use of private property constitutes a taking if it deprives the owner of all economically viable uses of the property and the property owner can no longer obtain a reasonable return on his investment.

In a 1992 landmark decision by the U. S. Supreme Court, *Lucas v. South Carolina Coastal Council* (120 L. Ed. 2d 798, 1992), the court found that a regulation allowing a taking under eminent domain is unconstitutional if it prohibits the building of any habitable or productive improvement on the owner's land and eliminates all economically beneficial use of the land.

You Should Know **The difference between police power and eminent domain.**

A requirement for an eminent domain taking always implies just compensation to the affected property owner. A government's right under police power is to decide and legislate matters related to real property for the public benefit. It does not imply compensation to the property owner. This fact forms the basis of numerous lawsuits.

TABLE 10.1 Taxation, eminent domain, and escheat.

	DEFINITION	PRIVATE OR PUBLIC RIGHT	COMPENSATION TO PROPERTY OWNER	LEGAL POWER
Property Taxation	Right to levy tax according to property value	public	No	A specific involuntary lien
Eminent Domain	Right to take property for public use	public	Yes	Involuntary title conveyance for the public good
Escheat	Property goes to the state if there are no heirs or will	public	No	Involuntary conveyance of title

Power of Escheat

If an owner dies intestate (without having a valid will) the decedent's property is distributed to heirs in accordance with New York statutory provisions. *If there are no located heirs or creditors,* the state uses its power of **escheat** and *the property goes to the state.* (See Table 10.1.)

LOCAL AUTHORITY

Bundle of Rights and "As of Right Zoning"

The bundle of rights refers to the inherent rights that property owners may have in real property. The theory of "as of right zoning" is also implied in this bundle of rights. The court has held that when a zoning legislative body establishes the use of a particular zone, it cannot discriminate among different landowners in using the zone in a similar way. For example, if one property owner is allowed to build a two-family home in a residential zone, then every property owner may build a two-family house in that zone.

Zoning Classifications

Although New York has control over certain public lands and open spaces, planning and zoning are the province of local governments and their respective planning boards. Zoning, subdivision development, budgeting, site plan review, and even building codes are set by the local governments.

Areas in a community are divided into various classifications; these classifications may also have different uses within the zone. Certain zones are more restrictive than others.

Residential Zones

Residential zones can be subdivided into single-family homes and various levels of multifamily dwellings. **Accessory uses** of property are frequently found in residential zones. These uses are *incidental or subordinate to the main use of the property.* An example is an equipment shed on a residential lot. An **accessory apartment** could be *an in-law apartment in a residential home.* Residential property is sometimes used by an owner or a lessee for a small business or home occupation. A **home occupation** *may be conducted only by the residents of the dwelling and it must be incidental and secondary to the use of the dwelling.* The home occupation may not change the character of the dwelling and there must be no external evidence of the use except as permitted by the local zoning ordinance.

Much litigation has taken place over the years as to the establishment of group homes in residential zones. In today's society, there is a movement to remove individuals from institutional settings and relocate them into residential settings, such as large homes in residentially zoned communities. A **group home** is *a residential facility for five or more adults who have been institutionalized for various reasons and then released.* Halfway houses, established foster homes, and residential rehabilitation centers may also fit into the category. In some instances, residents may attempt to keep group homes out of their neighborhood claiming that only a family can reside in a single-family house in a residential zone. This brings up the question of what legally constitutes a family. The definition of a **family** in New York may be any one of the following:

- an individual, or two or more persons related by blood or marriage or adoption, living together in one dwelling
- a group of up to three people who are not married, or blood relatives, or adopted, who live together as a single housekeeping unit
- one or more persons living as a single housekeeping unit, as distinguished from a group occupying a hotel, club fraternity, or sorority house

In a lawsuit decided by the New York Court of Appeals in 1985, *McMinn v. Town of Oyster Bay* (66 NY2d 544 488 NE2d 1240), the court found that the town statute in question had an "over restrictive definition of a family which failed to provide for households functionally equivalent to a family," and that the statute violated the New York State Constitution and the New York Human Rights Law.

Other Zones

Commercial zones include retail stores, restaurants, hotels, service businesses, and other similar business.

Industrial zones may be composed of light or heavy manufacturing companies and warehouses.

Vacant land is land without buildings, or "unimproved." This includes land brought back to its natural state, or land that does not possess improvements that serve a purpose.

An *agricultural zone* is used for animal grazing and crop production. Zoning ordinances favor agriculture use, that has rarely been prohibited or limited.

Public open space is land that is not expressly developed for residential, commercial, industrial, or institutional use. Open space is owned by private individuals or the public (government) and includes agricultural and forest land, undeveloped shorelines, public parks, lakes, and bays. Land that is defined as open space depends on its surroundings. A vacant lot can be open space in a big city. A narrow pathway for walking is open space even though it is surrounded by public areas.

Park lands are public areas generally used for recreational activities and preserved for their ecological, aesthetic values, and education purposes. State and local governments administer and control open space and park land.

Recreation areas are supervised by DEC and OPRHP under the following categories: parks and shorelines; public fishing areas; trailways and greenways; and waterway access. Recreation areas are owned by individual municipalities and private individuals.

Institutional areas include hospitals, correctional facilities, courthouses, college and university campuses, and public schools. An institution such as a hospital may be permitted in a residential or commercial zone depending on the local zoning ordinance. Some institutions (for example, correctional facilities) are supervised by either the state or local municipality. Others, such as hospitals, may be publicly or privately owned.

Transfer of Development Rights

Inherent in a parcel of land are certain development rights. These development rights are not fully exercised with historic buildings and properties because the properties must be preserved. Therefore, the historic property can sell these rights to a developer, who, for example, wishes to erect a high-rise office or an apartment building, and whose development rights are not sufficient for the square footage desired for the structure. With this **transfer of development rights,** *the developer buys the development rights from the historic property (that cannot use them); the historic property then realizes income from the sale of these rights.* These development rights can also be transferred from other "underbuilt" properties. See Figure 10.2.

Types of Zoning

Incentive Zoning

This type of zoning offers *incentives* to developers and property owners to construct amenities that would provide uses and enjoyment for the residents of the municipality. The floor-to-area (FAR) ratio is often the incentive. FAR expresses the relationship between the amount of useable floor area permitted in a building (or buildings) and the area of the lot where it is situated. FAR is obtained by dividing the gross floor area of a building by the total area of the lot. A low floor-to-area ratio covers more of the lot area with building square footage. This is often economically desirable to developers. A municipality may grant a lower floor-to-area ratio if a developer agrees to provide amenities such as a daycare center, covered tunnels, or shops and service businesses in the building.

Cluster Zoning

Cluster zoning is *an example of multi-use zoning where a number of residential uses are allowed in one zone.* It allows a developer to place single-family houses, town homes, apartments, or other housing close together in exchange for leaving certain parts of the development open for the enjoyment of the community. The open space might be used for a swimming pool or for bike paths. *The cluster of housing may be composed of parcels of land that share a common border called* **abutting land**. Properties that are touching, bordering, or close together are known as *contiguous properties.* Figure 10.3 illustrates incentive and cluster zoning.

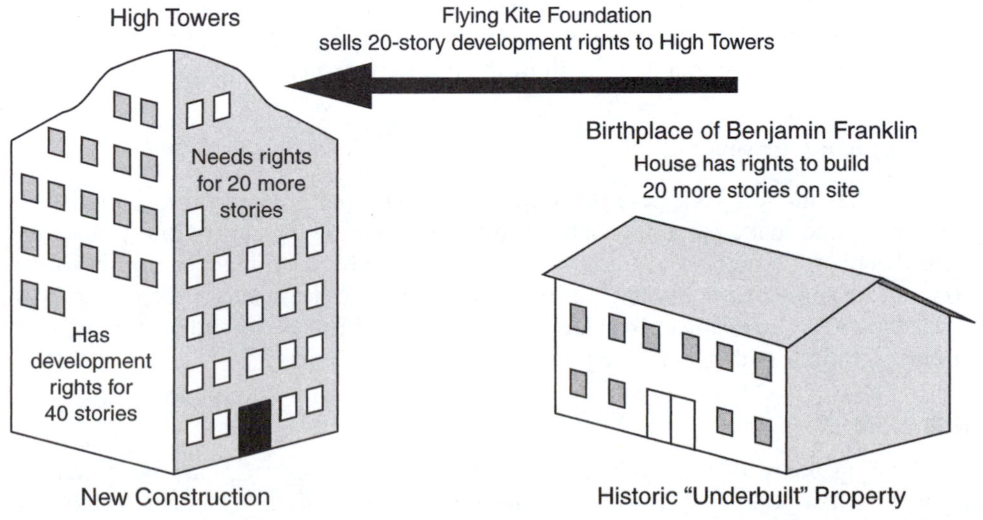

FIGURE 10.2
Transfer of development rights.

FIGURE 10.3 Incentive and cluster zoning.

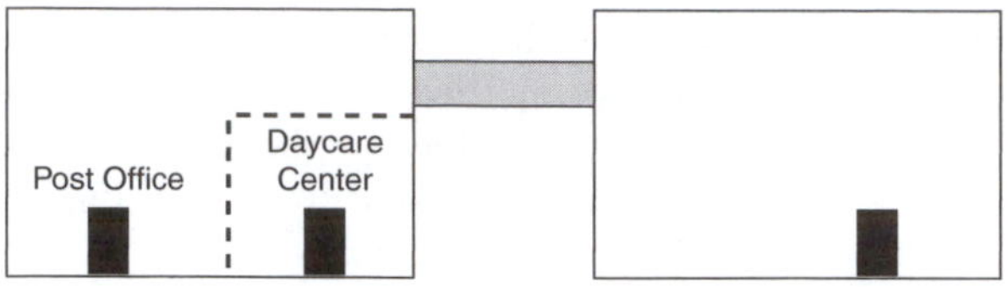

A post office, daycare center, and covered walkway to an adjoining building were constructed within the building so that the zoning authority would allow the developer to design a one-story structure with a low floor-to-area ratio.

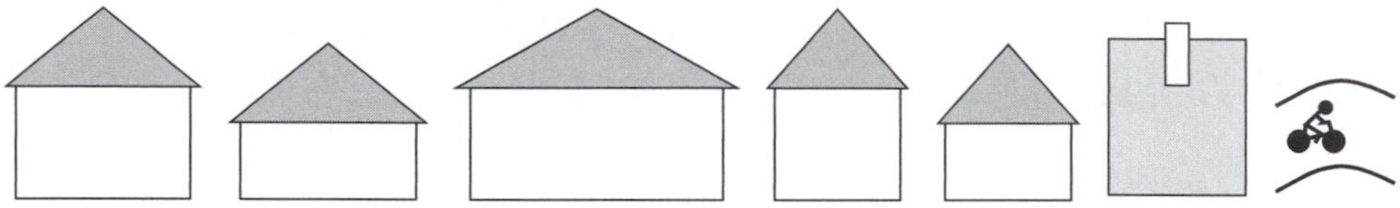

Properties are placed close together to make room for open space such as a pool and bike path.

Open Meeting Law (Sunshine Law)

The federal Freedom of Information Law (FOIL) provides that meetings of governmental agencies and departments be open to the public. It also provides that the public has reasonable access to records of these meetings. This is extremely important in land use proceedings because zoning boards, planning boards, and special sessions of the local zoning authority are open to the public.

LOCAL LAND USE PLANNING

Local land use measures may be legislated and carried out at several interrelated levels of government. Local planning boards decide the general layout of a specific municipality in a city, town, or village, and map the zones and uses allowed within each zone. Zoning boards of appeal hear and decide on variances and special use permits within the particular municipality.

The purpose of planning is to provide for the orderly growth of a community that will result in the greatest social and economic benefits to the people living there. In urban planning, the first step is typically to develop a *master* or *comprehensive plan* to determine the city make-up. Planners conduct a survey of the community's physical and economic assets. In the absence of such planning, haphazard development often ensues. Along with the plan, the community agrees on certain zoning requirements. The proposal is presented by referendum to all of the property owners in the community.

The Planning Board

Municipalities in New York have planning boards that hold public hearings and investigate, report, and make recommendations to the appropriate legislative body. Once they create the plan, zoning ordinances are established. Zoning ordinances consist of two parts: (a) the zoning map, that divides the community into designated districts, and (b) a text of the *zoning ordinance,* that sets forth the type of use permitted under each zoning classification, with specific requirements for compliance.

Subdivisions

The planning board of a municipality establishes *subdivision regulations.* A *subdivision* is land that is divided into lots for development purposes. Whether a subdivision is approved is based on many factors. The planning board must first consider the demographics of the community. **Demography** is *the study of the social and economic statistics of a community.* The planners must ascertain whether the community can support a new development. A census is a recordation of each individual and property in a municipality and includes statistical information that helps determine housing and service needs. **Census tracts** are designed for this statistical purpose. They are *small geographic areas established through cooperation between the local community and the Bureau of Census and have numerical identification numbers.*

New construction in a community causes increased *water usage, sewers, utilities, schools, roadways, medical services, and additional police and fire department support* that make up the community's **infrastructure**. An added burden of population will force the municipality to increase its services. Whenever development is proposed, new demands must be considered. A developer may be required to pay impact fees to the municipality to cover the extra cost for at least part of these services.

Zoning Actions

The planning board may make recommendations to the legislative body of the municipality to consider different types of zoning actions such as moratoriums, variances, special use permits, and rezoning. A **moratorium** imposed by a municipality *is a delay in allowing development of property within the municipality.* The reason may be that the municipality does not have the services available to support the new development. Some municipalities have plans that call for phased development. This is a process in which development is allowed when the additional support services are available. A moratorium also is an exercise of police power and must be initiated only for public welfare. Moratoriums are temporary. Eventually, a municipality must allow the property owner to use his land.

Capital Budget

Included in the master plan is a budget for the municipalities' expenditures—what they plan to acquire over the long term and when they plan to acquire it. For example, a municipality may develop a swimming pool and park area. It must budget monies as well as designate a date for initiating the project.

Plat, Density, Street, and Traffic Patterns

A developer must file a plat of subdivision with the municipality. The plat is a recorded map that shows a rendering of the lots, their sizes, and where they will be situated on the property. The size and shape of the lot determine the population density of the subdivision and therefore the types of structures that will be approved. *Density* is the occupancy restriction for the number of families that can inhabit a certain plot of land. Planning board rules governing density are set forth to avoid overcrowding residential areas. Considerations to control density may include a minimum lot size, setback and boundary requirements, and minimum size of the dwelling.

Contained in the plat is a legal description and any easements that run with the land. The plat illustrates the street and traffic patterns. Streets in a subdivision that are *dead ends and therefore do not connect to the main road* are known as **cul-de-sacs.**

Site Plan and Review

In New York, local planning boards have the authority to review site plans, an action that allows the board to evaluate a proposal's potential physical, social, and economic effects on the community. A site plan may be for either residential or commercial development. Other governmental agencies are involved in the review. The site plan must consider the **topography** of the land, that is, *the physical features and contours of the land.* It includes types of soil; the locations of water, such as wetlands or springs; and floodplains and the location of trees, rocks, and other vegetation. These features are relevant to how and where dwellings will be situated, where utilities and pipelines will be located, and the overall look of the completed subdivision. The plan includes available utilities and implementation of new utility systems, drainage, easements running through the property, zoning surrounding the site, open spaces, configurations of streets and sidewalks, types of structures that will be built, environmental considerations, and marketing.

A *survey,* that measures the boundaries and the total physical dimensions of the property, is part of the site plan. The developer must present the entire plan for a proposed site for review by the planning board.

Federal Housing Administration (FHA) Approval

FHA is a federally backed agency that insures lenders against default by borrowers. If there is a default, FHA pays the lender the amount due on the borrower's mortgage. The FHA creates minimum building standards for properties whose mortgage is approved and insured. Therefore, if the houses in a subdivision have FHA financing, the developer must follow its regulations and guidelines.

The Zoning Board of Appeals

The *zoning board of appeals* has the power to review administrative rulings made by the planning board or other legislative body, grant or deny exceptions and special permits, and process applications for variances. The zoning board of appeals is an administrative agency, but only *quasi-judicial.* Its decisions are subject to review and change in the state and federal courts. The zoning board does not make policy. It is a local administrative appeal agency and an interpreter of the zoning ordinance. The zoning board of appeals perfects and ensures the validity of zoning and safeguards the rights of property owners. It also ensures the fair application of zoning regulations and serves as a safety valve for the zoning system. If a property owner wishes to obtain an exception to the zoning ordinance, the owner may appeal to the board for a variance or special use permit. If the request is denied by the zoning board of appeals, the property owner may petition the New York Supreme Court through an *Article 78 proceeding.* An Article 78 proceeding is an appeal brought forth because of a ruling by a government agency. Lawsuits involving zoning ordinances are common, and some cases have been decided by the U. S. Supreme Court.

New York City

In New York City, the planning and the zoning board is combined and is known as the Board of Standards and Appeals. Zoning applications go through the planning commission. There is no separate zoning board of appeals. There are 12 members and one chairperson on the NYC planning commission.

Variance

A **variance** is *a permitted deviation from specific requirements of the zoning ordinance* (see Figure 10.4). For example, if an owner's lot is slightly smaller than the minimum lot-size requirement set by zoning ordinances, the owner may be granted a variance by petitioning the appropriate authorities. In New York, there are two types of variances: use variance and area variance. A **use variance** is *permission to use the land for a purpose that is prohibited under the current zoning restrictions.* A use variance must imply that the current zoning ordinance has caused the property owner an unnecessary hardship and should include all of the following:

1. The property owner is deprived of all economic use or benefit from the property. The property owner must give financial evidence to this effect.
2. The hardship is unique and not universal to the area or neighborhood.
3. The variance will not change the essential character of the neighborhood.
4. The alleged hardship is not self-created.

In the case of a use variance, the zoning board of appeals will grant the minimum variance necessary to address the unnecessary hardship while still protecting the character of the neighborhood and the health, safety, and welfare of the community. An example of a use variance is when the existing zoning allows one-family homes and a property owner receives a use variance to build a two-family home.

An **area variance** is *permission to use the land that is not normally allowed by the dimensional or physical requirements of the current zoning ordinance.* An area variance includes considering the benefit to the individual property owner as weighed against the detriment to the health, safety, and welfare of the neighborhood. The following are considered in granting an area variance:

1. undesirable change or detriment to nearby properties if granted
2. if the benefit sought can be achieved by other feasible means
3. if the requested variance is substantial
4. if it would have an adverse effect or impact on physical or environmental conditions in the neighborhood or district

FIGURE 10.4 Deviations from zoning ordinances.

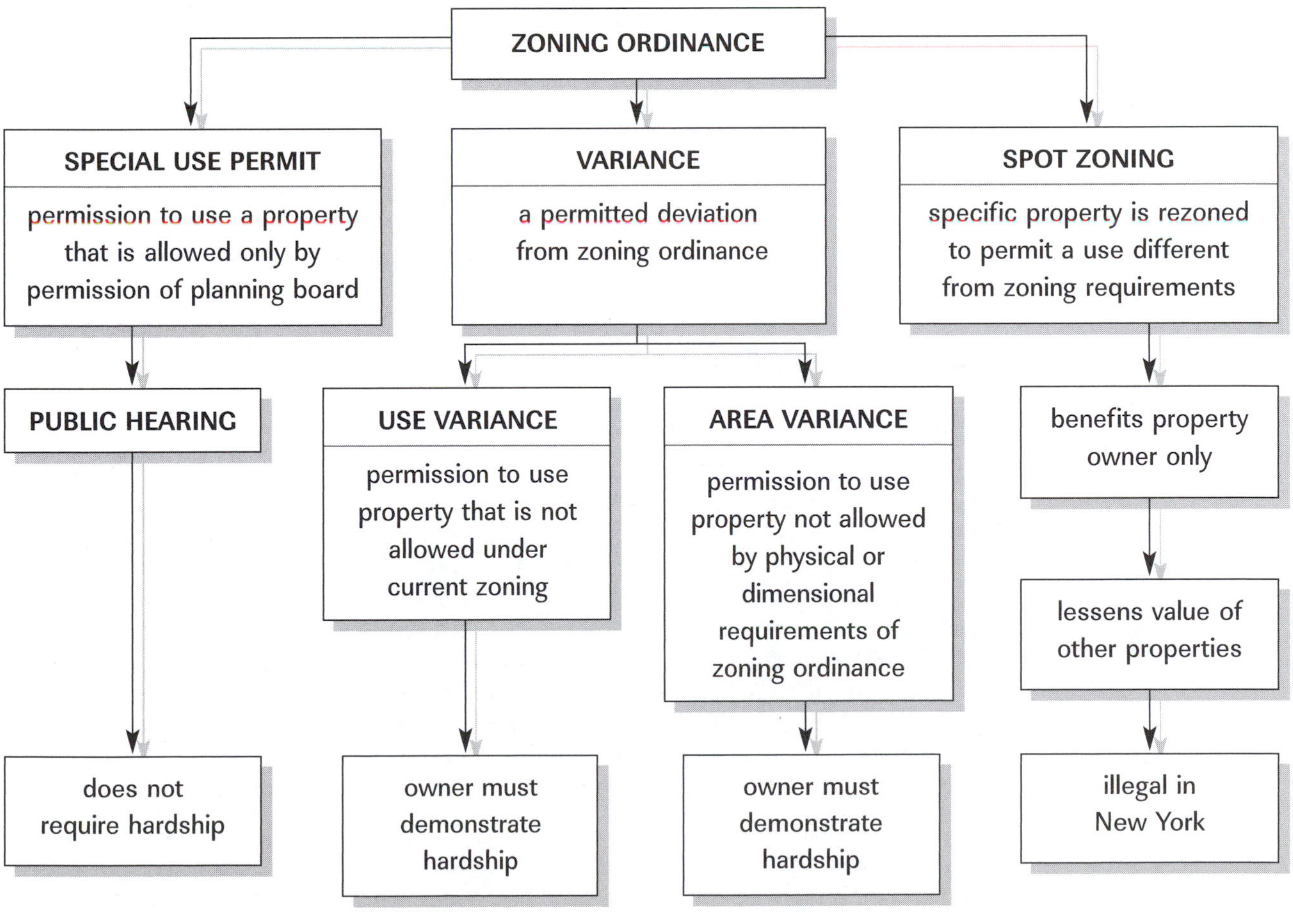

5. if the difficulty was self-created (even if the difficulty was self-created, it would not preclude granting the variance)

An example of an area variance is if the existing zoning ordinance mandates that lot square footage for a single-family home has to be 12,000 square feet and a property owner is given an area variance to build a home on the lot that is 11,850 square feet.

Special Use Permit

A special use permit is a use that is not permitted in the zone except with the special permission of the planning board or other legislative body. A special use permit cannot be granted without a public hearing in which the residents participate and voice their objections. Unlike a variance request, special use permits do not require that the property owner demonstrate undue hardship because of the current zoning. In New York, a special use permit can be authorized if the proposed use is in harmony with local zoning ordinances and laws, does not adversely affect the neighborhood, and is beneficial to the community.

Spot Zoning

With **spot zoning,** a *specific property within a zoned area is rezoned to permit a use different from the zoning requirements for that zoned area.* Spot zoning is illegal in New York. Property owners may try to rezone their land from residential to commercial or industrial use because this type of land is often more valuable. If the rezoning of a property is solely for the benefit of the property owner without a corresponding benefit to the entire neighborhood, or if the value of neighborhood properties would be decreased by the rezoning, this constitutes illegal spot zoning. Illegal spot zoning could occur, for example, if a property owner is allowed to build a manufacturing plant in a residential zone.

Nonconforming Use

When zoning is first imposed on an area or when property is rezoned, the zoning authority generally cannot require the property owners to discontinue a current use that does not now conform to the new zoning ordinance. A *nonconforming use* occurs when a preexisting use of property in a zoned area is different from that specified by the zoning code. This is called a preexisting nonconforming use or a "grandfathered" use. (See Figure 10.5 that illustrates zoning concepts.)

LOCAL ENFORCEMENT

Building Codes and Permits

Building codes provide another form of land use control to protect the public. *Building codes* require that a property owner obtain a *building permit* from the appropriate local government authority before constructing or renovating a commercial building or residential property. While construction is in progress, local government inspectors perform frequent inspections to ensure that code requirements are being met. After a satisfactory final inspection, a *certificate of occupancy* is issued, permitting occupation of the structure by tenants or the owner. Some cities require a certificate of occupancy based upon satisfactory inspection of the property, and prior to occupancy by a new owner or tenant, of any structure even though it is not new construction or has not been renovated. Inspection is required to reveal any deficiencies in the structure requiring correction before the municipality will issue a certificate of occupancy.

The New York State Uniform Fire Prevention and Building Code provides minimum standards for all types of buildings in New York, both residential and commercial. If a local code is more restrictive than the state code, then the more restrictive regulations would apply. If a municipality does not have a specific code, the

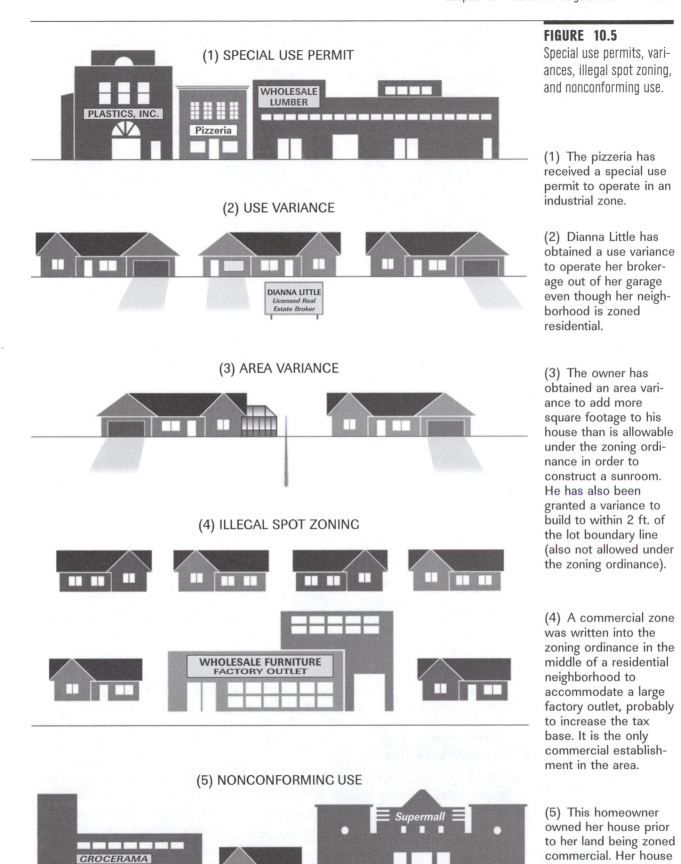

FIGURE 10.5
Special use permits, variances, illegal spot zoning, and nonconforming use.

(1) The pizzeria has received a special use permit to operate in an industrial zone.

(2) Dianna Little has obtained a use variance to operate her brokerage out of her garage even though her neighborhood is zoned residential.

(3) The owner has obtained an area variance to add more square footage to his house than is allowable under the zoning ordinance in order to construct a sunroom. He has also been granted a variance to build to within 2 ft. of the lot boundary line (also not allowed under the zoning ordinance).

(4) A commercial zone was written into the zoning ordinance in the middle of a residential neighborhood to accommodate a large factory outlet, probably to increase the tax base. It is the only commercial establishment in the area.

(5) This homeowner owned her house prior to her land being zoned commercial. Her house now sits among many commercial businesses.

New York code would apply. The code addresses construction, materials, safety, and sanitary standards for a building. It also includes standards for the "condition, occupancy, maintenance, rehabilitation and renewal of existing buildings."

Building departments. Building departments enforce the building code. Some have jurisdiction over large cities such as New York City; other departments oversee smaller municipalities. Their role is to protect the public by ensuring that code restrictions are adhered to and that work is performed by licensed and insured contractors. For example, the Department of Buildings in New York City oversees building construction, alteration and the enforcement of building and electrical codes, the State Multiple Dwelling Law, energy, safety, and labor laws related to construction. The approval, permission, and inspection of construction work, plumbing, elevators, electrical wiring, boilers, and licensing of trades people falls under its jurisdiction. The department inspects buildings under construction for compliance with public safety regulations and oversees more than 800,000 buildings.

Code violations. Many violations of building codes are possible. One example of a serious code violation in New York City is the creation of one or more illegal housing units without authorization from the Department of Buildings. An illegal conversion is the creation of a housing unit(s) without first receiving the approval of, and permits from, the New York City Department of Buildings. Often, a conversion involves the alteration or modification of an existing one- or two-family home by adding an apartment in the basement or attic. Sometimes, an illegal rooming house has been created in a building that was intended to be a one-family house. Illegal conversions reduce the quality of life in neighborhoods by enabling more people to live in an area than originally intended. Such unplanned growth causes a strain on local public services and results in the overcrowding of schools, public transportation, and sewer and sanitation systems. It also creates parking problems. The most serious aspect of this illegal construction is that often it creates substandard, potentially dangerous housing. Some of this housing also violates the zoning regulations for the area.

Professional Services

To control and develop land properly, the services of professionals specializing in various areas is essential. Civil engineers are employed to provide topographical descriptions of land and map out roadways. Environmental engineers evaluate environmental issues associated with land use to ensure lawful compliance. Surveyors provide detailed descriptions of the boundaries and divisions of land. Other experts, such as professional land use planners, may assist in the overall development and implementation of the master plan.

Local Courts

New York places most of the responsibility for overseeing local land use decisions with the courts. The courts usually, but not always, uphold municipal actions.

IMPORTANT POINTS

1. Private land use controls are in the form of deed restrictions and restrictive covenants.
2. Public land use controls include police power, taxation, eminent domain, and escheat.
3. New York Article 9–A protects state residents in the purchase or lease of vacant subdivided lands in and outside of New York purchased through installment land contracts.
4. The Interstate Land Sales Full Disclosure Act regulates the sale of unimproved lots in interstate commerce to prevent fraudulent schemes in selling land sight unseen.

5. Eminent domain is the right of government to take private land for public use.
6. If an individual dies without a will and no heirs or creditors, his property reverts to the state through the power of escheat.
7. Types of zones include residential, commercial, industrial, vacant land, agricultural, public open space, park lands, recreation areas, and institutional.
8. The planning board establishes subdivision regulations, creates a capital budget, and reviews site plans for new development.
9. The zoning board of appeals has the power to review administrative rulings made by the planning board.
10. A use or an area variance is a permitted deviation from specific requirements of a zoning ordinance.
11. Local support and enforcement of zoning ordinances and legislation include building codes, professional services, and the local court system.
12. The New York State Uniform Fire Prevention and Building Code provides minimum standards for all types of buildings.

How Would You Respond? CHAPTER REVIEW

Analyze the following situations and decide how the individuals should handle them in accordance with what you have just learned. Check your responses using the Answer Key at the end of the chapter.

1. Marjorie wants to open a woman's specialty clothing boutique in Syracuse, New York. Although she wants to locate her boutique in a commercial section of town, she also wishes to be near residential communities. How would you go about finding her the right location?

    ____

    ____

    ____

    ____

2. Roy wants to build a house on a lot you have shown him overlooking Saratoga Lake. The chalet he has designed is one foot too high for what is permitted. The extra foot provides the second story of the structure with a great view of the lake and would increase the property's value. No neighboring homes exist behind the lot. What might you suggest?

    ____

    ____

    ____

    ____

KEY TERM REVIEW

Fill in the term that best completes each sentence and then check the Answer Key at the end of the chapter.

1. The right of government to take private property for public use is called ______________________.
2. ______________________ is the actual taking of private property for public use.
3. ______________________ enables government to fulfill its responsibilities to provide for the public health, safety, and welfare of its citizens.
4. If an individual dies and leaves no heirs, the state uses its power of ______________________ to claim property left by the deceased.
5. A(n) ______________________ is an example of the control of private property.
6. An individual who wishes to open a business in a house that is used for living purposes only and is located in a residentially zoned area may have to apply for a(n) ______________________.
7. According to the ______________________, if landowners are lax in protecting their legal rights, they may lose them.
8. The delay in allowing development of property within the municipality is called a(n) ______________________.

MULTIPLE CHOICE

Circle the letter that best answers the question and then check the Answer Key at the end of the chapter.

1. Which of the following is an example of the private control of land?
   A. zoning
   B. building codes
   C. restrictive covenants
   D. environmental controls

2. Restrictive covenants are enforced by:
   A. zoning
   B. condemnation
   C. police power
   D. injunction

3. A permitted deviation from the standards of a zoning ordinance is called:
   A. special use permit
   B. spot zoning
   C. certificate of occupancy
   D. unlawful nonconforming use

4. Rezoning of a specific property for the owner's benefit only, without considering the welfare of the community is called:
   A. variance
   B. nonconforming use
   C. spot zoning
   D. unlawful nonconforming use

5. Which of the following statements concerning the Interstate Land Sales Full Disclosure Act is false?
   A. it regulates sales of unimproved lots across state lines
   B. it is administered by HUD
   C. the developer is required to record a property report in the county clerk's office
   D. subdivisions of fewer than 25 lots are exempt

6. With regard to vacant subdivided land, Article 9–A protects residents of New York State in the:
   A. purchase or lease of land located both in New York and other states with any type of purchase agreement
   B. purchase of land only
   C. purchase of land in New York and other states when it is purchased through an installment land contract
   D. purchase of land in New York that is obtained through eminent domain

7. Before a planning board will approve a subdivision, the developer must:
   A. purchase the land
   B. hire a construction crew
   C. apply to the zoning board of appeals
   D. submit a site plan for review by the planning board

8. When a developer buys development rights to allow more square footage in a structure, these rights are often:
   A. purchased from the municipality
   B. purchased from the owners of a historic property or other underbuilt structures
   C. mandated by a zoning ordinance
   D. allocated by enabling acts of the state legislature

9. A use that is incidental to the main use of a property is termed a(n):
   A. multi-use
   B. special use permit
   C. accessory use
   D. use variance

10. The federal agency that administers funding of federal money for housing is:
   A. Department of Housing and Urban Development
   B. Army Corps of Engineers
   C. New York Department of State
   D. Department of the Interior

ANSWER KEY

How Would You Respond?

1. An excellent reference for salespersons is the zoning map of the area in which you are marketing. You can illustrate where each zone is located, what zones are adjacent to one another, and other details regarding allowed uses. With the zoning map, you can easily show Marjorie the busy retail sections and their relationship to the residential sections.
2. Roy may be able to obtain an area variance since no neighbors live behind the structure who would be affected by the one-foot height difference. Also, one foot is not a major deviation from allowable dimensions. Roy suffers a hardship, as the property's value would be greatly diminished without the lake view.

Key Term Review

1. eminent domain
2. condemnation
3. police power
4. escheat
5. deed restriction
6. use variance
7. doctrine of laches
8. moratorium

Multiple Choice

1. C
2. D
3. A
4. C
5. C
6. C
7. D
8. B
9. C
10. A

Chapter 11

KEY TERMS

amperage
bearing wall
building envelope
circuit breakers
eave
fascia
flashing
footing
foundation wall
frieze board
fuse
girder
header
joist
lally column
pitch
rafter
R-factor
ridge beam
septic system
sheathing
sill plate
slab-on-grade construction
soffit
stud
voltage

LEARNING OBJECTIVES

Classroom hours: 3

1. Distinguish between land use as it relates to plans, specifications, building codes, building permits, and certificates of occupancy.
2. Explain New York State requirements on wells, sanitary wastewater systems, and energy codes.
3. Identify the use of various sites for drainage, shading, walkways, and landscaping.
4. Discuss basic construction knowledge of footings, foundation walls, wood framing, beams, girders, studs, and other structural components.
5. Identify types of insulations and proper location.
6. Demonstrate knowledge of the importance of ventilation and the systems employed to provide proper ventilation.
7. Know and identify the components in major heating, air conditioning, plumbing, and electrical systems.

Introduction to Construction

IN THIS CHAPTER A licensees' knowledge of construction and the systems that comprise a house can be the catalyst that makes or breaks a sale. Moreover, because a seller's Property Condition Disclosure form is generally part of the transaction, knowledge of construction principles is essential. This chapter provides an explanation of the principles, terminology, and methods of residential construction, and reviews the construction process from *top to bottom*.

LAND USE

Plans and Specifications

To comply with building codes, contractors or developers must file plans and specifications with the appropriate governmental body, usually the local building department and/or planning board. The *building plan,* also known as a *blueprint,* is a detailed architectural rendering of the structure that usually includes the plans for the mechanical systems. In New York, blueprints must be stamped by a licensed architect or engineer. The plan includes a layout of the rooms, their exact sizes, the location of doorways, windows, bathroom fixtures, and major kitchen appliances. The plan includes renderings of the outside appearance and dimensions including front, back, and side elevations. This blueprint provides the "map" that the builder and subcontractors will follow.

Building specifications are written narratives that explain the building plan. The specifications may include the materials used in the construction; an explanation of the various systems in the structure (heating, air conditioning, and plumbing); any particular design features not entirely visible in the plan; and landscaping plans, including existing vegetation that will remain. Mechanical and structural engineers and soil experts may be involved in the design.

NEW YORK STATE SITE REQUIREMENTS

On-Site Well Requirements

Many rural areas in New York are supplied with a private water supply such as a well. The New York State Department of Health (NYSDOH) has regulations for sanitary and safe water that act as the guideline for well water. Guidelines for site location for a well include the following:

1. The well should be constructed in an accessible location not subject to flooding.
2. It should be situated at a good distance from potential sources of pollution on the owner's property or any adjoining properties. NYSDOH has suggested a minimum distance between water supply and wastewater disposal units. Figure 11.2 illustrates a layout pattern for a house in relationship to the well water and wastewater disposal system.
3. When a well is located next to a building, it must clear any projection from the building by at least five feet.

On-Site Sanitary Waste System Requirements

Appendix 75–A of the New York Public Health Law covers all guidelines for on-site individual wastewater treatment systems. Some of the important guidelines regulating the site of wastewater treatment systems include the following:

1. If individual wastewater systems overlay a drinking water aquifer, the local health departments may establish population density limits and minimum lot sizes.
2. There must be four feet of usable soil available above rock for the installation of the absorption field (defined later).
3. Soils with rapid *percolation rates* must be blended with other less permeable soils to slow down the infiltration rate. *Percolation* is the movement of water through soil.
4. Wastewater systems must be separated from buildings, property lines, and wells and waterways according to specified minimum distances (see Figure 11.2). For example, a septic tank must be at least 50 feet from a well and the absorption field must be at least 100 feet from the well. These minimum distances can be changed only if plans are submitted by a design professional or an engineer and if approved by the local health department.
5. An additional usable area of 50 percent of the size of the system must be set aside for future replacement or expansion of the system whenever possible.

FIGURE 11.1
An onsite sanitary waste system (septic system).

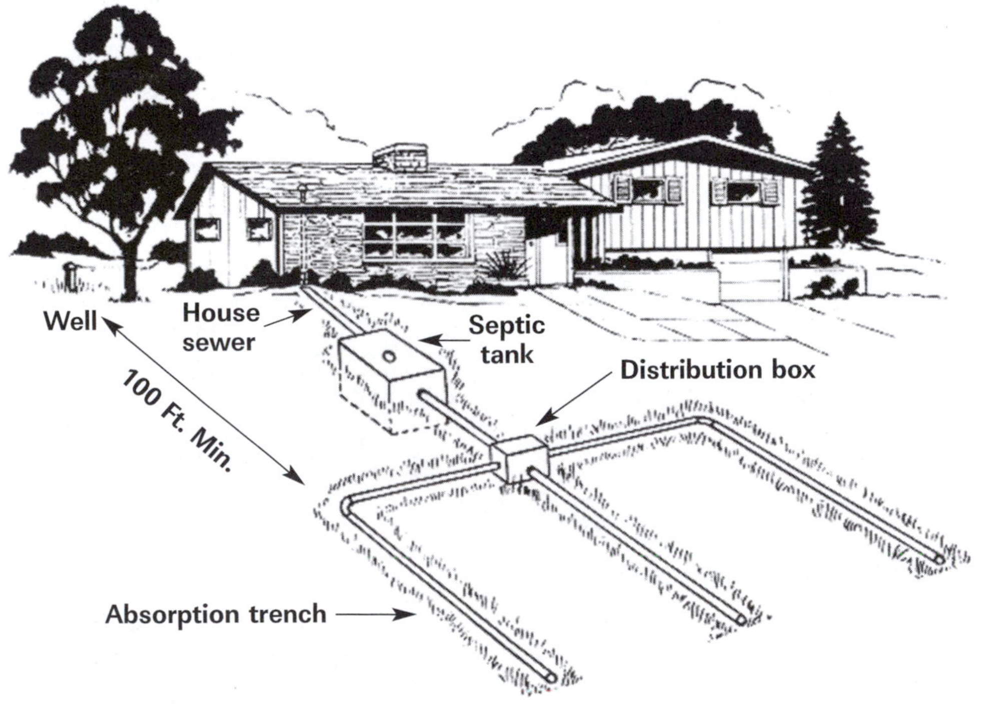

Source: New York State Department of Health.

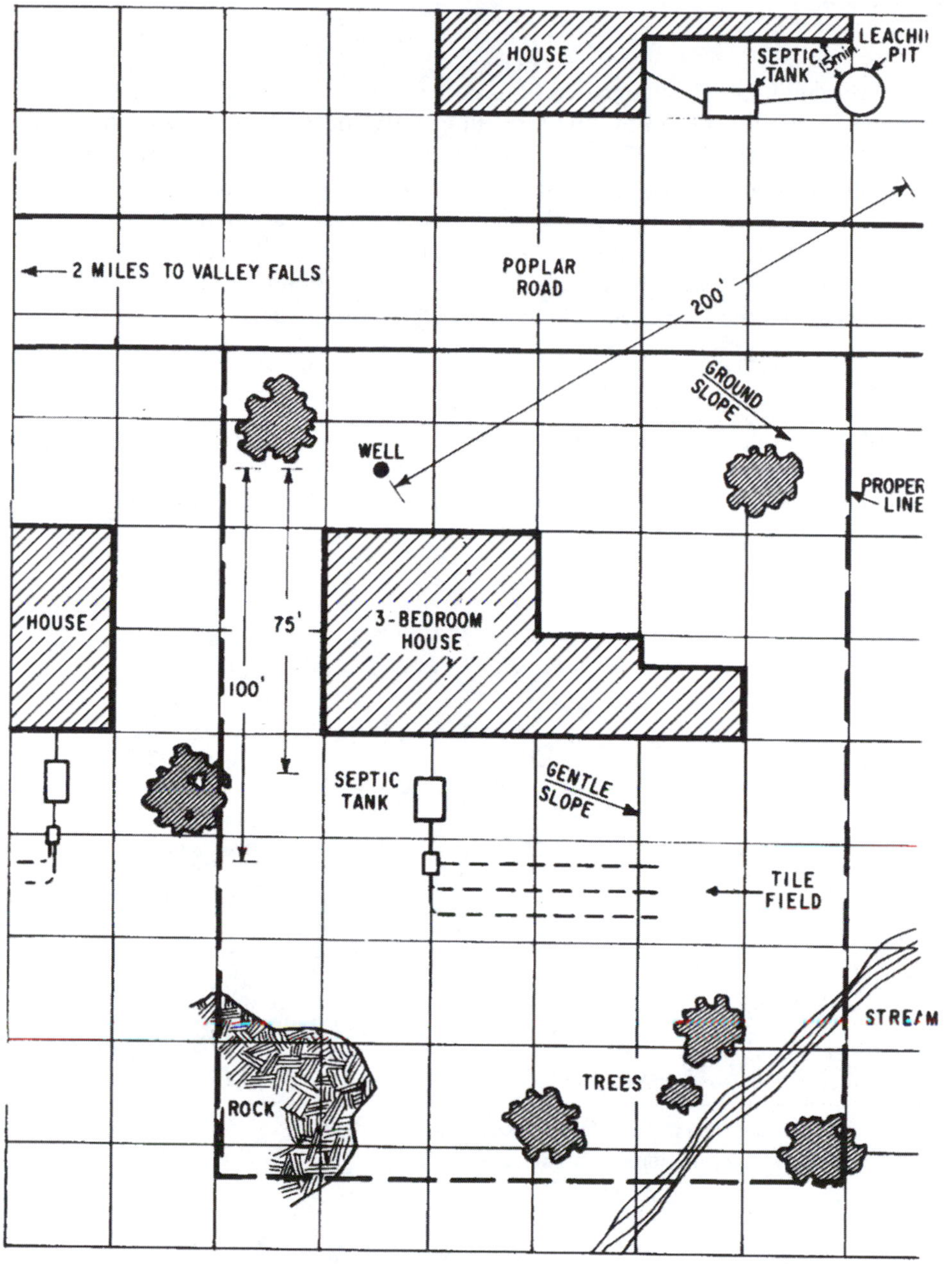

Source: New York State Department of Health.

FIGURE 11.2
A well location sketch.

Prior to construction, an environmental assessment must determine that the development of the site with the system is consistent with the overall development of the area and will not cause adverse environmental effects.

Energy Code

The *New York State Energy Code* sets minimum requirements for the design of all new buildings and renovations or additions to existing buildings. The code regulates building envelopes, HVAC, hot water, electrical and lighting systems, and equipment for efficient use of energy. The **building envelope** is *the building materials that enclose the interior and through which heating, cooling, or fresh air passes.* Local codes may be more restrictive than the statewide code and historic buildings are exempt.

SITE USE

Drainage

Drainage is one of the first considerations in preparing a construction site (Figure 11.3). A site that is composed of slightly rolling hills and valleys provides more natural drainage than do flat or very steep sites. Grading of the site, which is the arrangement and preparation of the soil for construction, places drainage areas where appropriate for water runoff. Proper grading must ensure that surface water is directed away from the foundation. Footing drain tile is used around all concrete or masonry foundations enclosing habitable or usable space, below grade (Figure 11.4). Crawl spaces under homes must be graded to ensure positive drainage.

Landscaping

Besides aesthetic appeal, landscaping can conceal unsightly areas, serve as a noise barrier, define certain spaces, prevent soil erosion, and remove pollutants. Natural vegetation, such as mature trees, may be on the site before excavation. The developer may wish to keep them

FIGURE 11.3
Draining problems–site located at the base of an incline.

In this illustration, water running down the incline washes the soil particles down the slope. This eventually causes full or partial erosion of the entire slope.

Source: From *The Home Inspection Book: A Guide for Professionals*, by Marcia Darvin Spada. © 2002. Reprinted with permission of South-Western Publishing.

FIGURE 11.4
Footing drain tile.

The footing drain tile is a perforated pipe laid around the perimeter of the foundation wall along the footing.

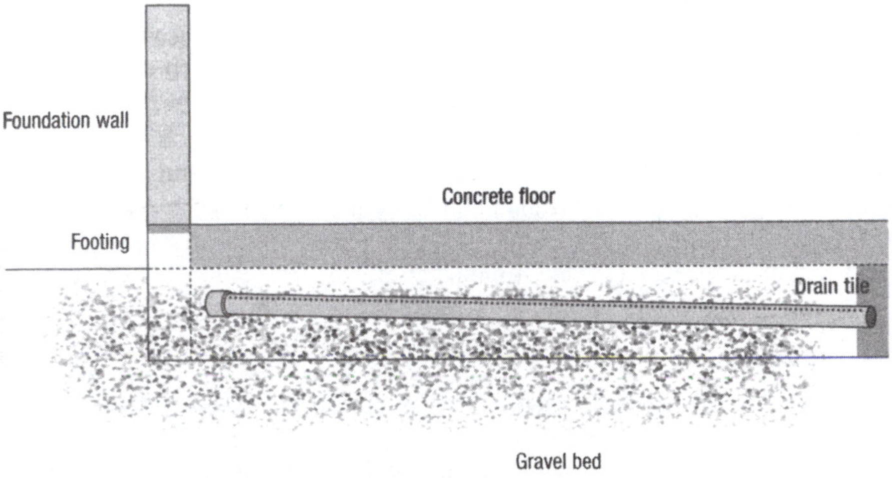

Source: From *The Home Inspection Book: A Guide for Professionals*, by Marcia Darvin Spada. © 2002. Reprinted with permission of South-Western Publishing.

in place. It is recommended that the house be situated at least 20 feet from any existing vegetation, especially mature trees that are to be preserved, so as not to disturb the root system. Surveys have shown that older trees around a house can improve value and salability.

In addition, the placement of trees and other landscaping can provide shade to certain areas of the house. The placement of the structure on the property determines the structure's exposure to sunlight at different times of the day.

Walkways and Paths

Generally, building code requirements call for a walkway from the front door of the house to the street or driveway. The minimum property standards set forth by HUD require walkways to all dwellings and other facilities within a development. Concrete, brick, or tile may be used for walkways. As part of the approval process, the planning board of the municipality may require the developer to construct walkways around or through the subdivision for public use. Within a specific lot, the site plan also may call for utilitarian and decorative walkways and paths. In addition to any code requirements, a developer, as part of the site plan for a subdivision, may have to dedicate to the municipality certain areas for public use (See Chapter 10).

STRUCTURE

Although a house is composed of many different components that may be unfamiliar, each basic part is necessary and relates to another. As you read through this section, refer to Figure 11.5 in order to visualize the complete structure.

FIGURE 11.5 The basic parts (structure) of a house.

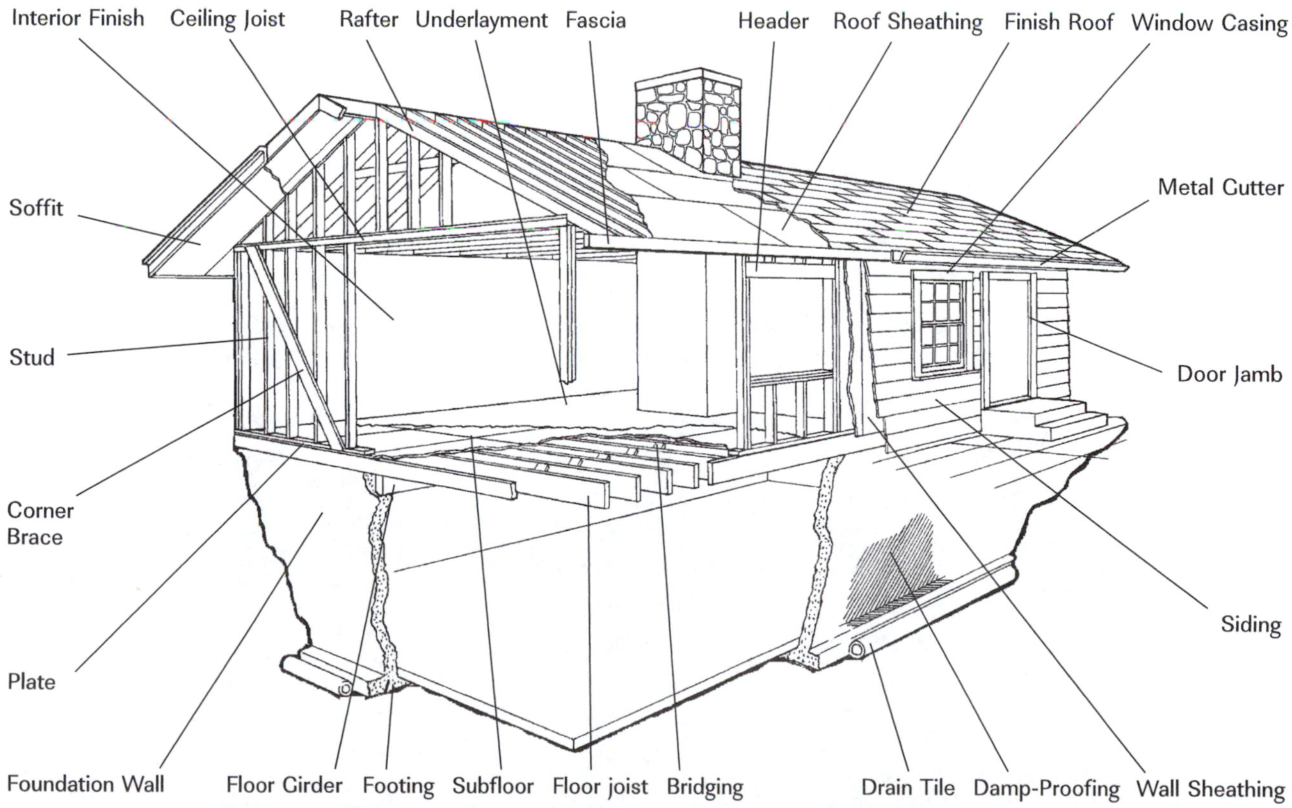

Source: From *The Home Inspection Book: A Guide for Professionals*, by Marcia Darvin Spada. © 2002. Reprinted with permission of South-Western Publishing.

Footings

The most important foundation building block is the footing. The **footing** is *the concrete base below the frost line that supports the foundation of the structure.* To construct the footings, the building lines are laid out with *batter boards,* temporary wood members on posts that form an L-shape outside the corners of the foundation. The width of the footing has to be at least twice the width of the foundation wall erected upon it. The depth of the footing is usually a minimum of eight inches (one- and two-story homes) and should be as deep as the foundation wall is thick. *The purpose of the footing is to support the foundation wall and, subsequently, the entire weight load of the structure.* The footings must provide an adequate base for the structure so as to prevent settling of the house. Figure 11.6 illustrates a typical residential footing and foundation.

Foundation Walls

Foundation walls in New York are generally *composed of poured concrete, masonry (concrete) block, or, sometimes, brick. The height of the foundation wall determines whether the structure has a full basement or a crawl space.* In masonry block foundation walls, the block forms the back half of the wall and is sometimes covered with a brick veneer on the front. Vertical masonry piers are built inside these foundation walls to provide additional support for the house. Of the three types of foundations built in New York (see Figure 11.7), full basements are most common (more than 80 percent), followed by slab-on-grade and crawl space.

The New York State Uniform Fire Prevention and Building Code requires that the foundation wall of the basement or crawl space and floors in contact with soil should

FIGURE 11.6 Footing and foundation.

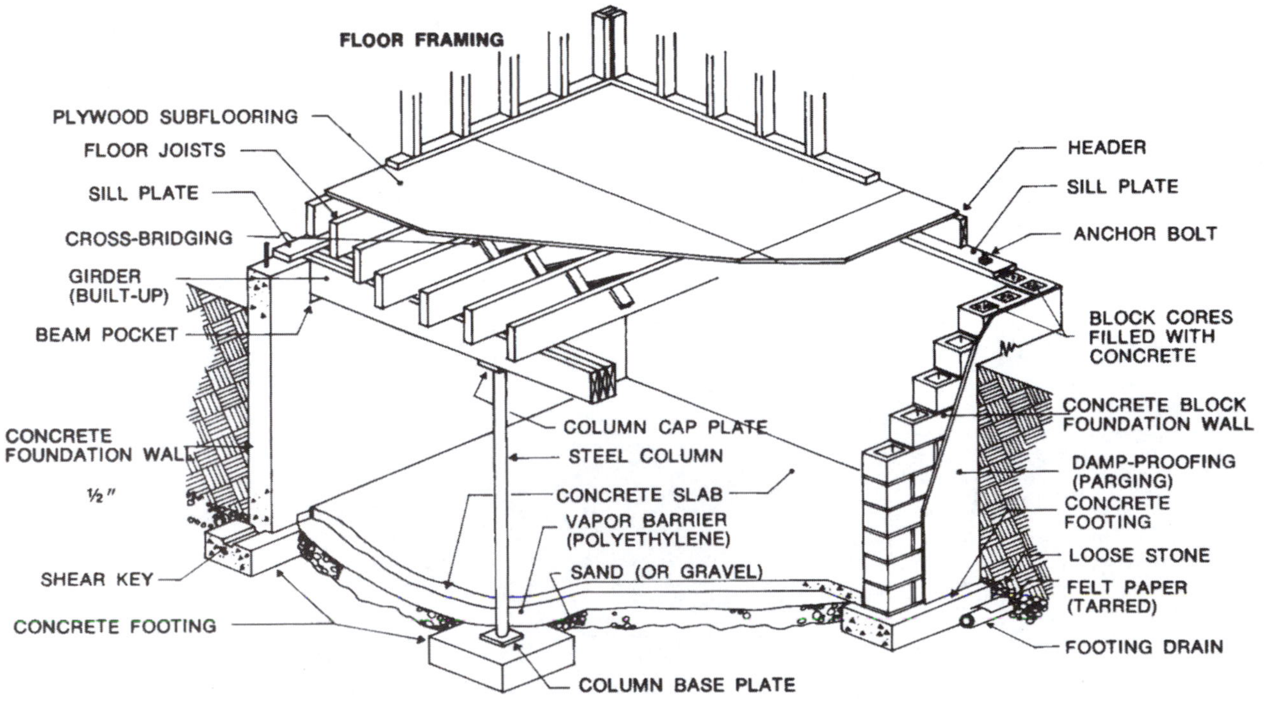

Source: *Houses, The Illustrated Guide to Construction, Design & Systems* by Henry S. Harrison, 3rd edition.

FIGURE 11.7 Common foundation types.

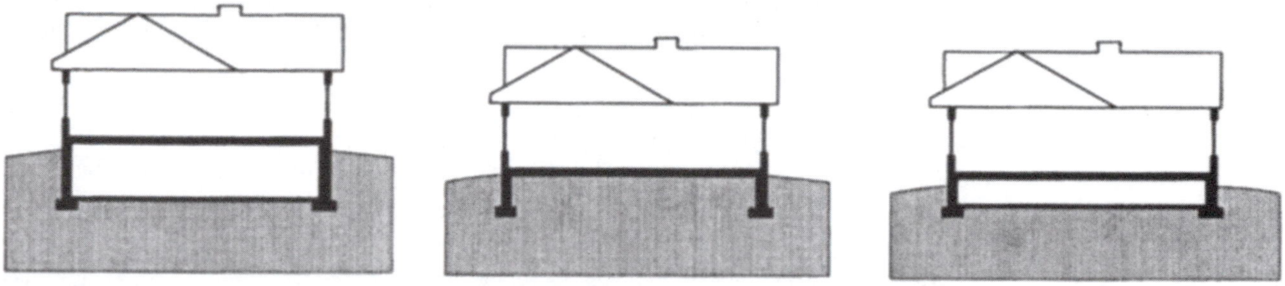

Of the three basic foundations built in New York State, full basements are most common (more than 80% of houses), followed by slab-on-grade and crawl-space foundations.

Source: *NY-STAR Builder Field Guide.* Copyright © NY-STAR, Inc.

be treated for penetration of ground and surface water. These vapor barriers can be heavy-duty plastic. Also, depending on local conditions, the New York code requires these areas be treated with termiticide.

Slab-on-Grade Construction

On level terrain, **slab-on-grade construction** is possible. The foundation is a concrete slab instead of a foundation wall. *The concrete slab is poured directly on the ground and therefore eliminates the crawl space or basement.* The slab provides the floor of the dwelling and the support for the exterior and interior walls. Slabs can be constructed by pouring the footing first and then pouring the slab. This is called a *floating slab.* If the footing and slab are poured at the same time, it is called a *monolithic slab.* The concrete slab method is less expensive than the foundation wall system or basement but is not practical in all building situations.

Wood Framing

Framing refers to the wooden skeleton of the home. *Wood-framing members* are lumber with a nominal dimension of 2" thickness. For example, a 2" × 4" is a piece of lumber 2" inches thick by 4" wide. These *framing members,* known also as **studs,** are commonly 2" × 4"s; 2" × 8"s, 2" × 10"s, or 2" × 12"s and are used vertically for wall construction. These wooden framing members are also used as **joists** for *floor and ceiling framing.* Usually 2" × 6"s or 2" × 8"s are used as **rafters** in the *roof framing system.*

Flooring

The top of the foundation wall is finished off with a course of solid masonry. On top of this rests the foundation sill plate. The sill plate is usually made up of a pressure-treated 2" × 6" or 2" × 8" piece of lumber. If pressure-treated lumber is not used for the sill, then metal flashing must be placed between the foundation wall and wooden member. The wooden sill is fastened to the foundation wall by anchor bolts. The **sill plate** is *the first wooden member of the house and used as the nailing surface for the floor system.*

The box sill, or banding, rests on the sill plate and is the same size wood member as the floor joists (2" × 8", 2" × 10", or 2" × 12"). The banding runs around the top of the foundation wall, attached to the sill plate.

The floor joists span the distance between the foundation walls and the girder and provide support for the subfloor. *The main carrying beam,* or **girder,** is *either a steel beam or several wooden members fastened together* (usually with 2" × 10"s, 2" × 12"s, or larger) *that spans the distance from one side of the foundation to the other.* The joists rest on the girder for support.

Lally columns may support the main carrying beam of the structure. *They are round steel columns filled with concrete that vary in diameter and rest on a base plate that is the column footing pad.* They are placed in the basement or crawl space, and their height is adjusted accordingly. The spacing of the lally columns is determined by the size and material of the main carrying beam.

Typical framing places wooden members at 16 inches on center. The phrase "16-inches on center" means that the center of one 2" × 4" stud is 16 inches away from the center of the next. Depending upon the area to be spanned, the joists are doubled or even tripled to support the load. Some modern construction methods use wooden floor trusses in place of single floor joists. A truss is a support member constructed in a factory by nailing a number of smaller members (2" × 4"s or 2" × 6"s) together in a number of triangular patterns to provide maximum strength. A plywood or particle-board subflooring rests directly on top of the joists.

STRUCTURAL TIE-IN OF ALL COMPONENTS

When all the framing members are assembled, the structure takes shape.

Walls

Wall framing forms the exterior and interior walls of the structure. The floor system serves as a stage or platform for the wall system. The walls are usually built of 2" × 4" studs, 16" on center. The **bearing walls** *support the ceiling and/or the roof and include the outside wall frame.* They are erected first. Nonbearing walls or partitions are walls that enclose interior space but do not support the structure.

A horizontal base plate, also called a *sole plate,* serves as the foundation for the wall system. A *double top plate* (Figure 11.8), also known as a *flitch beam,* is used to tie the walls together and provide additional support for the ceiling and roof system. The flitch beam is made up of two or more structural timbers bolted together with a metal plate sandwiched between for additional strength.

FIGURE 11.8 A wall double top plate or flitch beam.

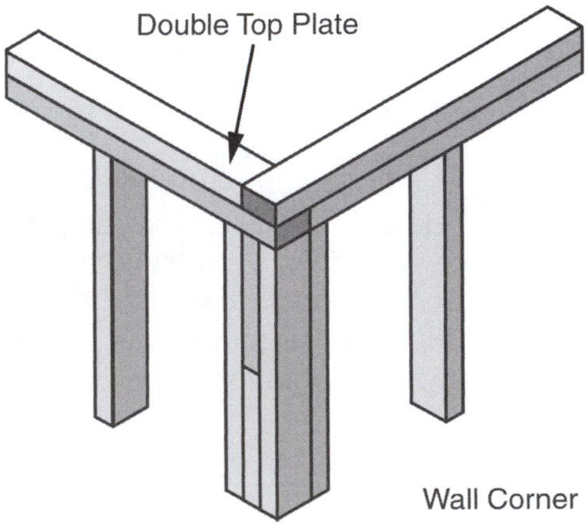

Openings in the wall for doors or windows must be reinforced to pick up the missing support for the vertical load. This process is done with 2" × 8"s, 2" × 10"s, or 2" × 12"s, known as **headers,** or *lintels,* erected over the top of the opening. Headers should form a solid wood bridge over the opening and extend to the bottom of the top plate. They actually support the ceiling and the roof over the door and window openings.

The type of framing described above is known as *platform framing,* because the framing of the structure rests on a subfloor platform. *Platform framing is the most common type of framing used in residential construction.*

An alternative to platform framing is *balloon framing.* This method uses a single system of wall studs that run from the foundation through the first and second floors to the ceiling support. This method is rarely used in residential construction.

A third type of framing is *post-and-beam framing.* These members are much larger than ordinary studs and may be 4" or 6" inches square. The larger posts can be placed several feet apart instead of 16" or 24" on center. Like balloon framing, this type of framing is seldom used in residential construction. Figure 11.9 shows the three types of framing.

FIGURE 11.9 Three types of frames.

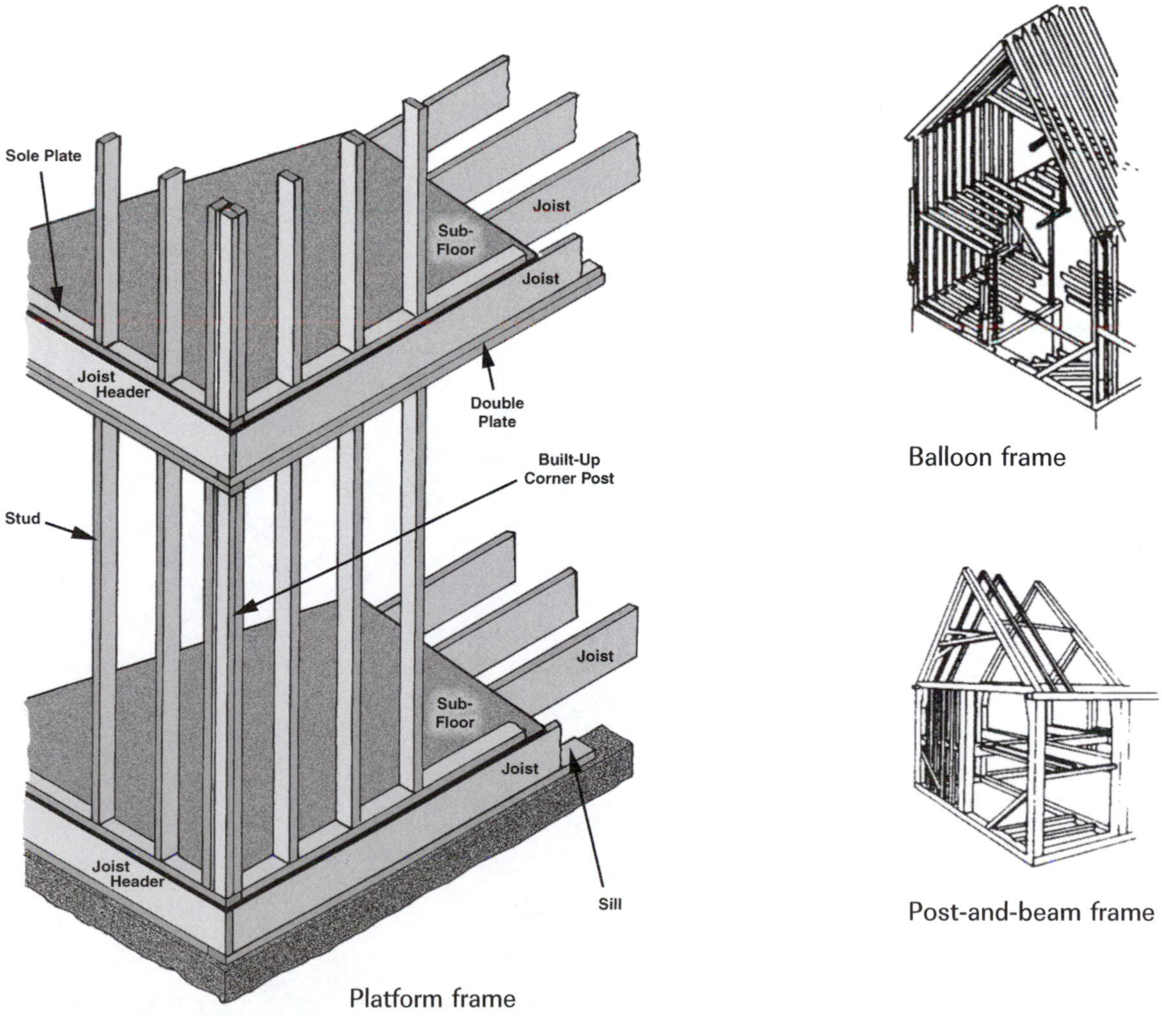

Ceiling Framing and Roof

The ceiling joists rest on the top plate of the wall. These joists should be placed directly over the vertical studs for maximum bearing strength. The joists span the structure between the outer walls. In traditional framing, these joists are usually 2" × 8"s, and the inner walls are important in helping to bear the load of the roof. This is different in the contemporary use of roof truss systems, in which the truss carries the load-bearing function to the outer walls. This feature provides freedom of placement of the inner walls. Since a roof truss is made up of a number of smaller members (usually 2" × 4"s), the attic space is almost completely lost. See Figure 11.10.

The **ridge beam** is *the highest part of the framing and forms the apex, or top line, of the roof. Rafters* are the long wooden members that are fastened to the ends of the ceiling joists and form the gables of the roof. Rafters are usually 2" × 6"s or 2" × 8"s. The rafters are fastened to the ridge at the peak of the gable. Most homes today are built with trusses (discussed above), therefore eliminating the ridge beam.

Characteristics to look for in roof identification include roof shape, or type, which includes the **pitch.** *The pitch is the slope of the roof.* Construction technique, style, and customized forms are other identifying factors. The roof is one of the most easily identifiable components of a house and often serves as a general description of the entire building. In contemporary residential construction, two varieties of roof styles are used: the traditional gable roof and the hip roof. Figure 11.11 includes an illustration of these and other common types.

The roof should extend at least 6" beyond the exterior of the structure. Common construction practices use a 12" overhang on the front and rear, with a 6" overhang on the side. These overhangs which are part of a sloped roof are known as the **eaves.** *The eaves are the lowest part of the roof which project beyond the walls of the structure.* The larger the overhang, the more protection exists from sun and rain for the exterior walls, windows, and doors. It is generally recommended that *flashing* strips be installed near the edge of the eave and other corners of the roof, such as around the base of the chimney. Mostly used in colder climates such as New York, **flashing** is *a*

FIGURE 11.10
A roof truss system.

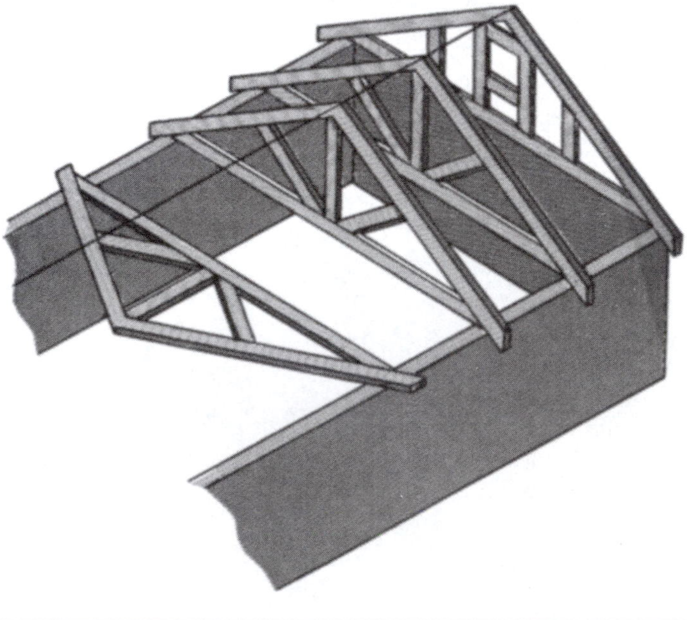

Source: From *Basics for Builders: Framing and Rough Carpentry*. Copyright R. S. Means Co., Inc., Kingston, MA 781-585-7880; All rights reserved.

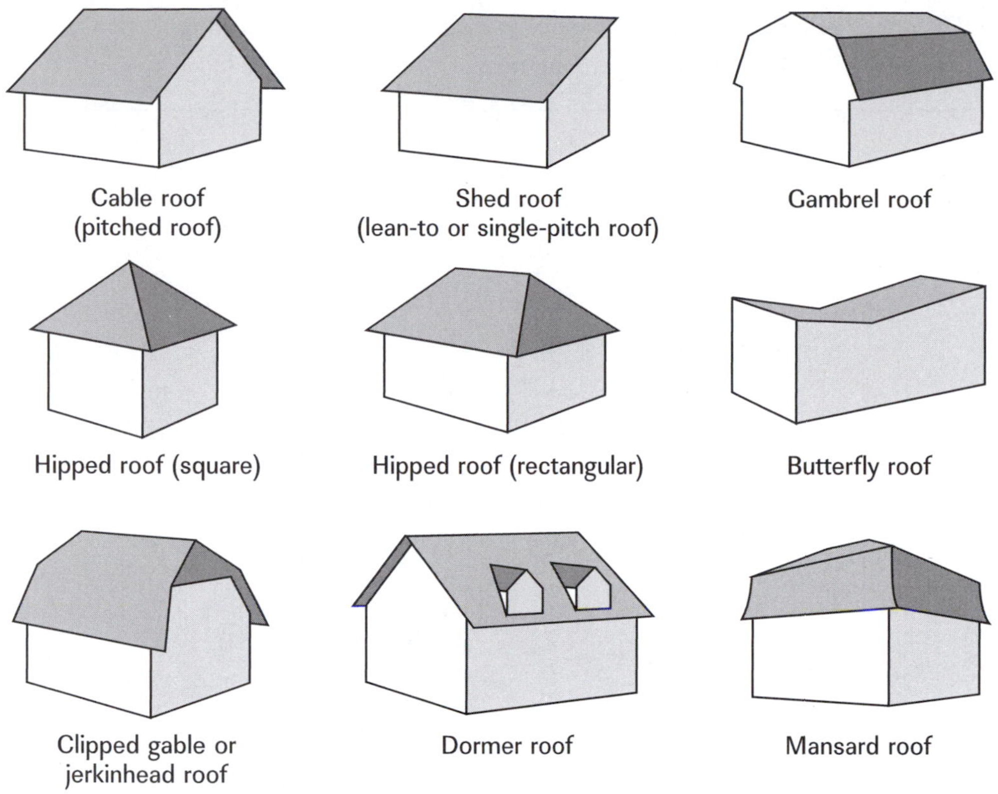

FIGURE 11.11
Common roof forms.

metallic material that is used in certain areas of the roof and walls to prevent water from seeping into the structure.

The overhang or eave is made up of three components: the soffit, the fascia, and the frieze board. The **soffit** is *the area under the roof extension.* This is made of wood, aluminum, or vinyl (depending upon the type of siding). *The area of material facing the outer edge of the soffit* is called the **fascia.** The fascia is typically a 1" × 6" or a 1"× 8" board and is perpendicular to the soffit. If guttering is installed on the roof, it is fastened to the fascia. The third component of the overhang is the **frieze board.** This is a *wooden member* (usually a 2" × 4", 2" × 6", or 2" × 8") *that is fastened directly under the soffit, against the top of the wall.* The purpose of the frieze board is both decorative and functional. The frieze board prevents wind and moisture from penetrating the junction of the soffit and sheathing. Once the structural skeleton of the roof system is in place, it is covered with either plywood or particle-board decking. On top of this, roofing paper is applied to aid in weatherproofing. On top of the roofing paper, shingles are applied. Most construction utilizes the fiberglass shingle, but tile and wood shingles are also used. Just as in the crawl space below the house, proper ventilation of the attic space is important.

Once all framing members are in place, including the roof rafters, a plywood covering called **sheathing** is *placed over the exterior framing members.* OSB board, also known as wafer board, may also be used for the sheathing. A final covering is placed over the sheathing; this covering is generally brick or siding in New York. *Siding* can be a metal, such as aluminum, wood, or vinyl. Often a combination of materials including fieldstone, brick, siding, or other materials is used. Some communities or subdivisions have regulations as to the outside materials of structures. Licensees working with new construction should be aware of any regulations. For the interior walls of the structure, a material known as sheetrock, wallboard, or plasterboard may be used, and special sheathing materials are also used for insulation.

PUTTING IT TO WORK Fill in the parts of the house as best as you can. Refer to the diagram of a house (Figure 11.5, p. 257) to check your answers.

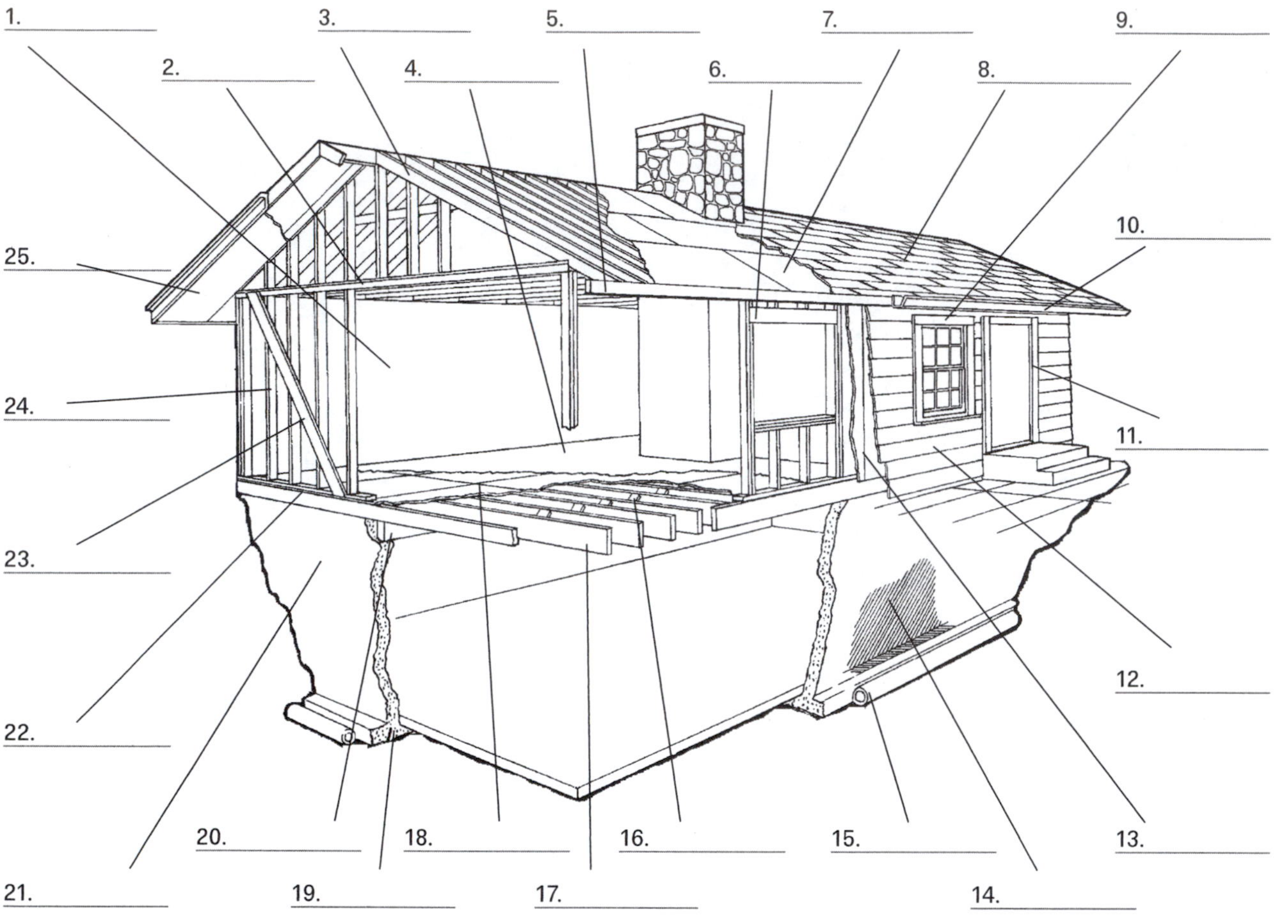

Source: From *The Home Inspection Book: A Guide for Professionals*, by Marcia Darvin Spada. © 2002. Reprinted with permission of South-Western Publishing.

ENERGY EFFICIENCIES

R-Factor

The primary purpose of insulation is to resist the flow of heat from one area to another. It provides the double benefit of preventing heat loss in the winter and protecting against heat load in the summer. The ceiling, walls, and floor must be insulated. Insulation is rated via an R-factor. Since the **R-factor** means *the degree of resistance to heat transfer of the walls* (heat is kept in or out), the larger the R-factor, the greater the degree of insulation. Most brand-name insulation products are marked with their particular R-factor.

Types and Location of Insulation

Once the structural components of the house are completed and the exterior walls are in place, the insulation is installed. Insulation is available in a variety of forms and falls into five categories: flexible, loose fill, rigid or wallboard, reflective, and sprayed. Flexible insulation is available in two types: blanket (or quilt) and batt.

- *Blanket insulation* is anywhere from 1" to 3" thick and comes in rolls of fiberglass or other fibrous material in 15½"-wide rolls. The insulation is stapled or nailed between the studs and under the rafters or over the ceiling. It is designed to fit in the space between the framing members such as joists and studs. Blanket insulation is enclosed in paper covers. One side may be treated for a vapor barrier to help keep moisture out of wall cavities. This cover sheet is often surfaced with aluminum foil or other reflective insulation that helps to keep out the heat.
- *Batt insulation* is made of fibrous material such as fiberglass and may range from 2" to 6" thick; it is widely used in New York. See Figure 11.12 for an illustration of batt insulation installed between studs.
- *Loose-fill insulation* is composed of lightweight materials such as perlite, vermiculite, wood paper, or cotton fibers. It can be poured or blown in to fill spaces between studs on a horizontal surface or in hard-to-reach areas. It is often used on attic floors.
- *Rigid insulation* is fibrous material in the form of lightweight wallboards that combine strength with heat and acoustical insulating properties. These boards can be used in roof and wall sheathing and concrete slab flooring.
- *Reflective accordion insulation* (Figure 11.12) receives its value not from the thickness but from its reflective surface. It must be exposed to an air space to be effective and can be installed in up to four layers that are opened up to provide the air space.

  Unfazed rolls (without paper covering) and loose blown-in insulation can be added on top of existing attic insulation to improve the energy efficiency of homes.
- *Spray-on insulation* is a hot, viscous mixture that is sprayed into the inside of the sheathing where it becomes solid. Urea-formaldehyde foam insulation (UFFI), an example of this type of insulation, is no longer used (see Chapter 14).

FIGURE 11.12
Two types of insulation.

(A) **Batt insulation.** The cavity is completely filled leaving no room for air movement.

(B) **Reflective accordion-type insulation.** The flat insulation is "opened up" to form spaces between the surfaces when installed.

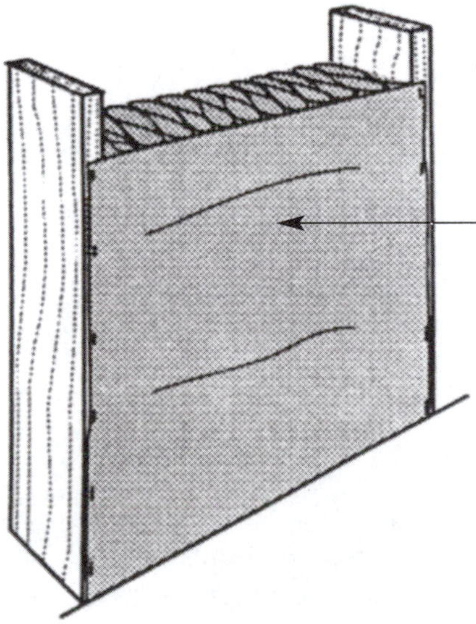

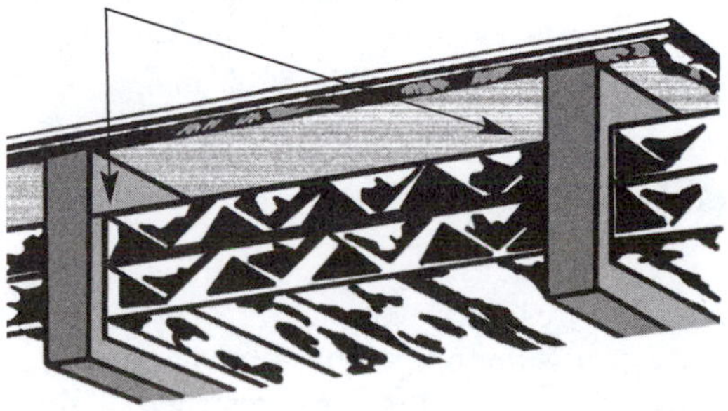

(A) *Source: NY-STAR Builder Field Guide.* Copyright © NY-STAR, Inc.

FIGURE 11.13
Insulation placement.

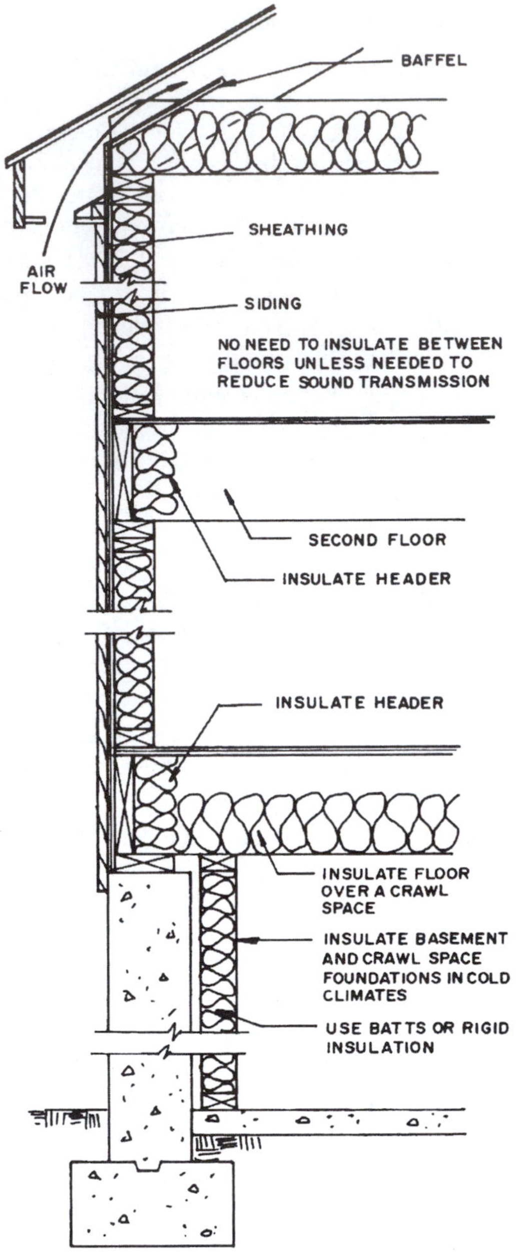

Insulation Requirements

The New York Energy Code mandates minimum R-values for insulation in various parts of a residential structure and designates the areas where insulation must be installed. Insulation is placed wherever the interior walls, ceilings, or floors are exposed to exterior temperatures such as roofs, ceilings, floors, foundation walls, and slab edges. (See Figure 11.13.) The code also regulates the glazing and caulking around windows and skylights and entrance doors. The required performance of the insulation depends on the type of heating system.

The New York Energy Code requires that all building envelope materials that can absorb moisture must be protected by a vapor barrier on the insulation applied to the warm (inside) wall of exterior walls. The vapor barrier is important in preventing the warm interior air from mixing with the cold exterior air and forming condensation within the wall. Should condensation occur, the structure, in effect, "sweats," and causes the wood framing members to rot and also damages other construction components.

MAJOR MECHANICAL SYSTEMS

Heating and cooling systems, plumbing systems, and electrical systems are run through the walls, floors, and ceilings. The local building inspector inspects these systems before they are enclosed with with insulation and wallboard. Heating and cooling systems are referred to as *HVAC systems.* HVAC stands for heating, ventilation, and air conditioning.

Heating

Types of heating systems. Home heating systems are usually one of the following types: hot water, steam, forced warm air, and electric.

1. *Hot water system.* Whenever liquids such as water are heated or cooled, the process is referred to as a *hydronic* system. A hot water system consists of pipes, a boiler, and room-heating units such as a radiator or convector. The water is heated in the boiler and then propelled through the pipes by one or more circulator pumps to the radiators or convectors, where the heat is transferred to the air in the various rooms. Convectors are the more common heating medium. A convector is a heat-emitting unit where heat is produced by the movement of air around a metal surface. Older homes have upright convectors that look something like radiators. The more common type is the finned tube baseboard convectors that usually run along the baseboards. One or more walls may have convectors depending on a room's size and configuration. (See Figure 11.14.)

2. *Steam system.* A steam system consists of a boiler, where steam is produced, and a system of pipes that conveys the steam to radiators, convectors, or other types of room-heating elements. Steam can produce a large amount of heat with a small amount of circulating fluid. The most common types of steam systems are one-pipe systems in which the steam and condensation (evaporation) are carried in one pipe; a two-pipe system in which the steam and condensation are carried in two different pipes; and a vapor steam system, which is a low-pressure two-pipe system. Steam heat is usually found in older homes.

3. *Forced warm air system.* A forced warm air system consists of a furnace that contains a fan or blower, a heat source such as gas or oil, and filters (Figure 11.15). The system works by extracting cool air from in and out of doors and passing this cool air through the heat sources. The warmed air then flows through ducts to the various rooms. The system can be designed to provide cooling as well as heating through the same ducts. Depending on the system size, forced warm air systems can be adapted for residential, commercial, and industrial applications.

4. *Electric heating system.* Residential electric heating is usually in the form of baseboard heaters placed directly along the walls of a room. When electricity passes through a wire, the molecules are stirred up and this creates heat. The unit consists of three basic elements: a resistor, which is the material used to produce heat by passing current through it; insulated protective metal sheathing where the resistor is embedded; a terminal that connects the unit to the power supply. Electric heat installation is economical as it does not require a furnace or duct work, but the cost in New York is generally more expensive than other types of fuel.

5. *Radiant panels.* Radiant panels are composed of tubes that carry electricity, steam, or hot water as a heat source. These tubes can be embedded in the ceiling, walls, or floor. Heat is transferred evenly to the surrounding objects and people rather than to the air.

Types of heating fuel and power. In most heating systems, a furnace is used to heat the air that is then discharged into the space being heated directly or through ducts. All warm-air furnaces consist of a blower, a heat exchanger, a casing, and controls. There are three types of air furnaces: electric, oil-fired, and gas-fired.

1. *Electric heat.* An electric furnace has a resistance heating element that either heats the circulating air directly or through a metal sheath enclosing the element. There are several styles of electric furnaces depending on the areas that need to be heated and where the furnace is located. Rising utility costs over recent years have made the electric furnace less economical than in the past.

2. *Oil-fired heat.* Oil-fired furnaces (Figure 11.15) include a burner and controls and are also available in a variety of shapes and styles. Oil-fired furnaces can be used to manufacture warm air or can be combined with an air cooling system. Oil-fired heat, although economical, requires the fuel to be delivered and stored. Oil may be stored in aboveground or underground tanks, or an oil company will deliver oil periodically. The regulation of above- and underground storage tanks is discussed in Chapter 14.

3. *Gas-fired heat.* In a gas-fired furnace, combustion takes place within a metal heat exchanger. The products of the combustion are conveyed through a flue or vent. Gas furnaces can burn either natural gas or liquefied petroleum air gases. Gas-fired heating is a popular form of heating in New York as it is economical and convenient because oil delivery is eliminated.

Ventilation

All ventilation systems have a central exhaust fan and ducts to remove stale air from various places in the house. This fan is usually installed in the basement or attic, keeping fan noise away from the living space.

Systems differ in how fresh air is introduced to replace exhausted air and depend upon the type of heating or air-cooling system in the home. All systems have a central exhaust fan that pulls stale air out of the kitchen, bathrooms, and other locations where pollutant concentrations are usually highest. The systems differ in how fresh air is introduced and circulated throughout the house.

Building science and indoor air quality experts have determined that at least 15 cubic feet per minute (cpm) of fresh air are required per person in a residential building. This standard was developed by the American Society of Heating, Refrigeration, and Air Conditioning Engineers (ASHRAE) and is used in many building codes.

FIGURE 11.14
Types of fin-tube convectors.

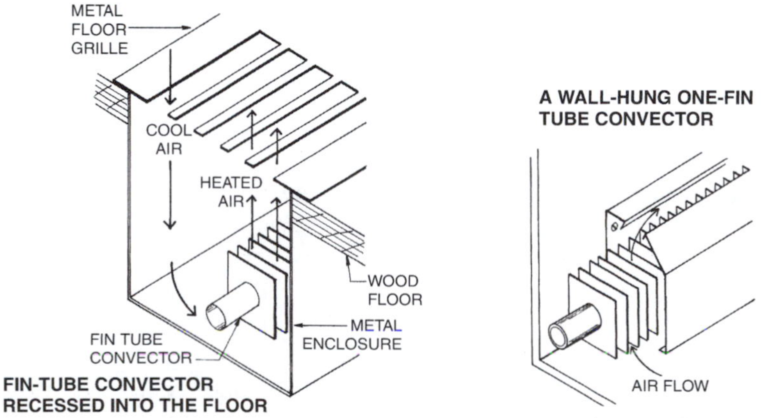

Source: From *Construction Materials, Methods, and Techniques* 1st Edition by SPENCE ©1998. Reprinted with permission of Delmar Learning, a division of Thomson Learning: *http://www.thomsonrights.com.* Fax 800-730-2215.

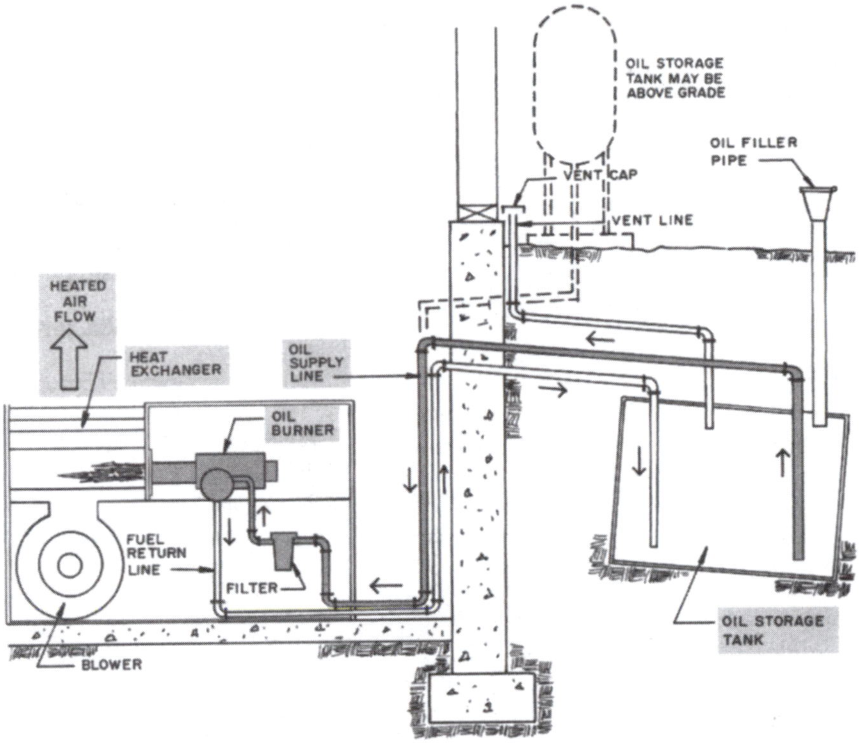

FIGURE 11.15
An oil-fired warm air furnace.

Source: From *Construction Materials, Methods, and Techniques* 1st Edition by SPENCE ©1998. Reprinted with permission of Delmar Learning, a division of Thomson Learning: *http://www.thomsonrights.com.* Fax 800-730-2215.

Air Conditioning

Central air conditioning. With the integration of HVAC systems into home construction, central air conditioning is fast becoming standard equipment. Central air-conditioning units are located outside of the air-conditioned space and can be placed indoors, in the basement of a building, outside on the roof, or adjacent to the outside walls of the structure.

Major air conditioning components. The mechanical components of an air conditioner are liquid refrigerant, evaporator, compressor, and condenser. A refrigerant is any substance that produces a cooling effect by absorbing heat as it vaporizes (disperses into the air). The refrigerant must be nontoxic and nonflammable. The most common refrigerant used in air conditioners is freon. The evaporator takes heat from the air surrounding it and brings it to the refrigerant. The compressor then creates a flow of refrigerant from one part of the system to the other. The condenser liquifies the refrigerant gas by cooling it.

Integral systems with forced air. Because an air-conditioning unit *conditions* air, a single forced-air heating system can also include cooling, ventilating, and dehumidifying systems. *Cooled air, fresh air from outdoors, and dehumidified air can travel through the same ducts as the heated air.* Because the same duct work is used for all functions, this is one of the most economical types of installations.

Air-cooled and water-cooled systems. Whether the system is *air-cooled* or *water-cooled* depends on the type of condenser used in the system. An air-cooled condenser consists of a fan or a natural draft that blows air across a large surfaced coil. This type of condenser is used in smaller units. In a water-cooled condenser, water circulates through tubes or coils inside of a shell. Refrigerant circulates through the space between the tubes or coils. The water-cooled condenser is suited to medium-sized units. Sometimes air-conditioning condensers are a combination of water-cooled and air-cooled and are called evaporative condensers.

BTU Ratings

Most components of an HVAC system are assigned a BTU rating. *BTU* stands for *British thermal unit*, a measure of heat energy, and is the amount of heat required to raise the temperature of one pound of water by one degree Fahrenheit. The capacity of an air-conditioning unit is rated in tons of refrigeration, and 12,000 BTUs are equal to a one-ton capacity. Therefore, an air conditioner rated at 12,000 BTUs per hour would melt one ton of ice per day, and it takes 40 BTUs to cool one cubic foot of space.

Heat Pumps

Another type of heating and cooling system is the heat pump. *Air source heat pumps* extract heat from the outside, even in moderately cold weather, and transfers the heat into the home. This heat transfer cycle is reversed in the warmer months to extract heat from the interior of a building and transfer it to the outdoors, and produce air conditioning (cooling).

Heat pumps are distinguished from one another according to how they draw on the heat source. *Air-to-air heat pumps* draw on the outside air as a heat source. *Ground-source heat pumps* (Figure 11.16) draw on the consistent temperature of the ground to bring heating and cooling into the house. In most of New York State, ground-source heat pumps are more efficient than air-source heat pumps.

FIGURE 11.16 The inside unit of a ground-source heat pump.

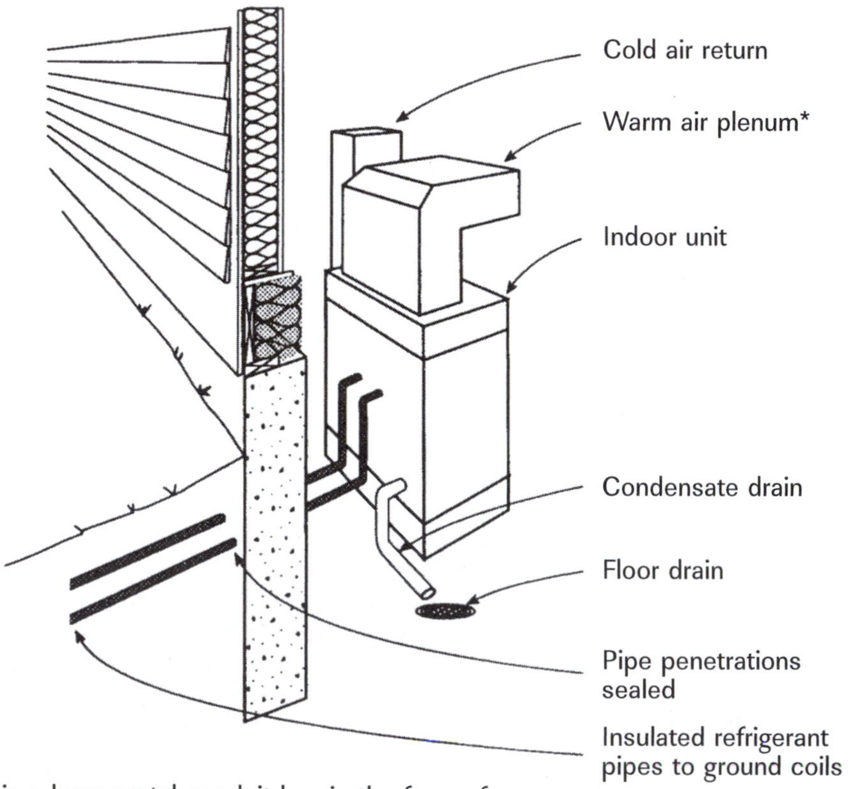

* A plenum is a large metal conduit box in the form of a duct located inside the heat system.

Source: *NY-STAR Builder Field Cuide.* Copyright © NY-STAR, Inc.

A disadvantage of both types of heat pump is that they can operate only in moderate climates. When the temperature drops below 0 degrees as it frequently does during New York winters, the heat pumps are ineffective. The limitation of the air-to-air heat pump system is that the temperature of the air outside is typically the lowest when the need for heat inside is the greatest. The ground-source system is troublesome in winter because the frozen ground around the pump insulates it and prevents it from extracting heat.

Another drawback to the heat pump is that the heat coming out of the vent feels cooler than that generated by a furnace. In climates with cold winters, homeowners who use a heat pump often have a back-up heating system to maintain a comfortable living environment. The advantage of the heat pump is that the air cooling and heating systems are built into the same unit.

Plumbing Systems

The plumbing system may seem to some to be a mysterious complex of pipes, fittings, valves, and fixtures. Actually, it consists of two systems: the water supply system, used for drinking, cooking, and washing; and the drainage system for wastewater. These systems must be separated from each other to prevent contamination. Local building codes are very specific as to the system's structure and materials.

Hot-Water Heaters

Several types of hot-water systems are found in residential construction. Gas and electric water tanks are common, as are systems that are connected to the heat source. Typically, single-family homes require at least a 40- to 50-gallon hot-water tank.

Gas hot-water heaters. Gas hot-water heaters consist of a vertical storage tank enclosed in an insulated metal tank. The gas is automatically controlled by a thermostat inside of the tank so that the incoming cold water turns on the gas. When the water is heated, the thermostat lowers the flame.

Electric hot-water heaters. Electric hot-water heaters are also insulated tanks. With this type of tank, a heating element is immersed inside the tank and heats the water. Electric heaters can be constructed to take 120 or 240 volts of electricity; 240-volt currents are more efficient and economical. (See Figure 11.17)

Summer-winter hookup. Summer-winter hookup is a method of heating water that can sometimes be found in residential construction. A copper coil is immersed in the hot water of the house-heating boiler. Pipes connect this coil to a hot-water storage tank. Water flows from the pipes that connect the boiler to the storage tank, where it is then stored. In this type of hookup, the tanks are horizontal rather than vertical as in the gas and electric water tanks. In addition, some houses have a hot-water system that has no hot-water storage tank. Hot water is supplied by immersing a large number of coils directly into the boiler water. This is called a *tankless coil system.*

Solar hot water heaters. Using a closed loop antifreeze system, this system has three major components: the solar collectors, a storage tank, and a heat exchanger. A back-up electric, oil, or gas system is sometimes necessary and activates when the system does not provide the full amount of hot water desired. Solar water systems can also be used with radiant floor heating systems.

Sanitary Waste Systems

The sanitary waste system or drainage system of a house carries wastewater and used water from the house and deposits it into the public sewer system or private septic tank. Within the house, waste and water from the plumbing fixtures move down the fixture drain through soil pipes to the main soil stack. The main soil stack connects to the house drain, where the waste leaves the system.

FIGURE 11.17
An electric water heater.

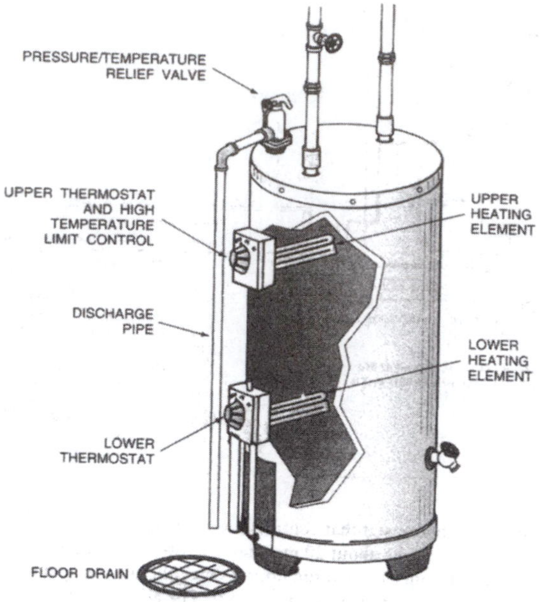

Source: From *Electrical Wiring: Residential—HC* 13th Edition by MULLIN ©1999. Reprinted with permission of Delmar Learning, a division of Thomson Learning: *http://www.thomsonrights.com.* Fax 800-730-2215.

On-site wastewater treatment systems. In most rural and some suburban residential areas, individual household wastewater treatment systems are used to dispose of household wastes. A typical household wastewater treatment system consists of a *house sewer, septic tank, distribution box, and an absorption field or seepage pit.* This is known as a **septic system.** Figure 11.1 diagrams a typical septic system.

In a household septic system, the house sewer is the pipeline connecting the house to the drain and septic tank. Untreated liquid household water will clog the absorption field if not properly treated; therefore the septic tank provides this needed treatment. The *distribution box* distributes the flow from the septic tank evenly to the absorption field or seepage pits. The *absorption field* is a system of narrow trenches partially filled with a bed of washed gravel into which perforated joint pipe is placed. The discharge from the septic tank is distributed through these pipes into the trenches and surrounding soil. The *seepage pit* is a covered pit with a perforated or open-jointed lining through which the discharge from the septic tank infiltrates the surrounding soil. According to health department regulations, if soil and site conditions are adequate for absorption trenches, seepage pits cannot be used.

House sewer construction, including materials, must comply with the New York State Uniform Fire Prevention and Building Code.

Municipal wastewater systems. With houses that are part of a municipal wastewater system, the wastewater drains through the house drainage system into a house sewer. The house sewer extends from the house drain and connects to the municipal main sewer system.

Domestic Water Systems

Incoming services: Well and town. Most suburban and municipal areas in New York have access to public water supply systems. These systems are regulated by the local health department and are the recommended source of water supply. A public water supply system can be a municipality such as a city, village, or town. The water supply

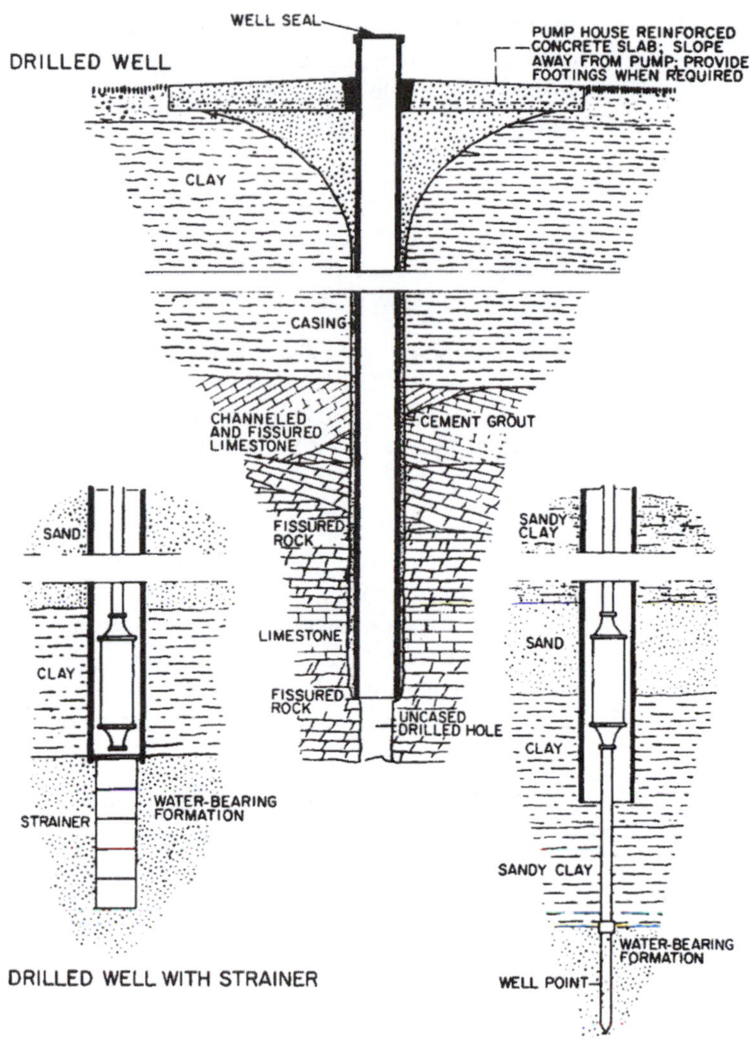

FIGURE 11.18 A cross section and detail of a drilled well.

Source: New York State Department of Health.

system in the house delivers hot and cold fresh water to all the fixtures. Water is brought under pressure from a municipal water main or a private or community well into the house pipes. All water fixtures should have separate cutoffs so that a repair can be made without shutting down the entire system. Homes in rural areas of New York may depend on individual and community well-water supplies.

Well water: New York State requirements. The New York Department of Health furnishes guidelines for the proper location, construction, and protection of well water. If guidelines are not followed or an area becomes heavily populated, the sanitary quality of the well water can be jeopardized. There are several types of wells: drilled, dug, and springs. *Studies have shown that drilled wells are the better type.* Dug wells can be excavated by hand or by mechanical equipment. Springs are classified as rock or earth springs, depending on the source. For satisfactory water, one must find the source and develop it properly. Figure 11.18 illustrates a cross section of a drilled well.

Some of the health department specifications for well water include:

1. Wells should be built at a depth of more than 20 feet below the ground surface.
2. After construction and before the water is issued, wells must be disinfected according to health department guidelines.

3. Well owners must be alert for any change in the appearance or taste of the water since this can be a sign of contamination. If the well is found to be polluted, it should be filled in or made inaccessible. A sanitary survey of the surrounding area should be made to find the cause of the pollution.

Types of Pipes

Pipes for water supply and house drainage systems come in a range of types and have advantages and disadvantages. Older homes contain different materials used in piping than those that are common today. The main types that appear in water distribution and plumbing systems include cast iron, galvanized steel, copper, PVC (plastic), and brass.

Cast-iron pipe. This type of pipe is typically used for underground plumbing in the house drainage system because it is strong and durable. It is available in light and heavy weights, and building codes usually specify the required weight for the application. The disadvantage of cast iron pipe is that it is heavy, time-consuming to install, and eventually can rust on the inside.

Copper pipe. This type of pipe is used for both water supply and drainage systems. Copper pipe is longer lasting than brass or steel pipe, is corrosion resistant, and is easy to work with. In the water supply system, copper pipe is used for hot- and cold-water lines and for branch pipes to house fixtures, such as sinks and washing machines. In the drainage system, copper pipe is used for the main soil stack, soil pipes, and vent pipes. For plumbing applications, copper pipe is available in rigid or flexible form in different thicknesses. Building and plumbing codes generally determine what type of tube should be used for a certain application.

Plastic pipe. This pipe is more often used than previously in plumbing systems and is approved by building codes for different applications. When first developed, it was used only for cold water supply, outdoor sprinkler systems, and swimming pool plumbing. The older plastics were not as resilient or heat resistant as metal pipes. For home plumbing, essentially three types of plastic pipe are used: PVC, ABS, and CPVC.

Plastic is lightweight, economical, resistant to corrosion, and easy to install. When compared to metal pipe, however, plastic is less resistant to heat, expands and contracts more when heated and cooled, has less crush resistance, withstands less internal pressure, and may require more support because of its flexibility. ABS pipe is used in one- and two-family homes for drainage, but according to New York State code cannot be used in multifamily dwellings or commercial/industrial applications because it contains a flammable petroleum product. CPVC is sometimes used for hot-water pipes. However, according to the New York State Uniform Fire Prevention and Building Code, plastic pipe cannot be used for drinking water.

Brass pipe. Brass pipe is no longer used in many plumbing installations. Brass is expensive and has been replaced by other materials that do the job just as efficiently. In some homes, brass pipe can still be found in exposed pipes that have been chrome-plated. It is still sometimes used where there is a hard-water problem.

Steel pipe. Steel pipe was used extensively 40 or more years ago for the water supply and less frequently, house drainage systems. It has been replaced by brass. In water supplies, steel pipe can be used for hot and cold water and for branch pipes to fixtures. It is infrequently used in the drainage system and for the main soil stack, soil pipes from fixtures, and vent pipes. Steel is not used for underground plumbing.

Pipe Size for Adequate Pressure

The minimum acceptable pressure in a water distribution system is the lowest pressure that permits safe, efficient, and satisfactory operation. The maximum acceptable pressure is the highest pressure that will not cause damage to the system. Building codes stipulate the minimum pressure for various plumbing fixtures as well as maximum allowable pressure.

A pipe that is sized too small will not allow the available water pressure to flow through to the fixture. Sometimes problems occur in older houses where the pipes become clogged, particularly with a buildup of mineral deposits over a long period.

Water pressure can also be regulated through systems within the house. A booster pump or other similar systems can be used to increase water pressure. A pressure regulating valve (PRV), also called a pressure reducing valve, is used to reduce and automatically maintain the pressure of water within predetermined parameters.

Venting Requirements

A vent system consists of pipes installed in a sanitary wastewater drainage system to provide a flow of air to and from a drainage system. These vent pipes allow air to circulate to ensure rapid and silent flow of waste and stop back pressure. Vent piping permits gases and odors to circulate up through the system and escape into the air.

Every plumbing fixture is connected to a vent pipe that is then connected to a roof vent pipe. The main vent is the top of the main soil stack and connects to all the toilets in the house. Secondary vents connect to other fixtures such as sink traps. Building codes specify venting requirements. (See Figure 11.19)

Electrical Systems

The proper design, scope, and layout of electrical outlets and components ensures that the system is adequate to handle present and future requirements. A voltage service of 120/240 volts is standard; less voltage does not meet the requirements of residential property. Most residential service is a minimum of 100 amps, but new construction generally has 150 to 200 amp service.

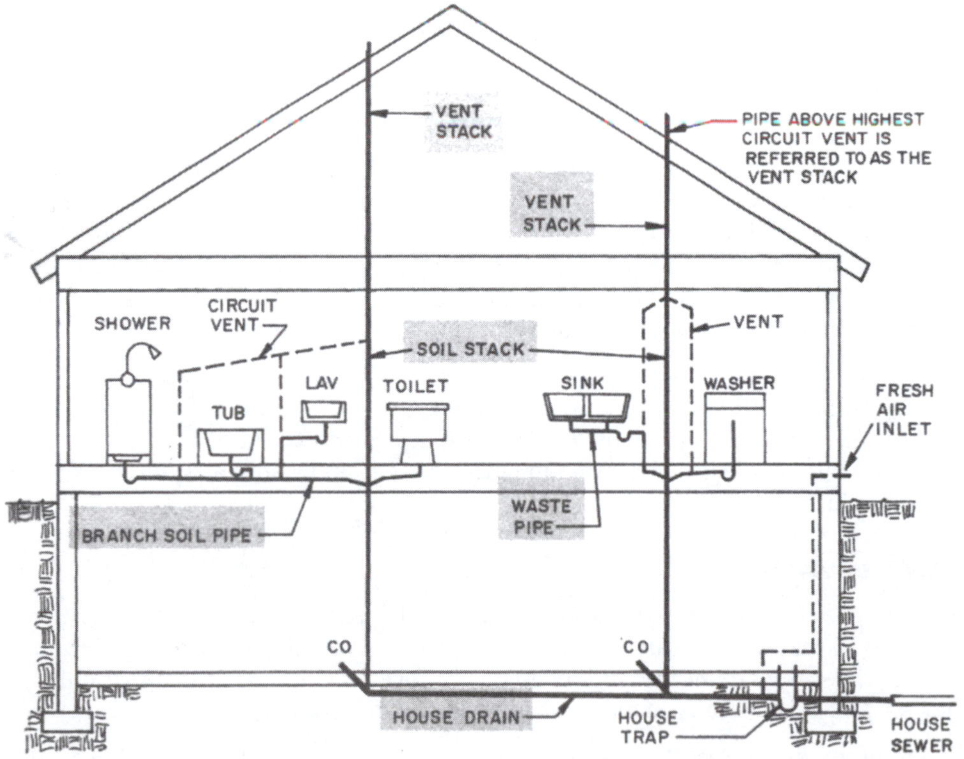

FIGURE 11.19
A residential piping system.

Source: From *Construction Materials, Methods, and Techniques* 1st Edition by SPENCE ©1998. Reprinted with permission of Delmar Learning, a division of Thomson Learning: *http://www.thomsonrights.com.* Fax 800-730-2215.

The electrical distribution panel should be located in a utility room, basement, or garage for ease of access to reset circuit breakers and to perform maintenance. The home should be wired with sufficient electrical wall outlets. Utility areas such as garages and bathrooms require the installation of dedicated circuit breakers to prevent accidental electrical shock.

Incoming Services

Electrical power is brought to the house through outside cables and is then delivered through a series of conductors to the house wiring system. Two types of services exist: some houses are located in areas that have *aboveground* cables; others have *underground* or buried cables.

Aboveground cables, which come from the nearest pole connecting to the service entrance conductors of the building, are called the *service drop.* Underground wiring connecting the house is called the *service lateral.*

Utility Company and Landowner Responsibilities

The utility company's responsibility is to bring electricity to the service drop or lateral of the house. The property owner is responsible for every other aspect of the service beyond that point of entry. For example, property owners are responsible for all inside wiring, blown fuses, and, in most cases, the electric meters that measure usage.

Voltage and Amperage

Voltage is *the electrical pressure that pushes through the wires.* Voltage is very similar to water pressure; it is the push. Although 120 volts are standard voltage for lighting and small-appliance loads, 240-volt usage is needed for heavy residential and commercial applications. **Amperage** is *the amount of current or electricity flowing through the wire.*

Electrical capacity requirements are determined when a house is built and are normally delineated in watts or kilowatts. Amperage required for different electrical usage is calculated in watts or kilowatts. House electrical circuits are installed according to these kilowatt requirements.

If the wire size or service is not strong enough for the electrical needs of the house, the circuit will overheat, causing fuses to melt or circuit breakers to trip and therefore interrupt the electrical service. A **fuse** is *a device that will melt and open the circuit, causing electrical power to stop when overheating occurs.* Melted fuses must be replaced with new ones. After melting, they are no longer usable. Fuses also can be mishandled and therefore expose individuals to high voltages.

Circuit breakers are more convenient and safer than fuses. **Circuit breakers** will trip; that is, *they will switch the electrical power for a given circuit off if the current increases beyond the capacity of the system.* They do not need to be replaced every time the system overloads. Houses built since about 1960 usually have circuit breakers rather than fuses.

Identifying Amperage

The *main panel board* or *distribution panel* may have an amperage rating written on it; the rating may be the same as or larger than the actual service. The distribution panel is where the circuit breakers or fuses are located (Figure 11.20). The only sure indicator of service size is found on the service entrance cables.

Therefore, the size of the electrical service in a house cannot necessarily be identified by the number of fuses or circuit breakers on the distribution panel. Individual branch circuits can be anywhere from 15 to 50 amps. Each *circuit breaker* or fuse must be identified as to its ampere rating, that is, the amount of amperage it can carry, as specified in the National Electric Code (discussed below). Conductors (wires) of specific sizes must have the proper-sized fuse or circuit breaker to carry the electrical current.

GFCI's (Ground Fault Circuit Interrupters)

GFCI's are highly sensitive circuit breakers that sense extremely small current leakages across a circuit and are used to protect against electrocution hazard. They are generally located where water may be present such as bathrooms, kitchens, basements, garages, outdoor receptacles, and swimming pools. The National Electric Code specifies where these devices should be used.

Wiring Materials

House wiring, or branch circuit wiring, runs from the distribution panel through the walls of the building to the outlets where the current is used. Outlets can be any type of opening including a plug, a switch, or a light fixture. Various conductor sizes and materials are used inside and outside the house. Figure 11.20 depicts two types of distribution panels.

Aluminum versus copper wiring. Aluminum wiring is used today primarily where the current is heaviest. This is essentially at the point where the current is fed into the house. It is also used for heavy appliances such as air conditioners or clothes dryers. If a house was built between 1965 and 1972, branch circuit aluminum wiring may have been used. Branch circuit wiring runs to the switches and outlets within the house. Experts found that aluminum wiring caused a great deal of overheating in outlets and switches. Those houses in question should be inspected by a qualified electrician to correct problems.

(A) Typical main panel with 200-ampere fusible pullout, suitable for use as service equipment.

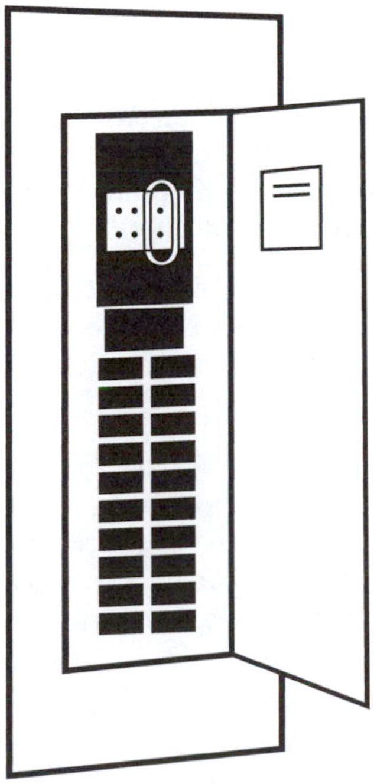

(B) Service entrance panel equipped with circuit breakers.

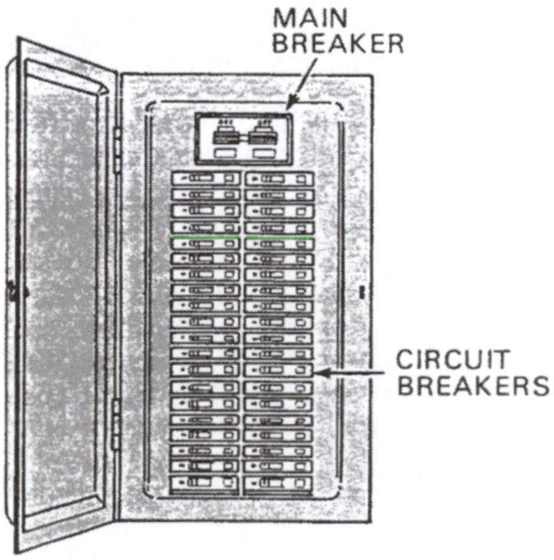

FIGURE 11.20
Two types of distribution panels.

(B) Source: *Electrical Wiring,* 5th edition. Published by the American Association for Vocational Instructional Materials, Winterville, Georgia.

Copper wire works better than aluminum wiring. Copper is a stable medium that does not overheat and can carry both large and small amperages. Most new construction uses copper wires except wiring at the service entrance to the house, where aluminum works best.

BX cable. This wiring type is a generic name (named after the Bronx, New York) for a type of armored electric cable. Armored cable is an assembly of insulated conductors (wires) in a flexible metallic enclosure. This type of cable is used when the wires must be protected from physical damage; it is generally found in branch circuit wire that feeds the outlets.

Romex cable. This cable is a nonmetallic sheath cable that is essentially the same as BX cable *except it is plastic-coated* and is therefore moisture resistant and flame retardant. Romex cable is less expensive than BX cable and is easier to install. Most houses built before 1950 use BX cable, however.

Conduit. This is a pipelike enclosure, made of galvanized steel, plastic, or aluminum, used to house current-carrying conductors (wires). Conduit can be made of either galvanized steel or plastic. The wires are enclosed inside the conduit to protect them from damage if BX or Romex cable is not being used. Conduits can be found at the service entrance to a house and are used both above and below ground. *Although BX and Romex cable are used for branch circuit wiring only, conduit can be used in all house electrical applications.*

Greenfield conductors. This is another type of conduit that looks a lot like BX cable; however, there are no conductors (wires) inside until they are put in. The distinguishing characteristic of Greenfield conductors is that they are a *flexible rather than rigid metal.* Greenfield conductors are used for connecting air conditioners, clothes dryers, and other large appliances where BX or Romex cable is not used. Greenfield conduit can be used only in dry, interior places. Greenfield conduit is useful in many applications because its flexibility allows it to withstand vibrations, whereas a rigid metal might break. It is also easier to work with, especially in a confined space.

National Electric Code

The *National Electric Code* is a national standard for electrical installation and service written to safeguard people and property from hazards arising from the use of electricity. The code was developed by the National Fire Protection Association so that consumers, local code enforcement agencies, insurance companies, and other organizations would have a uniform standard of electrical performance and safety.

The code is renewed every three years and is used for all electrical installations and remodeling projects and must be adhered to by qualified personnel. It sets minimum requirements; however, municipalities may have more restrictive requirements.

New York Board of Fire Underwriters

According to the New York State Uniform Fire Prevention and Building Code, all electrical installations, whether on new or existing construction, must be inspected for compliance with the National Electric Code. Local municipalities can choose a qualified inspection organization to determine whether installation complies with code requirements.

The New York Board of Fire Underwriters, a privately owned organization created by an act of the New York legislature in the early 1900s, is one of the oldest companies that is available to inspect electrical installations. Once the building is approved, the organization issues a certification that the installation is in compliance with the National Electric Code. In New York, other companies, such as Atlantic Inland and Syracuse North, also perform these inspections.

MANDATED GUARANTEES, WARRANTIES, AND INSTALLATIONS

Home Improvement Contracts

Article 36–A of the New York General Business Law provides that home improvement contractors who enter into contracts exceeding $5,000 must deposit all payments received prior to completion into an escrow account. The contractor also has the option of providing a bond or letter of credit guaranteeing the payment. If a payment schedule is arranged according to a specified amount of work completed, the contract must provide a payment schedule indicating the amount of payment due and the corresponding work completed, including materials. An owner may cancel a home improvement contract, through a written notice to the contractor, up to three business days after the contract was signed. The cancellation policy can be forfeited if an owner has initiated the contract for an emergency repair and furnishes the contractor with a written statement waiving the right to the three-day cancellation.

If an owner enters into a contract as a result of fraudulent representation, the owner may sue the contractor, and if the court determines in the owner's favor, the owner may recover a penalty of $500 (plus attorney's fees) and other damages as determined by the court. (If the owners do not prevail, the contractor may be awarded attorney's fees.) Contractors who violate the deposit provisions of this law may be fined up to $250 or 5 percent of the contract price not to exceed $2,500.

Warranties on Sales of New Homes

According to Article 36–B of the New York General Business Law, implied in all contracts of sale for new housing is a one-year builder's warranty against defects in construction; a two-year warranty for all plumbing, electrical, heating and air conditioning systems; and a six-year warranty covering material defects.

Carbon Monoxide Detectors

The Uniform Fire Prevention and Building Code was amended (2003) to establish standards for the installation and maintenance of carbon monoxide detectors. Regulations require that at least one functioning carbon monoxide detector be installed near the bedrooms in all one- and two-family properties including condos and co-ops that are constructed or offered for sale.

Life Expectancies

Life expectancies of all components of HVAC, plumbing, and electrical systems depend on a number of factors, including level of usage, standards of routine maintenance, and location. Each of these systems should be inspected annually by a professional who is familiar with the type of system. Malfunctioning parts should be replaced and systems should be kept free of dust and debris whenever possible.

Before buying a property, purchasers should have professionals inspect the HVAC, plumbing, and electrical systems. Required seller property condition disclosure mandates sellers to closely evaluate the status of their property and disclose any problems or defects on a prescribed form. Seller agents can furnish the form to all sellers as part of the listing presentation. Prospective purchasers are entitled to read this form before entering into a contract of sale. (See Chapter 1)

IMPORTANT POINTS

1. In New York, all residential and commercial structures must comply with state and local building codes. The New York State Uniform Fire Prevention and Building Code supplies the minimum requirements.
2. New York has laws and regulations that govern on-site well regulations and on-site sanitary waste systems. The New York Energy Code governs types of insulation and energy efficiencies.
3. Other site considerations in the planning stage include drainage, landscaping, shading, and walkways.
4. Footings support the foundation wall and, subsequently, the entire weight of the structure.
5. Foundation walls may be poured concrete, masonry block, or, sometimes, brick. The height of the foundation wall determines if the house has a crawl space or full basement.
6. Framing is the wooden skeleton of a structure. Framing members are lumber with a nominal dimension of 2" thick.
7. The floor system starts with the sill plate nailed to the foundation system. Wood joists support the subfloor material.
8. Wall framing is almost exclusively 2" × 4" studs placed 16" on center. The most common wall-framing system is the platform method. Alternative methods are balloon or post-and-beam framing.
9. The roof structural skeleton is usually built with 2" × 8" ceiling joists and 2" × 6" or 2" × 8" rafters.
10. The primary purpose of insulation is to resist the flow of heat from one area to another. Insulation is rated on an R-factor; the larger the R-factor, the greater the degree of insulation.
11. HVAC stands for heating, ventilation, and air conditioning. Some systems use fuel oil or natural gas for energy, while others use electricity.
12. Heating systems found in the home are usually hot water, steam, forced warm air, or electric. The heat pump is another type of heating system.
13. Forced air heating and cooling systems use a central fan or blower to distribute the heated or cooled air throughout the house. Hot water heating systems use circulator pumps to propel the heated water through pipes to the convectors.
14. Air conditioning units may be placed inside or outside the house. Components of an air conditioner include liquid refrigerant, evaporator, compressor, and condenser.
15. The plumbing system consists of two systems: the water supply system that is used for drinking, cooking, and washing; and the drainage system, where wastewater goes.
16. Hot-water systems commonly found in residential construction include gas and electric water tanks as well as other types of systems that are connected to the heat source.
17. The sanitary waste system or drainage system of a house carries wastewater and used water from the house and deposits it into the public sewer system or private wastewater treatment system.
18. Electrical power is brought to the house through outside cables and delivered through a series of conductors to the house wiring system.
19. The New York General Business Law contains provisions to protect consumers who enter into home improvement contracts. This law also provides for a one-year builder's warranty against construction defects.
20. Recent New York regulations require that at least one functioning carbon monoxide detector be installed near the bedrooms in all one- and two-family properties including condos and co-ops that are constructed or offered for sale.

How Would You Respond? CHAPTER REVIEW

Analyze the following situations and decide how the individuals should handle them in accordance with what you have learned. Check your responses using the Answer Key at the end of the chapter.

1. Enzo represented the buyers, the Defreezes, in the purchase of a home. The Defreezes moved in September, and when they turned on the heat in October, found that the furnace was dead. They informed Enzo that they intend to sue him, the sellers, and the seller agent for the cost of replacement. The Defreezes bought the property "as is" but subject to a structural and systems inspection contingency. Analyze this situation and figure out the parties, if any, that may be liable.

 ____

 ____

 ____

 ____

2. Justine and Hans are about to put up their 50-year-old, wood-exterior, Victorian-style house for sale. They know that the house is not in perfect condition, but realize that lots of people would enjoy its charm and spaciousness and would not mind improving it. They call agent Kim, whose expertise is marketing older properties. What suggestions might Kim make to market the property?

 ____

 ____

 ____

 ____

KEY TERM REVIEW

Fill in the term that best completes each sentence and then check the Answer Key at the end of the chapter.

1. The ____________ is the concrete base below the frost line that supports the foundation of the structure.
2. The ____________ is the first wooden member of the house and is used as the nailing surface for the floor system.
3. ____________ support the ceiling and the roof over the door and window openings.
4. The ____________ consists of the materials of a building that enclose the interior and through which heating, cooling, or fresh air passes in and out.
5. The ____________ support the ceiling and/or the roof.
6. The ____________ is the highest part of the framing and forms the apex, or top line, of the roof.

7. The area of material on the roof facing the outer edge of the ________________ is called the ________________.

8. ________________ is the electrical pressure that pushes electricity through the wires, and ________________ is the amount of current or electricity flowing through the wires.

MULTIPLE CHOICE

Circle the letter that best answers the question and then check the Answer Key at the end of the chapter.

1. Which of the following is NOT regulated by the New York Energy Code?
   A. HVAC systems
   B. electrical and lighting systems
   C. building envelopes
   D. setback requirements

2. The most common type of framing used in residential construction is:
   A. platform
   B. floating
   C. post-and-beam
   D. balloon

3. The overhang of the house roof is made up of which of the following?
   A. trusses, rafters, ridge beam
   B. header, joist, stud
   C. soffit, fascia, frieze board
   D. sill plate, sheathing, header

4. Of the following one-family residential heating choices, which is the most economical and efficient for New York weather?
   A. the heat pump
   B. a forced warm-air system
   C. baseboard electric heat
   D. solar heat

5. The main carrying beam of a structure is also known as a:
   A. sill plate
   B. joist
   C. girder
   D. header

6. The most common gas used for cooling in air conditioners is:
   A. freon
   B. radon
   C. propane
   D. carbon dioxide

7. A disadvantage of oil-fired heating is:
   A. it is the most expensive heat source
   B. it requires delivery and storage of the oil
   C. heating systems requiring oil cannot be used in residential applications
   D. heating systems requiring oil emit toxic fumes

8. Framing members used for wall construction are called:
   A. rafters
   B. lally columns
   C. beams
   D. studs

9. Which of the following is NOT part of a typical household septic system?
   A. house sewer
   B. absorption field
   C. drilled well
   D. distribution box

10. Studies have shown that the best type of well is a(n):
    A. drilled well
    B. dug well
    C. springs well
    D. O well

11. A type of pipe typically found in a house drainage system is:
    A. brass
    B. aluminum
    C. PVC
    D. cast iron

12. Which of the following is FALSE regarding venting or plumbing fixtures? It:
    A. provides a flow of air to and from a drainage system
    B. ensures rapid and silent flow of waste and stops back pressure
    C. does not work in a house that has more than two floors
    D. permits gases and odors in the drainage piping to escape into the air outside the house

13. Amperage required for different electrical usage is calculated in:
    A. voltage
    B. watts or kilowatts
    C. cubic feet per minute
    D. lateral drops

14. Which of the following is FALSE regarding residential electrical systems?
    A. the distribution panel is where circuit breakers or fuses are located
    B. the minimum electrical service required is 100 amps
    C. electrical wiring must be installed according to requirements in the National Electric Code
    D. most houses today use fuses rather than circuit breakers

15. Which of the following type of electrical wiring is NOT found in residential construction?
    A. Greenfield cable
    B. steel wire
    C. copper wire
    D. Romex cable

ANSWER KEY

How Would You Respond?

1. When the Defreezes purchased the house, they bought it "as is" according to their contract of sale. This means the sellers do not have to guarantee the condition of the property or its major components. The notable exception to this is that sellers must divulge any material defects in the property. This information should be included in the sellers' mandatory Property Condition Disclosure form (required for the sale of one- to four-unit properties). In this case, if the sellers knew the furnace did not work, then they were required to make that clear when the Defreezes were considering the purchase. However, if an older furnace was in operating condition, there is no seller financial responsibility to guarantee its continued operation. The Defreezes did make their offer to purchase contingent upon an inspection of the major components and systems of the property. However, in this case, the inspection did not indicate that the furnace was about to stop working. It is possible that the furnace could break down after occupancy, and if there is no reason to believe the sellers knew this would happen, then the Defreezes would not be able to recover damages from the sellers. If the Defreezes are certain that the sellers knew the furnace was defective, then the Defreezes could choose to sue for damages in small claims court. The situation is similar with Enzo, the Defreezes' agent. If Enzo knew about the furnace, then he must give that information to all prospective buyers. If he had no reason to believe that anything was wrong, he is not liable.

2. National statistics show that the highest resale value results from interior repainting and recarpeting. Next comes furnace replacement, fireplace additions, and exterior painting. Besides making these basic improvements, Kim asks Justine and Hans to hire a home inspector, not only to assess the workability of the construction and major house systems but also to point out the beneficial construction features that may not appear in newer homes. Items such as hardwood floors, solid-oak kitchen cabinets, mature landscaping, a wraparound porch, and a cobblestone fireplace are some of the possible selling features.

Key Term Review

1. footing
2. sill plate
3. headers
4. building envelope
5. bearing walls
6. ridge beam
7. soffit/fascia
8. voltage/amperage

Multiple Choice

1. D
2. A
3. C
4. B
5. C
6. A
7. B
8. D
9. C
10. A
11. D
12. C
13. B
14. D
15. B

Chapter 12

KEY TERMS

appraisal
assessed value
comparative market analysis
cost
cost approach
depreciation
direct cost
evaluation
external obsolescence
functional obsolescence
income approach
indirect cost
insured value
investment value
market value
mortgage value
plottage
price
sales comparison approach
valuation
value in use

LEARNING OBJECTIVES

Classroom hours: 3

1. Distinguish between a comparative market analysis and an appraisal.
2. Discuss the definition of market value.
3. Distinguish the differences in value, price, and cost.
4. Illustrate and explain how a CMA is used.
5. Demonstrate how to analyze a property for a CMA.
6. Perform a practice CMA.

The Valuation Process

IN THIS CHAPTER Accurate valuation is of supreme importance in marketing a property in a timely and effective manner. It often takes some experience for new licensees to extract and analyze appropriate comparables, and create a comparative market analysis (CMA). Computer generated multiple listing service reports greatly streamline the procedure. (See Figure 12.1)

CHARACTERISTICS OF REAL PROPERTY

Real property has specific characteristics that set it apart from other marketable and valuable commodities. These characteristics are both physical and economic. The physical characteristics of real property are:

1. immobility
2. indestructibility (permanence)
3. nonhomogeneity (uniqueness)

The economic characteristics of real property are:

1. scarcity/limited availability
2. permanence of investment
3. location (situs)
4. modification by improvement

The physical characteristics pertain to the land itself. The economic characteristics pertain to value and change in value of the land. As a result of the interplay of all the characteristics, physical and economic, the real estate business is constantly changing.

Physical Characteristics

Immobility

A physical characteristic of vast importance is the immobility of land. This is the primary difference between land and tangible personal property, which is highly mobile. Land cannot be relocated. The characteristic of immobility is a major reason the location of real estate is so important.

FIGURE 12.1
A multiple listing CMA.

CMA One-Line Report

Comparative Market Analysis
Active Single Family Listings

St		MLS#	Address	SC	SBA	List Price	BR	BA	Gar	Bas	Style	Age	Acres
ACTV		2310371	5 MEDINAH CT		129	$311,730	4	2.1	2	FULL	COL		.640
ACTV		2311003	23 CHERRY TREE RD		131	$319,900	5	2.1	1	PART	COL	65	
ACTV		2220784	BRIGHTON		133	$329,900	4	2.1	2	RECRM	COL		

Total 1F Active Listings: 3	**Average List Price: $320,510**
	Average DOM: 233

Off-Market Single Family Listings

St		MLS#	Address	SC	SBA	List Price	Off Date	DOM	BR	BA	Gar	Style	Age
WITH		2218874	5 LIBERTY WAY		132	$319,900	09/13/02	73	4	2.1	2	COL	14

Total 1F Off-Market Listings: 1	**Average List Price: $319,900**
	Average DOM: 73

Pending Single Family Listings

St	MLS#	Address	SC	SBA	List Price	Pend Date	DOM	BR	BA	Gar	Style	Age
PEND	2220383	167 OLD NISKAYUNA RD		133	$325,000	12/15/02	161	4	2.1	2	COL	
PEND	2226635	14 COPENHAGEN CT		134	$328,900	12/27/02	1	4	2.1	2	CONT	
PEND	2311582	50 DUTCH MEADOWS DR	EXCLUSIVE AGENCY	135	$295,000	02/06/03	3	4	2.1	2	COL	

Total 1F Pend Listings: 3	**Average List Price: $316,300**
	Average DOM: 55

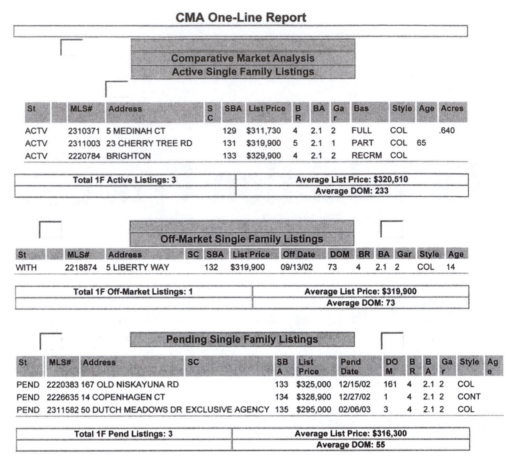

This is a computer generated comparative market analysis. It was based on a search of active, withdrawn, pending, and expired listings in the range of $310,000–$330,000 within a given area within the past 180 days.

Indestructibility

Land is a permanent commodity and cannot be destroyed. It may be altered substantially in its topography or other aspects, but it remains. The indestructibility of land makes it attractive as a long-term investment.

Uniqueness

Nonhomogeneity means that no two parcels of land are identical. A *parcel* is *a specific portion of land, such as a lot.* In agricultural land, fertility varies from location to location. In urban real estate, accessibility and zoning differ. Each parcel of real estate has its own topography, soil type, zoning, size, and shape.

Economic Characteristics

Scarcity/Limited Availability

An important economic characteristic of real property is its *scarcity,* or its availability. Scarcity follows the principle of supply and demand, that states the greater the supply of any commodity in comparison to demand the lower the value. Land is a commodity in *fixed supply;* no additional supply of land is being produced to keep pace with increasing population.

Permanence of Investment

Ownership of land is considered an investment because land is permanent. Because land is indestructible and immobile, landowners are willing to invest large sums of money to improve it. Permanence means that ownership of land is economically desirable. Investment in real estate, however, is not always a short-term investment because it is *illiquid,* or *difficult to readily convert to cash.* An investment in stocks, however, can be readily converted to cash and is thus considered a liquid investment.

Location (Situs)

Of all the characteristics of land, location has the greatest effect on property value. The physical characteristic of immobility dictates that the *situs,* or *location of a parcel of land,* is both unique and permanent. Therefore, if the land is located in an area where land is scarce, that land has a substantially higher value. Conversely, if the land is inaccessible from a practical standpoint or is located in an area with little demand, the economic value is depressed.

Modification by Improvement

Improvements to the land can greatly affect its value. As a parcel of real estate is transformed from a plot of vacant land to a completed dwelling, the appeal of the land increases, resulting in increased value. Improvements are not limited to buildings and can include landscaping, grading, clearing, installing connection utilities, and creating improved road access.

APPRAISAL, VALUATION, EVALUATION, AND MARKET VALUE

Appraisal

An **appraisal** is *an unbiased estimate of the nature, quality, value, or utility, based on factual data, of an interest in or aspect of identified real estate and related personalty as of a certain date.* Also affecting the opinion is the reason or purpose for the appraisal, also called the problem. The opinion is supported in writing with collected data and logical reasoning.

Appraisal versus Comparative Market Analysis

An appraisal uses collected data and applies three approaches to value: sales comparison, cost, and income. Each approach may yield a different value. The appraiser reconciles the differing values, applying accepted appraisal principles and methods. In some cases, one or more of the approaches may not be utilized. For example, the income approach is not commonly used in appraising single-family residential property.

The Three Appraisal Approaches to Value

Sales comparison approach. This is the primary approach for estimating the value of single-family, owner-occupied dwellings and vacant land. *It involves comparing the property that is the subject of the appraisal with other similar properties that have sold recently.* These are called comparables, or comps. No two properties are exactly alike; however, many are similar in desirability and utility (use). Adjustments are made to the comparables to account for the differences. For example, if the subject home has a closed garage and comparable 1 has a carport, the price for comparable 1 is adjusted up by the dollar amount that a closed garage would have added to the sale. A minimum of three comparables is absolutely necessary. If available, as many as six comparables are appropriate. Comparables should be as similar as possible to the subject property in all respects.

After making all adjustments, the net adjustment amount for each comparable is calculated and the result is applied to the price for which the comparable sold, to arrive at an adjusted price. The three adjusted prices are correlated or reconciled to arrive at an indicated market value for the subject property.

Cost approach. *This is the main method for estimating the value of properties that have few, if any, comparables and are not income-producing.* Examples of the types of structures appraised by this method are schools, hospitals, and government office buildings. Virtually any new construction can be appraised using the cost approach. The cost approach relies heavily on depreciation of a property.

Depreciation is defined as *a loss in value from any cause.* The loss in value is estimated by the difference in the present market value and the cost to build new. Depreciation results from the following: physical deterioration, functional obsolescence, and economic obsolescence.

Physical deterioration is caused by: (1) unrepaired damage to the structure caused by fire, explosion, vandalism, windstorm, or damage caused by wood-boring insects; or (2) wear and tear resulting from normal use of the property and lack of adequate maintenance measures to keep the property in good condition.

Functional obsolescence refers to *flawed or faulty property, rendered inferior because of technical advances and changes,* such as:

- inadequacy of wiring, plumbing, heating and cooling systems, and insufficient number of bathrooms or closets
- outdated equipment
- exposed wiring or plumbing; lack of automatic controls for furnaces and hot-water heaters; inadequate insulation
- faulty design
- a superadequacy such as an overimprovement (too costly for the general market area)

Economic obsolescence refers to property that is outdated for external, environmental, or locational reasons, such as:

- **external obsolescence** where there are *changes in surrounding land-use patterns resulting in increased traffic, air pollution, and other hazards and nuisances*
- failure to adhere to the principle of highest and best use
- changes in zoning and building regulations that adversely affect property use
- reduction in demand for property in the area caused by local economic factors

The first step in the cost approach is to estimate the value of the site as if it were vacant. The *site value is estimated by the sales comparison approach that uses comparable parcels of land to arrive at the value estimate.* To estimate the land value, the site is compared to comparable parcels of land that have sold recently. The second step is to estimate the cost of reproducing or replacing the structure. *Reproduction cost* is the price to construct an exact duplicate of the property when it was new. *Replacement cost* is based on constructing a building of comparable utility using modern building techniques and materials. If the subject property was constructed many years ago, estimating the cost of reproducing that property today may be impossible. The materials and craftsmanship may not be available. Therefore, the basis of the cost approach for older structures is replacement cost new. Reproduction cost new may be used for properties that have been constructed recently.

Income approach. This approach, also called appraisal by capitalization, is *the primary method used to estimate the present value of properties that produce income.* The value of the property is estimated by converting net annual income into an indication of present value by application of a capitalization rate. It is sometimes difficult to arrive at the proper capitalization rate. A number of complex methods are used to establish this rate. They are beyond the scope of this discussion. In essence, the capitalization, or cap rate, is the rate that other investors are achieving on like investments in the market area. The rate of return, or percentage of income per money invested that the investor gets back on an investment, includes a consideration for a risk factor. The greater the risk of loss, the greater potential rate of return the investor is entitled to expect.

The Uniform Residential Appraisal Report (URAR) is the most common appraisal form used by appraisers. This form gives a brief overview of the property and the site, a neighborhood analysis, and a fairly detailed analysis of all three approaches. On the URAR form, the most attention and emphasis are given to the sales comparison approach. Appraisers also use longer narrative reports that are particularly common in commercial appraisals.

A **comparative market analysis (CMA)** is *an analysis of the competition in the marketplace that a property will face upon sale attempts. This procedure is not an appraisal.* A CMA takes into consideration other properties currently on the market, as well as properties that have recently sold, and in many cases, expired or withdrawn listings. A CMA is similar in concept to the sales comparison approach of an appraisal as it is a comparison of properties; however, the analysis and procedural techniques used to arrive at value for the property are different. An example of a written CMA is shown in Figure 12.3.

Valuation

Valuation of a property establishes an opinion of value utilizing a totally objective approach. It is *the process of estimating the market value of an identified interest in a specific property as of a given date.* The valuation is based upon facts relating to the property, such as age, square footage, location, cost to replace, and so on. A valuation is usually done to determine the property's market value.

Types of Value

The most common purpose of an appraisal is to estimate the market value (discussed later) of the particular property. Different types of value are listed in Figure 12.2. In addition to market value, the following values may be the purpose of an appraisal:

Investment value. **Investment value** is determined by *the amount of return on a certain dollar investment a property will produce.* Therefore, if an investor requires a 20% return and a property returns $20,000, the investment value is $100,000.

Insured value. This value estimates the value of property as a basis for determining the amount of insurance coverage necessary to protect the structure adequately against loss by fire or other casualty. Insurance companies are concerned with the cost of replacing or reproducing structures. **Insured value** is *the cost of replacing or reproducing the structure in the event of a total loss because of an insured hazard.*

Value in use. **Value in use** is *the value of the property based on its usefulness to an owner or investor.* Value in use is defined more for its value to the owner and not for its value if placed on the market. Usefulness, in this case, is defined as its utility, income, or other amenities. For example, a second home used for vacation purposes for the owner's family is an amenity for the family only. Its usefulness is expanded if this owner also rents the second home when the family is not using it. Another value, income value, can then be attributed to the property.

FIGURE 12.2
Different types of value.

1. Market value
2. Investment value
3. Insurance value
4. Value in use
5. Assessed value
6. Mortgage value

Assessed value. The **assessed value** of real property is determined by a local or state official. It is *the value to which a local tax rate is applied to establish the amount of tax imposed on the property.* The assessed value, as set by statute or local ordinance, is normally a percentage of market value. This percentage may be up to 100 percent. A combination of the assessment and the tax rate as applied to the property determines the annual tax bill. Assessed value is calculated by using the formula market value $\times$ assessment rate $=$ assessed value.

Mortgage value. In making a mortgage loan, the lender is interested in the value of the property pledged as security for the debt or loan. In the event of a foreclosure, the lender must recover the debt from sale of the property. Consequently, the **mortgage value** is *whatever the lender believes the property will bring at a foreclosure sale or subsequent resale.* Some lenders make a conservative value estimate; others are more liberal. Mortgage value almost always differs from the market value.

Evaluation

Evaluation is a study of the nature, quality, or utility of certain property interests in which a value estimate is not necessarily required. Evaluation studies include the following types.

Marketability studies. This type of analysis examines whether or not a given property can be effectively presented and marketed given current conditions.

Feasibility studies. When considering large-scale projects such as residential subdivisions, shopping centers, office complexes, and industrial parks, prudent investors must first statistically analyze the market. They must analyze all facets of the project and compare the data with similar projects. This detailed statistical analysis is called a *feasibility study.* Factors considered are the cost of site development (including environmental factors), available financing, cost of financing (including prevailing interest rates), tax considerations, rates of return on similar-type investments, and the benefit to the community and its acceptance of the project.

Supply-and-demand studies. The economic principle of supply and demand is applicable to the real estate industry just as it is to other economic activities in the free enterprise system. This principle states that the greater the supply of any commodity in comparison to the demand for that commodity, the lower its value. Conversely, the smaller the supply and the greater the demand, the higher the value.

Land utilization studies. Land utilization studies may interpret the **plottage** value of land. *This theory examines the increase in value and utility when small plots of land are combined to form a larger plot.* An example might be a subdivision development where smaller parcels of land are bought up, possibly from different owners, to form the larger parcel needed for the subdivision. Commercial developments, such as shopping centers, may also have to be developed by a similar process.

Highest and best use studies. The concept of *highest and best use* is extremely important in real estate. It refers to the use of land aimed at preserving its usefulness, providing the greatest income, and resulting in the highest land value. To achieve the highest and best use, land is improved by the use of capital and labor to make the land productive. Along with the concept of highest and best use, the appraiser must consider three other related aspects of use: possible use, permissible use, and feasible use.

1. *Possible use* considers the physical characteristics of the property.
2. *Permissible use* is that legally available for the land.
3. *Feasible use* refers to the physical characteristics of the property and legal controls that make land appropriate for the market, neighborhood, and economic conditions.
4. *Highest and best use* is the feasible use that will produce the highest present value. The highest and best use in the context of market value is the most probable use. It may or may not be the present use of the property.

Evaluation of a property does not result in an estimate of value as does valuation.

Market Value

Market value is defined as *the most probable price, as of a specific date, in cash or in other terms, for which the property should be sold after reasonable exposure in a competitive market, under conditions requisite to a fair sale, with the buyer and seller acting prudently, knowledgeably, and for self-interest, and assuming that neither is under undue duress.*

Market value is the most probable price a property will bring if:

1. Buyer and seller are equally motivated. However, the seller is not under duress to take the first offer that comes along.
2. Both parties are well informed or well advised, and each is acting in what they consider their own best interests.
3. A reasonable time is allowed for exposure in the open market.
4. Payment is made in cash or its equivalent.
5. Financing, if any, is on terms generally available in the community as of the specified date and is typical for the property type.
6. The price represents a normal consideration for the property sold, unaffected by special financing amounts or terms, services, fees, costs, or credits incurred in the transaction.

Market value implies a nonrelated buyer and seller; that is, an arm's-length transaction. Related-party sales or sales in which one party is in a distress situation obviously are not indicative of fair market value.

Comparing Market Value, Price, and Cost

While obtaining the correct market value for one's property is the ideal situation, the actual price finally attained does not necessarily equal the value. **Price** is *the amount a particular purchaser agrees to pay and a particular seller agrees to accept under the circumstances surrounding the transaction.* This may or may not equal the value. Many factors may cause a purchaser to pay either more or less than the market value. A seller under duress, for example, may be an individual who must move quickly because of a job transfer. Another example is a family that inherits property through a will and cannot afford to keep it.

Cost is quite different from both value and price and is composed of a number of factors, that, when added together, equal the total dollar expenditure to construct the property. **Cost** is defined as *the total dollar expenditure for labor, materials, legal services, architectural design, financing, taxes during construction, interest, contractor's overhead and profit, and entrepreneurial overhead and profit.* Entrepreneurial costs refer to those expenditures involved in a project requiring financing, start-up costs, overhead, and other expenses. Market value is defined as what the market will pay for the property. It is possible for cost to be equal to, above, or below market value. If the cost is equal to the market value, this simply means that the property was sold for the market value, which was equal to the cost of constructing the property. In some instances, the cost of constructing a property turns out to be more than it is worth in the marketplace, and therefore the cost would be above market value. This often occurs when there are financing problems, unmet time schedules, and other unforeseen construction problems. In other cases, a property, because of aesthetic features, location, or historical value, may be worth more in the marketplace than it did when it was built. Think of examples in your community.

There are two types of costs:

1. **Direct costs** are also called *hard costs, and they include the cost of labor and materials.*
2. **Indirect costs** are *the costs that create and support the project.* They include architectural and engineering fees; professional fees, such as those rendered by surveyors, attorneys, and appraisers; financing costs; administrative costs; filing fees; and other miscellaneous costs. In New York, deeds, mortgages, and subdivided land sold through the installment plan require recording and therefore filing fees.

COMPARATIVE MARKET ANALYSIS

Part of the listing process involves recommending a market price to the owner that will be the listing price. This price is determined by a comparison of the property with other similar properties that have sold recently and those currently listed for sale. No two properties are exactly alike. However, many are comparable or similar in quality, location, and utility. In comparing the listed property and the selected comparables, allowances are made for differences in lot size, age, number of rooms, square footage, number of baths, and so on.

Comparables should be as similar as possible to the subject property. Comparables are found in office real estate files, town or county assessor's files, MLS closed sales data, current listings available through an MLS, and from appraisers. If a computerized MLS is used, an information sheet about the property must be completed so that the information may be imputed to the multiple listing service (MLS). This information, together with a photo of the property, is made available to all member agents of MLS. This method might eliminate the exact format of the CMA illustrated in Figure 12.3. The more recent the date of sale of the comparable, the more valuable the comparable. Emphasis should be given to the similarity between the physical characteristics and location of the comparables to the subject property. In addition to knowing what has sold recently, the seller should be told what is currently available. Knowing the competition may influence pricing and marketing strategies.

Analyzing a Property for a CMA

Figure 12.3 illustrates a completed comparative market analysis.

- *Section 1* indicates the date prepared, the parties for whom the analysis is prepared, the competitive price range, and the recommended list price. These numbers are a result of the research that is contained in the analysis.
- *Section 2* gives the address and particulars of the subject property.
- *Section 3* analyzes five properties that were recently sold. These properties are comparable to the subject property in age, size, and number of rooms. Notice that all the properties took a relatively short time to sell and the prices of the properties sold range from \$117,500 to \$129,000. The number of days it takes to sell a prop-

FIGURE 12.3 A completed comparative market analysis form.

1

DATE	PREPARED FOR	PHONE	PREPARED BY
10/10/99	Betsy and Josh Dupree	458-1234	

COMPETITIVE PRICE RANGE	RECOMMENDED LIST PRICE	RECOMMENDED TERMS
$ 118,000 TO $ 125,900	125,900	

2

PROPERTY ADDRESS	NO. OF ROOMS	NO. OF ROOMS	BED-ROOMS	BATH	GARAGE	BASE-MENT	AGE	APPROXIMATE SQUARE FT.	LOT SIZE	HEAT A/C	DAYS ON MARKET	CURRENT LIST PRICE	TERMS	MISCELLANEOUS
49 Rose Crest	Col	6	3	1	1	FL	60		60x100	OHW				

3

PROPERTY RECENTLY SOLD

PROPERTY ADDRESS	NO. OF ROOMS	NO. OF ROOMS	BED-ROOMS	BATH	GARAGE	BASE-MENT	AGE	APPROXIMATE SQUARE FT.	LOT SIZE	HEAT A/C	DAYS ON MARKET	CURRENT LIST PRICE	DATE SOLD	PRICE	TERMS	MISCELLANEOUS
9 Violet Way	Col	7	3	2	2c	FL	62		60x100	GAS	92	123,900	5/11/99	123,900		
32 Blossom Ln.	Col	8	3	1.5	1c	FL	62		50x115	GHA	111	129,900	2/2/99	129,000		
7 Cherry Drive	Ranch	6	3	1	1c	FL	32		60x133	GHA	115	127,900	9/22/99	127,900		
40 Plumtree Ct.	Col	9	3	2	1c	slab	60		40x125	GHA	126	122,900	6/16/99	117,500		
41 Aster Lane	Col	8	3	2	1c	FL	60		40x120	Oil	97	122,500	8/23/99	117,500		

4

COMPETING HOMES

PROPERTY ADDRESS	NO. OF ROOMS	NO. OF ROOMS	BED-ROOMS	BATH	GARAGE	BASE-MENT	AGE	APPROXIMATE SQUARE FT.	LOT SIZE	HEAT A/C	DAYS ON MARKET	CURRENT LIST PRICE	ORIGINAL	TERMS	MISCELLANEOUS
80 Hydrangea	Col	7	3	1.5	1c	FL	67		48x120	OHW		118,900			
2 Bluebell Ln.	Col	6	3	2	1c	slab	60		50x100	GHA		129,400			
6 Bluebell Ln.	Col	6	3	2	1c	slab	60		48x120	GHA		122,400			
25 Bluebell Ln.	Col	6	3	2	1c	slab	60		50x115	GHA		132,400			

5

EXPIRED LISTINGS

PROPERTY ADDRESS	NO. OF ROOMS	NO. OF ROOMS	BED-ROOMS	BATH	GARAGE	BASE-MENT	AGE	APPROXIMATE SQUARE FT.	LOT SIZE	HEAT A/C	DAYS ON MARKET	CURRENT LIST PRICE	ORIGINAL	TERMS	MISCELLANEOUS
16 Rose Crest	Col	6	3	1	1c	FL	60		48x120	GHA	180	135,900			
10 Bluebell Ln.	Col	6	3	2	2c	FL	62		50x115	GHA	180	133,400			
15 Peony Street	Col	6	3	1.5	1c	FL	62		60x100	GHA	180	131,600			
42 Columbia St.	Col	6	3	1	1c	FL	60		48x120	GHA	180	130,500			

6

CONDITIONS	REMARKS
AREA CONDITIONS: EXCELLENT	For rapid sale, price at 122,900
MARKET CONDITIONS: EXCELLENT	
MORTGAGE MARKET CONDITIONS: EXCELLENT	

The statements and figures presented herein, while not guaranteed, are secured from sources we believe authoritative.

Although this form has generally been replaced by computer forms, it provides another means of generating a CMA.

erty often depends on the listed price. For a faster sale, a property may be priced on the lower end of the price range. It is important to note the differences between the listed price and the sales price. In this example, only two of the properties—40 Plumtree Court and 41 Aster Lane—sold for significantly less than the listed price. The analysis must consider these differences in determining an appropriate price range for the subject property. For example, if most of the sold properties were listed at $122,500 but sold for $117,500, and they are comparable to the subject, then the analysis should adjust by lowering the price range of the subject.

- *Section 4* analyzes competing properties that are currently being marketed. They too are similar in age, size, number of rooms, and lot size.
- *Section 5* delineates the expired listings. These properties were listed for approximately six months and did not sell. Although the features of these listings are comparable to the subject, notice the price range of these expired listings: $130,500 to $135,900. Compare these expired listings to the properties recently sold. The price range of the recently sold properties is much lower; this factor, no doubt, accounts for their timely sale.
- *Section 6* addresses the area conditions; that is, the conditions in the neighborhood where the subject property is located, the market conditions, and the mortgage market (financing). In the "Remarks" section, there is room to note special comments or advice. In this example, although the analysis states that the recommended list price should be $125,900, the remarks indicate that the property would sell more rapidly if priced $3,000 less, at $122,900.

RESIDENTIAL MARKET ANALYSIS

A residential market analysis is a careful study of the individual property being listed as it stands on its own and also *in light of the conditions in the marketplace.* These conditions determine how the property should be marketed. The more knowledge a licensee has of these conditions, the better his chances of selling the property in an appropriate time frame at or near market value. Certain elements are considered in the residential market analysis to derive a listing price. They are discussed below.

Recently Sold Properties

Recently sold properties should be located in the same general vicinity as the subject property and be similar as to age and living area. Anywhere from three to six sold properties in the same neighborhood are analyzed and compared as to type of structure, age, size and number of rooms, lot size, location, condition, number of days on the market, the listed price, and the final selling price. Other items such as landscaping or air conditioning can be compared as well.

Current Competing Properties

The history of competing properties are analyzed considering questions such as:

- How long have the properties been on the market?
- How many competing properties are on the market?
- Has the original listing price been reduced?
- If so, what is the adjusted price?
- Has the price been adjusted more than once?

In the case of pending sales, the sold price may not be available, but the most recent listing price can be used to obtain an idea of the most current price of the property under contract. It is not generally accepted practice to compare properties yet to be built with existing homes. New construction does not have the same value as existing properties because there is a waiting time before they are ready for sale.

PUTTING IT TO WORK 1

As a listing agent, you will research and create CMAs. There is stiff competition for these valuable listings. The accuracy of your findings, along with the effectiveness of your presentation, will help secure the listing. Use the following information and the blank CMA worksheet in Figure 12.4 to practice producing a CMA. After filling out the information, determine a competitive price range and a recommended list price. You may also fill in applicable remarks. Check your responses using the model in the Answer Key at the end of the chapter.

You are preparing this CMA for Donna and Carl Shakes. The date of the listing is 10/10/04. All of the properties, including the subject, are ranch style with 6 total rooms including 3 bedrooms, a 1-car garage, full basement, and gas hot-water heat.

Subject property:

- 310 Lenox Avenue; 2 full bathrooms; age 45; lot size 52′ × 205′

Properties recently sold:

- 18 Crystal Way: 1 bathroom; age 16; lot size 66′ × 138′; 10 days on market; list price $107,500; date sold 3/5/04; sold price $105,000
- 421 Saucer Court: 1 bathroom; age 35; lot size 50′ × 134′; 134 days on market; list price $105,000; date sold 9/12/04; sold price $99,000
- 213 Pepper Street: 1 bathroom; age 40; lot size 70′ × 160′; 7 days on market; list price $105,500; date sold 1/13/04; sold price $100,000
- 29 Stoneware Drive: 1.5 bathrooms; age 40; lot size 51′ × 100′; 58 days on market; list price $112,500; date sold 9/9/04; sold price $100,000
- 245 Corning Lane: 1 bathroom; age 37; lot size 50′ × 115′; 38 days on market; list price $99,900; date sold 3/10/04; sold price $98,000

Competing homes:

- 14 Chinaberry Lane: 1 bathroom; age 45; lot size 50′ × 100′; 15 days on market; list price $105,000
- 6 Teacup Circle: 1.5 bathrooms; age 10; lot size 60′ × 100′; 117 days on market; list price $104,000
- 80 Sugarbowl Drive: 1 bathroom; age 55; lot size 50′ × 100′; 111 days on market; list price $104,900
- 17 Lemon Road: 1 bathroom; age 57; lot size 40′ × 138′; 8 days on market; list price $99,900

Expired listings:

- 19 Spoon Road: 1.5 bathrooms; age 45; lot size 52′ × 205′; 180 days on market; list price $113,200
- 26 Placemat Circle: 1.5 bathrooms; age 40; lot size 50′ × 200′; 180 days on market; list price $112,500
- 42 Silver Way: 1.5 bathrooms; age 47; lot size 45′ × 210′; 180 days on market; list price $111,900
- 64 Salty Drive: 1.5 bathrooms; age 45; lot size 50′ × 155′; 180 days on market; list price $109,000

Area conditions: Excellent

Market conditions: Good

Mortgage market conditions: Excellent

FIGURE 12.4 Blank comparative market analysis form.

DATE	PREPARED FOR	PHONE	PREPARED BY
COMPETITIVE PRICE RANGE $ TO $	RECOMMENDED LIST PRICE	RECOMMENDED TERMS	

	PROPERTY ADDRESS	NO. OF ROOMS	NO. OF ROOMS	BED-ROOMS	BATH	GARAGE	BASE-MENT	AGE	APPROXIMATE SQUARE FT.	LOT SIZE	HEAT A/C	DAYS ON MARKET	CURRENT LIST PRICE	TERMS			MISCELLANEOUS
PROPERTY RECENTLY SOLD														DATE SOLD	PRICE	TERMS	
COMPETING HOMES														ORIGINAL	TERMS		
EXPIRED LISTINGS														ORIGINAL	TERMS		

AREA CONDITIONS	REMARKS
MARKET CONDITIONS	
MORTGAGE MARKET CONDITIONS	

Recently Expired Properties

Expired listings are properties that have not sold within the time of the listing agreement. Often, these listings were priced too high for market conditions. A careful research of the prices of these expired listings along with the full history of the listing can reveal valuable information regarding an acceptable price range for the subject property.

Buyer Appeal

Buyer appeal is subjective and has much to do with visual aspects of the property. A property that appears larger from the street, compared with one that looks smaller but is actually the same size inside, may have greater buyer appeal. Buyers also look at the distance from the house to the road, the landscaping, the entry or approach to the house, the color, and the construction materials. Some properties have so-called inferior curb appeal, and yet they may offer better amenities than more visually appealing ones.

Market Position

This refers to the number of similar properties that are available in the same price range. A good residential analysis must ask how the subject property is different from these other properties and what the marketing strategy is to make this difference known in the marketplace.

Assets and Drawbacks

Certain assets that buyers look for in a property are universal: a property in good to excellent condition; a desirable location; and a tolerable traffic pattern. In general, cul-de-sacs, which are dead-end streets, have more appeal than through-streets because there is less traffic noise. In analyzing the marketplace, the assets of the subject property should be compared with competing properties.

Most properties, however, are not perfect and may have some undesirable features. High-traffic areas, lack of trees or landscaping problems, and close proximity to other properties are some of the drawbacks that can affect a property's marketability.

When evaluating current competing listings, expired listings, and sold properties, licensees should analyze the assets and drawbacks for each of the properties to see how they have affected the sale, price range, or final sales price of these properties.

Area Market Conditions

Market conditions fluctuate greatly. They depend on the economy in general, on supply-and-demand factors, as well as on seasonal considerations. Supply and demand implies that if properties are in short supply, there will be greater demand for those few available. *If properties are plentiful, there will be more competition.* Seasonal considerations include holidays, weather, back-to-school times, and other similar factors. In light of these considerations, licensees must draw up a plan to market the property. If market conditions are favorable, the property will likely sell in a shorter period of time. A good indication of time and corresponding market conditions is a thorough examination of pending and sold properties.

Recommended Terms

The more favorable the terms are to a buyer, the more quickly a property will sell. Some of the circumstances involved in the terms of sale are:

1. Will the house be available immediately on transfer of title or are the sellers buying a home not available until a later date? This sometimes occurs with new construction where there may be delays.
2. What are the financing terms? Is the mortgage assumable and are the interest rates favorable? Are mortgages readily available with terms that are attractive to purchasers? Will the sellers offer financing directly to the buyer?

Market Value Range

After researching the market, a price range for the subject property is determined. A market analysis may consist of a high, middle, and low price. *In a higher-priced property, the span or price range may be greater than that of a lower-priced property.* A price is usually determined for the time frame that the property will remain on the market. The seller can be offered a choice. For example, a property will sell more quickly if the property is placed in the low end of the price range and more slowly if the property is marketed on the high end. The price should be continuously evaluated and adjusted to ensure continued market activity.

If the sellers are reluctant to accept a suggested price range after well-researched market analysis, the licensee should consider refusing to market the property. A listing that does not take into account the conditions of the marketplace would be unlikely to produce a timely sale.

Salesperson's Role

Certain professional characteristics and responsibilities are essential in the residential market analysis process:

Competence

A salesperson should be able to handle all aspects of marketing competently. If the client has questions in certain areas that a salesperson cannot answer, the salesperson will look toward his broker for guidance. At the onset, a well-researched listing presentation should be communicated to the sellers with appropriate examples from the marketplace. The salesperson should be prepared with justifiable and appropriate data and be able to verify the data with a knowledge of the area being marketed and the nature of the competition.

Diligence

Diligence involves doing your homework. Once a salesperson has a listing, he must follow through to ensure that the property is correctly marketed. This involves contacting agents who showed the property and obtaining feedback both from the agents who showed the property and their prospective purchasers. This helps to evaluate the property's assets and drawbacks. Diligence also refers to communicating with the sellers and informing them as to the activity on the property, and tracking the market, continuously analyzing the activity of the competing properties and readjusting the marketing focus.

Documentation

The salesperson must keep records of agents who showed the house, records of preview caravans (groups of agents viewing the property) from both the salesperson's firm and other companies, lists of people who appear at open houses, and notes of follow-up interviews with them. The salesperson should document and review new listings daily, noting those that are competitive and also noting competitive older listings that have sales pending. From this daily documentation, the salesperson may wish to adjust the list price if a similar house is under contract for a lower price than the subject property.

Effective Communication

This refers to the salesperson's ability to provide information to the seller in a professional manner, keeping the sellers informed about the market activity on their property, communicating with other agents who have shown the property and obtaining feedback from them, and relating this information to the sellers.

PUTTING IT TO WORK 2

Many sellers believe that they can properly value and market their homes without the professional services of a licensee. Shape your response to the following scenario* so that the prospective sellers will understand the value of your services. Compare your response to the model in the Answer Key at the end of the chapter.

We are selling our home and leaving the area. What should we consider when establishing the asking price? By the way, we are determined to sell without a real estate agent, so don't try to talk us into hiring one.

IMPORTANT POINTS

1. Real property has certain physical characteristics including immobility, indestructibility (permanence), and nonhomogeneity (uniqueness). It also has certain economic characteristics: scarcity (limited availability), permanence of investment, location, and modification by improvement.
2. An appraisal is an estimate of value based on factual data as of a specific date for a particular purpose on a specified property.
3. Appraisals commonly use three approaches to value. They are the sales comparison approach, the cost approach, and the income approach. The Uniform Residential Appraisal Report (URAR) is the most common appraisal form used by appraisers to report these approaches to value.
4. Valuation is the process of estimating the value of an identified interest in a specific property as of a given date. Besides market value, other types of value include value in use, insurance value, investment value, assessed value, and mortgage loan value.
5. Market value is the amount of money a typical buyer will give in exchange for a property.
6. Evaluation, as compared with valuation, is a study of the quality or utility of a property without reference to a specific estimate of value.
7. Various evaluation studies include marketability, feasibility, supply and demand, land utilization, and highest and best use. In the context of market value, highest and best use is the most probable use. It may or may not be the present use of the property.
8. Price is the amount a purchaser agrees to pay and a seller agrees to accept under the circumstances surrounding the transaction.

---

*Source: James A. Ader, "Real Estate Spotlight." Copyright © The Albany *Times Union.* Reprinted by permission.

9. Cost is composed of a number of factors that equal the total dollar expenditure to construct the improvements. Included are direct costs, such as labor and materials, and indirect costs, such as professional fees, filing fees, and other items inherent in the construction process.
10. A comparative market analysis (CMA) is an analysis of the competition in the marketplace that a property will face upon sale attempts.
11. A residential market analysis consists of a study of the following: recently sold properties, currently competing properties, recently expired properties, buyer appeal, market position, assets and drawbacks of the property, area market conditions, recommended terms, and price range.
12. The degree of competence, diligence, documentation, and effective communication skills on the part of the licensee is integral to effective marketing of the property.

CHAPTER REVIEW

KEY TERM REVIEW

Fill in the term that best completes each sentence and then check the Answer Key at the end of the chapter.

1. An unbiased estimate of the nature, quality, or utility value, based on factual data, of an interest of real estate as of a certain date is a(n) ______________.
2. The probable price that a property will bring in a competitive and open market is ______________.
3. Labor and materials in a construction project are considered to be ______________.
4. ______________ is a study of the usefulness, quality, or utility of a property without reference to the specific estimate of value.
5. ______________ is the value to which a local tax rate is applied to establish the amount of tax imposed on a property.
6. The total dollar value to construct a property is its ______________.
7. A value of a property based on its utility to the owner is ______________.
8. ______________ is the actual cash value or replacement cost of a totally destroyed property.

MULTIPLE CHOICE

Circle the letter that best answers the question and then check the Answer Key at the end of the chapter.

1. The basis of market value is most typically:
   A. utility value
   B. book value
   C. subjective value
   D. value determined between a willing buyer and willing seller

2. The amount of money a property will bring in the marketplace is called:
   A. extrinsic value
   B. intrinsic value
   C. market value
   D. value in use

3. Which of the following is FALSE regarding market conditions? They:
   A. fluctuate greatly
   B. tend to remain the same year after year
   C. are dependent on the economy in general
   D. are influenced by supply and demand factors

4. Which of the following is NOT a type of evaluation study?
   A. land utilization studies
   B. feasibility studies
   C. highest- and best-use studies
   D. historical valuation studies

5. Essie and John must sell their house quickly as John has received a job transfer. They need the cash from their current home to purchase a new home. Which of the following best applies?
   A. they are sellers under duress and may have to accept less than market value for their home
   B. they will likely receive full market value for their home
   C. it is impossible for them to sell their house at market value
   D. they will have to sell their home at cost

6. Which of the following factors is NOT defined as cost?
   A. financing
   B. entrepreneurial profit
   C. the price a purchaser agrees to pay for the property
   D. taxes during construction

7. Direct costs are also known as:
   A. administrative costs
   B. locational costs
   C. overhead factors
   D. hard costs

8. Which of the following is NOT included in a market analysis?
   A. appraisal
   B. current competition in the marketplace
   C. recently sold listings
   D. expired listings

9. If a listed property does NOT sell within a six-month time period, the property:
   A. should sit on the market at the listed price for six more months
   B. has a listed price that is probably above market value
   C. has a listed price that should be increased to meet a greater market demand
   D. should probably be taken off the market by the sellers

10. Expired listings:
    A. are never used in comparative market analysis
    B. are often indicative of properties that were priced below market value
    C. are properties that were not sold during the term of their listing
    D. yield little or no information that is useful to marketing a subject property

ANSWER KEY

Putting It to Work 1

Comparative Market Analysis

DATE	PREPARED FOR	PHONE	PREPARED BY
10/10/04	Donna & Carl Shakes		
COMPETITIVE PRICE RANGE		RECOMMENDED LIST PRICE	RECOMMENDED TERMS
$ 97,500 TO $ 107,500		105,000	

	PROPERTY ADDRESS	STYLE	NO. OF ROOMS	BED-ROOMS	BATH	GARAGE	BASE-MENT	AGE	APPROXIMATE SQUARE FT.	LOT SIZE	HEAT A/C	DAYS ON MARKET	CURRENT LIST PRICE	TERMS			MISCELLANEOUS
	310 Lenox Avenue	Ranch	6	3	2	1c	FL	45		52x205	GHW						
PROPERTY RECENTLY SOLD														DATE SOLD	PRICE	TERMS	
	18 Crystal Way	Ranch	6	3	1	1c	FL	16		66x138	GHW	10	107,500	3/5/04	105,000		
	421 Saucer Ct.	Ranch	6	3	1	1c	FL	35		50x134	GHW	134	105,000	9/12/04	99,000		
	213 Pepper St.	Ranch	6	3	1	1c	FL	40		70x160	GHW	7	105,500	1/13/04	100,000		
	29 Stoneware Dr.	Ranch	6	3	1.5	1c	FL	40		51x100	GHW	58	112,500	9/9/04	100,000		
	245 Corning Ln.	Ranch	6	3	1	1c	FL	37		50x115	GHW	38	99,900	3/10/04	98,000		
COMPETING HOMES														ORIGINAL	TERMS		
	14 Chinaberry Ln	Ranch	6	3	1	1c	FL	45		50x100	GHW	15	105,000				
	6 Teacup Cr.	Ranch	6	3	1.5	1c	FL	10		60x100	GHW	117	104,000				
	80 Sugarbowl Dr.	Ranch	6	3	1	1c	FL	55		50x100	GHW	111	104,900				
	17 Lemon Rd.	Ranch	6	3	1	1c	FL	57		40x138	GHW	8	99,900				
EXPIRED LISTINGS														ORIGINAL	TERMS		
	19 Spoon Road	Ranch	6	3	1.5	1c	FL	45		52x205	GHW	180	113,200				
	26 Placemat Cr.	Ranch	6	3	1.5	1c	FL	40		50x200	GHW	180	112,500				
	42 Silver Way	Ranch	6	3	1.5	1c	FL	47		45x210	GHW	180	111,900				
	64 Salty Drive	Ranch	6	3	1.5	1c	FL	45		50x155	GHW	180	109,000				

AREA CONDITIONS: EXCELLENT	REMARKS: 310 Lenox Avenue has extra bath worth $1,500 for rapid sale price at 103,500
MARKET CONDITIONS: GOOD	
MORTGAGE MARKET CONDITIONS: EXCELLENT	

The statements and figures presented herein, while not guaranteed, are secured from sources we believe authoritative.

Putting It to Work 2

Pricing at a realistic level from the start may be the most important factor in the quick sale of your home. Often, sellers price their property based upon what neighbors recently received for their home or on information from friends. Many subtle factors should be considered when determining your asking price: the recent sales prices of homes similar to yours in the same neighborhood; the asking price of homes that were on the market but did not sell; the asking price of homes currently on the market competing with yours. Be careful about estimating the value of improvements you have made: What was a must have for you might be a must remove for a potential buyer. You will want to conduct a CMA to determine the asking price. Although you may not want a real estate agent, you should understand that agents are trained to analyze your property in light of all of the above factors. Because they can determine an appropriate listing price for your property, you will probably realize a greater profit than if you attempted to market it on your own.*

*Source: James A. Ader, "Real Estate Spotlight." Copyright © The Albany *Times Union.* Reprinted by permission.

Key Term Review

1. appraisal
2. market value
3. direct costs
4. evaluation
5. assessed value
6. cost
7. value in use
8. insured value

Multiple Choice

1. D
2. C
3. B
4. D
5. A
6. C
7. D
8. A
9. B
10. C

Chapter 13

KEY TERMS

Americans with Disabilities Act
blockbusting
cease and desist list
cease and desist zone
Civil Rights Act of 1866
Department of Housing and Urban Development (HUD)
disability
Fair Housing Act of 1968
familial status
filtering down
marital status
multiple dwelling
New York State Human Rights Law
nonsolicitation order
redlining
steering
testers

LEARNING OBJECTIVES

Classroom hours: 4

1. Explain why fair housing laws are necessary based on history and background.
2. Identify what kind of behavior is likely to create problems in this area.
3. List what people are in protected classes and explain why protected classes were created.
4. Describe the various fair housing laws.
5. Outline responsibilities of licensure concerning advertising, the taking of listings, and the showing of homes and apartments to all individuals.
6. Describe what cease and desists are and why they are used.
7. Describe the concept of nonsolicitation orders and broker and salesperson's responsibility to comply with each order.

Human Rights and Fair Housing

IN THIS CHAPTER Licensees should be well informed about discrinination laws. Not only is discrimination socially offensive but it can also jeopardize a transaction, your license, and expose you to liability. Violation of fair housing laws carry stiff penalties on both the federal and state levels.

> Among the most cherished of civil rights is the right to live where one chooses. It is through the exercise of this right that one defines the environment in which one will raise a family, invests the largest part of one's resources, and generally lives out one's life. It is the existence of free housing choice that distinguishes the neighborhood from the ghetto and the home from a prison.*

EQUAL HOUSING OPPORTUNITY TODAY

Many people believe that the issue of fair housing has long been resolved through actions such as the civil rights movement of the 1960s. Despite the intention of both the 1866 and the 1968 civil rights acts to provide equal housing opportunity for all citizens, this goal has not been achieved in practice. Here are some examples of discriminatory postures that you may encounter as a licensee:

- owners and sellers who request only specific types of people be shown their housing
- sellers' concerns about what the neighbors will think, say, or do if a family of a particular race, religion, or ethnic origin moves into their home
- discriminatory statements by buyers and renters about certain parts of the community
- buyers and renters asking pointed questions of a discriminatory nature about the community
- buyers and renters refusing to be shown houses if certain types of people live in that part of the community

Broker's Responsibility to Uphold Fair Housing

Legal statute, HUD regulations, NAR recommendations, and court rulings all define the broker's responsibility to comply with fair housing policy.

---

*Source: William D. North, "Fair Housing in the 90s: A Historical Perspective," in *Facilitator's Guide to Fair Housing in the 90s.* Copyright © National Association of REALTORS®. Reprinted with permission of the National Association of REALTORS®.

Broker's Responsibility for Acts of Sales Agents

Under the law, brokers have a responsibility to supervise their salespersons, provide fair housing training, and take appropriate steps to insure compliance. However, a broker's liability for the acts of salespersons is often scrutinized by the courts. An important U.S. Supreme Court case, *Meyer v. Holley*, (January, 2003) ruled that individual broker-owners are not personally liable for the acts of agents who commit fair housing law violations. In this case, a racially mixed couple sought relief under the Fair Housing Act to make the owner of a real estate firm personally responsible for the actions of one of its agents who had allegedly made disparaging remarks about the couple. The court found that innocent officers and owners of residential real estate corporations are not personally liable for the unlawful conduct of the corporation's employees or agents. It further held that vicarious liability principles permitted only the corporation, and not the individual owner and officer of the corporation to be liable for acts of the corporation's agents.

Office Procedures

To ensure fair housing compliance, NAR recommends that agents sign a policy statement that includes an affirmative commitment to equal opportunity. To further comply, the firm should designate a fair housing officer, either the broker or another agent. This individual oversees fair housing training, keeps up-to-date on fair housing developments, tracks the firm's compliance, and finds answers to policy questions. In addition, office procedures should outline the initial contact with customers and clients including discussing the services offered by the firm, assigning agents to the customer, and obtaining initial customer information.

Fair Housing Poster

An amendment to the Fair Housing Act of 1968 requires all offices to prominently display the fair housing poster distributed by HUD. Upon investigation of a discrimination complaint, failure to display the poster could be proof of failure to noncompliance with federal law.

Salesperson's Responsibility to Uphold Fair Housing

Fair Housing Training and Resources

Real estate agents should regularly engage in fair housing training obtained in the classroom or online, through programs offered by NAR, (*http://www.realtor.org*), the NYS Division of Human Rights, state and local boards, and proprietary schools. Subject matter should include prohibited discriminatory behavior, fair housing laws, procedures for providing equal service, and good record keeping.

Equal Service

Activities such as greeting people, obtaining listings, holding open houses, record keeping, and follow up procedures should be performed so that each individual receives the same measure of professional treatment. The housing needs and wants should be emphasized and limited to the price, size, special features, and location of a property. The agent should determine if the customer knows what they are financially able to purchase. (See Figure 13.1) Discussion should be limited to information on housing availability, methods of finance, and items such as schools, hospitals, transportation, or employment.

Record-keeping

A record of conversations regarding housing choices should be written down and kept by the agent. Notes should include the housing request, the housing options offered by the agent, and the services provided to the customer. (See Figure 13.2)

PUTTING IT TO WORK

Salesperson responsibilities for fair housing compliance includes:

- know fair housing laws
- always act in accordance with the law
- learn excellent record-keeping skills
- attend fair housing training seminars
- know how to report fair housing misconduct

FIGURE 13.1 Needs and wants checklist.

NEEDS AND WANTS CHECKLIST

Date ________

Name(s) ________

Present Address ________

Telephone No. ________

Urgency ________

Motivation ________

Reason for Contacting You ________

Affordable Purchase Price ________

Type of Home

[ ]	Ranch	[ ]	Colonial	[ ]	Cape Cod
[ ]	Split Level	[ ]	Townhouse	[ ]	Condonminum

Age of Home

[ ]	New	[ ]	1-3 years	[ ]	4-6 years
[ ]	7-10 years	[ ]	10-20 years	[ ]	Over 20 years

Features:
Number of bedrooms ________
Number of bathrooms ________
Type/size of kitchen ________
Type/size of dining room ________
Type/size of living room ________
Family room ________
Office/den ________
Fireplace ________
Basement ________
Garage/Carport ________
Yard ________

Other:
Convenient to shopping ________
Convenient to schools ________
Convenient of recreation ________
Decorating plans ________
Family hobbies ________
Other ________

Attach to ESR and place in customer file

This form allows the agent to qualify prospects and focus on their needs and wants.

FIGURE 13.2 An Equal Service Report form.

BOARD OF REALTORS®
EQUAL SERVICE REPORT

DATE ________
TIME ________

FIRM NAME ________ LOCATION ________
SALES AGENT ________

INFORMATION DATA*
HOMESEEKERS NAME ________
ADDRESS ________ TELEPHONE ________
EMPLOYER ________ SOCIAL SECURITY NO. ________
AGE ____ SEX ____ RACE: MINORITY ________ NON-MINORITY ________

HOUSING PREFERENCE INFORMATION
☐ SALE ☐ RENTAL
PRICE RANGE PREFERENCE ________
GEOGRAPHIC AREA OR LOCATION PREFERENCE ________

SIZE AND FEATURE PREFERENCE ________
NO. OF BEDROOMS ________ NO. OF BATHROOMS ________
GARAGE ____ BASEMENT ____ OTHER ________

HOMES SHOWN

	GEOGRAPHIC AREA OR LOCATION	ADDRESS	LISTING PRICE	DATE SHOWN
1.				
2.				
3.				
4.				
5.				

ORIGIN OF INQUIRY
WALK IN ________ SIGN ________ NEWSPAPER ________
TELEPHONE SOLICITATION ________ MAIL SOLICITATION ________
REFERRAL ________ BY WHOM ________

DISPOSITION ________

I (the Homeseeker) have been advised of the proximity and availability of public transportation, schools, shopping, community services and potential sources of employment as well as alternative methods of financing.

SIGNATURE ________ DATE ________

* Information pertaining to homeseekers age, sex and race is requested in connection with the NATIONAL ASSOCIATION OF REALTORS® Affirmative Marketing Agreement, which was accepted by the Department of Housing and Urban Development on December 16, 1975, and are consistent with requirements for mortgage financing included in regulations issued by the Board of Governors of the Federal Reserve System pursuant to the Equal Credit Opportunity Act and as published in Vol. 41 No. 140 of THE FEDERAL REGISTER on July 20, 1976.

EQUAL HOUSING OPPORTUNITY

REALTOR®

141-566 **WHITE,** SALES AGENT COPY . . . **CANARY,** CUSTOMER COPY . . . **PINK,** LISTING BROKER COPY

This form assists the agent in record-keeping and fair housing compliance.

FEDERAL ANTIDISCRIMINATION LAWS

Federal laws that prohibit discrimination in housing are the Civil Rights Act of 1866, the Civil Rights Act of 1964, and the Fair Housing Act of 1968, with its important 1974 and 1988 amendments. Several important U. S. Supreme Court decisions also shaped civil rights policy. Another federal antidiscrimination law, the Americans with Disabilities Act of 1992, protects rights of individuals with disabilities.

You Should Know

Documenting and reporting fair housing misconduct

Salespersons should maintain notes regarding discussions they had with prospective purchasers and sellers in which questions or statements of a possible discriminatory nature arise. Salespeople should be careful about how they respond to questions of this nature. You will have some practice with these questions in the role-playing exercises in this chapter. Many brokers have forms for phone conversations, in-person interviews and conversations, open-house activity, listing and contract presentations, with sellers and prospective purchasers. These documents are important in case a discrimination charge or lawsuit is brought against a firm or an agent.

Salespersons and associate brokers should immediately report behavior or conversations of a discriminatory nature to their broker. If a prospective seller or prospective purchaser cannot be dealt with according to the law, then a salesperson should not agree to represent this individual. In New York, illegal discriminatory behavior can be reported to either the New York State Division of Human Rights, or, in New York City, to the New York City Commission on Human Rights.

The Civil Rights Act of 1866

The first significant statute affecting equal housing opportunity is the federal **Civil Rights Act of 1866.** Far from being obsolete, this statute has had a major impact on fair housing concepts mainly because of a landmark case in 1968, the year the Federal Fair Housing Act became law. Although the 1968 Act provides for a number of exemptions, the 1866 law has no exemptions and contains the blanket statement that *all citizens have the same rights to inherit, buy, sell, or lease all real and personal property.* This statute is interpreted to prohibit all racial discrimination.

1. C+S sexual orient
2. D.O.S. FHA.
3. Attorney General
'vindicate public's interest'

In the 1968 case of *Jones v. Alfred H. Mayer Company,* the U. S. Supreme Court applied the older Civil Rights Act of 1866 to prohibit any racially based discrimination in housing. This court ruling is important because the Federal Fair Housing Act provides exemptions under certain circumstances. Because of the court's determination in *Jones v. Mayer*, exemptions in the Fair Housing Act cannot be used to allow racial discrimination under any circumstances. Note that this 1866 law prohibits racial discrimination in the purchase, sale, or lease of both housing and personal property.

Supreme Court Decisions

The Civil Rights Act of 1866 guaranteed the right of *all citizens* to "purchase, lease, sell, hold, and convey real and personal property." The following important Supreme Court issues shaped U. S. policy during the 100 years after the Civil Rights Act of 1866 was passed.

***Plessy v. Ferguson* (163 U. S. 537).** In this 1896 case, the Court ruled that *separate but equal* was legally acceptable. Therefore, as long as separate housing accommodations or facilities for African-Americans and whites were deemed equal, they were legal.

***Buchanan v. Warley* (245 U. S. 60).** At the turn of the century, local zoning laws were passed that required block-by-block segregation. Many states ascribed to these ordinances. In the Buchanan case, the court decided that city ordinances that denied minorities the right to occupy housing in blocks where many of the houses were occupied by whites were unconstitutional. Despite this 1917 decision, many communities tried to keep racial zoning laws on the books into the 1950s.

Brown v. Board of Education. In this 1954 landmark decision, the Supreme Court reversed its ruling on *Plessy v. Ferguson.* It found that separate facilities were, by their nature, *unequal.* This case was significant in causing the integration of public schools.

Civil Rights Act of 1964

Initiatives by the federal government to promote fair housing occurred in 1962, when President John F. Kennedy issued an Executive Order guaranteeing nondiscrimination in housing for FHA and VA loans. Shortly afterward, Title VI of the *Civil Rights Act of 1964* was enacted, which prohibited discrimination in any program receiving federal money. These laws, unfortunately, did not apply to privately financed housing.

The Federal Fair Housing Act of 1968

Originally enacted by Congress as Title VIII of the Civil Rights Act of 1968, the **Fair Housing Act** *prohibits discrimination in housing on the basis of race, color, religion, or national origin.* An amendment in the *Housing and Community Development Act* of *1974* added the prohibition against discrimination on the basis of gender. The Fair Housing Amendments Act of 1988 added *provisions to prevent discrimination based on mental or physical handicap or familial status.*

1988 Amendments to Fair Housing Act

Although the Fair Housing Act of 1968 established broad responsibilities in providing fair housing for the nation's citizens, it essentially lacked clout for enforcement. Until 1988, the role of the **Department of Housing and Urban Development** (HUD) was limited to that of a negotiator, trying to effect a voluntary conciliation between the affected parties through persuasion. *HUD is a federal regulatory agency through which civil rights violations can be reported.* Although aggrieved parties could always take their complaints to a federal court and seek civil damages, they rarely did because of the burden of legal expense on the discriminated party.

In addition, Congress found that although racial complaints were becoming less frequent, a major problem in housing was discrimination against families with young children as well as people with disabilities. To address these concerns, Congress passed sweeping amendments to the act, which became effective March 12, 1989, adding new protected classes and new enforcement provisions to the act.

New Protected Classes

Persons with disabilities. Protected classes now include individuals with mental or physical impairments that impede any of their life functions. Owners must allow tenants with disabilities to make reasonable modifications to an apartment, at the tenant's expense, to accommodate their special needs. Tenants, for example, must be allowed to install a ramp or widen doors for a wheelchair or install grab bars in a bathroom. At the end of their tenancy, they must return the premises to their original condition, also at their own expense. New York law also provides for similar housing modification for people with disabilities and calls for "rules, policies, practices, and services" to afford the disabled individual "equal opportunity and enjoyment" of the housing accommodation.

According to the federal Fair Housing Act, new multifamily construction must provide certain accommodations for people with disabilities, for example, switches and thermostats at a level that can be operated from a wheelchair, reinforced walls to install grab bars, and kitchen space that will permit maneuverability in a wheelchair. New York law also provides that multifamily dwellings, or **multiple dwellings** *(residences that contain three or more families)* that were first occupied after March 13, 1991, must allow accessibility for persons with disabilities. For instance, all doors that allow passage into and throughout the premises must be wide enough to allow an individual in a wheelchair to pass through. The design and construction of the multiple dwelling must also conform to the New York State Uniform Fire Prevention and Building Code.

Familial status. Another added protected class is **familial status.** Familial status is defined as *an adult with children under 18, a person who is pregnant, or one who has legal custody of a child or who is in the process of obtaining such custody.* Therefore, landlords are prohibited from using advertising with the words "adults only" in most circumstances. The amendments, however, provide for elderly housing if (a) all units are occupied by individuals age 62 or older, or (b) 80 percent of the units have persons age 55 or older and the facility has services to accommodate the physical and social needs of the elderly.

Types of Discrimination and Prohibited Acts

Under current law, discrimination against protected classes is illegal in the sale or rental of housing or residential lots, advertising the sale or rental of housing, financing housing, and providing real estate brokerage services. The act also makes blockbusting and racial steering illegal (discussed later).

A few special exemptions are available to owners in renting or selling their own property. In the absence of an exemption, the following discriminatory acts based on race, color, religion, gender, national origin, handicap, or familial status are prohibited:

1. Refusing to sell or rent housing or to negotiate the sale or rental of residential lots. This includes representing to any person on discriminatory grounds "that any dwelling is not available for inspection, sale, or rental when in fact such dwelling is available." It is also illegal to refuse to sell or rent after the making of a bona fide (good faith) offer or to refuse to negotiate for the sale or rental, or in any way deny or make housing unavailable to protected groups based on discrimination. Examples of violations are:

- Advising a prospective buyer that a house has been sold, because of the prospect's national origin, when it has not.
- Refusing to accept an offer to purchase because the offeror is a member of a certain religion.
- Telling a rental applicant that an apartment is not available for inspection because the applicant is a female (or male), when the apartment is actually vacant and available for inspection.
- Refusing to rent to a person confined to a wheelchair or make reasonable modifications (at the tenant's expense) to an apartment to accommodate the wheelchair.
- Refusing to rent to a family with children.

2. The act makes it illegal to discriminate in the terms, conditions, privileges of sale or rental of a dwelling, or in providing services or facilities. Examples of violations in this category are:

- The manager of an apartment complex routinely requires tenants to provide a security deposit in an amount equal to one month's rent except when the rental applicant is Hispanic, in which case the required deposit is increased to two months' rent.
- The owner of a condominium includes in the purchase of a condo apartment a share of stock and membership in a nearby country club, provided the purchaser is not Jewish.
- A landlord charges a larger deposit to a couple with young children than to a couple without children.
- A landlord charges a higher than normal rent to a person in a wheelchair.

Blockbusting

The act specifically makes **blockbusting** illegal. Blockbusting occurs *when real estate salespersons induce owners to list property for sale or rent by telling them that persons of a particular race, color, national origin, gender, religion, handicap, or familial status are moving into the area, or when real estate firms sell a home in a neighborhood to a person from one of the protected classes with the sole intent to cause property owners to panic and place their property for sale at reduced prices.* In New York, blockbusting is also prohibited by the human rights laws and DOS regulations.

Steering

In **steering,** another violation resulting from the acts of real estate licensees, licensees *direct prospective purchasers from culturally diverse backgrounds to presently integrated areas to avoid integration of nonintegrated areas.* The prohibition against steering falls under the general prohibition of refusing to sell, rent, or negotiate the sale or rental of housing or residential lots. Examples are:

- showing a white prospect properties in areas populated by white people only
- showing African American prospects properties in integrated areas only or in areas populated only by African Americans
- showing Polish prospects properties in areas populated only by Poles
- placing tenants with disabilities in a separate building

Discriminatory Advertising

Discriminatory advertising directed at any of the groups protected by the Fair Housing Act is prohibited. It is illegal to make, print, or publish, or cause to be made, printed, or published any notice, statement, or advertisement concerning the sale or rental of a dwelling that discriminates against the protected groups. Examples are:

- an advertisement for the sale of condominium units or rental apartments containing pictures that show owners or tenants of only one race on the property, or
- an advertisement stating that the owner prefers tenants who are male college students

Financing of Housing—Redlining

In the past, areas populated by culturally diverse persons were "redlined." Prior to enactment of the Fair Housing Act, some lending institutions circled certain local areas with a red line on the map, refusing to make loans within the circled areas based upon

PUTTING IT TO WORK

The intent of the message and whether any particular groups are excluded should be considered when creating ads. Discrimination includes specific directions to a property that refer to well known racial, ethnic, or religious landmarks, or other landmarks that indicate a preference for a specific type of person or community. Advertisements should not be targeted to one specific segment of a community. Discriminatory advertising may not be used in any electronic or print media; not only newspapers, but radio, T.V., billboards, application forms, flyers, signs, posters, or banners. Certain words or phrases regarding disabled people or families with children are also prohibited including: adult buildings, blind, crippled, deaf, exclusive, mature persons, mentally ill, restricted community, retarded, singles, board or membership approval, exclusive, integrated, restricted, private, or traditional.

some characteristic of property owners in the area. The act prohibits lending institutions from **redlining,** or *refusing to make loans to purchase, construct, or repair a dwelling by discriminating on the basis of race, color, religion, gender, national origin, handicap, or familial status.*

The prohibition against discrimination also applies to those who deny a person a loan or financial assistance for the purchase, construction, improvement, repair, or maintainence of residential property. The prohibition applies to individuals who discriminate in fixing terms of a loan, including interest rates, duration of the loan, or any other terms.

The Community Reinvestment Act (CRA) (1977, revised 1995), also known as the Fair Lending Law, was enacted to encourage lenders to help meet the credit needs of communities where they are located, including low- and moderate-income neighborhoods. The CRA requires that each lender's record in helping meet the credit needs of its entire community be evaluated periodically. In a process known as **filtering down,** *properties in formerly middle- or upper-income neighborhoods decline in value,* thereby allowing people with lower incomes to purchase these properties. If lenders do not make loans available to lower-income purchasers, these communities can deteriorate rapidly.

Real Estate Brokerage Services

The Fair Housing Act makes it illegal to deny membership, special terms, or conditions of membership in any real estate organization on discriminatory grounds. This prohibition extends to access to multiple listing service. The New York Human Rights Law contains a similar provision.

Exemptions

The Fair Housing Law provides exemptions to *property owners* under certain conditions. Some of the exemptions in the federal law are not allowable in New York because of restrictions in the New York Human Rights Law (discussed later). Exemptions from the 1968 Fair Housing Act include:

1. An owner in the sale or rental of up to three single-family dwellings at any one time is exempt. If the owner was not living in the dwelling at the time of the transaction or was not the last occupant, the owner is then limited to only one exemption in any 24-month period.
2. An owner of an apartment building containing up to four units is exempt in the rental of the units provided the owner occupies one of the units as a personal residence.
3. Properties owned and operated by religious organizations for the benefit of their membership and for noncommercial purposes may give preference to members of their own religion provided that membership in the religion is not restricted on account of race, color, national origin, gender, handicap, or familial status.
4. A private club that does not operate for commercial purposes is exempt as long as it provides lodging for the benefit of its members only and not to the general public.

None of these exemptions is available if either of the following has occurred: (a) discriminatory advertising has been used, or (b) the services of a real estate licensee or any person in the business of selling or renting dwellings are used.

A person is deemed to be in the business of selling or renting housing if (a) the individual has, within the preceding 12 months, participated as principal in three or more transactions; (b) participated as an agent (excluding the sale of personal residence) in providing sales or rental facilities or services in two or more transactions; or (c) is the owner of any housing intended for occupancy by five or more families.

Enforcement and Penalties

The Fair Housing Act may be enforced in three ways:

1. By administrative procedure through the Office of Equal Opportunity, Department of Housing and Urban Development. HUD may act on its own information and initiative. HUD must act in response to complaints. New York does *not* have an agreement to receive or investigate complaint referrals from HUD. However, individuals may file a separate complaint with both HUD and the New York Division of Human Rights. Complaints must be in writing and state the facts upon which an alleged violation is based. If the case is referred to HUD and HUD is unable to obtain voluntary conciliation, a charge will be filed and the case referred to an administrative law judge, unless either party elects to have the case tried in a civil court.

   The judge may impose a civil penalty of up to $10,000 for a first offense, $25,000 if another violation occurs within five years, and $50,000 if three or more violations occur in seven years. An individual can be fined $25,000 or $50,000 without limitation of time periods if he engages in multiple discriminatory practices.

2. The aggrieved party, with or without filing a complaint to HUD, may bring a civil suit in a federal district court within one year of the alleged violation of the act unless a complaint has been filed with HUD, in which case the period is two years. If the aggrieved party wins the case, the court may issue an injunction against the violator and award actual and punitive damages with no limitation by the statute.

3. The U. S. attorney general may file a civil suit in any appropriate U. S. district court where the attorney general has reasonable cause to believe that any person or group is engaged in a pattern of violation of the act and, as such, raises an issue of general public importance. The court may issue an injunction or a restraining order against the person responsible and impose fines of up to $50,000 to "vindicate the public interest." A first-time fine of $50,000 may be imposed where a "pattern of practice" of discrimination is discovered.

HUD has four offices in New York State (Region II). The New York City office address is: 26 Federal Plaza, Suite 3541, New York, NY 10278-0068; (212) 264-1161; (212) 264-3068; *http://www.hud.gov*.

The Americans with Disabilities Act

The **Americans with Disabilities Act,** which took effect in 1992, specifically *protects the rights of individuals with disabilities.* **Disability** is defined in USC 42, Sec. 12101, as a *physical or mental impairment that substantially limits one or more of the major life activities of a person.*

Under this law, individuals with disabilities cannot be denied access to public transportation, any commercial facility, or public accommodation. This act applies to all owners and operators of public accommodations and commercial facilities, regardless of the size or number of employees. It also applies to all local and state governments.

Public accommodations are defined as private businesses that affect commerce and trade, such as inns, hotels, restaurants, theaters, convention centers, bakeries, laundromats, banks, barbershops, attorneys' offices, museums, zoos, places of education, daycare centers, and health clubs. Commercial facilities are those intended for nonresidential use and affect commerce, such as factories.

To comply with this law, public accommodations and commercial facilities are to be designed, constructed, and altered to meet the accessibility standards of the new law if readily achievable. "Readily achievable" means easily accomplished and able to be carried out without much difficulty or expense. Considerations in determining if the commercial facility or public accommodation can be made accessible are:

1. nature and cost of the needed alteration
2. overall financial resources of the facility involved and number of persons employed
3. type of operation of the entity

Public accommodations must remove structural, architectural, and communication barriers in existing facilities if the removal is readily achievable. Examples of barriers to be removed or alterations to be made include placing ramps, lowering telephones, making curb cuts in sidewalks and entrances, widening doors, installing grab bars in toilet stalls, and adding raised letters on elevator controls. Commercial facilities are not required to remove the barriers in existing facilities. Beginning January 1993 in the construction of new public accommodations and commercial facilities, all areas must be readily accessible and usable by individuals with disabilities. The act also requires new multifamily housing developments with at least four units to have easy access for people with disabilities and the elderly.

The Americans with Disabilities Act is enforced by the U. S. attorney general. Punishment for violating this law includes injunctions against operation of a business, a fine of up to $50,000 for the first offense, and $100,000 for subsequent offenses. Individuals with AIDS, alcoholism, or mental illness are included in the category of people with a mental or physical disability that impairs any life functions.

NEW YORK ANTIDISCRIMINATION LAWS

In addition to the federal Fair Housing Law, Article 15 of the New York Executive Law, the Human Rights Law, the New York City Commission on Human Rights, and local legislation, afford New York residents protection against discrimination in the sale, lease, or rental of housing, land, and commercial space.

New York Human Rights Law

The **New York State Human Rights Law** is substantially broader in scope than the federal laws as it *prohibits discriminatory practices in many other areas besides housing.* The law created a *Division of Human Rights* to *"eliminate and prevent discrimination"* in employment, public accommodations, places of amusement such as movie theaters and parks, educational institutions, housing accommodations, commercial space, land, and credit transactions. In addition to the groups protected under federal law, New York has three more protected classes: age (persons 18 years or older), marital status, and sexual orientation. **Marital status** is defined as *individuals who are either married or divorced.* Also, New York law covers discrimination in the *sale, lease, and rental of commercial space* as well as residential and public housing. The Sexual Orientation Non-Discrimination Act (SONDA) (2002) added sexual orientation as protected class under the Human Rights Law. New York law has fewer exemptions than federal law and the exemptions themselves are more restrictive. The administrative offices of the Division of Human Rights are located at 55 West 125th Street, New York, NY 10027; (212) 870-8400; *http://www.nysdhr.com*. There are eleven regional offices located throughout the state.

In transactions involving housing, land, and commercial space, it is unlawful for an owner, lessee, or agent (including real estate salespersons and brokers) to "refuse to sell, rent, lease, or otherwise deny any person or group of persons because of race, creed, color, national origin, gender, age, disability, marital status, or familial status." Discrimination regarding the terms or conditions of the sale, lease, or rental is also unlawful. In addition, any statement, advertisement, publication, or application form may not directly or indirectly discriminate.

PUTTING IT TO WORK

As a real estate practitioner, you may be confronted with discriminatory behavior by a seller or buyer. These scenarios* offer examples that may occur in which the buyer or seller asks you a question or requests you to do something that is discriminatory. Although the following questions might present some moral dilemmas for you, they do unfortunately occur.

To role-play these exercises, work with a partner. One should assume the role of the salesperson and the other the role of buyer or seller. Compare your role-plays with the model in the Answer Key at the end of the chapter.

a. You have shown this house five times to a single mother, an African American male, a Hispanic family with four children, an elderly couple, and a white family of four. The African American male has made the offer. Your seller asks, "Which buyer is this contract from?"

b. An African American couple, one a computer programmer, the other a commodities trader, have made an offer on the house. Your seller asks, "What color are they?"

c. Mr. and Mrs. Sanchez are Hispanics. They are financially qualified and have made an offer on a house that is within $1,000 of the asking price. You have shown the house a number of times and think that an offer from the O'Briens, or possibly another white family, might be forthcoming. Your seller asks, "Can I wait for Mr. and Mrs. O'Brien to make an offer? The Sanchez family just doesn't seem to be the type I want to buy my home."

d. Mr. Jones, the prospective buyer, is African American. The house in which he is interested has been shown only three times in three months, and no one else seems interested. Your seller asks, "If I take my home off the market, how long do I have to wait before I can sell it again?"

e. You have a new listing in a community that is a white pocket in a mixed-race county. Your seller asks, "Are you aware that there is a bonus for selling my home to the 'right people'?"

f. Your seller is an elderly African American college professor who lives in an upper-class section of town. She is interested in seeing that the neighborhood stays integrated. She asks, "Why must I sell my house to people I don't like, white or African American? Why don't I have freedom of choice? How about my rights?"

g. Your sales territory covers the entire south side of a major metropolitan area. You are showing homes to a family of Asian descent. Your buyer asks, "What is the racial composition of the neighborhood?"

h. Your prospective buyers are an elderly couple. Your area covers urban, suburban, and rural areas, with pockets of high crime in the urban area, while the suburbs tend not to suffer from major crimes. There are some adult communities in your area with walls and security guards. Your buyers ask, "Why don't you just pick out some nice properties in a safe area for us?"

---

*Source: *Fair Housing in the 90's Facilitator's Guide,* November, 1990, prepared by Office of Equal Opportunity of the National Association of REALTORS®. Copyright © National Association of REALTORS®. Reprinted with permission.

Exemptions

Like the federal Fair Housing Law, the New York Human Rights Law contains exceptions in certain situations. It is important to remember, however, that the law has *no exemptions for discrimination based on race.* Exemptions exist in the following circumstances:

- in the rental of a duplex (two-family house), if the owner or member of the owner's family lives in one of the housing accommodations
- when the restriction of the rental of all rooms in a housing accommodation is to individuals of the same gender
- in the rental of a room or rooms in a single-family house, if the rental is by the occupant or by the owner
- with respect to age, in the sale, rental, or lease of housing accommodations, land, or commercial space exclusively to persons 55 years of age or older. Federal law also provides for similar exemptions
- public housing that addresses the special needs of a particular age group, such as people age 55 or older

Note that, unlike the federal law, the New York law has *no exemptions for the sale of single-family housing.* In New York, exemptions exist only for the rental of a two-family (duplex), owner-occupied dwelling, whereas the federal law permits exemptions for the rental of up to four-family owner-occupied residential units. Salespersons and brokers in New York may not participate in the exemptions listed above except those that allow restriction of the sale, rental, or lease of housing accommodations, land, or commercial space exclusively to persons 55 or older.

Credit for Housing, Land, or Commercial Space

The Human Rights Law provides sanctions against discriminatory practices with respect to obtaining credit for the *"purchase, acquisition, construction, rehabilitation, repair or maintenance"* of housing accommodations, land or commercial space. Applicants may not be discriminated against because of race, creed, color, national origin, age, gender, marital status, sexual orientation, or disability.

Stockholders, officers, or employees of the applicant are also covered under the law, as well as prospective tenants or occupants of the housing, land, or commercial space. Discrimination in the "granting, withholding, extending of or renewing credit or fixing of credit rates is prohibited." Furthermore, it is also unlawful to use an application form for credit that records or inquires either directly or indirectly about information that is discriminatory. For example, credit applications that contain boxes where individuals are asked to check whether they are married or single, their age, or religion, are examples of unlawful discrimination.

Enforcement and Penalties

A complaint alleging discriminatory behavior must be filed with the New York State Division of Human Rights within one year. Individuals may also elect to bring an action in New York Supreme Court within three years of the alleged discriminatory act. The New York attorney general or the Division of Human Rights may also file a complaint. The Division of Human Rights will investigate the complaint and, if it is not dismissed, a hearing is held within 270 days after the complaint was filed. Disputes may first be submitted to voluntary arbitration if all the parties to the complaint agree. However, the parties involved must pay for the cost of the arbitration.

If an individual is found guilty of discrimination, an order requiring the guilty party to *cease and desist* from engaging in the discriminatory practice may be issued. In addition, an order may be issued requiring the guilty party to initiate *affirmative action* to right the discriminatory act, such as granting credit, if that was the subject of the complaint. Compensatory damages may be awarded; that is, repayment to the person who was harmed by the discriminatory act. In housing discrimination only, punitive damages not exceeding $10,000 may be awarded to the complainant. New York may also require repayment to the state of profits obtained because of the discriminatory activity. If the Division of Human Rights finds that the respondent is still committing discriminatory acts after an agreement has been reached, it may petition the Supreme Court for a restraining order. An injunction forcing the respondent to stop the discriminatory behavior may be issued. The Division of Human Rights, within one year, will investigate whether the respondent is in compliance with the terms of any agreement or court order and will take appropriate action to ensure compliance if this is not the case.

New York Real Property Law and DOS Regulations

The Real Property Law prohibits evicting a tenant if the tenant becomes pregnant or has a child while occupying the premises. This law also prohibits landlords from refusing rental to families with children. The law also covers mobile home parks.

The Department of State (DOS), Division of Licensing Services, may investigate complaints of discriminatory behavior on the part of its licensees and may suspend or revoke a license charging incompetency and untrustworthiness in accordance with the provisions of Article 12–A of the Real Property Law. In the past, the Secretary of State could issue a **nonsolicitation order** *prohibiting licensees from soliciting listings for the sale or purchase of real property in certain specified areas of the state.* This order is issued to stop the practice of blockbusting. However, in a lawsuit brought forth by the New York Association of REALTORS® against DOS, the court found that nonsolicitation orders violated the constitutional rights of licensees.

The Secretary of State can, however, establish a **cease and desist zone** after *determining that some homeowners within a certain geographic area have been subject to intense and repeated solicitation by real estate agents.* Upon establishment of the cease and desist zone, homeowners may file a request with DOS to be placed on a **cease and desist list,** indicating that they *do not desire to sell, lease, or list their residential property and do not wish to be solicited by real estate agents.* If real estate agents solicit these homeowners, DOS can take disciplinary action.

New York City Commission on Human Rights

New York City residents living in the five boroughs are governed by the *New York City Commission on Human Rights.* Like the state law, New York City law also covers discrimination in the sale, rental, or lease of housing, land, and commercial space. The commission has, however, defined three additional protected groups: *alienage or citizenship status, lawful occupations, and sexual orientation.* Alienage or citizenship status is defined as the citizenship of any person or the immigration status of any person who is not a citizen or national of the United States. Sexual orientation is defined as heterosexuality, homosexuality, or bisexuality. Two-family owner-occupied housing is exempt from the law in New York City only if the housing has *not* been made available through advertising, real estate listings, or some other kind of public notice. The rental of rooms in an owner-occupied housing accommodation other than publicly assisted housing is also exempt. Individuals alleging discriminatory behavior must file their complaint with the commission within one year. Under the law, complainants must choose to file their complaints with either the New York City Human Rights Commission *or* the Division of Human Rights.

The New York City Commission on Human Rights is located at 40 Rector Street, New York, NY 10006; (212) 306-7500. There are also two neighborhood field offices each in the Bronx, Brooklyn, and Queens.

LEGAL RESPONSIBILITIES

Table 13.1 summarizes the protected classes under federal, New York State, and New York City laws. Note that other municipalities besides New York City also have more restrictive laws and regulations than the state law.

Megan's Law

Megan's Law (1996), an amendment to the 1994 federal Violent Crime Control and Law Enforcement Act, requires a public registry of known sex offenders. In New York, law enforcement officials as well as real estate agents have a duty to disclose the presence of sex offenders in a neighborhood. However, the extent of this disclosure responsibility for real estate agents has been tested by the courts.

In *Glazer v. LoPreste*, (278 A.D. 2nd 198), the court dismissed a lawsuit by the buyers against the sellers and sales agents where the buyers were not informed that a convicted sex offender lived across the street. The court ruled that, under the doctrine of "caveat emptor," (buyer beware), neither the sellers nor the sales agents had a duty to disclose this information to the buyers since there was no active concealment and the information was available to the buyers in newspapers. New York courts uphold the doctrine of caveat emptor. This means that unless there is a confidential or fiduciary relationship between the parties, there is no duty for the seller or seller's agent to furnish information about the property. However, in this case, there was no specific inquiry made by the purchasers regarding the existence of a sex offender. If they had

TABLE 13.1

A summary of protected classes under the civil rights and fair housing laws.

	LAWS					
PROTECTED CLASSES	Civil Rights Act of 1866	Federal Fair Housing Act of 1968	Housing and Community Development Act of 1974	Fair Housing Amendments Act of 1988	New York State Human Rights Law	New York City Commission on Human Rights
Race	✓	✓			✓	✓
Color		✓			✓	✓
Religion		✓			✓	✓
National Origin		✓			✓	✓
Gender			✓		✓	✓
Disability				✓	✓	✓
Familial Status				✓	✓	✓
Age					✓	✓
Marital Status					✓	✓
Alienage or Citizenship						✓
Lawful Occupation						✓
Sexual Orientation					✓	✓

asked, the agent would have to respond or refer the purchaser to local law enforcement. In addition, a buyer's broker, who has a fiduciary relationship with the buyer, would have a duty to disclose the sex offender's presence.

Testers

One means of enforcing the law is through an organized program of testing. **Testers**, either volunteers, employees of federal programs, or people from civil rights groups, *visit real estate offices posing as prospective homebuyers to see if race influences the information or services offered by the broker or salesperson.* There are often four testers, a white couple and an African American couple, matched as to buyer qualifications such as income and down payment. After each couple visits a particular real estate office, they compare the treatment received to see if it was equal with respect to the price, location, and number of listings offered, the quality of service, and the attitudes of the broker or salesperson.

Testers look for unlawful racial steering practices. Investigations by testers have been recognized by the U. S. Supreme Court and the DOS, as a legitimate method of gathering evidence of alleged housing violations.

Emotional Results of Housing Discrimination

The stringent legal penalties and fines imposed because of violation of fair housing laws is a major deterrent to discriminatory behavior. However, laws alone are not enough. All of us are aware of the emotional divisiveness, anger, and societal upheaval that occurs as a result of a segregated and divided community.

An individual who is the target of discriminatory behavior is not the only victim. Discrimination pulls us all down. The Reverend Martin Luther King, Jr., said, "I have a dream that one day this nation will rise up and live the true meaning of its creed." As we celebrate each April the passage of the Fair Housing Act of 1968, we must hope that real estate professionals will renew their ongoing commitment to the spirit and intent of the law.

PUTTING IT TO WORK

Many of us may have been victims of housing or other types of discrimination or have witnessed the damage that discriminatory behavior can do. If you feel comfortable, this is a good opportunity to discuss your experiences.

CASE STUDY

The following case study details how testers, who were actually employees of DOS, "tested" a real estate firm in Long Island. As you read the case study, analyze whether you think discrimination has occurred and, if so, why. See *To the Student,* "Case Studies," which explains the terms and format of the DOS administrative hearings.

Department of State, Division of Licensing Services, Complainant, against Respondents Town House Realty, Real Estate Broker; Harold Klarnet, Representative Real Estate Broker; and Elliot Klarnet, Real Estate Broker.

Allegations. The Complainant alleges that the Respondents engaged in acts that constituted discrimination based on race and racial steering.

Findings of fact. As part of a series of tests by the Division of Licensing Services to uncover racially discriminatory practices by real estate brokers, two teams of testers (one African American, one white) visited the office of Town House Realty. Each team posed as a married couple seeking to purchase a home that had been advertised in the newspaper in the price range of $170,000 in Valley Stream, Long Island, then a predominantly white community. When the team of African American testers arrived, they were told that this particular house was sold. The testers then asked to see other properties in Valley Stream. Respondent Elliot Klarnet showed the African American testers one house in Valley Stream and, at the same time, advised the testers that he believed a person should get a house based on eligibility, but, in fact, that Valley Stream was "strange" and they " . . . might have doors closed in their faces." Respondent offered to show them properties located in the areas of Elmont and Malverne, stating that the prices and the school districts were better in those racially integrated areas. On the same day, the white testers arrived and were told by a salesperson that the advertised house was sold. Respondent then showed the white testers three houses for sale in the Valley Stream area (including the one property shown to the African American testers). Respondent informed the white couple that the area schools were good and suggested they place a binder on one of the properties in which they expressed an interest.

Opinion. First, it is established legal precedent that real estate licensees can be held accountable for unlawful discrimination against testers. In order to establish a case of discrimination based on steering, DOS must prove (a) that the prospective purchaser was a member of a racial minority, (b) purchaser had applied for and was financially qualified to purchase the property involved, and (c) purchaser was rejected because of being a member of a racial minority. Respondent claimed that he acted in good faith and it was his duty to inform an African American potential home buyer of what racially motivated events have occurred in the community. DOS found, based on legal precedent, that Respondent exceeded the guidelines of permissible behavior, as he voluntarily offered his own evaluation of the level of racial bias in the community. Regardless of the intent of Respondent, the effect of his actions were to both discourage the prospective home buyers from purchasing a house in the predominantly white community of Valley Stream and to encourage the home buyers to purchase a home in the racially integrated areas of Elmont and Malverne.

Conclusions of law. The evidence established that Respondent engaged in unlawful discrimination based on race and racial steering.

Determination. The court ruled that Respondent had demonstrated incompetence and the penalty was that his license would either be suspended for two months or, in lieu of suspension, Respondent would pay a fine of $1,000 to the Department of State.

IMPORTANT POINTS

1. The Civil Rights Act of 1968, also known as the Fair Housing Act, prohibits discrimination in housing because of race, color, religion, gender, national origin, age, handicap, or familial status.
2. Discrimination is prohibited in (a) sale or rental of housing, (b) advertising the sale or rental of housing, (c) financing of housing, and (d) provision of real estate brokerage services. The act also forbids blockbusting.
3. Four exemptions to the federal Fair Housing Act are provided to owners in selling or renting housing: (a) owners who do not own more than three houses, (b) owners of apartment buildings that have no more than four apartments and in which the owner occupies one of the apartments, (c) religious organizations, as to properties used for the benefit of members only, and (d) private clubs, as to lodging used for the benefit of members only. The owners' exemptions are not available if the owner used discriminatory advertising or the services of a real estate broker.
4. The Civil Rights Act of 1964 prohibited discrimination in any housing program receiving federal money but did not cover privately financed housing.

5. The Civil Rights Act of 1866 prohibits discrimination only on the basis of race. The prohibition is not limited to housing but includes all real estate transactions. The act may be enforced only by civil suit in federal court. This law has no exemptions.
6. Supreme Court decisions such as *Plessy v. Ferguson* (1896), separate but equal; *Buchanan v. Warley* (1917), disallowing block-by-block segregation; and *Brown v. Board of Education* (1954), separate but unequal; shaped much of U. S. policy.
7. Enforcement of Title VIII of the 1968 Civil Rights Act was amended significantly in 1988. Enforcement procedures now include: (a) administrative procedure through the Office of Equal Opportunity of HUD, which first attempts voluntary conciliation and then can refer the case to an administrative law judge, who can impose financial penalties of $10,000 to $50,000; (b) civil suit in federal court; and (c) action by the U. S. attorney general, who may file a suit in federal court and impose penalties of up to $50,000 on the first offense in a "pattern of discrimination."
8. The Americans with Disabilities Act provides that individuals with disabilities cannot be denied access to public transportation, any commercial facility, or public accommodation. Barriers in existing buildings must be removed if readily achievable. New buildings must be readily accessible and usable by individuals with disabilities.
9. New York is governed by Article 15 of the Executive Law, called the Human Rights Law. This law adds three protected classes not included in federal law—marital status, age, and sexual orientation—and covers the lease and sale of commercial space and land as well as residential housing. New York law offers no exemptions for the sale or rental of single-family housing.
10. The antidiscrimination enforcement agency in New York is the Division of Human Rights. Complaints must be filed with the division within one year of an alleged discriminatory act.
11. The New York City Commission on Human Rights is the enforcement agency for antidiscrimination policy in the five boroughs that compose New York City. New York City law includes two more protected classes in addition to those covered by New York State law: citizenship or alienage, and lawful occupation.

CHAPTER REVIEW

KEY TERM REVIEW

Fill in the term that best completes each sentence and then check the Answer Key at the end of the chapter.

1. The first federal civil rights statute, known as the ______________________, specifically prohibits discrimination based on race.
2. A real estate broker sells a home to a person of a particular national origin with the sole intent of forcing neighborhood residents to panic and sell. This practice is called ______________________.
3. A building with three or more residential units is defined in New York as a(n) ______________________.
4. Inducing homeseekers to a particular area based on race, color, or national origin is called ______________________.
5. A lending institution's refusal to grant loans for repairs or improvements to the property in a particular area based on the ethnic composition of the neighborhood is called ______________________.
6. To comply with the federal Fair Housing Act of 1968, all real estate brokers must prominently display the ______________________ in their place of business.

7. Two of the important 1988 amendments to the federal Fair Housing Act were to outlaw discrimination based on ________________ and ________________.

8. In New York, the ______________________ is the agency that regulates and enforces antidiscrimination law.

9. Volunteers who pose as prospective homeseekers to investigate discriminatory practices in real estate brokerage firms are called ______________________.

10. The New York Department of State, Division of Licensing Services, may issue a(n) ______________________ in a certain geographical area to prevent the practice of blockbusting by licensees.

MULTIPLE CHOICE

Circle the letter that best answers the question and then check the Answer Key at the end of the chapter.

1. A major difference between the New York Human Rights Law and the Federal Fair Housing Act of 1968 is:
   A. the New York law allows exemptions to real estate brokers and the federal law does not
   B. the New York law has fewer protected classes than the federal law
   C. the New York law covers both residential and commercial sales and rentals
   D. the New York law allows discriminatory advertising and the federal law does not

2. Which of the following is NOT a basis of discrimination prohibited by the 1968 act?
   A. race
   B. national origin
   C. occupation
   D. religion

3. The Whitleys, who live in Albany, New York, refuse to accept an offer on their single-family home from Nancy Delaney, a financially qualified buyer who is divorced. The Whitleys are:
   A. exempt from selling to Ms. Delaney under the New York Human Rights Law
   B. not exempt under the New York Human Rights Law
   C. protected by the Civil Rights Act of 1866
   D. allowed under the law to sell their home to whomever they please

4. Our Town Multiple Listing Service refuses to accept a listing because the home's owner is Russian. Which of the following is correct?
   A. a multiple listing service does not come under the 1968 act because it is a private nonprofit organization
   B. the 1968 act does not prohibit discrimination against Russians
   C. the listing broker's membership in the MLS may be terminated for taking the listing
   D. the MLS is in violation of the 1968 act for denying access to the service because of the owner's national origin

5. A property manager refuses to rent an office because the rental applicant is an African American. The applicant has legal recourse under the:
   A. Federal Fair Housing Act of 1968 only
   B. Civil Rights Act of 1866
   C. Fair Housing Amendment of 1988
   D. Civil Rights Act of 1974

6. In an advertisement offering the other unit in her duplex for rent in West Seneca, NY, the owner states that she will give preference to renters who are white females, pay cash, and are members of the Catholic religion. She subsequently refuses a rental because the offeror is a male Presbyterian. Which of the following is correct?
   A. the renter is taking advantage of an exemption in the New York Human Rights Law
   B. because the advertisement is discriminatory, the owner is not exempt under the law
   C. because the seller's main purpose was to receive cash, the refusal is not discriminatory
   D. the owner must allow him to rent the duplex because she cannot discriminate on the basis of gender

7. A real estate salesperson shows white prospects homes only in all-white areas. This discriminatory practice is called:
   A. redlining
   B. blockbusting
   C. steering
   D. directing

8. Which of the following is exempt from the provisions of the Federal Fair Housing Act of 1968?
   A. an owner of four houses
   B. an owner occupying one of four apartments in his building
   C. a religious organization renting one of 16 apartments it owns and operates for commercial purposes
   D. an owner who has listed a residential lot with a real estate broker

9. Which of the following is NOT an enforcement procedure for the Federal Fair Housing Act of 1968?
   A. a civil suit for damages in federal court
   B. administrative procedures through HUD
   C. action by the U. S. attorney general
   D. arbitration with the National Labor Relations Board

10. A homeowner, not living in New York, avails herself of the exemption provided by the 1968 act and refuses to accept an offer because the prospect is a white person. The prospect may do which of the following?
    A. bring suit in federal district court under the Civil Rights Act of 1866
    B. nothing, because the offeror is white
    C. bring suit in federal district court under the Federal Fair Housing Amendment of 1988
    D. ask for arbitration with HUD

11. The following ad appears in a local New York newspaper: "Rooms for rent in my home; limited to nonsmoking female; 2 bedrooms; 1 bath." Which of the following is correct? The ad:
    A. does not violate the New York Human Rights Law
    B. violates the Civil Rights Act of 1866
    C. is only allowable for public housing
    D. violates the Fair Housing Amendments of 1988

12. A person confined to a wheelchair requests that an apartment be modified to meet her physical needs. Which of the following is correct?
    A. the owner must make appropriate modifications at the owner's expense
    B. at the end of the tenancy, the renter must pay for returning the premises to their original condition
    C. the owner may refuse to rent to the disabled tenant because of the needed modifications
    D. the owner may charge increased rent because of the needed modifications

13. When Donna Sheehan signed her rental agreement for Valley View Apartments, a 50-unit complex, the rental agent told her that because she had two children, she would have to pay an extra months' security deposit instead of one. Which of the following is correct?
    A. the rental agent's request was legal according to the Federal Fair Housing Act
    B. the rental agent's request was in violation of New York law only
    C. the rental agent's request was in violation of federal and New York State human rights laws
    D. only New York City human rights laws were violated

14. The owner of a movie theater in New York refuses to lower his one pay phone in the lobby to accommodate persons in wheelchairs. Which of the following is correct?
    A. he is in violation of the Americans with Disabilities Act
    B. he must lower his pay phone within four years of the date of the Americans with Disabilities Act
    C. movie theaters are exempt from the Americans with Disabilities Act, so he is not in violation
    D. pay phones do not have to be accessible to people in wheelchairs under the Americans with Disabilities Act

15. Omar Prince, an African American, wants to open a vegetarian restaurant in Syracuse, New York. A leasing agent tells him that minority applicants must fill out a special addendum to the lease guaranteeing 12 percent of their gross to the leasing company instead of the 6 percent required of other applicants. The leasing agent is in violation of:
    A. New York law only
    B. the Fair Housing Act only
    C. the Civil Rights Act of 1866 only
    D. the New York Human Rights Law and the Civil Rights Act of 1866

16. A complaint alleging discriminatory behavior must be filed with the New York Division of Human Rights within:
    A. one year
    B. three years
    C. five years
    D. an unlimited period of time

17. Carlos Ortega, a Hispanic, has paid the mortgage on his townhouse in the Bronx and wishes to take out a loan to repair his roof. Although he has a steady income and perfect credit record, he has applied to four local banks for a $2,000 loan and has been turned down. He has been told that he is not credit-qualified, but is offered no further explanation. If Carlos sues these banks, what might be the grounds?
    A. that discrimination based on race has occurred
    B. that discrimination on a credit application has occurred
    C. that the banks are guilty of redlining
    D. all of the above

18. Sunny Life Properties proposes to build a planned unit development (PUD) limited to people 55 years old and older. The PUD, located in Buffalo, New York, will include housing, retail stores, and movie theaters. Which of the following does NOT apply to Sunny Life Properties?
    A. it is in compliance with New York Human Rights Law and the Fair Housing Act of 1968
    B. it will have to comply with the Americans with Disabilities Act
    C. real estate salespersons and brokers may participate in the sale of units in the development
    D. it is in violation of the Federal Fair Housing Act of 1968

19. The Dohertys receive a phone call from Penny, at Let Us Sell Realty, who states that an African American family is moving to their neighborhood. Penny also mentions that she has heard rumors that a family with 12 unruly children is moving in next door. She asks the Dohertys if they would like to list their home. Penny is guilty of:
    A. racial steering
    B. blockbusting
    C. redlining
    D. nothing—she is well within her rights to solicit listings

20. The Purple Medallion Club, a private club in Binghamton, New York, allows its members to lodge at the club for a small fee, but the club does not allow nonmembers to stay there. The Purple Medallion Club:
    A. is in violation of the Civil Rights Act of 1866
    B. must open its lodgings to the public to comply with federal and state laws
    C. is operating within the federal and New York laws that allow the limitation of a club's lodging to its membership
    D. is in violation of the New York Human Rights Law

ANSWER KEY

Putting It To Work*

a. This offer is from Mr. John Jones; you may remember, the computer salesman from Akron. (NEVER: The offer is from Mr. John Jones—remember, the African American man.)

b. (1) Before I try to answer your question, I need to know why you are asking it. As you know, our listing agreement provides that this property is offered without regard to color. If you intend to violate that agreement, I need to know upfront so that we can save ourselves and each other a great deal of litigation and liability. I must protect myself and my company, and, I hope, protect you.

(2) Under the terms of our listing agreement and under the law, I am really reluctant to have you ask that question or to try to answer it. The color of the prospective buyer is really irrelevant, isn't it, to your desire to sell your property at the price and on the terms you consider fair? If you want one of those terms to be a buyer of a certain race, then, frankly, we can't represent you and no other real estate broker in town can legally do so and keep his license.

(3) Mr. Seller, I don't want to answer that question because whatever answer I give you will make the marketing of your property a great deal more complicated and costly for both you and me. You and I are both obligated by law to offer your property without regard to color. If I answer your question, how are we ever going to be able to prove that we have fulfilled our legal obligation? No matter whether the buyer is African American or white or some shade in between, we will have a lot of trouble proving that race was *not* a factor in your final decision to sell. And, really, it shouldn't be a factor if we can get you the price and terms you are looking for.

c. (1) Ms. Seller, I don't understand why you don't believe Mr. and Mrs. Sanchez are the type you want to buy your home. They have made a good offer and are financially qualified. What type are you looking for? [If the response reveals that they are looking for a white buyer, the broker should advise the seller of her legal and contractual obligation *not* to discriminate.]

(2) Ms. Seller, I certainly appreciate your desire to have the opportunity to consider all offers, and I will try to get a firm offer from the O'Briens immediately. But the Sanchezes' offer is a good one and I would hate to see you lose out by delaying. Also, I really don't understand why you don't consider the Sanchezes to be the type to buy your home. [Where the basis for deferring decision is ambiguous but could be discriminatory, it is important that the broker attempt to remove the ambiguity by forcing the seller to articulate the concern. If the concern is founded in bias, the broker is able to take action to remove or overcome the bias or repudiate any support for it. On the other hand, the concern may be the product of considerations or impressions that the broker can either clear up or explain in nondiscriminatory terms.]

d. (1) Mr. Seller, you must understand that if you withdraw this property in order to avoid selling it to Mr. Jones (an African American), you risk serious legal liability and you may be unable to sell your property indefinitely. I strongly suggest you consult with your counsel before you take this action. As for me and my firm, I certainly cannot agree to the termination of our listing agreement for this reason.

(2) Mr. Seller, I am very uncomfortable with your decision to withdraw your property from the market. I realize this is your decision, but I am concerned that it will appear to be merely an excuse not to sell to Mr. Jones (an African American). Perhaps you should rethink your decision.

---

*Source: *Facilitator's Guide to Fair Housing in the 90s.* Copyright © National Association of REALTORS®. Reprinted with permission.

(3) Mr. Seller, I understand the reasons you feel you need to withdraw your property from the market. However, Mr. Jones may feel that they are merely an excuse for not accepting his offer because he is African American. I think it would be helpful to you and Mr. Jones, and it might avoid hard feelings, misunderstanding, and possible litigation, if I brought Mr. Jones by and let you explain your decision to him personally. [Face-to-face meetings between seller and offerees from culturally diverse backgrounds have several values: First, the broker is relieved of the problem of articulating and explaining the reasons for the withdrawal; second, the offeree is able to see that it is the seller and *not* the broker who has made the decision; third, the mere bringing of seller and offeree together for a "final discussion" supports the objective role of the broker; and, fourth, the prospect of confrontation may well discourage the seller, whose reasons for withdrawing the property are not substantive or honest.]

e. (1) I appreciate the offer of a bonus, but it would be both unethical and illegal for me to accept it when it is conditioned on the race, national origin, religion, handicap, familial status, gender, age, or marital status of the buyer I am able to bring you. Such an arrangement would subject both of us to very serious liability.

(2) Your offer of a bonus for bringing you offers from the "right" people is inconsistent with our agreement that I am to market your property without regard to the race, religion, national origin, handicap, familial status, gender, age, or marital status of the homeseeker. I must insist on holding to our agreement.

f. (1) Professor Seller, I don't think it is appropriate for me to try to answer these questions for you. If you believe you have the right to discriminate on the basis of race, religion, national origin, handicap, familial status, gender, age, or marital status, I can only urge you to have a talk with your attorney.

(2) From my standpoint, and that of my firm, we know we are prohibited by law and by our code of ethics from marketing property on a discriminatory basis. Moreover, it is difficult for us to understand how people can dislike a whole race, religion, nationality, gender, family status, age, marital status, or handicap. How can someone hate you without knowing you? What does being Jewish have to do with being a good neighbor? What does being Italian have to do with the price you want for your property?

(3) We can do a good job of selling your property to a qualified buyer at the price and on the terms you specify. But we cannot do that job unless we have your consent and support to market your property on a nondiscriminatory basis.

g. We have a host of demographic information back at the office. You can review it when we return. It would not be wise for me to guess. If you'd like to research this matter, I have the telephone numbers of the city's planning department and the Bureau of Census. They have additional information.

h. (1) We have many homes in our market area to choose from. Perhaps we should inspect a few to see which ones best fit your needs.

(2) Our office does not compile crime statistics. Let's go through our multiple listing of homes and select some that fit your requirements. While we're out inspecting homes, we can stop at the village police department if you would like to. Also, I can put you in touch with several security services who would undoubtedly be able to discuss your concerns in depth.

Key Term Review

1. Civil Rights Act of 1866
2. blockbusting
3. multiple dwelling
4. steering
5. redlining
6. HUD poster
7. familial status, disability or handicap
8. Division of Human Rights
9. testers
10. nonsolicitation order

Multiple Choice

1. C	6. B	11. A	16. A
2. C	7. C	12. B	17. D
3. B	8. B	13. C	18. D
4. D	9. D	14. A	19. B
5. B	10. A	15. D	20. C

Supplemental Reading

1. *Fair Housing Guide.* This guide is available online at the New York State Division of Human Right's website: *http://www.nysdhr.com/fairhousing.html.* The guide defines who is protected under the law, what is prohibited, the housing covered, and fair lending.
2. Fair Housing Sales: *Shared Neighborhoods Equal Opportunities Pocket Guide.* This guide reviews commonly asked questions by customers and clients and how agents should answer them. The reasoning behind the answer is explained. These guides are available in packages of five for $19.95 from the National Association of Realtors. To order, call 1 (800) 874-5000.
3. *Fair Housing Handbook.* The National Association of Realtors publishes this booklet. This booklet is a complete overview of fair housing laws and practice and includes a detailed interpretation of HUD advertising regulations. To order this publication and access other fair housing information, go to NAR's website: *http://realtor.org.*
4. *National Fair Housing Advocate.* This newsletter reports fair housing and fair lending litigation. To be added to the mailing list write to: National Fair Housing Advocate, 825 W. Jefferson Street, Room 100, Louisville, KY 40202. (502) 583-3247.

Chapter 14

KEY TERMS

asbestos
chlordane
chlorofluorocarbons (CFCs)
due diligence
electromagnetic field
environmental impact statement (EIS)
freon
friable
groundwater
lead
polychlorinated biphenyls (PCBs)
radon
State Environmental Quality Review Act (SEQRA)
underground storage tanks
urea-formaldehyde foam insulation (UFFI)
wetlands

LEARNING OBJECTIVES

Classroom hours: 3

1. Identify long-standing and contemporary environmental issues relating to real estate.
2. Recognize possible future environmental issues relating to real estate.
3. List each of the long-standing issues, such as water, septic systems, and termites, and identify actions that could be taken to determine or limit problems.
4. Describe the contemporary issues and the health effects of each.
5. List the steps required to properly disclose the existence of lead paint per federal mandate.

Environmental Issues

IN THIS CHAPTER Knowledge of certain problematic issues will enable you to help buyers make informed choices about their investment. This chapter gives an overview of environmental concerns and offers a starting point to learn more about issues related to your market area.

TODAY'S MAIN ENVIRONMENTAL ISSUES

The study of the environment as it relates to real estate can be divided into two categories:

1. *Long-standing issues.* Although the issues of clean water, wastewater treatment facilities, and pest infestation have been dealt with over the years, state and local laws are evolving to meet changing problems, increased awareness, and modern technology. Environmental concerns also include preserving our natural resources, such as wetlands.
2. *Contemporary issues.* These concerns include the use of chemical contaminants in houses and buildings, such as asbestos, lead, radon, indoor air quality, and PCBs. Because of these ever present contaminants, environmental assessments may be necessary to investigate and remediate.

   Other present concerns are the impact on health and the environment of man-made chemicals and other phenomena that are by-products of today's progressive society. Underground storage tanks and electromagnetic fields can impact the sale of real property, and chlorofluorocarbons found in refrigerator and air conditioning equipment threaten the ozone layer. Planning and legislation concerning these issues are ongoing. (See Figure 14.1)

Longstanding Issues:	**Contemporary Issues:**
Drinking water	Chemical contaminants: asbestos, lead, radon
Wastewater treatment	Indoor air quality
Pest infestation	PCBs
Wetland preservation	Underground storage tanks
	Electromagnetic fields
	Chlorofluorocarbons

FIGURE 14.1 Today's main environmental issues.

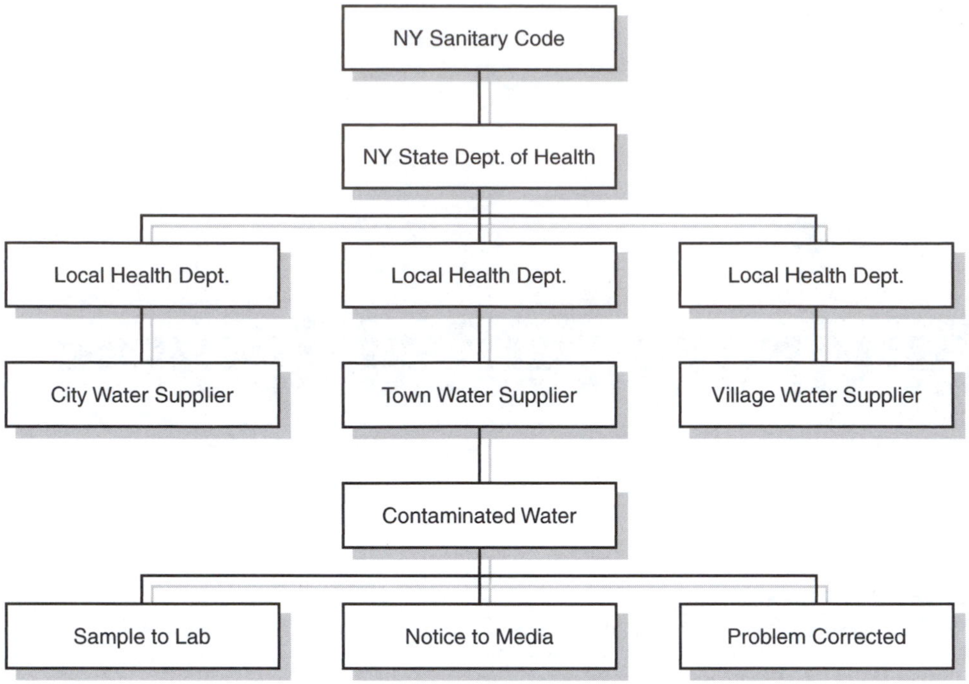

FIGURE 14.2
New York's public water supply system.

LONG-STANDING ISSUES

Drinking Water

Public Municipal Water Supply

The federal *Safe Drinking Water Act of 1974* is the guideline for New York's drinking water regulations. The New York State Department of Health (NYSDOH) is the regulatory agency that oversees the safety of drinking water. Local health departments are agents of NYSDOH and may have laws that are more restrictive.

A public water supply system can be a municipality such as a city, village, or town. The New York Sanitary Code lays out specific maximum contaminant levels and standards, establishes design criteria for systems, requires licensing of operators, and enforces the code to make sure the water supply meets federal requirements. When a contaminant level in the water is violated, the supplier must notify NYSDOH. Public notification through the media may be issued. The water supplier then submits a water sample to a laboratory analysis and, based on the findings, corrective measures are taken.

Private Water Supply

Individuals may own their own water supply. NYSDOH guidelines suggest that privately owned systems meet the same standards as publicly owned systems. A private water system is usually a well.

Private wells. Public health standards maintain that public water supplies are the most reliable and should be used in preference to individual wells. Many people, however, rely on wells until a public supply becomes available. Outside of New York City, more than 2,500,000 people in the state depend on individual well-water. A well utilizes **groundwater,** that is *water from underground.* A private well may serve one home in a rural area. NYSDOH furnishes guidelines for the construction of wells. Drilled wells are recommended over dug wells, or springs, as they are less likely to become contaminated and are a more dependable water source.

Community wells. Community wells refer to two or more wells that may serve several different residences. If a community well serves 25 or more people or it has more than five service connections (five homes, for example), it is regulated by NYSDOH and the New York State Department of Environmental Conservation (NYSDEC). In New York City, all of the water supply is public except for a few private wells in Staten Island.

Health Effects

The New York Sanitary Code recommends frequencies for water monitoring and tests for the following:

Bacteria. Bacteria consists of microbiological organisms. These organisms are the most frequent contaminant in the water supply and cause the greatest amount of illness. The public water supply is tested every day for bacterial contamination. NYSDOH establishes the contaminant level for both inorganic and organic substances in the water.

Mineral content. The goal of the water supply is water that is not devoid of minerals but does not have an overabundance of minerals.

Corrosiveness versus noncorrosiveness. Water hardness is not directly monitored in drinking water. The corrosiveness of the water, which includes its pH level, and the number of minerals in the water are measured. The pH of water measures its degree of alkalinity; a high pH means that the water is very alkaline; a low pH means that the water is more acidic. Water that is noncorrosive is soft water with a low pH and low number of total dissolved substances (TDS). Total dissolved substances are the number of different minerals in the water. Corrosive water is hard water with a high pH and a large number of TDS. *One of the biggest concerns about the safety of water is that highly corrosive water may contain dangerous amounts of lead.* A 1986 amendment to the Safe Drinking Water Act establishes guidelines for the safe amount of lead and copper in the water supply.

Testing and Remediation

The only way to know whether the water in a home is contaminated is to test it. If tests reveal that a state drinking water standard has been violated, the supplier must move to correct the situation and notify the state or local department of health. If the home is supplied with water from its own private well, laboratory testing of a water sample is the only way to determine if the water supply is contaminated. In New York, a special sanitary survey and water sampling service is available to residents of some counties. On request, a trained health specialist from the county health department makes a sanitary survey of the area surrounding a private water supply. When homes are supplied by private wells, analysis and treatment of the contaminated water may solve the problem. The NYSDOH offers assistance for decontamination of private water sources. A contract for purchase and sale in New York generally includes a contingency for the determination of well-water flow and quality when there is a private water supply.

Individual Wastewater Treatment Systems

The installation and approval of individual residential on-site wastewater treatment systems of less than 1,000 gallons per day in New York are regulated by NYSDOH.

NYSDEC standards apply to buildings or residences that process 1,000 or more gallons of wastewater per day. NYSDOH also reviews and approves plans for wastewater treatment systems in residential subdivisions (discussed below). Minimum standards for individual residential wastewater treatment systems include site requirements and design and construction guidelines for different types of septic systems. NYSDEC approves plans for community and public wastewater.

Septic Systems

In most rural and some suburban areas, individual wastewater treatment systems are used. This system is usually in the form of a septic system. Plans for wastewater treatment systems, other than specifically outlined in the New York regulations, must be designed and submitted to the health department for approval by a design professional such as a NYS licensed engineer or architect. *The design professional must submit as-built plans of the system.* These are drawings or renderings of the finished system. The construction must also be supervised by the design professional, who must certify that the system was built in accordance with the approved plan.

Prior to construction, an environmental assessment must determine that the development of the site with the system is consistent with the overall development of the area and will not have an adverse environmental impact. In New York, contracts for purchase and sale may include a septic system contingency agreement, which provides for a test of the system by a qualified professional or health department inspector.

Subdivision and Individual Lot Approval

According to the public health law, a subdivision falls under the jurisdiction of NYSDOH if it has five or more lots that are leased, sold, or offered for sale for residential building within any three-year period. A residential lot is defined as a parcel of land five acres or less. In Suffolk County, this law also applies to commercial or industrial building lots. Before a building permit is issued, the water supply and wastewater treatment systems must be approved by the local or state health department. In New York, realty subdivision maps cannot be filed in the county clerk's office without health department approval. The map must show the methods for obtaining and furnishing an adequate and satisfactory water supply and wastewater treatment facilities for each proposed lot. Proposed Suffolk County projects must also be filed with the County Department of Environmental Control. The owner of one parcel of land in an unapproved subdivision also must have plans for water supply and septic systems approved by the department of health. If land does not fall within the above definition of subdivision or if a lot is not in a subdivision, then approval is not required by the state health department. However, local zoning ordinances, building codes, and/or county health department regulations may apply. NYSDEC retains responsibility for the review, approval, and regulation of plans for public (municipal) and community wastewater treatment facilities.

Testing and Remediation

Health department personnel will go on the site before the subdivision is approved and witness percolation and deep-hole tests to make sure the ground is suitable for a wastewater treatment system. Deep-hole tests determine groundwater elevations and the suitability of the soil to treat wastewater. Percolation tests are used to determine the absorption of the soil. The state and county department of health staff as well as local code enforcement officers and design professionals may inspect the site during construction. Some areas of New York have inspection programs to monitor wastewater treatment sites after they are constructed.

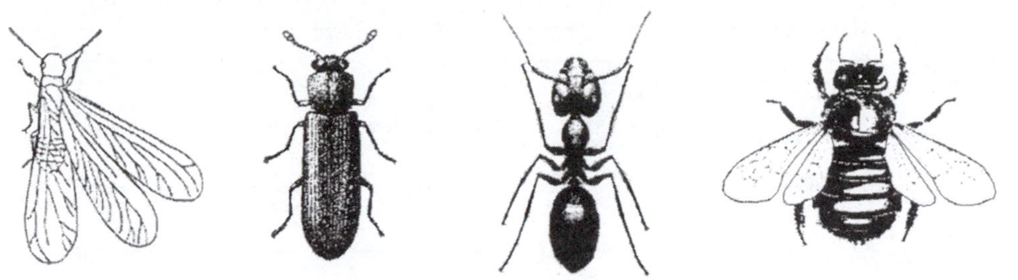

FIGURE 14.3
A termite, powderpost beetle, carpenter ant, and carpenter bee.

Source: USDA.

Chlordane — **You Should Know**

Chlordane is *a chemical insecticide and termiticide that was banned in the early 1980s because of its toxicity and persistence*. Its use as a termiticide in the home can negatively affect indoor air quality

Pest Infestation

Termites, carpenter ants, powderpost beetles, and carpenter bees (Figure 14.3) are insects that eat wood. Wood eating pests have been known to eat into the wood-frame construction of a house, the wood flooring, and other items. As they infest and multiply, they can cause considerable damage that can cost thousands of dollars to repair.

Testing and Remediation

An unlicensed individual may test for pest infestation. The affected area can be examined for both infestation and damage. *Only an individual licensed by NYSDEC may apply pesticides*. Contracts for purchase and sale in New York may be contingent upon pest inspection, and if infestation is found, the purchaser has the right to cancel the contract within a set period of time.

Wetland Regulations

Wetlands are also known as marshes, swamps, bogs, wet meadows, or flats. *Wetlands are protected areas because they provide flood and storm water control, surface and groundwater protection, erosion control, pollution treatment, a place for fish and wildlife habitats, open space, and natural beauty.* In New York, wetlands are protected under Article 24 of the Environmental Conservation Law, also known as the Freshwater Wetlands Act (1975).

The agency that oversees wetland protection is the *NYSDEC.* Wetlands protected under the act must be larger than 12.4 acres and may also include any smaller wetlands of unusual appearance. An adjacent area of 100 feet is also protected, to provide a buffer zone.

The act requires NYSDEC to map all protected wetlands. Certain activities are specifically exempt from regulation and do not require a permit. Other activities require either a permit or a letter of permission (see Figure 14.4). The act allows local governments to assume jurisdiction for regulating wetlands once NYSDEC has filed a map for their area. Under the act, activities in wetlands that require a permit are restoring, modifying, or expanding existing structures; draining, except for agriculture; installing docks, piers, or wharves; constructing bulkheads, dikes, and dams; installing utilities; and applying pesticides. Figure 14.5 diagrams alternative layouts for a house and septic system located near a wetland.

FIGURE 14.4 NYSDEC and Army Corps Joint Application for permit.

JOINT APPLICATION FOR PERMIT

95-19-3 (8/00) pfp

New York State
United States Army Corps of Engineers

Applicable to agencies and permit categories listed in Item 1. **Please** read all instructions on back. Attach additional information as needed. Please print legibly or type.

1. Check permits applied for:

NYS Dept. of Environmental Conservation

- Stream Disturbance (Bed and Banks)
- Navigable Waters (Excavation and Fill)
- Docks, Moorings or Platforms (Construct or Place)
- Dams and Impoundment Structures (Construct, Reconstruct or Repair)
- Freshwater Wetlands
- Tidal Wetlands
- Coastal Erosion Control
- Wild, Scenic and Recreational Rivers
- 401 Water Quality Certification
- Potable Water Supply
- Long Island Wells
- Aquatic Vegetation Control
- Aquatic Insect Control
- Fish Control

NYS Office of General Services
(State Owned Lands Under Water)

- Lease, License, Easement or other Real Property Interest
- Utility Easement (pipelines, conduits, cables, etc.)
- Docks, Moorings or Platforms (Construct or Place)

Adirondack Park Agency

- Freshwater Wetlands Permit
- Wild, Scenic and Recreational Rivers

Lake George Park Commission

- Docks (Construct or Place)
- Moorings (Establish)

US Army Corps of Engineers

- Section 404 (Waters of the United States)
- Section 10 (Rivers and Harbors Act)
- Nationwide Permit (s)
  Identify Number(s)

For Agency Use Only:
DEC APPLICATION NUMBER

US ARMY CORPS OF ENGINEERS

2. Name of Applicant (Use full name) | **Telephone Number** (daytime)

Mailing Address

Post Office | **State** | **Zip Code**

3. Taxpayer ID (If applicant is not an individual)

4. Applicant is a/an: (check as many as apply)
Owner Operator Lessee Municipality / Governmental Agency

5. If applicant is not the owner, identify owner here - otherwise, you may provide Agent/Contact Person information.
Owner or Agent/Contact Person Owner Agent /Contact Person | **Telephone Number** (daytime)

Mailing Address

Post Office | **State** | **Zip Code**

6. Project / Facility Location (mark location on map, see instruction 1a.)
County: Town/City/Village: Tax Map Section/ Block /Lot Number:

Location (including Street or Road) | **Telephone Number** (daytime)

Post Office | **State** | **Zip Code** | **7. Name of Stream or Waterbody** (on or near project site)

8. Name of USGS Quad Map: **Location Coordinates:**
NYTM-E NYTM-N 4

9. Project Description and Purpose: (Category of Activity e.g. new construction/installation, maintenance or replacement; Type of Structure or Activity e.g. bulkhead, dredging, filling, dam, dock, taking of water; Type of Materials and Quantities; Structure and Work Area Dimensions; Need or Purpose Served)

10. Proposed Use: Private Public Commercial | **11. Will Project Occupy State Land?** Yes No | **12. Proposed Start Date:** | **13. Estimated Completion Date:**

14. Has Work Begun on Project? (If yes, attach explanation of why work was started without permit.) Yes No | **15. List Previous Permit / Application Numbers and Dates:** (If Any)

16. Will this Project Require Additional Federal, State, or Local Permits? Yes No If Yes, Please List:

17. If applicant is not the owner, both must sign the application
I hereby affirm that information provided on this form and all attachments submitted herewith is true to the best of my knowledge and belief. False statements made herein are punishable as a Class A misdemeanor pursuant to Section 210.45 of the Penal Law. Further, the applicant accepts full responsibility for all damage, direct or indirect, of whatever nature, and by whomever suffered, arising out of the project described herein and agrees to indemnify and save harmless the State from suits, actions, damages and costs of every name and description resulting from said project. In addition, Federal Law, 18 U.S.C., Section 1001 provides for a fine of not more than $10,000 or imprisonment for not more than 5 years, or both where an applicant knowingly and willingly falsifies, conceals, or covers up a material fact; or knowingly makes or uses a false, ficticious or fraudulent statement.

Date __________ Signature of Applicant ______________________________ Title ______________

Date __________ Signature of Owner ______________________________ Title ______________

Source: New York State Department of Environmental Conservation.

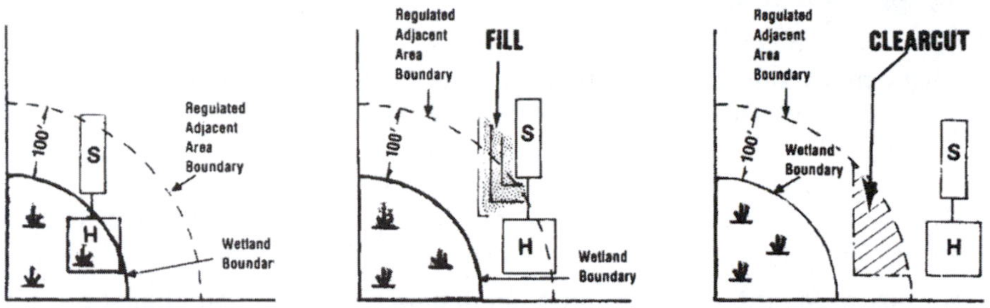

Incompatible (P(X))
- Disposal of sewage in adjacent area
- House construction in wetland

Usually Incompatible (P(N))
- Fill in adjacent area
- House construction in adjacent area

Usually Compatible (P(C))
- Clear-cutting timber in adjacent area
- House and septic outside of regulated area

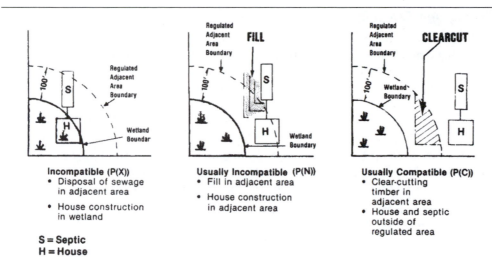

S = Septic
H = House

FIGURE 14.5 Alternative layouts for a house and septic system near a wetland.

Note: The "usually compatible" diagrams comply with New York environmental law and codified rules and regulations. Alternative layouts are possible. "Usually compatible" projects are most likely to gain approval.

Source: New York State Department of Environmental Conservation.

CONTEMPORARY ISSUES

Asbestos

Asbestos is *a fibrous mineral found in rocks and soil throughout the world.* Asbestos has been used in construction applications because it is strong, durable, fire retardant, and an efficient insulator. Alone or in combination with other materials, asbestos is found in a variety of products, such as flooring, walls, ceiling tiles, exterior housing shingles, and insulation or fire retardant for heating and electrical systems. According to the EPA, many homes constructed prior to 1973 probably do contain asbestos products. Since then, the use of asbestos has become more and more restricted until 1988 when it was no longer allowed in residential construction. Generally, if the material is in good condition and is located where it is not likely to be disturbed, the asbestos-containing material should be left in place. Over the years, the EPA and the Consumer Product Safety Commission (CPSC) have taken several steps to reduce consumers' exposure to asbestos.

Health Effects

Home health risks arise when age, accidental damage, or normal cleaning, construction, or remodeling activities cause the asbestos-containing materials to crumble, flake, or deteriorate. The term **friable** refers to this flaky or crumbly texture of asbestos *when hand pressure is applied.* As a result, *it is likely to emit fibers when disturbed.* Asbestos has been identified as a carcinogen (cancer-causing agent). Once ingested or inhaled, asbestos fibers lodge in the lungs or intestines, and can cause lung and other types of cancer. Experts are unable to provide assurance that any level of exposure to asbestos fibers is safe.

Asbestosis is a chronic disease of the lungs that is directly caused by the inhalation of asbestos fibers. Breathing becomes progressively more difficult, and the disease can lead to death. Mesothelioma is a cancer of the chest and abdominal membranes. This illness almost never occurs without exposure to asbestos. These diseases may not show up until 20 to 40 years after exposure.

Testing and Remediation

Qualified contractors, who can test for asbestos, are accredited through EPA or New York State-approved training courses. All buildings greater than four units must employ trained and certified individuals for asbestos repair or removal. Removal workers are protected under federal regulations that specify training, protective clothing, and special respirators. The federal Asbestos Hazard Emergency Response Act (AHERA) that became effective in 1988 requires that building owners of two-family or larger dwellings complete an asbestos survey before renovation or demolition.

Asbestos may be detected through air monitoring, bulk sampling of suspected materials, or wipe sampling suspected materials. In addition, the manufacturer may be able to tell, based on the model number and age of a product, if it contains asbestos.

The repair or removal of asbestos-containing products from a home is generally a complicated process. Once asbestos is detected, there are several methods of response. In some cases, a maintenance plan is developed to ensure that asbestos-containing materials are kept in good condition. If asbestos is found in pipe or boiler covering, the covering is repaired. Other remedies include encapsulation, enclosure, and removal. Encapsulation is a process where the material is covered with a sealant to prevent fiber release. Enclosure consists of placing a barrier around the material. There are special procedures for removal. Total removal of even small amounts of asbestos-containing material is usually the last alternative.

Lead

Lead is *a metallic element found worldwide in rocks and soils.* The toxic effects of lead have been known since ancient times. Lead can be present in drinking water, in interior or exterior paint, in dust within a home, and in soil around the home.

Lead-based paint. Lead can enter the air within a home when surfaces covered with lead-based paint are scraped, sanded, or heated with an open flame in paint-stripping procedures. Once released into the home atmosphere, lead particles circulate in the air and can be inhaled or ingested through the mouth and nose. The EPA estimates that lead-based paint was applied to approximately two-thirds of the houses built before 1940, one-third of the houses built between 1940 and 1960, and a smaller portion of houses built since 1960.

Lead-based paint disclosure. The Residential Lead-Based Paint Hazard Reduction Act of 1992 sets forth the procedures to be followed in disclosing the presence of lead-based paint for sales of properties built prior to 1978. In 1996, HUD and the EPA released rules to implement Section 1018 of the 1992 act. According to this law, a real estate licensee will generally not be held liable for failure to disclose to a prospective purchaser the presence of lead-based paint if the hazard was known by the landlord or seller but not disclosed to the licensee. Licensees who act on behalf of a purchaser or lessee and are paid exclusively by the purchaser or lessee, are not required to comply. However, a selling agent who is working with a buyer would be required to comply with the requirement for placing a clause in the contract giving the buyer 10 days to inspect the property (if the selling agent is preparing the contract).

Penalties for noncompliance include the payment of up to three times the amount of damage incurred by a purchaser or lessee, up to a $10,000 fine, and criminal penalties for repeat offenders. The Act applies to what is known as *target properties.* In addition to sole owners of single family residential property, the Act defines sellers of target housing to include partnerships, individuals or entities that transfer shares in cooperative apartments, and individuals or entities that transfer leasehold interests. In the transfer of individual cooperative apartments both the tenant–shareholder and the cooperative corporation would be required to comply. Certain types of residential housing are exempt, such as senior citizen housing.

You Should Know

Disclosure requirements under the Residential Lead-based Paint Hazard Reduction Act

- Sellers, lessors, or their agents must disclose the presence of known lead-based paint and/or lead-based paint hazards.
- Sellers, lessors, or their agents must distribute a lead hazard pamphlet and disclose any known information to the buyers or their agent concerning lead paint. EPA and HUD have a prepared pamphlet that may be distributed (see Figure 14.6). In many cases, these pamphlets are distributed through local boards of REALTORS®.
- Sellers and lessors must provide purchasers and lessees with copies of any available records or reports pertaining to the presence of lead-based paint and/or lead-based paint hazards.
- There is a mutually agreeable 10-day period for a lead paint assessment before a purchaser becomes obligated under the contract (see Figure 14.7, A Lead-Based Paint Inspection Contingency Form). During this time, the purchaser may conduct a risk assessment or inspection for the presence of lead-based paint or lead-based paint hazards. The purchaser, however, may agree to waive the assessment.

Sales and lease contracts must include specific disclosure and acknowledgment language. (See Figure 14.8, Disclosure Form for Lead-Based Paint.)

FIGURE 14.6 EPA/HUD lead-based paint pamphlet.

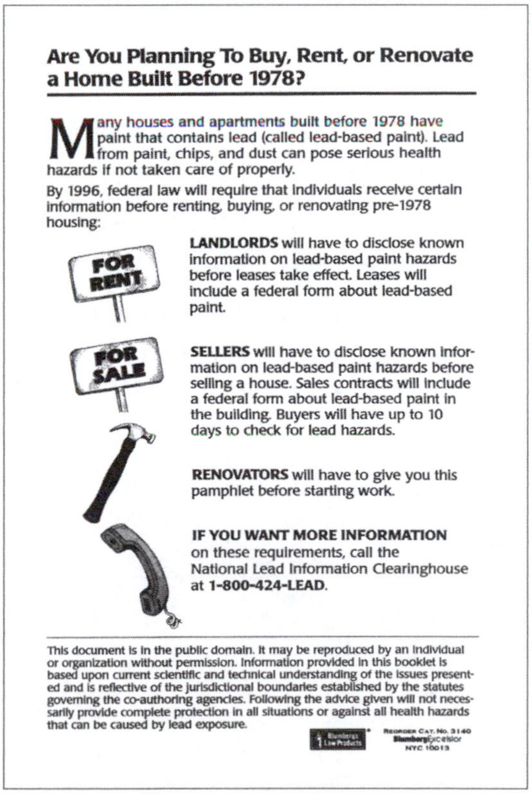

Are You Planning To Buy, Rent, or Renovate a Home Built Before 1978?

Many houses and apartments built before 1978 have paint that contains lead (called lead-based paint). Lead from paint, chips, and dust can pose serious health hazards if not taken care of properly.

By 1996, federal law will require that individuals receive certain information before renting, buying, or renovating pre-1978 housing:

FOR RENT

LANDLORDS will have to disclose known information on lead-based paint hazards before leases take effect. Leases will include a federal form about lead-based paint.

FOR SALE

SELLERS will have to disclose known information on lead-based paint hazards before selling a house. Sales contracts will include a federal form about lead-based paint in the building. Buyers will have up to 10 days to check for lead hazards.

RENOVATORS will have to give you this pamphlet before starting work.

IF YOU WANT MORE INFORMATION on these requirements, call the National Lead Information Clearinghouse at **1-800-424-LEAD**.

This document is in the public domain. It may be reproduced by an individual or organization without permission. Information provided in this booklet is based upon current scientific and technical understanding of the issues presented and is reflective of the jurisdictional boundaries established by the statutes governing the co-authoring agencies. Following the advice given will not necessarily provide complete protection in all situations or against all health hazards that can be caused by lead exposure.

Reorder Cat. No. 3140 BlumbergExcelsior NYC 10013

Source: U. S. Environmental Protection Agency. U. S. Consumer Products Safety Commission.

FIGURE 14.7 Lead-Based Paint Inspection Contingency form.

Addendum #________ **LEAD-BASED PAINT TESTING CONTINGENCY**

THIS IS A LEGALLY-BINDING CONTRACT. IF NOT UNDERSTOOD, WE RECOMMEND CONSULTING AN ATTORNEY BEFORE SIGNING.

ADDENDUM TO CONTRACT FOR PURCHASE AND SALE
OF REAL ESTATE BETWEEN

______________________________ (Purchaser)

and

______________________________ (Seller)

Regarding the property located at: ______________________________

This contract is contingent upon a risk assessment or inspection of the property for the presence of lead-based paint and/or lead-based paint hazards[1] at the Purchaser's expense until 9:00 P.M. on the tenth calendar day after ratification or until ______________________________.
This contingency will terminate at the above predetermined deadline unless the Purchaser (or Purchaser's agent) delivers to the Seller (or Seller's agent) a written contract addendum listing the specific existing deficiencies and corrections needed, together with a copy of the inspection and/or risk assessment report. The Seller may, at the Seller's option, within ________ days after Delivery of the addendum, elect in writing whether to correct the condition(s) prior to settlement. If the Seller will correct the condition, the Seller shall furnish the Purchaser with certification from a risk assessor or inspector demonstrating that the condition has been remedied before the date of the settlement. If the Seller does not elect to make the repairs, or if the Seller makes a counter-offer, the Purchaser shall have ________ days to respond to the counter-offer or remove this contingency and take the property in "as-is" condition or this contract shall become void. The Purchaser may remove this contingency at any time without cause.

[1]Intact lead-based paint that is in good condition is not necessarily a hazard. See EPA pamphlet *Protect Your Family From Lead in Your Home* for more information.

Purchaser	Date	Seller	Date
Purchaser	Date	Seller	Date

6/21/96
Capital Region Multiple Listing Service, Inc.

Source: Capital Region Multiple Listing Service, Inc. (CRMLS). Reprinted by permission.

FIGURE 14.8 Disclosure form for lead-based paint.

DISCLOSURE OF INFORMATION AND ACKNOWLEDGMENT
LEAD-BASED PAINT AND/OR LEAD-BASED PAINT HAZARDS

Lead Warning Statement

Every purchaser of any interest in residential real property on which a residential dwelling was built prior to 1978 is notified that such property may present exposure to lead from lead-based paint that may place young children at risk of developing lead poisoning. Lead poisoning in young children may produce permanent neurological damage, including learning disabilities, reduced intelligence quotient, behavioral problems, and impaired memory. Lead poisoning also poses a particular risk to pregnant women. The seller of any interest in residential real property is required to provide the buyer with any information on lead-based paint hazards from risk assessments or inspections in the seller's possession and notify the buyer of any known lead-based paint hazards. A risk assessment or inspection for possible lead-based paint hazards is recommended prior to purchase.

Seller's Disclosure *(initial)*

________ (a) Presence of lead-based paint and/or lead-based paint hazards *(check one below):*

☐ Known lead-based paint and/or lead-based paint hazards are present in the housing *(explain):*

____

____

☐ Seller has no knowledge of lead-based paint and/or lead-based paint hazards in the housing.

________ (b) Records and Reports available to the seller *(check one below):*

☐ Seller has provided the purchaser with all available records and reports pertaining to lead-based paint and/or lead-based hazards in the housing *(list documents below):*

____

____

☐ Seller has no reports or records pertaining to lead-based paint and/or lead-based paint hazards in the housing.

Purchaser's Acknowledgment *(initial)*

________ (c) Purchaser has received copies of all information listed above.

________ (d) Purchaser has received the pamphlet *Protect Your Family From Lead in Your Home.*

________ (e) Purchaser has *(check one below):*

☐ Received a 10-day opportunity (or mutually agreed-upon period) to conduct a risk assessment or inspection of the presence of lead-based paint or lead-based paint hazards; or

☐ Waived the opportunity to conduct a risk assessment or inspection for the presence of lead-based paint and/or lead-based paint hazards.

Agent's Acknowledgment *(initial)*

________ (f) Agent has informed the seller of the seller's obligations under 42 U.S.C. 4852 d and is aware of his/her responsibility to ensure compliance.

Certification of Accuracy

The following parties have reviewed the information above and certify, to the best of their knowledge, that the information they have provided is true and accurate.

Purchaser	Date	Seller	Date
Purchaser	Date	Seller	Date
Agent	Date	Agent	Date

6/21/96
Capital Region Multiple Listing Service, Inc

Source: Capital Region Multiple Listing Service, Inc. (CRMLS). Reprinted by permission.

Lead in drinking water. Many homes built prior to 1988 contain plumbing systems that use lead-based solder in pipe connections. In such systems, lead can enter drinking water as a by-product when plumbing fixtures, pipes, and solder are corroded by drinking water. In these instances, lead levels in water at the kitchen tap can be far higher than those found in water at treatment plants.

Lead in soil. If a house was built prior to 1950, there is a good chance that lead from exterior surface paint has accumulated in surrounding soils. The grounds surrounding the home should be well landscaped to minimize the likelihood of children being exposed to contaminated dust.

Health effects. When ingested, lead accumulates in the blood, bones, and soft tissue of the body. High concentrations of lead in the body can cause death or permanent damage to the central nervous system, the brain, the kidneys, and red blood cells. Even low levels of lead may increase high blood pressure in adults.

Infants, children, pregnant women, and fetuses are more vulnerable to lead exposure because lead is more easily absorbed into growing bodies as their tissues are more sensitive. Because of a child's smaller body weight, an equal concentration of lead is more damaging to a child than to an adult.

Testing and Remediation

Lead-based paint. The only accurate way to determine if paint in a home contains lead is to remove a sample of the paint and have it tested in a qualified laboratory. It is best to leave lead-based paint undisturbed if it is in good condition and there is little possibility that children will ingest it. Other procedures include covering the paint with wallpaper or other material, or completely replacing the painted surface.

Lead in water. *The Safe Drinking Water Act* established a maximum contaminant level for lead in drinking water, and 1986 amendments banned further use of materials containing lead in public water and in residences connected to public water. Lead-based solder in plumbing applications within homes and buildings is prohibited. While many newer homes rely on nonmetallic plumbing lines, the majority of faucets and plumbing fixtures used today can contribute some lead to home water supplies. However, the presence of lead can be eliminated effectively by running the faucet for 15 seconds before drawing drinking water. The only way to determine lead levels in water is to test a water sample. If lead is suspected, local, county, state health, or environmental departments will refer individuals to qualified testing laboratories. If a household renovation includes replacement of aging water pipes with copper or metal piping, the renovating contractor can ensure that lead solder was not used in pipe joints.

Radon

Radon is *a colorless, odorless, tasteless, radioactive gas found worldwide as a by-product of the natural decay of uranium present in the earth.* Radon can be found in the soil surrounding a home or in well water. Radon from surrounding soil enters a home through small spaces such as cracks in concrete, floor drains, sump pump openings, wall and floor joints in basements, and the pores in hollow block walls. See Figure 14.9, Some ways that radon enters a house.

Radon can seep into groundwater and remain entrapped there. Therefore, if a home is supplied with water from a groundwater source, there is greater potential for a radon problem. The likelihood of radon in the water supply is greatly reduced for homes using a municipal water supply. When radon gas and its decay products enter the home, it circulates in the enclosed air. Outdoors, radon is not a problem because the gas diffuses into the atmosphere.

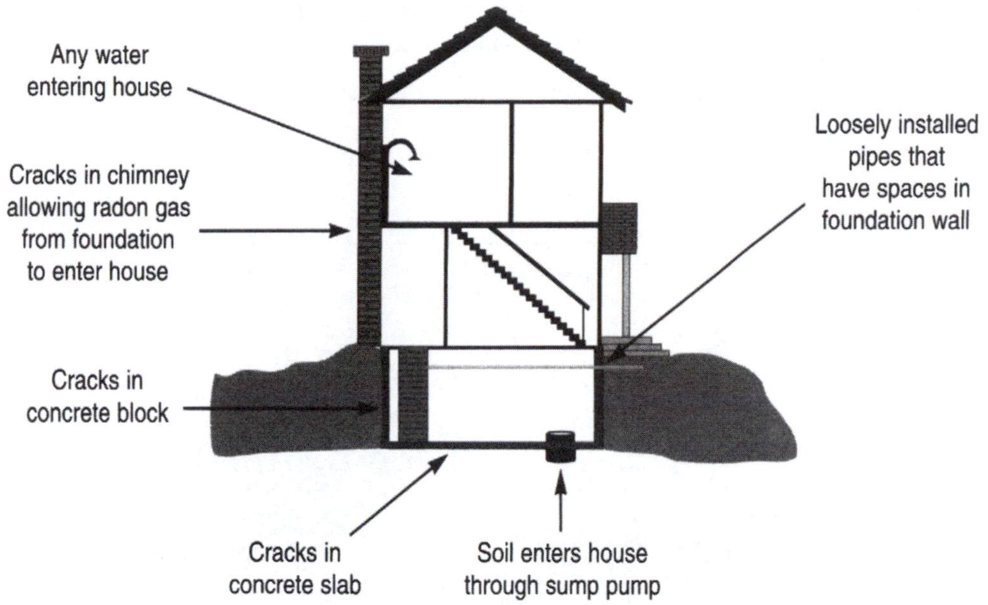

FIGURE 14.9
Some ways in which radon enters a house. Radon is present primarily in soil and water. The soil enters the house through various cracks and openings.

Health Effects

Radon gas breaks down into radioactive particles (called decay products) that remain in the air inside the home. As people breathe these particles, they can become trapped in the lungs and cause damage that may lead to lung cancer.

The concentration of radon in air is measured in units of picocuries per liter of air (pCi/L). Estimates suggest that most homes will contain from one to two picocuries of radon per liter of air. If preliminary tests indicate radon levels greater than four picocuries per liter of air in livable areas of the home, the EPA recommends that a follow-up test be conducted. No level of radon is considered safe; there are risks at very low levels.

Testing and Remediation

The only way to detect radon is to test for it. Radon levels vary depending on the house construction and the surrounding soil. Radon-detection kits are available (in the form of canisters) and must be certified by the Environmental Laboratory Accreditation Program. Short- and long-term testing kits can be purchased from the local or state department of health, accredited laboratories, and hardware stores. If testing is done by an individual, the person must send the canister to an accredited laboratory to be analyzed. Testing can also be done by a certified laboratory. Short-term testing (ranging from a few days to several months) is one way to determine if a potential problem exists. Long-term testing (lasting for up to one year) is a more accurate way to determine if radon is present. Tests that measure radon in water require a sample of tap water to undergo laboratory analysis.

There are many effective and relatively inexpensive methods of reducing radon levels in a home. If radon is present in water supplies, it can be removed altogether or reduced by the installation of filter systems. The cost of installing radon-reduction equipment ranges from several hundred dollars to several thousand dollars. If the system chosen involves fans, pumps, or other appliances, operating costs for these devices may increase the monthly utility bills (see Figure 14.10). When a homeowner is seeking a contractor to assist with a radon problem, the state or local department of health can be consulted for recommendations of certified radon-reduction contractors and laboratories.

New York abides by EPA guidelines regarding safe radon levels and has no statewide code.

FIGURE 14.10 Radon reduction in a single-family home. A ventilation stack draws air and any radon gas out from under the basement slab.

Source: *A Citizen's Guide to Radon.* U. S. Environmental Protection Agency, U. S. Department of Health and Human Services, and U. S. Public Health Service.

Indoor Air Quality

Various substances can contaminate the air in the home. Several of the major air pollutants are discussed below.

Urea-Formaldehyde Foam Insulation (UFFI)

Formaldehyde is a colorless, gaseous chemical compound that is generally present at low, variable concentrations in both indoor and outdoor air. Formaldehyde is an ingredient in foam that was used for home insulating, especially in new construction, until the early 1980s. **Urea-formaldehyde foam insulation (UFFI)** *contains large amounts of formaldehyde.* While contractors have voluntarily stopped using UFFI, the material is still present in many homes that were originally insulated with UFFI. Since 1985, the federal government, through HUD, has enforced regulations that sharply curtail the use of materials containing formaldehyde, requiring instead lower-emitting products. However, use of formaldehyde compounds is still widespread in the manufacture of furniture, cabinets, and other building materials.

Health effects. Formaldehyde has been shown to cause cancer in animals, but there is no definitive evidence linking the chemical to cancer in humans. Higher-than-normal levels of formaldehyde in the home can trigger asthma attacks in susceptible individuals. Other health hazards attributed to formaldehyde include skin rashes; watery eyes; burning sensations in the eyes, throat, and nasal passages; and breathing difficulties. Most persons will first react when the levels are in the range of 0.1 to 1.1 parts per million. Some individuals acquire a reduced tolerance to formaldehyde following their initial exposure. In these instances, subsequent exposures to even small amounts will cause reactions.

Testing and remediation. Reducing formaldehyde levels in the home can be a simple or complex task depending on the source of the gas. Initial procedures include steps to increase ventilation and improve circulation of outside air through the home. Because formaldehyde emissions from building materials decrease as the materials age (particularly over the first two or three years), older urea-formaldehyde building materials probably are not a significant problem.

If purchasers suspect the presence of formaldehyde, they may wish to hire a qualified building inspector. In addition, home monitoring kits are currently available for testing formaldehyde levels. The testing device should be operated for a minimum of 24 hours to ensure a representative sampling period.

Biological Agents and Allergens

Biological contaminants include bacteria, mold, mildew, viruses, mites, pollen, and animal dander. Many of these pollutants are found in all types of structures. Mold and mildew growth is increased by damp conditions resulting from high humidity and water-pipe leaks. Dust mites can grow in a warm, damp environment but are commonly found in carpets and upholstery. Respiratory illnesses can be caused by inhaled viruses or bacteria. In addition, allergic reactions to mold, mildew, and mites are possible.

Sick Building Syndrome

In some situations, large numbers of people in a commercial building fall ill with a variety of complaints ranging from allergic reactions to flulike systems to more serious complaints. If no other outside cause is evident, a chemical illness may be the cause. *This phenomenon may be blamed on the air quality inside the building and is known as sick building syndrome.* The state or local health department may be called in to investigate and identify the cause if it is a public building. Privately owned commercial buildings require a private consultant. The building is tested, and appropriate measures are taken.

Polychlorinated Biphenyls (PCBs)

Polychlorinated biphenyl is *a manmade, liquid organic compound.* PCBs are used with electrical transformers as a cooling and insulating medium. Several years ago, it was found that PCBs from a chemical plant in Fort Edward, New York, leaked into the Hudson River. PCBs also leak into the ground from electrical transformers. This chemical has been known to appear in groundwater and soil. PCBs are a suspected carcinogen that can accumulate in human fatty tissue.

Testing and remediation. If PCBs are suspected, EPA or NYSDEC test groundwater or soil samples at the site. If the tests are positive, soil containing PCBs can be removed to special incinerators and landfills especially made to handle them.

Environmental Assessments

Under the **State Environmental Quality Review Act (SEQRA)** (1976), the state environmental quality review (SEQR) is a *process* that requires all levels of state and local government *to assess the environmental significance of actions for which they have discretion to review, approve, fund, or undertake.* For example, if a developer wants to create a subdivision, this requires *approval* by the local planning board; therefore the SEQR process is necessary. The SEQR process applies to residential, commercial, and industrial structures. The agency that coordinates the investigation is called the *lead agency.* If a property is simply transferred from owner to owner and the use is not changed so that governmental approval is not necessary, the SEQR process does not apply. The process begins with a three-part environmental assessment form. (See Figure 14.11)

The **environmental impact statement (EIS)** is a report that *describes and analyzes a proposed action that may have a significant effect on the environment.* The SEQR process uses the EIS to consider ways to avoid and reduce adverse environmental impacts related to a proposed action and to consider its alternative. There is a minimum 30-day comment period, and a public hearing can then be held. The lead agency reviews all comments. The final environmental impact statement is the culmination of all material relating to the action and becomes the lead agency's final document.

Due Diligence

Under the *Comprehensive Environmental Response, Compensation, and Liability Act* (*CERCLA*) (1980) a program exists to identify sites containing hazardous substances, seek reimbursement from the responsible party, and ensure cleanup by the parties responsible or by the government. The Superfund Amendments and Reauthorization Act (SARA) (1986), an amendment to CERCLA, expanded the definition of persons liable for clean-up costs. If a property is transferred, liability for environmental contamination could be passed on to the new owners. Liability may include the cost of cleaning up the property. *In the sale of large tracts of land or other types of commercial property, because of this liability, lenders, purchasers, and tenants often conduct* **due diligence** *reviews of the property;* these reviews are written up and evaluated by the parties.

These assessments or audits can be conducted by a private engineer or consultant. The assessments may go through four phases. These phases are not necessarily uniform and may depend on what parties (lender, purchaser, tenant) initiate the assessment. Phase I is the *investigative phase,* when the due diligence work takes place. Not only is the property examined, but a review of records pertaining to the history of the property is also conducted. In addition, properties surrounding the subject property may be examined. For example, if there are transformers on the property,

FIGURE 14.11 A NYSDEC short environmental assessment form.

PROJECT ID NUMBER

617.20
APPENDIX C
STATE ENVIRONMENTAL QUALITY REVIEW

SEQR

SHORT ENVIRONMENTAL ASSESSMENT FORM
for UNLISTED ACTIONS Only

PART 1 - PROJECT INFORMATION (To be completed by Applicant or Project Sponsor)

1. APPLICANT / SPONSOR	2. PROJECT NAME
3.PROJECT LOCATION: Municipality	County

4. PRECISE LOCATION: Street Addess and Road Intersections, Prominent landmarks etc

5. IS PROPOSED ACTION : ☐ New ☐ Expansion ☐ Modification / alteration

6. DESCRIBE PROJECT BRIEFLY:

7. AMOUNT OF LAND AFFECTED:
Initially acres Ultimately acres

8. WILL PROPOSED ACTION COMPLY WITH EXISTING ZONING OR OTHER RESTRICTIC
☐ Yes ☐ No If no, describe briefly:

9. WHAT IS PRESENT LAND USE IN VICINITY OF PROJECT? (Choose as many as apply.)
☐ Residential ☐ Industrial ☐ Commercial ☐ Agriculture ☐ Park / Forest / Open Space ☐ Other (describe)

10. DOES ACTION INVOLVE A PERMIT APPROVAL, OR FUNDING, NOW OR ULTIMATE
AGENCY (Federal, State or Local)
☐ Yes ☐ No If yes, list agency name and permit / approval:

11. DOES ANY ASPECT OF THE ACTION HAVE A CURRENTLY VALID PERMIT OR APPR(
☐ Yes ☐ No If yes, list agency name and permit / approval:

12. AS A RESULT OF PROPOSED ACTION WILL EXISTING PERMIT / APPROVAL REQUIRE I
☐ Yes ☐ No

I CERTIFY THAT THE INFORMATION PROVIDED ABOVE IS TRUE TO THE BEST OF MY

Applicant / Sponsor Name Date:

Signature________________________________

If the action is a Coastal Area, and you are a state agency, complete the Coastal Assessment Form before proceeding with this assessment.

(continued)

FIGURE 14.11 Continued.

PART II - IMPACT ASSESSMENT (To be completed by Lead Agency)

A. DOES ACTION EXCEED ANY TYPE I THRESHOLD IN 6 NYCRR, PART 617.4? If yes, coordinate the review process and use the FULL EAF.
☐ Yes ☐ No

B. WILL ACTION RECEIVE COORDINATED REVIEW AS PROVIDED FOR UNLISTED ACTIONS IN 6 N\
declaration may be superseded by another involved agency.
☐ Yes ☐ No

C. COULD ACTION RESULT IN **ANY** ADVERSE EFFECTS ASSOCIATED WITH THE FOLLOWING: (Answers may be handwritten, if legil

C1. Existing air quality, surface or groundwater quality or quantity, noise levels, existing traffic pattern, solid w
potential for erosion, drainage or flooding problems? Explain briefly:

C2. Aesthetic, agricultural, archaeological, historic, or other natural or cultural resources; or community or nei

C3. Vegetation or fauna, fish, shellfish or wildlife species, significant habitats, or threatened or endangered sp

C4. A community's existing plans or goals as officially adopted, or a change in use or intensity of use of land or oth

C5. Growth, subsequent development, or related activities likely to be induced by the proposed action? Expla

C6. Long term, short term, cumulative, or other effects not identified in C1-C5? Explain briefly:

C7. Other impacts (including changes in use of either quantity or type of energy? Explain briefly:

D. WILL THE PROJECT HAVE AN IMPACT ON THE ENVIRONMENTAL CHARACTERISTICS THAT CAU
ENVIRONMENTAL AREA (CEA)? (If yes, explain briefly:
☐ Yes ☐ No

E. IS THERE, OR IS THERE LIKELY TO BE, CONTROVERSY RELATED TO POTENTIAL ADVERSE EN
☐ Yes ☐ No

PART III - DETERMINATION OF SIGNIFICANCE (To be completed by Agency)

INSTRUCTIONS: For each adverse effect identified above, determine whether it is substantial, large, important or c
effect should be assessed in connection with its (a) setting (i.e. urban or rural); (b) probability of occurring; (c) duration; (d) irreversibility; (e)
geographic scope; and (f) magnitude. If necessary, add attachments or reference supporting materials. E
sufficient detail to show that all relevant adverse impacts have been identified and adequately address
yes, the determination of significance must evaluate the potential impact of the proposed action on the en

Check this box if you have identified one or more potentially large or significant adverse impacts which **MAY** occur. Then proceed directly to the FULL EAF and/or prepare a positive declaration.

Check this box if you have determined, based on the information and analysis above and any supporting docu
WILL NOT result in any significant adverse environmental impacts **AND** provide, on attachments as necessary, the reasons supporting this determination.

Name of Lead Agency	Date
Print or Type Name of Responsible Officer in Lead Agency	Title of Responsible Officer
Signature of Responsible Officer in Lead Agency	Signature of Preparer (If different from responsible officer)

Source: NYS Department of Environmental Conservation.

they will be checked for PCB leakage. Responsibility for the transformers is determined and the owner contacted to participate in remediation activities.

If the investigation shows that testing should be done, Phase II, the *testing phase,* is initiated. The appropriate party or agency goes to the property to determine if there is a problem. If testing does not show any significant problems, then the assessment ends. However, if a problem is ascertained, Phase III is initiated. This is when coordinated *clean-up efforts* take place. Clean-up activity may involve a number of different parties, including state, federal, and private organizations, depending on the nature of the problem and where the responsibility lies. Phase IV, the *management phase,* includes periodic monitoring by responsible parties to check the site and to remediate any future problems.

OTHER PRESENT CONCERNS

Underground Storage Tanks

NYSDEC regulates the bulk storage of chemicals and petroleum both aboveground and underground. As of 2002, DEC reports that there are 43,000 petroleum bulk storage facilities in New York with a total of 92,000 registered storage tanks. New York must abide by federal regulations that are overseen by EPA that apply to underground storage only. **Underground storage tanks** are *utilized by business and industry because the tanks are out of sight and also are protected against vandalism and fire.*

Underground Storage of Chemicals

NYSDEC has listed over 1,000 chemicals that are considered hazardous, ranging from chlorine used in pools to fertilizers, acids, alkalis, and pesticides. Most of the facilities where these tanks are stored are commercial or industrial businesses that use chemicals. NYSDEC sets the standards for storage and handling; NYSDEC does not determine the site of the tanks. Sites must comply with local zoning ordinances.

Concerns of Leaking and Testing and Remediation

EPA regulations require that contaminated UST sites must be cleaned up to restore and protect groundwater resources and create a safe environment for people who live or work near these sites. Gasoline and other petroleum products contain a substance called MTBE that at certain concentrations, renders groundwater unpleasant and unsafe to drink. Releases of the substance can also cause fire and explosion as well as produce long-term negative health effects. As of 2002, EPA estimates that there are about 150,000 sites that require clean up.

Older tanks, worn by age, can suffer from corrosion due to their chemical content or from a reaction between the tank and the soil. NYSDEC has the right to inspect for leakage. Owners of underground tanks are required to test the tanks periodically to determine if they are leaking and must report their findings to NYSDEC. It is sometimes difficult to tell if a tank is leaking. However, if leakage is present, the owners must call the spill hotline within two hours. The product must be removed from the tank and the tank repaired or replaced. Restoration of the environment may become necessary if the area has become contaminated. The NYSDEC, Division of Spills Management, oversees and assists with the clean-up process.

Petroleum Bulk Storage

NYSDEC regulates petroleum bulk storage (PBS) facilities that have a combined storage capacity of over 1,100 gallons for tanks both aboveground and underground. The

EPA mandates guidelines for smaller underground storage tanks for gasoline, diesel fuel, and waste oil. New York has delegated its petroleum bulk storage program to four counties: Nassau, Suffolk, Rockland, and Cortland. Other counties in New York are regulated directly by the state program.

EPA Exemptions to Petroleum Storage

Neither EPA nor NYSDEC regulates small heating oil tanks for on-site consumption such as those used in residences. In Nassau and Suffolk counties, however, some regulations do apply and are administered through the local health departments. However, all leaks or spills should be reported and remediated. Stored amounts of farm and residential motor fuel of less than 1,100 gallons, used for noncommercial purposes, are not regulated by EPA or NYSDEC. Owners of regulated storage tanks containing petroleum and chemicals must register with NYSDEC, pay a fee, provide information about the site, and indicate the material that is stored there. NYSDEC provides standards for storage, handling of the material, closure, and standards within new construction. The agency maintains a 24-hour daily hotline number to report oil and chemical spills: (800) 457-7362. The hotline number to answer questions regarding bulk storage is (800) 342-9296.

Electromagnetic Fields (EMFs)

Electromagnetic fields *occur wherever there is electricity*; near radio and microwave towers, high voltage transmission lines, low power electrical distribution lines, household appliances, and office electrical equipment. *The term electromagnetic fields generally refer to the high frequency radio waves in which the electric and magnetic fields are inseparable.* At low frequencies, including the 60-Hertz at which electric power is delivered to our homes and factories, electric and magnetic fields are independent and measured separately. An electric field exists when an appliance is "plugged-in." The magnetic field only exists when the appliance is "turned on" and operating. No federal laws currently regulate EMF emissions. In 1978, New York adopted a *prudent avoidance policy.* That is, New York advises people to exercise caution and to avoid exposure to these fields when possible. New York has no regulation for small power lines in neighborhoods or households. However, for the protection of the public health, in 1990 the New York Public Service Commission enacted a limit of 345 kilovolts for a given power line. Kilovolts are a measure of voltage or *juice* flowing through a power line. Magnetic field strength (measured in milligauss) is limited to a strength of 200 milligauss at the edge of a right of way. (The right of way is the strip of land on which a power line is built.)

Health Effects

The New York State Power Lines Project, as well as numerous other groups has found that EMFs may be possibly related to a number of health problems including certain cancers. However, these studies are not conclusive and are ongoing.

Testing and Remediation

Some power lines are stronger than others. Exposure decreases with distance. Electric fields can be shielded by walls, trees, or hills. Magnetic fields cannot be shielded. To reduce exposure, distance is the key. To reduce exposure in the home, electrical appliances should not be placed close to where people sleep, work, or sit. Computer users should sit at arm's length from a terminal, or pull the keyboard back still further, since magnetic fields fall rapidly with distance. VDT screens should be turned off when not in use. Some local power companies offer home testing, or a private consulting engineer can be hired. Because opposing magnetic fields can cancel each other out, a knowledgeable electrician can rewire a home to reduce magnetic fields.

Chlorofluorocarbons (CFCs)

Chlorofluorocarbons are *manmade chemical substances that were used in hundreds of applications, including refrigerators and air conditioners, Styrofoam products, aerosol dispensers, and cleansing agents. Hydrochlorofluorocarbons (HCFCs), also known as* **freon**, *are used in most home air conditioning units.* Chemically, CFCs and HCFCs are nontoxic and extremely stable.

Air Conditioning and Aerosols

Most car air conditioners use CFCs as a cooling agent, while HCFCs are used in most home air conditioning units. CFCs were used in aerosol spray cans but have been banned since the late 1970s.

CFCs are expelled into the air and migrate some 30 miles above Earth to the upper atmosphere, where they enter the stratospheric ozone layer. The ozone layer is a layer of gas that screens us from the sun's ultraviolet (UV-B) radiation. Since CFCs are chemically stable, they may last for 100 years or more. In the stratosphere, the ultraviolet rays of the sun break up the CFCs and the chlorine portions are expelled into the stratosphere, breaking up ozone molecules and forming an *ozone hole.* In 1985, a giant ozone hole was discovered over Antarctica, and scientific data have revealed that the ozone layer over the North Pole is currently being depleted. In addition, the ozone layer is eroding above North America, Europe, and other populated areas. The thinner ozone layer allows more of the UV-B radiation to reach Earth. As a result, an increase in cases of skin cancer and cataracts may occur. Damage to crops and marine ecosystems, which in turn reduces our food supply, can also occur.

In 1990, an amendment to the federal *Clean Air Act* dramatically curtailed the use of CFCs. The amendment calls for an end to the production of all chemicals that deplete the ozone layer. CFCs have not been produced since 1995. Under the law, HCFCs can replace CFCs in some air conditioning systems and may be produced until 2030. The Clean Air Act bans the release of CFCs and HCFCs during the service, maintenance, and disposal of air conditioners and other equipment that use refrigerants. Refrigerants must be recovered from the appliance before disposal. Individuals who work on such equipment must follow EPA regulations for ozone-safe practices including the recovery and recycling of refrigerant. EPA is authorized to assess fines up to $25,000 per day for violation of this act.

Remediation

About eight million refrigerators and freezers are thrown away each year and, without refrigerant recovery, about four million pounds of ozone-depleting chemicals escape from these appliances. The national program to protect the ozone layer requires CFC and HCFC recycling, developing substitute chemicals, banning nonessential uses, and enforcing product labeling. Technicians may no longer simply open a valve and vent refrigerant when servicing a unit. Refrigerant recovery machines are used to draw the refrigerant into a holding tank where it is purified and sold for reuse. The appliance can then be discarded without harming the ozone layer.

FIGURE 14.12 Environment-related legislation.

LAW	YEAR	NEW YORK STATE	FEDERAL	PURPOSE
Clean Air Act (CAA) and Amendments	1970 and after		✓	Federal regulation of air pollution; phased-in ban of HCFCs and CFCs
Safe Drinking Water Act	1974		✓	Imposed minimum contaminant levels for drinking water
State Environmental Quality Review Act (SEQRA)	1976	✓		Calls for preparation of an environmental impact statement on actions that may affect environment
Comprehensive Environmental Response, Compensation and Liability Act (CERCLA)	1980		✓	Solutions to uncontrolled disposal of waste
Superfund Amendments and Reauthorization Act (SARA)	1986		✓	Expanded liability of persons liable for hazardous waste cleanup
Residential Lead-Based Paint Hazard Reduction Act	1992		✓	Disclosure of lead-based paint in pre–1978 residential properties

IMPORTANT POINTS

1. Long-standing environmental issues relative to real estate include drinking water, wastewater treatment, and pest infestation. Contemporary issues include the use of chemical contaminants such as asbestos, lead, radon, and PCBs. Other present and future concerns include underground storage tanks, electromagnetic fields, and the release of chlorofluorocarbons.
2. Federal and state legislation provide regulations and guidelines for the implementation of environmental policy.
3. The federal Safe Drinking Water Act is the guideline for New York's drinking water regulations. The New York Department of Health oversees the safety of drinking water and the installation and approval of individual on-site wastewater treatment facilities of less than 1,000 gallons per residence in New York.
4. Federal law mandates that in the sale or lease of pre-1978 residential properties, sellers or their agents must distribute a lead hazard pamphlet and disclose any known information to the buyers or their agent concerning lead paint. The parties must agree to a 10-day period for a lead paint assessment before a purchaser becomes obligated under the contract. Sales and lease contracts must include specific disclosure and acknowledgment language.
5. Asbestos, a carcinogen, is found in a variety of building products that have numerous applications within the building industry.
6. Lead can be present in drinking water, in interior and exterior paint, and in dust, and soil in and around the home.
7. Wetlands are protected and overseen by the New York State Department of Environmental Conservation. Construction can take place on or near a wetland but builders must obtain approval for regulated activities from the state through local and federal government (Army Corps).
8. Radon from surrounding soil enters a home through small spaces and openings. The only way to detect radon is to test for it.
9. The Clean Air Act gives EPA the power to regulate air pollution, identify air-polluting substances, and mandate the states to implement protective measures.

10. One source of air pollution in the home may be urea-formaldehyde foam insulation (UFFI), which contains large amounts of formaldehyde.
11. Another source of home air pollution is insecticides, including chlordane, which is a chemical insecticide and termiticide that has been banned since the early 1980s.
12. Bacteria is a source of possible air pollution in homes and buildings. Sometimes large numbers of people in a commercial building fall ill from a chemical illness known as sick building syndrome.
13. A PCB is a toxic, manmade, liquid organic compound that has been found in New York's soil and waterways.
14. The state environmental quality review (SEQR) is a process that requires all levels of New York state and local government to assess the environmental significance of actions that they have discretion to review, approve, fund, or undertake.
15. The environmental impact statement (EIS) describes and analyzes a proposed action that may have a significant effect on the environment.
16. Because of liability for environmental clean-up, lenders, purchasers, and tenants often conduct due diligence reviews of property before transfer.
17. NYSDEC regulates the bulk storage of chemicals and petroleum both aboveground and underground. These tanks must be monitored for leakage.
18. Electromagnetic fields are present where there are power lines. New York has adopted a prudent avoidance policy.
19. Chlorofluorocarbons are manmade chemical substances used in refrigerators and air conditioners. The release of these chemicals threatens the ozone layer.

How Would You Respond? CHAPTER REVIEW

Analyze the following situations and decide how the individuals should handle them in accordance with what you have just learned. Check your responses using the Answer Key at the end of the chapter.

1. Yvonne wants to purchase a 20-acre parcel of land in a rural town in upstate New York and develop a 10-residential-lot subdivision. Yvonne wants to know if she will need environmental approval. Second, she is concerned as to how she will furnish the drinking and wastewater treatment since the land is distant from municipal water and sewer lines. She has engaged a buyer's broker, Lester, to advise her. What will Lester tell her?

2. Nadia is purchasing a large estate in Rome, New York. Nadia's mother recently read an article about the dangers of radon in homes and warns her not to buy any home without having it tested. Nadia is set on buying the home but has found from past experience that mother is *sometimes* right. Nadia is represented by a buyer's broker, Maria, and voices her concerns about radon. How might her broker handle the concern?

3. Wayne is purchasing an industrial plant in Gloversville, New York, to manufacture chemicals for swimming pools. The plant owns five underground storage tanks. Wayne does not plan to expand the plant in any way or add more storage tanks. However, he is concerned that he will have to undergo complicated environmental assessment reviews by both the city government and his lender before he can close the deal. What are your thoughts?

____

____

____

____

KEY TERM REVIEW

Fill in the term that best completes each sentence and then check the Answer Key at the end of the chapter.

1. A toxic metallic element found worldwide in rocks and soils that was widely used in the manufacture of paints is ____________________.
2. ____________________ has been used in architectural and construction applications, particularly pipe insulation, ceiling tiles, and flooring because it is strong, durable, fire retardant, and an efficient insulator.
3. ____________________ is a toxic, colorless, odorless gas that is present in soil or well water and is a by-product of the natural decay of uranium.
4. ____________________ contains large amounts of formaldehyde and was widely utilized as insulation in houses.
5. A known carcinogen that has appeared in soil and groundwater, ____________________ (is/are) used with electrical transformers as a cooling and insulating medium.
6. A(n) ____________________ describes and analyzes a proposed action that may have a significant effect on the environment.
7. ____________________ are chemical substances that are manmade and were used in hundreds of applications, including refrigerators, air conditioners, Styrofoam products, and aerosol dispensers.
8. Whenever electricity flows through a wire, ____________________ are created.

MULTIPLE CHOICE

Circle the letter that best answers the question and then check the Answer Key at the end of the chapter.

1. The federal law that provides guidelines for the clean-up of hazardous wastes is the:
   - A. National Environmental Act
   - B. Comprehensive Environmental Response, Compensation and Liability Act
   - C. Clean Air Act
   - D. National Recovery Act
2. The responsibility for safe drinking water in New York rests with the:
   - A. Department of Agriculture
   - B. Department of State
   - C. Department of Health
   - D. Office of OSHA

3. Sick building syndrome is:
   A. an imaginary phenomenon
   B. a result of chemical pollutants and bacteria
   C. due primarily to a large number of sick and tired employees
   D. a result of poor building insulation

4. Urea-formaldehyde foam insulation is:
   A. not toxic and is not of concern to home buyers
   B. not found in any homes today
   C. a possible health hazard to many people
   D. still being used by contractors to insulate homes

5. The SEQR process applies to:
   A. all property transactions in New York
   B. property transactions that transfer private property between two or more parties
   C. industrial property only
   D. real estate projects that require approval by a government agency

6. An environmental impact statement:
   A. is always necessary for the transfer of real property in New York
   B. becomes necessary if the SEQR process finds that further evaluation of the property is needed before a project can take place
   C. is a voluntary environmental assessment
   D. is needed only for hazardous waste sites

7. Underground storage tanks can pose a threat to the environment because:
   A. their contents can leak into the surrounding soil
   B. their contents always release noxious fumes into the air
   C. they are illegal
   D. they are not regulated in New York

8. Which of the following does NOT apply to electromagnetic fields?
   A. studies have been inconclusive as to their effect
   B. they are created whenever there is electricity
   C. distance is a key factor in reducing exposure
   D. power lines must be buried in residential neighborhoods in New York

9. If a property is found to be termite-infested:
   A. it must be rebuilt from the ground up
   B. it can be treated with termiticide and structurally repaired if necessary
   C. it cannot be placed for sale in New York
   D. a real estate licensee is not allowed to disclose information regarding termite infestation, if known, to prospective buyers

10. PCBs are:
   A. used as insulating material in homes
   B. not found in soil
   C. used as insulating material in electrical transformers
   D. not found in New York's waterways

ANSWER KEY

How Would You Respond?

1. Because the project requires approval from a governmental body, Yvonne will need to file a short (or long) environmental assessment form as required by the State Environmental Quality Review Act. Based on the findings in this assessment, a determination will be made as to the necessity of further action. If it is determined that impact to the environment is significant, then an environmental impact statement must be prepared. The size of the subdivision falls within the definition of a subdivision according to the public health law. Therefore, the plans for the subdivision must be approved by the local or state department of health. The rural location of the subdivision will probably necessitate individual wastewater treatment facilities for each property. Local or state health department staff will visit the site; observe percolation and deep-hole tests; and review, approve, or disapprove plans for proposed residential development.

2. Maria should suggest that Nadia attach a radon inspection contingency along with the contract for purchase and sale. This contingency provides for a qualified inspector to test for and measure the radon level of the property. If radon is present and the level is above four picocuries, the seller must take action to remediate the problem. If the seller refuses to remediate the problem, Nadia can terminate the contract.
3. Because Wayne is not planning to expand or change the plant in any way, governmental approvals are not necessary. Therefore, according to SEQR, environmental assessment is not necessary. However, because of legal due diligence requirements that mandate that the property owner is responsible for clean-up if a property is environmentally threatened or damaged, the lender will probably require an environmental assessment beginning with a Phase I inspection and investigation of the property, including the tanks, before lending mortgage money. If leakage is found, the assessment will proceed through further phases and tests, remediation of any damage, and ongoing management and remediation of the property as necessary.

Key Term Review

1. lead
2. asbestos
3. radon
4. urea-formaldehyde foam insulation (UFFI)
5. PCBs
6. environmental impact statement (EIS)
7. chlorofluorocarbons (CFCs)
8. electromagnetic fields

Multiple Choice

1. B
2. C
3. B
4. C
5. D
6. B
7. A
8. D
9. B
10. C

REFERENCES

1. The NYS Department of Health website: *http://www.doh.state.ny.us* and the NYS Department of Environment Conservation website: *http://www.dec.state.ny.us* contain useful information.
2. *The NYS Conservationist*, a very informative and aesthetically pleasing publication, is available by prescription. $12 per year. Call 1-800-678-6399 or go to the DEC website.

Chapter 15

KEY TERMS

employee

independent contractor

LEARNING OBJECTIVES

Classroom hours: 1

1. Describe the nature of the independent contractor relationship between a real estate broker and salesperson.
2. Identify the elements of the independent contractor laws in New York State.
3. Discuss the consequences for the real estate broker and salesperson in the event of noncompliance with the independent contractor laws.

Real Estate Salesperson: Independent Contractor or Employee

IN THIS CHAPTER Generally, real estate salespersons and associate brokers work under the broker in an independent contractor relationship. One of the most important distinctions of the independent contractor employment arrangement is that these individuals do not receive a set salary on any regular basis. Salespersons and associate brokers are not required to be independent contractors to practice real estate. Ultimately, the payment arrangement and employment status are decided between the licensee and the broker.

INDEPENDENT CONTRACTOR VERSUS EMPLOYEE

It is sometimes difficult to classify whether a worker is an *independent contractor* or an *employee.* From the standpoint of the Internal Revenue Service and New York law, the most important aspect of an **independent contractor** relationship is a *worker situation in which the employer does not have the right to control the details of a worker's performance.*

Other issues that are considered when determining independent contractor status are whether the worker (a) receives any instructions or training from his employer, (b) has work hours set by his employer, (c) is required to do the work at a specific location, (d) is paid by the job, (e) is required to do the work in a set order, (f) must pay his own expenses, and (g) must have his own tools.

The issue of whether a worker is an independent contractor or an employee affects how the worker is paid. If the worker is classified as an **employee,** then *the worker's employer(s) must withhold federal, state, and social security taxes (FICA). The employer also must pay federal unemployment (FUTA) and state unemployment taxes, prepare quarterly reports (941) and annual reports (W-2, W-3, and Form 940), and make required deposits of income taxes withheld and FICA taxes. The employer also must pay workers' compensation and disability insurance.*

However, if a worker is classified as an independent contractor, none of these taxes or deposits must be made, and no money is withheld from the worker's paycheck. If the worker earns $600 or more, the employer must file only a Form 1099 misc. with the IRS to report the worker's earnings for the year. The worker must also pay self-employment taxes. In addition, a worker classified as an employee may receive other benefits that an independent contractor does not, such as pension plans, paid vacation and sick days, and health care.

Case Law, IRS, and New York

The classification of an employee versus an independent contractor has evolved through a combination of the IRS code (federal law); New York law, which generally follows the guidelines set forth by IRS; and case law, in which statutory law is interpreted through lawsuits. For federal employment tax purposes, there are four categories of workers:

1. *Independent contractor.* This is a worker who does not work under the direct supervision of his employer.
2. *Common-law employee.* The trade or profession of this worker has generally been accepted as holding employee status.
3. *Statutory employee.* The work, trade, or profession of this worker is written into legal statutes as holding employee status.
4. *Statutory nonemployee.* The trade or profession of this worker is written into legal statutes as holding *nonemployee* status. *Workers who hold nonemployee status under the law are classified as independent contractors.*

Internal Revenue Code Section 3508 (a)(b)

According to IRS code, real estate agents are statutory nonemployees and are therefore independent contractors. To be qualified under this category, the real estate agent must be licensed, and all monies received for services rendered must be related to sales or other output, not to the number of hours worked. The code also states that *there must be a written contract between the broker and the sales associate and the contract must state that the licensee will not be "treated as an employee for federal tax purposes."* The salesperson and his broker must review the independent contractor agreement once every 12 to 15 months. This is to ensure that the activities of the salesperson fall within the parameters of independent contractor guidelines.

1986 New York Independent Contractor Laws

In 1986, additions to the New York labor law and workers' compensation law further defined the role of the salesperson in the independent contractor relationship. The 1986 law requires that the contract between broker and sales associate *not be executed under duress.* Note that both federal and state law require a written contract between broker and sales associate. See Figure 15.1 for an illustration of an independent contractor agreement.

You Should Know

The independent contractor relationship

1. Commissions are paid without deductions for taxes and are directly related to output.
2. There is no remuneration for the number of hours worked.
3. Salespersons are permitted to work any hours they choose.
4. Salespersons can work from home or a broker's office.
5. Salespersons are free to engage in outside employment.
6. Brokers can provide office facilities and supplies, but salespersons are responsible for expenses.
7. The broker supervises but does not direct and control the activity of the salesperson.
8. Either party may terminate the relationship at any time.

FIGURE 15.1
An independent contractor agreement form.

REALTOR®

INDEPENDENT CONTRACTOR RELATIONSHIP AGREEMENT

THIS AGREEMENT, (hereinafter "Agreement") made and entered into this _____ day of ______________________, 200___, by and between ______________________________ (hereinafter "Salesperson") and ______________________________ (hereinafter "Broker").

WHEREAS, the Salesperson and the Broker are both duly licensed pursuant to Article 12-A of the Real Property Law of the State of New York; and

WHEREAS, the Salesperson and Broker wish to enter into this Agreement in order to define their respective rights, duties and obligations.

NOW THEREFORE, in consideration of the terms, covenants, conditions and mutual promises contained herein, and other good and valuable consideration, it is hereby stipulated and agreed as follows:

1. The Salesperson is engaged as an independent contractor associated with the Broker pursuant to Article 12-A of the Real Property Law and shall be treated as such for all purposes, including but not limited to Federal and State taxation, withholding, unemployment insurance and workers' compensation; and
2. The Salesperson (a) shall be paid a commission on his or her gross sales, if any, without deduction for taxes, which commission shall be directly related to sales or other output; (b) shall not receive any renumeration related to the number of hours worked; and (c) shall not be treated as an employee with respect to such services for Federal and State tax purposes; and
3. The Salesperson shall be permitted to work any hours he or she chooses; and
4. The Salesperson shall be permitted to work out of his or her home or the office of the Broker; and
5. The Salesperson shall be free to engage in outside employment; and
6. The Broker may provide office facilities and supplies for the use of the Salesperson, but the Salesperson shall otherwise bear his or her own expenses, including but not limited to automobile, travel and entertainment expenses; and
7. The Broker and Salesperson shall comply with the requirements of Article 12-A of the Real Property Law and the regulations pertaining hereto, but such compliance shall not affect the Salesperson's status as an independent contractor nor should it be construed as an indication that the Salesperson is an employee of the Broker for any purpose whatsoever; and
8. This contract and the association created hereby may be terminated by either party hereto at any time upon notice give to the other; and
9. This Agreement is deemed to have been entered into in, and will be construed and interpreted in accordance with the laws of the State of New York; and
10. BY SIGNING BELOW THE UNDERSIGNED STIPULATE AND AGREE THAT THEY HAVE COMPLETELY READ THIS AGREEMENT, THAT THE TERMS HEREOF ARE FULLY UNDERSTOOD AND VOLUNTARILY ACCEPTED BY THEM AND THAT THIS AGREEMENT IS NOT SIGNED UNDER DURESS.

IN WITNESS WHEREOF, the parties hereto have executed this Agreement as of the day and year first above written.

____
SALESPERSON

____
BROKER

Negotiating an Employment Contract

Before negotiating an agreement with any brokerage firm, new licensees should first evaluate their goals, both short- and long-term. If licensees know what they are looking for, it will be much easier to find it. Brokerage firms differ in regard to the employment terms offered to salespersons. These differences are due to the size of the firm, the types of properties marketed, the location of the firm, and other factors. The following are questions to consider when seeking work through a particular brokerage firm.

- What is the specific focus of the firm: sales, leasing, or property management? Is it primarily residential, commercial, or industrial? Is it local only, a part of a franchise, or international? Are there many offices or one? What is the referral system, if any?
- What is the commission or fee schedule and what is the commission split for sales agents in various agency relationships (such as listing agent, for example)?
- What specific office duties, such as floor or phone duty, are required and how often? Will there be specific workspace available on a daily basis?
- Does the firm belong to MLS, and if so, what are the costs, responsibilities, and computer linkage, if any?
- What are the start-up costs including MLS, business cards, and other such items, and will special equipment such as computers, cell phones, cameras, etc. need to be purchased?
- What types of leads will there be, if any?
- What is expected with regard to production in the first six months or year?
- What specifically will the broker and the company do to assist with *your* goals?

The above are only a few of the many topics that should be discussed with the broker prior to signing an agreement. It is also a good idea to meet and talk to the other agents in the firm for further feedback.

Consequences of Noncompliance

Classification of a worker as an independent contractor rather than an employee can save the employer a large sum of money that would otherwise go toward employment taxes. Because of this, an employer can incur large tax penalties if a worker is incorrectly classified as an independent contractor. Therefore, salespersons who are deemed independent contractors must work in compliance with the rules stated above. If the broker–sales associate relationship becomes one of employer–employee, then the broker must pay all federal and state taxes and insurance premiums, as discussed earlier.

If the sales associates are not deemed independent contractors, then they will not be able to file Schedule C of the federal income tax form 1040 and deduct the expenses incurred during the year. The lump sum compensation received during the year would also be subject to withholding taxes.

Review of Recommended Forms

Sales associates should track earnings and expenses carefully and should file yearly federal and state tax returns. The broker must prepare and file IRS Form 1099 misc. for all sales associates who earn $600 or more. The sales associate should receive a copy of Form 1099 misc., which reports the total earnings for the year. A copy of this form must be filed with IRS. To protect the independent contractor relationship, all brokers and sales associates should enter into an independent contractor agreement.

Supervision of Salespersons by Broker

DOS Regulation 175.21, based on Section 441, 1(d) of the New York Real Property Law, states that the supervision of a salesperson by a broker "shall consist of regular, frequent and consistent guidance, instruction, oversight and superintendence." Although no legal duty exists to supervise an independent contractor, it is nevertheless required by New York license law and regulations. Moreover, even though entering into an independent contractor agreement fulfills one of the legal requirements to maintain independent contractor status, the broker must still supervise salesperson activities.

Records of Transactions to Be Maintained

DOS Regulation 175.23 states that "each licensed broker shall keep and maintain for a period of three years records of each transaction effected through his office concerning the sale or mortgage of one- to four-family dwellings." In addition to keeping records of the parties to the transaction and other items, the broker must maintain records showing the amount of commission or gross profit realized through the transaction as well as the *net profit* or *commission "and the disposition of all payments."* These payments include commissions or fees paid to salespersons. Again, this regulation may imply the type of activities such as recording and tracking earnings, which are considered employer–employee activities. However, in abiding by license law and regulations, this activity must still be a part of the salesperson–broker relationship.

Implications for the Future

Will licensees become employees? Many considerations are involved in evaluating the employee versus independent contractor relationship and the different interests involved. On the part of the licensee, although the employer saves money in an independent contractor relationship, the licensee bears some of the burden because she must then pay social security self-employment tax to make up for the FICA (social security taxes) not withheld from her pay. The licensee also gives up (in most cases) other benefits of an employee relationship, such as pensions, sick pay, and so on.

The broker, within the context of the independent contractor relationship, still has a duty to supervise and can be held accountable by New York law and regulations for the activity of sales associates.

As previously discussed, the IRS code allows independent contractor status for sales associates despite the fact that boundaries have crossed into an employer–employee relationship. It is possible, therefore, that the status quo will be maintained in the future unless the statutory legal definition of the independent contractor–real estate associate is changed by federal law or regulation.

IMPORTANT POINTS

1. Real estate salespersons and brokers are classified under the IRS code as independent contractors. To qualify under the law for this employment arrangement, the real estate agent must be licensed and the broker and sales associate must enter into a written contract.
2. As independent contractors, licensees do not receive sick pay or medical benefits and must file a Form 1099 misc. with IRS. They must also pay self-employment taxes.
3. Even though sales associates are independent contractors, their brokers still have a duty to supervise their activities under DOS Regulation 175.21.

CHAPTER REVIEW

MULTIPLE CHOICE

Circle the letter that best answers the question and then check the Answer Key at the end of the chapter.

1. Which of the following is a requirement under the IRS code for a salesperson–broker independent contractor relationship? The salesperson must:
   A. be at least 21
   B. enter into a written independent contractor agreement with the broker
   C. have five years experience in the real estate business
   D. demonstrate at least $10,000 in gross commissions during a one-year period

2. The most important aspect of the independent contractor relationship is that the:
   A. worker has specific work hours each day
   B. worker earned below $600 per year
   C. employer does not have the right to control the details of a worker's performance
   D. employer must file a quarterly 941 report with IRS

3. According to the IRS code, real estate licensees are classified as:
   A. statutory employees
   B. common-law employees
   C. laborers
   D. independent contractors

4. In an independent contractor relationship, salespersons may NOT do which of the following?
   A. work any hours they choose
   B. work without broker supervision
   C. work from their home or the broker's office
   D. obtain outside employment

5. Ben is the only licensee working for Gloria, the owner of a small real estate firm. Ben is so competent that Gloria is taking off a year to travel in the Far East. She is leaving Ben in charge of the office. Gloria believes that Ben does not require her supervision because Ben is an independent contractor. Which of the following is correct?
   A. Gloria can leave the office in Ben's hands if she leaves written instructions
   B. Gloria has a duty to supervise Ben only if he is a salesperson, not a broker associate
   C. Gloria has no duty to supervise Ben because he is an independent contractor
   D. Gloria must supervise Ben's activities despite his independent contractor status

6. A real estate broker must maintain records of the sales transactions of one- to four-family dwellings for:
   A. one year
   B. two years
   C. three years
   D. four years

7. Which of the following tax forms must be completed by the broker if a salesperson who works as an independent contractor earns $600 or more?
   A. Form 1040
   B. Form 1099 misc.
   C. Schedule C
   D. Form 941

8. Even though licensees may be paid through a commission arrangement based on sales activity, the broker is responsible for which of the following?
   A. tracking and recording the number of hours worked by each licensee
   B. filing quarterly FICA payments for each licensee with IRS
   C. maintaining records as to the gross and net profit of all transactions
   D. keeping records of any outside employment of the licensee

9. Though Jared is an independent contractor, he works approximately 35 hours per week. Jared believes he is entitled to sick and vacation pay because of the hours he puts in. Which of the following is correct? Jared:
   A. is entitled to sick and vacation pay
   B. would only be entitled to sick and vacation pay if he worked 40 or more hours a week
   C. is not entitled to sick and vacation pay
   D. is entitled to sick and vacation pay only if his gross sales per month exceed the cost of this pay

10. E.R. is an independent contractor who wishes to terminate his employment arrangement with his broker. Which of the following is true?
    A. he may do so at any time
    B. he may do so only with the permission of the Department of State
    C. his broker may refuse to terminate the contract
    D. he must reapply to retake his license exam before he leaves his broker

ANSWER KEY

Multiple Choice

1. B
2. C
3. D
4. B
5. D
6. C
7. B
8. C
9. C
10. A

Chapter 16

KEY TERMS

acre
commission
front foot
gross income
income
interest
net operating income
point
principal
rate
tax rate
value

LEARNING OBJECTIVES

Classroom hours: 3

1. Solve problems using percentages.
2. Compute area, length, and volume.
3. Calculate problems involving rates.
4. Describe a balloon payment and calculate problems determining payment.
5. List the various reasons points are charged and calculate point payments based on the loan.

Real Estate Mathematics

IN THIS CHAPTER Real estate licensees need an understanding of arithmetic fundamentals. Using these fundamentals, you need to master certain mathematical calculations related to real estate. Some people have difficulty with math. The practice exercises in this chapter along with your future experiences will be helpful. The multiple choice questions indicate which chapters they correspond to.

GENERAL PRACTICE IN REAL ESTATE MATHEMATICS

Percentages

In the real estate business, many calculations involve percentages. For example, *a real estate broker* **commission** *is often a percentage of the sales price.* A percentage is a number that has been divided by 100. To use a percentage in a calculation, you must change the percentage to its decimal equivalent. The rule for changing a percentage to a decimal is to remove the percent sign and move the decimal point two places to the left (or divide the percentage by 100). Examples of converting a percentage to a decimal are:

98% = 0.98		1½% = 1.5% = 0.015
1.42% = 0.0142		1¼% = 1.25% = 0.0125
0.092% = 0.00092		¾% = 0.75% = 0.0075

To change a decimal or a fraction to a percentage, simply reverse the procedure. Move the decimal point two places to the right and add the percent sign (or multiply by 100). Some examples of this operation are:

1.00 = 100%	½ = 1 ÷ 2 = 0.5 = 50%
0.90 = 90%	⅜ = 3 ÷ 8 = 0.375 = 37.5%
0.0075 = 0.75%	⅔ = 2 ÷ 3 = 0.667 = 66.7%

Formulas

Almost every problem in a real estate transaction uses the format of something × something = something else. In mathematics language, factor × factor = product. Calculating a real estate commission is a classic example:

sales price paid	×	percentage of commission	=	commission
\$80,000	×	7%	=	\$5,600

In most real estate problems, two of the three numbers are provided. Calculations to find the third number are required. If the number missing is the product, the calculation or function is to multiply the two factors. If the number missing is one of the factors, the calculation or function is to divide the product by the given factor.

Solving for product:	**Answers:**
43,500 × 10.5% = ________	(43,500 × 0.105 = 4,567.50)
100,000 × 4% = ________	(100,000 × 0.04 = 4,000)
51.5 × 125 = ________	(6,437.50)
Solving for factor:	**Answers:**
43,500 × _____ = 4,567.50	(4,567.50 ÷ 43,500 = 0.105 = 10.5%)
______ × 4% = 4,000.00	(4,000.00 ÷ 0.04 = 100,000)
51.5 × _____ = 6,437.50	(6,437.50 ÷ 51.5 = 125)

Commission Problems

Problems involving commissions are readily solved by the formula:

sales price × rate of commission = total commission

Sales

1. A real estate broker sells a property for \$90,000. Her rate of commission is 7%. What is the amount of commission in dollars?

Solution: sales price × rate = commission
\$90,000 × 0.07 = ________
product missing: multiply

Answer: \$6,300 commission

2. A real estate broker earns a commission of \$6,000 in the sale of a residential property. His rate of commission is 6%. What is the selling price?

Solution: sales price × rate = commission
________ × 0.06 = \$6,000
factor missing: divide \$6,000 by 0.06 = ________

Answer: \$100,000 sales price

3. A real estate broker earns a commission of \$3,000 in the sale of property for \$50,000. What is her rate of commission?

Solution: sales price × rate = commission
\$50,000 × ________ = \$3,000
factor missing: divide \$3,000 by \$50,000 and convert to percentage

Answer: 6% rate

Rentals

4. A real estate salesperson is the property manager for the owner of a local shopping center. The center has five units, each renting for \$24,000 per year. The center has an annual vacancy factor of 4.5%. The commission for rental of the units is 9% of the gross rental income. What is the commission for the year?

Solution: gross rental × rate = commission
gross rental = $24,000 × 5 minus the vacancy factor
vacancy factor = $120,000 × 0.045 = $5,400
$120,000 − $5,400 = $114,600
$114,600 × 0.09 = ________
product missing: multiply

Answer: $10,314 commission

Splits

5. A real estate salesperson sells a property for $250,000. The commission on this sale to the real estate firm with whom the salesperson is associated is 7%. The salesperson receives 60% of the total commission paid to the real estate firm. What is the firm's share of the commission in dollars?

Solution: sales price × rate = commission
$250,000 × 0.07 = ________
product missing: multiply
$250,000 × 0.07 = $17,500
100% − 60% = 40% is the firm's share
$17,500 × 0.40 = $7,000

Answer: $7,000 firm's share of commission

6. A broker's commission is 10% of the first $50,000 of sales price of a property and 8% of the amount of sales price over $50,000. The broker receives a total commission of $7,000. What is the total selling price of the property?

Solution:

Step 1: sales price × rate = commission
$50,000 × 0.10 = ________
product missing: multiply
$50,000 × 0.10 = $5,000 commission on first $50,000 of sales price

Step 2: total commission − commission on first $50,000 = commission on amount over $50,000
$ 7,000 − $5,000 = $2,000 commission on selling price over $50,000

Step 3: sales price × rate = commission
________ × 0.08 = $2,000
factor missing: divide
$ 2,000 ÷ 0.08 = $25,000

Step 4: $50,000 + $25,000 = $75,000

Answer: $75,000 total selling price

Estimating Net to Seller

The formula used to estimate the net dollars to the seller is:

sales price × percent to seller = net dollars to seller

The percent to the seller is 100% minus the rate of commission paid to the real estate agent.

7. A seller advises a broker that she expects to net $80,000 from the sale of her property after the broker commission of 7% is deducted from proceeds of the sale. For what price must the property be sold?

Solution: 100% = gross sales price
100% − 7% = 93%
93% = net to owner
$80,000 = 0.93 × sales price
factor missing: divide
$80,000 ÷ 0.93 = __________

Answer: $86,022 sales price (rounded)

Estimating Partial Sales of Land

8. A subdivision contains 400 lots. If a broker has sold 25% of the lots and his sales staff has sold 50% of the remaining lots, how many lots are still unsold?

Solution: 0.25 × 400 = 100 sold by broker
400 − 100 = 300
300 × 0.50 = 150 sold by sales force
400 − 250 sold = 150 unsold

Answer: 150 lots still unsold

Interest Problems

The **principal** is also known as the *loan balance.* Annual **interest** on *a loan is calculated by multiplying the rate of interest as a percentage times the principal balance.* The number resulting from the calculation is the annual interest. The annual interest calculation also may be used in amortizing a loan on a monthly basis. The annual interest is divided by 12 (number of months in a year) to determine the monthly interest. The monthly interest then is subtracted from the monthly loan payment to determine what amount of the monthly payment paid applies to reduce the loan principal.

Simple Interest

Interest calculations use the formula:

loan balance × rate of interest = annual interest

1. A loan of $30,000 is repaid in full, one year after the loan is made. If the interest rate on the loan is 5.5%, what amount of interest is owed?

Solution: loan × rate = annual interest
$30,000 × 5.5% = __________
product missing: multiply

Answer: $1,650 interest

Principal and Interest

2. On October 1, a mortgagor makes a $850 payment on her mortgage, which is at the rate of 6%. Of the $850 total payment for principal and interest, the mortgagee allocates $600 to the payment of interest. What is the principal balance due on the mortgage on the date of the payment?

Solution: $600 × 12 mo = $7,200 annual interest income
principal × rate = annual interest
__________ × 6% = $7,200

factor missing: divide

\$7,200 ÷ 0.06 = ________

Answer: \$120,000 mortgage balance on date of payment

3. If an outstanding mortgage balance is \$50,000 on the payment date and the amount of the payment applied to interest is \$250, what is the rate of interest charged on the loan?

Solution: \$250 × 12 mo = \$3,000 annual interest

principal × rate = annual interest

50,000 × ________ = \$3,000

factor missing: divide and convert to percentage

\$3,000 ÷ \$50,000 = ________

Answer: 6% interest rate

Points

Lenders may charge discount **points** in making mortgage loans. *Each point is equal to 1% of the loan amount.* The formula for calculating the dollar amount owed in points on a loan is:

loan × number of points (percentage) = dollars in points

1. A house sells for \$60,000. The buyer obtains an 80% loan. If the bank charges 3 points at closing, how much in points must the buyer pay?

Solution: loan × number of points (%) = dollars paid

(\$60,000 × 0.80) × 0.03 = ________

\$48,000 × 0.03 = ________

product missing: multiply

Answer: \$1,440 points payment

2. Cameron borrows \$64,000. If he pays \$4,480 for points at closing, how many points are charged?

Solution: loan × number of points (%) = dollars paid

\$64,000 × ________ = \$4,480

factor missing: divide

Answer: 7 points

Appreciation and Depreciation

An increase in property value is known as *appreciation.*

1. A property valued at \$150,000 appreciates 3% each succeeding year. What is the value of the property after three years?

Solution:

Step 1: original value × % of appreciated value = new value

150,000 × 0.03 = 4,500

The percentage of appreciation is added to the property value at the end of each year

4,500 + 150,000 = 154,500 first year appreciation

Step 2: 154,500 × 0.03 = 4,635

4,635 + 154,500 = 159,135 second year appreciation

Step 3: 159,135 × 0.03 = 4,774.05

159,135 + 4,774.05 = 163,909.05 third year appreciation

Answer: \$163,909.05

Depreciation is a loss in value from any cause. The examples of depreciation that follow represent the types of problems a real estate practitioner may encounter. In the first problem, the present value of a building is given and the requirement is to calculate the original value. The second problem provides the original value to be used in arriving at the present depreciated value.

Depreciation problems use the formula:

original value × % of value NOT lost = present value

2. The value of a 6-year-old building is estimated to be $450,000. What was the value when new if the building depreciated 2% per year?

Solution: 6 yrs. × 2% = 12% depreciation

100% (new value) − 12% = 88% of value not lost

original value × % not lost = present value

_________ × 88% = $450,000

factor missing: divide

$450,000 ÷ 0.88 = _________

Answer: $511,364 (rounded) value when new

3. A 14-year-old building has a total economic life of 40 years. If the original value of the building was $75,000, what is the present depreciated value?

Solution: 100% ÷ 40 yrs. = yearly depreciation rate

1.00 ÷ 40 = 0.025, or 2.5% year depreciation

14 yrs × 2.5% = 35% depreciation to date

100% − 35% = 65% not lost

original cost × % not lost = remaining dollar value

$75,000 × 0.65 = _________

product missing: multiply

$75,000 × 0.65 = _________

Answer: present depreciated value is $48,750

AREA CALCULATIONS

It is often necessary to determine the size of an area in square feet, cubic feet, and number of acres. In taking a listing, the broker should determine the number of square feet of heated area in the house. To establish the lot size, the number of square feet should be determined so it may be translated into acreage, if desired. Table 16.1 provides a list of measures and formulas.

The area of a rectangle or square is determined by simply multiplying the length times the width. In a square, the length and width are the same. The area of a triangle is calculated by multiplying one-half times the base of the triangle times the height of the triangle.

Formula for rectangle: area = length × width or A = L × W

Formula for square: area = side × side or A = S × S

Formula for triangle: area = 0.5 × base × height

TABLE 16.1
Measures and formulas.

LINEAR MEASURE
12 inches = 1 ft
39.37 inches = 1 meter (metric system)
3 ft = 1 yd
16½ ft = 1 rod, 1 perch, or 1 pole
66 ft = 1 chain
5,280 ft = 1 mile

SQUARE MEASURE
144 sq inches = 1 sq ft
9 sq ft = 1 sq yd
30¼ sq yd = 1 sq rod
160 sq rods = 1 acre
2.47 acres = 1 hectare or 10,000 square meters (metric system)
43,560 sq ft = 1 acre
640 acres = 1 sq mile
1 sq mile = 1 section
36 sections = 1 township

FORMULAS
1 side × 1 side = area of a square
width × depth = area of a rectangle
½ base × height = area of a triangle
½ height × ($base_1$ + $base_2$) = area of a trapezoid
½ × sum of the bases = distance between the other two sides at the mid-point of the height of a trapezoid
length × width × depth = volume (cubic measure) of a cube or a rectangular solid

CUBIC MEASURE
1,728 cubic inches = 1 cubic foot
27 cubic feet = 1 cubic yard
144 cubic inches = 1 board foot (12" × 12" × 1")

CIRCULAR MEASURE
360 degrees = circle
60 minutes = 1 degree
60 seconds = 1 minute

TAX VALUATION
Per $100 of Assessed Value (AV): Divide the AV by 100, then multiply by tax rate.

$$\frac{\text{assessed value}}{100} \times \text{tax rate}$$

Per Mill: Divide the AV by 1000, then multiply by tax rate.

$$\frac{\text{assessed value}}{1000} \times \text{tax rate}$$

Square Footage

1. A rectangular lot measures 185 feet by 90 feet. How many square feet does this lot contain?

   Solution: A = L × W
   _____ = 185 × 90

   Answer: 16,650 sq ft

2. A room measures 15 feet by 21 feet. Prospective buyers want to purchase wall-to-wall carpeting and need to calculate the exact amount of carpeting required.

   Solution: Carpeting is sold by the square yard, so we need to convert square feet to square yards. The number of square feet per square yard is 3 × 3 = 9 square feet per square yard. Therefore, to convert size in square feet to size in square yards, we need to divide by 9.
   Area × 15 × 21 = 315 sq ft
   sq yd = 315 ÷ 9 = _______

   Answer: 35 sq yd of carpeting

3. A new driveway, 115 feet by 20 feet, will be paved. The paving cost is $0.65 per square foot. What will be the minimum cost for paving?

Solution:

Step 1: A = L × W
A = 115 × 20
A = 2,300 sq ft

Step 2: cost = 2,300 × $0.65

Answer: $1,495

Price per square foot

4. A house measures 28 feet wide by 52 feet long and sells for $64,000. What is the price per square foot?

Solution:

Step 1: calculate the area
A = 28 × 52 = 1,456 sq ft

Step 2: divide the sales price by the area
$64,000 ÷ 1,456 = ______

Answer: $43.96 per sq ft

Irregular Lot or Building Size*

A plot of ground or a building may be a combination of triangles, squares, and rectangles (see Figure 16.1). To find the area of a plot or floor space of a building, divide the shape into triangles, squares, and rectangles, and then find the area of each separate figure and add all the areas together.

FIGURE 16.1 Irregular lot or building sizes.*

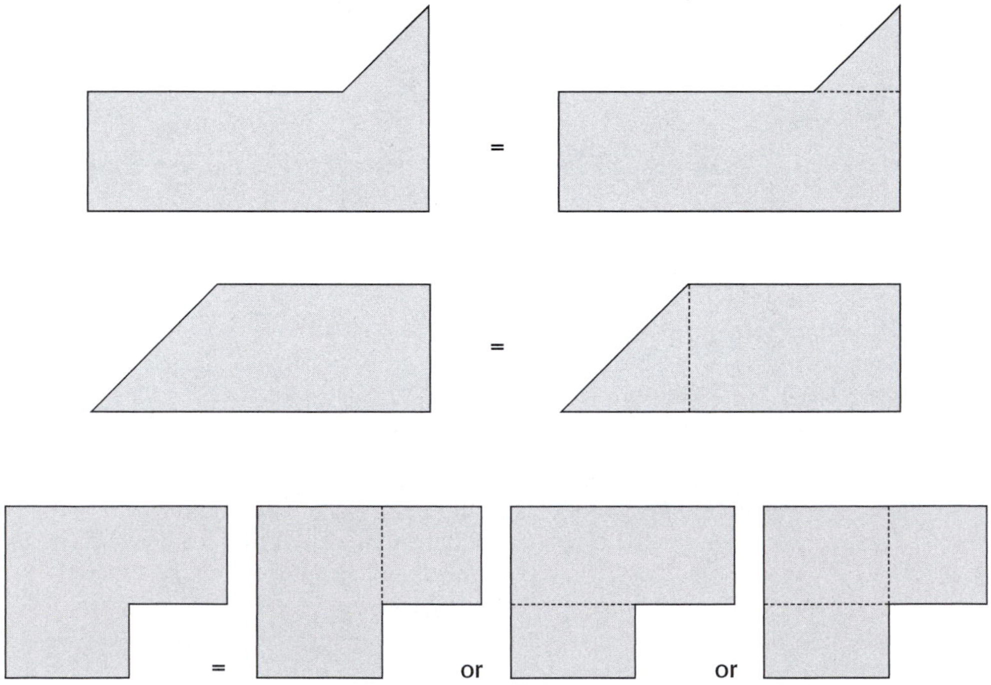

*From *Practical Real Estate Math,* 2nd ed., by Armbrust et al., © 1995. Reprinted by permission of South-Western Publishing, Cincinnati, OH.

1. Find the number of square feet in the floor plan of a home with the measurements given:

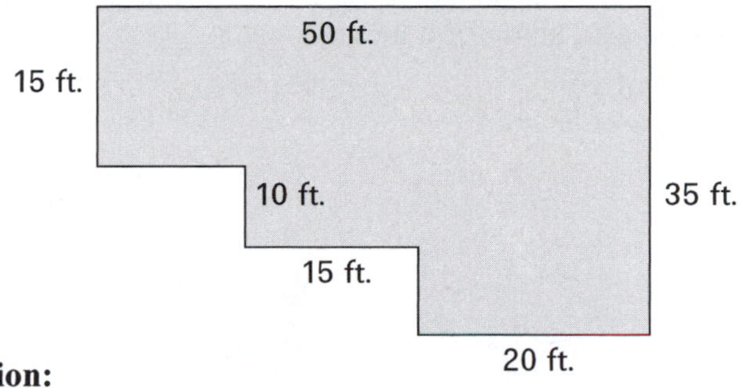

Solution:

Step 1: Divide into rectangular regions I, II, and III.

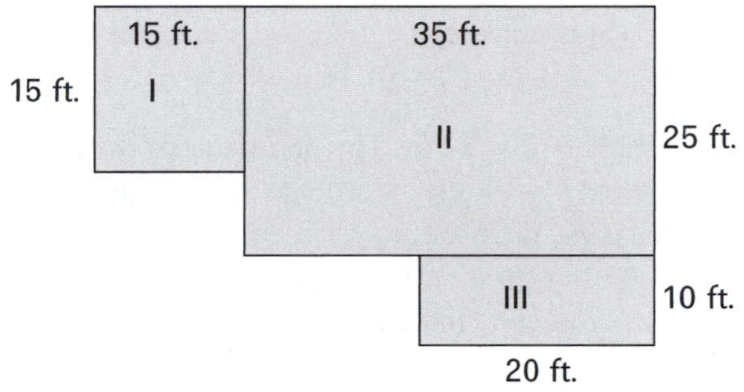

Region I is a square 15 ft by 15 ft
Region II is a rectangle 35 ft by 25 ft
Region III is a rectangle 20 ft by 10 ft

Step 2: A = LW for a rectangle and a square.
Area region I: A = 15 × 15 = 225 sq ft
Area region II: A = 35 × 25 = 875 sq ft
Area region III: A = 20 × 10 = 200 sq ft

Step 3: Total area: 225 sq ft + 875 sq ft + 200 sq ft = 1,300 sq ft

Answer: The number of square feet contained in the floor is 1,300 sq ft

Front Foot

The **front foot** is *a linear foot of property frontage on a street or highway.*

1. The owner of a rectangular parcel of land measuring 600 feet wide (front) by 145.2 feet long is offered $15 per front foot or $4,000 per acre. What is the amount of the higher offer?

Solution: 600 ft. × 145.2 = 87,120 sq ft
87,120 sq ft ÷ 43,560 sq ft/acre = 2 acres
2 acres × $4,000 = $8,000 acreage basis

Answer: $15 × 600 ft. = $9,000 front-foot basis

2. A triangle tract is 4,000 feet long and has 900 feet of highway frontage, which is perpendicular to the 4,000-foot boundary. How many square yards does the tract contain?

Solution: ½ × base × height = area of a right triangle
½ × 900 ft × 4000 ft = 1,800,000 sq ft

Answer: 1,800,000 sq ft ÷ 9 sq ft/sq yd = 200,000 sq yd

Perimeter*

The *perimeter* is the entire outer boundary of a figure such as a plot of land or the measure around a figure, such as a house or building.

1. Find the perimeter of each figure:

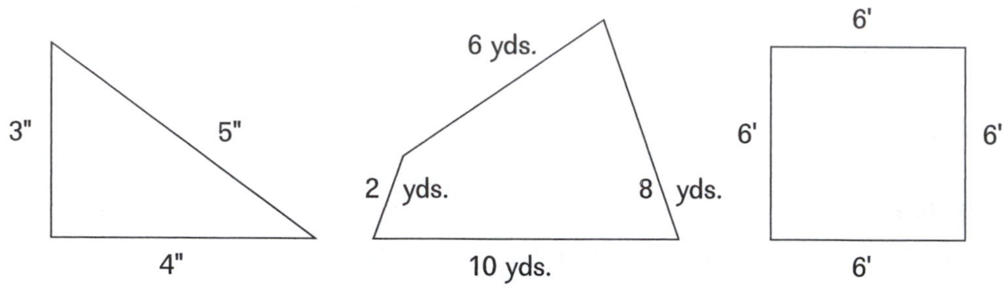

(a) triangle (b) quadrilateral (c) square

Solution: a. 4 in + 5 in + 3 in = 12 in. The perimeter of the triangle is 12 in.
b. 2 yds + 6 yds + 8 yds + 10 yds = 26 yds. The perimeter of the quadrilateral is 26 yds.
c. 6 ft + 6 ft + 6 ft + 6 ft = 24 ft Since every square has four equal sides, you can find its perimeter by multiplying the length of the side by 4: 6 ft × 4 = 24 ft The perimeter of the square is 24 ft.

2. Find the perimeter of a lot whose length is 20 feet and whose width is 15 feet.

Solution:

Step 1: Draw the four-sided closed figure with four right angles and opposite sides equal.
From the figure, the perimeter is
20 ft + 15 ft + 20 ft + 15 ft = 70 ft

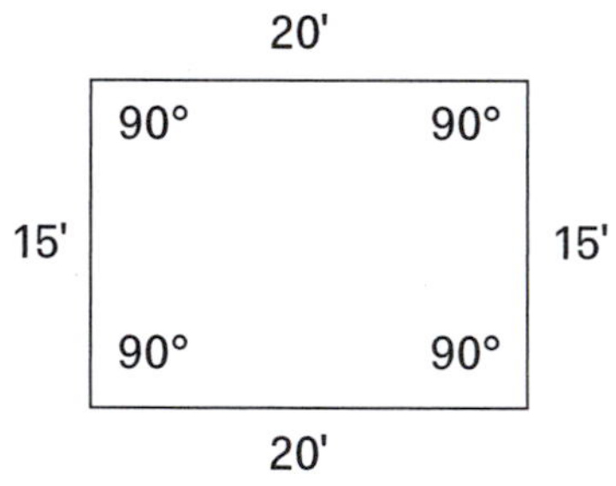

Step 2: Note that there are two 20-foot measures and two measures of 15 feet.
We could also find the perimeter:
2 × 20 ft + 2 × 15 ft
40 ft + 30 ft = 70 ft

Answer: The perimeter of the lot is 70 feet.

Acreage

1. An acre of land has a width of 330 feet. If this acre of land is rectangular in shape, what is its length? An **acre** *contains 43,560 square feet.*

Solution: A = L × W
43,560 = ________ × 330
factor missing: divide
43,560 ÷ 330 = ________

Answer: 132' long lot

*From *Practical Real Estate Math,* 2nd ed., by Armbrust et al., © 1995. Reprinted by permission of South-Western Publishing, Cincinnati, OH.

2. If a parcel of land contains 32,670 square feet, what percent of an acre is it?

   Solution: 32,670 square feet is what % of an acre?
   32,670 = ____% × 43,560
   factor missing: divide and convert decimal to percent
   32,670 ÷ 43,560 = 0.75

   Answer: 75% of an acre

Hectare

The metric system is a decimal system of measures and weights based on the meter and kilogram. A *hectare* is equal to 10,000 square meters and approximately 2.47 acres in U.S. equivalent measurements.

1 How many approximate hectares are there in a 30-acre tract of land?

   Solution: Divide the total acres by 2.47.
   30 ÷ 2.47 = 12.15

   Answer: 12.15 hectares

FINANCIAL CALCULATIONS

Typical arithmetic calculations pertaining to real estate finance include annual interest, debt service on a loan, loan origination fees, loan-to-value ratios in qualifying for a loan, and amortization of a loan.

Debt service is the annual amount to be paid to retire or reduce a loan or mortgage balance. The annual debt service on a mortgage is the monthly mortgage payment times 12 (number of months in a year). Lending institutions use loan-to-value ratios to determine the maximum loan to be issued on a given parcel of real estate. The loan-to-value ratio also can be stated as a percentage of the value of the real estate; in fact, the ratio is much more commonly expressed as a percentage. Some lending institutions lend up to only 90% of the appraised value of the property (a 9:10 ratio). If a lending institution approved a loan of 100% of the value, the loan-to-value ratio would be 1:1. If a lending institution approved a loan that was only 70% of the value, the loan-to-value ratio would be 7:10.

Debt Service

1. The monthly amortized mortgage payment Darcy owes is $1,450. What is her annual debt service on this loan?

   Solution: debt service is monthly payment × 12
   $1,450 × 12 = __________

   Answer: $17,400 annual debt service

2. A mortgage loan of $50,000 requires monthly payments of principal and interest of $516.10 to fully amortize the loan for a term of 20 years. If the loan is paid over the 20-year term, how much interest does the borrower pay?

   Solution: 20 years × 12 mo payments = 240 payments
   240 × $516.10 = $123,864 total amount paid
   total amount paid − principal borrowed = interest
   $123,864 − $50,000 = __________

   Answer: $73,864 interest paid

Loan Origination Fee

3. Marie and Manuel borrow $55,000 at 6% interest for 30 years. The bank requires 2 months' interest to be placed in escrow and a 1% loan origination fee to be paid at closing. What is the amount of interest to be escrowed? What is the amount charged for the loan origination fee?

   Step 1: Interest escrow

   Solution: $55,000 × 0.06 = $3,300 annual interest
   $3,300 ÷ 12 = $275 monthly interest
   $275 × 2 = __________

   Answer: $550 interest escrow

   Step 2: Loan origination fee

   Solution: $55,000 × 0.01 = __________

   Answer: $550 loan origination fee

Loan-to-Value Ratios

4. In problem 3 above, the appraised value of the home purchased is $68,750. What is the loan-to-value ratio?

   Solution: loan ÷ value = ratio
   $55,000 ÷ $68,750 = 0.80
   0.80 = 80:100

   Answer: 80% loan-to-value ratio

5. The Montorris apply for a loan. The purchase price of the home is $80,000. The bank authorizes a loan-to-value ratio of 90%. What is the amount of loan authorized?

   Solution: $80,000 × 90% = loan

   Answer: $72,000 loan

Basic Mortgage Qualifying

For a borrower to qualify for a loan, the ratios of the borrower's housing and total debts to income must meet the lender's requirements. The typical housing debt-to-income ratio for conventional loans is 25–28%. The typical total debt-to-income ratio for conventional loans is 33–36%. The 25–28% means that for the borrower to qualify, PITI (principal, interest, taxes, insurance) must not be more than 25–28% of the borrower's monthly gross income. The 33–36% means that for the borrower to qualify, the total monthly expenses (including housing expense) must not be more than 33–36% of the borrower's monthly gross income.

1. Romeo and Jane have a combined total monthly income of $2,500. If the lender requires a debt-to-income ratio of 25:33 for housing and total expenses, what is the maximum house payment they will qualify for? What is the maximum total monthly expenses besides PITI that will be allowed?

   Solution:

   Step 1: housing: $2,500 × 0.25 = $625
   Step 2: total expenses: $2,500 × 0.33 = $825
   $825 − $625 = __________

   Answer: $200 other than PITI

ANNUAL INTEREST RATE	YEARS TO FULLY AMORTIZE LOAN 15	20	25	30
6.00	8.44	7.17	6.45	6.00
6.50	8.71	7.46	6.75	6.32
6.75	8.85	7.60	6.91	6.49
7.00	8.99	7.75	7.07	6.65
7.25	9.13	7.90	7.23	6.82
7.50	9.27	8.06	7.39	6.99
7.75	9.41	8.21	7.55	7.16
8.00	9.56	8.36	7.72	7.34
8.25	9.70	8.52	7.88	7.51
8.50	9.85	8.68	8.05	7.69
8.75	9.99	8.84	8.22	7.87
9.00	10.14	9.00	8.39	8.05
9.25	10.29	9.16	8.56	8.23
9.50	10.44	9.32	8.74	8.41
9.75	10.59	9.49	8.91	8.59
10.00	10.75	9.65	9.09	8.78

Note: The above is an abbreviated amortization chart intended for example. It is used to estimate the monthly principal and interest payment by multiplying the mortgage rate. The monthly payment (multiplier) is shown per thousand therefore the total principal is first divided by 1000. For example, a principal of \$150,000 at 6.50% for 15 years = 8.71 × 150 = \$1,306.50 principal and interest per month. A mortgage calculator or software is also used to compute principal and interest payments.

FIGURE 16.2
An abbreviated amortization chart.

Amortization

Many mortgages are paid through a type of installment plan each month known as *amortization.* A portion of each payment is applied first to the interest and the remainder then reduces the principal. Amortization charts (see Figure 16.2) and amortization tables (Table 16.2) are used to compute the payout of the mortgage. To use the amortization chart, two factors must be known: the interest rate and the term of the loan. Most real estate professionals rely on financial calculators or computer programs to compute amortized mortgage payments.

Figure 16.2 illustrates the payments for a mortgage based on a certain interest rate and number of years for payout. Figure 16.2 does not separate interest and principal, nor is it based on a specific mortgage amount as is the amortization table in Table 16.2.

Balloon mortgages

One type of mortgage payment arrangement is the *balloon mortgage.* This payment arrangement provides for installment payments that are not enough to pay off the principal and interest over the term of the mortgage. Therefore, the final payment, called a balloon payment, is substantially larger than any previous payment. A balloon mortgage is also known as a *partially amortized mortgage* because the loan does not amortize out at the due date.

Sometimes, a balloon mortgage may have payment based upon a longer term, for example 15 years, and then the remaining balance has to be paid over a shorter term, for example, one year.

TABLE 16.2 An amortization table.

Amortization Table

Initial Data

LOAN DATA		TABLE DATA	
Loan amount:	$300,000.00	Table starts at date:	
Annual interest rate:	7.00%	or at payment number:	1
Term in years:	15		
Payments per year:	12		
First payment due:	1/1/04		

PERIODIC PAYMENT

Entered payment:	$2,650.00	*The table uses the calculated periodic payment amount unless you enter a value for "Entered payment".*
Calculated payment:		

CALCULATIONS

Use payment of:	$2,650.00	Beginning balance at payment 1:	300,000.00
1st payment in table:	1	Cumulative interest prior to payment 1:	0.00

Table

No.	Payment Date	Beginning Balance	Interest	Principal	Ending Balance	Cumulative Interest
1	1/1/04	300,000.00	1,750.00	900.00	299,100.00	1,750.00
2	2/1/04	299,100.00	1,744.75	905.25	298,194.75	3,494.75
3	3/1/04	298,194.75	1,739.47	910.53	297,284.22	5,234.22
4	4/1/04	297,284.22	1,734.16	915.84	296,368.38	6,968.38
5	5/1/04	296,368.38	1,728.82	921.18	295,447.19	8,697.19
6	6/1/04	295,447.19	1,723.44	926.56	294,520.63	10,420.63
7	7/1/04	294,520.63	1,718.04	931.96	293,588.67	12,138.67
8	8/1/04	293,588.67	1,712.60	937.40	292,651.27	13,851.27
9	9/1/04	292,651.27	1,707.13	942.87	291,708.40	15,558.40
10	10/1/04	291,708.40	1,701.63	948.37	290,760.04	17,260.04
11	11/1/04	290,760.04	1,696.10	953.90	289,806.14	18,956.14
12	12/1/04	289,806.14	1,690.54	959.46	288,846.67	20,646.67
13	1/1/05	288,846.67	1,684.94	965.06	287,881.61	22,331.61
14	2/1/05	287,881.61	1,679.31	970.69	286,910.92	24,010.92
15	3/1/05	286,910.92	1,673.65	976.35	285,934.57	25,684.57
16	4/1/05	285,934.57	1,667.95	982.05	284,952.52	27,352.52
17	5/1/05	284,952.52	1,662.22	987.78	283,964.74	29,014.74
18	6/1/05	283,964.74	1,656.46	993.54	282,971.20	30,671.20
19	7/1/05	282,971.20	1,650.67	999.33	281,971.87	32,321.87
20	8/1/05	281,971.87	1,644.84	1,005.16	280,966.71	33,966.71
21	9/1/05	280,966.71	1,638.97	1,011.03	279,955.68	35,605.68
22	10/1/05	279,955.68	1,633.07	1,016.93	278,938.75	37,238.75
23	11/1/05	278,938.75	1,627.14	1,022.86	277,915.90	38,865.90
24	12/1/05	277,915.90	1,621.18	1,028.82	276,887.07	40,487.07

PRORATIONS AT CLOSING

Prorations at closing involve the division between seller and buyer of annual real property taxes, rents, homeowner's association dues, and other items that may have been paid or must be paid. Proration is the process of dividing something into respective shares.

In prorating calculations, the best method is first to draw a time line with the beginning, ending, and date of proration, then decide which part of the time line you need to use. In calculating prorations for closing statements, the amount is figured to the day of closing. Therefore, in problems that require calculating a daily rate, the monthly rate is divided by the number of days in the month.

An alternative approach to proration is to reduce all costs to a daily basis. Assuming 30 days in every month and 12 months per year, we can assume 360 days per year for our purposes (and most standard exams). One other rule to remember in prorating various costs for closing statements is that the day of closing is charged to the seller. In the "real world," be sure to check with an attorney about local customs regarding prorations.

1. In preparing a statement for a closing to be held August 14, a real estate broker determines that the annual real property taxes in the amount of $360 have not been paid. What will the broker put in the buyer's statement as her entry for real property taxes?

Solution: $360 ÷ 12 = $30/mo

$30/mo ÷ 30 days = $1/day

7 mos × $30 = $210

$210 + $14 = $224

Answer: $224 buyer credit (this is the seller's share of the real property taxes to cover the 7 months and 14 days of the tax year during which he owned the property).

2. A sale is closed on September 15. The buyer is assuming the seller's mortgage, which has an outstanding balance of $32,000 as of the date of closing. The annual interest rate is 8%, and the interest is paid in arrears. What is the interest proration on the closing statements the broker prepares?

Solution: $32,000 × 0.08 = $2,560 annual interest

$2,560 ÷ 12 = $213.33 interest for September (rounded)

1/2 × $213.33 = $106.67 interest of ½ mo

or

$2,560 ÷ 24 = $106.67 interest for ½ mo

Answer: $106.67 buyer credit

$106.67 seller debit

Because the interest is paid in arrears, the buyer is required to pay the interest for the full month of September when making the scheduled monthly payment on October 1. Therefore, the buyer is credited with the seller's share of a half-month's interest for September in the amount of $106.67. The entry in the seller's closing statement is a debit in this amount.

Rates

Title Transfer Taxes (Revenue Stamps)

New York imposes a *real property transfer tax* on the conveyance of title to real property and requires the seller to pay this tax. The amount of tax is based on the consideration the seller receives in selling the property.

The amount of transfer tax charged on the purchase price in New York is at a rate of $4 per $1,000 of the purchase price. New York subtracts the amount of any mortgage being assumed, or "old money," and therefore charges the tax only on the "new money" brought into the transaction, above the amount of the assumed loan.

New York City real property transfer tax. In addition to the New York State transfer tax, for the sale of residential property, New York City imposes an additional transfer tax of 1% of the selling price. If the selling price is over $500,000, the New York City transfer tax is 1.425%. For other types of property, the rate is 1.425% of the selling price, and if the consideration is more than $500,000, the transfer tax is 2.625% (also see Chapter 8).

1. A property sold for $250,000 in Albany, New York. The purchaser assumed a $100,000 mortgage. What is the amount of transfer tax to be paid by the seller?

Solution: Transfer tax applies to $150,000 of new money.
Rate = $4.00 per thousand
Multiply new money × rate
$150,000 × .004 = $600

Answer: $600 transfer tax

Mortgage Recording Tax

In New York, the mortgage recording tax is three-quarters of a percent of the mortgage amount in certain counties. In counties where there is a regional transportation system, the amount is 1 percent. In this case, in the sale of one- to six-family residential properties, three-quarters of the mortgage recording tax typically is paid by the purchaser and one-quarter is paid by the lender. If there is no outside lender involved in the transaction, then the purchaser must pay the entire mortgage recording tax.

2. In a certain county in New York, the mortgage recording tax is at a rate of ¾% of the mortgage. The Santiagos have obtained a mortgage in the amount of $125,000. What is the amount of mortgage recording tax that they will have to pay?

Solution: Rate = ¾% of the total mortgage
Rate = .0075% of the total mortgage
.0075 × 125,000 = $937.50

Answer: $937.50 mortgage recording tax

AD VALOREM PROPERTY TAXES

Certain terminology applies to real property tax valuation. Assessed value is the value established by a tax assessor. The assessed value usually is a percentage of the estimated market value of the property and may be up to 100% of market value. The amount of tax is calculated by multiplying the assessed value by the tax rate, which is expressed either in dollars per $100 of assessed value or in mills (one mill is one-tenth of a cent) per $1,000 of assessed value. The tax rate is determined by the amount of the tax levy. The rate must be sufficient to provide the revenue required to accomplish the budgetary requirements of the local government unit. The formula for calculating property tax is:

assessed value × tax rate = annual taxes

1. If the assessed value of the property is $80,000 and the tax value is 100% of the assessed value, what is the annual tax if the rate is $1.50 per $100?

Solution: assessed value × tax rate = annual taxes

$\$80{,}000 \times \frac{\$1.50}{100} =$ ________

product missing: multiply

$80,000 × 0.0150 = $1,200

Answer: $1,200 annual taxes

2. A property sells at the assessed value. The annual real property tax is $588.80 at a tax rate of $1.15 per $100 of tax value. The property is taxed at 80% of assessed value. What is the selling price?

Solution: assessed value × tax rate = annual taxes

________ $\times \frac{\$1.15}{100} = \$588.80$

factor missing: divide

$588.80 ÷ 0.0115 = $51,200 assessed value

assessed value is 80% of selling price

$51,200 = 0.80 × ________

factor missing: divide

$51,200 ÷ 0.80 = selling price

Answer: $64,000 selling price

3. If the assessed value of property is $68,000 and the annual tax paid is $850, what is the tax rate?

Solution: assessed value × tax rate = annual taxes

$68,000 × ______ = $850

factor missing: divide, then convert to per $100 of value

$850 ÷ $68,000 = $1.25

Answer: $1.25 tax rate per $100 of tax value

4. If the market value is $70,000, the tax rate is 120 mills, and the assessment is 80%, what is the semiannual tax bill? (To calculate mills, divide by 1,000.)

Solution: assessed value = 0.80 × $70,000

assessed value = $56,000

assessed value × tax rate = annual taxes

$56,000 × 120 mills = ________

annual tax bill = $6,720

semiannual tax bill = $6,720 ÷ 2

Answer: $3,360 semiannual tax bill

5. The real property tax revenue required by a small hamlet is $140,800. The assessed valuation of the taxable property is $12,800,000. The tax value is 100% of the assessed value. What must the tax rate be per $100 of assessed valuation to generate the necessary revenue?

Solution: assessed value × tax rate = annual taxes

$12,800,000 × ________ = $140,800

factor missing: divide and convert to per $100 of value

$140,800 ÷ $12,800,000 = $0.011 (rate per $1.00)

$0.011 × 100 = $1.10 per $100

Answer: $1.10 tax rate per $100 of assessed value

REAL ESTATE INVESTMENT

Analysis of Income, Rate, and Value

Income is defined as *the amount of money one receives.* The most common application of income is commission, rents, or other moneys in your pocket. Although income can be received on a monthly basis, for purposes of this section, all monthly income must be converted to annual income. To do that, simply multiply the amount by 12 if it is not already converted to the annual figure. **Gross income** is *income received without subtracting expenses.* **Net operating income** is *gross income less operating expenses.*

Rate is defined as *a percentage.* The most common application of rate will be an interest rate, a capitalization rate, or a commission rate. Once again, remember that rate is always calculated on an annual percentage.

Value is defined as *the total amount of worth or cost of the unit.* The most common applications of value will be the principal balance of a mortgage and the sale price of a house.

In calculating either income, rate, or value, you must know two of the three variables to solve for the third. For example, if the sale price of a home is $400,000 (the value), and the commission rate is 6% (the rate), what is the income? To solve this, one could simply multiply $400,000 by 6% and get the answer. This is a fairly simple application, but it can be achieved in the same way using IRV.

To calculate IRV, use this table:

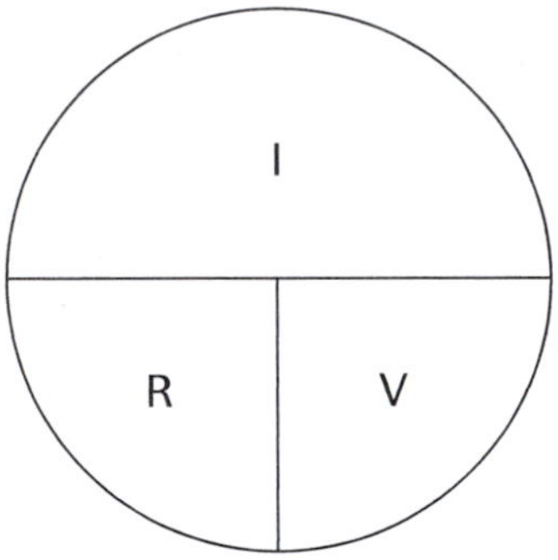

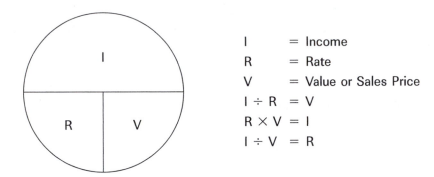

I = Income
R = Rate
V = Value or Sales Price
$I \div R = V$
$R \times V = I$
$I \div V = R$

For example, the net monthly income of a five-unit apartment building is $2,250. The capitalization rate the lender uses is 7%. Use the IRV formula to find the value of the building.

To solve for this, using IRV, you would multiply the income by 12 (to bring it to an annual figure) and divide by the rate: $2,250 × 12 = $27,000 ÷ .07 = $385,714.

Profit/Loss on Sale of Real Estate

Profit or loss is always based upon the amount of money invested in the property.

The formula for profit is:

investment × percent of profit = dollars in profit

The formula for loss is:

investment × percent of loss = dollars lost

1. Edward buys a house for investment purposes for $175,000. He sells it six months later for $200,000 with no expenditures for fix-up or repair. What is Edward's percentage of profit?

Solution: investment × percentage of profit = dollars in profit
$175,000 × ________ = $25,000

factor missing: divide and convert decimal to percentage
$25,000 ÷ $175,000 = ________

Answer: 7% (rounded) for the six months; 14% (rounded) for the year.

2. Devora purchases some land in 2000 for $35,000. She puts up a fence in 2002 costing her $15,500. In 2004, she sells the land for $46,000. What is her percentage of loss?

Solution: investment × percentage lost = dollars in loss
$50,500 × ______ = $4,500
factor missing: divide and convert decimal to percentage
$4,500 ÷ $50,500 = _____

Answer: 8.91%, rounded to 9%

3. An owner purchases his home at 8% below market value. He then sells the property for the full market value. What is the rate of profit?

Solution: market value = 100%
100% − 8% = 92% purchase price
8% ÷ 92% = rate of profit
0.08 ÷ 0.92 = ________

Answer: 8.7% profit

Capitalization

The *capitalization rate* is the percentage of the investment the owner will receive back each year from the net income from the property. This rate is based upon the dollars invested and the annual net income from the property.

1. In appraising a small produce store, the appraiser establishes that the store produces an annual net income of $97,500. The appraiser determines the capitalization rate to be 13%. What should be the appraiser's estimate of market value for this business?

Solution: investment × rate = annual net income or value
________ × 13% = $97,500
factor missing: divide
$97,500 ÷ 0.13 = ________

Answer: $750,000 market value

CHAPTER REVIEW

Circle the letter that best answers each question and then check the Answer Key at the end of this chapter. *Note: The review problems presented here are divided according to subject matter in the applicable chapters in the textbook.*

Commissions and Sales (Chapter 2, Law of Agency)

1. A real estate broker earns a commission of $4,900 at a rate of 7%. What is the selling price of the property?
   A. $24,000
   B. $44,000
   C. $65,000
   D. $70,000

2. A real estate salesperson earns $24,000 per year. If she receives 60% of the 7% commissions paid to her firm on her sales, what is her monthly dollar volume of sales?
   A. $33,333.33
   B. $45,000.00
   C. $47,619.08
   D. $90,000.00

3. An owner lists a property for sale with a broker. At what price must the property be sold to net the owner $7,000 after paying a 7% commission and satisfying the existing $48,000 mortgage?
   A. $49,354
   B. $56,750
   C. $57,750
   D. $59,140

4. A triangular lot measures 350 feet along the street and 425 feet deep on the side perpendicular to the street. If a broker sells the lot for $0.75 per square foot and his commission rate is 9%, what is the amount of commission earned?
   A. $ 5,020.31
   B. $ 6,693.75
   C. $10,040.63
   D. $14,875.00

5. A broker's commission is 8% of the first $75,000 of the sales price of a house and 6% of the amount over $75,000. What is the total selling price of the property if the broker receives a total commission of $9,000?
   A. $ 79,500
   B. $ 93,000
   C. $105,000
   D. $125,000

6. A buyer pays $45,000 for a lot. Five years later she puts it on the market for 20% more than she originally paid. The lot eventually sells for 10% less than the asking price. At what price is the house sold?
   A. $44,100
   B. $48,600
   C. $49,500
   D. $54,000

Prorations (Chapter 8, Title Closing and Costs)

7. A sale is closed on February 12. The buyer is assuming the seller's mortgage, which has an outstanding balance of $28,000 as of the closing date. The last mortgage payment was made February 1. The annual interest rate is 7.75%, and interest is paid in arrears. What interest proration appears in the buyer's closing statement?
   A. $ 72.36 credit
   B. $ 77.52 credit
   C. $180.83 debit
   D. $253.19 credit

8. A buyer is to assume a seller's existing loan with an outstanding balance of $20,000 as of the date of closing. The interest rate is 6%, and payments are made in arrears. Closing is set for November 10. What will be the entry in the seller's closing statement?
   A. $33.30 credit
   B. $33.30 debit
   C. $22.00 debit
   D. $22.00 credit

Principal, Interest, Points (Chapter 9, Real Estate Finance [Mortgages])

9. If the monthly interest payment due on a mortgage on December 1 is $570 and the annual interest rate is 6%, what is the outstanding mortgage balance?
   A. $ 61,560.00
   B. $ 63,333.33
   C. $114,000.00
   D. $131,158.00

10. A house sells for $165,000. If the seller agrees to pay 5.5% discount points on a VA loan of $155,000, and the broker's fee is 6%, how much will the seller net?
    A. $146,575
    B. $148,275
    C. $156,575
    D. $158,375

11. On February 1 a mortgagor makes a $638 payment on her mortgage, at the rate of 6.5%. The mortgagee allocates $500 to payment of interest. What is the principal balance due on the mortgage on February 1?
    A. $ 82,450.38
    B. $ 92,307.69
    C. $ 97,402.47
    D. $102,344.89

Area Calculations: Land (Chapter 10, Land Use Regulations)

12. A rectangular lot measures 40 yards deep and has a frontage of 80 feet. How many acres does the lot contain?
    A. 0.07
    B. 0.21
    C. 0.22
    D. 0.70

13. The owner of a rectangular unimproved parcel of land measuring 600 feet wide (front) by 145.2 feet long is offered $15 per front foot or $4,000 per acre. What is the amount of the higher offer?
    A. $2,187
    B. $7,680
    C. $8,000
    D. $9,000

Area Calculations: Improvements to Property (Chapter 11, Construction)

14. The outside dimensions of a rectangular house are 35 feet by 26.5 feet. If the walls are all 9 inches thick, what is the square footage of the interior?
    A. 827.5 sq ft
    B. 837.5 sq ft
    C. 927.5 sq ft
    D. 947.7 sq ft

15. A property owner is having a concrete patio poured at the rear of the house. The patio is to be rectangular and will be 4 yards by 8 yards. The patio is to be 6 inches thick. The labor cost for the project is $3.50 per square yard, and the material cost is $1.50 per cubic foot. What will be the total cost of the patio?
    A. $112
    B. $198
    C. $328
    D. $552

Ad Valorem Taxes (Chapter 10, Land Use Regulations; Chapter 12, Valuation Process)

16. A parcel of land is sold at market value. The market value and the tax value are the same. If the tax value is 100% of assessment value, the tax rate is $1.50, and the annual tax is $540, what is the selling price of the land?
    A. $24,000
    B. $27,700
    C. $36,000
    D. $81,000

17. If the tax value is 100% of the assessed value and the assessed value is $63,250, what are the annual taxes if the rate is $2.10 per $100?
    A. $ 132.83
    B. $1,328.25
    C. $3,011.90
    D. $3,320.16

18. A lot was assessed for 60% of market value and taxed at a rate of $3.75 per $100 of assessed value. Five years later the same tax rate and assessment rate still exist, but annual taxes have increased by $750. By how much has the dollar value of the property increased?
    A. $ 8,752.75
    B. $20,000.00
    C. $33,333.33
    D. $38,385.82

19. A house has an assessed value of $142,000. The property is taxed at 80% of assessed value at a rate of $2.12 per $100. If the assessed valuation is to be increased by 18%, what is the amount of taxes to be paid on the property?
    A. $2,638.49
    B. $2,841.82
    C. $3,119.84
    D. $4,232.50

20. A real estate sale closes on February 20. The real property taxes have not been paid. Assessed value of the property is $67,500, and the tax value is 80% of assessed value. The tax rate is $1.50 per $100 of tax value. What is the proper entry on the seller's settlement statement regarding real property taxes?
    A. $112.50 credit
    B. $112.50 debit
    C. $697.50 credit
    D. $697.50 debit

Profit and Loss (Chapter 7, Leases; Chapter 12, Valuation Process)

21. A percentage lease stipulates a minimum rent of $1,200 per month and 3% of the lessee's annual gross sales over $260,000. The total rent paid by the end of the year is $16,600. What is the lessee's gross business income for the year?
    A. $73,333.33
    B. $260,000.00
    C. $333,333.33
    D. $553,333.33

22. A group of investors purchase two tracts of land. They pay $48,000 for the first tract. The first tract costs 80% of the cost of the second tract. What is the cost of the second tract?
    A. $9,600
    B. $28,800
    C. $60,000
    D. $125,000

23. A lease specifies a minimum monthly rental of $700 plus 3% of all business over $185,000. If the lessee does a gross business of $220,000, how much rent is paid that year?
    A. $6,000
    B. $9,450
    C. $11,550
    D. $12,600

24. A parking lot containing 2 acres nets $12,000 per year. The owner wishes to retire and sell his parking lot for an amount that will net him $12,000 per year by investing the proceeds of the sale at 8½% per annum. What must the selling price be to accomplish the owner's objective?
    A. $96,000
    B. $102,000
    C. $120,000
    D. $141,176

25. A building under rent control allows a property owner to increase the rent on apartments by 2.25% of the cost of improvements. The landlord spends $1,200 per unit for improvements, then raises the rent from $380 to $415. By how much has the owner exceeded the guidelines?
    A. $8
    B. $15
    C. $26
    D. $35

ANSWER KEY

Commissions and Sales

1. sales price × rate = total commission
   _______ × 7% = $4,900
   factor missing: divide
   $4,900 ÷ 0.07 = $70,000, or (D)
2. 24,000 is 60% of total commission
   $24,000 = 60% × total commission
   factor missing: divide
   24,000 ÷ 0.60 = $40,000
   sales price × rate of commission = total commission
   _______ × 7% = $40,000
   factor missing: divide
   $40,000 ÷ 0.07 = $571,429 per year in sales
   divide by 12 to get monthly volume of sales
   $571,429 ÷ 12 = $47,619.08, or (C)
3. $7,000 + $48,000 = $55,000
   100% − 7% commission = 93%
   $55,000 ÷ 0.93 = $59,140 (rounded), or (D)
4. area of a triangle = 0.5 × base × height
   0.5 × 350 ft × 425 ft = 74,375 sq ft
   74,375 sq ft × 0.75/sq ft = $55,781.25 sales price
   $55,781.25 × 0.09 = $5,020.31, or (A)
5. $75,000 × 0.08 = $6,000 commission on first $75,000
   $9,000 − $6,000 = $3,000 commission on price over $75,000
   sales price × rate = commission
   _______ × 6% = $3,000
   Factor missing: divide
   $3,000 ÷ 0.06 = $50,000 sales over $75,000
   $75,000 + $50,000 = $125,000, or (D)
6. $45,000 × 1.20 (120%) = $54,000 asking price
   $54,000 × 0.90 = $48,600 sold price, or (B)

Prorations

7. $28,000 × 0.0775 = $2,170/yr
   $2,170 ÷ 12 mos = $180.83/mo
   $180.83 ÷ 30 days = $6.03/day
   $6.03 × 12 days = $72.36 used portion, or (A)
   (as payments are made in arrears, this amount is a credit to buyer and a debit to seller)
8. loan balance × rate of interest = annual interest
   $20,000 × 0.06 = _______
   product missing: multiply
   annual interest = $1,200
   $1,200 ÷ 12 mos = $100/mo
   $100 ÷ 30 = $3.33/day
   10 × $3.33 = $33.30 debit to seller, or (B)

Principal, Interest, Points

9. loan balance × rate of interest = annual interest
   _______ × 6% = ($570 × 12)
   factor missing: divide
   $6,840 ÷ 0.06 = $114,000, or (C)
10. expenses of sale and closing are points and commission
    points: loan × number of points as percentage = dollars in points
    $155,000 × 0.055 = _______
    product missing: multiply
    dollars in points are $8,525
    commission: sales price × rate of commission = total commission
    $165,000 × 0.06 = _______
    product missing: multiply
    total commission = $9,900
    $9,900 + $8,525 = total expenses
    $165,000 − $18,425 = $146,575 net to seller, or (A)
11. loan balance × rate = annual interest
    _______ × 6.5% = $6,000
    factor missing: divide
    $6,000 ÷ 0.065 = $92,307.69, or (B)

Area Calculations: Land

12. 40 yd × 3 ft/yd = 120 ft
    120 ft × 80 ft = 9,600 sq ft
    9,600 sq ft ÷ 43,560 sq ft = 0.22 acres, or (C)
13. 600 ft × 145.2 ft = 87,120 sq ft
    87,120 sq ft ÷ 43,560 sq ft/acre = 2 acres
    2 acres × $4,000 = $8,000 acreage basis
    $15 × 600 ft = $9,000 front-foot basis, or (D)

Area Calculations: Improvements to Property

14. 9 inches thick on each of two ends = 1.5 ft
    35 ft − 1.5 ft = 33.5 ft
    26.5 ft − 1.5 ft = 25 ft
    33.5 ft × 25 ft = 837.5 sq ft, or (B)
15. 4 yd × 8 yd = 32 sq yd
    32 sq yd × $3.50/sq yd = $112 labor costs
    0.5 ft × 12 ft × 24 ft = 144 cu ft
    144 cu ft × $1.50 = $216 material costs
    $112 + $216 = $328, or (C)

Ad Valorem Taxes

16. assessed value × tax rate = annual tax
    $\_\_\_\_\_\_ \times \frac{\$1.50}{100} = \$540$
    factor missing: divide
    $540 ÷ 0.0150 = $36,000, or (C)
17. assessed value × tax rate = annual tax
    $63,250 × 0.0210 = ______
    product missing: multiply
    annual taxes: $1,328.25, or (B)
18. $750 increase ÷ $3.75 = 200 ($100 units)
    200 ($100 units) × $100/unit = $20,000 tax value
    $20,000 ÷ 0.60 = $33,333.33, or (C)
19. $142,000 × 1.18 = $167,560 increased valuation
    $167,560 × 0.80 = $134,048 new tax basis
    assessed value × tax rate = annual taxes
    $134,048 × 2.12/100 = ______
    product missing: multiply
    $134,048 × 0.0212 = $2,841.82 (rounded), or (B)
20. seller owes for 30 + 20 days = 50 days
    $67,500 × 0.80 = $54,000 tax value
    tax value × rate = annual taxes
    $54,000 × 0.0150 = $810
    $810 ÷ 12 = $67.50/mo
    $67.50 ÷ 30 = $2.25/day
    $2.25 × 50 = $112.50 debit to seller, or (B)

Profit and Loss

21. 12 mos × 1,200 = $14,400 minimum annual rent
    $16,600 − 14,400 = $2,200 above minimum
    $2,200 is 3% of what amount?
    $2,200 = 3% × ______
    Factor missing: divide
    $2,200 ÷ .03 = $73,333.33 over $260,000
    $260,000 + $73,333.33 = $333,333.33 total sales, or (C)
22. 80% of second tract = first tract
    .8 × ? (2nd tract) = $48,000
    2nd tract = $48,000 ÷ .8
    2nd tract = $60,000, or (C)
23. $700/mo x 12 mo = $8,400/year base rent
    $220,000 − $185,000 = $35,000 (earnings over $185,000)
    $35,000 × .03 = $1,050
    $8,400 + $1,050 = $9,450, or (B)
24. Investment × rate of return = annual net income
    ______ × 8½% = $12,000
    Factor missing: divide
    $12,000 ÷ .085 = $141,176 (rounded), or (D)
25. $1,200 × .0225 = $27 maximum allowable increase
    $415 − $380 = $35 increase
    $35 − $27 = $8, or (A)

Appendix

The following questions are weighted in number according to the percentage of classroom hours allotted for each topic. Note that this is a diagnostic exam to help you pinpoint areas in which you may need further study. The New York State licensing exam contains 50 questions.

I. License Law and Regulations (3 hours) 7 questions

1. Which of the following statements about license laws is incorrect?
   A. license laws are an exercise of the police power of the state
   B. the purpose of the license laws is to protect the general public
   C. obtaining a license is a privilege and not an automatic right
   D. the federal government establishes the license laws

2. In New York, an individual may obtain a salesperson license at age:
   A. 17
   B. 18
   C. 19
   D. 21

3. A salesperson licensee may receive commissions from which of the following?
   A. cooperating broker
   B. buyer
   C. seller
   D. employing broker

4. Which of the following is a legal activity according to the license law?
   A. failing to submit all written offers to the listing seller
   B. advising a prospective buyer that the seller will take a certain price for a property that is less than the listed price
   C. failing to obtain an accepted offer during the term of the listing
   D. failing to account for all funds belonging to other persons that come into the licensee's hands

5. Which of the following does NOT apply to a salesperson's license?
   A. it is issued to and maintained in the custody of the broker with whom the salesperson is associated
   B. it need not be prominently displayed by the broker
   C. it authorizes the salesperson to work under a broker and not independently
   D. it authorizes the salesperson to work in a reciprocal state without broker sponsorship

Sample Salesperson Exam

6. In the process of preparing an offer for commercial property, a broker was asked by two potential purchasers to recommend the most beneficial way for them to take title to the property. Which of the following should the broker recommend?
   A. tenants in common
   B. in severalty
   C. ask an attorney
   D. ask the listing broker

7. Upon the broker's recommendation, a seller accepted an offer that was 8% below the listed price. The broker did not disclose to the listing seller that the buyer was the broker's brother-in-law. Which of the following is correct?
   A. the broker violated his obligations as agent of the seller
   B. the fact that the buyer is related to the broker is not required to be divulged to the seller
   C. the broker has done nothing wrong as long as he doesn't take any commission
   D. the broker has done nothing wrong if the appraised value of the home matches the offered price

II. Law of Agency (8 hours) 15 questions

8. Which of the following types of listing contracts gives the broker commission entitlement if anyone sells the listed property during the listing term?
   A. net
   B. open
   C. exclusive agency
   D. exclusive right to sell

9. A real estate salesperson advises a prospective buyer that the property the buyer is considering is scheduled for annexation into the city limits. This disclosure constitutes which of the following?
   A. disloyalty to principal
   B. misrepresentation
   C. required disclosure to buyer
   D. violation of disclosure of information by agent

10. After inspecting a property, a prospective buyer tells the salesperson that she will not pay the listed price of $235,000. Knowing that his client, the owner, is eager to sell, the salesperson suggests that the prospective buyer make an offer of $210,000. Which of the following statements is correct?
    A. the salesperson is violating his obligation as a special agent
    B. because the salesperson knows the owner is eager to sell, he is acting correctly
    C. the salesperson is violating his obligations as a universal agent
    D. the prospective buyer can be found guilty of conversion

11. A salesperson receives two offers for a listed property within a 10-minute period. One offer is 2% less than the listed price, and the other is 6% less than the listed price. The salesperson should present to the seller:
    A. neither offer
    B. both offers
    C. the highest offer
    D. the lowest offer

12. A salesperson associated with Lighthouse Realty effects a sale of property listed in the MLS with a universal offer of subagency by Point Hazard Realty. In this transaction the salesperson is a subagent of which of the following?
    A. seller
    B. Lighthouse Realty
    C. buyer
    D. seller and buyer

13. According to the Real Property law, a broker may:
    A. never accept compensation from more than one party to a transaction.
    B. only accept compensation directly from a principal
    C. never split commissions with brokers from other states
    D. accept compensation from more than one party to a transaction only with the full knowledge and consent of all parties to the transaction

14. An agent is a:
    A. fiduciary
    B. principal
    C. consideration
    D. contractor

15. An owner lists his property with three brokerage firms. In each case he retains the right to sell the property himself without being obligated to pay a commission. The type of listing contract is called:
    A. exclusive right to sell
    B. open
    C. multiple
    D. net

16. A listing contract creates an agency relationship in which the:
    A. broker is a general agent
    B. seller is the principal
    C. seller is a general agent
    D. broker is the principal

17. The type of listing that ensures the real estate agent a commission if the agent sells the property and no commission if the seller sells the property is called a(n):
    A. net listing
    B. exclusive right to sell listing
    C. exclusive agency
    D. multiple listing

18. When a real estate agent or seller conceals a known defect, this is an example of:
    A. mutual mistake
    B. unintentional misrepresentation
    C. positive misrepresentation
    D. mistake of law

19. When a real estate firm attempts to represent both the buyer and seller in the same transactions, what type of agency has arisen?
    A. single agency
    B. dual agency
    C. broker agency
    D. seller agency

20. According to New York Real Property Law, listing agreements for one- to four-unit residential property must be accompanied by a(n):
   A. disclosure regarding dual agency form
   B. exclusive right to sell agreement
   C. payment of a partial fee or commission to the listing agent
   D. informed consent to dual agency form

21. A written listing agreement is an example of:
   A. implied agency
   B. ratification
   C. express agency
   D. estoppel

22. If all broker members of a particular real estate board agree to charge a commission of not less than 10% of the purchase price of a property, this is:
   A. a violation of antitrust law
   B. a violation of agency law
   C. allowable under New York law
   D. allowable under New York law in the sale of commercial property only

III. Estates and Interests (2 hours) 4 questions

23. The owner(s) of real property may NOT hold title as:
   A. tenants in common
   B. lessees
   C. owner in severalty
   D. joint tenants

24. An estate created for the life of a person other than the life tenant is called a life estate:
   A. in remainder
   B. pur autre vie
   C. by dower
   D. in reversion

25. Freehold estates that are not inheritable are called:
   A. defeasible estates
   B. leasehold estates
   C. life estates
   D. fee simple estates

26. A piece of personal property that has become real property by permanent attachment is called a(n):
   A. fixture
   B. trade fixture
   C. chattel
   D. emblement

IV. Liens and Easements (1.5 hours) 3 questions

27. Which of the following statements is correct?
   A. an easement provides right of possession
   B. an easement in gross has no servient tenement
   C. an easement is a fixture to real estate
   D. an appurtenant easement can be obtained by necessity

28. Which of the following is a right in the land of another by the owner of adjoining land?
   A. profit
   B. easement appurtenant
   C. license
   D. easement in gross

29. Liens that are given the highest priority are:
   A. real property tax liens
   B. judgment liens
   C. income tax liens
   D. mortgage liens

V. Deeds (1.5 hours) 3 questions

30. Which of the following provides the grantee with the greatest assurance of title?
    A. bargain and sale deed
    B. deed of gift
    C. full covenant and warranty deed
    D. grant deed

31. Which of the following is a benefit of recording a deed?
    A. it prevents any liens from being filed against the property
    B. it protects the grantee against the grantee's creditors
    C. it protects the grantee against future conveyances by the grantor
    D. it makes a mortgage lien subordinate

32. Of the following types of deeds, which provides the grantee with the least assurance of title?
    A. bargain and sale
    B. quitclaim
    C. grant
    D. full covenant and warranty

VI. Contracts (2 hours) 4 questions

33. Which of the following clauses in an accepted offer to purchase protects buyers from losing their earnest money in the event financing is not obtained?
    A. habendum
    B. contingency
    C. defeasance
    D. subordination

34. Mutual promises supply which of the following?
    A. consideration
    B. competency
    C. contingency
    D. collateral

35. Sara Seller is satisfied with all of the terms of an offer to purchase her property from Bill Buyer except the date of possession, which she changes from April 9 to April 10. Which of the following is correct?
    A. Sara's acceptance creates a valid contract
    B. Sara cannot make a counteroffer
    C. Sara can always accept Bill's original offer if the April 10 date is not accepted
    D. Sara has counteroffered Bill's offer

36. Which of the following is NOT a remedy upon breach of the contract?
    A. specific performance
    B. liquidated damages
    C. estoppel
    D. compensatory damages

VII. Leases (2 hours) 4 questions

37. When a lessee installs trade fixtures, these are:
    A. a permanent part of the real estate
    B. owned by the lessor
    C. the personal property of the lessee
    D. real property

38. Which of the following is NOT provided by a lease?
    A. legal title to the property
    B. equitable title to the property for the duration of the lease
    C. exclusive right to possession and control of the property
    D. quiet enjoyment of the property during the term of the lease

39. An action or inaction by the lessor resulting in the property being unusable is:
    A. actual eviction
    B. assignment
    C. percentage lease
    D. constructive eviction

40. A tenant who breaches the lease but refuses to vacate the premises is a:
    A. trespasser
    B. tenant at will
    C. tenant at sufferance
    D. periodic tenant

VIII. Title Closing and Costs (1 hour) 3 questions

41. A buyer purchased a rental property and closed the transaction on July 20. The tenant had paid rent for the month of July in the amount of $540 on July 1. The rent should be shown as a:
    A. debit to buyer of $180
    B. debit to seller of $180
    C. debit to seller of $360
    D. credit to buyer of $360

42. The amount of a purchase money mortgage appears in the closing statement as:
    A. seller credit only
    B. buyer debit only
    C. seller debit; buyer credit
    D. seller credit; buyer debit

43. The amount of earnest money deposit appears on closing statements as a:
    A. credit to buyer
    B. debit to seller
    C. credit to seller
    D. debit to buyer

IX. Real Estate Finance (Mortgages) (5 hours) 12 questions

44. Which of the following most accurately describes the major purpose of a mortgage?
    A. to secure the payment of a note
    B. to convey a title to the trustee
    C. to provide for equity of redemption
    D. to prevent assumption

45. The acceleration clause provides for which of the following?
    A. equity of redemption
    B. prepayment penalty
    C. right of lender to require immediate payment of principal balance when borrower is in default
    D. alienation by borrower

46. Which of the following liens has priority over mortgage foreclosure sale proceeds?
    A. mortgage lien
    B. income tax lien
    C. real property tax lien
    D. mechanics' lien

47. An alienation clause makes a mortgage:
    A. defeasible
    B. unassumable
    C. incontestable
    D. adjustable

48. The mortgagee is the:
    A. lender
    B. borrower
    C. escrow agent
    D. purchaser

49. A mortgage that is subordinate to another mortgage is called a(n):
    A. first mortgage
    B. junior mortgage
    C. mortgage satisfaction
    D. negative amortization

50. A blanket mortgage usually contains which of the following?
    A. closed-end clause
    B. release clauses
    C. good faith estimate
    D. due-on-sale clause

51. Which of the following regulates the advertisement of credit terms available for a house offered for sale?
    A. RESPA
    B. Fannie Mae
    C. Equal Credit Opportunity Act
    D. Regulation Z

52. Brantley Buyer obtained an FHA-insured loan to purchase a home. The difference between the purchase price and the loan amount was $3,100. Which of the following statements about the $3,100 is correct?
    A. Brantley must pay this amount from his existing assets, borrow on the security of another asset such as his stocks, or acquire it as a bona fide gift from a close relative or friend
    B. Brantley may satisfy this amount by giving the seller a purchase money second mortgage
    C. Brantley may borrow the $3,100 from a relative at 6% interest
    D. Brantley may obtain the money by giving a lending institution a second mortgage

53. Brian and Betty Brown execute and deliver a $50,000 mortgage to Ajax Financial Associates at 10:30 A.M. on April 1. At 11:30 A.M. on the same day, they give a $10,000 mortgage pledging the same property to Fidelity Finance, Inc. Fidelity's mortgage is recorded at 1:10 P.M. that day, and the mortgage to Ajax is recorded at 1:42 P.M. on April 1. Which of the following statements about these mortgages is correct?
    A. because the mortgage to Ajax was executed and delivered first, Ajax holds the first mortgage
    B. Fidelity has the second mortgage because it was executed and delivered after the mortgage was given to Ajax
    C. Ajax and Fidelity will be co–first-mortgage holders because both mortgages were signed on the same day
    D. because the mortgage to Fidelity was recorded first, Fidelity holds the first mortgage

54. In the sale of their home, Van and Vera Vendor were required to satisfy their existing first mortgage of $40,000 so the buyers could obtain a first mortgage to finance their purchase. The Vendors' closing statement contained a debit in the amount of $800 because the Vendors paid off their loan prior to the full term. From this information, it can be determined that the Vendors' mortgage contained a(n):
    A. habendum clause
    B. alienation clause
    C. prepayment penalty clause
    D. defeasance clause

55. An agreement that is a financing instrument and a contract of sale is called a(n):
    A. option
    B. lease
    C. installment contract
    D. exclusive agency

X. Land Use Regulations (2 hours) 4 questions

56. Which of the following statements about zoning is correct?
    A. spot zoning is illegal in New York
    B. if a nonconforming structure is destroyed, it may be replaced by another nonconforming structure
    C. all nonconforming uses are illegal
    D. a preexisting nonconforming use requires a variance

57. Deed restrictions enforced by a suit for damages or by an injunction are:
    A. conditions
    B. conveyances
    C. covenants
    D. considerations

58. A property owner in a recently zoned area is permitted to continue to use his property in a manner that does not comply with the zoning requirements. This use is described as:
    A. spot zoning
    B. deviation
    C. nonconforming use
    D. private control of land use

59. The state took part of an owner's property for construction of a building. Which of the following statements about this event is correct?
    A. the property owner must be compensated for the difference in market value of the property before and after the partial condemnation
    B. the building to be constructed may be used for the sole use and benefit of a private corporation
    C. the property owner has no recourse to challenge the state's taking his property
    D. the value established is the average of the owner's desired value, the state's desired purchase price, and an independent appraisal

XI. Construction (3 hours) 7 questions

60. Written narratives that explain the building plan of a structure are known as:
    A. blueprints
    B. building specifications
    C. building codes
    D. building permits

61. Guidelines for safe and sanitary well water are provided in New York under regulations promulgated by the:
    A. Department of State
    B. Department of Energy
    C. Department of Health
    D. Office of General Services

62. The materials of a building that enclose the interior and through which heating and cooling pass in and out are known as the:
    A. foundation walls
    B. framing members
    C. facade
    D. building envelope

63. The most important foundation building block is the:
    A. lally column
    B. concrete slab
    C. footing
    D. foundation wall

64. The most common type of framing in residential construction is:
    A. platform framing
    B. post-and-beam framing
    C. ridgeform framing
    D. balloon framing

65. The amount of current or electricity that flows through a wire is called:
    A. voltage
    B. kilowatt strength
    C. amperage
    D. electromagnetic field

66. Of the types of foundations built in New York, the most common is:
    A. full basement
    B. slab-on-grade
    C. crawl space
    D. concrete block

XII. Valuation Process (3 hours) 7 questions

67. When listing real property for sale, a real estate agent should:
    A. do a comparative market analysis
    B. make an appraisal to estimate market value
    C. estimate residual income
    D. correlate reproduction cost

68. Which of the following is NOT included in a comparative market analysis?
    A. properties that have sold recently
    B. properties currently on the market
    C. properties sold at foreclosure
    D. recently expired listings

69. Which of the following will *decrease* a seller's chances of selling at market value?
    A. buyer and seller are equally motivated
    B. payment is made in cash or its equivalent
    C. a reasonable amount of time is allowed for exposure in the open market
    D. seller is eager to sell at any price

70. Comparative market analyses are based on the supposition that:
    A. many properties are exactly alike
    B. no two properties are exactly alike
    C. many properties are similar in quality, location, and utility
    D. the law of supply and demand governs comparable property selection

71. An arms length transaction implies:
    A. buyers and sellers who are not related to each other
    B. buyers and sellers who are related to another
    C. commercial transactions only
    D. a form of adjustable rate mortgage financing

72. The value of a property based on its utility to the owner or investor is called:
    A. value in use
    B. insurance value
    C. mortgage loan value
    D. assessed value

73. Which appraisal approach to value is the most similar to a comparative market analysis?
    A. cost approach
    B. income approach
    C. highest- and best-use analysis
    D. sales comparison approach

XIII. Human Rights and Fair Housing (4 hours) 10 questions

74. Which of the following properties, if rented, need NOT abide by the Federal Fair Housing Act of 1968?
    A. office space
    B. apartments
    C. single family houses
    D. duplexes

75. Which of the following is legally allowable according to the Fair Housing Act of 1968 ?
    A. discriminatory advertising
    B. use of brokerage services
    C. steering
    D. redlining

76. Inducing an owner to list property by telling the owner that people of a certain national origin are moving into the neighborhood is called:
    A. steering
    B. redlining
    C. blockbusting
    D. profiteering

77. Which of the following does NOT cause exemptions to the Fair Housing Act of 1968 to be lost?
    A. use of discriminatory advertising
    B. use of a broker
    C. use of a sign that states "Room for Rent"
    D. use of a REALTOR®

78. Which of the following is NOT exempted under the New York Human Rights Law?
    A. the sale of a single-family house by the owner
    B. the rental of a duplex by an owner who resides in the other unit
    C. the rental of rooms in a single-family house if the rental is made by an owner
    D. the rental of apartments in a building exclusively to persons 55 years or older

79. Redlining applies to which of the following?
    A. brokers
    B. developers
    C. lenders
    D. landlords

80. Which of the following is NOT covered under New York State Human Rights laws?
    A. discrimination in the sale or rental of commercial space
    B. age as a protected class
    C. marital status as a protected class
    D. citizenship status as a protected class

81. Real estate agents' directing prospective purchasers to integrated areas to avoid integration of nonintegrated areas is called:
    A. redlining
    B. blockbusting
    C. steering
    D. directing

82. The Fair Housing Amendments Act of 1988 added which of the following protected classes?
    A. sex
    B. creed
    C. familial status and disability
    D. alienage

83. The Supreme Court case, *Brown vs. the Board of Education,* was important because it:
    A. ruled that antitrust activities are illegal
    B. formed the basis of the Americans with Disabilities Act
    C. found that separate but equal facilities are unequal
    D. ruled that block by block zoning discriminates

XIV. Environmental Issues (3 hours) 7 questions

84. Lead is NOT found in which of the following places?
    A. drinking water
    B. soil around the home
    C. paint from either the exterior or interior of the home
    D. fabric-covered home furnishings

85. Which of the following substances contain fibrous particles that can irritate the lungs?
    A. radon
    B. freon
    C. chlordane
    D. asbestos

86. The importance of the New York State Environmental Quality Review Act is that it provides for:
    A. funding for environmental projects
    B. review of safe drinking water
    C. radon contingencies in real estate contracts
    D. environmental impact statements

87. Which of the following is NOT mandated under the Clean Air Act ?
    A. fines of $25,000 per day for violations of CFC disposal requirements
    B. a ban on production of CFCs since 1995
    C. lawful venting of CFCs or HCFCs into the air
    D. recovery of refrigerant before disposal of the appliance

88. The Residential Lead-based Paint Hazard Reduction Act set procedures to be followed in disclosing the presence of lead in:
    A. residential properties built prior to 1978
    B. all residential properties offered for sale
    C. new residential construction only
    D. residential properties built prior to 1998

89. A colorless, odorless gas that enters the home through surrounding soil that is dangerous to people because inhalation may cause lung cancer is known as:
    A. lead
    B. freon
    C. radon
    D. krypton

90. Environmental reviews by lenders, tenants, or purchasers to protect against liability for environmental hazards that may transfer with title are known as:
    A. lender qualifying statements
    B. emergency tenant and purchaser protection reviews
    C. fact finding missions
    D. due diligence reviews

XV. Real Estate Salesperson: Independent Contractor or Employee (1 hour) 3 questions

91. Real estate agents are classified by IRS as:
    A. employees
    B. independent contractors
    C. special agents
    D. double agents

92. The IRS form that independent contractors should receive from their supervising broker if they earn more than $600 per year is known as form:
    A. W-2
    B. 941
    C. 1099 misc.
    D. 940

93. In an independent contractor relationship, the salesperson is entitled to which of the following?
    A. paid vacations
    B. health benefits
    C. compensation based on hours worked
    D. compensation directly related to sales output

XVI. Real Estate Mathematics (3 hours) 7 questions

94. If a salesperson lists and sells a property for $90,000 and receives 60% of the 7% commission paid to the employing broker, how much does the salesperson receive?
    A. $2,520
    B. $3,780
    C. $5,400
    D. $6,300

95. At the time of listing a property, the owner specifies that he wishes to net $65,000 after satisfying a mortgage of $25,000 and paying a 7% brokerage fee. For what price should the property be listed?
    A. $90,000
    B. $94,550
    C. $96,300
    D. $96,774

96. The monthly payment of principal and interest on a 30-year home equity loan at 10% for $40,000 is $351.03. How much interest will the borrower pay over the 30-year term?
    A. $40,000
    B. $86,371
    C. $126,371
    D. $160,000

97. A triangular tract of land is 8,000 feet long and has highway frontage of 4,000 yards. If Ajax Realty lists this property at 9% commission and sells it for $1,600 per acre, what amount of commission does Ajax receive?
    A. $105,785
    B. $158,678
    C. $218,160
    D. $317,355

98. If the closing date is November 10 and the seller had paid the real property taxes of $2,880 for the current tax year of January 1 through December 31, which of the following is the correct closing statement entry for taxes?
    A. seller's credit of $400
    B. seller's debit of $2,480
    C. buyer's credit of $400
    D. buyer's debit of $2,480

99. A property with a market value of $80,000 is assessed at 75%. What is the tax rate per $100 if the bill is $900?
    A. $1.125
    B. $1.50
    C. $11.25
    D. $15.00

100. If a lease specifies the rent to be 2% of the gross sales per year, with a minimum annual rental of $8,000, what is the rental if gross sales are $1,200,000?
    A. $8,000
    B. $12,000
    C. $24,000
    D. $28,000

ANSWER KEY

I. License Law and Regulations

1. D
2. B
3. D
4. C
5. D
6. C
7. A

II. Law of Agency

8. D
9. C
10. A
11. B
12. A
13. D
14. A
15. B
16. B
17. C
18. C
19. B
20. A
21. C
22. A

III. Estates and Interests

23. B
24. B
25. C
26. A

IV. Liens and Easements

27. D
28. B
29. A

V. Deeds

30. C
31. C
32. B

VI. Contracts

33. B
34. A
35. D
36. C

VII. Leases

37. C
38. A
39. D
40. C

VIII. Title Closing and Costs

41. B
42. C
43. A

IX. Real Estate Finance (Mortgages)

44. A
45. C
46. C
47. B
48. A
49. B
50. B
51. D
52. A
53. D
54. C
55. C

X. Land Use Regulations

56. A
57. C
58. C
59. A

XI. Construction

60. B
61. C
62. D
63. C
64. A
65. C
66. A

XII. Valuation Process

67. A
68. C
69. D
70. C
71. A
72. A
73. D

XIII. Human Rights and Fair Housing

74. A
75. B
76. C
77. C
78. A
79. C
80. D
81. C
82. C
83. C

XIV. Environmental Issues

84. D
85. D
86. D
87. C
88. A
89. C
90. D

XV. Real Estate Salesperson: Independent Contractor or Employee

91. B
92. C
93. D

XVI. Real Estate Mathematics

94. B
95. D
96. B
97. B
98. A
99. B
100. C

Glossary

This glossary contains terminology from this textbook as well as general terminology that is useful to the real estate professional.

abandonment The surrender or release of a right, claim, or interest in real property.

absorption field A system of narrow trenches through which the discharge from a septic tank infiltrates into the surrounding soil.

abstract of title A history of a title and the current status of a title based on a title examination.

abutting land Parcels of land next to each other that share a common border.

acceleration clause A provision in a mortgage or deed of trust that permits the lender to declare the entire principal balance of the debt immediately due and payable if the borrower is in default.

acceptance Voluntary expression by the person receiving the offer to be bound by the exact terms of the offer; must be unequivocal and unconditional.

access The right to go onto and leave a property.

accession Property owners' rights to all the land produces or all that is added to the land, either intentionally or by mistake.

accessory apartment For example, an in-law apartment in a residential home.

accessory uses Uses that are incidental or subordinate to the main use of a building such as a laundromat.

accord and satisfaction A new agreement by contracting parties that is satisfied by full performance, thereby terminating the prior contract as well.

accretion The gradual building up of land in a watercourse over time by deposits of silt, sand, and gravel.

accrued expenses Expenses seller owes on the day of closing but for which the buyer will take responsibility (such as property taxes).

acknowledgment A formal statement before an authorized official (e.g., notary public) by a person who executed a deed, contract, or other document, that it was a free act.

acquisition The act of acquiring a property.

acquisition cost The basis used by the FHA to calculate the loan amount.

acre A land area containing 43,560 square feet.

act of waste Abuse or misuse of property by a life tenant.

action to quiet title A lawsuit to clear a title to real property.

actual age Chronological age.

actual eviction The removal of a tenant by the landlord because the tenant breached a condition of a lease or other rental contract.

actual notice The knowledge a person has of a fact.

adjoining lands Lands sharing a common boundary line.

adjustable rate mortgage (ARM) One in which the interest rate changes according to changes in a predetermined index.

adjusted sales price The amount realized minus fix-up expenses.

administrative law judge (ALJ) A judge who hears complaints and makes decisions regarding statutory violations of law.

administrator A person appointed by a court to administer the estate of a one who has died intestate.

administrator's deed One executed by an administrator to convey title to estate property.

administratrix A woman appointed by a court to administer the estate of a person who has died intestate.

ad valorem Latin meaning "according to value"; real property is taxed on an ad valorem basis.

adverse possession A method of acquiring title to real property by conforming to statutory requirement; a form of involuntary alienation of title.

affirmative action Policy expressed in some form of legislative act with respect to the handling of certain public or private acts or conduct.

affirmative easement A legal requirement that a servient owner permit a right of use in the servient land by the dominant owner.

agency The fiduciary relationship between a principal and an agent.

agency disclosure form *See* disclosure regarding agency relationships form.

agent A person authorized to act on behalf of another person.

agreement A contract requiring mutual assent between two or more parties.

agricultural districts Created and protected by New York statute; these areas are used for animal grazing and crop production.

air rights Rights in the airspace above the surface of land.

alienage The citizenship or immigration status of any person who is not a citizen or national of the U.S.

alienation Transfer of title to real property.

alienation clause A statement in a mortgage or deed of trust entitling the lender to declare the entire principal balance of the debt immediately due and payable if the borrower sells the property during the mortgage term. Also known as due-on-sale clause.

allodial system The type of land ownership existing in the United States whereby individuals may hold title to real property absolutely.

alluvion Increased soil, gravel, or sand on a stream bank resulting from flow or current of the water.

Americans with Disabilities Act A federal law protecting the rights of individuals with physical or mental impairments.

amortization Applying periodic payments first toward the interest and then toward the principal to eventually pay off a debt.

amortization schedule Designation of periodic payments of principal and interest over a specific term to satisfy a mortgage loan.

amortized mortgage One in which uniform installment payments include payment of both principal and interest.

amperage The amount of current or electricity flowing through the wire.

annexation Addition of an area into a city.

annual percentage rate (APR) The actual effective rate of interest charged on a loan expressed on a yearly basis; not the same as simple interest rate.

anticipation The principle that property value is based on expectations or hopes of the future benefits of ownership.

antitrust violations Any business activity where there is a monopoly, a contract, a conspiracy, or a combination that negatively impacts an individual's or a company's ability to do business.

apartment information vendor A licensed individual who is paid to provide information concerning the location and availability of residential real property.

apartment sharing agent A licensed individual who is paid to arrange and coordinate meetings between current owners of real property who wish to share their housing with others.

apportionment The division of expenses between buyer and seller.

appraisal An estimate of value of particular property, at a particular time for a specified purpose.

appraisal report Documentation containing an estimate of property value and the data on which the estimate is based.

appraiser One who estimates the value of real property.

appreciation An increase in property value.

appurtenances All rights or privileges that result from ownership of a specific property and move with the title.

appurtenant easement *See* easement appurtenant.

area variance Permission to use land in a manner that is not normally allowed by the dimensional or physical requirements of a zoning ordinance.

arrears Delinquency in meeting an obligation; or, paid at the end of a period (e.g., at the end of the month) for the previous period. Payments in arrears include interest for using the money during the previous period.

Article 9-A A section of the New York Real Property Law addressing the purchase or lease of vacant subdivided lands sold through an installment contract within or without New York.

Article 12-A The section of the New York Real Property Law pertaining to real estate salespersons and brokers.

Article 78 proceeding An appeal brought forth because of a ruling by a government agency.

asbestos A fibrous mineral found in many building materials and when improperly disturbed can cause serious lung illnesses.

"as is" Words in a contract of sale indicating that a property is sold without warranty as to condition.

assessed value The dollar amount of worth to which a local tax rate is applied to calculate the amount of real property tax.

assessment A levy against property.

assessor An official of local government who has the responsibility for establishing the value of property for tax purposes.

assignee One to whom contractual rights are transferred.

assignment Transfer of legal rights and obligations by one party to another.

assignment of lease Transfer by a lessee of the entire remaining term of a lease without any reversion of interest to the lessee.

assignor The person transferring contractual rights to another.

associate real estate broker A licensed real estate broker who chooses to work under the name and supervision of another licensed broker.

assumable mortgage One that does not contain an alienation clause and can be transferred from one party to another.

attorney-in-fact A person appointed to perform legal acts for another under a power of attorney.

auction A form of property sale in which people bid against one another.

availability An economic characteristic of land denoting that land is a commodity with a fixed supply base.

avulsion Sudden loss or gain of land as a result of water or shift in a bed of a river that has been used as a boundary.

balloon framing Method of construction that uses a single system of wall studs that run from the foundation through the first and second floors to the ceiling support.

balloon mortgage One in which the scheduled payment will not amortize the loan over the mortgage term; therefore, to fully satisfy the debt, it requires a final payment called a balloon payment, larger than the uniform payments.

bargain and sale deed A form of deed with or without covenants of title.

base rent The fixed or minimum rent portion in a percentage lease.

bearing walls Walls that support the ceiling and/or roof.

beneficial title Equitable title to real property retained by a mortgagor or trustor conveying legal title to secure a mortgage debt.

beneficiary (a) Recipient of a gift of personal property by will. (b) Lender in a deed of trust.

bequest A gift of personal property by will.

bilateral contract An agreement based on mutual promises that provide the consideration.

bill of sale An instrument transferring ownership of personal property.

binder A written document for the purchase and sale of real property that does not generally contain all of the essential elements of a valid contract.

blanket mortgage One in which two or more parcels of real property are pledged to secure payment of the note.

blind ad An ad for real property placed by a real estate broker that does not indicate that the advertiser is a broker and does not include the name of the broker and telephone number.

blockbusting For profit, to induce or attempt to induce any person to sell or rent any dwelling by representations regarding the entry or prospective entry into the neighborhood of a person or persons of a particular race, color, religion, sex, or national origin.

blueprint A building plan that is a detailed architectural rendering of the structure.

board of directors Governing and decision-making board of a cooperative.

bona fide In good faith.

book value Dollar worth as it appears on the owner's books, usually for tax purposes; also known as historic value.

breach of contract Failure, without legal excuse, to perform any promise that forms the whole or part of a contract.

bridge loan A loan for a short duration of time.

brokerage The business of bringing buyers and sellers together and assisting in negotiations for the terms of sale of real estate.

broker's agent One who is hired through a broker to work for the principal.

BTU Abbreviation for *British thermal unit*. The amount of heat required to raise the temperature of one pound of water by one degree Fahrenheit.

building codes Public controls regulating construction.

building envelope The materials of a building that enclose the interior.

building permit Permission from the appropriate local government authority to construct or renovate any type of property.

building specifications Written narratives that explain the building plan.

bundle of rights The rights of an owner of a freehold estate to possession, enjoyment, control, and disposition of real property.

buydown The voluntary paying of discount points by a borrower to reduce mortgage interest rate at the time the loan is made.

buyer agent A real estate agent who works in the best interests of a buyer.

buyer brokerage An agency relationship between a buyer and a broker.

capital gain The profit realized from the sale of a real estate investment.

capital improvement An item that adds value to the property, adapts the property to new uses, or prolongs the life of property. Maintenance is not a capital improvement.

capitalization rate The percentage of the investment the investor will receive back each year from the net income from the property.

cash flow Income produced by an investment property after deducting operating expenses and debt service.

caveat A warning or caution that may be addended to a contract of sale such as a disclosure that a property lies in an Agricultural District.

caveat emptor Latin, meaning *let the buyer beware*. Does not apply when there is a fiduciary relationship.

cease and desist list A list of homeowners compiled by DOS in a cease and desist zone who do not wish to be solicited by real estate agents.

cease and desist zone A designation given by DOS to a certain geographic area that has been subject to intense and repeated solicitation by real estate agents. *See* cease and desist list.

census tract Small geographical areas established through cooperation between the local community and the Bureau of Census.

certificate of occupancy A document issued by a local government agency, after a satisfactory inspection of a structure, authorizing that the structure can be occupied.

certificate of title opinion A report, based on a title examination, setting forth the examiner's opinion of the quality of a title to real property.

cession deed A deed used to relinquish real property to a municipality for a road or something of that nature.

chain In land measurement, a distance of 66 feet.

chain of title Successive conveyances of title to a specific parcel of land.

change The principle stating that change is continually affecting land use and therefore continually altering value.

chattel Personal property.

chlordane Chemical insecticide and termiticide that was banned in the early 1980s.

chlorofluorocarbons (CFCs) Manmade chemical substances that were used in hundreds of applications including refrigerators and air conditioners.

chronological age Actual age of an item.

circuit breaker Devices that switch off the electrical power for a given circuit if the current is above the capacity of the system.

civil action A lawsuit between private parties.

Civil Rights Act of 1866 A federal law that prohibits all discrimination on the basis of race.

Civil Rights Act of 1964 Law that prohibited discrimination in any housing program receiving federal money.

Civil Rights Act of 1968 *See* Fair Housing Act of 1988.

Clayton Antitrust Act Federal legislation including the imposition of civil and punitive damages for antitrust activities.

client The principal of the agent.

closed mortgage One that imposes a prepayment penalty.

closing costs Expenses incurred in the purchase and sale of real property paid at the time of settlement or closing.

closing statement An accounting of the funds received and disbursed in a real estate transaction.

cloud on a title A claim against a title to real property.

cluster zoning A form of zoning providing for several different types of land use within a zoned area.

Coastal Zone Management Program A program coordinated by DOS to preserve and protect New York's coastline.

Code of Ethics A standard of conduct required by license laws and by the National Association of REALTORS®.

codicil A supplement or an appendix to a will either adding or changing a bequest.

coinsurance clause A requirement of hazard insurance policies that property be insured for a certain percent of value to obtain the full amount of loss.

collateral Property pledged as security for payment of a debt.

color of title The deceptive appearance of claim to a title.

commercial property Property producing rental income or used in business.

commercial zones Uses that allow retail stores, restaurants, hotels, and service businesses.

commingling Mixing money or property of others with personal or business funds or other property.

commission A fee paid for the performance of services, such as a broker commission.

commissioner's deed A form of judicial deed executed by a commissioner.

commitment A promise, such as that by a lending institution to make a certain mortgage loan.

common areas Property to which co-owners hold title as a result of ownership of a condominium unit.

common elements *See* common areas.

common law Law by judicial precedent or tradition as contrasted with a written statute.

common law dedication An act by an owner allowing the public use of the property.

community-based planning A form of land use control originating in the grassroots of a community.

community planning A master plan for the orderly growth of a city or county to result in the greatest social and economic benefits to the people.

community property A form of co-ownership limited to husband and wife; does not exist in New York.

comparative market analysis An analysis of the competition in the marketplace that a property will face upon sale attempts.

compensatory damages The amount of money actually lost, which will be awarded by a court in case of a breached contract.

competent parties Persons and organizations legally qualified to manage their own affairs, including entering into contracts.

competition The principle stating that when the net profit a property generates is excessive, very strong competition will result.

complete performance Execution of a contract by virtue of all parties having fully performed all terms.

condemnation Exercise of the power of eminent domain; taking private property for public use.

condemnation value Market value of condemned property.

condition Any fact or event which, if it occurs or fails to occur, automatically creates or extinguishes a legal obligation.

condominium A form of ownership of real property, recognized in all states, consisting of individual ownership of some aspects and co-ownership in other aspects of the property.

condominium declaration The document that, when recorded, creates a condominium; also called a master deed.

conforming loans Those processed on uniform loan forms and according to FNMA/FHLMC guidelines.

conformity Homogeneous uses of land within a given area, which results in maximizing land value.

consent decree A compromise in civil lawsuits where the accused party agrees to stop the alleged illegal activity without admitting guilt or wrongdoing (called nolo contendere in criminal cases).

consideration Anything of value, as recognized by law, offered as an inducement to contract.

construction loan A short-term loan, secured by a mortgage, to obtain funds to construct an improvement on land.

construction mortgage A temporary mortgage used to borrow money to construct an improvement on land.

constructive eviction Results from some action or inaction by the landlord that renders the premises unsuitable for the use agreed to in a lease or other rental contract.

constructive notice One in which all affected parties are bound by the knowledge of a fact even though they have not been actually notified of such fact.

consumer price index (CPI) An index of the change in prices of various commodities and services, providing a measure of the rate of inflation.

contingency A condition in a contract relieving a party of liability if a specified event occurs or fails to occur.

contract An agreement between competent parties upon legal consideration to do, or abstain from doing, some legal act.

contract buyer's policy Title insurance that protects contract buyer against defects in contract seller's title.

contract for deed A contract of sale and a financing instrument wherein the seller agrees to convey title when the buyer completes the purchase price installment payments; also called installment land contract and installment plan.

contract rent The amount of rent agreed to in a lease.

conventional life estate One created by intentional act of the parties.

conventional mortgage loan One in which the federal government does not insure or guarantee payment to the lender.

conversion Change in a form of ownership, such as changing rental apartments to condominium ownership.

convey To pass to another (as in title).

conveyance Transfer of title to real property.

cooling-off period A three-day right of rescission for certain loan transactions.

cooperating broker or agent One who participates in the sale of a property.

cooperative A form of ownership in which stockholders in a corporation occupy property owned by the corporation under a lease.

co-ownership Title to real property held by two or more persons at the same time; also called concurrent ownership.

corporation A form of organization existing as an entity.

corporation franchise tax A tax calculated on the net profit of the corporation.

cost The total dollar expenditure for labor, materials, and other items related to construction.

cost approach Appraisal method for estimating the value of properties that have few, if any, comparables and are not income-producing.

counteroffer A new offer made by an offeror rejecting an offer.

covenant A promise in writing.

covenant against encumbrances A promise in a deed that the title causes no encumbrances except those set forth in the deed.

covenant for further assurances A promise in a deed that the grantor will execute further assurances that may be reasonable or necessary to perfect the title in the grantee.

covenant of quiet enjoyment A promise in a deed (or lease) that the grantee (or lessee) will not be disturbed in the use of the property because of a defect in the grantor's (or lessor's) title.

covenant of right to convey A promise in a deed that the grantor has the legal capacity to convey the title.

covenant of seisin A promise in a deed ensuring the grantee that the grantor has the title being conveyed.

covenant of warranty A promise in a deed that the grantor will guarantee and defend the title against lawful claimants.

credit In a closing statement, money to be received or credit given for money or an obligation given.

creditor One to whom a debt is owed.

cubic-foot method A means of estimating reproduction or replacement cost, using the volume of the structure.

cul-de-sac A dead-end street with a circular turnaround at the dead end.

cumulative-use zoning A type of zoning permitting a higher-priority use even though it is different from the type of use designated for the area.

curtesy A husband's interest in the real property of his wife.

customer The party the agent brings to the principal as seller or buyer of the property.

damages The amount of financial loss incurred as a result of another's action.

debit In a closing statement, an expense or money received against a credit.

debt service Principal and interest payments on a debt.

decedent A dead person.

declaration Master deed containing legal description of the condominium facility, a plat of the property, plans and specifications for the building and units, a description of the common areas, and the degree of ownership in the common areas available to each owner.

declaration of restrictions The instrument used to record restrictive covenants on the public record.

decree A court order.

dedication An appropriation of land or an easement therein by the owner to the public.

dedication by deed The deeding of a parcel of land to a municipality.

deductible expenses Costs of operating property held for use in business or as an investment. These expenses are subtracted from gross income to arrive at net income.

deed A written instrument transferring an interest in real property when delivered to the grantee.

deed in lieu of foreclosure Conveyance of title to the mortgagee by a mortgagor in default to avoid a record of foreclosure. Also called friendly foreclosure.

deed restriction Limitation on land use appearing in deeds.

default Failure to perform an obligation.

defeasance clause A statement in a mortgage or deed of trust giving the borrower the right to redeem the title and have the mortgage lien released at any time prior to default by paying the debt in full.

defeasible Subject to being defeated by the occurrence of a certain event.

defeasible fee A title subject to being lost if certain conditions occur.

deficiency judgment A court judgment obtained by a mortgagee for the amount of money a foreclosure sale proceeds were deficient in fully satisfying the mortgage debt.

delivery and acceptance The transfer of a title by deed requiring the grantor to deliver and the grantee to accept a given deed.

demise To convey an estate for years; synonymous with lease or let.

demography The study of the social and economic statistics of a community.

density Number of persons or structures per acre.

Department of Housing and Urban Development (HUD) *See* U.S. Department of Housing and Urban Development.

depreciation (a) Loss in value from any cause. (b) Deductible allowance from net income of property when arriving at taxable income.

descent The distribution of property to legally qualified heirs of one who has died intestate.

description by monument A legal description sometimes used when describing multiple-acre tracts of land and may refer to permanent objects such as a stone wall, large trees, or boulders.

description by reference A valid legal description that may be found on a deed that references a plat of subdivision or other legal document.

devise A gift of real property by will.

devisee The recipient of a gift of real property by will.

direct cost The cost of labor and materials.

disability The impairment of any life function.

disclosure and informed consent Explanation by a real estate agent of his position in the agency relationship and the verbal and written consent of the relationship by the client or customer.

disclosure of information The prompt and total communication to the principal by the agent of any information that is material to the transaction for which the agency is created.

disclosure regarding real estate agency relationships form Pursuant to Section 443 of the New York Real Property Law, this document must be presented by a licensee and signed by all parties at the first substantive meeting with prospective purchasers or sellers.

disclosure statement An accounting of all financial aspects of a mortgage loan required of lenders to borrowers in residential mortgage loans by Regulation Z of the Federal Reserve Board.

discount points A percentage of the loan amount the lender requires for making a mortgage loan.

discriminatory advertising Any advertising that states or indicates a preference, limitation, or discrimination on the basis of race, color, religion, sex, national origin, handicap, familial status, marital status, or age in offering housing or commercial property for sale or rent.

disintermediation The loss of funds available to lending institutions for making mortgage loans, caused by depositors' withdrawal of funds for making investments that provide greater yields.

distribution box A part of a septic system that distributes the flow from the septic tank evenly to the absorption field or seepage pits.

distribution panel The location of circuit breakers or fuses.

doctrine of laches Loss of legal rights because of failure to assert them on a timely basis.

dominant tenement Land benefiting from an easement appurtenant.

dower A wife's interest in her husband's real property.

dual agent A broker/salesperson who attempts to represent both buyer and seller in the same transaction.

due diligence Investigation and review of a property to determine any legal liability.

due-on-sale clause *See* alienation clause.

duress The inability of a party to exercise free will because of fear of another party.

duty of disclosure A responsibility for revealing all information that affects the agency agreement.

earnest money deposit A deposit a buyer makes at the time of submitting an offer to demonstrate the true intent to purchase; also called binder, good faith deposit, escrow deposit.

easement A nonpossessory right of use in the land of another.

easement appurtenant A right of use in the adjoining land of another that moves with the title to the property benefiting from the easement.

easement by condemnation Created by the exercise of the government's right of eminent domain.

easement by grant Created by the express written agreement of the landowners, usually in a deed.

easement by implication Arising by implication from the conduct of the parties.

easement by necessity Exists when a landowner has no access to roads and is landlocked.

easement by prescription Obtained by use of the land of another for the legally prescribed length of time.

easement for light and air A type of negative easement restraining a property owner from developing his or her property so as to block the view of another.

easement in gross A right of use in the land of another without the requirement that the holder of the right own adjoining land.

eave The lowest part of the roof that projects beyond the walls of the structure.

economic depreciation Physical deterioration of property caused by normal use, damage caused by natural and other hazards, and failure to adequately maintain property.

economic life The period of time during which a property is financially beneficial to the owner.

economic obsolescence Loss in value caused by things such as changes in surrounding land use patterns and failure to adhere to the principle of highest and best use.

effective interest rate Actual rate of interest being paid.

egress The right to leave a parcel of land entered (ingress) by law.

electromagnetic field (EMF) Created when electricity flows through a wire.

Emergency Tenant Protection Act A law governing rent control and rent stabilization in New York.

eminent domain The power of government to take private property for public use.

enabling acts Laws passed by state legislatures authorizing cities and counties to regulate land use within their jurisdictions.

encroachment Trespass on the land of another as a result of intrusion by some structure or other object.

encumbrance A claim, lien, charge, or liability attached to and binding upon real property.

enforceable A contract in which the parties may be required legally to perform.

environmental impact statement (EIS) A requirement of the State Environmental Quality Review Act prior to initiating or changing a land use that may have an adverse effect on the environment.

Environmental Protection Agency (EPA) A federal agency that oversees land use.

Environment Policy Act A federal law that requires filing an environmental impact statement with the EPA prior to changing or initiating a land use or development.

Equal Credit Opportunity Act (ECOA) A federal law prohibiting discrimination in consumer loans.

equitable title An interest in real estate such that a court will take notice and protect the owner's rights.

equity The difference between the value of a property and its liabilities.

equity of redemption The borrower's right to redeem the title pledged or conveyed in a mortgage or deed of trust after default and prior to a foreclosure sale by paying the debt in full, accrued interest, and lender's costs.

erosion The wearing away of land by water, wind, or other processes of nature.

escheat The power of government to take title to property left by a person who has died without leaving a valid will (intestate) or qualified heirs.

escrow The deposit of funds or documents with a neutral third party, who is instructed to carry out the provisions of an agreement.

escrow account (a) An account maintained by a real estate broker in an insured bank for the deposit of other people's money; also called trust account. (b) An account maintained by the borrower with the lender in certain mortgage loans to accumulate the funds to pay an annual insurance premium, a real property tax, or a homeowner's association assessment.

estate at sufferance Continuing to occupy property after lawful authorization has expired; a form of leasehold estate.

estate at will A leasehold estate that may be terminated at the desire of either party.

estate for years A leasehold estate of definite duration.

estate from year to year A leasehold estate that automatically renews itself for consecutive periods until terminated by notice by either party; also called estate from period-to-period or periodic tenancy.

estate in fee An estate in fee simple absolute.

estate in real property An interest sufficient to provide the right to use, possession, and control of land; establishes the degree and duration of ownership.

estoppel Preventing a person from making a statement contrary to a previous statement.

estoppel certificate A document executed by a mortgagor or mortgagee setting forth the principal amount; executing parties are bound by the amount specified.

estovers The right of a life tenant or lessee to cut timber on the property for fuel or to use in making repairs.

evaluation A study of the usefulness or utility of a property without reference to the specific estimate of value.

eviction A landlord's action that interferes with the tenant's use or possession of the property. Eviction may be actual or constructive.

exclusive agency listing A listing given to one broker only (exclusive), who is entitled to the commission if the broker or any agent of the listing broker effects a sale, but imposes no commission obligation on the owner who sells the property to a person who was not interested in the property by efforts of the listing broker or an agent of the listing broker.

exclusive right to rent This contract is between an owner or a lessor and a broker/agent in the rental of residential property.

exclusive right to sell listing A listing given to one broker only, who is entitled to the commission if anyone sells the property during the term of the listing contract.

exclusive use zoning A type of zoning in which only the specified use may be made of property within the zoned district.

executed contract An agreement that has been fully performed.

execution Signing a contract or other legal document.

execution of judgment Judicial proceeding in which property of a debtor is seized (attached) and sold to satisfy a judgment lien.

executor A male appointed in a will to see that the terms of the will are carried out.

executory contract An agreement that has not been fully performed.

executrix A female appointed in a will to see that the terms of the will are carried out.

exercise of option Purchase of optioned property by the optionee.

express agency An agency relationship created by oral or written agreement between principal and agent.

express contract One created verbally or in writing by the parties.

extended coverage An insurance term referring to the extension of a standard fire insurance policy to cover damages resulting from wind, rain, and other perils.

external obsolescence Changes in surrounding land-use patterns resulting in increased traffic, air pollution, and other hazards and nuisances.

Fair Housing Act of 1968 A federal prohibition on discrimination in the sale, rental, or financing of housing on the basis of race, color, religion, gender, or national origin.

Fair Housing Act of 1988 A federal prohibition on discrimination in sale, rental, financing, or appraisal of housing on the basis of race, color, religion, gender, national origin, handicap, or familial status.

Fair Housing Amendments Act of 1988 A law adding to the Fair Housing Act provisions to prevent discrimination based on mental or physical handicap or familial status.

fair market value A price for property agreed upon between buyer and seller in a competitive market with neither party being under undue pressure.

familial status Defined under Fair Housing Law as an adult with children under 18, a person who is pregnant, one who has legal custody of a child, or who is in the process of obtaining custody.

family An individual, or two or more persons related by blood or marriage or adoption, living together in one dwelling; or a group of up to three people who are not married, or blood relatives or adopted, living together as a single housekeeping unit; or one or more persons living together in a single housekeeping unit as distinguished by a hotel or club.

Fannie Mae The shortened name for the Federal National Mortgage Association (FNMA), a privately owned corporation that purchases FHA, VA, and conventional mortgages.

fascia In house construction, the area of material facing the outer edge of the soffit.

Federal Housing Administration (FHA) The U.S. agency that insures mortgage loans to protect lending institutions.

Federal Reserve System The U.S. banking system that regulates monetary policy and, thereby, the money supply and interest rates.

Federal Trade Commission An administrative body that has the power to declare trade practices unfair, particularly with regard to antitrust legislation.

fee simple absolute An inheritable estate in land providing the greatest interest of any form of title.

fee simple on condition A defeasible fee (title), recognizable by words "but if."

FHA-insured loan A mortgage loan in which payments are insured by the Federal Housing Administration.

fiduciary A person, such as an agent, placed in a position of trust in relation to the person for whose benefit the relationship is created; essentially the same as a trustee.

filtering down The decline in value of properties in neighborhoods that were once middle or upper income.

finance charge An amount imposed on the borrower in a mortgage loan, consisting of origination fee, service charges, discount points, interest, credit report fees, and finders' fees.

fire insurance policy *See* homeowner's policy.

first mortgage One that supersedes later recorded mortgages.

first substantive meeting The first contact or meeting by a licensee when some detail and information about the property is shared with parties who express some interest in the real estate transaction.

fixed expenses Expenditures such as property taxes, license fees, and property insurance; subtracted from effective gross income to determine net operating income.

fixed lease One in which the rental amount remains the same for the entire lease term; also called flat, straight, or gross lease.

fixed-rate mortgage **One** in which the interest does not change.

fixture Personal property that has become real property by having been permanently attached to real property.

flashing A metallic material used in certain areas of the roof and walls to prevent water from seeping into the structure.

flat lease One in which the rental amount does not change during the lease term.

flexible payment mortgage A loan that allows smaller mortgage payments in the first years after purchase and then increases the amount of payment later on.

flitch beam A double top plate used to tie the walls together and provide additional support for the ceiling and roof system.

floating slab A type of foundation constructed by pouring the footing first and then pouring the slab.

footing The concrete base below the frost line that supports the foundation of a structure.

forbearance The act of refraining from taking legal action for payment of a mortgage despite the fact that it is due.

foreclosure The legal procedure of enforcing payment of a debt secured by a mortgage or any other lien.

forfeiture Relinquishing a portion of title to the government without compensation.

forfeiture clause A statement in a contract for deed providing for giving up all payments by a buyer in default.

formal will A will, in writing, signed by the testator or testatrix in front of two witnesses.

foundation walls Poured concrete, masonry block, or brick sides of a structure.

framing members Lumber with a nominal dimension of 2" thick used for constructing the wooden skeleton of a building.

fraud An intentional false statement of a material fact.

Freddie Mac A nickname for Federal Home Loan Mortgage Corporation (FHLMC), a corporation wholly owned by the Federal Home Loan Bank System that purchases FHA, VA, and conventional mortgages.

freehold estate A right of title to land.

free market An economic condition in which buyer and seller have ample time to negotiate a beneficial purchase and sale without undue pressure or urgency.

freon A nontoxic substance used in most home air conditioning units which if released into the air can cause damage to the ozone layer.

friable A quality of some asbestos that causes it to crumble, allowing toxic particles to escape into the air and lodge in the lungs.

frieze board The wooden member fastened under the soffit against top of wall.

front foot A linear foot of property frontage on a street or highway.

full covenant and warranty deed A deed containing the strongest and broadest form of guarantee of title.

fully amortizing mortgage One in which the scheduled uniform payments will pay off the loan completely over the mortgage term.

functional obsolescence Flawed or faulty property rendered inferior because of advances and change.

fuse A device that is part of a wiring system that will melt and open the circuit, causing electrical power to stop when overheating occurs.

future interest The rights of an owner of an estate who will vest at some upcoming time.

gender Either male or female

general agent One with full authority over one property of the principal, such as a property manager.

general lien One that attaches to all of the property of a person within the court's jurisdiction.

General Obligations Law *See* Statute of Frauds.

general partnership The partners are personally liable for partnership debts exceeding partnership assets.

general warranty deed A deed denoting an unlimited guarantee of title.

Ginnie Mae A nickname for Government National Mortgage Association (GNMA), a U.S. government agency that purchases FHA and VA mortgages.

girder The main carrying beam of a house that spans the distance from one side of the foundation to the other.

good faith estimate Lender's estimate of borrower's settlement costs, required by RESPA to be furnished to borrower at time of loan application.

government loan Mortgage guaranteed, insured, or funded by a government agency.

grace period In a mortgage, a specified time frame in which the payment may be made without the borrower being in default.

graduated lease One in which the rent changes from period to period over the lease term in stair-step fashion. Used for new business tenant whose income increases over time.

graduated payment mortgage (GPM) One in which the payments are lower in the early years but increase on a scheduled basis until they reach an amortizing level.

grant A transfer of title to real property by deed.

grantee One who receives title to real property by deed.

granting clause The statement in a deed containing words of conveyance.

grantor One who conveys title to real property by deed.

gross lease One in which the lessor pays all costs of operating and maintaining the property and real property taxes.

ground lease A long-term lease of unimproved land, usually for construction purposes.

groundwater Water obtained from underground.

group boycott A conspiracy wherein a person or group is persuaded or coerced into not doing business with another person or group.

group home A residential facility for five or more adults who have been institutionalized and then released.

habendum clause The statement in a deed beginning with the words "to have and to hold" and describing the estate granted.

habitable Suitable for the type of occupancy intended.

headers Wooden reinforcements for the placement of doors and windows.

hectare Metric system equivalent to the U. S. measurement of 2.47 acres

heirs Persons legally eligible to receive property of a decedent.

heterogeneous A variety of dissimilar uses of property; nonhomogeneous.

highest and best use The use of land that will preserve its utility and yield a net income flow in the form of rent that, when capitalized at the proper rate of interest, represents the highest present value of the land.

holding period The length of time a property is owned.

holdover tenant A tenant who remains in possession of property after a lease terminates.

holographic will One handwritten by the testator.

Home Buyer's Guide A booklet explaining aspects of the loan settlement required by RESPA.

home equity loan A loan against the equity in a home.

home occupation A small business or occupation that may be conducted only by the residents of the dwelling and must be incidental and secondary to the use of the dwelling.

homeowners' association An organization of owners having the responsibility to provide for operation and maintenance of common areas of a condominium or residential subdivision; also called property owners' association.

homeowner's policy An insurance policy protecting against a variety of hazards.

homeowner's warranty (HOW) An insurance policy protecting against loss caused by structural and other defects in a dwelling.

homestead The land and dwelling of a homeowner.

homogeneous Similar and compatible, as in land uses.

HUD Form No. 1 A standard settlement form required by RESPA.

Human Rights Law *See* New York State Human Rights Law.

HVAC An acronym that stands for heating, ventilation, and air conditioning.

hydronic system A process in a heating system where liquids such as water are heated or cooled.

hypothecate To pledge property as security for the payment of a debt without giving up possession.

illiquid An investment that is not easily convertible to cash.

immobility Incapable of being moved; fixed in location; an important physical characteristic of land.

implied agency Agency that exists as a result of actions of the parties.

implied contract One created by deduction from the conduct of the parties rather than from the direct words of the parties; opposite of an express contract.

implied warranty One presumed by law to exist in a deed, though not expressly stated.

improvements Changes or additions made to a property, such as walls or roads, and so on. These typically increase the value of a property, except in some cases of overimprovement.

incentive zoning Offers incentives to developers and property owners to construct amenities that would provide certain types of uses and enjoyment for the residents of the municipality.

income approach The primary method used to estimate the present value of properties that produce income.

income property One that produces rental income.

incompetent Describes a person who is not capable of managing his or her own affairs, under law.

incorporeal Intangible things such as rights.

indemnification Reimbursement or compensation paid to someone for a loss already suffered.

independent contractor Workers who hold nonemployee status under the law.

indestructibility A physical characteristic of land describing that land as a permanent commodity that cannot be destroyed.

index lease A method of determining rent on long-term leases where the rent is tied to an economic indicator such as an index.

indirect cost Costs that support a construction project, such as architectural fees.

industrial zones Uses that allow light or heavy manufacturing and warehouses.

inflation An increase in money and credit relative to available goods resulting in higher prices.

informed consent Agreement by a buyer or seller to a type of agency relationship after considering the various alternatives.

infrastructure Services and systems that support a community, such as hospitals, schools, and roadways.

ingress The right to enter a parcel of land; usually used as "ingress and egress" (both entering and leaving).

injunction A court instruction to discontinue a specified activity.

installment land contract *See* contract for deed.

installment sale A transaction in which the seller receives the sale price over a specified period of time.

instrument A written legal document such as a contract, note, or mortgage.

insurable interest The degree of interest qualifying for insurance.

insured conventional loan One in which the loan payment is insured by private mortgage insurance to protect the lender.

insured value The cost of replacing a structure completely destroyed by an insured hazard.

interest (a) Payment for the use of someone else's money. (b) An ownership or right.

interim financing A short-term or temporary loan such as a construction loan.

interspousal deed Conveys real property from husband to wife or wife to husband.

Interstate Land Sales Full Disclosure Act A federal law regulating the sale across state lines of subdivided land under certain conditions.

intervivos trust A trust set up while the parties are living.

intestate The condition of death without leaving a valid will.

intestate succession Distribution of property by descent as provided by statute.

invalid Not legally enforceable.

investment The outlay of money for income or profit.

investment syndicate A joint venture, typically controlled by one or two persons, hoping for return to all investors.

investment value The highest price an investor would pay in light of how well he believes a given property would serve his financial goals.

involuntary alienation Transfer of title to real property as a result of a lien foreclosure sale, adverse possession, filing a petition in bankruptcy, condemnation under power of eminent domain, or, upon the death of the titleholder, to the state if no heirs.

involuntary lien An act wherein a creditor places a claim on real and/or personal property of another to obtain payment of a debt.

irrevocable That which cannot be changed or canceled.

joint tenancy A form of co-ownership that includes the right of survivorship.

joint venture Participation by two or more parties in a single undertaking.

joists Wooden framing members used in the construction of floors and ceilings.

judgment A court determination of the rights and obligations of parties to a lawsuit.

judgment lien A general lien resulting from a court decree.

judicial deed One executed by an official with court authorization.

judicial foreclosure A court proceeding to require that property be sold to satisfy a mortgage lien.

junior mortgage One that is subordinate to a prior mortgage.

jurisdiction The extent of authority of a court.

kickback Payment by a broker of any part of a compensation to a real estate transaction to anyone who is not licensed or who is not exempt from the license law.

laches *See* doctrine of laches.

lally columns Round steel and/or concrete columns that support the main carrying beam of a structure

land The surface of the earth, the area above and below the surface, and everything permanently attached thereto.

land contract *See* contract for deed.

land grant Conveyance of land as a gift for the benefit of the public.

landlease A type of lease that allows a lessee the right to use land for any purpose for a specified period of time.

landlocked Describes property with no access to a public road.

land patent Instrument conveying public land to an individual.

land trust Type of trust in which title to land is held by a trustee for the benefit of others.

land use controls Governmental restrictions on land use (e.g., zoning laws and building codes).

lead A toxic metallic element found in some homes in paint, dust, and water.

lead agency The governmental agency that oversees the environmental impact process and makes final decisions.

lease A contract wherein a landlord gives a tenant the right of use and possession of property for a limited period of time in return for rent.

leased fee Lessor's interest in leased property.

leasehold estate Nonfreehold estate; of limited duration, providing the right of possession and control but not title.

leasehold mortgage One in which a leasehold (nonfreehold) estate is pledged to secure payment of the note.

legacy A gift of personal property by will.

legal capacity The ability to contract.

legal description A description of land recognized by law.

legal entity A person or organization with legal capacity.

legality of object Legal purpose.

legatee Recipient of the gift of personal property by will.

lessee A tenant under a lease.

lessor A landlord under a lease.

leverage The use of borrowed funds; the larger the percentage of borrowed money, the greater the leverage.

levy Imposition of a tax, executing a lien.

license A personal privilege to do a particular act or series of acts on the land of another.

lien A claim that one person has against the property of another for some debt or charge, entitling the lienholder to have the claim satisfied from the property of the debtor.

lienee One whose property is subject to a lien.

lien foreclosure sale Selling property without consent of owner who incurred the debt resulting in a lien, as ordered by a court or authorized by state law, and title conveyed to purchaser by judicial deed.

lienor The one holding a lien against another.

life estate A freehold estate created for the duration of the life or lives of certain named persons; a noninheritable estate.

life estate in remainder A form of life estate in which certain persons, called remaindermen, are designated to receive the title upon termination of the life tenancy.

life estate in reversion A form of life estate that goes back to the creator of the estate in fee simple upon termination.

life estate pur autre vie An estate in which the duration is measured by the life of someone other than the life tenant. *See* pur autre vie.

life tenant One holding a life estate.

limited partnership An organization consisting of one or more general partners and several partners with lesser roles.

liquidated damages Money to be paid and received as compensation for a breach of contract.

liquidity The attribute of an asset's being readily convertible to cash.

lis pendens Latin, meaning *a lawsuit pending*. *See* notice of lis pendens.

listing contract A contract whereby a property owner employs a real estate broker to market the property described in the contract.

litigation A lawsuit.

littoral rights Rights belonging to owner of land that borders a lake, ocean, or sea.

loan commitment Obligation of a lending institution to make a certain mortgage loan.

loan origination fee Financing charge required by the lender.

loan-to-value ratio The relationship between the amount of a mortgage loan and the lender's opinion of the value of the property pledged to secure payment of the loan.

location (situs) An economic characteristic of land having the greatest effect on value in comparison to any other characteristic.

L.S. Abbreviation for *locus signilli*, a Latin term meaning "in place of the seal."

margin Measure of profit.

marital status Either married or single.

marketable title One that is free from reasonable doubt and that a court would require a purchaser to accept.

market allocation agreement An agreement between competitors dividing or assigning a certain area or territory for sales.

market value A property's worth in terms of price agreed upon by a willing buyer and seller when neither is under any undue pressure and each is knowledgeable of market conditions at the time.

master deed The instrument that legally establishes a condominium; also called condominium declaration.

material fact Important information that may affect a person's judgment.

materialmen's lien *See* mechanics' lien.

mechanics' lien A statutory lien available to persons supplying labor (mechanics) or material (materialmen) to the construction of an improvement on land if they are not paid.

meeting of the minds A condition that must exist for creation of a contract.

merger The absorption of one thing into another.

merger clause Clause in a real estate contract wherein the contract is fulfilled and the conveyed deed supersedes the contract.

metes and bounds A system of land description by distances and directions.

mill One tenth of a cent.

mineral rights A landowner's ability to take minerals from the earth or to sell or lease this right to others.

minor A person who has not attained the statutory age of majority; in New York, age 18.

misdemeanor A crime punishable by up to a year in prison and/or a $1,000 fine.

misrepresentation (a) A false statement or omission of a material fact. (b) In real estate, making an intentionally false statement to induce someone to contract.

monolithic slab A type of foundation in which the footing and slab are poured at the same time.

moratorium A delay in allowing development of property within the municipality.

mortgage A written instrument used to pledge a title to real property to secure payment of a promissory note.

mortgage assumption The transfer of mortgage obligations to purchaser of the mortgaged property.

mortgage banker A form of organization that makes and services mortgage loans.

mortgage broker One who arranges a mortgage loan between a lender and a borrower for a fee.

mortgagee The lender in a mortgage loan, who receives a mortgage from the borrower (mortgagor).

mortgagee's title insurance policy A policy that insures a mortgagee against defects in a title pledged by a mortgagor to secure payment of a mortgage loan.

mortgage insurance premium (MIP) A payment for insurance to protect the lender and/or insurer against loss if default occurs.

mortgage loan value The value sufficient to secure payment of a mortgage loan.

mortgage principal The amount of money (usually the loan amount) on which interest is either paid or received.

mortgage satisfaction Full payment of a mortgage loan.

mortgaging clause The statement in a mortgage or deed of trust that demonstrates the mortgagor's intention to mortgage the property to the mortgagee.

mortgagor The borrower in a mortgage loan who executes and delivers a mortgage to the lender.

multiple dwelling Residence rented to three or more families.

multiple listing service (MLS) An organized method of sharing or pooling listings by member brokers.

mutual assent The voluntary agreement of all parties to a contract as evidenced by an offer and acceptance.

mutual mistake An error of material fact by both parties.

National Association of REALTORS® (NAR) The largest and most prominent trade organization of real estate licensees.

National Electric Code National standard for electrical installation and service.

negative amortization When a loan payment amount is not sufficient to cover interest due, the shortfall added back into principal, causing the principal to grow larger after payment is made.

negative covenant *See* restrictive covenant.

negative easement A right in the land of another prohibiting the servient owner from doing something on the servient land because it will affect the dominant land.

negligence Legal term describing failure to use the care that a reasonable person would use in like circumstances.

net lease One in which the lessee pays a fixed amount of rent plus the costs of operation of the property.

net listing Not a type of listing but a method of establishing the listing broker commission as all money above a specified net amount to the seller; illegal in New York.

net operating income Gross operating income less expenses.

New York City Commission on Human Rights Deals with discrimination in the sale, rental, or lease of housing, land, and commercial space.

New York Real Property Law *See* Article 12-A.

New York State Association of REALTORS® (NYSAR) Umbrella board for all of the real estate boards in New York and member board of the National Association of REALTORS®.

New York State Department of Environmental Conservation (DEC) An agency whose purpose is to protect the quality of land, water, scenery, and the health and diversity of fish and wildlife and their habitats in New York State.

New York State Energy Code Regulations that set minimum requirements for the design of energy efficiencies for new buildings and renovations to existing buildings.

New York State Human Rights Law Created to eliminate and prevent discrimination in residential and commercial real estate as well as in employment, public accommodations, places of amusement, and educational institutions.

New York State Office of Parks, Recreation, and Historic Preservation (OPRHP) Oversees public recreational areas and administers federal and state preservation programs authorized by federal and state law.

New York State Uniform Fire Prevention and Building Code Provides minimum standards for the construction and renovation of all types of buildings in New York.

nonconforming use Utilization of land that does not conform to the use permitted by a zoning ordinance for the area; may be lawful or unlawful.

nonfreehold estate Leaseholds; estates with a length determined by agreement or statute; establishes possession of land as opposed to ownership in fee.

nonhomogeneity A physical characteristic of land describing that land as a unique commodity.

nonpossessory An individual does not occupy a property; easements imply a nonpossessory interest in land owned by another.

nonrecourse note A note in which the borrower has no personal liability for payment.

nonsolicitation order An order issued by the secretary of state prohibiting licensees from soliciting listings in certain areas of the state.

notary public A person authorized by a state to take oaths and acknowledgments.

notice of lis pendens A statement on the public record warning all persons that a title to real property is the subject of a lawsuit and any lien resulting from the suit will attach to the title held by a purchaser from the defendant.

novation Substitution of a new contract for a prior contract.

null and void Invalid; without legal force or effect.

obligee One to whom an obligation is owed.

obligor One who owes an obligation to another.

obsolescence Loss in property value caused by economic or functional factors.

occupancy Physical possession of property.

offer A promise made to another conditional upon acceptance by a promise or an act made in return.

offer and acceptance Necessary elements for the creation of a contract.

offeree One to whom an offer is made.

offeror One making an offer.

open-ended listing contract One without a termination date.

open-end mortgage One that may be refinanced without rewriting the mortgage.

open listing A listing given to one or more brokers wherein the broker procuring a sale is entitled to the commission but imposes no commission obligation on the owner in the event the owner sells the property to someone who was not interested in the property by one of the listing brokers.

open mortgage One that does not impose a prepayment penalty.

operation of law The manner in which rights and liabilities of parties may be changed by application of law without the act or cooperation of the parties.

opinion of title *See* certificate of title opinion.

optionee One who receives an option.

optionor One who gives an option.

option to purchase A contract whereby a property owner (optionor) sells a right to purchase his or her property to a prospective buyer (optionee).

option to renew A provision setting forth the method and terms for renewing the lease.

oral will A will usually restricted to the granting of personal property because it conflicts with the Statute of Frauds, which states that the conveyance of real property must be in writing.

ordinance A law enacted by a local government.

origination fee A service charge by a lending institution for making a mortgage loan.

overimprovement An improvement to land that results in the land not being able to obtain its highest and best use.

ownership The right to use, control, possess, and dispose of property.

ownership in severalty Title to real property held in the name of one person only.

owner's title insurance policy A policy insuring an owner of real property against financial loss resulting from a title defect.

package mortgage One in which personal property as well as real property is pledged to secure payment of the note.

package policy Insurance coverage for property damage and liability loss all within one premium.

parcel A specific portion of land such as a lot.

parens patriae The right of government to litigate and therefore protect in the name of the public good.

parol evidence rule A concept allowing that oral explanations can support the written words of a contract but cannot contradict them.

participation mortgage *See* shared equity mortgage.

partition A legal proceeding dividing property of co-owners so each will hold title in severalty.

partnership A form of business organization in which the business is owned by two or more persons, called partners.

party wall A common wall used by two adjoining structures.

payment cap If the interest rate on the loan changes and therefore the monthly payments increase, the lender allows a payment cap in which the monthly payment remains the same and the money for the higher interest rate is added to the principal.

percentage lease One in which the rental amount is a combination of a fixed amount plus a percentage of the lessee's gross sales.

percolation The movement of water through soil.

percolation (perc) test A test of soil to determine if it is sufficiently porous for installation of a septic tank.

periodic tenancy A lease that automatically renews for successive periods unless terminated by either party; also called an estate from year to year.

per se illegal Legal doctrine that states that an activity is specifically not allowable under the law.

personal property All property that is not land and is not permanently attached to land; everything that is movable; chattel.

physical deterioration Loss in value caused by unrepaired damage or inadequate maintenance.

pitch The slope of a roof.

PITI Acronym denoting that a mortgage payment includes principal, interest, taxes, and insurance.

planned unit development (PUD) A form of cluster zoning providing for both residential and commercial land uses within a zoned area.

planning A program for the development of a city or county designed to provide for orderly growth.

plat A property map, recorded on the public record in plat books.

platform framing The most common type of framing in residential construction in which the framing of the structure rests on a subfloor platform.

pledge To provide property as security for payment of a debt or for performance of a promise.

pledged account mortgage The down payment is deposited in a savings account with the lender and the borrower makes escalating payments to which are added withdrawal forms from the savings account.

plottage Combining two or more parcels of land into one tract that has more value than the total value of the individual parcels.

pocket card Identification card issued by the Department of State to real estate licensees.

points *See* discount points.

police power The power of government to regulate the use of real property for the benefit of the public.

polychlorinated biphenyls (PCBs) A manmade, odorless, liquid organic compound and carcinogen appearing in groundwater and soil.

population density The number of people within a given land area.

positive misrepresentation A person's actual statement that is false and known to be false.

possession One who either actively or constructively occupies a property; implies constructive notice that the possessor has certain legal rights

possessory The act of occupying a property which implies certain rights. *See* nonpossessory.

post-and-beam framing A type of construction in which the framing members are much larger than ordinary studs and larger posts can be placed several feet apart instead of 16" or 24" on center.

power of attorney An instrument appointing an attorney-in-fact; creates a universal agency.

prepaid expenses Costs the seller pays in advance but were not fully used up (such as utility payments or property taxes due) shown as a credit to the seller and debit to the buyer.

prepaid items Funds paid at closing to start an escrow account, as required in certain mortgage loans; also called prepaids.

prepayment penalty clause A financial charge imposed on a borrower for paying a mortgage prior to expiration of the full mortgage term.

prescription A method of acquiring an easement by continuous and uninterrupted use without permission.

prescriptive easement One obtained by prescription.

price The amount a purchaser agrees to pay and a seller agrees to accept under the circumstances surrounding a transaction.

price fixing Competitors in a group or industry conspiring to charge the same or similar price for services rendered.

prima facie case A suit that is sufficiently strong that it can be defeated only by contrary evidence.

primary financing The loan with the highest priority.

primary mortgage market The activity of lenders' making mortgage loans to individual borrowers.

prime rate The interest rate a lender charges to the most creditworthy customers.

principal (a) In the law of agency, one who appoints an agent to represent her. (b) Amount of money on which interest is paid or received.

principal residence The home the owner or renter occupies most of the time.

priority liens Special liens that receive preferential treatment (such as mechanics' liens).

private land use control Regulations for land use by individuals or nongovernmental organizations in the form of deed restrictions and restrictive covenants.

private mortgage insurance (PMI) A form of insurance coverage required in high loan-to-value ratio conventional loans to protect the lender in case the borrower defaults in the loan payment.

private property That which is not owned by government.

privity of contract An agreement that exists only between lessor and lessee for the right to demand and receive the specific benefit.

probate The procedure for proving a will.

procuring cause The basis for a direct action that results in successfully completing an objective.

profit The right to participate in profits of another's land.

promissory note A written promise to pay a debt as set forth in the writing.

promulgate To put in effect by public announcement.

property condition disclosure form A comprehensive checklist pertaining to the condition of the property including its structure and any environmental hazards in and around the property.

property description An accurate legal description of land.

property management Comprehensive, orderly, continuing program analyzing all investment aspects of a property to ensure a financially successful project.

property manager One who manages properties for an owner as the owner's agent.

property report Disclosure required under the Interstate Land Sales Disclosure Act.

proprietary lease A lease in a cooperative apartment.

proration Division of certain settlement costs between buyer and seller.

prudent avoidance policy New York advises people to avoid exposure to EMF fields when possible.

public grant A grant of a power, license, or real property from the state or government to a private individual.

public land use control Regulation of land use by government organizations in the form of zoning laws, building codes, subdivision ordinances, and environmental protection laws.

public open space Land that is not intensely developed for residential, commercial, industrial, or institutional use.

public property That which is owned by government.

public record Constructive notice, for all to see, of real property conveyances and other matters.

punitive damages Court-ordered awards for extremely bad behavior by a party; intended to punish and indicate that the behavior will not be tolerated.

pur autre vie Latin meaning *for the life of another*. A life estate measured by the life of someone other than the life tenant.

purchase money mortgage A mortgage given by a buyer to a seller to secure payment of all or part of the purchase price.

qualified fee simple A defeasible fee (title), recognizable by words "as long as."

quasi-judicial Rulings that are subject to review and change in the state and federal courts.

quiet enjoyment Use or possession of property that is undisturbed by an enforceable claim of superior title.

quiet title action A lawsuit to remove a cloud on a title.

quitclaim A deed to relinquish or release a claim to real property.

quitclaim deed A deed of release that contains no warranty of title; used to remove a cloud on a title.

radius Distance from the center of a circle to the perimeter; part of a metes and bounds description.

radon A colorless, odorless, radioactive gas present in the soil that enters a home through small spaces and openings.

rafters Wooden framing members used in the roof.

rate cap With adjustable rate mortgages, limits on interest rates during the lifetime of a loan.

ratification Affirming an implied agency by approving a broker's actions.

ready, willing, and able Describes a buyer who is ready to buy, willing to buy, and financially able to pay the asking price.

real estate Land and everything permanently attached to land.

real estate broker A person or an organization acting as agent for others in negotiating the purchase and sale of real property or other commodities for a fee.

real estate investment trust (REIT) A form of business trust owned by shareholders making mortgage loans.

real estate market A local activity in which real property is sold, exchanged, leased, and rented at prices set by competing forces.

real estate salesperson A person performing any of the acts included in the definition of real estate broker but while associated with and supervised by a broker.

Real Estate Settlement Procedures Act (RESPA) A federal law regulating activities of lending institutions in making mortgage loans for housing.

reality of consent Mutual agreement between the parties to a contract; meeting of the minds; to exist and be free of duress, fraud, undue influence, and misrepresentation.

realized gain Actual profit resulting from a sale.

real property The aggregate of rights, powers, and privileges conveyed with ownership of real estate.

real property tax lien Taxes levied against real property by the local government and which have priority over all other liens.

REALTOR® A registered trademark of the National Association of REALTORS®; its use is limited to members only.

realty Land and everything permanently attached to land.

reciprocity Mutual agreement by certain states to extend licensing privileges to licensees in each state.

recognized gain The amount of profit that is taxable.

reconciliation (a) The process of checking accounting of the settlement statement. (b) The adjustment process in appraising, whereby comparables are adjusted to the subject property.

recordation Written registration of an owner's title in public records to protect against subsequent claimants.

recording Registering a document on the public record.

rectangular survey system A type of land description utilizing townships and sections.

redemption *See* equity of redemption.

redlining The refusal of lending institutions to make loans for the purchase, construction, or repair of a dwelling because the area in which the dwelling is located is integrated or populated by culturally diverse people.

re-entry The owner's right to regain possession of real property.

referee's deed Used to convey real property when a court appointed individual (referee) acts as directed by the court in a bankruptcy or similar case.

referral fee A percentage of a broker commission paid to another broker for sending a buyer or seller to him or her.

reference to a plat A description on a deed that may refer to a plat map and lot number as part of a recorded subdivision.

refinancing Obtaining a new mortgage loan to pay and replace an existing mortgage.

reformation A doctrine that permits the court to correct a mistake and to rewrite a contract to express the true intentions of the parties.

Regulation Z Requirements issued by the Federal Reserve Board in implementing the Truth-in-Lending Law, which is a part of the Federal Consumer Credit Protection Act.

reject To refuse to accept an offer.

release clause A provision in a mortgage to release certain properties from the mortgage lien when the principal is reduced by a specified amount.

remainder interest A future interest in a life estate.

remainderman One who has a future interest in a life estate.

remise To release or give up.

repossession Regaining possession of property as a result of a breach of contract by another.

rescission Cancellation of a contract when another party is in default.

Residential Leadbased Paint Hazard Reduction Act Sets forth procedures to be followed in disclosing the presence of leadbased paint for sale of properties built prior to 1978.

restrictive covenant Restriction placed on a private owner's use of land by a nongovernmental entity or individual.

reverse annuity mortgage Used by older people who need additional income and want to take advantage of the equity in their homes.

reversion Return of title to the holder of a future interest, such as the grantor in a life estate not in remainder.

reversionary interest A provision stating the owner's interest—that possession of property will go back to owner at end of lease.

revocation Withdrawal of an offer.

R-factor A wall's degree of resistance to heat transfer. Also R-value.

rider Addendum to cover supplemental issues of an agreement.

ridge beam Highest part of framing of a building; forms the apex of the roof.

right of assignment Allows lender to sell mortgage at any time and obtain money invested rather than wait for completion of loan term.

right of first refusal A statement in a lease or condominium articles of association that provides for a lessee or an association to have the first opportunity to purchase the property before it is offered to anyone else.

right of inheritance The right for property to descend to the heirs of the owner as set out by will or by intestate succession.

right of survivorship The right of an owner to receive the title to a co-owner's share upon death of the co-owner, as in the case of joint tenancy and tenancy by the entirety.

right-of-way An easement allowing someone to use the land of another.

riparian rights The rights of an owner of property adjoining a watercourse such as a river, including access to, and use of, the water.

risk factor The potential for loss.

risk management Controlling and limiting risk in property ownership.

rule of reason Legal doctrine that means that if an activity is reasonable, then it is allowable under law.

running with the land Rights moving from grantor to grantee along with a title.

sale and leaseback A transaction in which a property owner sells a property to an individual who immediately leases back the property to the seller.

sales comparison approach Appraisal approach for estimating the value of single-family dwellings and vacant land; it compares the subject property with other similar properties that have sold recently.

sales contract An agreement between buyer and seller on the price and other terms and conditions of the sale of property.

satisfaction of mortgage Legal instrument signifying a mortgage has been paid in full.

scarcity (a) An economic characteristic of real property. (b) In appraisal, supply of property in relation to effective demand.

secondary mortgage market The market in which lenders sell mortgages.

second mortgage One that is first in priority after a first mortgage.

security deposit A sum of money that the landlord requires of the tenant prior to the lease, to be refunded at the end of the lease based upon the condition of the premises.

seepage pit A covered pit through which the discharge from the septic tank infiltrates into the surrounding soil.

seisin (seizin) Possession of a freehold estate in land.

self-dealing Illegal activity that can occur when a broker has an undisclosed interest in a property.

seller agent A listing agent, subagent, or broker's agent who works in the best interests of the seller.

separate ownership Ownership in severalty by one's spouse.

separate property Any property acquired by one spouse during marriage by gift or inheritance or purchased with the separate funds of a husband or wife.

septic system A household wastewater treatment system consisting of a house sewer, septic tank, distribution box, and absorption field or seepage pit.

service drop Aboveground electrical cables that come from the nearest pole connecting to the service entrance conductors of a house.

service lateral Underground electrical wiring connecting to a house.

servient tenement Land encumbered by an easement.

setback The distance from a front or interior property line to the point where a structure can be located.

severalty Ownership by only one person.

Sexual Orientation Non-Discrimination Act (SONDA) Law that added sexual orientation as protected class under the New York Human Rights Law.

shared equity mortgage A type of mortgage used in commercial lending where the lender participates in the profits generated by a commercial property.

sheathing A material such as plywood or sheetrock, which covers the framing members of a structure; also a type of insulation material.

Sherman Antitrust Act Federal legislation including imposition of civil and punitive damages for antitrust activities.

sick building syndrome A chemical illness that may be caused by the air quality inside a commercial building.

sill plate The first wooden member of a structure used as the nailing surface for the floor system.

single agent An agent who works only for the buyer or the seller.

situs Location of land.

slab-on-grade construction A type of concrete flooring that is part of the foundation and is poured on a prepared and graded surface.

soffit A wood, vinyl, or aluminum material placed under the roof extension of a structure.

sole plate A horizontal base plate, which serves as the foundation for the wall system.

sole proprietorship A business owned by one individual.

SONYMA (Sonny Mae) State of New York Mortgage Agency, which raises money from the sale of New York tax-free bonds and uses these funds for mortgage loans.

special agent Agent with limited authority to act on behalf of the principal, such as created by a listing.

special assessment A levy by a local government against real property for part of the cost of making an improvement to the property, such as street paving, installing water lines, or putting in sidewalks.

special purpose real estate Category of real property created as a result of combining both the land and its improvements for a singular highest and best use.

special use permit A permit for a use that is not permitted in the zone except with the special permission of the planning board or other legislative body.

specific lien One that attaches to one particular property only.

specific performance A court instruction requiring a defaulting party to a contract to buy and sell real property to specifically perform her obligations under the contract.

spot zoning In New York, the illegal rezoning of a certain property in a zoned area to permit a different type of use than that authorized for the rest of the area.

Standards of Practice Established practices set out in the Code of Ethics established by the NAR.

State Environmental Quality Review Act (SEQRA) A New York law requiring preparation of an environmental impact statement on any projects that require government approval and that may have a significant effect on the environment.

Statute of Frauds A law in effect in all states; in New York, the General Obligations Law, requiring real estate contracts for more than one year to be in writing.

Statute of Limitations Law establishing the time period within which certain lawsuits may be brought.

statutory dedication When a property owner files a plat marked with portions of the property dedicated to public use.

steering The practice of directing prospective purchasers toward or away from certain neighborhoods to avoid altering the racial/ethnic make-up of these areas.

straight-term mortgage A loan in which the borrower pays interest only for a specified term and, at the end of the term, is required to pay the principal.

studs Wooden framing members used for forming the wall skeleton of a structure.

subagent A person appointed by an agent with permission of the principal to assist in performing some or all of the tasks of the agency.

subchapter S corporation Corporate formation whereby corporate income and expenses flow through to shareholders as if a partnership.

subdivision regulation (ordinance) Public control of the development of residential subdivisions.

sublease The transfer of only part of a lease term with reversion to the lessee; a lesser lease estate.

subordinate Lower in priority.

subrogation of rights The substitution of the title insurance company in the place of the insured for filing a legal action.

substitution The principle providing that the highest value of a property has a tendency to be established by the cost of purchasing or constructing another property of equal utility and desirability provided that the substitution can be made without unusual delay.

subsurface rights Rights to the area below the earth's surface.

supply and demand The principle stating that the greater the supply of any commodity in comparison to demand, the lower the value; conversely, the smaller the supply and the greater the demand, the higher the value.

survey Document showing measurements, boundaries, and area of a property.

survivorship The right of the surviving co-owner automatically to receive the title of a deceased co-owner immediately without probate.

suspension Right of the Department of State to deactivate a broker or salesperson license for wrongdoing.

swing loan A type of interim loan wherein a borrower uses the equity in one property to obtain the money necessary to buy another property.

take-out loan Permanent financing arranged to replace a short-term construction loan.

taking The act of a government body obtaining a property under its power of eminent domain.

taking title subject to a mortgage Accepting a title pledged to secure a mortgage and with no personal liability for payment of the note.

taxation A power of government to tax, among other things, real property.

tax-deductible expense An amount of money that may be deducted from gross income in arriving at net taxable income before depreciation, if any.

tax deed A deed conveying title to real property to a new owner that a municipality obtained from the original owner's failure to pay real estate taxes.

tenancy by the entirety A form of co-ownership limited to husband and wife, with the right of survivorship.

tenancy in common A form of co-ownership that does not include the right of survivorship.

tenant relocator A person who arranges, for a fee, the relocation of commercial or residential tenants from buildings that are to be demolished, rehabilitated, or remodeled.

tenements Right of ownership of real estate held by a person.

term mortgage One that requires the mortgagor to pay interest only during the mortgage term, with the principal due at the end of the term.

testamentary trust A trust set up within a person's will and effective upon the death of the person who created the trust.

testate To have died leaving a valid will.

testator A male who has died and left a valid will.

testatrix A female who has died and left a valid will.

testers Volunteers from state or private agencies who enforce fair housing by claiming to be homeseekers, thereby finding out if brokers deal fairly with all clients or customers.

tie-in arrangement Agreement between a party selling a product or service with a buyer that as a condition of the sale, the buyer will buy another product from the seller, or the buyer will not buy a product or use a service of another.

time is of the essence A phrase indicating that closing must take place on or before the exact date stipulated in the contract.

title Evidence of the right to possess property.

title closing The consummation of a real estate contract; a meeting in which the buyer, seller, and closing agent meet for execution of documents and disbursement of funds.

title examination A search of the public record to determine the quality of a title to real property.

title insurance An insurance policy protecting the insured from a financial loss caused by a defect in a title to real property.

title transfer tax A tax imposed on the conveyance of title to real property by deed.

topography The physical features and contours of land.

Torrens system A method of title recordation.

tract An area of land.

trade fixtures Items that are installed by a commercial tenant and are removable upon termination of the tenancy.

transferability The ability to transfer property ownership from seller to buyer.

transfer of development rights Purchase of the development rights of another property such as those of a historic property that cannot make use of them.

trespass Unlawful entry on the land of another.

triple net lease One in which the lessee pays all the expenses associated with the property in addition to the rent.

trust A legal relationship under which title to property is transferred to a person known as trustee.

trustee One who holds title to property for the benefit of another called a beneficiary.

trustor One who conveys title to a trustee.

Truth-in-Lending Simplification and Reform Act (TILSRA) *See* Regulation Z.

underground storage tanks Tanks located underground and utilized for the bulk storage of chemicals and petroleum.

underimprovement Use of land that is not at its highest and best use and thus does not generate the maximum income.

underwriting The act of reviewing loan documentation and evaluating borrower's ability and willingness to repay the loan and sufficiency of collateral value of the property.

undisclosed principal A principal whose identity may not be disclosed by an agent.

undivided interest Ownership of fractional parts not physically divided.

undue influence Any improper or wrongful influence by one party over another whereby the will of a person is overpowered so that he is induced to act or prevented from acting according to free will.

unencumbered property Property that is free of any lien.

unenforceable contract One that appears to meet the requirements for validity but would not be enforceable in court.

Uniform Commercial Code (UCC) A standardized and comprehensive set of commercial laws regulating security interests in personal property.

uniform irrevocable consent and designation form Allows the courts to serve a summons or other legal documents on the New York secretary of state in place of personal service on out-of-state licensees.

unilateral contract An agreement wherein there is a promise in return for a specific action, which together supply the consideration.

uninsured conventional loan One in which the loan payment is not insured to protect the lender.

unintentional misrepresentation An innocent false statement of a material fact.

unity of interest Created when co-owners all have the same percentage of ownership in a property.

unity of possession Created when all co-owners have the right to possess any and all portions of the property owned, without physical division.

unity of time Created when co-owners receive title at the same time in the same conveyance.

unity of title Created when co-owners have the same type of ownership in a property.

universal agent Agent that has complete authority over any activity of principal; for example, power of attorney.

urea-formaldehyde foam insulation (UFFI) A type of foam containing formaldehyde, a gaseous compound used for home insulating until the early 1980s.

U.S. Army Corps of Engineers A division of the U.S. Army that oversees navigation, water resource activities, flood control, beach erosion, and dredging projects.

U.S. Department of Housing and Urban Development (HUD) A federal agency that administers funding for projects related to housing.

useful life The period of time that a property is expected to be economically useful.

use variance Permission to use the land for a purpose which, under the current zoning restrictions, is prohibited.

usury Charging a rate of interest higher than the rate allowed by law.

utility Capable of serving a useful purpose.

vacancy rate A projected rate of the percentage of rental units that will be vacant in a given year.

vacant land Unimproved land that could include land brought back to its natural state, or land that does not possess improvements necessary to serve some kind of purpose.

VA-guaranteed loan A mortgage loan in which the loan payment is guaranteed to the lender by the Department of Veteran Affairs.

valid contract An agreement that is legally binding and enforceable.

valuable consideration Anything of value agreed upon by parties to a contract.

valuation Establishes an opinion of value utilizing an objective approach based on facts related to the property, such as age, square footage, location, cost to replace, and so on.

value in exchange The amount of money a property may command for its exchange; market value.

value in use The present worth of the future benefits of ownership; a subjective value that is not market value.

variance A permitted deviation from specific requirements of a zoning ordinance because of the special hardship to a property owner.

vendee Buyer.

vendor Seller.

vendor's affidavit Document signed under oath by vendor stating that vendor has not encumbered title to real estate without full disclosure to vendee.

vesting options Choices buyers have in how to acquire property.

vicarious liability A person's being responsible for the actions of another.

voidable contract An agreement that may be voided by the parties without legal consequences.

void contract An agreement that has no legal force or effect.

voltage The electrical pressure that pushes through the wires.

voluntary alienation The transfer of title freely by the owner.

voluntary lien A type of lien in which individuals consent to placing a security against themselves or their property.

wetlands Federal and state protected transition areas between uplands and aquatic habitats that provide flood and storm water control, surface and groundwater protection, erosion control, and pollution treatment.

words of conveyance Wording in a deed demonstrating the definite intent to convey a specific title to real property to a named grantee.

wraparound mortgage A junior mortgage in an amount exceeding a first mortgage against the property.

writ of attachment Court order preventing any transfer of attached property during litigation.

yield The return on an investment.

zoning A public law regulating land use.

zoning board of appeals A local appointed board that has the power to review administrative rulings made by the planning board or other legislative body.

zoning map A map that divides the community into various designated districts.

zoning ordinance A statement setting forth the type of use permitted under each zoning classification and specific requirements for compliance.

Index